THE NEVER ENDING Quest

Dr. Clare W. Graves
Explores Human Nature

The Never Ending Quest

*A treatise on an emergent cyclical conception
of adult behavioral systems and their development*

edited and compiled by
Christopher C. Cowan and Natasha Todorovic

ECLET Publishing
Santa Barbara, California

© Copyright 2005 by Christopher Cowan and Natasha Todorovic
ECLET Publishing
All Rights Reserved

No part of this publication may be reproduced or transmitted in any form, by any means, electronic or mechanical, including photocopying, recording or by any information capture and storage system without written permission.

Second Printing

For permission to reproduce sections of this book, contact

ECLET Publishing
PO Box 42212
Santa Barbara CA 93140-2212
http://www.ecletpublishing.com

Graves, Clare W.
The Never Ending Quest / Clare W. Graves
Christopher Cowan and Natasha Todorovic, editors
ISBN 978-0-9724742-1-4

To the memory of Marian Graves,
to Sue and to Bob,
and to the extended family of students
in the legacy of Dr. Clare W. Graves

CONTENTS

Editors' Foreword i
Preface 1
Section I – What is Human Life All About? 9
   Chapter 1 – The Problem 11
   Chapter 2 – An Approach for Investigating the Problem 33
   Chapter 3 – The Basic Data 51
   Chapter 4 – Confusion and Contradiction Exacerbated 91
   Chapter 5 – New Problem, New Opportunity, New Task 133
   Chapter 6 – The Emergent Cyclical Model 159
Section II – The Levels of Existence 195
   Chapter 7 – The Autistic Existence – The AN State 199
   Chapter 8 – The Animistic Existence – The BO State 215
   Chapter 9 – The Egocentric Existence – The CP State 225
   Chapter 10 – The Absolutistic Existence – The DQ State 251
   Chapter 11 – The Multiplistic Existence – The ER State 307
   Chapter 12 – The Relativistic Existence - The FS State 337
   Chapter 13 – The Systemic Existence - The A'N' State 365
   Chapter 14 – The Intuitive Existence – The B'O' State 395
Section III – The Sum of All Our Days is Just a Beginning 403
   Chapter 15 – Verification 405
   Chapter 16 – The Broader Meaning of the Concept 475
Appendix 505
Bibliography 509
Index 543

TABLES and EXHIBITS

Table I a - Change Instigators 100
Table I b – Direction of Change 100
Table II – Psychometric Studies 122
Table III – Designation of Levels 169
Table IV – Six Levels and Subsystems 409
Table V – Harvey, Hunt, and Schroder Data 424
Table VI – Harvery, Hunt, and Schroder Data Rearranged 426
Table VII – E-C Theory Compared with Others 440-446
Table VIII – E-C Theory Compared to Ego Development............461
Table IX – Tachistoscope Data... 466
Table X – Mean Recognition Times 468

Exhibit I – Entering, Nodal, Exiting 56
Exhibit II – Rise and Fall of System Dominance......................... 113
Exhibit III – Organizational Structures 117
Exhibit IV – Conceptualization of Psychological Lifespace..........164
Exhibit V - E-C Psychosocial Development...............................168
Exhibit VI – Nesting Aspects of Adult Psychosocial Systems 171
Exhibit VII – E-C Model and Cultural Institutions 175
Exhibit VIII – Wave-like Development.......................................177
Exhibit IX – Progressive-Regressive Development 179
Exhibit X – Leading Edge Times 181
Exhibit XI – Existential Problems in Time 183
Exhibit XII – Double Helix Representation.................... 187, 376, 430
Exhibit XIII – Nomenclature 192
Exhibit XIV – Source of Existential States..................................193
Exhibit XV – DQ Subjects 468
Exhibit XVI – ER Subjects 469
Exhibit XVII – FS Subjects 470
Exhibit XVIII – A'N' Subjects 471
Exhibit XIX – Development of Existential States 479

Editors' Foreword

How to do justice to a man whose work, insights, contributions and observations have changed lives and transformed the way we see the world? One way is by continuing his work so as to bring it forth more broadly into that world so others might know the mind behind the theory and be thus mentored. What better than to share with the world the work and words of a brilliant and good man whose life was devoted to teaching, research and unraveling the riddle of human nature?

It is our privilege to help Dr. Clare W. Graves's endeavors continue to bear fruit, and to bring more of his perspective into more hands and minds. The interest in this kind of bridge-building approach is growing, just as he expected, because it adds necessary understanding of human affairs and connects many ways of figuring out why we do what we do, as we do, and what we might do next. Clare often said he was addressing questions which were not yet being asked in psychology or the sciences, for that matter, but that they would be one day. Now they are, in fields ranging from systems and cognitive psychology, to evolutionary developmental biology, to consciousness studies. He was a pioneer living a bit before his time, blazing trail for others to follow toward a common destination: understanding who and why we are.

To have the opportunity to share the Gravesian point of view so it can be more clearly understood, further elaborated, wisely used, and more sharply appreciated is a gift. This book is our way to honor Clare Graves and his profound influence. In the process, we fulfill a promise made to our friend and his life partner, Marian Graves, by ensuring that Clare's work might move forward through helping this volume and its companions come to be.

Thirty years have elapsed since Clare Graves began to put his ideas down in longhand on legal pads to be typed by his secretary in the old 'psych building' at Schenectady's Union College. Nearly twenty have passed since his death in 1986. Way back in 1951 he had set out on a quest for better understanding of human nature – who we are and who we are to become. It was an ambitious undertaking which culminated with the statement of a new theory and then a manuscript after nearly a quarter century of work. The original pages which remain are brittle, but the ideas are flexible and hold together better than ever. They have begun to be recognized for what they are: an elegant theory that pulls together a broad spectrum of approaches to human nature and helps bring them into focus. The beauty of Graves's work is its open-endedness, thus leaving room for all the discoveries made during those years between then and now in systems theory, the neurosciences, and even geopolitics. The concept—the bridge—is as fresh and vibrant today as it was in 1977, and provides a solid map to what lies ahead.

Graves did not set out to 'explain it all' or to provide all the answers to 'life's nagging questions.' He only sought to provide a framework with the explanatory power to pull our knowledge about ourselves and why we do as we do together with more elegance. He saw fragmentation and compartmentalization in psychology, in education, and politics. He also envisioned interconnected systems where others found compartments, and complementarity where others found competition. He sensed a deeper layer that could pull our understanding of the chunks closer together, a set of organizing principles that could draw the best from many viewpoints and resonate without eroding them. This theory was to be a statement for his peers and the world to consider – to accept, to build upon, or, perhaps, to shred and cast away. Today, many people, ranging from academics to successful bottom-line business executives, even New Age spiritual gurus, agree that he succeeded in opening a powerful new window through which to see the world differently. Gravesian thinking is an additive force in many domains.

Yet most of those opinions are based largely on secondary and tertiary reports of the Gravesian legacy and not the work, itself. When Clare died in 1986, his major project was shelved. Until this publication, only smatterings of the theory and the thinking behind it have been generally available. Thus, a number of reinterpretations, postulations, and even fabrications of what Dr. Graves intended have been tossed about along with accurate reports. This book will clear up some confusion. In Graves's own words, it gives those already interested in the material a means to cross-check what they've read and been told. It gives a Gravesian starting point to those who have not been prejudiced by renditions which might be distorted or which might be merely flying

Editors' Foreword

a flag of convenience, sometimes spreading nonsense under the name of Graves. And for those with a clear view of Gravesian theory already, it offers both foundational details and a direction for further work.

One of the editors of this book, Christopher Cowan, knew Dr. Graves quite well during the last decade of his life and had the opportunity to work closely with him, helping him prepare his last two summary papers in 1981 and 1982. Some of the materials blended herein are from his collection of Gravesian papers, as well as recordings and notes from sessions conducted jointly with Dr. Graves. Other pieces are from the collection of Gravesian archivist, William R. Lee.

In addition, Cowan is co-creator of what is arguably the most prominent commercial application of parts of the Gravesian point of view, Spiral Dynamics®, and co-author of the original book by that title, *Spiral Dynamics: Mastering Values, Leadership, and Change*. With the compilation of this manuscript and the learning that came with the process, however, he has also become a critic of some aspects of his own work from nearly a decade ago, recognizing how easy it is both to glibly over-simplify and to inject elaborations which are not appropriate. Thus, the publication of this "Graves" book is an opportunity to set some of the record straight, to confess some misunderstandings, and to redirect some confusion by accurately citing the source. We hope it provides a means for sincere students of the theory to lay down their own foundations on the bedrock of the Gravesian legacy—what it is and what it is not—and from there to raise their own challenges, find their own truths, and expand on a body of work better grounded on a more solid, accurate footing.

History

Every book has its history. If this one could speak, it would tell an adventure story of excitement, catastrophe, and separation involving an international border and hundreds of miles, both sides of a continent and at least four states and two provinces. It could speak of a wild ride through Canada avoiding moose and staying just ahead of a November blizzard, and of a paragraph found on the last page of an article in box #7 of the huge Carl Rogers archive at UCSB. It would celebrate what it is and ask readers to help it grow into what Graves wanted it to become.

When he began this project, Clare Graves's plan was to put out a definitive work. He envisioned an opus that would stand among the classics, a statement on human nature nothing short of revolutionary that might be a key to open minds to new thinking about psychology.

But there was a catch. Reportedly, he had seen Abraham Maslow "torn to pieces" by his colleagues at an APA seminar in the mid 1950's. Afterwards, Graves found Maslow hanging his head while slumped on a couch in the lobby of the hotel. Maslow was wondering why his friends and associates would treat him so shabbily and attack his point of view. He mourned: 'Why would they do that to me?'

That memory of an icon being lambasted and emotionally crushed by colleagues stuck with Clare Graves who seems to have vowed that he would never put himself in Maslow's position. Instead, he would conduct rigorous research and release his findings only when the theory was ripe and defensible in the face of the harshest criticism. It would be thorough and more. Thus, he published relatively little and held his work very closely while surrounded by the behaviorists and Freudians of his day.

His studies actually began in an effort to answer a student's semester-end question after a survey course in psychology: "OK, so which one is right?" From there he went on to try and rationalize Maslow's views and to prove them valid. He quickly came to discover, however, that the Maslowian approach was insufficient to frame his mounting piles of data, and that even the great Maslow's perspective was only brushstrokes on a much larger canvas of human nature. That picture was what he intended to reveal with this book.

The process of disclosure began in the 1960's when Graves was beginning to discuss his work and its implications more openly. He crafted statements for conferences and presentations (many of which are available on the www.clarewgraves.com website operated by the editors and William Lee). He had some success with an article in the *Harvard Business Review*[1] applying his viewpoint to managerial issues, and another in the *Journal of Humanistic Psychology*[2] laying out an initial statement of his theoretical perspective. A piece in Canada's *Maclean's Magazine*[3] suggested that his might just be "a theory that explains everything," though Graves was well aware that his, too, was only a work in progress without finale, just as is nature of *Homo sapiens*. Still, interest was growing. His approach was striking chords. A lengthy

---

[1] Graves, Clare W. (1966). Deterioration of Work Standards. *Harvard Business Review*, September/October 1966, Vol. 44, No. 5, p. 117-126.
[2] Graves, Clare W. (1970). Levels of Existence: An Open Sstem Theory of Values. *Journal of Humanistic Psychology*, Fall, Vol. 10, No. 2, p. 131-155.
[3] Steed, Nicholas (1967). A Theory that Explains Everything. *Maclean's Magazine*. October, 1967.

exposition of his point of view appeared in *The Futurist*[4], the publication of the World Future Society which has been active in support of this work for many years. (Graves's feelings about this piece were mixed since the text blends his own words with comments by the editor, some of which he liked and others which he found troubling.) There were study groups devoted to his point of view. He began sharing his ideas more broadly. And he commenced writing this, his major statement, as his star was beginning to rise.

Then, suddenly, a heart attack and problems in follow-on surgery halted that rise. Impaired eyesight and balance made reading and writing difficult. Graves was never able to resume his pace, though he did work on polishing parts of this manuscript for a time and also participated in a limited number of seminars, as well as consulting on several projects. The book project eventually went to sleep, a beginning and an end without a middle. It has waited a quarter century to awaken.

Drafts of large parts of sections I and III of this manuscript were ready in 1977, while other planned chapters remained unwritten. The project was shelved, due largely to frustrations created by impacts of his illness and in part to difficulties he never fully explained regarding his 'Canadian publisher.' He didn't even have copies of some of the pages he'd approved, only early pencil drafts. In truth, during the last years, it was unclear whether Clare was sad about the aborted attempt to complete this manuscript or if he was actually somewhat relieved that he was not required to bring the mammoth undertaking to fruition. (The latter was the opinion of his widow. It was also her opinion that what he had done needed to get out, despite his drive for completeness.)

So, the history of the book could have ended with Clare's passing in 1986. Co-editor Cowan helped Marian Graves to assemble his remaining papers which they donated to Union College's Library archives. Two years before, as his health was again deteriorating after several small strokes, Clare had decided to clean up the "mud room" one day and discarded his raw data and other writings to make room for harnesses from the barn. (In addition to being Union's golf coach, Clare and Marian loved Morgan trotters which gave the entire family such joy.) Thus, what remained in other filing cabinets were personal papers, articles, and rough copies of a few chapters of this book. There were pages scribbled in long hand on pads of legal paper; other sections were typed with scratch-outs; some were crinkled carbon paper copies. Conflicting versions and numbering made it nearly impossible to know

---

[4] Graves, Clare W. (1974). Human Nature Prepares for a Momentous Leap. *The Futurist*. April, p. 72-87.

what was to go where. It seemed the papers were merely of historical value as nuggets and small gems, nothing more.

Then, in 1999 the editors were fortunate in retrieving copies of additional chunks from a box stored away at the Quetico Centre in Canada, the organization which had been participating in the project earlier. In 2001 we found the table of contents which provided the intended order, along with some cassette audio tapes from the mid-1970's in which Clare discussed his book-in-progress. Those remarks provided sufficient direction to begin working on the puzzle. We have not given up on locating more pieces and, like Clare Graves's theory, this book is open-ended. But the picture is clear enough to move forward and live with a few missing pieces and unanswered questions.

Approaching the book

In reading Graves, remember that the Emergent-Cyclical (E-C) Levels of Existence theory (which he referred to as "the Emergent Cyclical, Phenomenological, Existential Double-Helix Levels of Existence Conception of Adult Human Behavior" in 1978 and "the Emergent, Cyclical, Double-Helix Model of Adult Human Biopsychosocial Systems" in 1981—the reason "E-C" is used herein) is the child of a multidisciplinary approach to human nature and behavior. Because it spans many fields, the theory cannot be collapsed into any one of them. Although not essential, the reader will benefit from familiarity with psychology, sociology, biology, education, systems theory, anthropology, history, and brain sciences. At the same time, study of any of these fields, including leadership, management, policy, politics, philosophy, or anything requiring understanding of human nature can benefit from exposure to this theory. Graves urges his readers to rise above established disciplinary boundaries, limits which often confounded his own studies, and to examine culture, adult behavior, thinking, motivation, management and learning from many points of view, each of which can hold elements of truth. He sees these not as different entities, but as multiple facets of the same diamond. This work pushes for broad rather than narrow views, and insists upon the recognition of interdependent relationships among ideas, fields, models, perspectives and concepts—a bridge.

Editors' Foreword

The book is in three sections.[5] In Section I, Graves asks the eternal question that leads to both war and peace while doggedly avoiding a single answer: 'What is human life about and what is it meant to be?' This question frames the entire work as he picks up human nature, holds it to the light, turns it, then examines it both under a microscope of individual development and from afar as an emergent process of our species.

In Chapter 1 he reviews various psychological approaches: behaviorism, psychoanalysis, and humanistic psychology, then proposes the Emergent Cyclical Levels of Existence Conception as a way to get beyond the confusion and contradiction in the field of psychology and culture with a new map. In Chapter 2 he explains how this conception emerged while glancing at other conceptualizers and what they seem to have overlooked. He outlines his basic research, then moves on to discuss his study of what adults had to say about the mature personality in Chapter 3. He weaves an intriguing story that would, were it not factual and a report of his activities, research and methodology, make for a good detective novel. As it is, he gives life to research and the suspense provides spice for the reader.

Chapters 4, 5 and 6 explore the building of a theory from a set of raw data. In Chapter 4 the evidence in the 'protocols'—statements about what the mature adult personality is like—provides clues to adult psychosocial development. The confusion in these data led Graves to search through other theorists' (and philosophers') work for explanations for what he had discovered and a way to frame it. Chapter 5 grapples with the idea that perhaps there is no such singular thing as psychological maturity, but that it is an emergent, open-ended process.

That leads to Chapter 6 wherein he lays out the Emergent, Cyclical, Double-Helix Model of Adult BioPsychoSocial Systems Development—the Levels of Existence theory (E-C)—and briefly compares it to other perspectives in personality, culture, change and maturity. (This summation chapter is required reading before getting to Section II lest the coping systems described here become a simple typology rather than a series of emergent relationships among existential factors from 'outside' and neurobiological equipment 'inside,' a trap many newcomers to Gravesian thinking fall right into.)

---

[5] Chapters 1-6 in Part I, as well as 14 and 15 in Part III, are from a near-final draft approved by Dr. Graves with only light editing and adjustment for this publication. The graphics appearing herein are either direct reproductions of drawings Dr. Graves used or reconstructions from rough copies in his other papers and notes.

Each chapter of Section II is devoted to describing one of the Gravesian Levels of Psychological Existence and some of its characteristics. This middle section—Chapters 7-14—was not written by Dr. Graves as it appears here. According to Marian Graves, he never completed these chapters, planning to leave them to the end of his project since they are artifacts of the theory, not the theory, itself. (Perhaps this was one of the issues between him and his publisher.)

Instead, Section II as presented here is mostly a compilation by the editors (Chris Cowan and Natasha Todorovic) of Dr. Graves's own words drawn from a number of original sources—both written papers and audio recordings. We have tried to concentrate on the phrasings and views presented in his later years when there was a choice or confusion as to his intentions. Since this theory was always a work in progress, Dr. Graves did change some aspects of it significantly over the years, while other pieces remained remarkably consistent down to the specific words. One idea that came in later, for example, is that there might be only six basic themes which then repeat in elaborated forms, producing the subsistence levels, the being levels, and, perhaps, compassionate levels (to borrow a term and idea from Anne Roe, John Calhoun, Maslow, and others).

We have included sections of the protocols and criteria Dr. Graves used to differentiate the levels and, where possible, sections on origins, management of the system, educational needs, reactions to stress, readiness for change and transitions to illustrate his thinking. One part – the recovered DQ/ER pages in Chapter 9 – demonstrate how rich this book would have been could he have completed it himself. There are examples of conceptions of the mature personality used to build the levels which Dr. Graves often cited, but no sample conceptions of the mature personality representing A'N' (Chapter 12) or B'O' (Chapter 13) because none remained among his papers, and he did not read them on tape or in seminars.

We decided to include practically everything Graves wrote and said about the B'O' level since it is one of the most controversial and curiosity-producing systems. He made it clear that his understanding of the eighth level was scant and speculative, and we insert this material only as historical notes, not a theoretical statement or description we can support today or with which he would necessarily agree. Readers can evaluate the evidence or lack thereof for the appearance of this level of psychological existence (and others) since 1977 for themselves. The open-ended nature of the theory certainly leaves room for the emergence of systems beyond B'O'. We leave this discussion for elsewhere and online since this book is a compendium of Dr. Grave's words then, and not our projections or opinions now. In any case, the core is the E-C theory and its derivation, not the levels.

Section III begins with a comparative analysis looking at other models of development, emergent systems, and evolutionary tracks. Chapter 14 includes discussion of similarities and differences with other theorists' work as verification or challenge to the E-C point of view. Comparison of Emergent Cyclical Theory to Maslow; Harvey, Hunt and Schroder; Loevinger; Schroder, Driver, and Streufert; Kohlberg; Perry; Isaacs; Calhoun; Drews; Aronof and more are all included within a table sampling and contrasting the models of twenty-five conceptualizers. The implications of this perspective to psychology, management, politics, social policy, education, foreign policy and various social transformations complete the book at Chapter 15.

The original bibliography and source list was lost. We have attempted to rebuild it as thoroughly as possible from citations in the manuscript (and other writings) which sometimes consisted of little more than a last name and, in a few cases, a last name with a page number. Very few titles of books or publications were included. With only a few exceptions—noted—we have located the books and scholars cited and tracked down quotations to source them. Our objective was to locate the writers and even editions which would have been available to Dr. Graves prior to 1977. In the process, we were exposed to some of the forgotten geniuses of his day, and to many ideas raised then which are being re-raised today as 'innovations'. Many of the authors he refers to have published considerably more; some have modified their positions; others stand by earlier works. A great deal has been learned in the neurosciences and cognitive systems post-Graves, for example. Yet even some of his ideas in this area which sound quaint on the surface stand up pretty well if one merely swaps the language for contemporary terms. Rather than include updates in this publication, though, we will rely on the technologies of today—online notes and discussion—to flesh it out and make corrections.

Dr. Graves obviously planned to include extensive explanatory footnotes. Some were intact in sections of the manuscript and notes. Those are marked "CWG:" in the text to indicate they are his own words, as found. The rest of the footnotes are our bibliographic references and, in a few cases, notes to explain events that would have been "current" in 1977 in America, but historic and mostly unfamiliar in 2005 and elsewhere around the globe to our international colleagues.

Reprints of many of his papers and biographical materials are available on our www.clarewgraves.com website. Fortunately, though, most of the material used in this book stands quite as well today as it did then. Even political examples are as apt now as three decades ago—change Presidents' names and things sound very much alike. That is one of the beauties of his point of view, of course, and why we are convinced that the theoretical work of Clare W. Graves stands even taller today than ever, and is even more useful now than then.

Acknowledgements, 2005

If this book could tell its story of excitement, frustration, abandonment, and renewal, it would speak of the many people involved in keeping it alive; for were it not for the pages stored, the papers filed, the tapes preserved, and the notes transcribed about the research conducted by Clare W. Graves, this could not be.

Thanks go to Linda Wiens, who worked with Clare at Quetico Centre and helped him in crafting these thoughts, along with others recognized later in the Preface. She kept the manuscript pages safe, waiting for the time to make them available as chapters. Dedicated archivist and Gravesian enthusiast William R. Lee had the interest, wisdom and foresight to collect and preserve every word, lecture and paper by Dr. Graves that he could as part of a Graves interest group in Washington, D.C., and then as teacher of the Gravesian legacy for 30 years to his own students at Arlington (VA) high school. In addition to his support of the ClareWGraves.com website, he has also assisted with checking this book and ensuring that it accurately reflects the authentic Gravesian perspective as well as possible. Ziza Todorovic waded through the noise of decaying cassette tapes to transcribe and check hours of recordings of Graves seminars, parts of which fill in large chunks of the missing chapters. We are indebted to her for weeks of effort, her reviews, and ongoing encouragement and enthusiasm.

Gratitude and respect to the many brilliant minds who laid down the ideas Graves built on and adapted, some of whose names appear herein, and to the creative legacy of many others unlisted. Our appreciation goes to Dr. O.J. Harvey for helping us to understand his work better and providing us with keys to Dr. Graves's inspiration. We are appreciative of Morris Stein, Robert Hawkins, and David Elkind

Editors' Foreword

who knew where their quotes came from, and from Mrs. William Gray who aided with her late husband's papers. All graciously took the time to respond to our queries. And special thanks go to Dr. Kenneth Isaacs who joined with us to explore where his work and Dr. Graves's coincide and differ.

In large measure, this book owes its existence to the support, friendship, advice and confidence of futurist Ed Edwards who has believed in the value of the Gravesian point of view for many, many years. While the editors fought with the pieces, dug through libraries, and doubted that it would ever come together, Ed always saw it as an important thing to make available to a wider public and generously facilitated that process. And, of course, this book is due to the friendship and blessings of the late Marian Graves and to the Graves's children, Sue and Bob, for their encouragement and endorsement.

But this book could not tell its story of human nature and our emergence were it not for the lifetime of work, research, dedication and persistence of the man who said and wrote it, Clare W. Graves, even though he is not physically present for the publication. This book is a sampling of his genius, passion and insight. We hope we have done justice to the work and to the man. We wish he could have been here through the process to clear his throat and say in his deep, resonant, professorial voice a protracted, "Welllll…" and then gently nudge for improvements and continue to turn on those light bulbs of revelation. We particularly wish he were here to discuss the innumerable questions that arose in its compiling and all the new ones an understanding of this point of view will surely pose. But those questions are now in your hands, gentle reader, and the answers forthcoming as you join with us move this work on.

ONLINE LINKS

To explore additional comments and elaborations on points made in this book, see the *online notes* at

http://www.neverendingquest.com

To read many of **Dr. Graves's papers** online and to learn more about the development of this theory, go to

http://www.clarewgraves.com

To learn more about the editors, their work and applications of Gravesian theory in seminars and consulting, go to

http://www.spiraldynamics.org

Preface[6]

The Sum of All Our Days is Just the Beginning

This is a book about the levels of human existence, those ever-emergent, ever-spiraling psychological way stations at which the adult human being may tarry and live out a psychological lifetime. Why and how this system's conception of adult human behavior came to be, what the systems are, how they operate and what they imply in the many faceted aspects of the mature human's life are the subject matter of this book.

It sketches a theoretical trellis upon which, it is hoped, the confusing behavior, the contradictory information and the conflicting explanations of adult human behavior can grow, with time, into an integrated network. It considers the adult behavioral system of the past, the systems of the present, and projects that new systems will appear infinitely in the future. It suggests that when, and only when, we have more knowledge of these adult behavioral systems and their hierarchical relationship to one another will we be able to more adequately describe,

---

[6] This preface was written by Dr. Graves in the late 1970's when he still expected to complete his book project. One working title was "The Sum of All Our Days is Just the Beginning" and is probably borrowed from Lewis Mumford. Others were "What is Human Life About? What is it Meant to Be?" and "The Existential Helix." Since this book is not what was planned, we have retitled it "The Never Ending Quest," a phrase drawn from Graves's writing.

understand, predict and manage the behavior of the adult individual, the operation of an organization, or the development of a society. It outlines the goals toward which the future of a person, organization or society should be pointed no matter the current position of that person, that organization or that society on a complex that is called a human existential helix.* And it suggests, within its framework, that there are ordered rules for dignifying or improving the state of existence of a person, or organization or a society so as to provide all human kind a future pregnant with hope rather than laden with the fear of our demise.

In these pages I take the position that human psychological development is an infinite process—that there is not, even in theory, any such thing as a state of psychological maturity. I say, instead, from the data of my studies, that one's conception of psychological maturity is a function of one's conditions for existence; and, I say that so long as humans continue to solve their problems of existence they will create new problems forever and on, and thus proliferate into new and higher-order forms of psychological being. And, I say that what our definition of psychological maturity is will change with each and every newly emergent form of psychological existence.

It is the thesis of this book that a human, though one biological organism, who does, in fact, develop biologically from a state of immaturity to a relative state of biological maturity which is maintained during the greater part of his or her individual existence, is an infinite number of psychological beings. And that our understanding of the human so far as ethics, values and purposes are concerned must be changed accordingly if we are to make any real inroads into the problems of human kind. We must reorganize our thinking and our approaches to man's problems to include the fact that there is no ultimate set of ethics, values, and purposes by which humans should live that will ever be revealed, laid down or discovered. There is instead, a hierarchically ordered, always open to change, set of ethics, values and purposes by which people can come to live. Thus, if we are to make progress in attacking our problems, our task is to learn how to live with an ever-changing process of values, ethics, and purposes rather than how to rear a person to live by "the right and proper" human values of ethics. Therefore:

- If you have almost despaired of making sense of human life, of the problems that we have and the people with whom you

---

* CWG: The existential helix is the basic construct utilized in this book to represent the emergent-cyclical adult behavioral systems.

have to deal, this book may bring you clarification and new hope because in it you may find new explanations of our past, new understandings of our present and new visions for our future.
- If you have asked yourself what is this militancy, this violence in so many of our people, or whether we are tearing apart at our moral seams, then you may find new and possibly even heretical thought in what I have to say.
- If you are a social planner concerned with the current and future goals of mankind, then the material in this book may open new horizons to your thinking.
- If, personally, you have asked, "Why can't I get along with my boss?" or if you are the boss, "Why are my subordinates so intractable?" then what this book says about the adult human being and the management of him at work may open new vistas for your thinking.
- If you are concerned with your organization and its viability, whether it be profit or non-profit oriented, then what is said about organizational decision-making may be something you need well to consider.
- If your interests are in basic social or behavioral sciences and if you are seeking regions for research which might extend man's knowledge, then the theoretical framework of this book may warrant your study and consideration.
- If you are an applied social scientist, an educator, or the like seeking new approaches to your problems, then you may find new avenues opened for application by what is said herein.
- If you are of the older generation trying to comprehend the young, or if you are one of the young trying to communicate your message of concern and hope, then this book may aid you to see the breadth of your problem.
- And finally, if you are just like me, simply a human being, wondering what human life is really like and what it is meant to be, then you may find what I have to say tantalizing. But if you are of another ilk, then what I have to say may be nothing less than scandalous.

The aim of this book is to attempt the impossible dream—to develop, in basic form, a theory of adult behavior, which:

- clarifies within its framework the many confusing, contradictory and controversial aspects of adult human behavior;
- is at one and the same time comprehensible to the layman and contributory to the worlds of pure and applied science;
- may someday coalesce into one explanatory framework the many diverse theories of human behavior which have been presented to date;
- will be applicable to any adult human being, regardless his culture;
- will reach into the past, carry through the present, and project into the future so as to help the reader make better sense of human behavior and see the totality of human life in clearer light;
- will provide a revised, enlarged and, in many respects, new theoretical framework within which the pure and applied scientist can reexamine and extend his knowledge of adult human behavior and cultural institutions;
- will provide the applied social scientist and social planners with a different means to the end of comprehending and approaching human problems than they have had at their disposal before;
- will provide the philosophically minded with new and needed goals for mankind, ethical wise and otherwise;
- strives differently to explain why you and the boss don't get along and what your organization can do to rectify such threats to its viability; and
- enables us to more fruitfully examine and constructively approach our adult educational problems.

The overriding intent of this book is to suggest, through its makeup, what human life is all about and what it is meant to be and to lay out through its blueprint what one might consider the goals for the future of mankind to be—the never-ending quest.

This book is another way station on my journey to and along the human existential helix. It is the outgrowth of more than twenty-four years of research, contemplation and writing. Therefore, a word of explanation is required as to how this work relates to what I have said in the past, in speeches delivered, papers read, classes and seminars conducted and articles published.

Some of my effort, scattered over the years, contain a certain amount of preparatory work and preliminary conception of adult human behavior. Some of this preparatory thought has been retained over the two decades of preparation. Some of the earlier thought has been discarded because, it seemed with time, it had aborted. Some of it has been revised as new data forced reconsideration. Thus, my earlier works reflect more the laborious process of an interpretive idea trying to be born than what my research leads me to say in this book.

Therefore, he who has had previous contact with my work may find much that is familiar but also some that is different from what I said before. The underlying conception of emergent psychosocial systems has been retained throughout the years, but the specifics of my conceptualization of adult behavior have changed and the underlying neurochemical, experiential explanation of their source will be quite new to many.

During the years of research and preparation some of my original sketches and interpretations have been attractive to others, even to the extent that some have been stimulated to do research within the confines of the preliminary conception expressed. Thus, I have been urged to hurry into print more of the details of my thinking. Grateful as I am for the acceptance the earlier expressions have received, and for the flattering request for more of my thinking, I must state what it has done. This very acceptance, use of, and call for more of my ideas has caused me to delay publication until such a time that I could feel my thinking was further developed, because even now, though it is being printed, it is far from mature and can become more mature only through the efforts of others.

Unfortunately, two years ago I was the victim of a surgical accident which damaged my brain. The accident left me considerably dysphasic and dyslexic and my conceptual capacities impaired. So the theory presented herein is not the product I had envisioned. It is a sketch with gaps and expressive deficiencies within.

In one sense, I apologize to those who sought more than I was, in pre-accident days, of a mind to scatter. On the other hand, I do not apologize, because then I did not feel that I was ready to stand on what I, too early, might have said. But now, even within my problem, I am ready to stand on what I say herein, but not on what I said before except in a basically general sense. What I said before was a part of an effort which produced the product contained herein. Even today it is not a finished product. Obviously it is incomplete and obviously there will be gaps and errors in my thinking. But when I say ON THESE WORDS I STAND, what I mean is this: If my conception of adult behavior is to be torn to shreds by criticism and even demolished by subsequent research, let it be the basics of the emergent cyclical levels of existence theory of adult behavior as I am able to present it herein that be criticized and torn apart. Let it not be that which I said or wrote while trying to conceive what is presented within the covers of this book. And let it not be the specifics of the conception that criticism dwell upon.

To the Philosophical or Behavioral Science Academician

This book should be useful as supplementary reading in any course which considers the nature of the human condition; the problem of ethics, morality and values; the management of human affairs, including education, management, per se; and psychotherapy. Also, it should find its place as a supplement in both graduate and undergraduate courses in Developmental and Life Span Psychology, Theories of Personality, and Organizational Behavior. Particularly, it could serve as a major text in that vast field of adult education where courses in the psychology of man are offered. It should fit all these areas and others because it is written in a language which requires no previous exposure to the jargon, specialized language, or way of thinking of psychology. So it is a book that can be profitably read by the interested layman, the beginning college student, the advanced undergraduate student, and still be thought-provoking to the new Ph.D. or the long established professor.

As for where this book fits into the world of philosophical and psychological thought, it is cast, philosophically, in the General Systems thinking of Joseph Lyons and Maurice Merleau-Ponty and other existentialists. On the psychological side, its deepest roots lie in the works of Heinz Werner, Jean Piaget and Kurt Goldstein. It is conceptually at home with the productions of Jane Loevinger, Lawrence Kohlberg, Abraham Maslow and the Maslowians, Fritz Heider, Peter Blos, Elizabeth Drews, Robert Peck and Robert Havighurst, O.J. Harvey, David E. Hunt, Harold Schroder, Jerome Bruner and the students of all of these. Its closest intellectual bedfellows are Gerald Heard's *The Five Ages of Man*, William C. Perry, Jr.'s *Intellectual and Ethical Development in the College Years,* and the work of John Calhoun.

As a contribution to the field of developmental psychology, this book might be seen as follows: Piaget's framework extends to 15 or so years. Harvey, Hunt and Schroder's work overlaps all of Piaget and extends into adulthood. The work of William Perry, Jr., adds an advanced period beyond Harvey, Hunt and Schroder and that of Eric Homburger Erikson whose last period begins in the thirties. This work overlaps all of these but picks up, particularly from where Perry and

Erikson leave off. The only other person, of whom I now know, who has the extending systems concept which I utilize is John Calhoun.

Theoretically, this book is a contribution to phenomenological, existential, humanistic and cognitive developmental emergent stage psychologies. As such, it attempts to meet some of the criticisms that have been directed at them. It attempts to bring some systematic toughness to the loose and discursive phenomenological and existential thinking. It attempts to move humanistic psychology away from its maudlin and sentimental view of human nature toward an empathic representation closer to the realities of being human.

As a contribution to cognitive-developmental stage theoretical psychology, it deals with at least five of the major criticisms directed toward them: (1) it offers an explanation of how constructs develop; (2) it presents a picture of what the process of development is like; (3) it hypothesizes what factors determine the hierarchical order of constructs; (4) it explains what determines the particular characteristics of constructs; and (5), it suggests how the constructs operate.

Herein, I should like to acknowledge those to whom I am in debt for aid in the preparation of this book. Thanks are extended to Clare Lumpkin, our departmental secretary, for her patience during the many hours and days she typed and retyped the basic manuscript. Thanks go as well to Richard Wakefield of Bethesda, Maryland, former President of the now disbanded Human Needs Foundation. I thank him as the only person who has provided moral support from the beginning of my first attempt to rationalize my data in 1961. As President of the former Human Needs Foundation, I thank him for the monetary support, which made possible the development of the figures and diagrams utilized to represent my thinking.

I desire, also, to express my thanks to the three people who contributed so much to the basic editing and layout of this book; Linda Wiens, Cliff McIntosh and Robert Michels of the professional staff of Quetico Centre. Without their aid, in a time of travail, this book could never have come to be. And finally, I wish to thank the Board of Quetico Centre, for offering the staff and facilities of Quetico Centre to me for the culmination of this book and its publication.

Section I

What Is Human Life All About?
WHAT IS IT MEANT TO BE?

Part I

CHAPTER 1

The Problem

Shaken by repeated threat to their established way of life, many people in this world are deeply troubled. But, is their concern properly directed? Are they correct when they see immaturities and immoralities in the behavior of their fellow man? Or are their concerns the offspring of misperception and delusion?

These are not idle questions just floating through a human mind because in the answer to them may lie the future of mankind. Nor are they new queries in the annals of man, for they were asked earlier by others when there were threats to the "established mature" ways of life. Threats to adult humans' establishment have been with us, so legend says, from the time of Eve and Adam. Yet every time man has faced a new tomorrow, the frightened ones have given forth their plaintive cry: "What the hell is going on? What is happening to people?"

"What is happening to people?" is a cry emitted not only by the frightened ones but by other people, as well. Some, more ashamed than afraid, cringe in shock at the "immature," "immoral" behavior of their fellow humans and proclaim how dreadful it is that the behavior which they see has ever arisen, or is allowed to be. Still others, more angered than frightened or ashamed, vehemently condemn those who question "the mature" ways for living and righteously defend the tenets of their personal conceptions of maturity. But I, for one, am not despaired by any questioning of man, nor am I troubled by the so-called "immature things" which many men are doing. I see, instead, that we live in a time for reappraisal—a time when we must reassess ourselves as one of nature's beings, a time when we must look again, but only after a re-centering of our focus. Then, and only then, may we see in a clearer light what the human is meant to be and what adult human life is all about. Then, and only then, may we see in newer ways what is the meaning in man's 'immaturities' and the misperceptions that lie in our current visions of them. And then, and only then, may we see in bold design new steps that we might take in order to survive that which keeps happening to people.

What does keep happening to the human being? Must humans always be tearing apart at their moral seams? Must they always be threatened with the decline of their established way of life—that (way of life) to which their existence owes its hope? Is there something cancerous in humanity that foredooms it to the kinds of disorder people seem so repeatedly to experience? Something happens; of this we can be certain. But, is this something bad? It is cancerous? Possibly it is, but perhaps it is not. Perhaps one's judgment of what keeps happening to humanity is a function of one's conception of the human organism. And perhaps those who repeatedly see breakdown in the behavior of certain people have conceptions of the human organism which should be questioned.

In the mid-twentieth century one could not deny that rifts in the behavior of adults came to exist. They were then to be seen at every point on the compass. From one direction, the American establishment's, the finger pointed at the psychedelic, confrontational, and sexual behavior of youth. From another, youth's direction, the finger pointed at the righteous protestations from those callous exploiters of our environment—the American industrialists. Businessmen and Presidents saw a breakdown in the work ethic as welfare rolls climbed, and they saw moral depravity in the slowdown and sabotaging activities of "the working people." But the "working people" pointed to questionable merchandising practices, budgetary manipulations, and political machinations as evidence of problems in our human decision makers. Dissenters were called immature when in the name of "civil rights" they frightened their fellow citizens, both here and abroad. Yet these same dissenters yelled immaturity at those who used "civil rights" as their shield while they carried on vicious, even murderous attacks upon those who were dissenting.

In China, in the sixties, under the banner of Maoism and a better life for all Chinese, the Red Guards attacked both the country and the towns. In Rhodesia and South Africa, the adult white man, while demanding the right of one's own decision, denied these same rights to his non-white countrymen. In Uganda, acting in the name of freedom and progress, Idi Amin[7] dispatched to exile or to death one after another of his countrymen.

In America, adult humans were so confused that they, in the name of peace, for ten years carried on a hopelessly futile war. They professed the need of equality for all, yet excluded many from the rights and privileges that some adults enjoyed. They spoke of the need to respect differences, both nationally and internationally, both in the school and in the factory, yet these same adult humans managed national and international affairs, the student, and the employee in ways more to deny that such differences did exist. And they professed concern for the poverty stricken but behaved toward them so as to precipitate riots born of their deepening despair.

In other realms, academics preached the sermon of integration of all knowledge, yet continued to devise curricula which fractionated all learning and failed to achieve the educational goals they so righteously proclaimed. Teachers acted to suppress the surge of "student power" yet took up the cudgel of the strike for their own, not just the public's welfare. And peculiar was the behavior of both labor leaders and labor members who condemned the strike behavior of those on the public payroll while they readily used the same weapon to further their own selfish interests. At the legislative level, legislators, both liberal and conservative, condemned youthful confrontation, sit-ins, and work stoppages while they righteously defended the right of filibuster and the right to slow the legislative process by committee machinations when to do so served their own selfish ends.

In still other regions of adult behavior, human thought and action was even more peculiar. Some professed an unshakable belief in God while other insisted that God was dead. Among the poor, apparently able-bodied people, living in the direst of circumstances, seemed to sit and complain rather than do something to improve their lot when it appeared that the opportunity to do so was provided them. But the everyday behavior of adults was not the only place where conflict and controversy, confusion and contradiction abounded.

---

[7] See Mittelman, James H. (1975). *Ideology and politics in Uganda : from Obote to Amin*. Ithaca, N.Y: Cornell University Press.

Confusion and contradiction pervaded the field of personality and culture theory, possibly more so than any other human realm. As one man, Ludwig von Bertalanffy said, "We have to realize at the start that personality theory is at present a battlefield of contrasting and controversial theories."[8] Another, Morris Stein, stated: "The problem is most pervasive. We encounter it when we survey the various theories of personality and the conflict between the theorists."[9] And Carl Rogers, writing particularly in respect to psychotherapy but touching on a theme applicable to all psychology, said:

> "The field of psychotherapy is in a mess. Therapists are not in agreement as to their goals or their aim in therapy. They are in deep disagreement as to the theoretical structures which would contain their work. They cannot agree as to whether a given experience for a client is healing or destructive, growth promoting or damaging. They are not in agreement as to what constitutes a successful outcome of their work. They cannot agree as to what constitutes failure. They diverge sharply in their views as to the promising directions for the future. It seems as though the field is completely chaotic and divided."[10]

On the cultural side, the anthropologists and sociologists presented no less confusion. Leslie White criticized Franz Boas for a cultural anthropology that he saw as "a philosophy of hodgepodgism."[11] Yet this same Leslie White insisted that investigators were ridiculous when they sought to learn whether the origin and the development of culture was an expression of human needs. He insisted that, "culture is a thing *sui generis*, that culture can be explained only in terms of culture."[12] Yet Malinowski, Parsons

---

[8] von Bertalanffy, Ludwig (1968). *General System Theory: Foundations, Development, Applications.* George Braziller, Inc., p. 105.

[9] Stein, Morris (1963). Explorations in Typology. In Robert W. White (Ed.). *The Study of Lives: Essays on Personality in Honor of Henry A. Murray.* Atherton Press, A Division of Prentice-Hall, Inc. p. 283.

[10] Rogers, Carl (1963). Phychotherapy Today or Where do we go from here? *American Journal of Psychotherapy.* Vol XVII, No. 1, p. 5-16.

[11] White, Leslie (1949).

[12] White, Leslie (1966). Social Organization of Ethnological Theory. *Monographs in Cultural Anthropology.* Rice University Studies, 52:4:1-66.

and Shils, and Kluckhohn and Murray among others, brought organismically based needs into their theories of culture.

All in all, conflict and confusion, contradiction and controversy lie everywhere in the world of adult humans. But are these problems reason for despair? Are they reasons for the condemnation of the human being or the designation of them as not mature, weak, immoral, selfish or worse? Is this what these problems are, or is there another explanation?

One could readily agree that such problems are reason for despair if the fears, premises, and the possible misconceptions of those who so see the behavior determined one's views. But before one agrees, some serious questions might be asked.

- Should we accept inferences which may be drawn from a narrow perceptual view—a field of view restricted by limited premises, narrowed by fear and constricted by an incomplete view of human nature?
- Is it perhaps true that those who believe adult human problems evidence only the improper shaping of them, or the baseness of their nature, really misperceive the human being?
- Are those who have concluded we are hopeless—are those who have concluded that we need better shaping—are those who have concluded that human problems are but a perversion of our basic human goodness blinded by interpretations of the past, illusions of the present and terrifying visions of the future?

Can it be that their minds are clouded by conceptions of humanity which may be false? Perhaps we should question the conclusion that our recurrent problems signify depravity or the breakdown of a solid and sound way of life which previously existed. And, perhaps we should question that such behavior signifies a failure to shape us into mature form, or that it is just a perversion of the urge toward maturity in our basic nature.

Suppose, instead, that in another framework, just as tenable (the framework of this book), such behavior could be seen as a positive sign, as a sign of growth rather than decay, as a sign of continuing maturation rather than improper shaping or perversion of our nature, as a sign of movement toward a more viable order rather than as a sign of disintegration of all that is good in life, as a sign of that which is necessary for human nature to survive, rather than the worst that is in it. Would not such a framework be interesting to explore?

For some, this may be strong stuff. It may border not only on heresy but also on the brink of irresponsibility and may seem to have within it more than a tinge of the crackpot. How, one may ask, can I take evidence as has been cited, twist it full around and come out with the bad as a sign of good, the immoral as a sign of growing toward more mature behavior, and the inconsistent as a sign of growth? And, one may ask, isn't this a rather extraordinary manipulation of data, or perhaps even a highly irresponsible and dangerous distortion of fact? How can I do this?

The answer is simple: I work from a different set of premises. I do so because it is not necessary to subscribe to only one set of premises when attempting to understand the behavior in question. Within the premise of some people, what is being said may indeed be a distortion, and what I am asserting will be a reprehensible and reproachable suggestion. But since there are other premises upon which understanding can be based, I intend to question whether it is wise to stay only in customary frames of reference when interpreting the adult behavior under consideration.

There are three major explanations of man's controversial behavior: the behavioristic, the psychoanalytic, and the humanistic or Third Force. Each is based on a premise consisting of three parts.

The Behaviorist Conception

The behaviorists and social learning theorists explain that controversial behavior results from improper shaping or modeling. Their point of view is as follows.

 1. The human is first and foremost a moldable organism.
 2. Moldable humanity can be shaped into good form or bad form provided one
     a. knows what to shape it into;
     b. knows how to do the shaping; that is, learns 'the powerful science of behavior'; and
     c. uses 'the powerful science of behavior' properly.

3. The immature behavior that has troubled so many people is evidence of
   a. failure, over time, to have experimentally determined the proper way to behave; and
   b. failure to learn the powerful science of behavior for shaping man (a Skinnerian phrase) and/or failure to use it properly (William Blatz).

This Lockean, Watsonian, Blatzian, Skinnerian, Bandurian, Walterian, Ullmanian, Krasnerian, Hawkinean point of view is the most prevalent and most enticing explanation of the immature behavior of people. It is the explanation of the American psychological establishment, the Russian Academy of Pedagogical Sciences and the Israeli Kibbutz. And it is the point of view which led Chairman Mao to say: "The outstanding thing about China's people is that they are poor and blank. On a blank sheet of paper, free from any mark, the freshest and most beautiful characters can be written."[13]

This is a most appealing explanation of the aberrations of human behavior. It appeals, at one and the same time, to the Utopians, the escapists, the simplistic-ists, and the moralists. For the Utopian it provides the way to the dream, not necessarily tomorrow or next year, but someday. The mature life for tomorrow is just waiting to be fashioned from within this conception of human nature. We need only search until we find it and then shape people to fit its design.

The escapists find it appealing because it enables them to place responsibility, particularly for their own aberrant behavior, outside of the self. From the reinforcement and modeling behavioristic point of view, the behavior troubling people has its source in what the shapers do or fail to do, and in no way does the responsibility for it lie within those whose behavior is condemned. It lies, by and large, in the molders of behavior, particularly in the parents who use behavior modification techniques to mold the human organism.

Robert Hawkins attests to this when he says in his paraphrase of Skinner:

"... it is not a matter of whether parents will use behavior modification techniques to produce mature

---

[13] Chairman Mao Tse-Tung. "Introducing a Co-operative." April 15, 1958.

behavior, but rather whether they will use these techniques unconsciously with unknown, unchosen results, or use them consciously, efficiently and consistently to develop the [mature] qualities they choose for their children."[14]

From the social behavioristic point of view, immature behavior has its source in improper modeling. The modeler does not properly take care to shape his or her self before placing that self in front of the one whose behavior he or she desires to influence. Those who seek quick answers to troublesome human behavior are enticed by the theoretical simplicity and Utopian possibilities in the behavioristic conception of humanity. All the troublesome behavior of humanity will waft away if you decide or learn what to shape a person into, learn how to do the shaping, and apply the rules for shaping properly. This is indeed an appealing solution to the many problems of mankind. Unfortunately, the behaviorists tend too quickly to glide past how complex it is, even within their conception, to implement into action what to teach, how to teach it, and how to properly do the teaching.

Seldom does one find, in behavioristic popularizations of their point of view, what they say in their professional articles. Seldom do they tell the larger public how their own conception says it may take a thousand years, and many abortive attempts along the way, before *even they* arrive on the threshold of what *they* believe mature human behavior should be. Seldom do they lay before the unsophisticated public that Skinnerian principles apply to an organism *in want,* and only to one confined in a Skinnerian box of life where only limited choice and limited opportunity to behave are provided. Reinforcement behavioristic principles are indeed *Beyond Freedom and Dignity*, in the Skinnerian sense, because they derive from studies in which the shaper restricts the degrees of behavioral freedom of the organisms being molded.

Beyond these problems with the behavioristic conception are still others which they tend to gloss over. Learning to do it properly is a complex business, so complex that merely learning how to reinforce behavior is very difficult. It is so difficult that few can be expected to properly learn to use this aspect of behavior

---

[14] Hawkins, Robert P. (1972). It's time we taught the young how to be good parents (and don't you wish we'd started a long time ago?). *Psychology Today,* 6, 11:28-40.

technology. Thus, there is considerable doubt that their attempts to implement their conception of maturity into action will make any real inroads upon the problems of humans.

This is true, also, of the social behavioral point of view, the point of view that promotes modeling as the way to tomorrow's mature behavior. Seldom do the social behaviorists point out the basic modeling problem: *To implement modeling requires an almost inhuman capability of people to monitor and change their own behavior so as to be sure the proper mode is placed before the imitator.* So, even this seemingly very simple solution to the production of maturity has incredible complexities in it.

But before you agree with this analysis, be careful. There is a way to conceive of implementing it into action. In fairness to the behavioristic conceptions, one can conceive that the few knowledgeable ones can do the shaping of the molders and thus effectuate this point of view. Thereby, the problems I have mentioned could be circumvented. However, one does not need to elaborate on the complexity of striving to accomplish the behavioristic aim by this means.

One of the values in the behavioristic conception, although this value creates a paradox, is that it does provide the escapist the opportunity to assign responsibility for his or her immature behavior to sources other than his/her own. Yet this same conception provides surcease for the moralist. Theoretically, it assigns the responsibility for the origin of troublesome behavior to the modeler or the shaper, but, ultimately in most adults, it places the responsibility for change in the person who is troubled or troublesome.

This can be seen in two lines of evidence. First, behavior technologists say that in most people, the final decision to submit the self for change lies in him or her whose behavior is troublesome. Secondly, the plethora of self-change manuals spawned by its protagonists is evidence of their belief that immature people should and can change themselves. But these basics in the behavioristic conception are less serious than those which stem not from *commissions* but from *omissions* within the conception.

Blithely, the reinforcement behaviorists cast aside any suggestion that new forms of consciousness emerge over time and changing conditions of existence. They do not see emergence as a worthy explanation of any of the things which keep happening to people. As one of them, Howard Kendler says: "Each person does not proceed through a predetermined sequence of stages, but instead learns important habits in certain situations in life."[15] Such statements, typical of behaviorists, suggest they are filtering out, rejecting, or oblivious to the reams of information suggesting *emergent stages* in the development of both individual and cultural man.

The non-emergent position is a tenable one to explore, but how does it explain the appearance of Black Muslim thinking in those in which it originally appeared, or Consciousness III[16] as a way that so many who were shaped to think otherwise now think today. Explanations based on accidentally chained responses, accidentally reinforced, or on accidental modeling are just not satisfactory ways to explain these changes in some of our people. Furthermore, how can such explanations handle the fact that public school teachers, once notorious bastions of respect for authority, suddenly turned to the strike cudgel in defiance of authority?[17] How does it explain that these previously authority dependent, authority respecting, authority promoting people suddenly came to demand, over and above salary, benefits and job protection, the right of autonomy in the performance of their jobs?

Beyond this there is a much more glaring omission in one of the behaviorist conceptions of man. It is particularly true of *reinforcement* behaviorism. This version of behaviorism expresses that reinforcement is the way to set proper behavior into man. Yet these behaviorists will admit that reinforcements oft times lose their potency for strengthening behavior, and they do so without having any adequate explanation of why this occurs. Beyond this, they do not sufficiently explain the casting aside of old values by those who have received much payoff for living by them. The behavioral position just does not explain a person's switch from one

---

[15] Kendler, Howard (1968). *Basic Psychology*, (2nd ed.). New York: Appleton-Century-Crofts, p. 497. [Slightly modified by Graves. The actual text is: "Each person does not proceed through a predetermined sequences of stages, but instead learns important habits in certain situations *of his early* life." ed.]

[16] From Reich, Charles (1970). *The Greening of America*. New York: Random House.

[17] Reference to the 1968 New York City teachers' strike which began with dismissals in the Ocean Hill–Brownsville area of Brooklyn and turned into a conflict involving workers' rights as well as race. See: Mayer, Martin (1968). *The Teachers Strike*. New York: Harper & Row, and Podair, Jerald E. (2002). *The Strike that Changed New York: Blacks, Whites, and the Ocean Hill-Brownsville Crisis*. New Haven: Yale University Press.

reinforcing agent to another—a problem which brings forth a third, though related, omission.

There is no way in the behavioristic conception of human nature to hypothesize the class of reinforcements to which one might switch when behavior is no longer responsive to that which previously brought it forth. The behavioristic conception offers no solid intelligence as to why a person shifts from what reinforces selfish, hedonistic, bodily-based values to that which reinforces altruistic, sacrificial, spiritual values. In other words, it does not explain the Piaget-like shifting of moral behavior which is found in the well-replicated cross-cultural studies of the Lawrence Kohlberg group. Or as Salvatore Maddi says in summing up his argument against the *total adequacy* of the behavioristic conception of human behavior:

> "To say that all behavior is the result of learning and then say nothing about developmentally common themes as to what is learned, is to do very little in the attempt to understand human life. To say that learning is dependent upon reinforcers and to 'give no basis for discovering or identifying reinforcers except as learning actually occurs,' is to damn us to a minute analysis of every event of human life that amounts to searching for a needle in a haystack."[18]

The *Homo Homini Lupus*:[19]
The Psychoanalytic Conception

Another conception of man which offers an explanation of his recurring immaturities is the *homo homini lupus* conception. This is the conception of certain religionists such as the Calvinists, the Orthodox, and early Freudian psychoanalysts. In this conception, man's recurrent problems are again mainly failures to transform immaturity to maturity. But it is based on a different premise, again consisting of three parts.

---

[18] Maddi, Salvatore R. (1976). *Personality Theories: A Comparative Analysis* (3rd Ed.). Homewood, IL: The Dorsey Press, p. 560.
[19] "Man is a wolf to man." Plautus, later cited by Thomas Hobbes.

1. Beneath it all, the human is a beast driven by original sin, aggressiveness, and a death instinct with a moderate capacity for conversion.
2. Since humans are so constituted, civilized human behavior, good values, mature behavior, can only be superimposed on people and, therefore, they must constantly be monitored and controlled lest their animalistic tendencies override their humanistic ones.
3. Ultimately these mature values, Judeo-Christian ethics, Buddhist principles, or the like can be fashioned in people so any failure to show them is evidence of faulty superimposition or lessened vigilance.

Logically within this three-part premise, current human problems are evidence of failure to properly transform, or of lessened vigilance, or in the parlance of psychology, permissiveness. In many respects this is a tenable explanation of recurrent immature behavior. But this explanation, like the behaviorist conception, is quite time bound in its origin and interpretation. It arose in times shortly before the birth of Christ and was a major explanation of human immaturity up through the third decade of the twentieth century. These were times when the conditions for human existence were quite precarious. Then nearly all men lived in a world of scarcity, and in a world of no chance for abundance.

Thus, it may be that this 'mine own self interest' concept of human nature is quite correct for explaining behavior when humans are in a state of want. But is it an adequate explanation when basic want is not the center of the human scene? It would make good sense for humans to behave in a selfish, not other-concerned way, if truly their lives depended on it; but the question is: Does this point of view explain the behavior of people whose life is more one of abundance than of want or threat of want? Does it handle the evidence that in sexually less-rigid youth one finds less prejudice, less material concern, less selfishness, and fewer signs of egocentrism?

It may seem odd to some, but very true to others, that a repeated complaint of the establishment toward some who dissent is, "*They* trust too much. *They* are going to lead us to complete anarchy if *they* get power and go around trusting people the way they do." As a former chairman of my academic division once said to me, "Graves, ever since you came here I have had a feeling there was something wrong with you. In today's meeting, I figured out what it is. You have a tendency to trust people—maybe not all—but you do have a tendency to trust. Don't you realize what will happen in this school if we trust *anything* those other people say?"

This is indeed a problem with the *homo homini lupus* conception of human nature. Even the very best in people, such as lack of prejudice, less materialism, less selfishness, trusting and the like, is always suspected to be bad. But beyond this, as shown in the annals of the psychoanalytic world, lies still more damning evidence. The Hartmans, the Krises, the Lowensteins, the Eriksons —all later day psychoanalysts—have found the early, orthodox psychoanalytic view not to fit many people living in the middle decades of the twentieth century.

The *homo homini lupus* conception of human nature does explain some of the troubling behavior of humans. One can see it in the behavior of those who go to any end to achieve, hold onto, and exercise power positions.

In many places where the eyes might fall, one can see Machiavelli's view: "For it may be said of men in general that they are ungrateful, voluble, dissemblers, anxious to avoid danger and covetous of gain ..."[20] But is this an immaturity or a failure to properly transform the bad into good? Or, is there another point of view? Does the *total evidence* support the Calvinist assertion that:

> "... Infants themselves are rendered liable to punishment by their sinfulness, not by the sinfulness of others. For though they have not yet produced the fruits of their iniquity, yet they have the seed of it within them, even their whole nature is as it were a seed of sin..."[21]

Or, must we include in our conceptualizing matrix what happens in man's behavior when the "sinfulness of others" is removed? What about that which happens when the "sinfulness of others" such as demeaning, degrading organizational practices are removed? What about all the evidence as to the appearance of positive work behavior when job enrichment supplants humanly demeaning job simplification as found by the Fred Herzberg group? Can this evidence be explained within the *homo homini lupus* conception of humanity? It is doubtful. Therefore, as with the

---

[20] Machiavelli, Niccolo (1903). *The Prince*. Chapter 17, Translation by Luigi Ricci.
[21] Calvin, John (1949). *Institutes of the Christian Religion*. (8th Ed.). Translated by John Allen. Grand Rapids: Eerdmans, I, 1, 8.

behavioristic position, one must question the total validity of this pessimistic conception of human nature. But in so doing one must not get lost on the other side, the side of the Humanistic or Third Force conception of the human being.

The Humanistic Conception: The Human is Neutral or Good

This third major explanatory conception of man is that of Condorcet and that of the early writings of Jean-Jacques Rousseau. It is the conception of Thomas Paine, Thomas Jefferson, and, in psychology, most who would call themselves humanists. Again, it bases its explanation of immature adult behavior on a premise consisting of three parts.

1. The human is either basically neutral or possibly an active, rational and positively good organism driven by an instinctive inner urge to come to know and to express his or her inherent potentials. Or, in the words of Abraham Maslow, "This inner nature, as much as we know of it so far, is definitely not 'evil,' but is either what we adults in our culture call 'good' or else it is neutral. The most accurate way to express this is to say that it is 'prior to' good and evil."[22]

2. Because humanness is neutral or active, rational and decent human behavior will be "good" unless it is deflected from its natural course by anti-human ways. Evil behavior is reactive rather than instinctive.

3. Therefore, immature adult behavior is evidence that man has been canalized into bad ways or has been deflected from behaving in accordance with his or her active, possibly rational and good nature.

This conception does not deny that humans can do some immature things, but its explanation is that humans do them in defense of the need to express their inner nature. Again as Maslow says:

---

[22] Maslow, Abraham (1962). *Toward a Psychoogy of Being*, Princeton, N.J.: D. Van Nostrand Company, Inc. p. 181.

"My opinion is that the weight of the evidence so far indicates that indiscriminately destructive hostility is reactive because uncovering therapy reduces it, and changes its quality into healthy self-affirmation, forcefulness, selective hostility, self-defense, righteous indignation, etc. In any case, the ability to be aggressive and angry is found in all self-actualizing people who are able to let it flow forth freely when the external situations "calls for" it."[23]

Thus, according to Maslow, immature adult behavior is defensive, reactive behavior. It is not from an inner wickedness in man. The critics of this point of view object not only to its conceptual looseness but to its idealistic conception of human nature. As one of these critics, Theodore Millon says:

"... The notion that man would be a constructive rational and socially conscious being, were he free of the malevolent distortions of society, seems not only sentimental but invalid. There is something grossly naive in exhorting man to live life to the fullest and then expecting socially beneficial consequences."[24]

Personally, I cannot accept that Millon's words, as expressed, are a valid criticism of the humanistic conception of human nature. His last sentence, in the quote above, too obviously extends from the *homo homini lupus* conception, a point of view I have already dismissed as not totally adequate for explaining human behavior. But rejection of this type of criticism does not mean that the conceptual basis is accepted—not at all, because I do have my objections to it.

Above all else, it is the conceptual looseness in the point of view to which I object—a looseness which makes it impossible to comprehend much of human behavior from within its framework. This is so in at least four ways. The first stems from Maslowian words as "... the ability to be aggressive and angry is found in self-actualizing people."[25] This type of statement, plus the admission that man can act in horrible ways, says to me that one of the potentials in man's nature—though Maslow chose to emphasize

---

[23] Maslow, Abraham H. (1962 &1968). *Toward a Psychology of Being* (2nd Ed.). Princeton, D. van Nostrand Company, Inc., p. 195.
[24] Millon, Theodore (1967). *Theories of Psychopathology*. Philadelphia: W.B. Saunders Co., p. 10.
[25] Ibid., (Maslow, p. 195).

calling it *ability*—is for bad behavior. No substitution of words, no semantic machination can wash away this conceptual looseness.

Secondly, it is absolutely imperative that any person seeking an explanation for man's behavior takes cognizance of another conceptually loose aspect of the humanistic position. Namely, if man is neutral or good, then how do the bad ways come to be? How does badness arise out of neutrality or goodness? Until the humanistic conceptualizers explain this better than as a reaction to barriers, their explanation of human ways must be suspect.

To understand the third conceptual problem in the humanistic position one must know that they divide human needs into two large categories: the deficiency or deficit needs and the abundance or growth needs. In respect to the former, immature humans behave in order *to get,* to get what they need to meet physiological needs, to get safety, to get love, belonging, approval and the like. In respect to the latter, the abundance or growth needs, one behaves in order *to be,* to become that which one is, in order to *express* his inherent potentials, to express the genetic blueprint. Within this need conception, they go on to derive, at least as currently stated, that any deficiency or deficit-oriented behavior is 'bad' or at least immature behavior except in the chronologically immature, as demonstrated by Maslow's words.

> "Immaturity can be contrasted with maturity from the motivational point of view, as the process of gratifying the deficiency needs in the proper order. Maturity or self-actualization, from this point of view, means to transcend the deficiency needs."[26]

Thus,

> "The psychological health of the chronologically immature is called healthy growth. The psychological health of the adult is called variously, self-fulfillment, emotional maturity, individuation, productiveness, self-actualization, authenticity, full humanness, etc."[27]

Unfortunately, there is a serious problem within this conception of healthy growth and/or maturity. It requires one to conclude that even successful deficiency oriented behavior in an

---

[26] Maslow, Abraham H. (1962 &1968). *Toward a Psychology of Being* (2nd Ed.). Princeton: D. van Nostrand Company, Inc., p. 202.
[27] Ibid., (Maslow, p. 196-197).

adult who lives in bad conditions for existence or the behavior of an adult who must struggle for need satisfaction is immature. In no ways does the humanistic conception of maturity deal with the question: Can there not be a mature way of adapting to a world in which necessity requires a deficiency need orientation? To avoid labeling many forms of man's behavior as immature, the humanists must reword the concept of actualization or include as mature the coping behavior of adults living in less than favorable human circumstances. Or as H.A. Witkin says, they must deal with the fact that:

> "... At any level of differentiation varied modes of integration are possible, although more complex integration may be expected with more differentiation. Adjustment is mainly a function of effectiveness of integration—that is, a more or less harmonious working together of the parts of the system with each other and of the system of the whole with its environment. Adequate adjustment is to be found at any level of differentiation, resulting from integrations effective for that level, although the nature of adjustment that may be considered adequate varies from level to level."[28]

The fourth conceptually loose aspect of humanistic psychology stems particularly from those humanists who think similarly to Carl Rogers. These humanists propose that need satisfaction from unconditional positive regard leads automatically to higher-level, more humanistic behavior. Those who think like Rogers break from the Maslowian position that frustration is necessary in life. They assert that the fulfillment of man's lower level needs leads automatically to the emergence of higher-level, more humanistic behavior.

They should consider that lower-level needs are just as much a part of being human as higher-level needs. To set off the higher needs in the Maslowian hierarchy as human needs, while the lower-level needs are seen as something else, is logical mish-mosh. But this criticism of this conceptual problem is trivial in comparison to their position that the only road to mature behavior is through need gratification brought about by unconditional positive regard.

---

[28] Witkin, H.A. (1962). *Psychological Differentiation: Studies in Development.* New York: Wiley, p. 10.

I will accept that need gratification is part of the way to mature behavior, but the evidence just does not support that it is *the road* to mature humanism. This position is just not explanatory of tribes like the Tasaday on the island of Mindanao.[29] Apparently, from what evidence we have, this tribe whose lower-level needs seem to have been relatively satisfied, for how long no one knows, still lives in a most primitive form of existence. They are reported as warm, friendly, compassionate people, full of love and interpersonal understanding. Yet, in their life, there is certainly no evidence of fulfilling their genetic blueprint, no evidence of their being fully functioning or self-actualizing persons. Thus, there must be more that brings forth higher-level behavior than just unconditional positive regard or lower-level need gratification. *Need satisfaction, alone, seems more to fixate* the behavior of man than to foster his development.

This brings us to the heart of this weakness in the humanistic position, a matter which is one aspect of the central core of this book. Even if need satisfaction *is the road* to higher-level behavior, the humanistic position does not:

- adequately map the road from lower-level, less mature to higher-level more mature behavior,
- adequately describe the means by which the road is to be traveled, or
- adequately handle the problem that there may be mature forms of behavior for less differentiated human beings.

Therefore many of the adult behaviors which so often trouble people would be classified as immature by the humanists when it is indeed possible there are mature ways of behaving for an adult human who has emerged only to a less differentiated psychological state. Thus, this Third Force view, like the others examined, seems to fall short of adequately conceptualizing the concept of maturity.

---

[29] Nance, John (1975). *The Gentle Tasaday: A Stone Age People in the Philippine Rain Forest.* Harcourt, Brace & Jovanovich.

The Emergent-Cyclical Levels of Existence Conception (E-C or ECLET)

Logically within the premises of first, second or third force psychologies, behavior such as I have mentioned represents either a breakdown of man's values and/or a failure to develop the values of a truly mature human being. But these are not the only premises from which we can look for conceptualization. There is another rapidly developing point of view based on a different three-part premise which casts a different light upon many so-called human immaturities. It is a marriage of the cognitive-developmental and existential systems of thought. I call it the Emergent-Cyclical Levels of Existence point of view (E-C). This premise holds that:

1. man's nature is not a set thing: it is ever-emergent, an open system, not a closed system.
2. man's nature evolves by saccadic, quantum-like jumps from one steady state system to another; and
3. man's psychology changes as the system emerges in new form with each quantum-like jump to a new steady state of being.

My version of this developing point of view is a revised, enlarged and, in certain critical aspects, new version of a hierarchical systems perspective, one of whose uniquenesses is that it is infinite rather than finite in character. According to this view, I am proposing the following in this book:

The psychology of the adult human being is an unfolding, ever-emergent process marked by subordination of older behavior systems to newer, higher order systems. The mature person tends to change his psychology continuously as the conditions of his existence change. Each successive stage or level of existence is a state through which people may pass on the way to other states of equilibrium. When a person is centralized in one of the states of equilibrium, he has a psychology which is particular to that state. His emotions, ethics and values, biochemistry, state of neurological activation, learning-systems, preference for education, management and psychotherapy are all appropriate to that state. If he were centralized in some other state he would think, feel and be motivated in manners appropriate to that state. He would have biochemical characteristics and a state of neurological activation particular to it. When in a certain state, he would have opened only certain systems for coping and learning. Thus, he would respond most positively to education, management, and therapy which is congruent with that state. And he would have to respond negatively to forms of education, management and therapy not appropriate to the state of his centralization.

An individual person may not be equipped genetically or constitutionally to change in the normal upward direction if the conditions of his existence become more favorable. Or, he may be genetically or constitutionally, even morphologically, prone to settle into or stay in a particular state unless extraordinary measures can be instituted to change the genetic, constitutional or morphologic disposition. He may move, given certain conditions (I see six of them) through a hierarchically ordered series of behavior systems infinitely on so long as his life exists, or he may stabilize and live out his lifetime at any one or a combination of the levels in the hierarchy. He may even regress to a position lower in the hierarchy. He may show the behavior of a level in a predominantly positive or predominantly negative fashion.

Thus, the theory to be presented in this book says an adult lives in a potentially open system of needs, values, aspirations, biochemistry, neurological activation, ways of learning, thinking, and the like, but he often settles into what approximates a closed system. When he is centralized within any level, he has only the degrees of behavioral freedom afforded him at that level. *If* the necessary conditions arise and he moves to another level, he lives by another set of psycho-organismic principles and will react negatively to the way he was previously managed. Thus, the behaviors cited at the beginning of this chapter can be interpreted within this framework as normal attempts on the part of humans to live according to their level of emergence rather than as they are interpreted when viewed from within the other frameworks I have examined.

If by now your opinions differ from mine, it is probably because of our premises. There is no doubt that other conceptions of man exist, and that other explanations of man's troubling behaviors stem from them. But from another angle of observation one can question that a fully adequate explanation of man's recurrent troubles has arisen during man's time on earth. From this angle of observation, one would have to doubt the comprehensive worth of some of the explanations which have come to be from other conceptions of man.

So, for the purposes of discussion, let this position be posed:

   a. that the data of history do not support that the recurrent problems of man are primarily signs of immature behavior; and
   b. that a different frame of reference allows one to interpret the behavior distressing to so many as necessary behavior, as a part of the laws of nature and as a heartening sign of man's growth and capacity for survival as an organism.

Actually, the position I shall present in this book is not based on what I know is the true nature of man. I do not possess such knowledge, nor does anyone else. The argument is based on a deduction, not without considerable evidence to support it, that there is a conception of adult humanity which allows one to interpret the recurrently disturbing behavior as necessary. And, the argument is that if this conception has substance, we should be more than pleased with what so many call immoral, unethical, and immature behavior. And the argument is that if this conception has substance, it might be well to understand it more fully and disseminate it more widely because in it may be not only new understandings of man's nature, but new insights into many of man's problems.

However, in our approach to the new we must not, on the way, destroy the old. We must incorporate it in the new because to me, as to David Elkind, "... it seems rather fruitless and unproductive to contrast theories which are more likely to be complimentary than contradictory."[30] Whether we are talking about Skinner or Freud, the blank slate or *homo homini lupus*, or a conception based on the goodness of man, "it is likely that each theory carries a certain measure of truth."[31] So, if we are to have a meaningful psychology of adult man, it must depict man as the being he is—as one who values, as one whose values change in peculiar ways, as one whose values rise from pylons rooted in the deep recesses of his biological

---

[30] Elkind, David (1971). Cognitive Growth Cycles in Mental Development. *Nebraska Symposium on Motivation, 1971.* Lincoln, NE: University of Nebraska Press.

[31] Ibid., Elkind.

nature. It must accept that in some manner all the established systems of psychology somehow represent the whole. Each of them, no matter how strange it may seem, is neither right nor wrong, but is a psychological datum, a part of the whole. But we cannot accept that an eclectic selection from each system is a way to the whole, because such a selection would disrupt the partial whole. The whole is the *all* of each, not the *best* of each. No condescending mixture of parts will be sufficient to represent the larger whole. There can only be one psychology of man in which somehow all the psychologies must be represented; and the body of this book is a suggestion in that direction.

But how did this framework come to be? What is its suggested nature? And what are its implications to *man in search of himself*,[32] and in search of new avenues of approach to his problems? Let us look first at how the framework of this book came to be.

---

[32] Likely paraphrase of Rollo May, "Man's Search for Himself."

CHAPTER 2

An Approach for Investigating the Problem

The emergent cyclical levels of existence conception of adult personality and cultural institutions began in a simple fashion. It started when I surmised that some of our adult problems exist because our means for managing them are based on erroneous conceptions of: 1) the psychological development of the adult human being; and, 2) the psychological development of the species *Homo sapiens*.

After years of working with adult behavioral problems, I concluded that erroneous conceptions of the psychological development of the adult and the psychological development of the species were producing more problems for us than they were producing effective means for coping with them. Therefore, I decided to consider that our management of adult behavior might be more effective if it were based on some conception of the psychological development of the adult individual other than the systematized conceptions then in existence. Particularly, it seemed our management of adult behavior might be better if our managerial means were derived from:

1. some conception more in line with our current knowledge of adult human behavior, and
2. some conception more inclusive of our recent information as to the organismic psychological nature of the human being.

Some Problems with Current Conceptions of Adult Human Behavior

Inge M. Ahammer, Paul B. Baltes and K. Warner Shaie, William Looft, Robert Havighurst and other Life Span investigators, as they are currently wont to call themselves, have reviewed, summarized, criticized and offered suggestions in respect to the existing conceptions of adult behavior. And, Joseph Katz and Nevitt Sanford have joined them in expressing dissatisfaction with all current conceptions of adult psychological development.[33]

Ahammer, particularly, has offered a statement of dissatisfaction when saying:

> "Adult development has typically been neglected by developmental psychologists
>
> 1. because of the psychoanalytic domination in the field of child psychology within the notion that personality traits are established in the first few years of life and only modifications thereof occur in the adult years;
>
> 2. because of the domination of the biological growth maturity model in the field of life-span psychology with the assumption that adulthood is a period of stability or maturity without systematic behavior change (see models by Buhler, 1933; Kuhlen, 1959); and
>
> 3. developmental state models, such as those of Piaget and Kohlberg, similarly preclude the study of adult development since they are tied to a maturational concept of development and since ... "it is not immediately obvious ... that there is a biological process indigenous to the adult portion of the life span that could impose such definite and strong constraints on (behavior) change (as there is in childhood)" (Flavell 1970, p. 279). These theories by definition conceived of adult behavior change as the stabilization of earlier achieved behavior change rather than as development to new qualitatively higher stages (Kohlberg, 1969; Kohlberg and Kramer, 1969)."[34]

---

[33] All of these investigators are in Baltes, Paul B. and Schaie, Warner, et al. (1973). *Life-Span Developmental Psychology*. Personality and Socialization Academic Press.

[34] Ahammer, Inge, in Baltes, Paul B. and Schaie, Warner, et al. (1973). *Life-Span Developmental Psychology*. Personality and Socialization Academic Press, p. 254.

Both Katz and Sanford agree that no conceptualization of adult behavior exists which includes the more recent information on the phenomenon of psychological growth in adults. In pointing this out Katz says: "The lives of some people show a pattern of continuing development not just in their teens but continuing into the thirties, forties, fifties and beyond."[35]

And Sanford, working with the same theme, says it is his observation that conceptual psychologists have overlooked an important point, namely, that psychological development can only be understood as a part of a continuing process of development not necessarily reaching a peak at 22, or thereabout, and then automatically sloping downhill to decay. He spotlights this problem by saying:

"Further elaboration and integration of personality can occur at any age. An adult's readiness for change and the occurrence of events that can upset equilibrium and induce new forms of behavior which are then integrated within a more complex structure are highly individualized matters. Our understanding of a particular adult's potential for further development and of how he or she might be assisted in overcoming and the various internal and external barriers to development is helped little by knowledge of psychological development in children."[36]

These words of Katz, Ahammer, et. al., point to definite deficiencies in the existing conceptualizations of the developmental psychology of the human adult. They do not point clearly to why this conceptual problem exists.

As I see it, the major reason for the lack of a more inclusive developmental psychology, one that

(1) includes the existing developmental psychologies in its framework,
(2) portrays adult development to continue into the forties, fifties, and beyond; and
(3) is potentially a developmental psychology not only of childhood and adulthood but of the life-span of the *species*,

is that we have not incorporated in our conceptual frameworks, whether they be developmental in character or otherwise, both some recent and

---

[35] Katz, Joseph in Baltes, Paul B. and Schaie, Warner, et al. (1973). *Life-Span Developmental Psychology*. Personality and Socialization Academic Press, p. 1.

[36] Sanford, Nevitt in Baltes, Paul B. and Schaie, Warner, et al. (1973). *Life-Span Developmental Psychology*. Personality and Socialization Academic Press, p. 2.

some earlier information as to the nature of the species *Homo sapiens* and its psychology.

Information Overlooked by Most Conceptualizers

Let me cite a few bits of information more or less overlooked by most conceptualizers of human psychology, and particularly adult psychology.

First, there is the information which indicates, as some of the authorities cited above said, that psychological development is a process which does not plateau or cease in the thirties, forties, fifties, and beyond. And there is the related information that the psychological development of the species has been preceding since its origin and is still in process today.

Second, there is the information pointing to the two-sided, objective-subjective aspects of man's neurological and psychological nature. Almost all conceptualizers have failed to weave this information into their systems. We have a plethora of one-sided objective, rational, positive conceptions of human behavior, but we have only a few, like those of Carl Jung and Vikor Frankl, wherein attempts have been made to include both the objective and subjective side of man's psychological being in a single conceptual framework.

A third body of information not adequately woven into existing conceptual frameworks is that indicating the hierarchical structuring of the human brain. John Sutherland[37] points to this when he says that a significant problem in conceptual psychology, largely overlooked, is that brains in both animals and humans must be viewed as hierarchical systems wherein causality tends to be unique in each system. He punctuates this by saying that the *modus operandi* associated with the brain stem does not imply knowledge of the cerebellum any more than knowledge of lower-order cognitive systems implies anything approaching knowledge of the cortical system. This type of information has just not been adequately woven into any of our psychologies let alone developmental ones.

A fourth bit of information passed over or overlooked suggests that the objective-subjective aspect of development is both hierarchical and cyclical. This is left unnoted in most conceptual systems. An outstanding exception is the work of Gerald Heard.

---

[37] Sutherland, John Derg (1959) *Psychoanalysis and Contemporary Thought.* New York Grove Press.

A fifth kind of information not sufficiently utilized suggests that the brain is not only hierarchically ordered, but systemically so. It seems that Gordon Bronson is one of the few persons who has called attention to this aspect of psychological brain organization. Bronson has not utilized it to further the conceptualization of adult behavior, but he does call attention to the systemic organization of neurological structures, learning processes, and critical periods of development in childhood.

A sixth bit of information passed by or overlooked by conceptualizers suggests human behavior is infinite rather than oriented toward some ultimate goal. This is of singular importance to conceptualizers because it requires one to question all conceptualizations which include in their framework concepts of ultimate fulfillment, *the* mature personality or *the* perfectibility of man. It appears to be only people like Ahammer and other social learning theorists who include this information in their conceptualizations.

And, finally, there is that bit of information which has been with us since the 1850's—the information about the extraordinary large size of the *Homo sapiens* brain. This fact led Alfred Russel Wallace to ask Darwin to explain, within Darwin evolutionary thinking, why the human brain is the size that it is.[38] By and large, Darwin ignored Wallace's question. And, by and large, our theories of adult development still ignore it today. We just do not have a developmental theory which explains, within its construction, why the brain of man contains far more structures than are necessary to provide, in a Darwinian sense, for the survival of the species.

A Suggested Social-Learning Substitute

With some of these criticisms of adult psychology in mind, Ahammer has suggested a social-learning paradigmatic substitute for the older conceptions of adult psychology. However, his suggested substitute is based on operant and classical conditioning, a choice which does not, in my judgment, sufficiently utilize all the seven kinds of information which are available to be used. Also Ahammer's social-learning substitute does not meet the suggestions of Looft and Baltes and Shaie[39] as to what a more adequate model of adult psychological development should include. Therefore, it appears that there is need for conceptualization which goes beyond Ahammer and

---

[38] Wallace, Alfred Russel (1891).
[39] Baltes, Paul B. and Schaie, Warner, et al. (1973). *Life-Span Developmental Psychology*. Personality and Socialization Academic Press, p. 339-395.

other past and current theorists. There is need for the development of adult psychological paradigms which meet not only the major criticism of Ahammer (namely that behavior changes throughout life have been neglected), but also depict the character of the development which takes place, how this development proceeds, why it takes place as it does and how this process of development can be influenced. This treatise is an effort in that direction.

Origin of the Study Behind the Emergent-Cyclical Conception

The emergent cyclical, levels of existence conception of adult psychology developed from a number of questions which arose in my mind in 1950-51, and in a series of studies which were begun in 1952.

In 1950-51, I was concerned with the contradiction and conflict, the confusion and controversy which pervaded the field of personality theory. As a means to the end of studying this conflicted state of psychological affairs, I chose to study the conflict and controversy in the area of conceptions of the mature personality. I started to study this area in the age-old way, that is, by examining what other people said was the nature and character of the mature human being. I read many theories in respect thereto, and by and large they suggested:

a. that research should be directed toward ascertaining *that state* or *that psychological condition* which is *the* psychologically mature state or condition, and

b. that research should be directed toward ascertaining what practical means could be utilized to implement *that state* or *that condition* into the people.

The thoughts expressed in the many theories required me to ask whether it is sufficient to assume that the mature personality is a describable state or condition which the human being conceivably can achieve. Or would we be better off if we think that mature personality is a process of becoming rather than the epitome of a state of being? In answer to this question, one must say that it is perfectly proper to assume that the mature personality is a state or a condition which does or can exist. And, it is just as proper to conduct research toward the possible description of the state. Such is, indeed, a legitimate scientific endeavor. In fact, the literature is replete with such endeavors and more.

Lay people and professionals alike raise their children; run their businesses; direct their educational enterprises; conduct their international relations; draw up, lobby for and pass laws; and order their societies so as to produce what is, in their minds, the mature adult personality, the viable business, the mature student, the mature state of national and international affairs, and the proper societal state made up of properly behaving people. The professionals go quite beyond the layperson. They not only conduct studies to ascertain the nature of the mature condition, both individually and societally, but they also write articles or books describing that state or that condition as they view it to be. And they go much further. The professional mental hygienist, the professional business manager, the professional educator, the professional legal expert, or the professional international relations practitioner extends efforts into the realm of therapeutic, managerial, educational, international relations and social welfare practices. They intervene, teach how to intervene, or administer the intervention into the lives of people, the activities of business, the process of adult education, or the practice of international and societal relations. They do so in order to change the psychologically or sociologically less-than-mature state into their conceived-to-be psychologically or sociologically mature state.

These people, these laymen, and these professionals, in lay circles or in professional circles, in mixed circles or in restricted circles, may argue as to what is the 'mature' personality; but seldom do they do that which needs to be done, namely, question whether the state should be considered to exist.

Although I accept that it is proper, for research purposes, to assume the existence of the ultimately mature state, I raise the question as to whether this theoretical state actually can exist? Perhaps the belief of so many people that this state not only exists but also is definable is a belief that is more mythical than true. It seems to me that a thorough investigation of how people conceive of *mature states* might clarify this confused and controversial region of human behavior, and that a clarification of psychological maturity as a process or as a state or a condition might resolve much of the conflict and contradiction in other regions of psychology and culture. Therefore, research toward this end might profitably examine:

1. What are the concepts of psychological maturity which actually exist?
2. Do the existing concepts suggest that psychological maturity should be viewed as a state or a condition, or should it be viewed as a process?
3. What is the actual nature of psychological maturity if research suggests that it is a state or a condition?
4. What is the nature of the process toward psychological maturity if research indicates that it should be viewed as a process?

Then, based upon the research of this point, one could ask:

- if psychological maturity is a state, what does the character of the state tell us about the practice of intervention into human affairs?
- if psychological maturity is a state, how can we diagnose human behavior in respect to that state?
- if psychological maturity is a state, what theory or theories of personality more appropriately relate to the properly- described state which is determined by research?
- if psychological maturity is a state, how can we relate our other knowledge of human behavioral problems indicated by research, to this state?

- if psychological maturity is a process, what does the character of the process tell us about the practice of intervention into human affairs?
- if psychological maturity is a process, how can we diagnose human behavior in accordance with the process?
- if psychological maturity is a process, how can we reconceptualize personality theory in order that it be consonant with the process, or are there theories of personality consonant with the process we might discover?
- if psychological maturity is a process, how can we relate our accumulated knowledge of human behavior, and our approaches to behavioral problems indicated by research, to a reconceptualization of personality based upon the evidence that psychological maturity is a process rather than a state or a condition?

But this was not all that I felt might come from a study of conceptualizations of mature personality. There is yet another set of problems of mature personality which might be clarified by investigation.

The other set of problems seems to arise from some peculiar inferences present in existing conceptualizations of the mature human being. These conceptions infer that a person who cannot take his basic needs for granted, who lives in an insecure world, who is much concerned with lovability or status, whose awareness or comprehension is limited cannot be a mature personality. Such inferences, it seems to me, demand that certain questions be asked. Among them are:

- Should we not consider that there might be something seriously wrong with the ways mature personality is conceptualized if such conceptions lead to the inferences that have just been noted?
- Must not we ask whether we should accept a conception which categorizes most living people as immature personalities?

These questions logically follow the inferences listed above, but beyond them there are other things to be considered.

It is entirely possible, if mature personality is a particular describable state or condition, that the questions above are irrelevant. Mature personality may be a state and, if it is, the decisions made there from must be accepted. However, it is equally possible that many people, dead or living, could be cast erroneously into the immature category simply by the nature of the conception of mature personality. This we can see if we focus on six reference points which are used by most definers of mature personality.

a. The attitude shown by the person toward his own self.
b. The style and degree of self-actualization.
c. The degree of personal integration achieved by the individual.
d. The degree of autonomy achieved by the person.
e. The adequacy of the person's perception of reality.
f. The degree of environmental mastery achieved by the person.

If one accepts, for purposes of argument, that some, or more probably all, of these six points define the mature personality, then he must answer the two questions asked above affirmatively. He must conclude:

1. that almost all biologically mature humans who existed in the past were immature personalities and,
2. that the vast majority of mankind who exist today are also immature personalities.

This he must do because the masses of humans who have lived have shown odd and peculiar attitudes toward their selves. Certainly they have shown a deficiency in self-actualization as the term is used today, although they may have achieved reasonable personal integration. Few alive today or in recent history, and still fewer in remote times, achieved autonomy or possessed an adequate perception of reality, and who knows if we possess one today? And only in very recent times have any number of people, whose total numbers are still few, achieved any reasonable degree of mastery of the environment.

How many people alive on this earth today have the mental hygienist's proper attitude toward the self? How many have approached self-actualization? In fact, is such approachable? Autonomy of the self is certainly lacking in the masses of currently living human beings. And the question of what is an adequate perception of reality is as much a matter for argument as it is a matter of accepted knowledge. Was and is a person psychologically immature because his world did not or does not permit him autonomy? Is the adult human necessarily immature who lives by a false perception of reality? Is it not possible that there is a mature form of existence for the human who cannot be autonomous; for one whose limited knowledge produces false perceptions of reality; for one who because of ignorance possesses peculiar attitudes toward the self?

These are very serious questions. They warrant careful and thorough consideration no matter what is the questioner's purpose. But, for this work, they are far more important because they led to the specific research questions I asked in my studies.

Questions Asked in the Studies

The first formulation of these questions was as follows:

1. How do biologically mature human beings conceive of what is the mature human personality?
2. Do adult humans have basically one identifiable conception of what is the psychologically mature adult?
3. Do adult humans have more than one conception of what is to be conceived of as the mature personality?
4. If they have several conceptions, are the various conceptions classifiable?
5. If the various conceptions are classifiable, how can they be classified?

a) Can they be classified by content? If so, how do they differ from one another in content?
b) Can they be classified structurally? If so, how can they be classified in a structural sense?
c) Can they be classified as to the manner in which they function? If so, how do they differ from one another functionally? How do people who possess the same or different conceptions operate in similar or in dissimilar situations? Do those who profess the same conception of psychological maturity behave similarly in relatively standard situations? Do those who profess different conceptions behave similarly or differently as the situation varies? If they behave similarly, what are the differences?
d) Will there be evidence that one conception of the mature personality stands out as superior to other conceptions of the mature personality?

Specifically the questions asked at the beginning of the series of investigations that led to my revised version of human and adult psychology were worked into the following form:

1. What will be the nature and character of conceptions of psychological maturity, in the biologically mature human being, produced by biologically mature humans who are intelligent but relatively unsophisticated in psychological knowledge in general, and theory of personality in particular?

2. What will happen to a person's characterization of mature human behavior when s/he is confronted with the criticism of his/her point of view by peers who have also developed their own conception of psychologically mature behavior?

3. What will happen to a person's conception of mature human behavior when confronted with the task of comparing and contrasting his/her conception of psychologically mature human personality to those conceptions which have been developed by authorities in the field?

4. Into what categories and into how many categories, if any, will the conceptions of mature human personality produced by intelligent, biologically mature humans fall?
5. If the conceptions are classifiable, how do they compare in content from category to category? How do they compare structurally and how do they compare functionally?
6. If the conceptions are classifiable, how do the people who fall into classes compare behaviorally as observed in quasi-experimental situations and in every day life?
7. If the conceptions are classifiable, how do the people who fall into one class compare to people who fall into other classes on standardized psychological instruments?

The Design of the Research Project

The basic studies which contributed to the development of this book were spread over nine years. Supplementary studies were done over another twelve years. The subjects in the basic studies were students in the author's classes in Normal Personality. Some were full-time day students in a men's college, some were graduate coed students in the field of teacher education and industrial management, and some were students in the evening division of a coeducational college for mature students. Most of the latter two groups had full-time jobs.

The class in which the students were enrolled was a fifteen-week course on The Normal Personality. In most cases this was a second course in Psychology taken by the students. There were more subjects in the lower age groups, and more of the subjects were male than female. However, these facts did not seem to affect appreciably the results of the studies. The investigation began with instructions given to the subjects on the first day of class. The instructions which led to Phase I of a four-phase study were:

Phase 1

During the first four weeks of this semester you will be expected to develop your own personal conception of what is the psychologically mature, biologically mature human being. No reading will be assigned to you during this time, and you are requested to do no reading on this subject during this four-week period. You are to develop your conception from what you now know, from that which you have experienced and from what you now believe.

During class time, we will discuss what personality is considered to be by various authorities and we will discuss what areas of human behavior need be considered as one thinks about what is psychologically mature behavior.

Outside of class you are to work toward the development of your *personal* conception of psychologically mature behavior.

At no time during the semester will I discuss with you what are my personal views about the subject. It is your conception of psychologically mature human behavior with which we will be concerned.

At the end of the first four weeks you will turn in to me your conception of psychologically mature human behavior. And since I must, at the end of five weeks, turn in grades, your conceptions will be graded on the basis of the following four criteria:

1. Breadth of coverage of human behavior.

2. Concurrence with established psychological fact.

3. The internal consistency of the conception.

4. The applicability of the conception.

When you turn your papers in to me at the end of four weeks, they will be read by me, and returned to you at a later class period.[40] You will then spend four weeks in small groups where each of you will, in turn, present and receive criticism of your point of view before and from your peers. After all have been presented and after all have received criticism, you will be required, in the ninth week, to develop a defense or a modification of your point of view elaborating on why you are defending, if you choose to do so, or explaining the reasons for your modification if that be your choice. This paper you will turned in to me at the end of the tenth week and I will return it to you at a later class period.[41]

After the second set of papers is returned, you will be reassigned to small groups in which you, with the groups, will spend the next four weeks studying the conceptions of mature personality which are in the literature. You will study the position of many authorities and you will compare and contrast your position to that of the various authorities. At

---

[40] CWG: The subjects were never aware that copies were made of their productions during this period of time.
[41] CWG: Again, these papers were copied.

the end of this experience, again, you will modify or defend your personal conception and give your reasons why.[42] After you have handed in your final papers, instead of a final written examination, I will first read your paper and then talk with you individually about the total experience.

From this basic design I was provided with three kinds of basic data produced in Phase 1 of the studies:

1. A phenomenological view of certain beliefs of the subjects—beliefs as to the nature of psychologically mature human behavior.
2. a) The reaction of the subject to peer criticism as shown in the modification or the defense of the original position.
   b) The reaction behavior of the subject under peer criticism, as observed unbeknown to the subjects, through one-way mirrors and an inter-communication system. (The physical arrangement of the investigator's laboratory provided several small rooms in which groups could assemble and which had an entry to observation booths outside the awareness of the subjects.) The coed college groups were observed in various classrooms.
3. The reaction to confrontation with the position of authority as shown in the final paper. Again, since the subjects were in small groups, it was possible to observe reaction to authorities of different kinds and of different points of view.
4. Interview data which came from a talk with the subjects after the final paper was turned in. These were data which enabled the investigator to double-check observations obtained from the papers and from the observation booths or rooms.

Phase 2

The second phase of the investigation involved classification of the most basic of the data, the original conceptions of psychologically mature behavior. This phase began in the second year and was continued on a cumulative basis each spring for the next eight years.

Independent judges, people not involved in the production of the conceptions of mature personality who knew nothing of the project, were assigned a task. They were handed the conceptions accumulated to date and were instructed to place them into categories if they found them to be classifiable.

---

[42] CWG: These papers were also copied.

They were instructed in a very simple manner: "Take these conceptions of mature personality, study them, then sort them into the fewest possible categories if you find them to be classifiable. Do not force any into categories. If some do not fit any category you decide upon, just place them into an unclassifiable group."

Each group of judges consisted of 7 to 9 people who had no relationship to the project. At first, each judge worked independently of all other judges. After each member of each year's group of judges had decided on his classification system, the group worked toward one classification system into which the conceptions could be classified by unanimous opinion. At no time was any conception forced into a class. If even one member disagreed as to placement of a conception, that conception was not used to establish classification types.

This phase produced the basic classes of mature adult behavior according to the judges who did the classifying.

Phase 3

Phase 3 of the investigation involved an exploration of the categories of conceptions of mature personality by means of a number of different techniques. Once groupings of conceptions of mature behavior were established, I made use of a fortunate coincidence which enabled me to explore the meaning of these categories.

Most of the subjects took another class with me the following semester. These were classes in Organizational or Industrial Psychology, Experimental Psychology and Abnormal Psychology. These classes were designed so that, where possible, students with like conceptions were grouped into small groups and placed in problem-type situations appropriate to the subject matter of the course they were taking.

Since some members of subsequent classes were not members of the experimental groups, they too, were grouped and taught through the same methodology. This served two purposes. It kept the experimental subjects from being aware that they were being treated in a special fashion and it served as a moderate control over the investigations in process.

The experimental groups were studied through the one-way mirror, as were the non-experimental groups. Special problems were designed for the Organizational and Experimental students. In the Abnormal Psychology class, many standard tests were administered under the guise of providing the student with knowledge of diagnostic instruments and providing self-insight, though these things they also did.

Phase 3, therefore, produced seven kinds of data for me:

1. How subjects who had similar conceptions of mature personality operated in certain problem situations.
2. How subjects who have similar conceptions organized to solve problems. (They were told, simply, what their goal was and that they would have to organize themselves to complete the assigned tasks.)
3. How subjects who had similar conceptions interacted with one another in the course of attempting to solve problems.
4. How subjects who had similar conceptions worked toward the solution of problems.
5. How long it took subjects who had a similar conception to solve problems.
6. How well subjects who had similar conceptions solved problems.
7. How subjects with similar conceptions performed on certain standard psychological tests.

Phase 4

Phase 4 of the investigation was a library research project which was carried on from 1960 up to the moment of this writing. From the classification, situation and test information, confusing data arose. Therefore, I combed the literature for any hints that I might get as to

a. how to make sense of the data, and
b. how to begin the conceptualization of adult behavior to which the data was pointing.

From this four-phase study, data was collected which seemed to say that many investigators have been living within an illusion—a misperception—of the nature of psychological maturity—an illusion which has created conflict and confusion for us where it does not need to be—an illusion which it seems must be swept aside if ever we are to truly comprehend the nature of man's being.

What then is this illusion which must be swept aside? What is this misperception by which we live that is creating consternation for us where it does not need to be? Have not many concluded from certain evidence before them that psychological maturity is a state which can conceivably come to be? Have they not concluded that psychosocial man, like biological man, grows from a state of relative immaturity through early stages or experiences, finally to arrive, in adulthood, as a fully developed, basically unchanging mature psychosocial system for the greater part of one's biologically mature years? Have not they concluded from this belief that if we can discern

- a. the underlying nature of man, and
- b. how to properly treat him in his developing years,

some day we will be able to live as truly mature psychological beings in a truly mature psychosocial system? And have not many conceptual explanations of man laid out, at least in theory, the road to man's Utopia? Has not Skinner done so in *Walden Two* and *Beyond Freedom and Dignity*? Did not Freud do so in his conception of the genital character? Has not Erikson done so in his eight stages of man and Maslow in his concept of the Self-Actualizing man?

Indeed they have, and yet from my data, doing so is to live in a world of misperception. From my data, it was necessary to conclude that the state or that condition which could be called psychological maturity or Utopian society cannot be theorized to exist and, further, to conclude that those writers, philosophers and scientists who have spent much time prospecting for or writing about the psychologically mature personality or the Utopian society were, or are, living within an illusion. It has been necessary because there are reams of evidence—mine and others—that negates the Utopian position and supports the assertion I have made. What these data were like, what problems they created, and how the problems were resolved is the subject matter of the next four chapters.

CHAPTER 3

The Basic Data

From the research project outlined, it should be apparent that the emergent cyclical theory of adult behavior did not arise capriciously, nor is it a product of armchair theorizing. I did not visit the Gods on Olympus nor have I stood on the mountaintop in Sinai to procure the substance in its words. It came to be in an arduous, systematic fashion.

As I sought some way to make sense of human life, of the confusion and contradiction of the conflict and controversy surrounding it, I came to have, in the language of the street, a 'monkey on my back.' This monkey consisted of data more confusing and contradictory than that which I had set out to clarify. The data could not, within my knowledge and efforts, be rationalized within any existing explanatory framework. Thus, I was driven by their nature to develop an explanatory framework which would make sensible, at least to me, the confusing data my efforts had amassed.

These data produced in me an experience similar to the one Darwin must have had when he visited the Galapagos Islands. As Darwin went from island to island in the Galapagos archipelago, he took note, in its confusing animal world, of the creatures that inhabited each of the islands. He observed subtle differences in the finches and iguanas and how these differences varied from island to island. These differences, it occurred to him, were part of a slow and developing process, the process he was to call evolution.

A similar experience happened to me in the course of my investigations. As a means of researching toward answers to my questions, I chose to study conceptions of mature personality and how those people who professed certain conceptions operated in a variety of situations. As I examined the basic data, the various conceptions of mature personality produced by my subjects, and how those who produced each type of conception operated, I moved from one conception of mature personality to another. I took notice of differences in the form of the conception, of the character of the conceiver's operation, and the way these changed with time and experience. My observations noted subtle differences in the conceptions of mature personality professed by the subjects who contributed basic data to my work. So studies were designed to investigate the nature of the conceptions and the character of the apparent differences. As the results came in, I seemed to see, as had Darwin, a slow and developing process, an observation which created a problem for me. The work had begun as an attempt to clarify the confusion and contradiction in adult conceptions of maturity and in the world of psychological information and theory. But soon I was faced not with clarification, but with exacerbation. The data, on the surface, seemed in no way to bring clarification to the muddled states of man, nor of his confused state of psychological affairs. It amplified them many-fold.

When this problem arose, time was taken to think through the situation created by the accumulated information. This period of contemplation directed me to reopen an age-old question – the question about the essence of human life. Pursuant to this train of thought I asked: "What is human life about? What is it meant to be?" If it is not, as I have questioned, a transformation of man's perversity into decency, if it is not a search for *the* proper way for man to live and for how to condition him to live that way, if it is not a search for one's self and for the expression of all of one's potential, then what is it? What is human life like and what is it meant to be? This is a question which needs to be answered if ever we are to understand mature human life and if ever we are to find more constructive approaches to the many of man's problems. But how are we to proceed toward an answer to it?

My approach began with a consideration of this question. Is human life a soul-trying, morality developing struggle up the mountainside only to experience, when the apex is reached, a character-destroying, institution-wrecking tumble down the other side? Or is it a trip fraught with heaven and hell that has a theoretical end in a benignant destination oozing with safety, security, freedom and abundance for all as B.F.

Skinner seems to want us to accept? Or is John Stambaugh correct when he says of human life:

> "... the historical cycle of the body politic indicates that man progresses from spiritual faith to courage, from courage to freedom, from freedom to abundance, then comes the waning, from abundance to selfishness, from selfishness to apathy, from apathy to dependency right back into bondage again."[43]

Or can we hope with Radoslav Tsanoff:

> "...that the twilight in which we seem to be moving today is a twilight not before night but before dawn: that we are reaching the end of the dark ages of materialism; that the modern mind, without surrendering the tools by which it has achieved its mastery of material nature, will now more fully vindicate its own self-recognition and achieve self-mastery and a more humane life individual and social?"[44]

Perhaps we can so hope, but perhaps to do so is a futile effort. The fact of the matter is we simply do not know which of these two men, if either, more correctly perceives the character of man's being or the future of mankind. But I do believe, from the data of my studies, that Tsanoff's hope is closer to the facts of human life than all the Stambaughs are. In fact, the latter poses a position which necessity requires that I debate. I do so because, from the information I have gathered, the strong suggestion has arisen that all such contradictory explanations of man's predicament exist because we have failed to solve a problem—a problem we have not as yet unriddled because we have not approached the goal James F.T. Bugental set down when he said:

> "Humanistic psychology has as its ultimate goal, the preparation of what it means to be alive as a human being. This is, of course, not a goal which is likely ever to be fully obtained, yet it is important to recognize the nature of the task. Such a complete description would necessarily include an inventory of man's native endowment, his potentialities of feelings, thought and action, his growth, evolution and decline, his interaction with various environing conditions (and here a truly complete

---

[43] This quotation is variously attributed and and frequently repeated. Its true provenance is unknown. A reference in John E. Stambaugh's has not been located.
[44] Tsanoff, Radoslav A. (1942). *The Moral Ideals of Our Civilization*. New York: E.P. Dutton & Co., Inc., p. 125.

psychology of man would subsume all physical and social sciences since they bear on the human experience actually or potentially), the range and variety of experience possible to him and his meaningful place in the universe."[45]

It seems to me that we have not approached this goal because we have lacked both the message of what human life is all about and a medium for its transmission. And it seems to me that we have lacked these because we have not had at our disposal an investigatory means sufficiently broad to bring forth all that human life seems to be. Also, it seems to me that the basic data from my studies may be a means through which is conveyed what adult human life is all about and what it is going to be. So let us see in this chapter how the conclusion came about.

When I asked adults, aged 18 to 61, to take four weeks of time to think through and develop, as best they could, their personal conception of the psychologically mature human being, the task was undertaken on the basis of three assumptions:

1. They would project themselves into their conception.
2. If I collected a considerable number of these conceptions, I would have a reasonably representative sample of what human beings see the best of human life to be.
3. With these ideas in hand, I might be able, through study of them and the people who produced them, to come closer to the goal of Bugental.

The assumption that the participants would project themselves into the conceptions was, I believe, well corroborated in my data. It was corroborated by my observation of them and by the fact that many openly said they were projecting. But I did not feel secure in this assumption until later, when Frank Barron of the University of California, supported it. He, after gathering together a group of his colleagues to attack the task of defining *healthy personality*, a task similar to mine, said:

" ... with some half-dozen psychologists arrayed in a circle and comfortably seated, it was natural enough that a sort of informal symposium should quickly organize itself. We listened as a group as each of us in turn presented his own ideas of what

---

[45] Bugental, James F. T. (1967). *Challenges of Humanistic Psychology*. Los Angeles: Psychological Service Associates, McGraw-Hill Book Company, p. 7.

the psychologically healthy person would be like. After a bit of listening, it became clear to me that I had fallen in with a group of rather noble souls for the traits, which they uniformly ascribed to the psychologically healthy person, were the sort that would earn anyone a reward in the afterlife. As I listened further, however, I began to realize that the catalogue of named virtues would be somewhat more appropriate to an effectively functioning person in the temperate zone than in the tropical or arctic zones. Then it came to me that the effectively functioning person had two rather locally determined restrictions imposed upon him; namely, like each and every staff member of the institute, he was a man rather than a woman and rather closer to middle-age than to adolescence. At the end of the first comfortable discussions, then, we had arrived at an excellent picture of an effectively functioning and notably virtuous man in his middle years in late summer at Berkeley, California."[46]

The second assumption was somewhat, but not completely, justified according to the data which came in. Originally four, then, with time, five major conceptions of mature human existence appeared. These five conceptions were easy to relate to established ways of life by which men live or have lived. But there were two forms of human existence not included in the data, those which some call the *tribalistic way of life* and the *pre-cultural ways* of man. Then, beyond these, an additional conception of mature behavior appeared which was not only different from any of the others but also did not relate to any established form of existence by which man has yet lived. Thus, eventually, to portray the picture of what the data from my studies said mature human life was all about, I had to move beyond existing conceptions of adult human psychology to construct the medium which I sought.

The third assumption—that the study of the conceptions of mature human behavior produced and study of the people who produced them would enable me to develop a medium for expressing what human life is all about—was, I believe, borne out because from it came the framework for the conception of adult human behavior presented in this book. Examining what my participants said can test the validity of this assertion.

---

[46] Barron, Frank (1963). *Creativity and Psychological Health*. Princeton, New Jersey, Toronto, London, New York: D. Van Nostrand Company, Inc., p. 2.

What Adults Say Mature Personality Is

The message transmitted through the conceptions and the reasons the emergent cyclical level of existence conception was developed can best be seen by an examination of what the participants said about mature personality. Soon you will find protocols of the conceptual types produced by my participants.

They produced conceptions which could be classified as *express-self* or *sacrifice-self* conceptions. These could be broken down into three kinds of *express-self* conceptions and two kinds of *sacrifice-self* conceptions. Each *express-self* or *sacrifice-self* type was further classifiable into an *entering* version, a *nodal* version and an *exiting* version as illustrated in Exhibit I.

Exhibit I

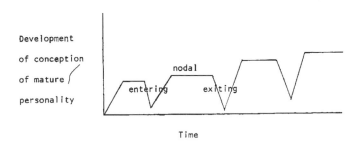

As you examine each conception, it may interest you to compare your thoughts about mature personality to my participants. If you do so, I offer a few words to keep in mind. There may be a conception which quite clearly portrays your ideas; but you may find your thoughts to be a mixture of more than one. Keep in mind that the protocols, as presented, represent a step-like progression from conceptions which develop earlier in human history to conceptions which develop later and later in time.

Also keep in mind that the protocols selected for presentation are ones which are more clearly *nodal* sub-types or more obviously transitional sub-types than ones which are mixed. The fact of the matter is that my participants produced what seemed to be clear *nodal* types, and obvious *entering* and *exiting* sub-types. But 40 percent of them produced types which were mixtures of several types or sub-types.

In cases of the purer *nodal* sub-types, almost all the person's thinking was centralized around the basic theme of the particular *nodal* type. In the sub-types almost all of the person's thinking consisted of two adjacent sub-types. In the mixed types, it is common to find at least 50 percent of a person's thinking stemming from one central theme with the remainder of the person's thinking varying over other types. Keep these things in mind *if* you compare your thinking to that of one of my contributors.

Now, as I present examples of five types and an *entering, nodal* and *exiting* version of each type, I will organize them around the type, the *entering* version of each type, the *nodal* version of each type, and the *exiting* version of each type. And I shall organize them in hierarchical order from types which appear earlier in adult human development to types which appear later in adult human development. The first is an *entering* sub-type of what I classified as 'the *express* self, to hell with others conception'. The second is a *nodal* version of this type and the third is an *exiting* version. These are followed by *entering, nodal* and *exiting* versions of the other four types.

Express Self, to Hell With Others Lest One Feel Shame— Entering Version

This is the conception of a tall, handsome, 24-year-old male. It, like all others, has been edited because space does not permit complete presentation. Editing removed only repeat examples of the person's thinking.

It is presented precisely as the participant wrote it. All errors, all rough language, all ungrammatical construction are unaltered:

> "Life is a jungle - one goddamned great big jungle. It is survival of the fittest and that is all. Anybody who does not recognize this is not or will never be a grown up person. Life is competition, it is fight and struggle and get and take and hang on. Some they have got it to fight there way through it and some they just don't have it. The grownup he survives, or he go down big in trying he's got it. He is the guy who fights to get what he needs and he keeps after it till he gest it. If he wants some chick he don't take no. He wears her down. One thing about him is he don't chicken, he don't let fear stand in his way.

If it has got to be done he does it he don't stay to think, he just does it. It don't matter who gets hurt thou it best it ain't him. There ain't no reason for him to feel guilty cause a man's got to live ain't he. This aint no picnik world in which he live. It better he do what have to be done cause he can't hold his head up if he ain't a man. That's the way life is any grown guy know it. He know its him or me and it sure ain't going to be me if hes healthy. He gets what he can from this world and no one pushes him around, even if the dice is loaded its up to him to make them shake his way. If he don't what kind of man is he --.

Now don't you set me down Doc for saying this. You said to put down what we believed. I believe this and don't you ever forget it."

This is the conception of a young man having his third try at college after having been, literally, thrown out of two other institutions. In it we see a frantic need to assert self, preferably for survival, but at least in order to be seen as manly. This was typical of all variants of the *express self regardless of consequences type*. In this conception, we see uncultivated language which was typical of this variant of this particular type of conception. Beyond these aspects, one can see a raw, idinal type of thinking, impulsive, amoral and uninhibited in character. There is no feeling of guilt in this thinking, but there is in it a strong element of fear of shame. Also, there seems to be an underlying aspect of heroism in the conception. It is as if the conceptualizer were saying: "If the dragon is there, then one must join battle with it, even if he dies in the action; otherwise he would be less than a man. If the dragon is not there, one must create it in order to prove that one has the right to survive, or live as a man." So, in this conception it is better to die in the glory of having tried rather than to live in the disgrace and humiliation of "being chicken." To die in the act of heroic living seems to enable this conceptualizer to live at least in the minds of the surviving who would say: "Sure he died. But, man! He had the guts to try. He was a man!"

Express Self, to Hell With Others Lest One Feel Shame – Nodal Version

To me, the second example of this type is quite like the first in basic content, but it is quite obviously a softer, more relaxed, not quite as barbarous version of the same theme:

> "Psychologically mature human behavior is that mental behavior that enables a human being not only to survive but also to succeed and win over his environment. The psychologically mature person is the one that fate has endowed with the natural human qualities to rise above the conditions of his being and to impose control over it and modify it as he sees fit regardless of what others think. Being an animal, the human being possesses certain natural qualities normal for his species. He is temperamental and impulsive, and thus given to violence, passion, stubbornness and irrational actions. He desires to mate but not just to produce children. He fights life as it is and he works most to survive.
>
> He senses that he is alone and endangered and seeing strength in numbers, he seeks to fit others to the needs of himself. The drive for self-preservation is instilled in him and the only way to be what he is, is to be selfish, placing his needs before all others with the "possible" exception of his own family. He must overcome his fears and inhibitions to his own satisfaction.
>
> He must fulfill his primal lusts and desires. A human being free from guilt and frustrations closely approaches the ideal of the mature personality. Unhampered expression of his impulses might lead to his destruction but it is necessary to his health. He must not temper his striving for pleasure.
>
> He performs when he is motivated for not to do would leave him less than a man. He is free from the threats and negative reactions of others and does not fear for his own psyche. In other words, he is confident of being a law unto himself, the source and inspiration of all of his actions and of good for others."

This is the conception of a male college sophomore attending a night school who has a full-time job as a self-tutored construction engineer. In this young man's conception is the same unabashed self-assertiveness of the first one. It is egocentric and survival-centered, as was its predecessor. It is hedonistic and impulsively oriented and has in it the element 'fear of shame least one be seen as less than a man.' But it seems as if this young man had come to peace with his conception, whereas the first young man was frantically attempting to achieve the way of life *'express self, to hell with others'*. Notice also that both young men deny that guilt should be a part of life's experience. It is as if guilt had not come to be as a part of their lives, an element which begins to change in the next variant of this *'express self to hell with others'* conception.

The following conception is one which maintains the 'express self to the benefit of self' theme, but a wee element of concern as to one's selfish impulsiveness enters the scene. It seems, developmentally, to be a mite beyond the way of thinking of the structural engineer, and to be one in which the conceptualizer is striving desperately to put tight hands upon that which the jungleistic young man in the first conception was striving to get into action. This type of change is an important aspect of all the conceptions of mature personality which were collected and, thus, warrants some attention at this time.

Once the data were collated, classified and studied, it seemed that each variant had a moment of rushing entrance onto the stage of life; each had a moment of calm, almost total take-over as if it were perceived as *the* way for the expression of life; and each had its moment of rigid, reluctant absenting from the scene. It is as if a new idea about life fights for existence, then takes over the ordering of existence, and then reluctantly rigidifies and loses its vitality before the next expression of life comes to be. So each way of life seems to come upon us in a rushing ground swell, then to have its moment of smooth sailing on the sea of life, only finally to break down from the weight of its own way of being. This latter aspect stands out particularly in the next concept where a rigidification of the *'express self to hell with others lest one feel shame'* theme takes place.

Express Self to Hell With Others—
Rigidifying Exiting Version

"My conception of the mature personality, as I suspect are all conceptions, is based on how this world is and the men we are. Though there are some who will profess to disagree with me, if they should really stop to think, they would agree that there are two facts of life upon which a conception of mature behavior must be based. One is men are not born equal, though they are born dependent on one another. The other fact is that the strong must use the weak to fight this world and its other people in order to survive. Therefore, the mature personality insists that the world take cognizance of those realities.

To me the mature personality organizes to maintain his existence and the right way of life taking into consideration only those he must in order to survive. He sees to it that he organizes his world so as to improve his chances. He takes over and assigns roles to those less able to decide and sees to it they know what their roles are and live by them. He is meticulously careful to take care of those lesser ones who can help him so long as they are helpful but he realizes, because of his superior powers, that they are more expendable than he in the mundane of life.

He takes seriously his duties to those who depend on him but he does not overdo it lest he raise wishes in them they are not competent to fulfill. He leads them to do what is right by outstanding examples in his own life.

He maintains his position in the world as is appropriate for one of his competence, by deed not by word, lest those who are dependent on him feel they be shamed in the eyes of others. He feels compassion for the fact that his dependent ones are not as he, but no undo qualms of guilt can enter into his decisions. His standards of action are high for himself and his kind but he readily recognizes the weaknesses in other men and his need to control them. So, he, through his superior competence sees to it that other people are organized so as to maintain the viability of that for which he is responsible. He enlarges his domain when it is to his advantage to do so and he is not overly hesitant as to how, if and when it becomes necessary.

He is ever watchful to his survival making arrangements whenever necessary, with whom ever necessary when they become necessary. These arrangements must take into consideration that the competent people in the world must care for the ones who are dependent on them.

He realizes the world could soon disintegrate into chaos if order were not impressed upon it. He knows the problem of unbridled lust in the lesser ones so he organizes so that normally the rules of living are quite strict upon them except as, through his largeness, he provides them moment uninhibited exultation. It is by example in his own life that he brings forth the force for implementing his will. For example, any man worthy of his name, any woman worthy of being called a lady serves their human desires but in a manner that is properly formalized."

This variant of the *express self lest one be ashamed for not being a man* theme is the conception of a 23-year-old black student reared in the British Colonial System. He is a Nigerian Ibo. This is, indeed, a most interesting conception. Within it we see all that is expressed in the two previous *'express self, regardless of consequences'* conceptions, but a new tone seems present within it. The self-assertiveness, the lust, the survival mode, the fear of shame are all present. But sneaking in seems to be the element of guilt, the tendency to feel there is something a bit wrong in not exercising at least some control over one's impulse life. Raw want is still there, but a questioning of its unbridled expression has crept into the scene. Along with this we see developing a peculiar sense of morality, but one that is imposed upon rather than derived from within. Particularly, we note the suggestion that chaos might be just around the corner. It is as if this person was desperately trying to hang on to the idea of self-assertive expression, but quite aware that such a way of life, if not bridled, can lead to disintegration. As a result, we see this conceptualizer declaring that this system for being does indeed exist, but only within rigidifying formalisms. It seems he is attempting to hold the old ways together with the glue of moralistic prescription. But we must ask: What does this moralistic, guilt-determined intrusion into this express self conception mean? Can it be the intruding germ that infects this way of life with its fatal disease? Can it be, at the same time, the herald preparing to trumpet the way of human life that is next to come to be? We shall see as we examine the next phase of the human existential helix.

Sacrifice Now to Get Reward Later—
Righteous Absolutistic Entering Into Version

The next conception of mature personality comes on with a rush like the jungleistic *express self to hell with others* conception, but this time its nature is an engulfing wave of righteousness. It seems the conceptualizer sees mature personality as that which is pounded into man's iniquitous soul. What is particularly central in this conception is almost diametrically opposed to the *'express self, to hell with others conception.'* Its centrality lies in the idea "nothing comes unless you put out first." It is a *'put out now to get reward later'* theme.

> "There is little doubt in my mind as to what makes mature personality. I learned that at the end of my old man's switch and I'm not likely to forget it. The grown-up learns[47] and particularly he learns nothing comes lest you put out first. Right is right and wrong is wrong and if you are going to be mature you better learn it, the sooner the better. It always has been this way and it will always be because that is the way it is. My old man learned it from his and his old man learned it from his father, and my kids are going to learn it from me because that is the law of the land.
>
> We were not put on this earth to get something for nothing. We were not put here to want or to wish for or to have evil thoughts. We were put here to do right and see to it that other people do right too. It is our duty to strike wrong whenever we find it. The mature personality knows what the rules are and he knows if he violates them he should get it. Life is a serious business with no place for frivolousness in it. He knows what he is allowed to wish for and he knows what is forbidden and he behaves accordingly. Any mature man has got his duties and he does them even if he does not want to because it would be wrong of him not to do so. If he does not the grown-up knows he should be punished. There is no place for self-serving sentimentally in becoming of age.
>
> One thing that bothers me about this work is what the kids said in class about God, heaven and the like. I didn't see a mature person seeing God as nice and loving. God is vengeful, he is to be feared. He is not some nice old grandfather-like guy. To me it is hell that you have got to fear more than you look for heaven. God says there are laws we must live by or He will see to it we pay for it in the future. That's what being fully grown is. The mature he is that guy who watches out for evil that is in us. He is the guy who learns to keep evil down and strive against it."

---

[47] CWG: Notice the language "learns" rather than the expected "knows."

This is the conception of a 19-year old male 'drafted' into college from his coalmining town in Pennsylvania. This conception seems to be a decidedly different form of thinking about mature, 'grown up' behavior and about what human life is meant to be. It is more an effort toward a conception than it is the culmination of one. We see the wee element of guilt that had crept into the previous conception become a central element in this morally righteous conceptions. It seems to say that the central aim of life is to make a person feel guilty for being what he or she is.

We see within it that the mature person is the one who learns to bind one's impulses within, rather than the heroic person of action of the previous conceptual type. Now the grown is one who has learned from the punitive action brought down upon him even for thoughts no more than entertained, let alone for actions taken.

In the previous conception one learned mature ways when positive results accrued from impulse driven, self-assertive, great risk taking venture. Now, in this morally righteous conception, the mature person quivers in fear lest action lead to condemnation and to pain. In the previous conception, the mature person acted in self-assured certainty that impulsive expression would produce pleasure from conquest if only it was fought through to the end of satisfaction. The least it could lead to was a heroic death as a reward for having tried. But this righteous conception seems to be the beginning of a major change in thinking about what is a mature human being. How major can be judged only as we see it relative to the previous conceptions presented to date, and to the ones which are to come.

The next conception is the first I shall present which was produced by a female, thus it raises a question. Is this because females, as some are wont to say, being more civilized than males don't think in more barbarous ways? Are they more moral than the male? My answer is, not at all. The presentation of a female protocol at this stage is purely an artifact, an artifact of the time and conditions under which the conceptions of my people were collected. The rawer thinking, rawer behaving females were simply not present in the college samples in the days when my data was being collected. In those days, education of the more idinal females, for one reason or another, was not being subsidized. Even rougher thinking males were not subsidized except in the case of athletic talent or in the case of emergent nation origin.

That this was an artifact and not a fact can be supported by a little time spent in a female prison or a big city street gang. The survivalistic, jungleistic females exist in such environs but don't make the error I made in an attempt to fill out my data. Do not try, as I did, to elicit written conceptions of mature personality from them. Never have I been so blistered, by language emanating from the mouths of humans, as I was blistered after requesting cooperation from females who think in the jungleistic fashion. They told me where to stick my request and they meant it.

The first female protocol to be presented was produced by a 27-year-old attractive-looking woman who was attending night school. She came to school from an office whose people said she was the epitome of secretarial competence. This fact is mentioned because certain aspects of her conception, recorded precisely as it was worded, takes on much significance when one knows she produced error free work when work was produced for others and not from within herself.

Sacrifice Now to Get Reward Later —
First Nodal Absolutistic Version

> "This assignment was to develop on our own, and in writing, our personal conception of what is the psychologically mature person in operation. Dr. Graves, I have found this to be a most difficult task. It is my honest belief that what is a mature personality is determined by that power which determines good and evil in the world. God created man and God has indicated in His Ten Commandments the principles by which the human should live. It is not for me to decide what God pretended [I believe the writer meant intended]. If God had wanted man to decide he would have indicated that. He would not have "commanded". As a result one cannot easily fulfill this assignment. I have thought very much about how I could fulfill this assignment. The only way it can be done is within God's design. Therefore, since God did give man free will to choose, in this context, to be mature or immature, I have decided the only way I can fulfill the assignment is to decry [I believe describe was intended] what I think God meant by each of his commandments. I do hope for your forgiveness if wrong or if this does not satisfy the requirements.
>
> Thou shalt have no other god before me.
>
> This commandment, in operation, questions the right of man to decide what the mature person is. This assignment, as

stated to us, would place man before God because it would not be God who determines the mature personality. The mature personality accepts what God commands. He does not, in arrogance take unto himself that which is not in his domain. The mature knows that God, in His omniscience, knows best. He lives for this rule.

Thou shalt not make any graven image.

The dictionary says this means one does not make an image of God in wood or in stone. This the mature person does not do. It is one reason why this assignment is an improper assignment, though I may be wrong, since the dictionary said no image in wood or stone. It seems to me if I sculptured my picture of the mature personality, I would be creating a graven image. This is because God created man in his own image. Thus an image of the mature human being would be a graven image of God.

Thou shalt not take the name of thy Lord thy God in vain.

This is what I have been trying [the "c" was crossed out and the "t" inserted] to say. The mature personality operates so, as not to take the name of God in vain. He does not question what is the mature person. He accepts that it is what God says it is, because God says that is the road to everlasting peace and contentment.

Remember the Sabbath, keep it holy.

The mature personality does on the Sabbath what holy means. He sets it apart and he devotes it to the service and worship of God. One sees that self is given to a sacred purpose.

Honor thy father and thy mother.

The mature personality does by word and deed honor his father and his mother. He does not criticize his parents since they are what God intended them to be. To criticize is to criticize God. The mature is thankful to his folks for having given him life and the opportunity to serve God in God's ways; he is not ungrateful like kids are today.

Thou shalt not kill.

The mature personality does not kill. This is why so many people are unhealthy. They add to the commandment, except in the service of God. This is not right. God commanded, "thou shalt not kill."

Thou shalt not commit adultery.

This should be the easiest of all to fulfill because God gave man the will to control his impulses. Man knows what it is for. It is to produce children. So the mature personality accepts this even, for example, if the wife is barren for if that happens, God intends that marriage to serve him in some other way.

Thou shalt not steal.

I have heard some kids say, "How can I serve God if I am dead?" Therefore, if I am hungry God will not condemn me if I steal bread. This is not the mature personality in operation. The mature follows this commandment even if it means to suffer with the hunger of children. God tests man in many ways to see if he is worthy.

Thou shalt not bear false witness.

Some who say they are mature personalities show they are *(not seems to have been omitted)* through this commandment. They do not realize that not to bear false witness means not to fail to tell the truth even if the truth hurts. Its only meaning is not, "Don't lie about a person." The mature personality tells the truth. He is honest all ways and at all times.

Thou shalt not covet.

To covet is to want, to desire. The mature personality does not covet. He suppresses desire and he does not question any why others have. If God intended him to have he would have given to him. If God gives, it is not because man needs or desires or wishes. It is because God has to see if it is used to serve God's purpose. The mature person does not covet, she accepts."

[Notice: though a female, this is the only use of *she* or *her*.]

In this conception, the mature personality accepts what the higher power prescribes. No questioning of it is permitted. The mature accepts that maturity is what the higher power says it is because a human is tested in many ways to see if s/he is worth—worthy that is, of the peace and contentment that comes in the after life. Such is the centrality of this conception: sacrifice the desires of self now, in order to get the reward of peace and contentment later.

Absolute obeisance to the prescriptions of an authority higher than the self is present in this conception. It stands in marked contrast to the 'express self, to hell with others' conception. Yet additional data to be presented in the next chapter indicates that the sacrifice now for reward later developed out of the 'express self, to hell with others' conception.

In the previous 'express self, to hell with others' conceptions, man made his own rules or went down in the glory of having tried. Mature behavior was aggressively striving behavior. Here, in this sacrifice now conception, mature behavior is that which is absolutely obeisant to the prescriptions of the higher order. Mature life is what one ought to do, what one must do. Previously, it was what one made it to be. Here that inkling of a guilty concern about one's impulses, which crept into the self-righteous version of the sacrifice now to get later conception, becomes the center of existence. Guilt is no longer a voice from the wings. Guilt is now stage center, so strong in fact that this conceptualizer suffered the torment of expected damnation for just trying to fulfill what was, to me, a simple classroom assignment.

The way this 27-year-old woman thinks is absolutistic almost beyond belief. Her thinking is all or none, black or white. It is categorical, rigid, dogmatic and redundant. She thinks in terms of accepting what is and not in terms of changing or even attempting to change what exists.

But there is a most interesting element present in this conception. This conceptualizer was known for her perfection as a secretary. Yet in several instances, in this and other similar conceptions errors, which look like Freudian slips of the keys, are present in the material handed in. Shades of *The Psychopathology of Everyday Life,* Freud's strict super ego bombarded by a relentless id seems unquestionably present in this type of conception.

A 24-year-old male refugee of the 1956 Hungarian revolt produced the conception, which follows. It is a most revealing document when it is seen in relation to the 27-year-old female's conception and the other conceptions presented so far. Not only does it reveal the same kind of thinking about mature behavior as the 27-year-old female, but also it reveals what came to be with time the most central of all my propositions for understanding adult human behavior—the proposition that it is not what a person thinks that reveals his or her psychology but it is how a person thinks that provides the central material for understanding a person.

In this Hungarian refugee's conception, the content is very different from the content of the thought in the 27-year-old female's conception of maturity. Yet, the way she thinks about maturity is the same as the way the 24-year-old male thinks about it. Each of these young persons thinks about maturity in an absolutistic, categorical black and white, obeisant to the higher order redundant, sacrifice of self manner.

A number of people have sought to develop "tests" which would assess a person's position in the levels of Human Existence hierarchy. Some have had a limited measure of success but some have reported that their efforts have not been as successful as their interpretation of my words have led them to hope. [48]

It is my considered opinion that this problem has arisen for one of two reasons: (1) the theory, which follows in this book, may be wanting. That is always a possibility in work of this type. But (2) this problem may arise because consumers of my words may fail to comprehend what it is that one must assess, if the theory in this book is to be put to the test of experiment and application.

With the case of the 27-year-old female and the 24-year-old Hungarian refugee, I present the first representation of what is central to assessment within the emergent cyclical theory of adult development. If you should be disposed to develop assessment instruments, in order to test or apply this theory, be certain you understand what is to be assessed.

Those who have tried to develop instruments have based them on what people think, do, or believe, which is not the proper base for assessment devices. They should be based not on what the person thinks but how s/he thinks, not on what people do or what they believe but how they do what they do, and how they believe that which they do believe.

The conceptions just presented, and the conception to follow, illustrate this problem. What the two *say* is mature personality is poles apart. How they *think about* mature personality is essentially the same.

Sacrifice Now to Get Later—
Second Example of Nodal Version

The former Hungarian says:

> "Maturity can be defined as a ripeness, as a fruition of determined potentialities, as a fullness of possible development. The word and the concept, as I see it, carries

---

[48] CWG: This fact is of prime importance to any who should aspire to develop assessment devices to test the propositions expressed in this book—a task which a number of people have attempted as a result of previous publications and papers read at professional meetings. They have missed the mark.

certain moral implications. When we say she or he is mature, we are passing judgments, the word carries an implied ought: maturity is good and one ought to be mature.

The mature ought to be what he can be and nothing more. The cardinal rule of maturity is that an individual must ever seek vainly and erroneously to compete [the "n" in never was left out; the "l" in complete was left out. Other than these two errors, this paper was letter perfect] himself falsely. He must never seek to find [lose himself] in the material world of things or hide himself in books or meaningless social activities. The mature individual never seeks to define himself strictly by roles. This, however, is only negative advice.

Positively speaking, the mature individual must (ought) transcend his animal desires and give its geist free range in order that it might seek the fullest possible actualization of its ideas. The mature individual must not repress his animality [here used in a neutral context] because man is both geist and body, and in fact they are one. An individual geist can only actualize itself through a body. The body ought therefore be appreciated, respected and cultivated to the fullest extent possible.

The mature individual must seek harmony between the symbolic system (as may be manifested by the intellectual rational ego), must realize its origins and limitations, while yet cultivating its powers. The mature individual must take stock of this emotive meaning structures and understand them. In this way the play of emotions and the subconscious will not produce existential anxiety in the mature individual and psychopathological stress will be avoided. The mature individual must take stock of his emotive meaning structures and understand them as opposed to vain attempts of others to comprehend, repress or ignore them.

The mature individual does not seek power or control of the environment. Since the mature personality realizes that his geist is but a particular manifestation of the Universal, he is aware that the same is true of all men.

Since personality is a process and develops through relationships, the mature individual must not bother himself with seeking absolute freedom. For him, it is a meaningless concept.

The mature individual realizes that the possibility of death lies always on the horizon and life per se is here and now. He will live his life, at any one moment, as if at the next death might bring an end to the projection of his ideals. This realization will not bring despair to the mature individual but rather will intensify his celebration of the joy of becoming. In the fullest sense, maturity is the ability to Be and Become; to know communion and realize the inevitability of reunion with the Universal."

This young refugee writes of maturity in a very different language than did the 27-year-old female. His words are couched in existential jargon. Hers were in the language of a Southern Baptist Lady, which she was. But the way they think about maturity is the same. In both, what is maturity is prescribed. In the case of the young man it was prescribed by the Universal order; hers were prescribed by God. Both are full of commandments. His are in the language of must and ought. Hers are in the language of "Thou Shall". He is redundant. She harps over and over on the same old theme. Her commandments are black and white. His are all or none. Both are categorical and both behave maturely in order to find peace and contentment, not to express themselves. And both are sacrifice now, in order to get reward later conceptions of maturity.

But it does seem that these two conceptions are about as different as conceptions can be from the 'express self, to hell with others' conceptions previously presented. They are so different that if, as my total data suggests, these conceptions follow the three previous ones on the developmental helix, then the people who produced them give evidence that they have taken a new, and qualitatively different view of what the best of human existence is all about. As a result, the curious person must ask: Is this change to an almost polar opposite form in two contiguous conceptions, a part of what the story of mature human life is all about? Is this one of the signals we must capture and decode if we are to translate conceptions of psychological maturity into the story of human existence? Perhaps it is and perhaps with its appearance, I should speculate as to certain other possibilities. In fact, if one carefully examines the data presented so far, limited as it is, one might ask four questions from the signals emitted to date. The first one has been noted before.

1. Does each conception of mature personality have its moment when it enters onto the stage of life, a moment when its theme

takes over centre stage and a moment when it exits as *the theme* for human existence?
2. Does each theme specify itself into many different ways?
3. Is there something to be learned from the data which says an express self is followed by a sacrifice-self theme?
4. Do themes change, first in a progressively quantitative fashion until, following a regressive movement, a qualitatively different way of thinking about maturity emerges?

It seems to me that the data so far presented answers each of these questions positively. And it seems to me, that these positive answers tentatively define the next three movements on man's existential helix.

According to the data to date, they should be: the rigidification of the sacrifice now, to get later theme; the beginning of a return to a self-assertive theme; to be followed by a nodal self expressive theme—in an assertive fashion somewhat different from the express self, to hell with others theme.

Sacrifice Now to Get Later—
Rigidifying Exiting Version

1. "I shall open my conception with a short statement which will lay before you the basic facts of what a conception of mature behavior should be. The statement will be about the assignment that we have been doing in class and the facts of my conception.
2. This class has been the worst of what I feared I would run into in college. It has been nothing but empty-headed theorizing and muddle-headed hemming and hawing. Why we have to spend four weeks talking about what proper instruction would cover in one good lecture, I don't know. [Note the display of anger toward the authority figure.]
3. It seems to me that it would be far more efficient for the facts of mature personality to be presented and then cover how to achieve it along with what happens if one does not. [Note that even within the anger expressed toward authority in 1 above, that there is dependence on authority displayed]

4. Several times I have asked why such nonsense is allowed, why the time is being utterly wasted and why the instructor will not tell us what mature personality is.
5. Therefore, at the risk of incurring the instructor's displeasure, sir, my conception is what any clear thinking person knows mature personality is.

The Mature Personality

The mature personality is the clear thinking person who makes decisions on the basis of fact. The mature does not let emotion overrule his reason.

The mature personality thinks about the things that are important, not about a lot of muddle-headed abstractions. He stands for the tried and true and against those who through their muddle-headed thinking would question the established purposes and virtue of man.

The mature personality does not go off on tangents, he is clearly focused.

The mature personality is loyal, he respects those who know better.

The mature personality has "his reach beyond his grasp." He works hard, he does not waste time, he knows that reward should come only for effort.

The mature personality sees to it he is known by his deeds, what he does, not what is said and he knows that it is right for him to do so.

The mature personality lives by the rules of proper living and requires that all others do so lest there be chaos.

The mature personality seeks always to better himself, he is never satisfied with half measure.

The mature accepts the laws for living because it is only through their existence that one can be free.

The mature has goals in life, he is not hampered in his goal seeking or decisions by uncertainties. He knows where he is going.

The mature is open-minded. He listens to all sides so that when he makes a decision he has all the information necessary to make the best decision, the one he knows is right.

The mature personality is he who achieves on his own, through his own efforts, by following the established rules.

The mature personality is one who respects the established order in life. He is one who knows that established order does exist and he is one who strives always to know and to guide his life by that established order.

The mature personality is respectful of his duty and he does it. If he does not subscribe to what is being done he seeks to achieve the position where he can institute right.

The mature has the will to work, he does not waste time, he always finds something worthwhile to do.

The mature controls his thinking. He keeps his mind on what he wants and off what he should not think about.

The mature strives to express only positive emotions - he uses negative emotions only to handle the evil in the world such as war or crime which he may need to hate so as to kill the evil.

The mature uses up surplus energy in work not in frivolity or sex or drinking or eating or the like.

The mature is undaunted by failure or misfortune. He believes success comes to he who keeps trying whatever his troubles may be. Every adversity has a benefit.

The mature is a master of his attitudes. He directs his thoughts and ordains through self-direction how to control his destiny.

The mature separates fact from fiction, fantasy from reality.

The mature believes the greatest value in life is to master the negative and animal emotions so as to do good for people even if they cannot or will not do good for themselves.

And finally -- whatever the mature has accomplished he recognizes it is not enough. To do right he must set his standards high and seek ever and ever to achieve more, so the *best* be better."

These axioms are but some of the righteous prescriptions for properly mature behavior laid down by this self-designated right thinking person. There seems little question that it is of the sacrifice now to get later type. But into it has crept an expressed disdain for an authority who does not act like an authority.

In the previous versions of the sacrifice now to get reward later theme in no way did the subjects question authority; in no way was the mature seen as one who asserted the self. Yet, here we find that this young person's mature individual quite definitely asserts self against what is perceived as deficiencies in the performance of authority. There is then, a new element in the 'sacrifice now for reward later' conception. But, it is not something new in the overall development of the human because assertion of the self was present before in the 'express self, to hell with others' conception.

In this particular conception, the 'express self' is of a different order than it was when previously we viewed it. Here the person asserts self by beginning to take opposition to those who react against authority, to those who see things in ways diverse from the conceptualizer. One can almost feel the scorn and derision directed toward those who would conceive of mature personality in a manner different from this participant. The mature person is absolutistic in knowing what is right. There is not a confused thought in his mind. He stands stubbornly against change unless he decides upon it. He is that well-intentioned person who rejects all those new-fangled ideas. The mature listens to all sides, yes! But not to change his views. Rather to learn how to argue so as to bring the dissidents to see that he is right.

Life to one who conceives of maturity in this manner is a matter of proper procedure. It is not a matter to be interpreted. There is no other better point of view. There is no other way to go. Life is not seen as a place for theoretical speculation. It is a no-nonsense business, a matter of dealing with the tangible and not with muddle-headed fuzziness.

To this conceptualizer, authority is still central in his life. But it is the authority of his own right thinking mind that is supreme. Respect is due to parents and the boss because they are the ones who show people both the light and the right. They have set before him the standards of what the mature person is like. They have taught him to believe in honest hard work to get in position to stand on one's feet. One gets there by following the dictates of authority as to how to become possessed of independence, not dependence; of certainty, not uncertainty; of knowing, not grasping to know.

One cannot avoid perceiving the 'he protesteth too much' quality in this conception. He fights so hard against those who question authority's established ways that it is obvious the germ of independent thinking is beginning to infect him with doubt. Why else would he be almost vicious with those who have come to peace with questioning? In others words, this is not the unquestioning obeisance to and accepting of authority shown in the 27-year-old woman's conception. Instead, it is the desperate attempt to hold onto belief when doubt has crept in. Opposition has taken a foothold in this thinking. Independent thought and action are not unthought of. They are, instead, a disturbing element in an inner world that is no longer a sea of tranquil certainty.

In the previous sacrifice conception, there was no diversity in thinking. In this one, diversity is present. However as seen by the conceptualizer, it is wrong and to be suppressed or eradicated. But present it is. Multiplistic thinking is aborning. Atomistic additive thinking has come to be thinking which is argumentative toward and oppositional to authority and is about to enter from the wings. It seems, indeed, that a leading edge of doubt is gnawing up from within, a fact which will become all the more apparent as we move to the next notch on the spiral of adult human existence.

The next protocol is another intriguing conception, particularly when one considers the background of the young woman who produced it. A 21-year-old daughter of a college professor of humanities developed it. Again this young woman prefaced her conception with a short statement as to how she felt about the assignment.

Express Self Calculatedly With Little Shame or Guilt—Entering Version

"I should like to preface my conception with a few words about the way this class is being conducted, and what I have to say is no shit. It is the straight stuff.

I'm a senior in college but I wonder how I got there. Maybe they did not want to embarrass the old man because I sure did not go for the crap those professors dished out the first three years. In fact, of all the time I have given to school this is the first class that ever acted as if there was some respect for the people who don't think the way profs or teachers do. This is what education ought to be, not that poll parrotting stuff we always get demanded. You would think no one knows anything except profs from the way most of them operate. But that is enough of that! What I believe mature personality is, is detailed below.

The mature woman can be seen through her analogue, the mature animal. She does not look for trouble but she is ever alert to its possibility. She has her antennae at the ready.

She takes nothing for granted. There's no certainties in the world so she organizes her domain so as to control and amplify her chances for success.

When others interfere with her domain she does not necessarily react to destroy or seriously harm them but to get them under control so as to drive them from her domain, but react with vigor and fury she can if necessary.

She gets away with what she can which will foster her chances lest she be considered a fool.

She is friendly with whoever are with her but watchfully so because she knows it is human nature to take people if you can.

She is too rational to ask for or take on that which is certain trouble but she will take advantage of any situation which is about to foster her success.

She is the one who has control of her world or whatever her organization is because she is not only one who can plan but is one who insists on running her affairs. She takes no shit.

She is able to shift attitudes as necessary. No fear, no doubt, no shame can stand in the way of her carrying out what she sees as the best.

She does not get bound up by the old virtues crap because she knows life is what you make it to be, not what the sayers say it is. She knows that that which is best for her is best for all.

The mature does not cast people into molds. She knows her opinion is as good as anyone's because nothing is certain except the certainty of one's own experience.

The last thing the mature would do would be to let others manage her affairs. It is she who looks out for herself and her interests.

She watches her impulses but she has no fear for using them if her own best interests are endangered.

She does not spend time contemplating who she is or what it is all about. She knows and she knows, she knows."

This is certainly a different conception from the three just previously presented. It is multiplistic[49] and dogmatic. Authority, which shackles the human in the *'sacrifice now to get later'* conceptions, is brusquely cast aside. In fact, what is present is that the authority of one's

---

[49] CWG: Multiplistic—the person accepts that there are a number of different views but believes that there is one *best* one.

own experience is substituted for the authority of some power higher than man. Thus, this is a conception more like the three *'express self, to hell with others'* conceptions than it is like the three sacrificial ones. But it is different from the *'to hell with others'* conceptions. It is not an *'express self, to hell with the consequences'* point of view. It is a wary conception. This young person's mature human is struggling more with the need to express self than recklessly doing so. It is a modulated form of self-expression which is more concerned with overcoming authority than with heroically overcoming the dragon.

Absolutism is gone from this conception. Nothing is for sure. There are as many value systems as there are people valuing, but she is in search of the *best* value system. This factor of professed multiplistic values may cause many to question whether this conception is further along on the spiral of life. Many may see it not as a notch further along but as a reversion backward toward the rawer, more brutish, more selfish, more egocentric, less civilized *'express self lest one be shamed'* conception. But before this conclusion is drawn one should examine it more carefully.

It is evident that this young woman's conception allows for differing value systems. Right is learned by careful testing rather than by arrogant assault. Right is something that humans in their actions establish rather than something a higher power decides. This conception speaks of expression as more than undisciplined assault, and of denial as less than the mature human displays. This conception lessens the pangs of shame and guilt but does not do away with them altogether. These are strong elements in the other conceptual systems we have examined.

It is evident that this conception has no firmer basis for valuing than one's own experience. It is true that it sees maturity in calculative, self-serving ways. And it is true that this young woman's conception allows for a chaotic multiplicity of values. But one can discern other significant things within it.

In this conception it is *the* authority which shackles the human that is cast aside. This young person sees maturity to be shown more in a person's struggle to be his or her self than in what an authority-prescribed set of rules says it should be. The human does not show maturity by restricting his or her behavior within the conditions for living into which s/he was dropped. The mature is the healthy animal staking out his territory for future existence. The mature is not one passively accepting that which is, or one roaring at restriction in uncontrolled defiance. The mature is the person who hungers for opportunity to express the self. The mature is the one who keeps grasping for something not quite in hand.

Certainly this conception takes an oppositional, possibly even negative attitude toward authority. And certainly the expression of self stands supreme within it. But whether it is or is not a further notch up on the helix of life is arguable—arguable to a degree that can be settled only by more information. Thus I turn, now, to the conception of a 35-year-old entrepreneur studying business administration.

Express Self Calculatedly With Little Shame or Guilt— Nodal Version

"After giving rational thought to what is the mature personality I have come to the following list of characteristics which add up to what it is.
1. The major characteristic of the mature person is that he is an independently operating individual. He goes it alone, so there is no such thing as a mature person. There are only people who behave maturely in their various ways.
2. The mature does what has to be done. He is not held back in his actions or judgments by that which other people do or believe.
3. The mature does not accept without questions existing data, theories or practices.
4. He is energetic, outspoken and expressive of what he believes regardless of where others stand.
5. The mature does for himself and thinks for himself. He does not look to others for their guidance or support and he does not need their acceptance or acclaim.
6. The mature person is absolutely objective. He does not let his emotions interfere with what has to be done. He is an acting person who keeps feelings out of his actions. He goes by the facts as they are not by sentimentality. He does not get entangled in emotional problems, his or others.
7. The mature personality is goal directed. He knows what he wants to do and does what he has to, to get there. He does not resign himself to his fate or surrender to the inevitable.
8. The mature person does not conform to arbitrary standards. He conforms to what he has established to be right. He goes

by his data until his data proves him wrong and then he changes however the data demand that he change.

9. The mature person is not afraid to do what has to be done. If a person has to be told his weaknesses, the mature person does so without being squeamish. He does not go out of his way to spare feelings. When people need to be shaped up, a mature person shapes them up. Wanting to be liked is not a weakness of the person who is mature.
10. The mature person does not feel guilty or ashamed for doing what rationally has to be done.
11. The mature person being rational and objective is a shrewd appraiser of that which is to his best interests.
12. The mature person accepts that he is human but he controls such tendencies when it is to his welfare to do so. He does not get sentimental and maudlin about such tendencies. He controls them himself.
13. The mature person has a reasoned, risk taking, calculating mind. He uses objective procedures to make his decisions. He places faith in that which he knows works, he does not get caught up in non-workable theory or speculation.
14. He is not afraid to stand alone, even in opposition to others, but he plans so as to have the best chance then goes ahead regardless of what others say or what effect it has.
15. The mature person is not afraid 'to get his hands dirty' in order to do what has to be done. He plays hard when he plays and he plays to win, but he does not waste his time in activities which he sees as hopeless.
16. He is not satisfied with yesterday's ways unless *he* has found them to work and he holds to them only so long as he sees them to work.
17. The mature person is not one who resigns himself to his fate or surrenders to the inevitable. He changes his course rather than accept what works against him. He never gives up control to his environment. He seeks rather to get the control that will enable him to do what he knows needs to be done."

This conception of maturity is indeed an express self type, but it is not the raw assertive form we saw in the first three conceptions. It is a conception which shows a lack of conscience and a disdain for empathy. It expresses that to get involved in interpersonal relations is to enter a very tenuous situation. This mature person seems to insist on maintaining one's self-evaluation even in the face of negative information. He represents maturity as being able to avoid modifying one's behavior except from one's own experience. This mature person never changes as a result of feedback from others.

In this conception of maturity, the mature person thinks not only disdainfully of empathy, but disdainfully of other people, as well. He thinks in terms of absolute self-sufficiency, of independent operation and cold quantitative evaluation. He thinks in terms of a multiplicity of values and a myriad of ways to do anything. So his way, if it works, is as good as anyone's way. But he does not normally think in ways that are overtly obstructive, destructive or over-reaching. Rather, he thinks mature behavior is shown in a high but not unrealistic level of aspiration. His thinking is that of the odds-calculating professional gambler, not that of a brash risk-taking fool.

The one who behaves maturely thinks in terms of leaving the field when the chances of winning the game become too slight. The mature operator is the one who thinks it is better not to enter the game than to risk self unduly in the playing. He truly lives by the dictum, 'to thine own self be true.'

To me, this is a conception which is developmentally beyond those previously presented, a position which is upheld by the data in the next chapter. It is not an *'express self, to hell with others'* conception. It is not a conception which sees denial or sacrifice of self as a sign of mature behavior. It is not a "let your reach exceed your grasp" conception. But it is a conception which seems excessively to see the maturely behaving person as an island unto himself.

Though I see this conception as further along the developmental trail than the others we have viewed, it does not seem to be as far along as the one I shall next present—an *exiting* version of the *'express self calculatedly'* conception. An 18-year-old English major who professed to be studying creative writing produced this. The following paragraphs are excerpts from her conception.

Express Self Calculatedly With Little Shame or Guilt – Exiting Version

"The psychologically mature person is the one who deals successfully with the environment, the one who has an unquestioned accurate and objective perception of one's environment and others and who is able to handle both successfully. The mature person takes both the conflicts and contradictions of life and turns them into experiences which are to her advantage.

Of course 'dealing successfully' and 'handling successfully' presupposes a wider range of abilities and competencies than one might think at first and thus will not be achieved by many. But it is the true sign of maturity. It means a superior ability to exercise one's emotions so that these volatile features enhance rather than harm one's ability to perceive and achieve goals. Indeed, perceiving clearly is probably the best way to deal with any environment and at this the mature personality is superior. One might be tempted to assert that dealing with other humans to fulfill one's personal need is really the only necessity in dealing with the environment. But I think other people are only one part of the environment, so the concept should include organizing other humans, the physical environment and one's own mind and one's own body to assure one's personal welfare.

The mature person is completely free of illusion. To her, mature means one must appraise others and self accurately, it means to be intelligent in any situation, even to being uninhibited as in sex, for it is intelligent to be so. The mature has that clear perception of reality which is based on objective evidence and her rational deductions. She must realize this reality and acts in her own best interests even if to do so requires her to take well thought out risks, even if it means to lose a friend.

The mature person says what needs to be said and does what needs to be done even if doing so may not be liked by others. The mature person is capable unto his or her self and does not need to depend on anyone. That is, the mature person adapts to the reality of the way things are but does not just accept them. If something isn't right or isn't working correctly as the mature person sees it, it is weighed against other factors. It is then labeled good, bad, right, wrong or whatever label is necessary. Then what the mature person does is to take intelligent action toward it, doing it if it is to one's advantage, avoiding it if it is not.

The truly mature person is the one who insists on total fulfillment with all actions determined by values directed at her own well-being. She would always recognize the necessity of developing herself as an entity while appearing to conform to the reality of the group. She would not do so out of fear of punishment or lest she feel guilty or ashamed but out of the realization that she must do so to employ the realities and personalities around her to her own ends without arousing them."

Here we have another conception which is quite obviously of the *'express self calculatedly'* type. But it is not a striving person that is mature, nor is it the calm operator who succeeds when the odds are good, but avoids when they are not who is mature. This mature person does not just strive. This mature person "deals successfully with" regardless of the odds. This mature person "has an unquestioned accurate and objective perception of his or her environment." Even the inevitable conflicts and contradictions of life give way to the superior talents and abilities of this person's mature human being.

In this conception, one feels again the element of protesting too much. According to this conceptualizer, the expression of the self is, should be, and will be unlimited. This person's idea of the expression of the self is extended almost to the realm of unreality. Even its element of optimism seems too strong for the real world, for it has within it almost an air of omnipotence. It emits the feeling that she is trying to grasp for herself a conception of maturity that is about to drift away. Her mature person "perceives with unquestioned clarity." Her mature person "is completely free of illusions." Her mature person is the accurate appraiser, possessed of the ability to be intelligent in any situation. She "says what needs to be said and does what needs to be done," and she is the judge of what is to be said or is to be done. But there are certain odd elements in this conception.

Her mature person denies the need to depend on anyone or anything other than her own competencies and abilities. This, she insists, "is the true sign of maturity." Self-expression is the be all and end all of maturity. She denies that the mature person is in any way constrained by the realities of being. Her mature one lives within an illusion of competence, and in the delusional world of "total self fulfillment."

But sneaking into this conception is the perception that maturity does not reside on an island unto itself, that the mature person at least "appears to conform to the reality of the group." A wee bit of sacrificialness is again present in this girl's conception of maturity. Some feeling for others, albeit selfishly conceived, seems to be reasserting itself in the core of her being.

Two other things are apparent in this conception. First it is obvious that this conceptual type overly insists on two key elements, expression of the self and rational, objective thinking. Secondly, it seems to see rationality as something which "enhances rather than harms one's ability to achieve goals." This latter point is possibly the most revealing of all, so far as this conception is concerned. This I say because its minor presence foretells what is to come in the next conception on the developmental helix of maturity.

The next is the conception of a 45-year-old male, civil service employee who was long an amateur and became a semiprofessional entertainer.

Sacrifice Self Now to Get Reward Now – Entering Version

> "I suspect as I start this, that each human being, as he sits back, alone with himself, considers his character to be fundamentally okay, or at least, headed in the right direction with good intention. In the social market place this attitude most assuredly gives way to a more self-critical state of mind, a consciousness in which ideals to be aimed at are evolved - however, it seems that solitude breeds a kind of tacit self-consent. My problem then becomes this: should I describe myself or what I would like to be? On the other hand, as I consider the vague presence of some sort of evaluative force which seeks by means of this document to classify my personality, I would imagine that if I describe what I think I am, it would in that way be aided. But the intent of the question with which I am faced, namely to define what I *consider* to be a psychologically mature human being, seems to point toward the ideals of the social market place, the psychological goals and aspirations of self-critical man. What I am driving at seems to be this: there appears to be a gap within the nature of this "evaluative force" of which I speak between its consideration of the personality itself and the intellectualizations of this personality, between actual behavioral skills and the sorts of fantasies which the behaving being aspires to.
>
> At this point, consideration of this question appears to me as crucial; yet for now a resolution of just who I should

describe shall have to wait and I shall acquiesce with the supposed intent of this project, attempting to imagine my psychological ideal.

I suppose the best way to approach such a consideration would be an outline of the dynamic sort of tendencies of the mature individual, then to be illustrated by the subject's attitude toward different realms of human experience - i.e. friendship, religion, authority, etc. Specifically, I envision the mature human as a vital, growing entity, potentially susceptible to change and influence at all times, experiencing happiness, suffering and developing. Since the self can only be a derivative of what is outside the self, since man's self consciousness, his "selfhood", seems necessarily to be socially founded, an obsession with individuality and autonomy appears a bit unrealistic, yet within its capacity as a reasoning entity, as an arbitrator of conflicting forces, the mature self finds its dignity, its separateness. Its peace is inner, unanxious over, and tempered to the realities of the outside. Social participation is motivated by enjoyment and a kind of personal curiosity, and not by a sense of quest. Emotionally, affection is esteemed, other emotions being a part of humaness. Rationality is valued as a means of growth, though owing to man's nature, by no means an exclusive means.

Regarding specific life's activities, physical activity, whether it be sport or manual labour, is seen as a fulfilling activity. Career goals of material, political or social nature are seen as insignificant."

Consistent with this sketch of an overall attitude seems to be these opinions:

On friendship - Inner security is such that friendships are not of a dependent nature. Friends are viewed more as "companions in the world" than as necessary to the satisfaction of need. Large circles of friends are sought but not required. The ability to be affectionate without expecting or requiring its return is also a sign of maturity.

On authority - Authority as a social expedient and necessity is recognized and accepted, though social mores will not mold the individual in the sense of ruling him; critical evaluation on the part of the individual is here the final judge. In the case of political and economic sorts of imperatives, having to abide by them is neither a matter of hardship or pleasure.

On the mystic urge - often deemed the religious attitude, the theological need to explain the unknown -mystic, a-rational, Zen-like attitudes toward reality are recognized as legitimate. The complimentary of this general state of mind with the tendency toward rational understanding is seen as a whole view of reality.

The concept of God as a moral force is virtually dismissed, and as a first cause determining force, respected though considered irrelevant for personal peace of mind.

As a final note, maturity also engenders a sort of overview of what such a paper as this has an object - i.e. something of a self-reflexive awareness of the relative nature of opinion; a recognition that although I can and must (because of my humanness) argue out of my own position, argumentation and opinion from other positions is equally valid in the sense of being understandable and defensible. But then again, it would appear that such a perspective cannot be humanly, vitally maintained and that we must therefore jump in and outside ourselves in the process of growth."

What stands out in the opening words of this contributor is his tentativeness. There is not the surety in his thinking that has been present in the conceptions previously reported. He really isn't sure what maturity is. He cannot describe himself as mature nor can he give in to describing an ideal. The closest he can come to an ideal is "the social market place." And he is torn between what he means by "the personality itself" (whatever he means by that phrase) and "the intellectualizations of this personality, between actual behavioral skills and the sorts of fantasies to which the behaving person aspires." What he conceives maturity to be seems obviously in a state of transition, between a state of categorical certainty and a state of relativistic thinking.

In his conception, he is prone to stop with the consideration of the question, but he reluctantly gives in to the nudge of authority (the task I assigned him). In other words, he is really not ready to commit himself. One gets the feeling that there was a time, in his mind, when he was more certain, but some change in his thinking is taking place. And it prevents him from writing about what was; at the same time, as it prevents him from writing about what is now.

He says, as he approaches the task, "I *suppose* the best way to approach the task would be to outline the dynamic *sort* of tendency." Even when he commits himself, he is not committed. Thus, as he enters into the task, he writes in the language of "I envision" not in the language of "I believe." He thinks in terms of wanting to be committed to a conception of mature personality, but all he can actually do is "envision" it.

Then, as he begins his envisioning, he discards inner absolutistic certainty and warns, as well, against "an obsession" with individuality and autonomy as bases for a conception. This type of thinking is not an *'express self, to hell with others'* conception; it is not a *'sacrifice self to the prescriptions of authority'* conception; it is not a conception in which the mature is in search of individuality and autonomy. These he dismisses as unrealistic thinking. Yet it is a conception which says, "the mature self finds itself, its dignity, as an arbitrator of conflicting forces." His is indeed a conception in transition with the stronger element being "inner, unanxious peace."

The rational conception of maturity is pushed to the back burner and positive emotional elements are placed in the front positions.

Rationality is only a part of mature thinking. It is by no means the dominant aspect of it. Maturity is other than materiality, other than the ascension to political power, and more than social interaction. But what it is, he cannot come to say. He seems on the verge of making a commitment he is not yet ready to make.

This contributor may not be certain of what maturity is, but he does know what it is not. Maturity has something to do with friendship but as companions not as confidants one can depend upon as in the previous sacrificial conceptions. Large circles are sought but a remnant of the 'go it alone,' 'friends are not necessary,' 'express self calculatedly' conception is left. And the sacrificial tone is back in this conception: "the ability to be affectionate without expecting or requiring its return is also a sign of maturity."

In it authority is a "social expedient" not a "ruling power." Acquiescence to imperatives is not a sign of maturity. The religious attitude is definitely an element, but not as a moral force. As such, God is virtually dismissed and replaced with a first cause concept and is irrelevant for personal peace of mind. Then, finally, he places the capstone on his thinking about maturity. It is something he will decide about. It is "something of a self-reflective awareness of the relative nature of opinion" wherein "an opinion from other positions is equally valid in the sense of being understandable and defensible." His position is tentative for, as he says, "it would appear that such a perspective cannot be humanly, vitally maintained."

As a conception of maturity these tentative words stand in marked contrast to the conception I shall now present. This conception, produced when the writer was a junior in college, is notable not only from the thought it contains, but from the story of what has happened to the woman who produced it. She has become a professional clinical psychologist and occupies herself today in the busy task of "growing personalities."

Sacrifice Self Now to Get Reward Now – Nodal Version

"I can say what is my conception of the mature personality in one sentence but it would take reams of paper to clarify what I mean. So I shall, in this endeavor, express my thoughts in one sentence and then elaborate only upon the basis of what I mean.

The mature personality is a participating, creative personality which in its operation does justice to every type of personality, every mode of culture, every human potential without forming anyone into typological molds.

The mature personality provides a means for bringing relations of reciprocity and willing amity to the entire family of human beings. The mature provides for the interchange and utilization of the entire experiences of humankind. He or she lives in a moral world which tears down manmade barriers of law and custom widening the means of communication and cooperation between humans.

The mature is a committed person, committing self to continuous self-development, and to intimate relations and cooperation with all people. He or she is one who believes in face to face interaction and assessment, one who believes friendly eyes are the indispensable mirror for reflecting what is. He or she believes in an absolutely open society where every nook, every corner is exposed to anyone who is curious. He or she behaves so as to demonstrate that every person may be freely heard.

The mature personality deliberately exercises choice which directs life toward allegiances which are beyond the boundaries of natural communities and the organized state and toward the ultimate hopes of mankind. He or she seeks to widen the ties of fellowship without respect to birth, caste or property, and disavows claims to special privilege or the exclusivity of leadership. He or she replaces Godly authority with the temporal authority of the time and the place. He or she softens the features which identify a person with a particular society or culture. To the mature, humanity is a unity of souls seeking salvation not a union of Catholics, High Episcopalians, Orthodox Jews or Baptists.

The mature is beyond sordid concern with his or her own survival and is focused on intensive cultivation of a belief in freedom, not a belief of freedom.

To the mature technology is for human needs, not power, productivity, profit or prestige and scientific endeavour is not for ruthless exploitation or desecration. Scientific endeavour is for depth exploration of all regions not just physical regions, so as to provide for the inner human knowledge that will assure human supremacy.

The mature indulges in the dematerialization of self, in self-transcending endeavours which reach beyond sordid concern with one's own survival, beyond the overrational and irrational, beyond mechanical uniformity toward a concept of organic unity. He or she operates by the belief that we are all one and should seek to enhance human expression to provide for a world society based on human values. He or she believes one should know both the objective and the subjective and show the ability to face one's whole self and direct every part of it to a more unified development.

In summary, and in Freudian terms, the mature personality accepts its id, but does not give it primacy, and fosters the super ego but does not allow it to depress the fullest expression of the ego."

CHAPTER 4

Confusion and Contradiction Exacerbated

To learn that adults believe in several types of mature personality is not particularly surprising. But to come upon a hint that the types emerge one out of the other in an ordered hierarchical way is quite a revelation. In addition, the apparent fact that these hierarchically ordered concepts of mature personality alternate with one another so that every other conception is like, yet not like, its alternating partners provided some most intriguing data. These data were so intriguing that I decided to explore in some detail the behavioral and psychosocial aspects of the people who produced them, and when this was done, I was in trouble.

I had collected and collated data with one end in mind, to clarify the confusion and contradiction, the conflict and controversy, in psychological fact and theory about mature human behavior. Now it was time to analyze the total data, to study it, to see what was contained therein. Much to my surprise and more to my dismay, these efforts took a most unwelcome turn. The efforts to study this representative realm of confusing and contradictory behavior so as to bring forth clarification did nothing of the sort. They served only to exacerbate an already muddled state of psychological affairs - a result which is the subject matter of this chapter.

In order to effectively present this exacerbation, I will begin with a short summary of the investigations and then develop, through a summary of the total results, the problem created by the data. But before this is done, a few words of explanation are in order.

Since the purpose in this chapter is to show how the results dictated a revised conceptual framework for explaining adult behavior, this chapter deals only with the results of the studies, not with the details of them. The details shall be dealt with at another time and in another place. These investigations were studying conceptualizations of mature personality and how those who professed conceptualization "A" versus conceptualization "B", versus conceptualization "C", operated in a variety of situations.

The subjects each developed, as a classroom exercise, his or her personal conception of psychologically mature behavior. At the beginning of a class in Normal Personality, the subjects were instructed to take four weeks to develop their conception. During these four weeks, the students were asked not to consult either authority or others and to develop only their own ideas. Classroom time was devoted to discussing the areas of human behavior, which might be included, and to providing factual information sought by the students.

At the end of each of nine semesters, these conceptions of mature personality were given to a group of seven to nine independent judges. The judges were instructed to sort them into the fewest possible internally consistent categories if they found them to be classifiable. The judges worked first independently of one another, then as a group. According to the judges, over sixty percent of the conceptions fell clearly into two major categories, one of three and one of two sub-types.

Category 1. Mature personality expresses self

Sub-type (a) - aggressive, heroic, exploitative, express self, to hell with the consequences, no feeling of guilt.

Sub-type (b) - dogmatic, express self with reasoned calculation for what self desires with little feeling of shame or guilt, and even at some expense to others but in such a way as not to raise undue reaction from those others.

Sub-type (c) - a quiet, undogmatic, express self with regard for others and never at the expense of others.

Category 2. Mature personality denies self

Sub-type (a) - denies self to prescriptions of higher absolute authority in order to get spiritual reward later.

Sub-type (b) - denies self to prescriptions of secular-valued other people in order to get approval and spiritual satisfaction now.

First Perplexing Result:
Two Opposed Categories

Later the process was repeated with other subjects. New judges were utilized. They classified the old and the new conceptions. From their work, the first mildly surprising result developed. It pertained to the *consistency* of results. I did not expect the extent of agreement that occurred over nine successive years. Overall, each group of judges agreed markedly both as to which documents were classifiable and the number of basic and sub-type categories to be established. In fact these judgmental runs resulted in many cases in each sub-type wherein *no* disagreement existed[50]. This I did not expect. This had not been my experience with previous psychological research - research which more often than not produced ambiguous data. Now I began to feel some trepidation. Now I started to doubt the secrecy of my design. I feared that somehow the judges might be trying to please me or even that they were in collusion. But as I thought it over, I dismissed this doubt from mind.

I simply could not see any way that the judges could be trying to please me because they knew nothing about what was being done except that I wanted them to classify the documents. They had practically no contact with the subjects who were also unaware of the nature of the project and each year's set of judges was gone from the scene before the next year's judges came to be. Also, there was no other source of information for them because not even my family, my department head, my administrators, my students, nor my colleagues knew I was involved in this research. In fact, in those years I was oft times chided for being 'nonproductive'. But this was not a crucial test of this problem. The crucial test was that each set of judges worked first of all with the new data of the current year. Yet with two exceptions, which I shall explain later, exceptions which in no way affected this crucial test, each year's set of judges came up with essentially the same classification system and roughly the same percentage of classifiable documents. Therefore, to my mind, there was nothing left to do but accept this mildly peculiar result as a psychological phenomenon suggesting that several discernible conceptions of mature personality do indeed exist.

---

[50] CWG: Only these cases were used in later behavioral and instrumental studies of the sub-type categories.

Second Perplexing Result:
Both Categories Functioned Well and Poorly

As time went on the peculiar aspects of the data became more and more apparent. The next perplexing results arose from clinical observations of the subjects - observations made over the two or three years that many of them continued as my students. Clinical judgment seemed to say (I have had many years' experience as a clinician) that something more was present in each sub-type category than simply the expression of a subject's belief as to what is a mature personality. In each sub-type category established by the judges I observed:

- the presence of subjects who seemed to function well and the presence of subjects who seemed to function poorly;

- subjects who displayed certain symptoms but not other symptoms; and

- subjects who were relatively free of symptomatic behavior.

These observations both intrigued me and confused me. I could not help but ask, what does it mean that two people who think alike psychologically, who have the same conception of mature personality, behave so differently? Why does one of the pair perform so poorly, and in a certain peculiar way? Why does the other perform so well, yet behave differently in other ways, too? Why does the former *never* turn in a paper without ridiculous errors, even when he has taken time and tried carefully to prepare it? Why is his work full of omissions, commissions, and obvious "slips of the tongue?" Why is this particularly true of one whose conception professes that maturity is the orderly, the rule-following, the carefully designed, authority respecting way of life? Why does he do that when his conceptual bed-fellow produces work which *is consistent* with his orderly, correct, rule-following, authority-respecting conception? But more than this, much more than this: Why do two representatives of the rational, calculating 'express self' conception of healthy personality behave similarly to the two 'sacrifice now for reward later' subjects in that one functions well, the other poorly, but well and poorly in a different way than the sacrificial subjects? Why do the two sacrificial subjects function so differently from the two 'express self' subjects when conceptual pair is compared to conceptual pair?

Why does the well-functioning *'sacrifice now for spiritual reward later'* subject follow the suggestions of the instructor as he produces his well-ordered conception? Why is the calculating risk taker driven to produce his well-ordered conception in a manner quite contrary to that suggested by the instructor? Why do both do so well when judged by the criterion "quality of performance?" Why do they behave so differently in the way that they do their work?

Why do two other conceptual antagonists show a similarity in that they both function poorly, yet behave so dissimilarly in the way they function poorly? For example, why does the *'sacrifice now to get spiritual reward later'* subject show his dysfunctional behavior in "silly" errors which punish self, when his conceptual antagonist becomes dysfunctional by interrupting his goal efforts with a mild to marked tirade directed toward others, usually his instructor?

What is different in the former that causes him, under stress, to take his frustration out on himself, while the latter takes it out on others, particularly authority? These results, accruing from my study of many such pairs, were bad enough, but the consternation they produced was minor in comparison to that which further study of them revealed, let alone what came to be when other sub-type pairs were studied. Soon I was to see that the similarity and dissimilarity between the *'sacrifice now for spiritual reward later'* sub-type and the *'rational calculating express self'* risk-taker was even more peculiar.

The *'sacrifice now to get spiritual reward later'* was not only punishing himself, he was also punishing me. When I returned his paper for correction stating it was returned for rewriting so that I could decipher it, the resubmitted paper took, relatively speaking, hours to decipher where previously it took minutes. In other words, this poorly functioning *'sacrifice now to get spiritual reward later'* subject hurt self directly, but me indirectly. Subtly, he made me pay for what he felt I had done to him. But the 'rational, risk taking express self' calculator's behavior was of a different order. There was nothing subtle in his direct attack upon me. He let me have it. But, at least from my point of view, he subtly attacked self by putting himself under the stress of much time lost in getting on toward the goal he was required to achieve.

When I moved on to examine the *'sacrifice now to get spiritual reward now'* type, my consternation increased, but it was trifling in comparison to the perplexity which developed when the *'express self but not at the expense of others'* data was encountered. The *'sacrifice now to get spiritual reward now'* displayed a tendency similar to the *'sacrifice now for spiritual reward later'* type. But once more, paradoxically enough, there was dissimilarity in the similarity of the two sub-types. As in the poorly functioning *'sacrifice now to get later,'* the poorly functioning *'sacrifice now to get now'* punished self directly and others indirectly. The poorly functioning representative of this type openly condemned self, damned self, and derogated self, but he was not aware that he punished others by making them suffer through his interminable self-condemnation.

On the well-functioning side, the *'sacrifice now to get spiritual reward now'* produced a well ordered, though different type of conception, but his modus operandi was very different from his well-functioning *'sacrifice now to get later'* counterpart. During the development of his papers he continuously sought the counsel and aid of his friends and he sought their approval of the final product; whereas the *'sacrifice now for reward later'* leaned on me and sought only my approval or leaned on some other authority he respected and sought his approval of the final product. Thus, the *'sacrifice now for reward now'* showed a dependency on his peers that was not the dependency on authority displayed by the *'sacrifice now for reward later'* type or the dependency on self of the *'express self with little shame or guilt'* subject.

Third Perplexing Result:
Poorly Functioning Produces Well

At this point, had I been predicting from the data studied to date how the "poorly functioning," *'express self but not at the expense of others'* would perform (poorly functioning must be in quotes for reasons which will soon be apparent), I would have said he will attack others directly and self indirectly, but in a new and different form because this was what I found in the other 'express self' category and because there was this kind of consistency in the two 'sacrifice-self' categories. And I would have predicted that he would produce an inferior product because that is what I found in each of the three categories studied to date. Had I done so, I would have been at one and the same time quite right but also very, very wrong,

I would have been right in that this 'express self' type did openly attack, and in that he did attack in a different form. But I would have been wrong because he did not attack other personalities. Subjects of this type did not attack people, nor did they displace their aggression on things. When they attacked, they bore down on *ideas*. Personalities were just not involved as they were in the 'calculating risk-taking' type. Thus, here, as with any set of my data, had I been predicting from one set to any other set *there would always be something I could predict, namely the general form of the behavior, but there would also be something I would never have predicted, namely its specificity.* That is, the behavior did not change just quantitatively; it also changed in a qualitative way. And more than this, at least in so far as the *'express self but not at the expense of others'* type was concerned, I would have missed one aspect of their behavior completely.

I would have predicted that this 'express self' type would harm self indirectly through failure to produce a satisfactory product, a product done well and also on time. Yet produce well and on time is precisely what he did, though one would never have predicted it from his means. When he was working on his conception or revision, he seemed at times both unsure of himself and at other times lethargic. What he did made no sense. Each task undertaken toward the goal seemed an insurmountable obstacle. But, always, out of lassitude and/or chaos and disorganization, an adequate, well-organized product emerged on the assigned delivery date. Hardly ever, except in most dire circumstances such as prolonged and incapacitating illness, did one of this type fail to produce not only on time but well.

This behavior of the poorly functioning *'express self but not at the expense of others'* brought my developing comprehension to a halt. Previous data had said poor functioning equals poor product, no matter the conceptualization of mature personality. Now I had to accept that for this category, this was not so. *Poor functioning* was not poor functioning. It only looked that way, even though in other psychological settings, other types of conceptions, poor functioning was poor functioning. These accumulating like and unlike results plagued me. They left me with the feeling that I was getting nowhere, and that I had to find some other approach to my data if clarification were to come.

This was most evident in the early stages of data analysis. For nine years I had collected data in the hope that it might help me clarify the confusing and contradictory world. Instead of fulfilling my hope, I had to face a fact. My data was screaming at me: "Psychology is a bigger muddle than ever you expected, and if you want to comprehend it you must find some other way than the one you are pursuing."

From this torment and from the peculiar kind of information now before me (similarity and dissimilarity both between major types and within sub-types and across type categories), the idea emerged that the conceptions represented something more than what some people thought was the psychologically mature person. The idea that the conceptions might represent personality systems in miniature came to be and the idea that psychological maturity was something other than a *state* or a *condition* came to be.

Are Mature Personality Conceptions *Personality Systems in Miniature*?

When the idea that psychological maturity and its parent, human personality, might be a systemically ordered process took root in my mind, I began to examine, from a systemic orientation, the quasi-experimental situations into which the subjects had been placed. Then the rumblings in my mind became a psychological avalanche which today has not subsided - an avalanche in which many feel my thinking should be buried because of what its slippage has uncovered. To see what this avalanche was and why so many think my findings should be rested deep within it, we need to take another backward look.

A Study of Change in Four Systems

After the subjects had developed their conceptions, without reference to the work of others and without reference to authority, each was required:

- to turn in a copy of his conception;
- to explain and defend his conception to a small group of co-subjects;
- to write either a revision or a defense of his conception, to cite the reasons for his defense and to turn it in to the instructor-investigator; and
- to study the conception of authorities as expressed in the literature.

Again, a defense or a revision was required along with reasons for the change or the defense.

Thus, there was the opportunity to observe for change or no change, an opportunity to observe for the direction of change if change took place, both when peer force was applied and when the force of authority was applied, and an opportunity to study what produced change. These data presented still more intriguing information. This we can see by looking at change as revealed in the early studies.

Change of one's conception of healthy personality, within the framework of the original four basic conceptual sub-types produced by the subjects and within the framework of the studies designed could be manifested in three major ways. They were:

1. no change;
2. peripheral change, that is change in the details of the conception but no change in the major premises; and
3. change centrally, that is, change in the major premise - progressive or regressive in nature.

In the course of the investigations, each of three major possibilities occurred. In the majority of the cases, the change was peripheral. When central change occurred the question was: Can one ascertain what precipitated this central change? To see how this was determined it is necessary to recall that the subjects were successively:

- put under peer pressure,
- required to modify or defend their conception and cite reasons for the change or the defense,
- put under the pressure of authority, and
- required to modify or defend their conception after being under the pressure of authority, and cite reasons for the change or the defense.

As checks upon the written reasons for change, subjects in each sub-type group were observed through a one-way mirror as they defended their conception in interaction with their peers and as they discussed their conception in relation to that presented in the literature by various authorities. Certain subjects were interviewed at the end of the course.

When the conceptions of the subjects who revised after either pressure situation were examined, it was found that some of the subjects in each category showed central change. When the cited reasons for this change were studied, it was found that certain reasons and not other reasons were given for change in each sub-type category. These reasons, again, tended both to differ and not to differ from sub-type category to sub-type category. When these data were crosschecked with the one-way mirror observation and interview data, the results listed in Table I appeared.

Table I – a
Change Instigators for Each Conceptual Sub-type of Healthy Personality

Type of Conception	Change Instigator
Sacrifice now for reward later	Pressure from respected authority
Sacrifice now for reward now	Pressure from valued important other
Express self for what self desires without shame or guilt	New information or experience, self procured
Express self but not at expense of others	New information, regardless of source

Table I – b
Direction of Change

Sacrifice now for reward later changed to:
Express self calculatedly for what self desires changed to:
Sacrifice self now for reward now changed to:
Express self but not at the expense of others.

Examination of Table 1 indicates that the sub-type *'sacrifice now for reward later'* conception changed centrally under the circumstance of pressure from external authority, a result which was not unexpected. It is quite customary for many humans to believe that authority should know and should direct, and for these humans to believe that authority exists in certain people but not in others - a fact which was clearly in the data. But here it was not only the pressure of authority that brought about the change; it was also a kind of external authority toward whom the subject already tended to feel respect. That is, a devout Catholic subject tended to respond to the thinking of a Catholic authority, but not to the thinking of a Jewish authority. A strong Jewishly oriented subject would be apt to respond to his kind of Jewish authority, but not to a Catholic authority, a Protestant authority, or a Jewish authority of a different ilk.

How the subjects knew who the authorities were is easily explained. In class sessions, before the student subject studied authorities, I presented an extended biography of each of those to be studied.

The sub-type category, *'sacrifice now to get spiritual reward now'* changed in a way similar but dissimilar from the *'sacrifice for spiritual reward later'* type. They, too, changed under the pressure of others, but their source was their valued peer. Authority did not come from *external higher* sources as in the *'sacrifice now to get later'* subjects. The latter did not respond to peer pressure, no matter what kind of people made up the peer group and no matter what was the peer group's orientation. Neither of these two sub-types changed centrally when straightforward factual information called into question the position they had taken. Instead, they questioned whether the information was factual. The *'sacrifice now to get later'* group called information a fact only when *their* authority said it was a fact, and the *'sacrifice now to get now'* subjects took information as gospel when their valued other accepted or provided it. These *'sacrifice now to get now'* groups did not ignore authoritativeness, nor did they disregard factual information. It was what they looked upon as authority and what they did with factual information that was different. They used the valued other as their authority, as the authority to pass judgment on whether factual information should or should not be accepted. If the valued other lent authoritativeness to the information, it was accepted and then, and only then, did central change ensue.

As I considered the meaning in this tidy bit of information, it became apparent that my psychological avalanche was now gaining momentum. Now, one sub-type said, "A fact is not a fact unless *my God* says it is so; but this same fact is not a fact if *your* particular God says it is." Another sub-type said, "A fact is not a fact when *anyone's* God so defines it. It is a fact only when my valued friends say so." But it isn't even a fact then, as we shall see as we look at the result of the 'express self rationally' sub-type.

The sub-type *'express self rationally but calculatedly for what self desires without shame or guilt'* accepted information as a fact in quite a different way. Thus, in this group the impetus to central change was of another order. These subjects paid no attention to what any authority said, least of all me. In fact, one day, a certain subject astonished me and his class when he demanded that I step aside and let him inform the class what his experience had told him were *the true* psychological facts. He and other sub-type subjects scoffed at peer opinion and disparaged all authority. When information peripherally modified their point of view, this information came to be and came to be "fact" only as a result of their own actions. They did something themselves the results of which signaled to them that their previous information did not work, and they did it alone. Their road to central change was pragmatic. These subjects went so far as to openly fight the design of the course. They insisted that they be excused from interaction with their peers and they even resisted studying authorities. They finally acquiesced to this part of the course only when I permitted them to demonstrate that from their own experience the authorities studied seemed to be wrong.

So now we have, from the 'express self rational calculators,' another interpretation of when information is a fact. It now becomes a fact if one's experience, and only one's experience, says it is. But I do not want to mislead the reader. There is nothing really new in the finding that there are filters in the minds of men.

However, there is something quite extraordinary in these data. It is the peculiar, similar-dissimilar aspect of the data in the first two sub-types which is not completely upheld in the third sub-type. Because of this, I wondered what I would find about a fact in the fourth sub-type, the 'express self, but not at the expense of others' group.

The fourth group related in their papers and stated orally that at times it was the word of authority which led them to change certain points in their conception. They reported and stated that other changes took place because of peer group experiences. And at other times, their data showed that some change arose from what the self alone did or what it alone thought. Thus, this group was again similar to the *'express'* types than the *'sacrifice'* types because information could become a fact for them regardless of its source. All this seemed to say that they were more open-minded.

Normally, we would readily explain the apparent open-mindedness of the *'express self concernedly'* subjects, particularly when the investigatory subject matter is conceptions of mature personality, in a very simple way. We would say that this sub-type is *the* psychologically mature state in operation. But before this conclusion is drawn, one should consider what it would leave unexplained in respect to the total data accumulated to date, a consideration which might leave you more confused.

One should recall that we have three other psychological states demonstrably different from each other, as well as different from the *'express self concernedly'* type. And one should recall that in each of these states, observation has indicated that people function well. Thus, if this fourth state is *the* psychologically mature state, then logically the other three are less mature states; and logically, there should be degrees of immaturity between the other three. But denoting the fourth as *the mature state* in no way explains the relationship of the other three to one another, nor why or how they are less mature. Therefore, it is necessary to entertain the idea that there is much more in the data than has been seen so far. And it is necessary to prepare ourselves for the possibility that designating the *'express self concernedly'* sub-type as *the mature state* may serve to lead us away from, rather than toward, an understanding of what human life is all about.

This is precisely the quandary I got into when the next set of data was examined.

My next set of data said almost unequivocally that the *'express self but not at the expense of others'* conception does not represent the mature psychological state in operation. In fact it demolished the idea that there is a conception of psychological maturity, a state of psychological being which can be researched for and someday described. It said that the *'express self concernedly'* is only one more state of being, one more in an endless chain. But these new data said much more, so much more, that the effect of what they revealed almost put me in a state of shock. My condition came to be as I examined the data for change in the centrality of conceptions and how, if it existed, such change came to be.

Six Factors in the Change Process

Change in the centrality of conception was not rare. When it was observed, the first thing which had to occur for change to another central conception to ensue was a solution of what I came to call *existential problems*. The evidence of this came about in a very peculiar manner. All of the subjects were students in my classes. All had the very real problem of not only passing the course but of achieving, or feeling they had a chance to achieve, the grade level to which they aspired. This problem of grading was a stumbling block to all until the first marking period in the course, the point at which the original conception was turned in. In order to demonstrate to the student-subjects that expressing self honestly would not damn them, I chose four criteria for grading their work. They were:

 a. Breadth of coverage of human behavior;
 b. Internal consistency of conception;
 c. Non-violation of established psychological fact (For example, it was indicated that if a conception said a human being was mature who did not feel emotion, this would violate fact.); and
 d. Applicability of the conception.

After setting up the criteria, I still had to prove, to the best of my ability, that personal bias as to mature behavior was not affecting the grading. I handled this by making lengthy comments and selecting certain papers to be read before the class with the comments appropriately related. Then, after the paper was read, the student was asked to tell the class what grade was recorded for him at the registrar's office. Some of the comments were almost brutal. For example, I might say, "If this is what you think a mature human being is, then when you leave this class, I hope I never see or meet you again." Or, "Ye Gods, what a horrible automaton you make of human life." The first might say he received an "A." The second might say he received a "D". We would then examine how the "A" came about through the application of the criteria and how the "D" seemed warranted in terms of the criteria set up for grading.

At the end of the course, when I interviewed those whose central position changed, they pointed out that solving the grade problem was essential to their readiness to think of change. But this, they said, served only to create the condition for change. It did not produce change.

When queried about what else was involved, they said one thing was that somewhere, somehow, in the course of time things were said or done which disturbed their complacency. They said that following this disturbance of their complacency some new ideas, some new thoughts which came from somewhere - they could not often express from where - started the change. And they said that at the right time the right person, seldom the instructor, encouraged them to explore their ideas further. But here the similarity from sub-type to sub-type ceased. For each sub-type the general factors listed above held, but the specific change factors varied.

For them to change, now translating into the technical language of this book, they had to experience certain general conditions which were:

1. potential,
2. solution of existential problems,
3. feeling of dissonance,
4. gaining of insights,
5. having properly timed and administered aid or non-interference - that is removal of barriers, and
6. opportunity to consolidate.

But, when they talked further, it became evident that these general change factors were particularized to each sub-type, a matter we shall now explain.

The meaning of having a chance to procure the grade desired meant something different to the subjects in each group. The *'sacrifice now to get now'* group felt it put them in good stead with the peer group. The *'express self at any cost without shame or guilt'* group felt it proved they had been right about this world all the while. And the *'express self but not at the expense of others'* said the grade meant little or nothing, but the fact that grading took place in a setting wherein they could think for themselves meant a lot.

That which disturbed the person's complacency, that is, that which produced dissonance also varied from sub-type to sub-type. The *'sacrifice self now to get reward later'* sub-type was disturbed when a respected authority questioned an idea the student believed his authority would never question. A Catholic subject might find a Catholic authority questioning whether sexual abstinence was good for psychological health. A *'sacrifice self now to gain now'* might find his valued other or valued others taking a position contrary to general group opinion, and he might find people who did not damn him if he differed with the group. The *'express self for what self desires without shame or guilt'* subject was particularly disturbed when I, as his instructor, disagreed with him violently and still gave him a good grade. He could not comprehend fair authority. The *'express self, but not at the expense of others'* became disturbed by reading over what he had previously said or he became disturbed by seeming to be too sure of himself.

The insights of each of the sub-types also varied. For example:

1. 'Sacrifice now for reward later group.'
   Insight - one can question authorities' established rules and not necessarily get into trouble.
2. 'Sacrifice now to get now group.'
   Insight - going against the group will not necessarily end in ostracism, if you have good information.
3. 'Express self calculatedly for what self desires without shame or guilt group.'
   Insight - others may help you express self, they are not always out to get you.
4. 'Express self but not at the expense of others group.'
   Insight - when I started this train of thought I felt I would find the answer; now that I see that any answer is a function of what information one has and of how he looks at the information, I see there is really no one answer.

When these six factors were studied in order to determine the role of each in change, I was far from prepared for what I was to find. When existential problems alone were solved, the person went only to a more complex version of his already existing way of thinking. It was as if he said unto himself, "Things have gotten better and better so long as I have thought this way; therefore, if I go further in this direction, things can't help but get better and better." In other words, solving one's existential problems alone was not sufficient reason for him to change his behavior. But as I continued, more and more insight into change came to be; but at the same time more and more confusion arose in my mind.

It so happened that some subjects who got good grades the first five weeks, who also extended and defended their original conception, produced a logical mishmash at the end of the second five weeks reporting period. Where this occurred, the subjects insisted on a resubmission so that their grade problem might be righted. At first, I simply acquiesced to their request and thus had an opportunity to observe what they would produce when existential problems had been solved (first five-week grade) and when dissonance came in to disturb what appeared to be an already existing solution of a problem. That the person was in a crisis stage was most apparent.

The first resubmission was simply an increase in what had worked well for the person originally, but had failed him later. After it failed him again, after the expected payoff was not forthcoming, all of these subjects came to progressively feel hopelessness and frustration. Some never got beyond this point; whereas others moved on into somewhat random trial and error behavior as if to say, "The old way isn't working; I'd better look for something new." But these people just did not make it back to where they were or forward to some other point of view. In other words, solution of existential problems and the arisal of dissonance, served either to cause a person's point of view to encyst or to cause the person to strive to change to a new functional point of view. Together, solution of existential problems and arisal of dissonance were not enough to establish a new behavioral form.

It was only when the insight specific to a category arose, along with potential, and was added to the solution of existential problems and dissonance that one could truly see a definitive change in conception taking place, definitive in terms of movement in the direction of a new conceptual form. But this alone, in the setting of this work, was not enough to rapidly change the conception. I say "in the setting of this work" because I still do not know if a person could have gotten there alone, because in the setting I helped the person as he demanded help. That is, wherever possible I removed *barriers* to his performance.

Two examples should illustrate this *barrier factor*. For the *'express self with little shame or guilt'* type, I had to completely remove intermediate evaluation of his performance. He would permit no evaluation of his work in process or evaluation of the way he was working. In the case of the *'sacrifice now to get later'* subjects, it was necessary to work toward change gently, protectively, and methodically in the beginning of the process to enable them to overcome the barrier of fear. When this was managed to their satisfaction, a second barrier arose in its place. The subjects were now blocked by any aid that I might proffer. Aid at this point was so frustrating that they told me to get off their back, to leave them alone, to let them work out the changed conception to their satisfaction whether it fulfilled the established criteria or not. When I learned to accept this change in them, they settled into the consummation of a new, different, and reasonably ordered conception which signaled the end of this change process.

Now I had a six-fold process of change. The first was potential - some never changed. The second was the solution of existential problems. The third was disturbance of the solution, that is dissonance, which precipitated a stage of regression. Then insight came into the picture as that which halted the regressive phase. This was followed by the need to remove barriers so that a quantum-like jump to a different way of thinking could occur. Then it was necessary for consummation of the change to take effect.

But in this overall process there was much complicating data. For each conception there were different kinds of dissonance, insights, barriers, etc. Now, all had to be combined with the previous data before I could think of rationalization. But this complication, though bad enough, was just a minor rumble from the avalanche that was now gaining mass and momentum—the avalanche that scr ambled all psychological data in its path.

The next data to be examined arose from the question: What is the nature of the change which ensues when central change occurs? These results became the most disconcerting ones to date because they so aggravated the developing confusion in the data—an aggravation which can best be reported by examples.

Examples of Central Change in Sub-type

Mike M. originally said in a part of his protocol:

"My idea of the psychologically healthy human may differ from others but here it is. First he does not have any glaring problems like the gambler. This includes certain kinds of addictions to habits which are not evil but wasteful, such as a sports "nut." Please don't confuse this with the sports buff. My definition of a sports nut is one who insists on watching the Sunday football game while the buff is one who likes football but disciplines himself to leave it alone. This is an example that the person would exercise control over his emotions and his actions. He lives by principles such as the Ten Commandments, by the religious ethical or moral principles prescribed in his world.

One of his most noticeable characteristics is his outwardly placid disposition protected by a thick emotional skin which allows him to remain unaffected by taunts, insults and other irritants in life. This placidity exists in the mature because he knows if he controls himself when others do not do so, it will be he in the long run who will profit. He is willing to sacrifice his own desires whenever possible and feels that were others to do so, it would be for the overall interests of society. He adheres to The Golden Rule—"Do unto others as you would have them do unto you."

He know that taking baths, and going to school, controlling his appetite is unpleasant to him but he knows the clear distinction between right and wrong and such things as temporary joy and sadness with respect to future joy and sadness. He does not live by what is good for him or will bring him momentary joy. He lives by what is right, by his raison d'etre, his reason for being almost invariably will be manifested in theism."

The centrality of this concept from Mike's original protocol (the totality is basically a repetition on the themes stated above) seems quite clear. He speaks of strong and disciplined control over his impulse life and wants; of sacrificing current desires for future reward; of living by an absolutistic, prescribed moral code generally theistic in origin; and in a subjective, qualitative way. But this is not the centrality in the conception he vigorously defended when the final presentation was made. Then he said:

> "I think now of what I said in the beginning of this course: 'My idea of the psychologically mature human may differ from others but here it is.' Now I would have to include myself among those others because something has happened to me. Even those who knew me in the past insist that what I say and do now is not what I said and did before. But somehow they just don't

understand. I don't deny that what I said then was me nor will I let anyone dispute that what I believe at this writing is the me that is.

I still believe that the mature personality disciplines himself but he does so to get control over the world of which he is a part; he does so to keep himself unwilling to submit to the arbitrary controls put upon him by rule and others; he does so in order that he can rationally and objectively question the validity of all ideas of the society.

Today to consider the issue of perfect psychological maturity one must accept the idea that behavior and character are interrelated and measurable. And, to be measurable, in two or more people, with the intent to compare the results are but a part of the end.

Each individual, ideally at least, should be governed by instincts and motivations which seem rationally to lead to his betterment and to his comfort. This is the only logical end one can attach to existence, the gratification of himself as an individual.

It is evident that in determining what is mature psychological behavior, we have based our conclusions on the prescriptions handed down to us by authority, judging men by values that were laid down "on Tablets of Salt." It was thus that our moral prescriptions for proper living and the means to their implementation developed. In the past it was generally accepted that the individual was subordinate to the cosmic whole, and hence the psychological traits of the mature person were based on value judgments concerning a collective rather than an individualistic analysis of human nature."

That is not how I see mature behavior today. Today it does seem to me that psychological well being is dependent upon man's ability to overcome the inhibitions to his own satisfactions, upon being free of guilt and free of shame and upon performing when he is motivated and not tempering his striving for pleasure. He is free from the threats and negative reactions of others. He does not fear his own psyche or the consequences of being a law unto himself. He is the source of inspiration for all of his actions, the determiner of what means are appropriate to his ends."

I doubt that anyone would deny that the centrality of Mike's final (final in the sense of the last class paper) conception is poles apart from his original presentation, though some might doubt that he meant what he said. I, however, had to proceed on the assumption, albeit tenuous, that the change was genuine.

Following that assumption I was able to conclude that Mike's revised conception centralized around the expression of self, the establishment of one's own rules, satisfaction of "human wants," shaping means to fit personal ends, and around objective materialistic, rational, quantitative thinking.

In some respects the character of the change in Mike M.'s conception did not surprise me. Experience would say that if one threw off a moralistic, absolutistic, self-sacrificing set of ideas, he would try in their place the unashamed expression of the self. But I had to ask myself: Would I have predicted that accompanying this "selfish expression of the self" would be a change from subjective, qualitative, spiritual thinking to objective, quantitative, thought processes? I know I would not have done so, and I doubt that others would have predicted the total change. Therefore, becoming more intrigued with each successive datum, I proceeded to the next, the change of the *'express self without shame or guilt'* to another central form. In this instance, the original conception of Linda S. proposed in the heart of her protocol:

> "If we view man's greatest concern as that of problem solving and decision making, the ability to make decisions rationally, objectively and decisively, without lingering doubt because it is backed by sound quantitative data, would be the basis of a psychologically mature mind. This ability to be decisive, to live without doubt, to be able to live for what one wants today, to be able to eliminate confusion regarding ends and the means necessary to reach those ends so as to decisively use the means necessary to the end, ranks as the number one requirement for a mature psychological mind. It helps prevent the establishment of misdirection and aimless behavior. The ability to prevent that which impedes logical, rational thinking which leads to worry, or guilt or shame, which in turn upsets the psychological soundness of the person, is one of the major qualities of the theory of decisiveness which helps lay the basis for judging a psychologically mature human being. If uncertainty and doubt are removed from the mind of man by objective, quantifiable information, if thinking can therefore be rational and logical, if ends (are established) and effective means established a psychologically sound human being is in the making."

Confusion and Contradiction

I believe it is apparent that the centrality of Linda's original conception is substantively the same as was found in the revised conception of Mike M. In her conception the central concern is with self, with ends over means, and with rational, objective, quantitative thinking—the same central elements we found in the conception of Mike. But now the question is: What is the character of the central change when Linda's concept evidenced revision? At the end of the course Linda said:

> "Not too long ago I might have hesitated to put down the words that now describe my feeling as to the psychologically mature mind. I have nothing of an objective or quantitative character upon which to base that which I now find myself disposed to believe.
>
> A few short weeks ago decisiveness was to me the key sign of maturity. Man had to observe, test, analyze and decide if he was to do the mature thing. But now I am not so certain, so certain as I was then that precise knowing is the means to the end of a sound psychological mind. It seems to me that the mature personality, the sound psychological mind cannot, need not, and should not be so calculating, so certain as then I conceived it to be. What then is the conception I now have? What is the psychologically mature mind? It is the mind that is alert, alert not only to fact, but also to feeling. It is the mind that recognizes facts may not be what the data says but the way they are interpreted.
>
> But I seem to be equivocating. I seem to be writing around rather than to the point. Tonight in contrast to my previous concern with decision making and objectively arrived at courses for action, I see the mature mind concerned with the effect decisions might have on others, with being with, rather than going it alone on the basis of evidence. I do not see how the mature mind can live as an island to itself. Nor do I see that it can exist solely in relation to its God. To be mature is to cast aside one's certainty, to be able to commune with others, to receive from them the signals for one's being rather than to live by one's own wants or the prescriptions of the past.
>
> Life is not a fact nor is it a set of rules. There is something more than believing, something more than knowing in the mind of him who is mature. There is, above all else, feeling, feeling with and feeling for and feeling that to be is to be as one with <u>the</u> others in our life, feeling that we must abrogate our wants if we are all to find the acceptance which we seek and which now and forever we

must have. I do now believe that becoming one with other men, leads more toward the maturity of man than all his certain knowing can."

These results, when first observed, were indeed disconcerting. When the moral, *'sacrifice self for reward later'* subjects changed centrally to the immoral, *'calculating, materialistic express self with little shame or guilt'* type it was not unexpected. But when I saw this materialistic view change into the *'sacrifice self now to get peace and approval now'* conception, I began to search for explanation. Then, when I searched for how the *'sacrifice some now for reward now'* changes, my capacities for explanation began to run out. It changed to the *'express self, but not at the expense of others'* type. As a pattern started to emerge, my dismay subsided. The pattern was that 'sacrifice-self' types, when they change centrally, change to 'express-self' types. But what of the other major category? What of the 'express-self' types? How do they change when the subject is not under stress? Now, still to my dismay, I was to learn that the pattern was repeating. The *'express self for what self desires with little shame or guilt'* type changed to *'sacrifice self for reward now.'* And, the *'express self but not at the expense of others'* rocked the total foundation of my beliefs. It changed to a new form, to *'maturity is accepting the realities of existence.'* Maturity is not trying to know the unknowable. Maturity is adjusting to man's existential dichotomies.[51] In other words, the *'express self but not at the expense of others'* changes to a new form of adjusting and became more like the two 'sacrifice-self' groups and less like the two 'express-self' types.

An interesting factor here is that in the latter part of the basic studies, a few subjects started to produce conceptions of this kind as their original point of view.

Systems Are Specific As Well As General

Now you can see a major peculiarity in the data. Now you can see that something remarkable has happened. The two 'sacrifice-self' groups, which look like one another in terms of being sacrificial, accepting systems, are also like one another in terms of shifting centrally to 'express-self' forms. But they are not like one another in terms of what they perceive to be their existential problems. They are not like one another in terms of what produces dissonance in the field, and they are

---

[51] CWG: Existential dichotomies, according to Eric Fromm, are: Why was I born? - Why must I die? Why was I born with more ability than can be used in a lifetime? Man is alone and related at the same time.

not like one another in terms of the insights they develop before and as other change takes place. The two 'express-self' categories are like one another in terms of changing centrally to 'deny-self' types of conceptions. They are unlike one another in the same way as are the sacrificial systems.

Now a cyclic, oscillating movement in adult development is suggested. It is, sacrifice self, express self, sacrifice self, express self, and so on. Next, the need for ordering this wavelike movement so that each wave is properly related to the other waves was required.

Exhibit II

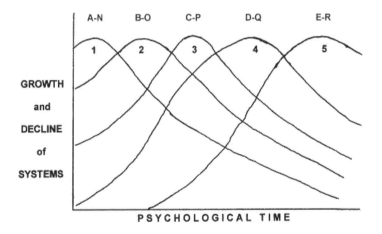

How this ordering should take place was suggested by another study, but before we look at it, we must examine some unfinished business.

What of the subjects who did not change, or what of those that changed in some other way than related above? Those who did not change seemed unaffected by the way I handled the grade problem. In other words, the power at my disposal could not solve any existential problem important to them. Any existential problems which had to be solved for them in order for them to be ready for change were problems I could not affect.

As to other forms of change, only one need be mentioned now. It is regressive change. As I look back, after the systems are ordered, I can see that some subjects changed regressively, not progressively. My opportunity to study this was limited because severe personal stress seemed to produce the regression and this seldom occurred in the course of the studies. It needs to be studied more, but since knowledge of it is not essential to the problem of deriving the conceptual idea, I will leave it at this point and return to the development of the idea of hierarchically ordered "systems" of adult behavior.

The Freedom to Behave Study

At this point, clinical inference again entered the field. By now I knew my subjects well, not only from their personal documents, but also from the behavioral situations. From this knowledge developed the impression that the *'express self but not at the expense of others'* subjects, of all the original subjects involved, were overall the freest subjects. In any situation they seemed to display more degrees of behavioral freedom. The *'sacrifice now to get reward later'* subjects seemed by far the least free of all. Therefore, another group of judges were assigned the task of observing the subjects in problem situations, to judge how free the subjects were to behave without restriction in a novel situation. They were instructed to order the conceptions from the least free to the most free.[52] The results corroborated the clinical judgment, and were further corroborated in later experimental studies.

The *'express self but not at the expense of others'* subjects were judged the most free and far freer than any others. The *'sacrifice self now to get now'* subjects were judged the next most free, followed by the *'express self for what self desires with little shame or guilt'* type. The least free was the *'sacrifice now to get reward later'* group.

Summary of Confusing Data

Now a most conflictual set of data had been collated. It is summarized below.

   a. The *'sacrifice now to get spiritual reward later'* was like the *'sacrifice self to get spiritual reward now'* in seeing mature personality as adjustive to external source and as denying the self.
   b. The *'sacrifice self now to get later'* was like the *'sacrifice now to get now'* group in terms of changing to an expression of self type when central change took place.

---

[52] CWG: The sacrifice self to existential realities were too few to study.

c. The *'express self for what self desires with little shame or guilt'* type was not like the *'express self but not at the expense of others'* in terms of taking advantage of others.

These conflictual data started to make some sense when the change data was combined with the data from the Freedom to Behave studies. Now, if one hypothesized that adult man moved from fewer degrees of behavioral freedom to more degrees of behavioral freedom, he had dictated to the hierarchy:

'sacrifice now to get later,' to
    'express self for what self desires with little shame or guilt,' to
        'sacrifice now to get now,' to
            'express self but not at the expense of others,' to possibly
                'adjust self to existential realities.'

But, this was still the germinal stage of an idea. It was necessary to explore further.

Supplemental Studies

When these data took the peculiar character noted above, several other studies were carried out in an attempt to see if further information might possibly clarify the conflict in the data and support the idea of adult personality systems. The first of them involved the Norman Maier type[53] problem solving situations but with some variations injected. For example, problems similar to Maier's were presented as problems for a group to solve rather than just on an individual basis. A group in each sub-type category was assigned not only the task of solving the problem but also they were told to organize themselves for the task. Five kinds of data were provided from these studies.

1. How each of the groups organized to carry out the assigned task.
2. How the members in each group interacted in the course of their attack upon the problem.
3. The degree to which the approach taken was relevant to the problem.
4. The quality of the solutions arrived at.
5. The quantity of solutions arrived at.

In a sense, the results of these studies did not clarify the previous data. Yet, in another sense, the new data made the older more

---

[53] CWG: These problems involved using objects in ways far removed from their normal use. [Ed.: The New Truck Dilemma, an exercise in group decision making]

meaningful, but not in the sense of removing any of the conflict in the previous data. These studies simply added more of the same. But, in the sense that they added more of the same, and thereby strengthened the developing belief that something quite peculiar lay in the data, the problem solving data was most helpful. We can see this by looking at each of the five sub-studies carried on in the problem solving setting. First, let us look at how each of the four basic groups organized to approach the problems. The results of how each group organized are shown in Exhibit III.

The groups varied in size from seven to fifteen. In each of the sub-type categories, the organization took a different form. The *'sacrifice self now in order to gain reward later'* regularly organized in pyramidal fashion, but never was just one pyramid formed. There were as many as four and as few as two. In each overall organization the members lined up under the direction of one they already considered an authority who began laying out an attack upon the problem. Some members quickly fell into line with and continued to carry out his/her instructions. But not all members fell in line with the one who was given the lead role. Before long, an obvious kibitzer or two emerged. The number of kibitzers in the pyramidal group varied. Some markedly challenged the position taken by the original leaders; other kibitzers did not. With time, other members, who waited first to follow, lined up under the original leader or a kibitzer. Still in most instances, one or two isolated or floating uncommitted appeared in this type of group.

The *'sacrifice self to gain reward later'* group, therefore, utilized a pyramid type of organization, but all members could not be drawn into one pyramid. The group organized itself basically into more than one pyramidally structured group.

The *'express self for what self desires with little shame or guilt'* group organized in a quite different fashion. Once the assignment was begun, an obvious vying for the leadership position took place. Each member seemed to be trying to get hold of the group. As the vying took place, argument increased. The whole atmosphere became charged. Epithets rolled; name-calling was the order of the day. The struggle continued until one party managed to subdue all objections to his taking the lead. Once he took the lead, he was not only the 'boss man' in the sense of thinking for the group as to how to approach the problem, but he also kept, so to speak, his finger constantly on the action and thought of all members of the group. He would allow no change from his approach.

Exhibit III

Diagramatic Representation of Organizational Structure Evolved by Four Sub-types in the Problem Solving Area

Sub-type	Sacrifice now to get later	Sub-type	Express self for what self desires without shame or guilt
Leadership assumed by Authoritarian		Leadership assumed after fight for power	

| More than one pyramidal System - some isolates | | Big wheel type - power figure directly controlled all others | |

Sub-type	Sacrifice now to get now	Sub-type	Express self but not at expense of others
Leadership avoided - taken only when group assigned		Leadership agreed on after lively discussion of possible approaches	

More than one flat type organization based primarily on previous acquaintanceship

Revolving type organization Leader change based on knowledge

Yet, he would change his approach suddenly at times, possibly in a direction some other member had previously tried to suggest. But seldom would he acknowledge that anyone had ever suggested a variation. This man acted like what some people call the "big wheel," a person who not only insists on leading the action, but also on being in on and controlling everyone involved in the action. Therefore, this was called "the Big Wheel" form of organization.

Our third group is the *'sacrifice now in order to get now'* group. Again, they operated in a fashion noticeably different from any other group. First of all, it was very difficult for them to get going. They insisted that time be taken for each to express himself as to how to approach a problem. They would express that they did not feel they should begin with any single person's approach until they were sure they were all in agreement, and no one seemed to take the lead. Gradually, as one or another expressed an opinion, form started to take place. Sub-groups developed as the members related to the idea of one person or the idea of some other member. The larger group, in other words, became organized into smaller groups. As each smaller group evolved, they again sought consensus and each again was reluctant to assume the lead. But with time *they* agreed on an approach and assigned a member or members the task of carrying it out. This type of organization was called the "Circle" organization because it reminded the author of Bavelas's work.[54]

The last group, the *'express self but not at the expense of others'* group, operated in a most intriguing fashion. As soon as the assignment was made, a squabble, sometimes more than just lively, tended to ensue. Each member, as soon as he had an idea, insisted that he be heard. He fought the ideas of others in order to get them to see his light but never fought a person personally. The fight always related to the merits of the idea. It was never reduced to epithets or name calling as in the other 'express self' group.

In this group, a person who seemed to be best equipped in terms of the problem, his knowledge, and his ideas emerged into leadership. But he made no attempt to dominate the work. He would present his ideas and he and the others would work them through. If his idea failed or when a new problem arose, he might or might not continue to lead. Whether he continued to lead seemed to be determined by whether the group continued to see him as more equipped. In other words, this group revolved leadership when, in their judgment, other knowledge should prevail. The leadership, then, tended to change, but failure never led to ostracism of the person whose approach did not work, as occurred in the other 'express-self' group. Because of this, it was called the "Revolving Leadership" organization.

Thus, as you can see from Exhibit III and the descriptions above, the two 'sacrifice-self' types are more like one another than they are like the 'express-self' types. But alike as they are, they are still *unlike* one another. This like but not like relationship holds for the 'self expressive' types as well. Therefore, we can see that the trend of the data in the organizational study follows the trend of the data from the previous

---

[54] Alex Bavelas, professor of psychology, MIT; founder of the Group Networks Laboratory in 1948; experimentor in communication and social networks.

studies cited. We can therefore see that we have, from the organizational studies, a reinforcement of the results of the previous studies.

The Interaction Studies

Some of the interaction data was obvious in the organizational studies related. Here I shall present only the salient results as they pertain to the developing conceptual idea.

Again, in these data I found the two 'sacrifice-self' groups similar and dissimilar at the same time, and I found them interacting quite differently from the 'express-self' groups. A most noticeable factor was the air of quiet control present in both sacrificial groups. Voices tended not to rise when disagreement was present. Politeness seemed to rule the scene. But here the similarity ended between the two sacrifice groups. This was most obvious when conflict ensued. When and if conflict ensued, in the *'sacrifice now to get later'* group it was between hierarchical leaders or between the same level of subordinates in their own or other hierarchies. By and large, conflict just did not ensue between levels in a hierarchy. When it did arise between hierarchies, it became ultimately the most vicious of the conflicts in all sub-type groups. It was not only irresolvable except by separation of the hierarchies within the particular *'sacrifice now to get later'* groups, but it lingered in spiteful and revengeful form far longer than in any other sub-type.

In the *'sacrifice now in order to get now'* group, conflict would arise in the form of mild disagreement, gently even almost apologetically expressed. But, as soon as it arose, nearly all members of the larger groups would try to conciliate the disagreement. It was as if they could not bear for any discord to break out. Disagreement might arise from any member of this group, even after the group established assigned leaders; but it was the group as a whole that operated to remove the disagreement even though the problem might not be solved. The group accepted that conflict might arise. That conflict should continue or should disrupt the group was beyond their ken. They interacted continuously in a compromising manner after conflict ensued in order to see that all finally agreed that the problem was resolved and that the conflict was eradicated.

In the self-expressive sub-type, I again found the similarity/dissimilarity operating. In the *'express self now for what self desires with little shame or guilt'* group, conflict was there from the beginning, and it was raucous conflict, not the quiet controlled form of the two sacrificial groups. The conflicts continued unabated until the more dominant won. Then the dominant person allowed no conflict once leadership was established. If his leadership failed, the conflict reappeared until a new pecking order ensued. It was only after leadership breakdown became apparent and new leadership was established that one could see only a sullen peace had intervened. The new leader was most vicious about the frailties of the fallen leader. The only similarities here to the *'express self but not at the expense of others'* group were that raucousness was present, that leadership changed and that a person central to all led the group.

In the *'express self but not at the expense of others'* group, raucousness was present, not only in the beginning, but almost all the time. They seemed, so to speak, to be having a ball while they argued. But there was no attempt of one to dominate another. Each had his say, and each by and large presented his say in a fervent manner. When it appeared that one person had a good idea, the others said, "Let's try it." If the idea failed, he did not necessarily lose his position. If he had another idea, as I said previously, it would be entertained with equal weight even though one of his ideas had just failed. He might well be kidded, but at no time was be reviled as was the fallen leader in the *'express self for what self desires with little shame or guilt'* group.

Again, one can see in these data the need to conceptualize adult behavioral systems so that certain of them are similar and dissimilar sacrificial systems at the same time. And we see again the need to view the 'express-self' systems as being quite different from the ones mentioned above, yet similar and dissimilar to one another. And, we will see in the remaining sub-studies more evidence to this effect piling up.

The Relevancy of Approach Study

In the problem solving situations I knew, of course, what attacks upon the problems were relevant and not relevant to the task before the subjects. Therefore, I was able to assess as I observed the process of attack upon the problem how relevant were the questions asked, and how much redundancy was present. That is, how much did a group tend to go at the problem in a progressively solving manner or in a manner that they had tried previously and found wanting.

Here it was found that the sacrificial groups approached the problem in a less relevant manner than the two 'express-self' groups. The approaches and questions of the sacrificial groups were also redundant. But the *'sacrifice now to get later'* group's approach was more irrelevant, more redundant than the *'sacrifice now to get now'* group. And the *'express self for what self desires with little shame or guilt'* group was more irrelevant and more redundant than the *'express self but not at the expense of others'* group which was the least redundant and most relevant of the four.

Quality and Quantity of Solutions

When I examined the quality of the solutions of the problems, all the groups did, in time, resolve most problems in ways which were considered to be reasonably good solutions, though the solutions of some were quite fragile. What varied most was the time to find a solution, the average time of solutions, and the number of the solutions. The sacrificial groups were slower than the 'express-self' groups. But the *'sacrifice self now to get later'* was the slower of the two and slower than the *'express self but not at the expense of others'* group. When the quantity and quality of solutions was considered, factors beyond the pairing of results appeared. Here the most significant data was that the *'express self but not at the expense of others'* found more solutions and better solutions than all the other groups put together.

A number of other studies were conducted, but with seven exceptions did not contribute anything new to the development of the basic conceptual idea. There were psychometric studies and, with the exception of the study of temperament, results are listed in Table II.

Table II
Results of Psychometric Studies of Four Conceptualizations of Healthy Personality per Sub-type

4 = s most of characteristic
1 = s least of characteristic
* = s significant difference in respect to other types as numbered immediately below

Instrument and 2nd Dimension Measured	Sacrifice now Reward later	Express at Cost	Sacrifice for Approval	Express self with Consideration
ACE and College Boards				
Intelligence	2.4	2.5	2.5	2.6
Adorno				
Authoritarianism	4	2	3	1
Rokeach				
Dogmatism	*2-3-4 4	*1-3-4 3	*2-3-4 2	*1-2-3 1.5
Gough-Sanford				
Rigidity	*2-3-4 4	1.5	3	*1-2-3 1.5
Edwards' Preference				
Deference	4	1.5	3	1.5
Autonomy	1	3.5	2	3.5
Affiliation	3	*3 1	*2 4	2
Change	*4 1.4	3.5	1.5	*1 3.5
Aggressiveness	2	4	2	2
Scott's Values				
Self control	*2-3-4 4	1.8 1	2.0	2.7
Honesty	*2-3 4	*1-3 1	3	2
Desire to be different	1	4	3	2
Kindness	*2 3.5	1	*2 3.5	2
Loyalty	4	1	3	2
Independence	1.5	4	1.5	3
Religiousness	*2-3-4 4	*1-3 1	3	2

The Dogmatism – Rigidity Studies

Representative members of each sub-type were administered the Gough-Sanford rigidity scale[55] and the Rokeach dogmatism scale.[56] On both, my confusion was again exacerbated. The developing pattern I have been describing was not confirmed. The plot thickened; the results were:

1. *'Sacrifice now to get later'* – most rigid, most dogmatic.
2. *'Express self for what self desires without shame or guilt'* – third most rigid, second most dogmatic.
3. *'Sacrifice self now to get now'* – second most rigid, third most dogmatic.
4. *'Express self but not at the expense of others'* – least rigid, least dogmatic.

These results on dogmatism and rigidity were statistically significant. Thus, these data produced a further conflict in the information. One measure, rigidity, varied wave-like, but the other measure, dogmatism, varied in a straight-line, quantitative fashion. This additional conflict thus had to be rationalized through some conceptual framework.

Other results, which we shall now look at, simply complicated this already confusing and contradictory picture of adult human behavior.

Other Psychological Test Results – The Intelligence and Temperament Studies

Representative subjects of each sub-type were administered the old ACE examination[57] and, where possible, were studied in respect to their College Board verbal and quantitative scales.[58] They were instructed, also, to score themselves on temperament in accordance with Sheldon's method of assessing temperament.[59] The results were that *no significant*

---

[55] Gough, H. G., & Sanford, R.N. (1952). "Rigidity as a Psychological Variable." Unpublished manuscript, University of California, Institue of Personality Assessment and Research, 1952.
[56] Rokeach, Milton (1960). *The Open and Closed Mind*. In collaboration with Richard Bovier et. al., New York: Basic Books.
[57] American Council on Education (ACE), One Dupont Circle NW, Washington, DC 20036.
[58] College Board verbal and quatitative scales, now known as the the SAT and administered by The College Board, New York.
[59] Sheldon, William and Stevens, S.S. (1942). *The Varieties of Temperament*. New York, London: Harper & Brothers.

differences were found between any of the sub-types studied so far as the intelligence or the temperament of the subjects was concerned. So, by now I had four, possibly five, behavior systems which varied in a cluster of two from another cluster of two which varied from one another in a system-specific fashion and which did not vary at all on some dimensions. But this did not bring to a close the confusion in the basic data, as the following information will show.

The Authoritarianism Study

Here the Adorno et al. F-scale[60] was administered to representative sub-type subjects. The results were that the pairing of categories was again confirmed. The two sacrifice-self groups were more authoritarian than the two express self groups. But again the *'sacrifice self to get later'* group was more authoritarian than the *'sacrifice to get now'* group and the *'express self but not at the expense of others'* was less authoritarian than the *'express self for self'* group.

The Preference Studies

The Edwards Preference Inventory[61] produced meaningful results from five factors: deference, autonomy, affiliation, change and aggressiveness, as seen in Table II. The results of measuring deference, autonomy, affiliation, and change corroborated the clustering of systems, but the measure of aggressiveness stirred up the pot of confusion once again. Only the *'express self for self with little shame or guilt'* type scored high—not only did it score high, but significantly high; beyond this there was no difference on aggressiveness between the other sub-type groups. Now, we have something in adult personality which related to a pattern and not to other patterns. We seem to have something system specific. Actually this result did not hold up with time because later another type appeared which was even more aggressive. This type later became positioned beneath the *'sacrifice now to get later'* group in the hierarchy of types. When it appeared, this particular system specificness disappeared, though system specificness was found in later

---

[60] Adorno, T. W., et al. (1950). *The Authoritarian Personality.* New York: Harper & Brothers.
[61] Edwards Preference Inventory (1967). Science Research Associates, Inc.

data. Nevertheless, at that time it brought forth a far more important conceptual question.

If at this time I had thought that another type of *express self* behavior was present in man, if I had thought it was a lower cyclic partner to the two other 'express self' types, and if I followed the cyclic oscillating trend, I would have said the *'express self but not at the expense of others'* would be less aggressive than its predecessors but more aggressive than the sacrificial types. But this would have been incorrect because the data did not support it. Therefore, I had to ask: What does it mean, conceptually, that aggressiveness seems to disappear with change in conception of mature personality? As we shall see later, the explanation for this psychometric variation is one of the most substantive aspects of the emergent cyclical conception of man.

The Study of Values à la Scott

This study was done after the ones I have reported, after W. A. Scott's 1965 scale was published. It is entered now because, as Table II shows, adult man's psychology is a crazy, mixed up thing. We have seen, by now, that my four sub-types seem to follow an ordered hierarchical plan. But one certainly would not normally expect, as Table II shows, that a higher order conception of mature personality would be less self controlled, less honest, less kind, and less loyal than a lower order conception which is both so and not so in the data. It is so in that the *'sacrifice self to get later'* conception is more controlled, kind, honest, and loyal than are any other types. But it is not so, at least not completely so, because the *'sacrifice now to get now'* is more honest than the 'express-self' types. Oh my! How confusion doth reign in the realm of adult behavior; and the further we go, the more confusing it all becomes. But let us add a little more confusion, another ingredient to the pot. Then, let us summarize and see what all of this has said about conceptualizing adult personality.

Added Conceptions of Maturity and Life

As I indicated previously, during nine years of basic data collection two additional categories of mature personality appeared to further confuse the picture. In both instances, the number of subjects producing these categories was too small to allow for studies of the type summarized above. Nevertheless, the appearance of these two categories again exacerbated the developing confusion in the data and intensified the need to search for a conceptual system to explain it. Because of them, one had to ask: What does it mean to the totality of the data that now there are six categories instead of four? And what does it mean that where five were always present from the beginning, though one was not originally noticed, that a sixth should appear first out of the study of change and secondly on its own, but late in the period of the investigations?

I have already mentioned one of these later appearing categories which first appeared when the *'express self but not at the expense of others'* changed in a central fashion. It is the category which appeared as an original conception five times in the years 1959 and 1960, the one titled, *'sacrifice the idea that one will ever know what it is all about and adjust to this as the existential reality of existence.'*

The other category, *'express self, to hell with others'* was present from the beginning of the investigations. It was not sorted out as a category per se until 1958 and after. It was only then that enough cases of its kind accumulated for the judges' attention to be drawn to it. It appeared six times, but never more than twice a year. It was, beyond question, according to the judges, an 'express self' category. But there was, according to the judges, a significant difference between it and the other two. This conception had centered in it the element of shame, but not of guilt. In essence, its theme was: "Thou shalt express self at all cost rather than suffer the unbearable shame of loss of face. Thou shalt express self at all cost in order to be praised as one who will live unashamed forever in the mouths of men."

When this express self category appeared, it brought with it a clarifying bit of information. Previously, there was much of human behavior which could not be related to any of the conceptions of mature behavior expressed by my subjects. None of the four conceptions they originally developed fitted, in any aspect, the way people thought in the ancient great civilizations of this world, nor the way people thought in the less developed cultures of the world. But as I examined this rarely appearing conception, the problem seemed to solve itself. I came to feel that I was reading something like the epics of old, that I was reading the state of mind expressed in the *Mahabarata,* Homer's *Odyssey,* or the *Ramayana*. Thus, the behavior of heroic man in the 'glorious' ages past or in certain of today's developing nations came to be represented as one of the ways of thinking expressed in my subjects' conceptions of mature personality.

Later, from library anthropological research and study of the works of others who have researched and thought along the lines of this book, evidence was found to indicate that this *'express self at all cost lest one be shamed'* category belonged in psychological time before the *'sacrifice now in order to get later'* category. So it became the third system in the hierarchy of adult ways of existence.

Then, the evidence from this continuing library research indicated that still another sacrifice-self way of life, *'sacrifice self to the traditions of one's elders, one's ancestors,'* had to be represented in the hierarchy of systems. This *'sacrifice self to the traditions of one's elders'* became the second system in the hierarchy of systems.

But at this point there seemed to be a logical gap in my developing hierarchy of systems. Logically, the first should be an *'express self to stay alive as an organism and perpetuate the species'* system. Such should be the beginning of the hierarchy of adult human psychological systems. This logical gap created a very real problem for me in the early nineteen sixties. Search as I could (and search I did), I turned up no anthropological evidence that supported the existence of this system of behavior which I deemed necessary to begin the hierarchy. So, in the early sixties, I had to hypothesize that this first system in man's psychological development had existed in man's past but that the evidence for it was buried in those past ages. Fortunately for me, the Tasaday of the island of Mindanao, in the Philippines archipelago, were discovered in the mid-sixties.[62] And this discovery gave credence to the systemic hierarchy my research had suggested.

So, by 1970 the basic data from nine original years of study and twelve years of supplemental study had produced some most disheartening data so far as the avowed purpose of my investigation was concerned. The investigation was undertaken to collect data which might clarify the confusion and contradiction in adult human behavior through a study of conceptualizations of psychological maturity. Now, they had led not to enlightenment but to confused consternation. Now, I had no evidence as to what really is mature personality and seemingly I had, instead, a hierarchy of highly defensible conceptions of mature personality which seemed to relate themselves to one another in most peculiar ways, which seemed to suggest that my investigations had aborted. But had I really failed? Had all this effort been to no avail? It was possible that it had. But it was possible that hidden within these

---

[63] See: Stone Age Men of the Philippines. *National Geographic Magazine*, August, 1972. See also: John Nance (1975). *The Gentle Tasaday: A Stone Age People in the Rain Forest.* Harcourt Brace Jovanovich.

data were signals. Though the signals were obscure, the light that I was seeking might emanate from them. So, I decided to summarize the basic data to see what would arise.

The data seemed to suggest that *eight central ways of being have emerged from within the nature of man* in his time on earth, and that eight basic conceptions of mature personality are related thereto. If these are numbered, and if the centrality of the way of existence is used to classify them, then the order of their appearance in the hierarchy is:

1. Express self in order to stay alive as a human and so as to perpetuate the species.
2. Sacrifice self to the established tribal ways of one's elders.
3. Express self at all cost lest one feel ashamed for not living forever in the mouths of humans.
4. Sacrifice now in order to get rewards later.
5. Express self for what self desires in a reasoned, calculating, not overly risky manner.
6. Sacrifice self now to valued peers in order to get rewards now.
7. Express self for what self desires but not at the expense of others.
8. Sacrifice self to the natural existential realities of life by adjusting to these realities.

But not all of the data fell into this hierarchy as it is ordered. If the systems are numbered 1 through 8, the odd-numbered states—1, 3, 5, and 7—are all *express-self* states. The even-numbered ones—2, 4, 6, and 8—are all *sacrifice-self* systems. The odd numbered states, though alike in being *express-self* systems, are different from one another in terms of how they believe expression should take place. The even-numbered states are different from one another in terms of how sacrifice should be carried out and what should be sacrificed.

These eight psychological systems differed from one another in still other ways. When certain personality dimensions were studied—rigidity, for example—there was a steady decrease from state to state. Yet intelligence did not show hierarchical relationship after the first two states.

The first six states had in common that they were driven by deficit or deficiency motivation [per Maslow], whereas states 7 and 8 were, in a sense abundance motivated.

The early data prior to 1962 brought forth what seemed to be only four states (states 4, 5, 6, and 7). Later data added three others at the bottom and one at the top of the current hierarchy. Thus, if at first there were four, then six, then seven, then eight, one must ask: Are there potentially, in the human being, even more than these? Also one must ask: If the first six share something in common–deficiency motivation–which is not present in states 7 and 8, and if 7 and 8 share something–abundance motivation–which is not present in the first six states, are states 7 and 8 the beginning of a second swing around a spiral staircase of life? And if there is a second swing around the spiral staircase, is there, off in man's future, assuming he continues to exist, a third, a fourth, an infinite number of swings?

This limited summation of the results of my studies seems to say that an appropriately inclusive conception of adult psychological development will include, at least, the 15 points listed below. It would:

1. See adult psychology as an infinitely emerging series of hierarchically ordered psychosocial systems.
2. Show the systems to alternate their focus in a cyclic, oscillating dominant, subordinate fashion.
3. Show the systems to focus first upon expression of attempts to control the external world and expand power over it, then upon the inner world and attempts to know and come to peace with it.
4. Show little variation over most systems for personality dimensions such as intelligence and temperament.
5. Show some personality dimensions to emerge at a particular position in the hierarchy with a decreasing or increasing quantitative dimension in subsequent systems. For example, ideological dogmatism enters first in the *'sacrifice now to get later'* system and decreases there after. On the other hand, cognitive complexity increases from the very beginning.
6. Show a particular dimension to emerge at a particular position in the hierarchy. Then show the dimension to vary quantitatively, by increase or decrease, in a cyclic, wave-like, in-and-out fashion. For example, guilt as a felt emotion seems to appear first in the *'sacrifice now to get later'* system, almost disappears in the next, the *'express self calculatedly'* system, reappears to a lesser degree in the *'sacrifice now to valued peer to get now'* system. Honesty, authoritarianism and

need for independence are other dimensions which show this cyclic, wave-like character.
7. Show every other system as like but, at the same time, not like its alternating partner. For example, all 'sacrificial' systems show a tone of obeisance to authority, but in the second system it is obeisance to the authority of one's tribal elders; in the fourth it is obeisance to a power higher than man; in the sixth it is obeisance to the opinion of the valued peer; and in the eighth it is obeisance to the existential dichotomies of life.
8. Show each system to have uniqueness, its system specificness. Examples of this are absolute belief in objectivity in the 'express self calculatedly' fifth system and fear of shame as the centralizing force in the 'express self to hell with others' third system.
9. Show there is a general, central theme for life characteristic of each system.
10. Show variations on the general theme particularized into an infinite number of peripheral ways of living. The *'sacrifice now to get later'* theme has been particularized into many different absolutistic monotheistic religious and absolutistic ideologies for living.
11. Show increasing degrees of behavioral freedom, that is, choices for behaving at each successive level in the hierarchy of living.
12. Show human psychology to be a symphony built on six basic themes which repeat themselves in higher order form as each new movement in the symphony of life comes to be with every seventh system. An example of this is that the first system for human being focuses on the establishment of viable existence in the natural conditions of human existence. The seventh, the first system in the second movement of the symphony of life, focuses on re-establishing viable existence in an earth system threatened by what has occurred during humankind's first six forms of existence. That is, show adult development is helical in character.
13. Show each system to develop from a specific set of existential problems to be solved and a specific set of neurological means capable of coping with the systems'

companion existential problems. That is, show that adult psychological development is a double helix.
14. Show that life is a process in which the human, as s/he solves each set of existential problems of a position in the hierarchy creates, by this solution, the next set of existential problems the person must face in his or her development.
15. Show that the movement from one system to another up the hierarchy takes place by slow accretion to a point of critical mass, then a jump in all things psychological: belief systems, perceptual systems, cultural systems, psychochemical brain properties, and activated neurological structures.

With this summation of the fruits of my efforts to date, one thing was now apparent. The efforts had not accomplished their original aim, but they had not aborted. They had produced, instead, a new problem to consider, a new opportunity for contemplation, and a new conceptual task. It is to this new problem, the opportunity it created, and the task which it defined that I turn to in the next chapter of this book.

CHAPTER 5

New Problem, New Opportunity, New Task

By now I had traveled the road to conflict and controversy into the by-road of consternation leading to despair. It seemed that my every effort to clarify mature human behavior had completely missed its goal. There seemed no clarification of these contradictory conceptions in the data. There was only exacerbation of it, a fact which became ever more apparent as new data came in and as it was collated and analyzed. Each new set of data, each succeeding analysis of it, made it more than obvious that this long-standing problem of psychology, in particular, and behavioral science in general, was being amplified by my every effort. Each new set of data, plus the old, made me painfully aware that *the total data* simply could not be rationalized within any existing conceptual system for explaining the many faceted aspects of mature man's behavior. Consequently, I was in a quandary. What now was I to do? Should I accept that the project had aborted and stop the effort, or should I go on? Were I to go on, how should I proceed? This was the problem I found in the waning months of 1960.

As the situation developed, four choices seemed ahead. One was to revise the whole attack, design anew, collect anew, and analyze new data. But I could not bring myself to do this. The situation was too intriguing, the predicament too tantalizing to let go. The truth of the matter was I was enjoying the mess I was in. It had all the enticement of Makaha[63] to suffer—all the lure of the hunt when the prey has just deviously slipped from view. So this choice was dismissed and the second was examined. This choice was to report the unrationalized results so that others might have their try at them—an action which, for me, would have taken all the fun from the game. Therefore, this choice became as none and therewith was dismissed.

The third choice seemed, on the surface, the most obvious of all. It was to let the data do the talking—let them dictate the conceptualization that should rationalize them. But this was easier said than done. For talking to occur, one must have a basic language within which the communication can take place, and this I had not found. I had not been able to find it in the language of any other theorist. As a result from this third alternative, and its problem offspring, an incestuous mating took place which produced the fourth of my choices. This choice was to search the more speculative, intuitionistic byways for the key to my Rosetta stone. So I turned to the literature, the speculative psychologist and the theoretical adventurer and there, in time, I came upon a basic language for a conceptual explanation of the data.[64]

The Problem Created by the Data

Four things stood out in the analysis of the basic data, my subjects' conceptions of mature human behavior. First, it was relatively easy to classify sixty percent of the conceptions the subjects submitted. They fell readily into distinguishable categories. Examination of the data by judges other than the investigator resulted in at first five, then six, and later eight kinds of logically well developed positions, only five of which

---

[63] Makaha: Hawaiian word meaning "in or through the breath of life;" a popular tourist destination with a prime surfing beach at the foot of a lush valley on the island of Oahu.

[64] CWG: As regularly happens in science, I was to learn later that others had come, in many respects, to a similar conceptual viewpoint at about the same time. Particularly this was true of some cognitive personality theorists such as Harvey, Hunt and Schroder (1961), or the historically minded Gerald Heard (1963) and the socially minded Louis Mumford (1957), and others. It was also apparent that in many respects the psychoanalytic ego psychologists were thinking along the line of my developing conception. This discovery created a language and organizational problem. Should these results and the derived theory be reported in one of the already existing languages or should the developing and existing language be transposed into that which I had spawned before the discovery was made? Ultimately the decision was made to incorporate the language of others into the language of this book. This was not done capriciously nor egocentrically.

will be utilized in the beginning of this discussion.[65] These positions were not determined by *what* the person thought as much as they were determined by *how* the person thought. It was not whether the person believed the mature human being should express his self that stood out; it was how the self should be expressed that differentiated certain conceptions from other conceptions. It was not whether the conceived form of mature personality believed in God or whether the mature personality did not believe in God that stood out; it was how the mature person related himself to the universe and to the idea of God that typified the conception. In other words, the conceptions of mature human behavior *had to be seen* in the light of Rokeach's statement that, "It is not so much what you believe that counts, but how you believe"[66] or the data had to be viewed in the light of Ionesco's words: "It isn't what people think that's important, but the reason that they think what they think."[67]

My data did not say categorically this is what life is all about or what it is meant to be. They seemed to say instead: "what life is seen to be depends." It depends upon the way one looks at things. What life is, what it is all about, and what it is meant to be, depends. I say this because, when I took a certain restricted point of view toward what life is about and what is the nature of the human, I could readily empathize with how the contributor viewed mature human behavior and the reasons why s/he thought the way s/he did. If I adopted another mental set as to what life is about and what human nature is like, then this

---

[65] CWG: It was done for a very substantive reason that is referred to in part in the 1961 book of Harvey, Hunt and Schroder. On page 89, there is a footnote referring to a state of development below the four cognitive stages theorized to exist in their book. My work, over and beyond the studies reported herein, suggested three nodal stages existing prior to the stages I - II - III and IV of Harvey, Hunt and Schroder and suggested another than just those of Mumford and Heard. My data required also that I hypothesize stages beyond those of any of these people or of others who were beginning to think this way. Since the first stage of adult human behavior, as per the data of my studies, can hardly be called a "cognitive" or "conceptual" stage, the decision was made to use a more comprehensive term—level of existence.

A similar reason led to the rejection of the psychoanalytic terminology of "ego defective" and "ego integrative" states. In one sense, the data of these investigations found "ego defective" and "ego integrative" states present in each conception of mature behavior. It should be noted, however, that earlier appearing conceptions are, in the sense of ability to deal with a complex world, "ego defective." But regardless of this, I stuck to my decision that the level of existence language was the more inclusive terminology.

[66] Rokeach, M. (1960). *The Open and Closed Mind*. In collaboration with Richard Bovier et. al., New York: Basic Books, p. 6.

[67] Ionesco, Eugene (1960). *The New Yorker*, p. 47.

different mental set applied well to some other category, but not to the remaining major classifications except that, in the sense of conformity or non-conformity, the conceptions fell into similar and dissimilar conceptions at one and the same time.

The second message in the data was as tantalizing as a love just touched, but still unknown. It said the surface aspects here are quite easy to perceive because the conceptions fall into an ordered hierarchy with "a" proceeding "b" and "b" preceding "c," etc. But, it also said there may be more here than surface aspects show because after "c" there is "d" and "e" and "f" and "g" and possibly others *ad infinitum*. In other words, the known serves only to point out that which is unknown, and psychological maturity is of this order. 'There is no such thing as psychological maturity' was this message in these data. There are only those forms of mature human behavior that have been conceived by humans to date, plus the newest one that is now coming to be. New forms of psychologically mature behavior are there just over man's horizon, there to come to be when their day and their hour arrives.

This message dictated, at least to me, that a conceptualization which would rationalize my data must start with a revised conception of human nature.

The third message in the data was a most salient one. It derived from the evidence that in each type of conception two basic forms appeared. One was a positivistic, almost vehement presentation of the conception of mature behavior which was followed by an uncompromising defense of it when the subjects were required to compare their conception to that of their peers or when they were defending their conception in comparison to authority. The other conceptual form, within a category, was a relaxed straightforward presentation which usually was peripherally modified after comparison to either peers or authority. These two intra-category forms differed markedly under critical evaluation. Those who produced rigid conceptions were most defensive when criticized; this tendency was not displayed in those who took a more relaxed attitude toward their creation. Thus, the message to date said: 'Seek a basic language that allows the meaning of life to change with time, a language that allows the meaning of life to change in an ordered hierarchical way, and which leaves the hierarchy open-ended. Then seek a language which allows for this normal open movement to become arrested and closed.'

From the third type of data another message emerged. Not all categories were as related above. One group, the fourth group in the hierarchy as it was seen at that time, which ultimately came to be the seventh, the *"express self-but-not-at-the-expense-of-others"* category, behaved in ways quite different from the ways of any other group. Basically, they held to their positions after comparing their conception to that of their peers or those of authority except in two respects. First, as they compared their position to others', they changed not from peer or authority pressure or the like, but only when their factual information was increased. And secondly, they demonstrated a great deal of sound intellectual doubt as to the validity of their position, argued their points fretfully, in many ways changing only when substantive new information came to them. Yet, in the long run, most of them retained a conception essentially close to the conception they had in the beginning. The few changed to a still broader conception.

Another set of data, how the groups organized for work, also showed a marked difference between this group and the three other groups. In the other three groups, organization finally took place around some individual. This never happened in the fourth group where organization took place around an idea and where leadership regularly revolved. How this group thought and behaved was radically different from any other group. So the part of the message was: 'Seek a language that allows for the most marked of changes to appear now and then.'

The fourth message in the data arose from a tangential observation. It soon became evident as I observed the subjects both in class and outside of class that if frank symptoms, undue anxieties, and seemingly unwarranted hostilities were shown in any of the subjects' behavior, that it was those whose presentations were more positivistic who tended more often to show the frank hostilities, anxieties, and symptoms. This observation required me to draw the conclusion that a peculiar relationship existed between the type of conception of mature human behavior and the presence or absence of pathological behavior in the person who produced the conception. Two people could conceive of mature human behavior in basically the same way, a way quite different from the way others conceived of mature human behavior. Yet, one of these persons would be obviously and overtly disturbed under stress and unable to function adequately, while the other would be a relaxed, relatively symptom-free, well-functioning person. Thus the message here was that I should seek a language which allows conceptions of maturity to be systemically organized and oriented. From these five results:

1. a logically sound position, provided one accepted certain premises of the conceptual constructor but radically different conceptions of mature behavior;

2. conceptions of psychologically mature behavior seemingly ordered into an open-ended hierarchy;
3. conceptions vehemently and defensively presented versus similar conceptions presented in an easy-going, relaxed, take-it-or-leave-it manner;
4. sudden *very* marked changes in conception and behavior; and
5. similar conceptions in those overtly disordered and overtly ordered;

and other accumulating evidence, my data had mired psychology and behavioral science further into their age-old morass—confusion and contradiction in experimental results. Resultantly, it was concluded that these basic data could not be rationalized within any existing psychological and/or behavioral science theoretical framework. So, I decided it was necessary to enter the more speculative world in order to seek some different language for a conceptualization of adult human behavior which would rationalize my accumulated data.

The Beginning of the Search for a More Inclusive Conception

Having deep respect for the perspicacity of the artist when it comes to divining the character of man's nature, I began a search through my mind's remembrances for what writers had said about the nature of man and the meaning of his life. Three particularly come to mind. They were Shakespeare, Keats, and Thoreau. Why these three were dredged out of the depths of my memories I do not know. But it was their words particularly which cast the first sliver of light upon my data.

The aid of Shakespeare's words is obvious if we see them in a slightly different way than he intended. "All the world's a stage—and each man in his time plays many parts,"[68] gave me aid. I saw this as suggesting that each of my subjects was conceptualizing an honest view. A view of how s/he thought one could best play the part of being a mature human and that I had to explain how these many honest views came to be. But the words of Keats and Thoreau were more to the point of my need than were the words of Shakespeare. In a letter penned to John Hamilton Reynolds in 1818, Keats said:

"I will put down a simile of human life as far as I now perceive it; that is, to the point to which I say we both have

---

[68] Shakespeare, William. *As You Like It,* Act II, Scene 7.

arrived at – 'Well – I compare human life to a large Mansion of many Apartments, two of which I can only describe, the doors of the rest being as yet shut upon me – The first step into what we call the infant or thoughtless Chamber, in which we remain as long as we do not think – We remain there a long while, and notwithstanding the doors of the second Chamber remain wide open, showing a bright appearance, we care not to hasten to it; but are at length imperceptibly impelled by the awakening of the thinking principle – within us – we no sooner get into the second Chamber, which I shall call the Chamber of Maiden-Thought, than we become intoxicated with the light and the atmosphere, we see nothing but pleasant wonders, and think of delaying there for ever in delight: However, among the effects this breathing is father of is that tremendous one of sharpening one's vision into the heart and nature of Man – of convincing one's nerves that the World is full of Misery and Heartbreak, Pain, Sickness and oppression – whereby This Chamber of Maiden – Thought becomes gradually darken'd and at the same time on all sides of it many doors are set open – but all dark – all leading to dark passages – We see not the balance of good and evil. We are now in that state..."[69]

These words of Keats comparing "life to a large Mansion of Many Apartments, two of which I can only describe, the doors of the rest being as yet shut upon me" were the keystone I was seeking. And the words of Thoreau, written in 1854, added fervor to my feeling for he said:

"The necessaries of life for man in this climate may be distributed under the several heads of food, clothing, shelter, and fuel; for not till we have secured these, are we prepared to entertain the true problems of life with freedom and a prospect of success. [After man has obtained these necessaries of life], what does he want next? Surely, not more warmth of the same kind, as more and richer food, larger and more splendid houses, finer and more abundant clothing, more numerous incessant and hotter fires, and the like. When he has obtained those things which are necessary to life, there is

---

[69] Keats, J. (1933). *Autobiography* (1818 letters). Compiled from his letters and essays by Carl Vonnard Weller; illustrated by Wm. Wilke. London: Stanford University Press, H. Milford, Oxford Univ. Press.

another alternative than to obtain the superfluities; and that is to adventure on life now, this vacation from humbler toils having commenced."[70]

These three writers, particularly Keats and Thoreau, gave support to my intuition that substance and not error lay in my data. And their words, when I recalled them, directed me to search beyond the artistic realm and into the speculative psychological realm for further help and aid. There the thoughts of two men, Abraham Maslow and Gardner Murphy were particularly helpful to me.

The Search in Psychological Speculation

Many investigators of human behavior were aware in the 1950's that the contradiction in psychological results and the confusion in psychological theory was increasing throughout the psychological world. They were aware that conceptually we needed to rethink theory in order to account for some new kinds of human behavior which were appearing. As Murphy said, "Human behavior is changing at an extraordinary pace—new kinds of humanity are coming into existence."[71]

One new kind of humanity, in the language of Murphy, which has become much more prevalent since Nietzsche's time was regularly represented in the conceptions of mature human behavior developed by my subjects, the adjust-to-the-existential realities kind. It is the kind of humanity sometimes written about by Tillich, Camus, the existentialists. How this kind of humanity thinks in general, or how it thinks in particular in my studies, as to the nature of mature human behavior seemed not explainable in the concepts of existing theological or scientific explanatory systems. From the data of these investigations, and from the data and explanations of others, it is a form of human behavior distinguishably different from the forms of human behavior which existed in the past. It seems to operate by psychological principles that are different from those by which other forms of human behavior that have existed or are appearing operate—the kinds that find or have found their reason for existence to be in their tribal beliefs or to be in the beliefs of their clan, to be in their gods or in their God, to be in their ideological systems, to be in their economic system, or to be in their

---

[70] Thoreau, H. D. (1854 letters). *Correspondence*. Walter Harding & Carl Bode, (Eds.). (1958). New York: University Press.
[71] Murphy, Gardener (1958). *Human Potentialities*. New York: Basic Books, Inc., p. 6.

social system—those that have found their reason for existence somewhere other than in the self.

The behavior of man in this existentially described emergent state is so foreign to the explanatory principles of existing behavioral theories that psychologists and other behavioral scientists have found it difficult to provide a satisfactory explanation of it. The older explanatory systems, the associative learning psychologists, the psychoanalytic psychologies, and the interpersonal psychologies either ignore it or explain it as an aberration. They either try to force it into existing conceptualizations, or to refurbish their old concepts in order to fit this new behavior into the existing scheme. But this has not been done by all psychologies. The phenomenologists, the existentialists, and some humanists have attempted to develop new conceptualizations to account for this emergent form of behavior; but as I see their efforts, there is a minor error in the effort they are putting forth. An error which is illustrated when May says:

> "I, for one, believe we vastly overemphasize the human being's concern with security and survival satisfactions … In my own work in psychotherapy there appears more and more evidence that anxiety in our day arises not so much out of fear of libidinal satisfactions (something he would not say from the data of my studies) or security, but rather out of the patient's fear of his own powers and conflicts that arise from that fear."[72]

May's criticism may hold increasingly for modern twentieth century man, as compared to nineteenth century man. But the phenomenological, existential, humanistic conceptualizers may tend to slight the fact that even now, insofar as the data of my studies demonstrates, there are more people who base their behavior and their conception of mature personality in the belief that God exists or in some other concept for living not based on the power of self than there are people who base their behavior and their concept of maturity in the belief that God is dead; that there are more people, now, even in our most advanced regions, whose chief concern is with security and survival satisfactions than there are people whose chief concern is with the search for self; that even now there are more people whose anxieties arise out of the fear of libidinal satisfactions than there are people whose anxieties arise from a fear of their own powers.

---

[72] May, Rollo (1961). *Existential Psychology*. New York: Random House, p. 18-19.

The data of my studies when first analyzed suggested that this is an error which must be avoided if one is to conceptualize mature human behavior so as to include all that my series of studies brought forth. It is an error which must be avoided if we are to conceptualize so that we explain not only all behavior that is emerging, but also all behavior that has existed before. If we are to conceptualize adequately, we must try to explain in one overall system not only the old systems of behavior, but also the systems of behavior that are new. And beyond this, it appears that psychological theorists must include within their conceptualizing matrix that there will be other, even newer, forms of humanity which will appear in the future.

The need to explain the new, and in so doing to avoid the errors of the past, suggested further the need for a new psychological frame of reference. But this was not the only problem that demonstrated a need to seek a new way of psychological thinking. The need to coalesce the conflict and contradiction between the results of studies, and the need to remove the conflict between theories, and the need to remove the confusion as to how to apply behavioral science knowledge were also present. Subsequently, it seemed that we might meet these needs if one took, as Gardner Murphy says, "...a closer look at human nature, its ways of development, its forms of control, and the direction it is moving."[73] It seemed that this closer look at human behavior—in this instance, the data of these studies—might provide a new model of adult human behavior that is more encompassing of the forms of humanity that have been; that is more cognizant of newly emergent behavior; and that is more anticipatory of the forms of adult-behavior which may come to be in the future.

Another factor which contributed to the thought that the data and the problem of psychology provided an opportunity to reconceptualize human behavior was another statement of Murphy which said that we need a...

> "...conception of science which represents man as genuinely capable of grasping certain aspects of reality and moving slowly toward grasping ever more because it would allow for a sort of deep staining of the mind of the observer, selectively bringing out that which was hidden before the stain was used. Man's interaction with the things of the world through the methods of the arts and through the methods of the sciences will produce more and more that is new in man as the centuries pass. The

---

[73] Murphy, Gardner (1958). *Human Potentialities*. New York: Basic Books Inc., p. 7.

very process of interaction with that which was previously unknown produced new content, new stuff, new realities, new things to understand and to love, as well as new instruments of observation, new ways of knowing, new modes of esthetic apprehensions. These will elicit changes in the nature of man not simply uncovering more that lies under the threshold of his immediate nature but by broadening the doorway through which he passes so that he may see more of the vista he approaches and may as he does so become a larger man. It is because of man's capacity for intimate union with the stuff of this world through the methods of the arts and through the methods of the sciences that he may hope to do more than transcend his existent being, may hope to become in each new emergent phase of his life a new kind of man."[74]

The idea that man was genuinely capable of "grasping certain aspects of reality and moving slowly toward ever more and more" seemed to be in the data gathered in these studies, and from there another part of an idea for removing the contradiction and confusion in psychological information gradually came to be.

It seemed that these words of Murphy's said my studies provided a chance to conceptualize adult behavior if one beginning assumption was made. It was an assumption which involved the conceptualizations produced in these studies, the existing systematic conceptualizations of human nature, and the existing theoretical explanations of man's behavior—conceptualizations with which and about which a theorist could contemplate the meaning of these activities of humans. It was an assumption which began to tie my data, and the data and conceptualizations of others, together. The assumption made should be acceptable to most authorities who study human behavior. It should be acceptable to authorities no matter what their discipline and no matter what the theoretical orientation to which they subscribe. The assumption was that, by and large, integrity exists in those people who have studied human behavior and conceptualized in respect thereto— both those whose efforts contributed to the studies reported herein and those whose approach is more sophisticated, more professional. More specifically, it was: *Let us assume that basically they have observed well, strived to report accurately, and tried to conceptualize adequately within the data available to*

---

[74] Murphy, Gardner (1958). *Human Potentialities.* New York: Basic Books Inc., p. 324-325.

them. That assumption enabled me to say one thing and to ask two crucial questions.

Within the assumption, I was able to say that most conceptualizers, my subjects, and professional theorizers have an explanatory system representing the human as he can and does sometimes believe and behave. I was able to say most conceptualizers are explaining a particular form of human behavior. This I could say because there is ample evidence that the major theorists have limited the source of their data just as, it seemed to me, had my subjects.[75] But it was not necessary to say that the conceptualizers are explaining all the forms of human behavior. What could be said was that within the limitations of that which the conceptualizer observed, that he observed well; that within the data open to him, his conceptualizations were warranted. What did not have to be said was that each observer saw representative samples of all possible forms of human behavior; nor was it necessary to say that the conceptualizations deduced were the only conceptualizations deducible from each person's data, at least when one person's data is viewed in conjunction with another person's data. And it was not necessary to say that each conceptualization allowed for all the forms of human behavior not observed. Thus, it was suggested to me that there was room for some one or some ones to conceive of human behavior in ways that allow for all the forms of human behavior that have existed, for all the forms of human behavior that do exist, and for all the forms of human behavior which may appear in the future. With such in mind, I went on to examine the two crucial questions which arose from the assumption.

The first crucial question was: Why, if we assume most conceptualizations are correct, is there so much argument as to whose conception is correct? Why has Eysenck[76] so offhandedly dismissed the psychoanalytic point of view? Why did Horney[77] so attack the biological underpinning of Freud? Why did Freud[78] become so antagonistic in respect to Adler's[79] assertions about human behavior? Why did

---

[75] Maskin, Myer (1960). Adaptation of Psychoanalytic Techniques to Specific Disorders. In Jules Massermar (Ed.), *Science and Psychoanalysis, Vol, III. Psychoanalysis and Human Values* (p. 321-352). New York: Grune & Stratton.

[76] Eysenck, Hans J. (1959). Learning Theory and Behavior Therapy. *Journal of Mental Science*. 105:61-75.

[77] Horney, Karen (1939). *New Ways in Psychoanalysis*. New York: W. Norton and Co., Inc..

[78] Freud, Sigmund (1933). *New Introductory Lectures on Psychonalysis*.

[79] Adler, A. (1927).

Tolman[80] so disagree with Spence[81] as to the task of psychology? Why are Skinner and Rogers [82] both admirable and meticulous investigators, both stimulating and creative conceptualizers, so at odds with one another's point of view? Why did Maslow[83] and Goldstein and Koch[84] take their predecessors and their colleagues so to task? Why did some subjects in my studies argue in utter disbelief when other contributors presented a conception of mature human behavior which the former thought was an impossible form of conception? One could go on and on listing such conceptual disputes in psychology, and one could even list the same in other fields; for example, anthropology.[85] But such would be of little avail. However, it would be of avail if one could have an answer which respects the integrity of each of the disputants—an answer which might lead the way to an explanatory behavioral framework which maintains the essential dignity of *each* existing conceptual system. The answer to which I came was that perhaps they were all roughly correct—an answer which obviously raised the second question. How could all of them possibly be correct? By what stretch of imagination could one fit all of them into the same conceptual framework—all of the conceptualizers who contributed to these studies and all of those professionals who have conceptualized as to the nature of adult personality?

The answer requires some explanation. The explanation suggested is that most conceptualizers have conceptualized more or less about and within or across particular systems of behavior; that most have correctly represented human behavior to the extent that their data and their phenomenology have permitted them to represent it. This explanation says that the data of each systematist does not represent an *inclusive* sample of human behavior. The answer asserts that the conceptualizer's phenomenology has permitted him to systematize only with respect to a certain system or systems of human behavior, but not in respect to *all*

---

[80] Tolman, E. C. (1951). Operational behaviorism and current trends in psychology. In E.C. Tolman. *Collected Papers in Psychology.* Berkeley: University of California Press, p. 89-103.
[81] Spence, Kenneth (1944). The Nature of Theory Construction in Contemporary Psychology. *Psychology Review.* 51, p. 47-68.
[82] Skinner, B. F. and Rogers, C. (1956). Some issues concerning the control of human behavior. A Symposium. *Science.* Nov. 30, Vol. 124, p. 1057-1066.
[83] Maslow, A. H. (1962) Some basic propositions of growth and self actualization psychology. *Perceiving, Behaving and Becoming. A New Form for Education.* Washington, D.C.: Yearbook of Association for Supervision and Curriculum, Development.
[84] Koch, Sigmund (1951, 1956).
[85] Kroeber, Alfred L. (1953). *Anthropology Today: An Encyclopedic Inventory.* Chicago: University of Chicago Press.

systems of human behavior. It says that each conceptualizer is writing about different levels of human existence, or a different system of human behavior. It says Pavlov and Eysenck, the more classical conditioning theorists, have been studying more and describing more the operation of one behavioral system, one level of human existence. It says that Spence and Skinner have been describing another behavioral system, the instrumental or operant system. It says that Mowrer (1947) in his two-factor learning theory, and the *orthodox* psychoanalysts are describing the same system regardless of Mowrer's long-standing feud with the orthodox analytical people.[86] The answer says that Mowrer and the orthodox psychoanalysts have been describing still a third level of human existence. This explanation says the Freudian-Mowrer human being can be a very different human being than the predominantly instrumentally conditioned human being who, in turn, is a quite different human being from the predominantly classically conditioned human being. And this explanation will say later that most human beings are combinations of these systems. According to the answer, Adler, because of his phenomenology, may have come upon yet another system of human behavior, the interpersonal theorists another, and Rogers and the self theorists still another system, another *level of human existence*. Thus, I thought that it was not at all fanciful to make the assumption that, by and large, all conceptualizers were correct, but systemically bound. And I thought, once this assumption was made, that my task as a model builder was laid out before me.[87]

The Task

Now my task was to develop, within the ways of scientific thinking extant, if possible, an overall model which would order the systemically

---

[86] CWG: In fact, Rokeach in his *Open and Closed Mind* brings forth the evidence that the closer the systematic form be belief the more vehement the conflict between those possessing such beliefs.

[87] CWG: Again, I should point out that the thinking of many was converging in this direction to the late fifties and early sixties. Myer Maskin (1960) writing on *Adaptions of Psychoanalytic Technique in Specific Disorders*, in Jules H. Masserman, (Ed.). *Science and Psychoanalysis*, Vol III "Psychoanalysis and Human Values." New York: Grune and Stratton, p. 321-352, point out that Jung, Rank, Freud, Sullivan et al. based their theoretical-models on certain types of behavior. And Morris I. Stein (1963), writing on "Explorations in Typology" in R.W. White (Ed.) *The Study of Lives*. New York: Atherton, p. 280-303, called attention to the problem solving behavior of some subjects he had studied. He said, in essence, one subject seemed to follow the principles of reinforcement, while another seemed to follow the principles of Gestalt psychology.

centralized behavior which I had observed. I had to develop a model which would enable one to see the totality of human behavioral systems in their proper relation to one another.

One observation is pertinent to this task. The data seemed to lend itself to hierarchical form. It seemed that the systems for conceptualizing mature human behavior were ordered on a scale running from considerable rigidity and dogmatism to less rigidity and dogmatism, on a scale from autistic thinking through absolutistic thinking to a type of relativistic thinking. Therefore, Maslow's[88] thinking on need hierarchies and Goldstein's[89] on behavioral hierarchies was recalled. I tried to order my data within Goldstein's thinking and the Maslowian "hierarchy of need." In fact, my first two published papers in 1962 and 1964[90] were cast in Maslowian terminology. But when these papers were read at conventions, questions from the floor caused me to doubt that Maslow's hierarchy as stated by him, or as revised by Ann Roe,[91] really handled some of the data I had collected. Therefore, it was necessary to research my data further so as to clarify what was the problem. It soon became apparent that the problem lay in the breadth of the Maslowian hierarchy, in his belonging and self-esteem need systems, in the lack of a cyclic factor in his hierarchy, and in the need for systems beyond self-actualization. I had by now eight levels; Maslow had five: the physiological, safety, belonging, self-esteem and self-actualization.

My data had, by this time, four systems in which *belonging* was salient. It had three systems in which *self-esteem* was a central factor. The central factor of valuing others, though in a different way, in each of my four belonging systems, and the valuing of self in the other systems, though again different in each of the three, alternated with one another. This problem could not easily be resolved through the Maslowian hierarchy. For example, my research indicated three quite different self-respect systems: the *self to hell with others*, the *self but be rational about it but don't feel guilty about or ashamed of experiencing it*, and the *self so long as others are also taken care of*. My valuing others systems were valuing one's

---

[88] Maslow, Abraham. A. (1943). Theory of Human Motivation. *Psychological Review*. 50, p. 370-396.

[89] Goldstein, Kurt (1940). *Human Nature in the Light of Psychopathology*. Cambridge, Mass.: Harvard University Press.

[90] Graves, Clare W. (1962). *Proceedings of the Third Annual Value Analysis Conference*, Schenectady, N.Y.: Value Analysis Inc., & Graves, Clare W. (1964). *Proceedings of the Fifth Annual Value Analysis Confer*ence, Schenectady, N.Y.: Value Analysis, Inc..

[91] Roe, Anne (1956). *The Psychology of Occupations*. New York: Wiley.

elders, valuing one's higher authority, valuing one's peers and valuing one's existential world.

Also, I had trouble with the meaning of Maslow's physiological or survival needs and the safety needs. The psychological need to survive, according to my data, became central only after cognitive awareness of the self came to be. It was, therefore, not the lowest-level need system. And safety was a marked element in the first three belonging systems, not just the second and not to the adjust-to-existential-realities subjects.

According to my data, the *express self but not at the expense of others* behaved in many respects like Maslow's description of the self-actualizing person. But, some of my so-called "self-actualizing" people changed in the course of my investigation to a new conception of maturity. And late in my basic studies, this same conception of mature behavior started to appear as the original concept of some subjects. When this previously not seen and unforeseen form of behavior appeared, obviously it was necessary to question what I then thought Maslow meant by the self-actualizing person. And it became necessary to accept the possibility that the human is an open system from whom higher and higher levels of behavior will forever emerge. Therefore, it was necessary to look beyond Maslow for a system for rationalizing my data. As a result of this failure, and what I have related about my data, I made another series of assumptions and added to them the twist of open-endedness.

I assumed that conceptions of mature human behavior, like any other behavior, grow and change with time. Like many other phenomena, such concepts may progress, fixate, or regress. It was assumed that there is something inherent in man which is triggered into operation as one or another behavioral system, in one or another form, under certain life circumstances. It was assumed that mature behavioral systems are growth phenomena which tend to develop through a series of definable but inclusive stages by an orderly progression from less complex to more and more complex stages. And, like any other growth phenomenon, it was assumed that once growth starts, there is no assurance that subsequent stages will emerge. Growth, such as studied in these investigations could, like a seed, progress on and on through its preprogrammed stages; or like the seed, it could become stunted, or even reorganize and take on a form not usually of its nature. And, finally, it was assumed that just as the seed will not grow to its higher form in adverse circumstances, so too, is man's adult behavioral form limited by the life circumstances in which the human lives. These assumptions put before me the broader aspects of my task; but it was still necessary to find a system of thought which would enable me to construct a model of human behavior which fitted the data and the assumptions.

Since a schematic basis for constructing such a model satisfactory to me could not be found in the older worlds of philosophical or scientific thought about behavior, a thorough review was made of the requirements of the needed way of thinking. The data indicated that the same phenomenon—conception of mature human behavior—must be thought about at one and the same time as an open system tending to change to another form, and as a closed system tending to alter only within the established form. The data suggested that one must think of levels of psychological maturity moving on a scale from low complexity to higher complexity. It indicated that one must think of a tendency toward organizing, stabilizing around a certain central core, and re-organizing around a different central core, possibly *ad infinitum*.

One must think of a conservative tendency—a tendency to maintain the existing structure—alternating with a reorganizing tendency—a tendency to alter the existing structure. This requirement was present because subjects who produced conceptions which were later called an even numbered system in the hierarchy of systems centralized their conceptions of mature personality around the need to *conform to some established order*. But what they conformed to was not the same in one even numbered system as that to which they conformed in some other even numbered system. Yet the central conforming tendency was always there.

And the same phenomenon was present in the conceptions which tended to centralize around altering the established order. These concepts, later numbered by odd numbers, could be called *non-conforming concepts of mature behavior*. Yet, just as that to which one conformed varied in the even-numbered systems, the nature of the non-conforming mature behavior varied from one odd-numbered system to another odd-numbered system. Thus, as I searched among the forms of scientific thinking and came upon the ways of thinking of the organicists and the ways of thinking of the General Systems theorists, it seemed natural that my data and my thoughts about the data made sense within the thought of Murphy, the organismic thinkings of Goldstein, Maslow revised, and the General Systems people. Therefore I proceeded to follow this train of thought to see where it might lead.

As a means of setting course into this train of thought, I shall cover in paraphrased form, with additions of my own, the thought of Gardner Murphy, who said in essence:

In the past our theories of personality and culture seem to have been based more on a part than on the totality of man's behavior. Therefore, barely in concept and barely in model can we be said to have solved the essential starting point from which a psychology—any kind of psychology—including a psychology of personality and culture can be written. A lingering aspect of this problem is that we do not know yet to what extent the principles operating in personality and culture are identical with general principles which operate elsewhere in the universe. Yet we continue to take one set of assumed general principles, those of classical physics, and continue to generalize them to develop most psychologies of man. We do this though it may be that some other set of general principles is more appropriate to our task. We have assumed that inert and purposeless matter somehow pushed and pulled until, quite fortuitously, it developed living forms and that these living forms reacted in accordance with physical properties until behaving man, as we know him, appeared. Having started with a purposeless and feelingless universe, and having striven to be scientific, we have come almost to deny the existence of these typically organismic behavioral modes. This we have done though the relation of purpose and feeling to the world of physics in almost as obscure as it was in the sixth century B.C.

Now, however, we are beginning to see, as the intellectual climate changes, from nineteenth century to twentieth century thinking, that our explanations of human behavior must also begin to change. We see the need to look at personality in a more extensive way. We are beginning to see that personality will be fixed only when man's intellectual climate ceases to change.

Today, these changes seem to evidence that one could conceive that human personality may best be understood as a set of systems, as a series of expressions of the irritability of the changefulness of biological organization. And we have started to see that a different set of general principles, possibly those of General Systems Theory, are more appropriate than those of classical physics. But, we have not organized this perception into a model which covers the broad spectrum of adult personality. We have not used it to develop a model which includes all forms of adult personality that are old, all forms that are current and all forms that might come to be.

We have, nevertheless, made a start. We are truly beginning to regard adult personality not as a state or form of organization but as a direction of development. We now see adult personality less as a recognizable cross section and more as a multidimensional trend phase of a complex developmental process. This approach to adult personality cautiously and modestly makes the most of similarities between cosmic evolution and human evolution with special reference to the principles of organization, centralization, differentiation and integration. This start takes note of the specialized ontogenetic growth and differs from other characteristic types of species development and from inorganic development. In this new view, it is natural and proper to give a specific form of adult personality context by stating its relation to the whole. It is equally proper to suggest the nature of the whole by reference to any specific part. In this new way of thinking, the fact is that a form, any form, of adult personality is relevant to trying to decide what the universe, personality, may be. In this way of thinking forms of personality organization beyond those emphasized in past or current personality organization may well lie ahead. This is so because in this new frame of thought, adult personality is relative. It takes on a different form when the organism/environment complex changes as space and time change. But this is not the sterile, culturally relativistic view of personality. It is more. It is more because another principle is relevant.

This other principle is the one of hierarchy. We do not have just culturally relative systems. We have instead, an ordered hierarchy of systems within and across culture, each earlier appearing system in the course of development, subordinated to and resting within. As we change our fixation upon adult personality as a state of form or organization and as we replace it with a conception of personality as a direction of development our approach to the myriad of psychological problems, also, changes. Still newer functional principles will be derived. New principles of and for personal and group evolution will appear and new forms of interaction between people will be observed. A changed concept of psychological health will develop and there will be a reordering of our knowledge of psychopathology. New types of contact with the cosmos will be released and new ethical concepts will be formulated. New insights across academic disciplines will emerge and some old barriers to interdisciplinary study will disappear. Basic research will of necessity change its form and new applications will become available and adult personality and the process of cultural evolution will be more understood. The future course of adult personality research, within this new and developing point of view, will not follow a continuation of the methods borrowed from physics, physiology or the older psychologies. But, it will not view the older methods as outmoded. Rather it will see them as more narrow, the newer as the more encompassing.

The newer methods which will be developed will bring us better time/space definitions of adult personality and will lead us into a more adequate evolutionary and cultural definition of man's being. Yet, even with these changes, two types of research and two types of theorization will continue in psychology. One will be that type which attempts to systematize and verify present day conceptions. The other will grope into the conceptual world beyond our past regions of effort—an aim which now became the purpose of this book.[92]

Thus, with Murphy's words and mine latched together, I turned to General Systems Theory for further aid. Overall, General Systems Theory promotes the appearance of structural similarities or isomorphies in different fields. It looks for correspondences in the principles which govern the behavior of entities which are intrinsically widely different. In particular, as it has reference to the data of the studies reported, it permits one to view behavior as an ordered revolution from some less organized state to some more organized state, and as being reached from different initial conditions. It allows one to think of adaptiveness as a series of step functions defining a system. According to General Systems thinking, a personality system arises, moves in a certain adaptive direction, and, after a certain critical condition is reached, the system jumps and moves to a new way of being. This form of thinking allows one to conceive of this movement as being from homogeneity to heterogeneity. It allows one to think of

---

[92] Paraphrasing Murphy, Gardner (1947). *Personality: A Biosocial Approach to Origins and Structure.* New York: Harper & Brothers Publishers.

states which strive to maintain the conditions of that state while at the same time, under certain conditions, it allows one to think of these states reorganizing and taking on another form. Since this way of thinking seemed to correspond so well with my observations and my thinking, I began to lean toward General Systems Theory. But I was still faced with some lingering conceptual problems before creation could begin.

With this in mind, I felt I must search for the "essential starting points" toward the solution of the conceptual problems. Then I must seek some insight that would combine these clues into the beginning of a revised conceptualization of first, human personality and later, individual psychology. Then, if that could be accomplished, I must begin to consider the general form that the more inclusive conceptualization might take.

Some Lingering Conceptual Problems

One place where I searched for the "essential starting points" from which a more inclusive adult psychology can be written is the lingering aspects of some age-old psychological problems of which Murphy said, as I related earlier:

"We do not know yet to what extent the principles operating within man [in the psychosocial world] are identical with the general principles which operate elsewhere in the universe."[93]

Yet, we continue to take one set of general principles, those of classical physics, and generalize them to develop most theories of culture and personality. We do this though it may be that some other set of principles is more appropriate to our task. Or, we take other proposed, but far less established sets of principles—those of the Drieschien[94] organicists, the Bergsonian[95] vitalists—and strive to develop some theory of man's behavior based on them. But most psychological

---

[93] Murphy, Gardner (1947). *Personality: A Biosocial Approach to Origins and Structure.* New York: Harper & Brothers Publishers, p. 916.
[94] Driesch, Hans (1925). *The Crisis in Psychology.* Princeton NJ: Princeton University Press.
[95] Bergson, Henri (1946). *Creative Mind.* New York Philosophical Library. Bergson, Henri (1944). *Creative Evolution.* Modern Library. Bergson, Henri (1955). *An Introduction to Metaphysics.* The Bobbs-Merrill Company, Inc.. Bergson, Henri (1912). *Matter and Memory.* London, George Allen & Co..

and cultural authorities work from the former, not the latter. Again as Murphy says:

> "It is often assumed ... that inert and purposeless matter pushed and pulled, until quite fortuitously, living forms have developed, and that these [living forms] have reacted in accordance with [classical] physical properties until [behaving] man as we know him appeared. Having started with a purposeless and feelingless universe, we are confronted with a thinking and feeling entity; we have tried either to deny the feelings and the thoughts or to derive them from the inert, non-sentient attributes described by physics."[96]

Murphy goes on to relate how having striven to be scientific, we have come almost to deny the existence of organic behavioral modes. This we have done, it seems, because along the way we got lost in a false conception of the whole and a metaphysical conception of the concept of purpose. We lost our way when mechanism as an explanation failed and when Driesch's monumental work erroneously replaced the failing concept of mechanism with the untestable concept of vitalism. But, perhaps we can find our way again because Spearman's[97] reconceptualization of the concept of the whole may point the way to a more adequate conceptualization of the behavior of adult man and the nature of his cultures. With Spearman's conceptual change we may be able to see our way out of both oversimplified mechanism and unscientific vitalism, at least so far as personality and culture is concerned.

For Driesch, the whole meant the typical end result which is the highest form of organization, and purpose was the subliminal striving toward the ultimate totality that the organism could become. In my mind, it was Driesch's conception of the whole which led organismically minded psychologists and many anthropologists into trouble with the concept of purpose. And, partially, it was our failure to develop an adequate concept of purpose and an adequate concept of the whole which fed our illusion both as to the nature of adult personality and our cultural ways of life. These problems led us astray when we tried to reconceptualize after the mechanism failed. The Drieschian concept of the whole led us to conceive of the mature adult personality and of the Utopian society as a describable, achievable state or condition—a

---

[96] Ibid., (Murphy, 1947, p. 917).
[97] Spearman, Charles E. (1927). *The Abilities of Man: Their Nature & Measurement.* New York: MacMillan.

conception which can be seen to be a myth when we conceive of them within Spearman's reconceptualization of what is the whole.

The whole, according to Spearman, is something quite different from Driesch's whole. To Spearman, the whole is the momentary total state of the system. It is not the typical end-state to be reached in the future. It is not the ultimate psychological or cultural state toward which man is striving, nor is purpose some magical striving for that distant, but theoretically achievable, highest form of organization. The whole, according to Spearman, is that maximum condition of harmonious organization which a given organism, in given conditions, can possibly achieve in these conditions. In the human, it is the organization that can now become a human *being*—what he is now and living in the circumstances he is in now. Purpose is the dynamic activity toward organization, as organization is now possible. It is not striving to become the ultimate perfect state. *Becoming is something that happens* as a result of dynamic possibilities. *It is not something sought* in some odd and mystical way. The whole is the organization that a personality or culture has come to be to date, a human being what s/he is, and living in the conditions that s/he is in. And, psychological or cultural maturity is the most harmonious organization of the current state, not the best possible organization that could ever come to exist.

With these conceptual changes, we can now begin to see that personality and culture can be conceived in a very different light. We can begin to see why Murphy said, as was related before, that they will be fixed only when man's intellectual climate ceases to change, only when knowledge no longer accrues to change the conditions of human existence;[98] that the rapidity of these changes are so manifestly apparent that only arrogance could conceive that man's personality will ever be discovered with finality, or that the best cultural system—democracy, communism, or whatever it might be—will ever come to be. And we can begin to see some basic criteria which a model of mature personality must meet to reflect the light transmitted in my studies. There are, at the least, ten of these basic criteria.

1. A model of mature personality must not concentrate on some one element of mature personality as if it could serve as a standard for evaluation of all behavior of the biologically mature human.

---

[98] Murphy, Gardner (1947). *Personality: A Biosocial Approach to Origins and Structure.* New York: Harper & Brothers Publishers, p. 917.

2. It must represent the phenomena observed. It must allow one to seek knowledge of that being represented. It must not destroy or distort the observation of the phenomena in order to try to fit previously established forms for explaining the phenomena and it must not set up mature personality as transcendent and exalted above human lives.
3. It must provide the possibility for explaining, within its confines, all existing intellectually substantive conceptions of mature personality because different well-founded conceptions of what is mature personality exist and are, therefore, a part of the data which any model must represent.
4. It must include within its form the possibility that the mature personality can exist. That is, that behavioral possibilities are finite. And it must include at one and the same time, that the emergence of newer and newer concepts of mature personality are forever possible—that is, that behavioral possibilities are infinite, not finite.
5. It must represent that certain people do believe that they know what is mature human personality, and it must explain why people believe so and why they express, and why they defend, widely divergent conceptions of mature personality.
6. It must allow one to develop, test and revise hypotheses and it must allow for refinement or discarding of aspects of the model as the data from the generated and tested hypotheses comes in.
7. It must allow one to describe the conceptions of mature human personality in some orderly way.
8. It must allow one to systematically seek the nature of adult human personality.
9. It must allow one to seek explanation for the emergence of behavioral systems.
10. It must allow one to explore for directionality of change and it must allow one to seek the conditions which determine such change.

Thus, as Gardner Murphy says:

"The task of writing a serious essay on the development of human potentialities consists largely of the capacity to perceive and describe the ways in which human nature transcends and fulfills itself by moving beyond the specific components which today constitute it."[99]

Or, as John Seiler states, the task of one who seeks to conceptualize mature human behavior is to portray how…

> "We seem to stay on plateaus of considerable stability for long periods, following accustomed patterns of behavior and thought. When the time is ripe—when that still somewhat mysterious condition of "readiness for change" arises—we leap up a steep incline of new, formerly untried behavior. This is a perilous time, because unfamiliar terrain makes us unsure of our direction and, often, we try routes which lead nowhere. We feel quite disoriented—sometimes exhilarated by the altitude, sometimes frightened and alone. If we don't slip and fall back, we find our way to a new plateau which, though it has some similarity to the old, displays many new characteristics. In time, we become as familiar with the higher elevation as we have been with the lower. We may stay on the new plateau for a considerable period of time, increasing our familiarity with it, and, in the process, our effectiveness. At the same time, we increase our sense of the limitations of our new patterns of behavior and thought, until we are ready to move on, once again."[100]

How this task was carried out is that to which I now shall turn.

---

[99] Murphy, Gardner (1958). *Human Potentialities*. New York: Basic Books Inc., p. 323.
[100] Seiler, John A. (1967). *Systems Analysis in Organizational Behavior*. Homewood, IL: Richard D. Irwin, Inc., p. 195.

New Problem, Opportunity, Task

CHAPTER 6

The Emergent Cyclical Model

The literature, the arguments of theorists, and the accumulated data clearly indicate that a theoretical need is present in the late twentieth century psychological world. It is the need for a reconceptualization of personality, culture, and the concept of maturity. This reconceptualization should depict in one model why and how the concepts of personality, culture, and maturity develop and change with time as environmental conditions, accruing knowledge, and current human activity alter the conditions of human existence for better or for worse.

Lately, efforts to meet this need have started to come to be. Investigators and theorists have come to perceive that personality and culture perhaps can be seen as sets of hierarchically ordered systems, as a series of emergent step-like expressions of the character of the human organism interacting with the established sociocultural conditions and the current state of environmental affairs. At this time, some are suggesting that the principles of General Systems Theory are more appropriate for conceptualizing these phenomena than principles like those of classical physics or vitalism. But according to my data, this movement toward a General Systems theoretical base is only in its beginning phase. It has not got beyond General Systems thinking to the specific concepts needed to build a model which strives to meet the discontent of others and explain the unrationalized data from my studies. This situation requires that concepts be developed to portray the needed conceptual system. So, it is to that task that I shall now turn.

Basic Concepts for an Emergent Cyclical Double-Helix Model

The first need is for a concept which represents time in a psychological, not a chronological sense. This concept should represent time in terms of the existential problems faced at the time the person is living rather than clock or calendar time. It should represent that existential problems normally arise in an ordered hierarchical way. (See Exhibit XI, p. 183) And it should represent that these problems can remain relatively constant, that old problems can reappear and new ones develop. Time, in this sense, I shall call *Psychological Time*.

A second and coequal need is for a concept which represents the character of the particular environmentosocial conditions the human is faced with in one region of geographical space in contrast to other regions of geographical space. These conditions I shall refer to as the *Psychological Space* for human living.

A third need is for a concept which expresses that a general, yet variable, *resultant* arises when certain organismic and environmentosocial forces of a critical amount meet at a particular moment in psychological time and in particular conditions of psychological space. This concept must allow for the normal pathological under- and over-development of a system. It must express that conceptions of what is personality, culture, and maturity grow normally and generally by quantum-like jumps in a hierarchical, step-after-step fashion according to an organismic developmental blueprint. It must express that these phenomena do not always achieve the form that normally appears later, and that their development may fixate, regress, and possibly take on a form not usually of their nature, or that the form may be not pure but mixed. The concept coined to meet this need I will call the *Levels of Existence,* a concept which fits well three conceptual needs indicated by the accumulated data:

1. The need to represent the psychology of the mature human organism as an emergent growth phenomenon changing as psychological time and psychological space change.
2. The need to represent this growth phenomenon as a double helix with intermediate forms developing in a saltatory

(leap-like) fashion on the way to later and later appearing forms of maturity, personality and culture.
3. The need to represent that a form might fail to emerge, might underdevelop, might overdevelop or that regression might occur.

At this point several other conceptual problems remain. One is the need to conceptualize the dual complex of determinants which provide the potentials in the *double-helix*. One of these sets of determining forces must represent the *environmental* side of development. The other needs to represent the *organismic* complex. The environmental side I shall conceive in terms of the living problems created by being a member of the species *Homo sapiens*, a member of a group, or an individual living in certain and not other conditions for existence. These problems I shall call the *Life Problems* of the species, group or individual. The other set of determinants, those which arise from the organismic factors in development, I will designate as the *Neuropsychological Equipment for Living* of the species, group, or individual.

Then there is the need to conceptualize that the problems of living of the species, group, or individual fall into six hierarchically ordered, hierarchically prepotent[101] sets of problems—six subsystems—which, as they are solved, spawn six sets of higher-order problems for living. To designate these potentials on the environmental side of the double-helix, I shall use the first six upper case letters of the first half of the alphabet: A, B, C, D, E, and F. And I shall prime and double prime these letters to designate higher order derived problems of living. Thus, I will conceive that the problems of living be symbolized by the letters A, B, C, D, E, and F, then A', B', C', D', E', and F'.

Following this is the need to conceptualize the organismic side of the double-helix, the neuropsychological equipment for living of the species, group or individual. This conceptual aspect must show that the organism's equipment for living is organized into *coping systems*: systems which *activate* the coping systems, systems which *support* the coping systems, and systems which *elaborate* the six basic coping systems into higher-order coping systems. The conceptual aspect must show that the coping systems are dynamic neurological systems which are organized in

---

[101] CWG: Prepotent—the problems of the first level take precedence over those of the second level; those of the second level take precedence over the third, etc. At any level, the problems of that level are more powerful than those of the preceding levels.

parallel with the problems for living. It must also show that the elaborating systems are built from originally uncommitted cells.

To accomplish this, I have chosen the upper case letters of the second half of the alphabet. The letters N, O, P, Q, R and S were chosen to represent the basic dynamic neurological coping systems. These letters N, O, P, etc. will be primed and double primed, etc., to signify higher order coping systems built upon the six basic coping systems. The letters X, Y, and Z will represent, respectively, the *activating systems*, the *supporting systems*, and the *elaborating system*. Thus, the organism will be conceived to consist psychologically of N, O, P, Q, R and S then N', O', P', Q', R', and S', plus X, Y, and Z.

From these conceptual decisions the need arises to represent not the overall potentials in the double-helix, but the *momentary operants* in each of the two sets of determining forces. To represent these momentary operants on the environmental side, I will use the phrase *The Conditions OF Exsitence* of the species, group or individual. The conditions of existence are the totality of environmentosocial forces setting the scene in which psychological being takes place.

To represent the momentary operants on the organismic side of the helix, I will use the term *The Conditions FOR Existence*. The conditions for existence thus are the activated psycho-neurological coping systems, the cognitive capacities, and the temperamental dispositions of the species, group, or individual.

Following from this decision arises the need to conceptualize the psychodynamic resultant of the momentary operants in each of the major force fields in the double-helix. On the environmental side, I will call this resultant *The Existential Problems* of the species, group or individual. On the organismic side, I will designate the resultant of the activated coping systems, the developed cognitive capacities, memory traces and the like and the temperamental disposition as *The Existential Means for Living* of the species, group or individual.

When the momentary resultants of each side of the double-helix are conceptualized as the existential problems of living and the existential means for living, there is a need to represent the psychodynamic resultant of the interaction of both sides of the double-helix. This resultant I will designate as *The Existential State* of the species, group, or individual. The existential state is the force field which must be discerned if one is to understand the psychological nature of the species, group, or individual. The existential state is that which produces the levels of existence of the species, the psychological positioning and organization along the double-helix of a group, and the psychosocial positioning and organization along the double-helix of the individual or culture.

And finally, there is the need to distinguish conceptually between certain gross classes of levels, between the levels of the first spiral of psychosocial development and those levels which appear later in psychological time. The first six together I will call *The Subsistence Level Systems*. Those of the second spiral I will name *The Being Level I Systems*. Those of later spirals, should they come to be, would be designated as *Being Level II Systems*, *Being Level III Systems*, etc.

Now, with the problem of specific concepts for a general systems model of adult psychosocial development resolved, it is time to sketch out a model which seems dictated by the information of others and the data resulting from my studies. It is time to take the concepts presented above and fashion them into a double helix model of the psychosocial development of the adult human being, the *emergent cyclical model* of adult human personality, culture, and maturity.

The Psychological Life Space of Emergent Cyclical Theory

In this section, the psychological life space of emergent cyclical theory is developed from the data and writings of others, my data, and the concepts defined at the beginning of this chapter. The theory is illustrated through a series of graphic designs and tables which depict personality, culture, and concepts of maturity as a double helix derivative of environmentosocial forces and the neuropsychological potentials in the organism. I begin with Exhibit IV [p. 164. See also Exhibit XIV, p. 193].

Exhibit IV is a broken-line ellipse which represents all conceivable forms of human behavior. The region within the broken lines represents all the systemic forms of adult behavior which have emerged at the time this book was written. The broken-line aspect represents the possibility that new adult behavioral forms will appear in the future which are, psychospatially, beyond those which have appeared to date.

Within the ellipse, but outside the representation of the brain cross-section, are regions A, B, C, D, E, F, A', B', etc., which represent the hierarchically ordered problems for human existence, the different *conditions of human existence* which a person may face in his or her lifetime. The conditions for human existence vary from those which produce and provide for simple subsistence needs (the problems of living A), to those which produce ever more complex conditions for existence (problems B, C, D, etc.). These conditions interact with the N, O, P, etc., forces arising from the neuropsychological structures of the organism *Homo sapiens.*

Exhibit IV

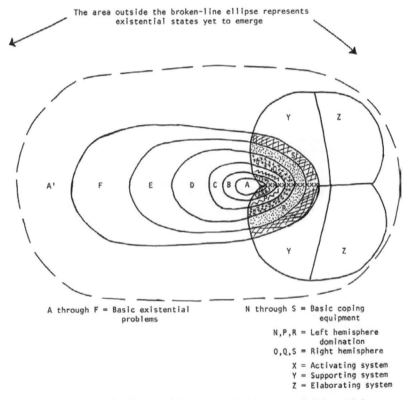

The neuropsychological potential of the adult human being is represented by the schematic of the horizontal median brain cross section. The brain as conceived consists of a series of hierarchically ordered dynamic neurological coping systems, à la the thinking of David Krech,[102] and three other major neuropsychological systems X, Y, and Z, the activating, supporting, and elaborating systems respectively. Each of the dynamic coping systems A, B, C, etc., is a region which operates according to its own laws. For example, each system has its own laws for learning, a point which will be elaborated later in each chapter in Part II.

It is conceived that each system is connected by a pressure-type neurochemical switching subsystem X which has the capacity to be off, partially on, or fully on. Its operation follows a J curve. As conceived, the lowest order coping system, N, possesses all the neurological equipment necessary to maintain the life of the individual and perpetuate the species. Each of the higher order dynamic coping systems contains different neuronal equipment which is specifically structured to sense and cope with each set of new and different life problems. The problems arise in hierarchical order, and the coping system can be triggered into operation if the associated conditions for existence come about.

If a higher order system is to be activated, increments of psychochemical force must be built up. For a time as these increments accumulate, a pressure-like valve opens very slowly. Then, when a critical amount of pressure from a particular composition of chemicals is reached, there is a spurt-like movement to dominant control by the laws of the next qualitatively and quantitatively different dynamic neurological system. The quantitative differences are represented by the size of the N, O, P, etc., regions. Varying forms of cross-hatching represents the qualitative differences.

It is important to note, on the A, B, C side that there are widely varying environmentosocial conditions of existence. On the N, O, P ... X, Y, Z side, there is widely varying capacity for sensing, reacting to, and coping with life's different environmentosocial conditions. On the A, B, C side, food and water may be readily available, or either or both may be most difficult to procure. Social mores and customs may also vary widely. On the organismic, the N, O, P ... X, Y, Z side, one person may have extraordinary equipment in the form of energy or capacity for coping with particular A or B or C, etc. problems. These general and specific aspects establish *thema* for existence and *schema*[103] for existence.

---

[102] Krech, David, & Crutchfield, R. (1948). *Theory and Problems of Social Psychology*. New York: McGraw-Hill.
[103] Bartlett (1932).

From this hypothesized life space, we see that psychosocial development AN, BO, CP, etc. results from the interaction of A, B, C with N, O, P. And we see that, in general, AN states are AN states and BO states are BO states; they are the same qualitatively from one culture or one human being to another. But they can vary significantly, in a quantitative way, from one culture or one human being to another.

It is important to note, on the A, B, C side that quantitatively the same general conditions for existence (amount of food available for consumption and its nutritional value, etc.) can be present in environmentosocial conditions which otherwise vary markedly. One person might receive no more food or no better food, nutritionally, than some other person, but the first might live in a warm and sympathetic atmosphere, the other in an emotionally cold and hostile world. Failure to consider these quantitative-qualitative differences in each of the major dynamics could lead one to overlook the breadth of meaning in the concepts *conditions for human existence* and *conditions of human existence*.

If a person misses this breadth of meaning, s/he may not comprehend why some people move to later levels of existence even when, on the surface, it looks as if they are living in poor *conditions of human existence*. Also, one might not comprehend why others do not move when conditions appear to be good. Many ghetto people, many in the world's disadvantaged lands might seem on the surface to be living in conditions too poor for movement unless the broader meaning in these two basic dynamics is understood.

So emergent cyclical theory represents psychosocial development as an environmentosocial-organismic field varying both quantitatively and qualitatively from one psychosocial system to another. Systems of personality and culture and concepts of maturity are only momentary systemic organizations of existential states in their current environmental circumstances. In emergent cyclical theory, concepts of personality, culture, and maturity depict the organization around a point in the flowing process that is human life. They represent where a species, a culture, or a person's development is now. But the point around which organization takes place or the form of the organization are not necessarily destined to remain as they are at any moment in time. On the other hand, they may fixate as they are. Thus, by focusing on the psychological life space of the species *Homo sapiens*, it is possible to see what have come to be the basic aspects of the emergent cyclical model of psychosocial development.

The Basics of the Emergent Cyclical Double-Helix Model

Exhibit V (p. 168) presents, in one diagram, the basic aspects of the emergent cyclical model of adult psychosocial development. It shows, as Exhibit IV says, that psychosocial systems develop as resultants of the interaction of a complex of two sets of determining forces: (1) the environmentosocial forces, the *problems of living* of the species, group, or individual—the forces, A, B, C, D, E, F; - A', N' etc. and (2) the organismic determinants, the forces N, O, P, Q, R, S; - N', O' etc. plus X, Y, and Z, *the neuropsychological* equipment for living of the species, group, or individual.

Existential problems A, the living problems associated with the environmentosocial conditions for satisfying or not satisfying the imperative, periodic, physiological needs, activate the neurological equipment N. This equipment, the first level neuropsychological equipment of the first spiral of existence, is structured specifically to sense and cope with life problems A. So if an adult exists in environmentosocial conditions A, the psychoneurological system N is activated within his or her brain. The person's existential state under this set of conditions is the AN state. A person in this state is to be known, comprehended, and managed through the dynamics and principles of the AN psychosocial system. This person cannot be known, comprehended, or effectively managed by the principles of any other existential state, any other level of existence.

Exhibit V
The Basic Complex of Emergent Cyclical Psychosocial Development Theory

The systems of psychosocial development arise as resultants of the interaction of a complex of two sets of determining forces.
1. The environment social determinants; THE EXISTENTIAL PROBLEMS OF LIVING of the species, group or individual; Forces A, B, C, D, E, F; - A', B' e
2. The organismic determinants; THE NEUROPSYCHOLOGCIAL EQUIPMENT FOR LIVING of the species, group or individual; Forces N, O, P, Q, R, S; - N', O' plus X, Y, and Z.

2.

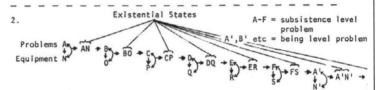

Existential States
A-F = subsistence level problem
A',B' etc = being level problem

Problems A
Equipment N

N-S = subsistence level equipment
N',O' etc = being level equipment

3. Diagram illustrates:
   i. Being level as a human being brings about <u>life problems A</u> which activates <u>neuropsychological equipment N</u>. A and N interact to produce psychosocial system, <u>level of existence AN</u>, the first system for existence. Living by psychosocial ways AN produces <u>life</u> problems B which activate <u>neuropsychological equipment O</u>. B and O interact to produce the <u>second existential state BO</u>. Living by ways BO <u>produces life problems C</u> which activate <u>neuropsychological equipment P</u> etc.
   ii. That <u>life problems A, B, C</u> ... are organized in parallel with the <u>neuropsychological equipment N, O, P</u> ...This is so because as the organism becomes more complex, its life problems become more comples.
   iii. That each set of determinants are hierarchically and prepotently organized.
   iv. That the resulting existential states AN, BO, CP ... are also hierarchically and prepotently organized.
   v. That the <u>life problems</u> and the <u>neuropsychological equipment</u> are organized into <u>subsistence level problems</u>, <u>subsistence level equipment</u> and <u>being level problems</u> and <u>being level equipment</u>.
   vi. That the <u>levels of existence</u> are organized into <u>subsistence level systems</u> and <u>being level systems</u>.

Table III

Designation of Levels of Existence, Existential State Nature of Existence per Level and Existential Problems per Level

Level of Existence	Existential State	Nature of Existence	Problems of Existence
Second Being	B'O'	Experientialistic	Accepting existential dichotomies
First Being	A'N'	Cognitivistic	Restoring viability to a disordered world
Sixth Subsistence	FS	Personalistic	Living with the human element
Fifth Subsistence	ER	Materialistic	Conquering the physical universe so as to overcome want
Fourth Subsistence	DQ	Deferentialistic	Achieving everlasting peace of mind
Third Subsistence	CP	Egocentric	Living with self-awareness
Second Subsistence	BO	Tribalistic	Achievement of relative safety
First Subsistence	AN	Automatic	Maintaining physiological stability

As A and N interact, the resultant is the automatic psychosocial way of living. This is a general way (*thema*) which can be specified into many particular forms (*schema*) of problems A, and many variances in the N neurological system. If the psychological space conditions provide relatively automatic and relatively continuous solution of the problems A, then a significant resultant occurs. Living will continue at the AN level forever with minimal activation of O, P, Q etc., neuropsychological equipment. (An example is the Tasaday of the Island of Mindanao in the Philippine archipelago.[104]) This is so because the N neuropsychological system is specifically structured to contain all the equipment necessary to maintain individual life and perpetuate the species when psychological space activates primarily the N neurological system. In appropriate conditions, an individual lifetime can be lived out and the species perpetuated through the automaticity of the N system and without O or any other neurological subsystem more than minimally activated.

If system N is deficient in some respect, which indeed is possible because of genetic, embryological, accident, or disease factors, then life

---

[104] Ibid., Nance.

will cease unless it is supported by artificial means. (This is done with the severely retarded, seniles, and some damaged by injury or disease.) This, as I have said, is because the N neuropsychological subsystem contains the structures for sensing and coping with the imperative, periodic, physiological needs.

On the other hand, if living by the ways of a particular AN form for existence changes the conditions in psychological space, if it depletes the food or water supplies, or if other social or environmental changes threaten the relatively automatic satisfaction of the imperative needs, then survival is endangered. In such circumstances, the very process of existing changes the facts of existence and generates a new sub-set of existential problems. Such changes create the problems of living B, the second level set of existential problems of the first spiral of existence. These are the problems of establishing safety and security in a region of psychological space which previously provided a relatively unthreatening world. (See Table III, column 4.)

To sense, perceive, and learn to deal with these new problems of existence, life problems B, neuropsychological equipment O must, first of all, be present in the organism. Sometimes it is not. (Recall the psychosocial definition of an 'idiot:' one who cannot sense or avoid the ordinary dangers of life.) If O is not present, or if it is disordered, then again life will cease unless it is supported by artificial means. If the neuropsychological system O, which consists, in certain major respects, of equipment for sensing and taking action in respect to danger, is present, it must be properly activated. Proper experience (the experience is specific to each subsystem) will activate the O neurological system and result in movement toward the BO existential state. Otherwise the usual psychosocial development does not occur. If system O is present and if it is properly activated to a critical degree, the human jumps to his or her second form for existence, the BO nodal state.

When the BO state emerges, the AN system is now embedded in and subordinated to it (Exhibit VI). There is now, when the BO system emerges, something old and something new in the adult's psychosocial makeup.

But now the question arises: What are the details of this change process? The research I have done and the work of others suggests that six factors control the process of change from one existential state to another. The first is obvious. It is *neuropsychological potential*. For change to occur, the higher order system must be present in the brain. But let us

Exhibit VI

Figurative Representation of the Subordination of Systems With Time. "The Nesting Aspects of Adult Psychosocial Systems."

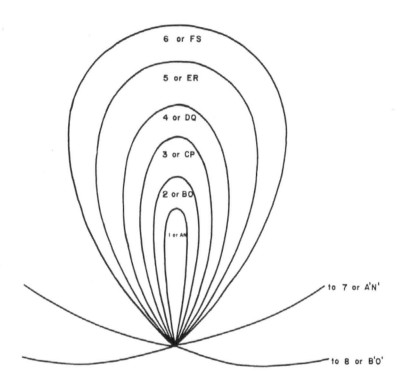

not pass by this point too quickly. To understand and manage some biologically mature adults—mild mental retardation, for example—we must recognize that their personalities will always be a variant on the AN existential state no matter the conditions for existence in the environmentosocial world.

If potential exists and if the other conditions are present, then the AN state changes to the BO system and psychosocial behavior becomes of another order. The five other conditions are:

1. There must be a *resolution of the existential problems* of the level where one is. This is necessary to produce free energy in the system through which change can be ready to occur.

2. Then *dissonance*, which can arise from inside or outside the person, must enter the field. There is no reason to change if dissonance does not occur. This dissonance arises from the creation of new existential problems in the field by living the AN way or by relative uniqueness in neurological equipment.
3. When dissonance occurs, some *insight* as to how to behave in order to meet the new problems B of existence must develop. This occurs when the X system, the activating system, produces the complex of organic chemicals necessary for activating the next level neuropsychological system, the system O.
4. Then there must be *removal of barriers* to the implementation of the insights which have developed.
5. And finally, there must be *consolidation of the new ways* for being so that survival can continue under the new conditions of existence.

The problems of existence which must be solved and the dissonance factors are specific to each of the levels. So are the insight factors and the barriers which must be removed.

If, as time passes, living by particular BO ways solves the problems B and from their solution creates dissonance in the form of problems C, then neuropsychological equipment P must be present and activated for the now-needed insights to develop. And the barriers to their implementation must be removed for psychosocial, not physical, development to continue. This is because the activation of neuropsychological structures P is not imperative for human survival.

P equipment is quite different from N or O equipment, as is the equipment of any other higher-order neuropsychological system. If equipment P is activated and the barrier factors are removed, the person begins to rapidly consolidate his or her progression to the next level of existence and begins to produce the next level of problems, problems D, and the process continues ad infinitum.

Careful consideration of this aspect of this conception of adult psychosocial development clarifies why I said earlier that there is, in emergent cyclical theory, no such thing as psychological maturity or Utopian society. Constant solution of existential problems, constant creation of new existential problems, and constant activation of more complex neuropsychological systems explains why emergent cyclical theory says that neither *the* mature way of being nor *the* Utopian society can ever come to be. The eradication of today's problems cannot result in *the* ultimate form for existence. It can serve only to produce the next set of existential problems.

Exhibit V-3-i represents the life problems as A, B, C, D, etc., and it depicts that the neuropsychological equipment is conceived as coping systems N, O, P, Q, etc., which operate in parallel with the life problems.

Exhibit V-3-ii and iii shows that each set of determinants—*the problems of living* and the *neuropsychological equipment for living*—are hierarchically and prepotently organized. And Exhibit V-3-iv shows that their resultant, existential states—AN, BO, CP, DQ, etc.—are also hierarchically and prepotently organized. But the diagram does not show two important factors which need to be considered.

One is that the problems of existence are plural, not singular. So living may produce solution of some but not all of the existential problems of a level. Therefore, partial psychosocial leaps are more the rule than total leaps to the next level of existence.

Secondly, the particular form of the AN, BO, CP state is determined in part by the particular problems of the particular psychological space in which living takes place. The particular character of the general N, O, P, etc., neuropsychological equipment for living of the species, group, or individual also determines them. This is important because it is through these aspects of emergent cyclical theory that one sees how this classification system is not a typological theory. It approaches such only in pure theoretical form which, of course, does not exist in the real world.

Section 3-v of Exhibit V depicts that the life problems are organized into sets of problems. But the exhibit, per se, does not explain *why* they are conceived as A, B, C, D, E, F – then A'N', that is as first order systems, second order systems, etc. They are so conceived because the human as s/he learns to solve the problems A, B, C, D, E, and F creates a new and higher-order set of survival problems. (For example, learning to survive through the use of fire, that is, fossil fuels, has created a new survival problem: How to live when all fossil fuels are exhausted.) These problems are the first level problems of the second spiral of existence (Exhibit V-3-v). Thus, if these are the beginning problems of a new spiral of existence and if the development of neuropsychological equipment parallels the development of existential problems, then the theory must allow for second order equipment, N', O', P' to develop *ad infinitum*. This, I propose, is accomplished through the elaborating system Z.

The existence of an elaborating system in the organism seems well supported by experimental evidence. Much data suggests that when the total brain is laid down in the young organism, many cells in the brain are not originally committed to systems N, O, P, Q, R, S, or systems X and Y. They are in system Z. The existence of a Z system is important because it offers an answer to the question Alfred Russel Wallace asked of Charles Darwin: 'Why does *Homo sapiens* have such a big brain? Why does the brain contain far more cells than are necessary for survival of the individual and perpetuation of the species?'

Emergent cyclical theory says the human has originally many uncommitted cells so they can be used in conjunction with the basic coping systems to develop the higher-order coping systems N', O', P', etc., of the later appearing levels of existence. The A cells combine with some uncommitted cells to form the A' system for coping when the survival problems of the second spiral of existence are produced by the combined results of having lived the AN, BO, CP, DQ, ER and FS ways of life. *Homo sapiens* has a large brain in order to be able to develop new coping systems for dealing with new existential problems, that is, in order to develop Being Level Systems I, II, III etc. (Exhibit V-3-vi).

The Psychosocial Double Helix

Exhibit VII shows that the psychosocial double-helix results from the continuing interaction of the emerging problems of human life and the hierarchical ordering of the neuropsychological equipment of the species, group, or individual. This continuing interaction produces, in order, the existential states of the first spiral of existence and those of the second spiral which are now beginning to appear. Theoretically, this spiraling can continue for as long as *Homo sapiens* exist because the elaborating system Z in the human brain is essentially infinite. (The brain contains 100 billion neurons ["11 or 12 billion cells" in 1977 text], with each brain cell having a potential capacity of some 10,000 interconnections with other brain cells.)

In Sections 2, 3, and 4 of Exhibit VII, we see the basic determinants specified through one model to the species *Homo sapiens*, a group of *Homo sapiens,* and an individual member of the species.

Section 2 of Exhibit VII shows that a unique set of life problems arise because of the very existence of *Homo sapiens*, and that the existence of *Homo sapiens* is maintained by the unique equipment for living of the species. The problems of living produce the conditions for existence of the species. The unique equipment provides the human with unique existential means. The existential problems of the species interact with

Exhibit VII

Emergent - Cyclical Double Helix Model of Adult Personality and Cultural Institutions

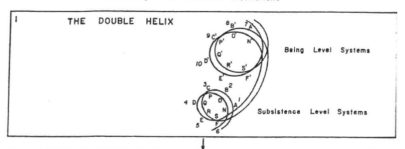

1	THE DOUBLE HELIX		
		Being Level Systems	
		Subsistence Level Systems	

---

2 Life Problems of Species Homo Sapiens   Neuropsychological Equipment for Living of Species
  (A,B,C,D,E,F;A',N',etc.)   (N,O,P,Q,R,S:N',O',etc. plus X Y Z)

CONDITIONS OF EXISTENCE OF SPECIES   CONDITIONS FOR EXISTENCE OF SPECIES

Existential Problems of Species   Existential Means of Species

EXISTENTIAL STATE OF SPECIES
(AN.BO.CP.DQ.ER.FS.A'N',B'O',etc.,or combination thereof)
Species Institutions and Personality Variables Observed (Conceptions of Maturity)

---

3 Life Problems of Group Members   Neuropsychological Equipment of Group Members
  (Group Problems Solved-A,B,C.etc.)   (Group Neuropsych Equipment Activated N,O,P.etc.)

CONDITIONS OF EXISTENCE OF GROUP   CONDITIONS FOR EXISTENCE OF GROUP

Existential Problems of Group   Existential Means of Group

EXISTENTIAL STATE OF GROUP
Group Forms of AN,BO,CP,etc., or combination thereof
Group's, Institution's, and Personality Variables Observed (Group's Conception of Maturity)

---

4 Life Problems of the Individual   Neuropsychological Equipment of the Individual
  (Individual Problems Solved-A,B,C.etc.)   (Individual Neuropsych Equipment Activated N,O.etc)

CONDITION OF EXISTENCE OF INDIVIDUAL   CONDITION FOR EXISTENCE OF INDIVIDUAL

Existential Problems of Individual   Existential Means of Individual

EXISTENTIAL STATE OF INDIVIDUAL
Individual Form of AN,BO,CP,etc., or combination thereof
Individual Institutional Behavior and Personality Variables Observed
(INdividual's Conception of Maturity)

---

the existential means of the species to produce the hierarchically ordered existential states of the species. From these states arise the levels of existence, and from them the many kinds of cultural ways of man and the personality variables which have appeared or may some day appear.

Section 3 of Exhibit VII shows that this same model can be used to describe, explain, and explore a group of individuals organized into a culture. Membership in a particular group, at a particular moment in psychological time, in a particular region of psychological space creates the particular life problems of the particular group of people. The equipment of a particular group may vary quantitatively from the equipment of members of another group and might even vary qualitatively. These probably different life problems of a group, and the possibly different neuropsychological equipment of group members, would and could produce different conditions of existence of the group and different conditions for its existence. Such could produce different group existential problems and group existential means. This could result in varying existential states for each group that exists. Thus, one could account for the many differences in social institutions and similarity in the personalities of group members.

Section 4 of Exhibit VII utilizes the same basic concepts of the emergent cyclical double-helix model to depict the psychosocial development of the individual. The life problems of the individual in need of solutions produce the conditions *of* existence of the individual. The person's individual neuropsychological equipment produces his or her conditions *for* existence. The conditions *of* existence of the individual produce the existential problems of the person. The conditions *for* existence of the individual provide the existential means for him or her to live. The latter two, the existential problems of the individual and the existential means of the person, interact to produce the existential state of the person. His or her existential state causes the development of the personal organization of the levels of existence. This personal organization of the levels of existence determines the particular institutional behavior of the person and his or her personality variables.

Exhibits VIII, IX and X elaborate some of the aspects of emergent cyclical theory previously covered. They illustrate certain aspects which cannot be seen through the previous diagrams. Exhibit VIII, particularly, shows that psychosocial development is, overall, a complex wave-like phenomenon. It is not, as previous words may have led you to believe, a discrete step-after-step movement that takes place. Slowly the movement begins. Then it picks up pace until it reaches a new nodal state, tarries at this stage for a while, then slowly (but never completely) recedes.

But Exhibit VIII is the representation of the sum of many sub-problems at a level that activate the many co-related neuropsychological subsystems when psychological space changes. For example, different sub-problems of the class A activate different structural parts of subsystem N. Thus, the wave illustration actually represents the average of all the movements in a particular phase of development. (See Exhibit VIII.) So when I say a person or a culture is positioned at a level, I am referring to the nodal position on the developing wave. This is clear when one examines, in Exhibit VIII, the vertical drop at the nodal point

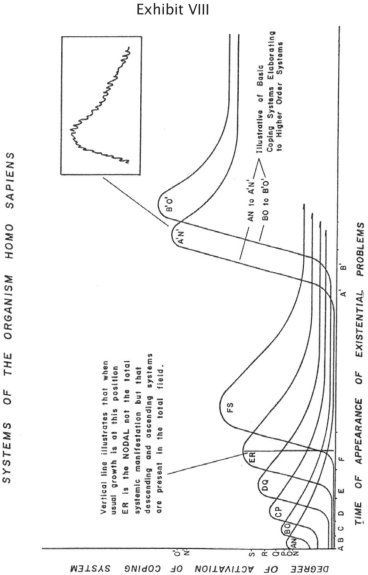

Exhibit VIII

of the ER system. At this point most behavior is ER, but DQ, CP, BO and AN behavior are present in decreasing amounts. FS behavior is also present in amounts about equal to DQ, whereas A'N' behavior has barely emerged.

The reason for the heavy lines of the AN and BO and A'N' and B'O' illustrate that movement to the second spiral of existence is not a complete break from the past. It is only a higher-order move in the complex spiral of life.

Overall, psychosocial development can indeed be seen as a complex wave-like phenomenon. But development does not occur in the smooth and flowing manner suggested by Exhibit VIII. It is more a spurt-like, plateau-like, more a progressive, steady state, regressive movement in which certain demarcation points can be identified in the flowing process. As systems of personality and culture come and go with changes in psychological time and alterations in psychological space, four demarcation points can be readily distinguished. This progressive, steady state, regressive development and the four demarcation points are shown in Exhibit IX.

The progressive, steady state, regressive path of development is shown in Exhibit IX by the line diagram of systems AN through B'O' The four demarcation points are indicated, for each successive level of existence, by the lower case letters a, b, c, d, and by priming and double priming them.

Lower case a, a', a'', etc., indicate periods of steady state functioning as represented by the plateaus in Exhibit IX. These periods exist when coping means are adequate to meet current existential problems. (These steady state periods, a for system AN, a' for system BO, etc., are shown as they represent the existential state of the species, not the individual. In the individual, in the modern world, the time scale is reversed.) During a, a', a'' periods, ways to cope with the existential problems produced by the psychological space are adequate.

When points b, b', b'' are reached, a change in psychological space has taken place. The change has produced new problems of existence and old ways are no longer adequate to the tasks of living. So points b, b', b'' stand out as times of crisis in the developmental process. They denote times when feelings of cognitive inadequacy arise as one attempts to solve newly appearing or newly created existential problems by old coping means. Such attempts produce states of anxiety and rigid functioning. As the anxiety increases, so does the rigid functioning. This

Exhibit IX

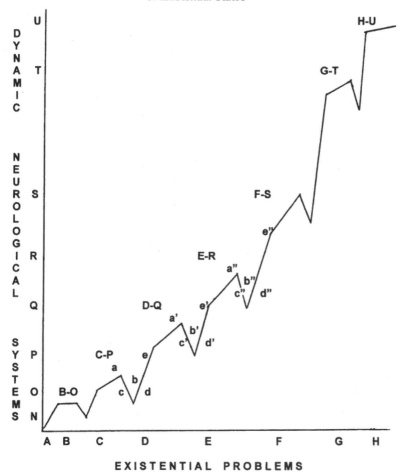

results in attempts to make older and older coping ways solve the newer and newer existential problems.[105] Thus, at points *b, b', b"* regression often takes place. During these times, depending on the amount of stress induced, fixation may occur. So, this is one place in the developmental process where pathology is apt to break out.

Functioning of a quite different character, susceptible to different kinds of pathology, arises at developmental points *c, c', c"*, etc. At these points, the dissonance created by the inadequacy of existing coping means has started the production of new chemicals in subsystem X, the activating system. These new chemical constituents have started the activation of the next set of neuropsychological equipment. This produces new ideas for coping which are able to solve the new existential problems. But these new insights may be blocked from implementation by the conditions in psychological space. Points *c, c', c"*, etc., are points at which a subjective state of anger and considerable labile functioning may occur. So this is another point in the development process at which fixation is apt to occur and from which regression to earlier forms of behavior might take place.

If conditions are right, if they provide for one to implement the new insights into action, then movement takes place to points *d, d', d"*. As new insights develop and provide new coping means, and as barriers are removed, the new existential problems are resolved. This results in very rapid movement and a quantum leap to the next steady state of being, the next level of existence.

To repeat, Exhibit IX applies, time-wise, to the species and not the individual. It illustrates, in one aspect, the length of time it took humankind to develop each new steady state *a, a', a"* for human existence. It took a longer period of time for *Homo sapiens* to move through the AN state of existence to the BO state than it took for movement from BO to CP. The leading edge of DQ existence took still less time to appear than the leading edge of the CP state. But this aspect of emergent cyclical theory can be viewed better through the diagram of Exhibit X.

Exhibit X shows a series of increasingly large quasi-concentric circles. The first, as illustrated, is confined to the lines of the "normal-sized" head. It represents the AN psychological space, the space in which all *Homo sapiens* lived until about 40,000 years ago. At that time changes in the conditions of human existence, probably climatic,

---

[105] CWG: Emergent cyclical theory sees the developmental process as Mehrabian sees it, except that he does not identify the systems or the determinants. [See: Mehrabian, Albert (1968). *An Analysis of Personality Theories*. Prentice Hall, p. 143-152.]

apparently triggered the appearance of the leading edge of BO thinking. This resulted in a considerable increase in the psychological space of *Homo sapiens*.

About 10,000 years ago, a new set of existential conditions—probably population numbers—came to be. As a result, the P system in the brain was activated in the leading edge of humankind. Another increase in psychological space occurred as the CP state of existence emerged.

Exhibit X

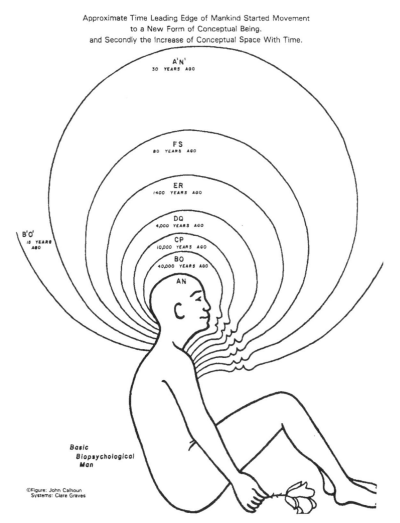

Approximate Time Leading Edge of Mankind Started Movement to a New Form of Conceptual Being, and Secondly the Increase of Conceptual Space With Time.

Basic Biopsychological Man

©Figure: John Calhoun
Systems: Clare Graves

Then about 4,000 years ago the D problems, probably full awareness of the fact that one must die, arose, activated the Q system, and produced another increase in psychological space. About 600 years ago, the conditions of existence for the leading edge of mankind changed again. He became aware that this is the only life he would ever have. These conditions activated the fifth level neuropsychological system, the R system, and the human began to operate in the ER manner.

But with the beginning of the realization that one is not an individual independent from all others, about 80 years ago, the psychological space changed again. The leading edge of humankind started its move to the FS state of existence.

And it was just some 30 years ago[106] that psychological space started to show its greatest change to date. This is portrayed by the A'N' system of Exhibit XII [p. 187]. It occurred when, for the first time in his existence, the leading edge of mankind truly realized that man is an *interdependent,* not an independent organism.

Exhibit XI illustrates, in a sense, all that this chapter has said to date about emergent cyclical psychosocial developmental theory. It lists in the horizontal table the first seven levels of existence—AN, BO, CP, DQ, ER, FS, and A'N'. Next to the letters designating each of the states is a thumbnail summation of some basic aspects of each associated existential state. The diagram shows that at the AN level, survival is on an automatic basis. There is no conscious awareness of self as different from any other human or any other animal. There is no differentiation of others, no differentiation between the inner and the outer world.

At the BO level, self is subsumed within others. Living is centered on sacrificing self to the "clan", "tribe," or group of others. The idea 'we as the group are one' is all-important, and the focus of life is on the attempt to control the inner self and come to peace with it.

When the CP system comes to be, consciousness of the self, as an identity, emerges. The person perceives that caring about others interferes with one's own existence. 'I, myself' emerges to be life's central concern. Others matter only inasmuch as they interfere with me. Overtly, in this state these become an 'express self, to hell with others' existence. The focus of living shifts to the external world and how to get control over it, so "I" can survive or at least go down to death glorified in the eyes of others.

---

[106] This was written in 1977, putting the approximate rise of A'N' at the end of World War II and the beginnings of the nuclear age.

Exhibit XI

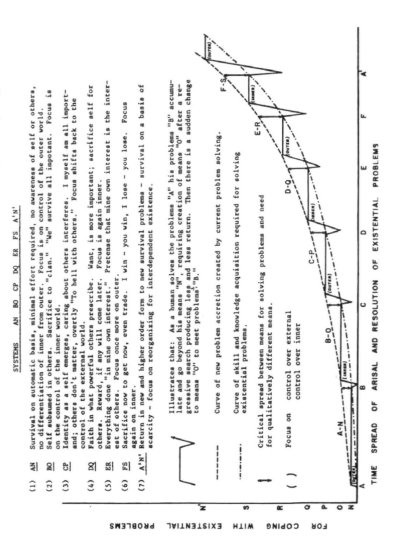

At the DQ level, faith prevails. "That which powerful others prescribe and want will make life what it would be for me" is the center of life. "Sacrifice self now to get later" becomes *the thema* for existence. One's higher power is the designer and the determiner of life. So, the focus for living shifts again back to the control of one's inner world and how to come to peace with all that is inside but cannot be expressed except in the way of the higher power.

The ER system again shifts its focus to the external world and how to gain control over it so one can acquire that which fulfills "mine own self interest." This system pretends that "mine own self interest" is really the interest of others. This is a characteristic of this express self system which is different from the CP express self system.

At the FS level, return is made to a sacrifice-self theme. But it is a "sacrifice now to get now" theme, not a "sacrifice now to get later" theme (DQ). The self, at this level, is a strong part of the total system, but the focus is again on knowing the inner world. The FS focus is different from AN and BO systems in which the idea of self had not emerged to a dominant position. It is also different from the CP external focus on the world and how to get around it, or the ER external focus on how to gain control over it. It has the inward focus of the DQ world but not on how to come to inner peace with the absolutistic prescriptions of authority. FS thinking seeks an even trade in life: 'If you win, I win. If you lose, I lose.' And central to it is: 'Whoever wins, whoever loses, let us not fight about it because that will only rob me of the time I need to come to know my inner world.' This dictum is lived to excess, as are all the dictums of subsistence level systems, and it is these excesses which lead to the emergence of the A'N' system, the first system of the second spiral of existence.

The A'N' system arises as a result of the excesses of the subsistence ways of living, as a result of over-denial and over-expression. Over-denial has led to the rape of self. Over-expression has led to the rape of others and of the world. This rape of others, the world, and the self has put sheer existence in jeopardy just as it was when human life began. Six ways of being—AN, BO, CP, DQ, ER, FS—have worked toward an epitome for living based on the total expression by the individual. Now, in the minds of some, this vision of life is perceived to doom *Homo sapiens* to go out of existence. So a new basis for living, the *interdependence* of all things, emerges as the perception upon which to start human life all over again. As Mumford says, the sum of all our days is but a new beginning.[107] The totality of this is shown in the two curves of Exhibit X.

In Exhibit XI, the solid line curve illustrates that as the human solves the problems A he gains the skills and knowledge through system N which are necessary to cope with problems A. But it shows that what

---

[107] Paraphrase of Lewis Mumford's (1956) optimistic remark, "The sum of all man's days is just a beginning." (*Transformations of Man*. p. 249).

accumulates from the solution of problems A creates problems B, etc., *ad infinitum*. These two curves are an abstraction superimposed on the progressive, steady state, regressive curve of Exhibit IX to remind the reader of the actual process of development.

In Exhibit XI, the [dashed line] – – – curve shows the accretion of new problems created by the current means for problem solving. The [dot-dash-dot] • – • curve shows the accumulation of knowledge and skills required for solving newly created problems. Life begins with the slow development of the skills and knowledge needed to solve problems A. As the skills and knowledge are accumulated, it begins to produce problems B. Thus, early in the process of living the AN way, the problems created are not in excess of the coping capacity of neuropsychological system N. So the person continues in the steady AN state. Later in psychological time, the ascending new problem (– – – curve in Exhibit XI) begins to exceed the capacity of the N system to cope. So a critical point in development is reached. It is shown at the end of each steady state by the double-headed arrows. When the spread between old problems solved and new problem accretion reaches a critical degree, there is a regressive attempt to force old ways to solve new problems. Forcing old solutions on new problems fails. The failure creates the dissonance which stimulates the activating system X to produce the chemical constituents necessary to activate higher level coping systems. These higher-level coping systems contain the kind of equipment necessary to deal with the kinds of excess problems created. Thus, the higher level is activated and the progressive, steady state development continues *ad infinitum*.

The exhibits presented so far illustrate the emergent side of emergent cyclical theory but they show nothing on the cyclical side. Exhibit XII is presented to fill this gap. Exhibit XII is, of all the illustrations presented, the one most pregnant with meaning. Therefore, I shall begin the narration in respect to it with some words about its derivation.

Exhibit XII derives from some of the data reported in Chapter IV. In particular I refer to the data which said:

1. Conceptualize adult psychosocial behavior as a hierarchical series of six upon six subsystems—the conceptions of maturity data.
2. Conceptualize adult psychosocial behavior so that each odd-numbered system in the hierarchy is more externally, more "change-the-environment" oriented and so that each

even-numbered system is more internally, more "adjust-to-the-environment" oriented—the "express-self/deny-self" data.
3. Conceptualize adult psychosocial behavior in a systemically alternating, cyclical, wave-like fashion allowing for repetition of general *thema* in a new and different way in every other system —the "change and organizational data."
4. Conceptualize psychosocial behavior so that every other system is similar to but at the same time different from its alternate—the "conceptions of maturity and change" data.
5. Conceptualize psychosocial behavior so that each system has its system specificness, so that each system has a quality all its own—the "interaction and learning" data.
6. Conceptualize psychosocial behavior so as to allow for quantitative variation in some dimensions—the "authoritarianism and dogmatism" data.
7. Conceptualize psychosocial behavior so as to allow for little or no variation in certain dimensions—the "intelligence and temperament" data.
8. Conceptualize psychosocial behavior so as to show increased degrees of psychological space in each successive system and particularly to show marked changes in psychological space every seventh system in the hierarchy of systems—the "freedom to behave" and the "problem solving" data.

Examination of these results indicates that a model of personality, culture and conceptions of maturity requires representation through two basic components in the mind of man (items 2, 3, and 4 above). So, in Exhibit XII, the broken line and the solid line represent these two components. The broken line represents the development of the mental component "focus on the external world and attempt to master it." The solid line represents the development of the component "focus on the inner world and attempt to come to peace with it." But whence come these two components? Emergent-cyclical theory proposes they derive from the two hemispheres of the brain. The externally focused component derives from the left hemisphere, the inner focused component from the right hemisphere. The recent experimental evidence which indicates that the two hemispheres function in different

Exhibit XII

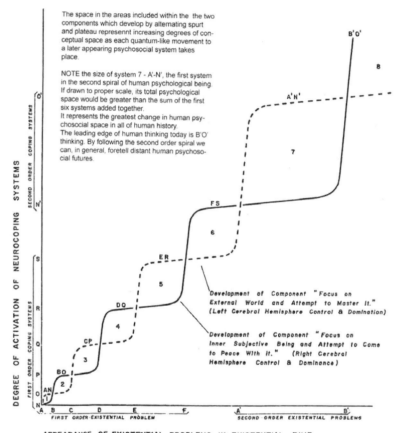

ways supports this.[108] So the dotted line, when in the upper position, represents domination of conceptual thinking by the functions of the

---

[108] Sperry, Roger W., Gazzaniga, M.S. and Bogen, J.E. (1969). Interhemispheric relationships: the neocortical commissures; syndromes of hemisphere disconnection. In Vinken, P. J. and Bruyn G.W. (Eds.), *Handbook of Clinical Neurology* (p. 273-290). Amsterdam: North-Holland Publishing Co., 4. Gazzeniga, M. S. (1970) *The Bisected Brain*. New York: Appleton. Ornstein, R. (1972). *The Psychology of Consciousness*. San Francisco: Freeman Co.

left cerebral hemisphere. The solid line represents domination by the functions of the right hemisphere.

But how can one represent the aspect of data 2, 3, and 4 which requires that systems of psychosocial behavior show an alternation between "externally oriented change systems" and "internally oriented come to peace with what is" systems? This is represented by the two curves in Exhibit XII developing by periods of spurt and plateau. As the two components vary in their rate of development, they produce a hierarchy of alternating systems. Systems 1, 3, 5, and 7—existential states AN, CP, ER and A'N' respectively—are externally oriented change systems. Their focus is on the external world and how to master and change it. System control and domination within each odd-numbered system is exercised by the left cerebral hemisphere. The even-numbered systems, 2, 4, 6, and 8—the existential states BO, DQ, FS, and B'O'—are internally oriented. This internal orientation is focused on achieving internal peace and dominated by the right cerebral hemisphere.

The spurt-like, plateau-like development of the two components produces the wave-like repetition of theme variation on theme required by my data. This alternation of growth of the components also illustrates the similar and dissimilar aspects of every other system.

The odd-numbered systems are represented by the broken line to indicate the tendency of these odd-numbered systems—AN, CP, ER and A'N'—to be more loosely bound. The even-numbered are represented by the ascending solid line to indicate that each even-numbered system —BO, DQ, FS, B'O'—is more tightly bound. The odd-numbered systems are more change systems. The even-numbered ones are more conservative.

The transition to new systems produced by the alternating, spurt-like, plateau-like development of the two basic components plus the nature of the cross hatching within each area of conceptual space represents each system to have a quality all its own. These representational requirements are also required by the data.

The data demand that one conceive of systemic development so that it shows increased degrees of behavioral freedom at each successive level in the hierarchy. This concept is included in Exhibit XII. It is included by allowing the space defined by the alternating lines to increase in size in each successive system. Also, the data demands that some dimensions of personality or culture be shown to vary little over all systems. The constant form of the systems illustrates this concept.

Looking further at Exhibit XII, we see that each even-numbered system is only slightly larger than its predecessor, but each odd-numbered system expands more over its preceding even-numbered system than the even expands over the preceding odd. This is included in the diagram to illustrate two things:

1. that the increases in conceptual space are greater in the odd-numbered systems and less in those that are even-numbered, and
2. that the odd-numbered systems are "growth, change the environment" systems while the even-numbered systems are "consolidating, adjust to the environment" systems.

But note also in respect to the increase in psychological space of each system the difference of the seventh system from all the preceding systems. The seventh system, the first system in the second spiral of existence, is proportionately much larger over FS than ER is over DQ. This portrayal indicates a marked expansion in psychological space, in conceptual and behavioral possibilities when this system emerges.

The A'N' system is represented to contain more psychological space than the sum of the six systems which precede it. This is required by my data. The part of my data referred to indicates that the A'N' existential state is much less rigid, far less dogmatic, etc., than earlier appearing states. Of all the subjects studied, the A'N' subjects, solved problems not only much more rapidly but they also found more answers than all the others added together. Relative to the others, the rapidity with which A'N' subjects could change their point of reference was almost unbelievable. Their differences from others were so obvious that I said in an unpublished 1961 paper, read at several meetings, that this signified something markedly important to personality and cultural theorists. I said:

> As man moves from the sixth level to the seventh, freedom to know and to do, a chasm of awesome significance is being crossed. The bridge from the sixth level to the seventh is the bridge between similarity to animals and dissimilarity to animals.
>
> Once we are able to grasp the significance of passing from the level of belonging to the level of to do and to know, we will see that we are able to explain the enormous differences between man and other animals. It will be seen that at this point we step over the line which separates those needs we have in common with lower animals and those needs which are distinctly human.

> Man on the step of the seventh level is on the threshold of the emergence of his human being. He is no longer just another of nature's species. He is now becoming a human being. And we in our times, in our moral and general behavior, are but approaching this threshold. Would that we not be so lacking in understanding and would that we not be so condemning that by such misunderstanding and such condemnation we block man forever from crossing the line between his animalism and his humanism.[109]

At another point in the same paper I said (slightly changed to update it):

> Modern man, at this moment in his history is approaching his great divide, the point between lower and higher behavioral systems. Across this psychological space he can become what only man is to be and his behavior can begin to be uniquely human behavior. It will be behavior that is good for life, not after life; that is good for all beings, not just for self; that is good for him, not just his boss; that is good for him not just his ego.
>
> On the other side of development he may be the doer of great things or lesser things. He will become infinitely himself. If ever the human leaps to this great beyond, there will be no vassalage, no peonage in behavior. There will be no shame in behavior for man will know it is human to behave. There will be no pointing of the finger at other men, no segregation, no depredation, and no degradation in behavior. The human will be striding forth on the beginning of his humanness rather than vacillating and swirling in the turbulence of partial blocked human behavior arrested forever from playing itself out on the sands of time.

Exhibit XII, as drawn, shows the developing B'O' system as the last system in the hierarchy at this moment in time. However, it is essential to note that the double-helix conception allows for the development of systems beyond B'O'. This illustrates another significant way in which the emergent cyclical conception of personality is different from many other conceptions. With the exception of John Calhoun's conception,[110]

---

[109] The source document has not been been found. However, these words were read at the 1971 Annual Meeting of the Association of Humanistic Psychology from "Levels of Existence: An Open System Theory of Values," and appear in that paper wherein Dr. Graves cites the original date as 1960 rather than 1961.

[110] Calhoun (1968, 1973).

B'O' is a system beyond any suggested by others who think in a systemic fashion. And it is a system, along with the A'N' system, which says that any conception of personality, culture, and maturity must be open minded.

The limited data I have on the B'O' system suggests that the central core of the B'O' existential state is: "One shall adjust to the existential realities of one's existence." One shall automatically accept the existential dichotomies of life of which Erich Fromm writes.[111] This central core is amazingly like the core of the second level of existence, the BO existential state. Similarly, A'N' is more like the AN state than it is like any of the five other subsistence level systems. Yet the B'O' state is unlike the BO state, just as the A'N' state is unlike the AN state. Thus, Exhibit X illustrates that the A'N' state is the beginning of a second spiral, a psychospatially very different spiral of existence, as the double-helix model suggests.

Thus we come almost to the end of the diagrammatic representation of emergent cyclical theory. All that is left is to present a diagram which identifies the major systems and subsystems which research should attempt to examine. These nodal systems and their entering and exiting subsystems are shown in Exhibit XIII.

The nodal systems—AN, BO, CP, DQ, ER, FS, A'N', and B'O'—have been designated before. But no words have been offered as to how the sub-systems are designated. The exiting sub-states and the entering sub-states are designated by a combination of upper case and lower case letters. In the case of the exiting states, the designation is BO/cp, DQ/er, etc., indicating a transitional system in which the BO component is stronger than the emerging cp component. The entering states are designated as bo/CP, cp/DQ, dq/ER, etc. This indicates a subsystem in which the bo component is subordinated to the strengthening CP component.

With this designation of the nodal systems and the subsystems, basic emergent cyclical theory has been presented. Now it is time to turn to a description of each of the existential states, the levels of existence of the organism *Homo sapiens*.[112]

---

[111] Fromm, Eric (1941). *Escape from Freedom*. Holt Rinehart and Winston.

[112] At this point there is a break in Dr. Graves's writing, explained on the pages which follow.

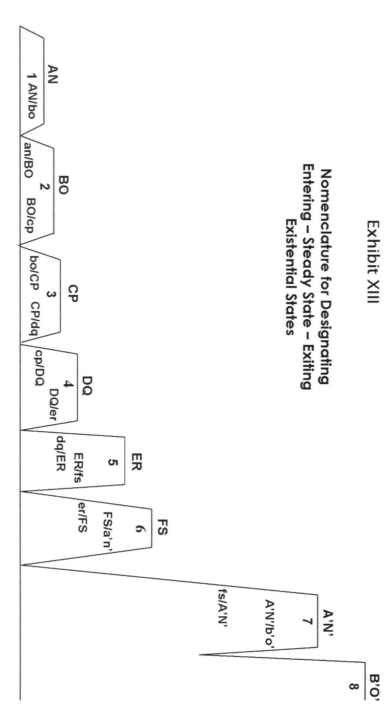

Exhibit XIII

Nomenclature for Designating
Entering – Steady State – Exiting
Existential States

Exhibit XIV

**SCHEMATIC REPRESENTATION OF THE SOURCE
OF EXISTENTIAL STATES - ADULT PERSONALITY
AS A COMPLEX OF BIO-SOCIAL ECOLOGICAL SYSTEMS**

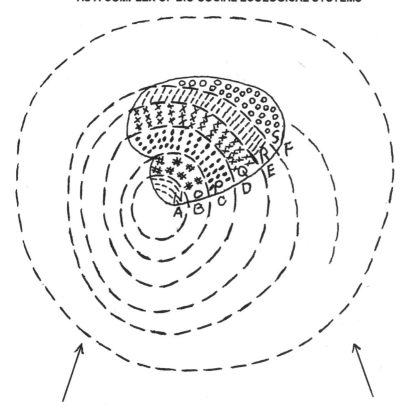

TOTALITY OF HUMAN BEHAVIORAL POSSIBILITIES EXTANT TODAY

A to F = Conditions for Existence – Existential Problems

N to S = Dynamic Neurological Systems

A-N, B-O, C-P, D-Q, E-R, F-S = Existential States

 = Qualitative Differences in Neurological Systems

Section II

Section II

The Levels of Existence along the Existential Staircase

We thought long and hard about whether to include the next part or not because we wanted to remain true to the work, the words and the manuscript. Dr. Graves either never completed most of the chapters for the following section, or they are lost. His widow believed he had not written them because, with his damaged eyesight, it became too burdensome to continue. He did complete some of the AN chapter, and one sample of his intended approach to the transition states does exist (the transitional DQ/ER chapter sub-section which is included within the DQ chapter, essentially intact). Thus, the chapters on from AN to B'O' are reconstructions by the editors from Dr. Graves's own writings with emphasis given to the phrasings of his later papers and summaries.

His table of contents made it clear that Dr. Graves wanted to include chapters on these levels of existence. Thus, the words in this section are those of Dr. Graves; only needed conjunctions have been added. However, the arrangement of ideas and the placement of sentences and phrases, compiled from various sources, is by the editors.

Some of the unpublished source documents are available online at www.clarewgraves.com for anyone wishing to search for specific phrases in the original context and are cited in the bibliography. A great many ideas appear in multiple papers over the years with only slight differences in wording, while others changed significantly as the theory evolved. Some of the comments included here come from transcriptions of recorded presentations and seminars. In addition to online documents, readers might want to locate a reprint of Dr. Graves's paper summarizing his views on management at the time from the *Harvard Business Review* (1966), as well as his preliminary remarks on theory in the *Journal of Humanistic Psychology* (1970); both of these should be viewed as works in progress.

The reader should be fully aware that this section is a compilation by the editors and not as organized by Dr. Graves. It is surely not what he had expected or hoped to produce, yet the work is so powerful, even in this reconstructed form, that we could not let it remain unexplored. Thus, the next eight chapters are included to elaborate on the important part – the theory in Sections I and III. The essence of the point of view, and the basis for further work, appears in those sections and stands up well without these details and illustrations. The reader should also keep in mind these cautionary words from Clare Graves's 1977 preface on page 25:

> So the theory presented herein is not the product I had envisioned. It is a sketch with gaps and expressive deficiencies within…In one sense, I apologize to those who sought more than I was, in pre-accident days, of a mind to scatter. On the other hand, I do not apologize, because then I did not feel that I was ready to stand on what I, too early, might have said. But now, even within my problem, I am ready to stand on what I say herein, but not on what I said before except in a basically general sense. What I said before was a part of an effort which produced the product contained herein. Even today it is not a finished product. Obviously it is incomplete and obviously there will be gaps and errors in my thinking. But when I say ON THESE WORDS I STAND, what I mean is this: If my conception of adult behavior is to be torn to shreds by criticism and even demolished by subsequent research, let it be the basics of the emergent cyclical levels of existence theory of adult behavior as I am able to present it herein that be criticized and torn apart. Let it not be that which I said or wrote while trying to conceive what is presented within the covers of this book. And let it not be the specifics of the conception that criticism dwell upon.

Over the years, many people who have adopted the Gravesian point of view have concentrated on the content of the levels—more as a typology and categories for differences—rather than focus on the E-C theory, itself. It was the emergent cyclical levels of existence perspective and the double helix, described in Section I and defended in Section III, which are the essence of this work. It is those chapters which are "The Graves Book." The next eight chapters are icing applied to his cake, made from ingredients he left and used with some consistency. They are, nonetheless, only our best approximation of what he might have baked. One of the motivations for making this text available is to suggest that further research and study is needed, how it might be pursued, and to make the basis of Dr. Graves's thinking available to those who choose further to explore human behavior—what it is, and what it is meant to be.

— the editors

CHAPTER 7

The Autistic Existence — The AN[113] State

The 1st Subsistence Level

The AN – Autistic, Automatic, Reactive Existential State

Theme: *Express self as if just another animal according to the dictates of one's imperative periodic physiological needs.*

Alternative theme: *Express self as if just another animal according to the dictates of one's imperative physiological needs and the environmental possibilities*

---

[113] In some of his writings, Dr. Graves used a hyphen to separate the letters in the pairs: A-N, B-O, etc. In other work he did not: AN, BO, CP, etc. The hyphen suggests and reinforces the link between the double-helix components. He used that in his later handouts. However, he did not include the hyphen in the 1977 manuscript and this text will adhere to that style for consistency. Readers should also note that Dr. Graves made it clear that his descriptions of the AN state were based on library research and, for obvious reasons, not from written conceptiosn.

Emergent cyclical theory depicts essentially eight major conditions of human existence that have or are emerging in man's history to date with a description of the characteristics of the human who typically lives within the confines of one of these levels of existence.

The first one is designated the AN level. The AN system is one by which all lived 40,000 or more years ago. It still exists in viable and functioning form today, though most often it is found in pathological cases. It exists in those conditions of existence which provide for automatic satisfaction of the A level problems of existence.

The A stands for the first set of conditions of human existence in which the human being lives. The N stands for the neurological system that is activated to deal with particular problems of existence confronting the individual. To have fixated into this form as a viable existence, the human conditions for existence must have provided for the automatic satisfaction of the imperative, periodic, physiological needs—the "A" - the individual and race survival problems of existence. Necessary information for survival of individual and species is sensed, processed, and reacted to through the automatic system and stored through the learning process of habituation, the learning equipment which automatically signals the on-off character of the degree of need. The "N" neuropsychological system, the neuro system specifically attuned to processing imperative, physiological need information, responds only to change in intensity of the imperative need and not to patterning.

According to E-C theory, this earliest-appearing system is based on the human's reaction to the presence or absence of physiological tension. The person, motivated only by the degree of satisfaction of the imperative, periodic physiological needs such as hunger, thirst, and sex is aware only of the presence and absence of tension. I sometimes call it the Autistic State, meaning that the person who lives at this level lives in a need-satisfying, wish-fulfillment manner; that the person is aware only of the presence and absence of tension. Sometimes I have called it the Animalistic Existence – humans behaving much as other animals do – and sometimes the Reactive Existence, for the individual just reacts to these tensions in the manner that will automatically take care of satisfying the particular need that has arisen out of the, to use a German term, *urangst* of the individual in this particular moment that he or she is living.

The absence of pain, that is tension, is what is good. Its presence is that which is bad. That which automatically reduces tension is good. That which increases the tensional level is bad. The tension arises and he automatically reacts in the direction of doing what he or she has learned will satisfy that particular tension. This is a process where the person learns to shut off stimulation. When he gets enough he stops. He learns to shut off and lives a life wishing for the cessation of that tension. Effort is expended in response to immediate needs or desires if awake, and he plays when surfeited.

As in infra-human animals there is no true self-awareness – no awareness of self as separate and distinct from the other animals, and no awareness of self as differentiated from others in this automatic reflexological existence. At the automatic level man is, by and large, unaware of his own subjectivity. He cannot distinguish his actions from environmental consequences. He is so little aware of what is going on that he tends not even to recognize that which is new or frustrating. He has no energy to mobilize into anger or fear, or hate or jealousy. He behaves more like the behaviorists' imprinted duckling than he does a 'human being.' Place a stimulus to which he is imprinted in front of him and he automatically responds so long as it is present. Put others in their place and it is as if they were not even there.

As in infra-human species, there is only a home territory concept of space, and imperative need-based concept of time, cause, space, and materiality of a very limited character. They don't know 'over the hill' or 'over yonder,' or 'down the river' or 'down the stream;' they have no concept of that nature. They live in some cave or depression they've found and crawled into. There is no concept of God, the gods, the universe or the like. This person lives as a herd, a herd of 12 to15 human beings in a group. They make no organized planned work effort. They show no concept of leadership. The only time they expend effort is in response to immediate need or desire. There is no formal organization or management of people who operate at this level. This man is not aware of his existence; he has no excess energy with which to plan, to organize or to foresee the future.

Life is either grubbing for that which will maintain the spark of life, or in the pathological cases, a signaling to the world of others "I am in need and if I am to continue to exist, then you must adjust to my signals." This, therefore, is the first of our 'adjustment of the environment to the organism' systems. Here man is striving to get the world of other people to adjust to his basic imperative needs, a matter, at this level, which is vital to his existence. For if they cannot be made to adjust, then he in this existential state ceases to be. He is soon dead.

Man the species, or man the individual, does not have to rise above this level to continue the survival of the species. Man can continue the survival of the species through the purely physiological aspect of the process of procreation existence. He can live what is for him, at the AN level, a productive lifetime—productive in the sense that his built-in response mechanisms are able to reduce the tensions of his imperative physiological needs—and a reproductive lifetime. But this level of existence seldom is seen today except in rare instances or in pathological cases.

Examples of AN Existence

This is the level of adult human behavior at which energies expended in the process of procuring food and conducting the tissue building and maintaining processes, the anabolic processes, are barely more, if more, than equivalent to the energies expended in the tissue destroying processes, the catabolic processes. There are no energies to activate man's usual psychological processes. There is energy for barely more than a physiological reflexological state of existence, only a sufficient amount for attendance to living in the most narrow sense of the phrase. The cells of the higher brain, if present, are alive but with the exception of those 'automatic' imprintable systems, there is little or no activation of cognitive brain substance. Even Pavlovian classical conditioning brain substance is minimally operant, and the intentional instrumental learning system just does not operate. Therefore, the behavior displayed by a person or group at this level is almost devoid of what we normally call human experience.

Man does exist at the bare subsistence level, but to say that he who is at this level actually "lives" would be to do him a grave injustice. He is alive—yes—and those neurological systems which maintain his physiological processes are operant; but existentially this can hardly be called human life, for it is a state of psychological non-existence. Cognitively, affectively and otherwise man at this level is almost without those experiences known to higher-level humans.

Today, this is the world of the adult psychological infant, possibly the world of the simplest of food gathering cultures, the world of the severe senile deteriorate, the world of he who has regressed severely under the stress of war, the world of he who has been kept alive by the compassion or guilt of his fellow man. At the extreme, he is more animal than human; barely more, if more, than a living vegetable. In fact, for many at this level it would be more appropriate to refer to them as in a state of vegetative existence.

In this state of being, the person does not have any awareness of him- or her self as being different from any other person, as being different from any other animal, as being different from a log or a tree or a rock or anything else. It's just a condition in which the individual is one with the world; but they will now and then perceive themselves as *a little* different. It's a state which is found rarely in the current world.

The research that came out in the mid 1960s corroborated that this state of existence *does* actually live on the surface of the globe at this particular time, and one finds them in the natural state, in a healthy state, and in the mature state in the Tasaday of the island of Mindanao in the Philippine Archipelago.[114] The Tasaday are people who have survived because of their particular conditions of existence—living way back in a verdant, rain forest, far and away from any other human being. The forest provides a continuous supply of food and water. There are natural limestone caves, so it naturally provides shelter from any inclement weather. They find a cave and they just move in.

People living at the first level of human existence—living the nodal way that is the way that maintains life and continues for them—don't need tools. They just go out in the stream and pick up a crawdad. Food is there to be gathered, to be plucked, to be picked. They don't have any concept of leadership; they don't have any concept of time; they have no concept of space other than the immediate little region in which they live. They live through the automatic equipment of the N neurological system which is specifically attuned to processing the imperative physiological needs. These people who are centralized at and have been living forever at the first level of existence have not gone on to higher levels of existence because they live in those verdant conditions. There has been no reason for them to go on.

They are not like other people who operate at lower levels of human existence who live, for example, in the Kalahari Desert[115] where it is necessary to search continuously for food. People like those who live on the Kalahari Desert have to find a more adequate way of existence than those who are like the Tasaday. So they at least begin movement out of the first level to the second level of existence; but these are only some examples of people who live at or close to the first level of existence today.

Sometimes people who once operated at considerably higher levels have had their conditions of existence worsened. Hence, their higher level systems were deactivated, turning on again and foreforcing the

---

[114] Ibid., Nance.
[115] Thomas, Elizabeth Marshall (1959). *The Harmless People*. New York: Alfred A. Knopf.

lower level systems. An example of this are the Ik, the nomadic African tribe that was forced out of its natural habitat into a static life in mountainous country insufficient to provide sustenance to meet even their periodic physiological needs or to enable these people to solve their problems of existence.[116] They have regressed probably to about the lowest level of human living that we have today.

It simply indicates, as I see it, that down underneath it all, if the human being is to survive, he must do whatever he can to survive. The human being is pretty bright. If it's necessary to steal the food out of the baby's mouth as the Ik does, do it. Now, let's get down to earth here, let's get down to the level which we were talking about and here, now, the lowest part of that level. At the first level the person does not differentiate self from any other animal. An animal gets hungry enough it will take what it must to live. A human will do the same thing; it's another animal; the Ik do that. Those who have written of the Ik—these are not my words—have described them as the most despicable human beings on the face of the globe.[117] They are simply trying to stay alive as human beings, and losing the battle.

Karl Jaspers related a regressed case of this kind in his book, *General Psychopathology*. A World War I German soldier related the state of mind to which he was reduced by the conditions for existence in which he was living. The soldier said:

> "We were reduced to having to wait and see. We were in immediate danger but our minds froze, grew numb, empty and dead. One gets so tired, so utterly weary. Thoughts crawl, to think is such a labor and even the smallest voluntary act becomes painful to perform. Even talking, having to reply, get ones thoughts together jars on the nerves, and it felt as sheer relief to doze and not to have to think of anything or do anything. The numbness may indeed grow into a dreamlike state, time and space disappear, reality moves off infinitely far, and while one's consciousness obediently registers every detail like a photographic plate ... feelings waste away and the individual loses all touch with himself. It is you who sees, hears and perceives or is it only your shadow?"[118]

---

[116] Turnbull, Colin M. (1972). *Mountain People*. New York, NY: Simon & Schuster.
[117] Ibid., Turnbull.
[118] Jaspers, Karl (1964). *General Psychopathology*. University of Chicago Press, p. 368-369.

Obviously, in the jargon of the day, this man is not 'with it.' He is not aware of time, space or materiality. There is no reality for him as many of us know reality. His psychological processes seem to have disappeared for, as he says, "our minds froze, grew numb, empty and dead." Intentional behavior is gone as is shown when he says, "Thoughts crawl, to think is such a labor and even the smallest voluntary act becomes painful to perform." All that operates in this state is basic reflexological behavior. Even emotions and one's concept of self disappear for as he says, "…feelings waste away and the individual loses all touch with himself."

Quite obviously this is the AN state in one of its pathological forms. But do not make an error at this point, for automatic behavior does not arise only from psychopathological or physiopathological conditions of existence. This is a normal state of existence, at least in our world today. This assertion is not one which it pleases me to make, for as you shall soon see, it need not be a normal state for man's being because there is much we could do about it. But for the moment, such regrets are not germane, for the AN state of existence is the life state of many non-pathological beings in our world today. So we must know its character if ever we are to take appropriate steps to lift man from this inhumane, human state of existence.

How many million adults in this world live at this level we do not know, but the lady whose case shall now be cited exists, lives, and is reproducing within the upper reaches of this state of human existence. First, let us examine the conditions for existence which surround her being today.

> Mrs. G. is the case. (Note: this was a white family.) She and her family live in one of the many decaying tenement row houses facing on the pock marked and trash littered pavement of __ St. The gutted sidewalk in front of the G. home is cluttered with broken glass that has collected throughout the litter of battered tin cans and soggy bags of garbage "air mailed" from the windows above. Worn dips in the steps of a wooden stoop and a swaying hand-railing lead into a hallway where the grit and grime underfoot and on a creaking stairway to the second floor also cling to the rickety banister.
>
> Grease coated walls in the kitchen and the damply dirty top of an outsized television set, long inoperative, revile the hand. The odor vaguely sensed but undefined in the hallway and up the stairs is unmistakable now. It is the smell of urine, dried and drying in the bare mattresses and in the sagging, stuffing-spilling

> sofas that are beds at night. The stench is present in the rumpled clothes that fill corners of the rooms and cover the floor of a bedroom. Nor are the fetid odors of cooking and the atmosphere of damp rot compounded by faulty plumbing dispelled by the open windows. There is no hot water to clean the clothes effectively or to cut the grease on top of the stove and the tabletop and in the skillet and in the scattered plates and dishes.

These conditions for human existence in both the German soldier and in Mrs. G's world certainly approach the A conditions hypothesized to trigger only the operation of the N neurological system. And, as we read further we will see how familiar is the psychology of our soldier and Mrs. G.:

> Next to the sink in the kitchen is a water heater. It would probably work, Mrs. G. thinks, because there is a hot water tap above the sink. But she ways, "We haven't got it hitched up yet. Maybe my husband will call the landlord or try to do it himself."

Notice the automatic registering of the world in Mrs. G's case—the same automatic registering of which our soldier wrote. But, notice also the absence of volitional behavior which the soldier said was too painful to even try. Going on we find:

> Mrs. G. is only vaguely sensitive to the squalor of her home. It has been this way for as long as she can remember. She would like things to be better, but she can't change things. She has no resources to call upon that might bring change.

Our regressed soldier said:

> "our minds froze, grew numb, empty and dead. One gets so tired, so utterly weary. Thoughts crawl, to think is such a labor and even the smallest voluntary act becomes painful to perform. Even talking, having to reply, get ones thoughts together jars on the nerves and it is felt as sheer relief to doze and not have to think of anything or do anything."

Are these not very similar existential states? Are not Mrs. G's conditions for existence but a little better than our soldier's? But is her psychology substantially different? Our soldier says, "the numbness may indeed grow into a dream like state, time and space disappear, reality moves off infinitely far." Our reporter says of Mrs. G.:

It is early afternoon but the children are only half-dressed. A three-year-old girl is wearing one of her brother's dirty undershirts and nothing else. None of the children is wearing shoes. Their feet are black with grime and look misshapen. The long hair of the girls is dirty, crumpled and knotted. There is no comb to be found today. Not even in the bedroom where a seven-year-old boy in a faded Cub Scout shirt lies sleeping. Mrs. G. is surprised to find her son asleep in the room. She thought he had eaten breakfast with the rest of the family and gone out to play—one of the children starts toward the door to go outside—"put shoes on." Mrs. G. tells her daughter. The child finds one laceless shoe. She goes out barefooted. Her mother is not looking.

"I don't even know the name of the woman next door. We lived here two years. No one lives on the first floor of this building. Those rooms come with the rent."

Certainly Mrs. G's mind has little comprehension of time, space and reality. But, again, let us not make an error. Mrs. G. can and has lived a reproductive lifetime at this level. She has 13 children, 13 children who are growing in this channel of human existence and who will be, at adulthood, in this level of existence unless their conditions for existence are changed.

This is the automatic, physiological reflexological, bare subsistence level of human behavior. It is the AN existential state in operation. This is the second to the lowest level of human living that we know of. The other one: it's a person maintained by machines, whose brain is essentially dead, but the body is kept alive. But people, like Mrs. G., are not idiots nor deteriorates who are necessarily bound to this form of existence. They are simply adult human beings who have taken on the form of existence which has the greatest survival value for them in their world; but they are also ones who are arrested at this level because certain societies will not do what is necessary to overcome the reasons for the arrestment.

Man at this level is an amoral being. Ethical thinking is not a part of his life, and God or religion is not there to be:

"In the moral sense this is an amoral system. There is no should or ought in behavior because man when centralized at this level does not operate cognitively. He only reacts. He does not think or judge or believe. Today, this value system, as the dominant system in man, is more theoretical than actual, more transitory than lasting. This is so because if man is to stabilize at the first, or any level, two conditions of existence would have to obtain. The external world would have to continue in a relatively undisturbed state and the cognitive component would have to be absent or inoperant. The latter might exist in the severely retarded, or during severe conditions of stress in infancy, but it is hardly conceivable in a mature, healthy adult. And even if the cognitive component were not operant, one can hardly conceive of a static external world, for nature is always indifferent to man's fate. Thus, these very conditions of human existence, the presence of an indifferent but ever changing external world and man's emerging cognitive component, inevitably challenge man to seek a higher level of living and a new and different value system. But, no man will ever be without some reactive values."[119]

Emotions play practically no role in his behavior; thus problems of the antisocial or immoral kind do not stem from automatic man. But this does not mean that this level presents no troublesome problems for higher level man today. Therefore, we must consider what its way of operation means to the totality of mankind.

Possibly, this automatic existential state is the product of some men's progression to at least the fourth, the "saintly" level of human existence. For it is very possible that the guilt which comes to be in man when he arrives at the fourth level has led him to create this possibly artificial form of human existence. When man at the third level becomes aware of life, and when at the fourth level he transcends living only for his self, he perceives as a part of his duty in life that he should care for "God's children." So he institutes saintly ways, "alms for Allah," welfare systems, institutions for the mentally retarded and the deteriorates which may, in reality, be the source of this AN existential state. Thus, today, any comprehensive, systematic framework for representing adult man's existential forms must include, within its body, room for this possibly artificially instituted form for existence.

If this is so, man in his fourth level "beneficence" has created here a problem of monstrous proportions. Assuming, as I do, that this state of existence is more artificial than natural, what does it mean that it has come to be? First of all, it means that much to the disbelief of some, our welfare programs have been successful—successful in the sense that they have made it possible for first level people to live rather than to die. But

---

[119] Graves, Clare W. (1970). Levels of Existence: An Open System Theory of Values. *Journal of Humanistic Psychology*, Fall 1970, Vol. 10, No. 2, p. 131-155.

they have been far from successful in enabling people at this level to move up to higher levels of existence. In fact, the very psychological state, the fourth level state, which brought this level into being and its parent and its offspring, third and fifth level psychology, have almost assured us that the AN state of behavior will be with us for some time.

As I have said, it is the guilt of fourth level man which causes him to institute the automatic existence into being as a state of human affairs. And it is another aspect of fourth level psychology which contributes to locking people like Mrs. G. into this inhumane AN state of existence. In the saintly, sacrificial system one of its systemic peculiarities is that the belief in the sacredness of life is coupled with the belief that it is wrong to tamper with the established order. Therefore, saintly sacrificial man, fourth level man, is on the one hand driven to create those institutional ways which keep marginal humans alive, though only in a state of psychological non-existence. While on the other hand, he is disposed not to tamper with that which has been decided, namely that it is his duty to keep them alive, but wrong to give more than needed for that. Thus he provides for the sustenance of life, but not for life's *being* or its *growth*.

Third level man, egoistic man, also contributes to the continuance of, rather than the emergence from, this state of existence. In his exploitative way, he wrings from their slum existence all that he can in the way of exorbitant rents, rigged food prices, poor food, etc. He steals from these people any chance which they might have, within existing institutional ways, to extricate themselves from this dungeon of life. But it is not the obsequious condescension of fourth level man or the exploitative rapaciousness of egoistic man that is most to blame for the continuance of this inhumanly condition. The arch criminal is fifth level man.

From his lofty position of relative worldly success and occupational superiority, he looks down in sneering condemnation on man at the first level. "If he had any gumption, he'd take himself in hand and get out of his conditions," says materialistic man in haughty condescension. "I did it. Look at me. I made it up here on my own. If he had anything on the ball, he would do it too." This belief of fifth level man that he made it on his own is one of the prime reasons why many of our poor are left to wither and die at the first level of existence. That this false belief exists in the mind of independent, materialistic man is a fact; but never was any human more deluded than he who professes this unfounded belief.

Fifth level man did not get there on his own. Only his blindness enables him to think he did. Fifth level man was brought to the materialistic doorstep because the humans who preceded him in man's historical development worked hard to move man through the lower levels of human existence. Humans who lived earlier in man's times solved the problems of the first four levels of human existence long before the night this self-righteous, smugly superior fifth level man was conceived. He did not get to the fifth level on his own. He was born on the threshold of that level and his family reared him in the channel of development which permitted him to emerge in adulthood ready to complete no more than the end of the transition from the fourth level to the fifth by his own efforts. Thus, he who is so scurrilous toward those who cannot do for themselves did not arrive at his high station for the reasons which he believes. He got most of the way there because he did not have to solve the existential problems faced by many people in a poverty stricken state.

As a result of this false belief, fifth level men in their haughtiness and fourth level men in their righteousness have been the main forces blocking the needed revisions in our welfare systems. People operating at these levels are prone to want to throw out most forms of protective maintenance, such as our welfare system. In fact, on a February 26, 1970, television program, Wilbur Mills of the House of Representatives said in essence: 'I believe a guaranteed income is wrong. I must go and pray and see if it should be.'[120] Such attitudes we must circumvent if we are to effectively manage in the AN state of existence so that higher states of being can emerge. We cannot promote emergence from the AN state so long as righteousness and haughtiness are roadblocks in our way.

Some validity is given to what I have been saying by the following letter sent to the editor of the Schenectady (N.Y.) *Gazette* on March 7, 1970[121]:

> I would like to add my vote for the stand taken by Mr.____ regarding the welfare situation. While it is true that we are commanded to be our brother's keeper and that we should not neglect the poor, the Scripture tells us we will

---

[120] Moynihan (1972) p.425: "On February 26 [1970] the committee [House Ways and Means] decided to report a bill and directed the staff to prepare a formal draft. In a news conference Mills said he was "going into retreat" to think through his own position, but added that even if he decided to vote against the measure on the floor, he would not lead a fight against it. On the other hand he would not be floor manager."

[121] *Schenectady Gazette*. Letters to the Editor. March 7, 1970, p. 14. Signed "Name Withheld." Writer unknown.

never be able to eliminate them—the poor ye will always have with you. It is possible to so persecute and tax the middle classes that the whole humanity will be low if a preacher is commissioned to preach, let him to do that very thing with all his heart. If he preached with dedication and conviction and left the social gospel to the do-gooders, he would receive fruits for his efforts and there would be no need of welfare as we see it today.

There should be a definite distinction made between those who can not work and those who will not. The Bible is unmistakenly clear on this point: he who will not work let him not eat. It is getting all out of hand when those who have not and will not contribute to society DEMAND the same benefits as those who have spent 40 years in laboring before they earn retirement.

Obviously those who possess such attitudes are the ones who are maintaining first level man in his arrested state today. And obviously, as now you shall see, this state of mind is contrary to the principles for managing the growth of man out of the AN state of existence.

The Management of the Automatic State

For automatic man, AN man, to emerge he must be managed by the principles of nurturant management, i.e., management concerned only with the maintenance of viability of life, management which seeks to provide unencumbered ministration to the human's imperative, periodic, physiological needs which are the only principles congruent with this state of existence. Failure to nurture will result in death of the managed.

There are virtually no ANs in the American work force. The first level is of less concern to the industrial or business manager in the United States than to officials who are trying to manage the government's attack on poverty. It is the behavior level at which man's energies are consumed in the process of staying alive, in maintaining a balance between catabolic and anabolic processes. Man's behavior at this level reflects only a vague awareness of his existence. He is aware of little more than the problems of sustenance, illness, reproduction, and disputes. As one man described this, he must be seen as akin to the neonate, the newborn baby, which has no resources to come by that which it needs in order to maintain its existence. And like the newborn baby, sustenance must be brought to him in sufficient amounts and in proper form if he is to gain that excess energy in his system necessary for him to take on a higher state of being.

To be specific, let me reiterate the two current practices which are quite at odds with the principles of nurturant management. Any kind of food-providing service which does not bring daily to these people that which they need to eat or to achieve vibrant health, not just existence, is just not going to do the job. Secondly, any kind of medical services which do not bring needed services to the door and into the home of these first-level people will be insufficient. And, thirdly let us look at our slum clearance practices.

First level man lives in a psychological world of no time and no space. He lives in a world where he behaves as an imprinted organism. Put a week's supply of food before him, at the beginning of a week, and he will just eat his way through it until none is left for later days in the week. Asking him to go to 'City General Hospital over on Thataway and Faroff Avenue,' when he has no comprehension of space, is ridiculous. Ask him to allow his home to be torn down and to move to some new area while his old area is to be rehabilitated is to threaten him beyond belief.

We must consider in addition to that above that even the New Jersey plan, the supplemental income plan, which guarantees a family a certain income if the paycheck does not reach that level, a plan which is a tremendous step forward in welfare planning, [122] is far too sophisticated for application to first level man. We must devise means which will utilize our usable young people in an all-out attack upon a problem of these dimensions. But even should we come to direct ourselves toward the use of nurturant managerial principles for first level man, we will only have stopped compounding the problem; we will not have righted it because, unfortunately, unless there is some remarkable biosocial breakthrough, we are faced with residual AN problems for a long time to come. This we now know because biological evidence tells us that when nutrition has not been good through pregnancy and the first six to eight months of life, cells just don't divide as they might. There just is not as much higher-level potential in those who have been nutritionally deprived as in those for whom life has been better. Thus, we must begin to think of both long-term, and shorter-term approaches to the problem of the AN existential state.

---

[122] See Theobald (1963), Moynihan (1973) and Pechman and Timpane (1975).

Transition

Fortunately for most humans who are living in this state today, the short-term attack can enable then to emerge out of the AN state. So we should concentrate our efforts in these directions to get the process of emergence underway. Then we can turn to their higher level human problems which come to be, problems which will become apparent to us as we proceed on through the levels of human existence.

No man will ever be without some reactive values[123] because he is always a physiological organism. When first-level man experiences change in the conditions of his existence, this challenge to his automatic state of being may change his focus on life and a new form of existence may develop. We say 'may' because the potential for change must be present in order for it to occur. Depending on the current conditions of his existence, reactive values may dominate his existence or they may be subordinated within emerging higher-level value systems. So long as the human lives in a completely provident, relatively unthreatened in respect to the satisfaction of the basic needs kind of world, the human has no reason to enlarge his or her conceptual space and move beyond this level of being.

As soon as man solves the problem of physiological existence, as soon as he can satisfy his imperative needs with a minimum of energy expenditure, he switches, if challenged, to solving the problem of survival in the broader sense of the word. He switches from basic manipulation of his world so as to provide protection from physical, animal, and human violence. If such happens, a new system begins to arise as man strives to reassure his state of physiological existence. He moves to the level of animistic living, the second subsistence level of behavior.[124] Man's quest is no longer for simple physiological existence.

He seeks now a primordial form of existence which he can control, not just one of automatic reactivity. He proceeds into a limited sensory-motor exploration of his world. From this exploration he finds himself rewarded or punished *a la* the principles of operant or instrumental conditioning. The effects of this operant conditioning are interpreted by a weak and undifferentiated cognitive component in an ego-centric way.

---

[123] Much of Dr. Graves's early approach was values-based. Thus, the terms "values" and "value systems" were used to describe what later became a level of psychological existence. This language was commonplace among many who tried to apply the Gravesian point of view. Conflation of the terms reulted in significant confusion of concepts and ideas.

[124] "Behavior" is another word extensively used by Graves in his writings and often used interchangeably with value system.

This weak cognitive component now perceives self as alive and as possessed of feeling – a state which is projected onto the conditioning objects in the external world. And, since man at this level feels pleasure or pain from his manipulation, he projects that the objects in the world also feel pleasure or pain from these same manipulations. To him objects feel, think, and act just as he feels, think, and acts. On this perception man structures his second form of existence and out of this structuring develops his second level value system. The *adjustment of the organism to the environment* component swings to ascendancy.

As soon as man, in his food-gathering wanderings, accrues a set of Pavlovian conditioned reflexes which provide for the satisfaction of his imperative needs, and as soon as he, in his wanderings, comes upon his "Garden of Eden," that place in space which is appropriate for *his* acquired Pavlovian behavior, he slides almost imperceptibly out of this stage into the second existential state, an established form of human existence, the *tribalistic way of life*.

And what I am saying to you is this: When you are working with the AN system, what you are attempting to do is not to get production or learning or anything like that out of the individual. That is not what the transition from the AN to BO is. The transition from AN to BO is the transition from the ragged edge of 'alive' into viable physiological life.

Chapter 8

The Animistic Existence — The BO State

The 2nd Subsistence Level

The BO – Animistic or Tribalistic Existential State

Theme: *Sacrifice self to the way of your elders*

Alternative Themes: *'Sacrifice one's desires to the way of one's elders'* and *'sacrifice self to the traditions of one's elders, one's ancestors'*[125]

---

[125] At the time of most of his writings, Dr. Graves had only theoretical contact with mature adult humans at the second level. Like AN, his descriptions of this state were derived primarily from library research. There were no BO conceptions represented in his data. Later in life he had experiences that put him more closely in touch with this level and validated what he had concluded earlier.

If the person by the very act of living successfully the first-level way, then by creating these new problems of existence by the first-level living, is to stay alive as a human being, there must be activated the second-level system; and so you have the second milestone on the map of human existence: the movement of the individual to the second level.

This is variously called the BO State, the Tribalistic State, the Animistic State, Second Level, and the Second Subsistence Level where we use different terminology for different purposes. This state first appeared approximately 40,000 years ago when cataclysmic climatic conditions changed markedly the source of food, water, shelter, etc., for humans. If one had the means with which to count, this would probably be the dominant system on the surface of the globe today.

Now the second level of human existence is quite a different kind of being. The human's brain is beginning to awaken and, as it awakens, many stimuli impinge on his consciousness but are not comprehended. The second level of human existence or the BO level—the animistic existential state - is a state produced when the B problems, that is safety and security and assurance problems, activate the second or the O neurological system that is specifically attuned to picking up, transmitting, and dealing with conditions which threaten one's existence - satisfaction of the non-imperative, aperiodic, physiological needs such as needs to avoid pain, cold, heat, etc., and escape harm from various dangers. The individual at this stage has progressed beyond a bare physiological existence.

This person, unlike the person at first level who lives very automatic form of existence and who has a very limited inner life, has a very full inner life, one which is full of indwelling spirits. The person at this level thinks animistically. Here he lives in a primeval world of no separation between subject and object, a world where phenomena possess no clear contours and things have no particular identity. He thinks in terms of an indwelling spirit of life in all things, animate or inanimate. Thus, the adult at this level is full of magical beliefs and superstition. Here one form of being can be transmuted into another for there is correspondence between all things. He thinks of the transmutation of self to other animals to other objects and the transmutation of other animals and objects to self and in terms of the continuing existence of disembodied spirits capable of exercising benignant or malignant influence. Yet he doesn't see self as one with all other human beings. He thinks in terms of there being a transmutable spirit in self, in others' selves, in animals, floods, stones, earthquakes, etc., and uses such to invoke continuance of what is, to ward-off harm, bring about favor, or control the unexpected. So the tree is alive and the tree has a spirit, and panther has a spirit and all the other animals have a spirit. "The stone did it to me." "The earthquake hurt me." "Why, mama, did that stick whack me?" They think that there are answers to those things. They think spatially in an atomistic, not wholistic, manner; thus, a name for each bend in a river, but none for the river.

The BO thinks ritualistically, superstitiously, and stereotypically. He lives by the prescriptions of totems and taboos, thus tries to manage life by incantation, using such to invoke continuance of what is or to control the unexpected. He strongly defends a life he does not understand. He believes that his tribal ways are inherent in the nature of things, thus is unchanging and unalterable, fixated and tenacious as he resolutely holds to and perpetuates things "as they are." At this level, man seeks social (tribal) stability. He also explains existence in a dichotomous way—good-bad—with only a dim awareness of a self merged with others. The individual is subsumed in "tribe."

They never question their way of existence: "This is the way one lives—that's all there is to it. You never raise any questions about it. You just live this way, the way the tribal elders have taught you to live; never in any way whatsoever do you change it." They have a 'Great Spirit' poorly defined concept as to why things are the way they are. They have a moderately increased degree of awareness in comparison to people at the first level of existence, and so they are aware that things do happen to them that help them or hurt them, that harm them or do not harm them, and so they try to propitiate the spirits in various rituals which they develop to continue to do the things that do them good and to get the spirits to bring a halt to the things that do them harm. They tend to fixate and hold tremendously to a totem and taboo way of life and work forever as if they were entirely restricted in their degrees of freedom by the particular taboos that are present in the world of which they are a part.

At the second subsistence level, man's need is for stability. He seeks to continue a way of life that he does not understand but strongly defends. This level of man has just struggled forth from striving to exist and now has his first established way of life. This way of life is essentially without 'awareness,' thought, or purpose, for it is based on Pavlovian classical conditioning principles by association without conscious awareness or intent. This learning without awareness, elder-dominated by the controller of lore and magic, produces the fixated, tenaciously-held-to, totem-and-taboo, tribalistic way of life.

So pervasive is the power of second-level values that they take on a magical character and force the person to observe them through ritualistic behavior. They tie the person to their meaning for him and result in over-reactional emotional response when questioned or threatened. As a result he holds tenaciously to unchanging and unalterable beliefs and ways, and strives desperately to propitiate the world for its continuance. Therefore, BO man believes his tribalistic way is inherent in the nature of things. The task of existence is simply to continue what it seems has enabled "my tribe to be."

At this level a seasonal or naturally based concept of time comes to be, and space is perceived in an atomistic fashion. Causality is not yet perceived because he perceives the forces at work to be inherent, thus linking consciousness at the deepest level. Second level man values that which experience or social transmission says will bring him the good will of his spirit world - traditionalistic values. He shuns that which will raise his spirits' ire. Here a form of existence based on myth and tradition comes to be, and being is a mystical phenomenon full of spirits, magic and superstition.

This person, having now experienced in his or her existence both the good and the bad of life - the good which enabled him or her to solve the problems of the first level of existence, and the bad having produced the problems of the second level which he was not ready to cope with, develops beliefs that things are either benignant or malignant, that they are for-you or against-you. He becomes very highly superstitious and believes that the whole world is filled with good and bad spirits which must be appealed to or avoided in order to stay alive, using such to invoke continuance of what is or to control the unexpected.

These people develop a way of living motivated on safety and security needs. They develop a way of living which is based upon supplication to the good spirits and forgiveness from the bad spirits. It's just one great big magical superstitious world in which they live. Now, they are quite different from the people at the first level. In fact they do have the beginning of what one might call religious beliefs; and they also have the beginning of very ritualistic ways of life. You do not have organized religions or religious groups, per se, at this particular level, as we think of an organized religion with set of dogma, or something of that nature. But, certainly, you find a great deal of this kind of thinking incorporated into the versions of Catholic religion in Texas, for example.

You see, when people at the first level get hungry, they just wander out and eat and they drink and they never have to have any set ways of doing it, because you walk out on this bush over here and eat, and go down to this stream here and drink, and crawl in that cave over there; so you don't have to have any set ways of life. But people at the second level have experienced loss and deprivation, and they know if they are to stay alive, to stay safe, and to stay secure, they've got to have some way of doing this, so they develop ritualistic ways full of totems and taboos which is their way to control by incantation and of assuring themselves that they are going to continue to have that which is necessary to take care of their basic needs.

If the person in this world lives the tribalistic way and is successful in this way of living as have been so many people in Africa (even up to recent times before the European man went there and started really disturbing things), they just go on living in that way. Many people on the surface of the globe today in the Amazon, on Luzon, and the like go on living in this way because they don't have to live any other way to stay alive. I found them in the tobacco hills of Virginia, in the coal-mine country of West Virginia, in the Arkansas hills, up in Northern Maine, with some of the French Canadians back in there. And I found them in Indian tribes in America and Canada.

The prime end value at the second level is safety and the prime means value is tradition. They are valued because here man's elders and their ancestors, though they cannot explain why, seem to have learned which factors foster man's existence and which factors threaten his well being. Thus, man's *thema* for existence at this level is "one shall live according to the ways of one's elders," and his values are consonant with this existential *thema*. But the schematic forms and values for existence at the second level are highly varied due to different Pavlovian conditionings from tribe to tribe, group to group. Each traditional set of phenomenistic values are tribally centered, concrete, syncretic, labile, diffuse, and rigid. The tribal member is locked into them and cannot violate them. At this level a value-attitude may contain several meanings because of the conditioning principles of generalization and differentiation. To the more highly developed man, the values may appear quite illogical. Here circumstances force the individual into a magical, superstitious, ritualistic way of life wherein he values positively that which will bring forth his spirit's favor. He shuns that which tradition says will raise his spirit's ire.

These people learn not by the process of habituation but predominant learning is by classical Pavlovian conditioning, Pavlovian reflexes - learning by association in time or place without conscious awareness or intent - a temporal overlap between innate reflexive states and the appearance of a concurrent stimulus condition. The simple straight-forward association between this and that causes them to learn what is going on, and so their learning takes place without knowledge in themselves, without awareness, and so they believe that whatever they experience is it, and that is all there is to it; nothing is learned by thought or logic.

At this second level, the neurological system is activated by changes, particularly sudden changes, in the mode or intensity of the stimuli associated with one of man's innate reflexive networks. This system, as the first, is not open to verbal assessment. Pavlov, Hudgins,[126] Menzies,[127] Doty,[128] Gerato,[129] – have demonstrated that there is a system in the brain where learning takes place without consciousness, intelligence or motivation. This is the BO system where conditioning follows the stimulation of certain sensory neurons in the brain. When followed by a specific motor or glandular response, when repeated sufficiently, the sensory pattern drives the motor-glandular response. Learning in this system is a consequence of many repeated stimulus-response experiences; no reward, no punishment, no intention, no consciousness, no intelligence, no motivation, is required on the part of the subject to affect behavioral change in the O system. Generally speaking, what I have found if you look at it culturally is that your hunting and gathering societies are societies in which the larger majority would evidence themselves to be operating in the BO state of existence and there would be a few, a minority, who would be beginning to see the life in the CP form.

Management of the state

The person centralized at BO is manageable within limits, but the limits are strict. A manager can get productive effort from the second level person only when the work is not negated by his superstitions or taboos; since his world is so replete with them, work effort is often spotty and sporadic. The model is the "friendly parent" who works alongside, shelters the person, makes the work fun and pleasant, and,

---

[126] Hudgins – not yet identified or sourced.
[127] Menzies, R. (1937). Conditioned vasomotor responses in human subjects. *Journal of Psychology*. 4, 75-120.
[128] Doty, R.W. (likely, but not confirmed as correct reference).
[129] Gerato – not yet identified or sourced.

above all, respects and observes the taboos. The manager must accept the individual's style of life and accommodate to it. He must adopt the person's way of thinking and acting. Then, after being accepted, the manager can get work done by presenting a model of what is desired which the person can then imitate. Extreme force is necessary to get a person to operate contrary to traditional ways, and even then it most often fails. Subordinates at the BO level must be isolated from anyone in the work group who will not accept the individual's way of life, who scoffs at the taboos, and who wants to be competitive.

But even if these approaches are followed, productive effort is very limited. Here, again, are employees who do not meet the needs of the typical U.S. enterprise - not unless the manager has a long-time, slow-to-accomplish goal in mind. Productive effort is limited in terms of typical industrial thinking because, in the relatively unawakened mind of the second level person, the concepts of time, space, quantity, materiality, and the like are woefully wanting. The close and immediate supervision required, the limited time span of work that can be expected, and other necessary accommodations do not provide a formula for productive effort. The portion of employees at this level in the American work force is less than a few percent. They find the job experience tremendously frightening in most situations and actively avoid it if at all possible. However, when properly managed, employees at this level will work hard and long. Understanding this level is important to organizations such as the Peace Corps.

Mismanagement at this level causes the subordinates to flee from the manager and organization. No attempts at disruption or sabotage will be made on the mismanaged persons' part. However, if the manager or organization attempts to coerce the second level person to a desired work behavior, the pressured individual is likely to "exorcise" the evil now so readily apparent.

We come now to a very important point. To a degree, managers can "negatively motivate" second level people by using (or threatening to use) sheer naked force; force will work so long as it does not come into conflict with strong second level taboos. However, *it will not work with first-level people.* They do not have enough energy to care about threats. Here is our first example of the necessity to use different forms of management with people who are at different levels of existence.

At this level man's welfare need is for protection from the evil spirits that can be accomplished only by accommodating to the way of life laid down by the elders of the tribe-like group. It is the tribal group's welfare that is important, and the individual does not count. Here the welfare worker must be as one of the group knowing all of its peculiarities and here he must work within, not against, the group's belief in malevolent magic.

The traditionalistic, tribal ways continue forever except as force now and then breaks and replaces old ways. The prime end value at this level is safety and the prime means is tradition. Man at this level becomes social, in the sense of being dominated by the traditions of his tribe. Things are valued because man's elders and ancestors seem to have learned what fosters man's existence and what threatens his well-being. Thus, the theme for existence at this level is "one shall live according to the ways of one's elders." The individual follows a magical, superstitious, ritualistic way of life.

Though these values seem mysterious, peculiar, odd, and unexplainable to some higher-level men, they do order man's BO state of existence. Eventually, however, the time comes when these values fail energetic youth who have not experienced the problems of their elders, or when other ways of life challenge the values of the tribe. Thus, boredom or challenge may lead man to attack the values of his first "establishment" and thus lead him on to the next level of existence. Living the tribalistic way where you are hemmed in by totems and taboos which, for example, say that even if you are starving to death you dare not eat this or dare not drink that because if you do, you are going to die, get themselves into very serious difficulty and create this third set of problems for a human being in his existence.

More by chance than by design, some men achieve relative control of their spirit world through their non-explainable, elder-administered, tradition-based way of life - a way of life which continues relatively unchanged until disturbed from within or without. When the established tribal way of life assures the continuance of the tribe with minimal energy expenditure by solving problems N by neurological means A, it creates the first of the general conditions necessary for movement to a new and different steady state of being. *It produces excess energy in the system which puts the system in a state of readiness for change.* But unless another factor such as *dissonance* or challenge comes into the field, the change does not move in the direction of some other state of being. Instead, it moves toward maximum entropy and its demise since it becomes overloaded with its accretion of more and more tradition, more and more ritual. If, however, when the state of readiness is achieved dissonance enters, then this steady state of being is precipitated toward a different kind of change. This dissonance arises usually in youth or certain minds not troubled by the memories of the past and who are capable of newer and more lasting insights into the nature of man's being. Or it can come to the same capable minds when outsiders disturb the tribe's way of life.

When such dissonance occurs it does not immediately produce a movement to a higher state of being. Instead, it tends to produce a regressive search through older ways before new insights come to be. This is a crisis phase for any established way of existence and is always the premonitor of a new state, provided three other conditions come to exist. The first of these three conditions is *insight*. The capable minds in any system must be able to produce new insights or be able to perceive the significance of different insights brought to the system's attention from outside sources. But insight alone does not make for change since, "full many a flower is born to blush unseen and waste its freshness on the desert air."[130] So there must also be a *removal of barriers* to the implementation of the insight - a matter not easy to achieve for, as can be seen, a period of confrontation arises. Then, if the insight can be effectuated through the removal of the barriers, *the consolidating factors* come into play enabling the new steady-state of being to be born.

When, at the BO level, readiness for change occurs, it triggers man's insight into his existence as an individual being - as a being separate and distinct from other beings - and from his tribal compatriots, as well. As he struggles, now *intentionally* since the operant or instrumental conditioning systems are opening, his need for survival comes to the fore.

With this change in consciousness man becomes aware that he is aligned against predatory animals, a threatening physical universe, other men who are predatory men, and even the spirits in his physical world - those who fight back for their established way of existence, or against him for the new way of existence he is striving to develop. Now he is not one-with-all, for he is alone, alone struggling for his survival against the "dragonic" forces of the universe. So he sets out in heroic fashion through his newly emergent operant conditioning learning system to build *a way of being which will foster his individual survival.*

Second-level values bring some order, albeit peculiar, to man in this undifferentiated cognitive state. They provide positive and negative landmarks for survival when he lives a regionalized, isolated, relatively undisturbed existence. But again nature provides no assurances, and man's developing cognitive component provides him no peace. As these values break down, man becomes a savage in the truest sense of the word. He attacks this world and all its beings as he demands that they be ordered to his personal needs. The wanton destruction in the awakening

---

[130] Gray, Thomas (1751). "Elegy Written in a Country Churchyard."

Congo[131] and the fire scarred ruins of American cities (1960s) demonstrate well this type of "breakdown of values." We have seen it also in "The Blackboard Jungle."[132] But savagery it is not; it is the plea of a desperate man – a man despairing the inadequacy of second level values. Man ceases to value that which has not provided, and his cognitive component perceives that there must be something more to life than to value that which provides only a miserable existence.

Now he is not one-with-all, for he is alone in his struggle for his survival against the "dragonic" forces of the universe. As this quest begins and takes hold, this searching man is accused of a breakdown in his moral and ethical ways. So he sets out in heroic fashion through his newly emergent operant conditioning learning system to build *a way of being which will foster his individual survival* - the CP existential state.

---

[131] See: Legum, Colin (1961). *Congo Disaster*. Baltimore: Penguin.
[132] Hunter, Evan (1954). *The Blackboard Jungle*. Simon & Schuster; see also: Richard Brook's 1955 film adaptation with Glenn Ford and Sidney Poitier.

Chapter 9

The Egocentric Existence – The CP State

The 3rd Subsistence Level

Theme: *Express self, to hell with the consequences, lest one suffer the torment of unbearable shame.*

Alternative Themes: *'Express self but to hell with others lest one suffer the torment of unbearable shame'*

Derived from the *'Express self, to hell with others'* Conceptions

> "Thou shalt express self at all cost rather than suffer the unbearable shame of loss of face. Thou shalt express self at all cost in order to be praised as one who will live unashamed forever in the mouths of men."

The egocentric existential state arises when the achievement of relative safety and security produces "P" problems of existence, the problems of boredom in a being as intelligent as the human, boredom from living an unchanging elder-dominated, 'shaman-controlled' way of life. The accumulating problems from living in this way produce expressive and survival problems for those whose capacities enable them to perceive the threats to the existence of their new-found selves if the old ways don't change. These problems activate the P system, that psychoneurological system which possesses the tissue specifically tuned to sense consciousness, and consciousness of self, and has the capacity to experience the feeling of shame. These survival problems activate awareness of self as a possibly powerful being separate and distinct from others; therefore, man no longer seeks merely for tensional relief or the continuance of his tribe's established way of life. He now feels the need to foster his own individual survival – a need which cannot dominate him until he becomes conscious of himself (as happens at this level). He now seeks a form of existence which he can control for his personal survival. He proceeds to explore his world and begins to manipulate it intentionally rather than merely passively accept it. This activates the risk-taking, chronological time and space perceiving equipment of the human. They experience the awakening of "selfism."

With this change in consciousness, man becomes aware that he is aligned against other men who are predatory men, those who fight for their established way of existence, or against him for the new way of existence he is striving to develop, against predatory animals and a threatening physical universe. In the CP state man must solve the problem of survival as an individual. So, he sets out in heroic fashion, through his newly emergent operant conditioning learning system, to build a way of being that will foster his survival and to hell with the other man.

They show a dominant-submissive type of psychology. They show stubborn resistiveness to power exercised by others, but obeisance to others when overpowered, when they are afraid, or until power over self is lost. The person on top of the hierarchy runs the show and the next person down bows to the top while the third person down bows to that one and right on down the line. The third person shows the tendency to try to make the fourth submit. The third always submits to the second. Thus, they think in terms of haves and have-nots.

Both the authoritarian and the submissive develop standards which they feel will insure them against threat, but these are very raw standards. The submissive person chooses to get away with what he can within the life style which is possible for him. The authoritarian chooses to do as he pleases. He spawns, as his *raison d'être,* the rights of assertive individualism. These rights become, in time, the absolute rights of kings, the unassailable prerogatives of management, the inalienable rights of those who have achieved positions of power, and even the rights of the lowly hustler to all he can hustle.

This is a world of the aggressive expression of man's lusts - openly and unabashedly by the "haves," more covertly and deviously by the "have-nots." But when this system solidifies into a stable feudal way of life, it creates a new existential problem for both the "have" and the "have-not." Each must face that his conniving is not enough, for death is there before the "have," and the "have-not" must explain to himself why it is that he must live his miserable existence. (As we shall see, out of this mix eventually develops man's fourth way of existence, the DQ way of life.)

Thinking at this level is totally self-centered, that is, egocentric in fashion. It is in terms of controlling or being controlled, in terms of intentions to assure that self will receive or be deprived, and to insure that self will always receive. Raw, rugged, self-assertive individualism comes to the fore. This is the level where "might makes right" thinking prevails. Every act they perform has as its intention 'taking care of me' with intentions to assure that self will receive, and to ensure that self will always continue to receive.

The individual thinks in terms of struggling to gain one's own satisfaction – 'to hell with others.' If you are aware that you live, and you believe in your own separate existence, and that the world is out to get you, then the only logical way for you to behave is in terms of snaring, entrapping and acting to avoid being caught while taking advantage of others. Because they see life in a very person affective way, inwardly they are a cauldron of strong negative emotional feelings such as shame, rage, hate, disgust, and grief. One of the most interesting aspects of human existence which stands out at this third level is that there is no guilt. The person operating at the third level of human existence, or any level below that, cannot feel guilt. He has no capacity to feel it. Whatever guilt is as a feeling in a human being, it has not yet been activated. So, the human being at the third level can do anything, no matter what it is, no matter how horrendous, how ornery, how onerous, and still feel that he is doing right. You have to arrive at the fourth level of human existence for the capacity to feel guilt to develop. At the third level, they don't give a damn about anyone else. They live by the credo: 'to hell with others; it is I who is important.' Really, when you look at it, these are not terribly pleasant human beings; but it is a very necessary stage of survival.

Coexistent in this person is the tendency to revel in hedonistic, pleasure-seeking pursuits to an orgiastic degree. They show strong emotional reactivity to the actions of others who are pleasing or not pleasing to their selfish desires with a generalized 'you are with me or against me' emotional response to others. They just smother you when you do something that pleases their selfish desires, and in the next moment they'll turn on you and pulverize you when you do something which does not satisfy them.

The person in the egocentric existential state lives a peculiar two-fold aim in life: to win or, at least, go down in the glory of having tried and live forever in the mouths and legends of others. As they put it over and over again, "I may die but by god they'll remember me. I will go down in the mouths of men as having been somebody." Thereby, they express such with no consideration of others. This spawns an exploitative form of management since there are no true two-way interpersonal relations.

Examples of the Egocentric Existential State

These are examples of people who are, in my way of thinking, operating at the third level:

Conception #1 –

> "Life is a jungle - one god-damned great big jungle. It is survival of the fittest and that is all. Anybody who does not recognize this is not or will never be a grown up person. Life is competition, it is fight and struggle and get and take and hang on. Some they have got it to fight there way through it and some they just don't have it. The grownup he survives, or go down big in trying he's got it. He is the guy who fights to get what he needs and he keeps after it till he gets it. If he wants some chick he don't take no. He wears her down. One thing about him is he don't chicken, he don't let fear stand in his way.
>
> If it has got to be done he does it he don't stay to think, he just does it. It don't matter who gets hurt thou it best it ain't him. There ain't no reason for him to feel guilty cause a man's got to live ain't he. This ain't no picnic world in which he live. It better he do what have to be done cause he can't hold his head up if he ain't a man. That's the way life is any grown guy know it. He

know its him or me and it sure ain't going to be me if he's healthy. He gets what he can from this world and no one pushes him around, even if the dice is loaded its up to him to make them shake his way. If he don't what kind of man is he. Now don't you set me down Doc for saying this. You said to put down what we believed. I believe this and don't you ever forget it."

Conception #2 -

"Psychologically mature human behavior is that mental behavior that enables a human being not only to survive but also to succeed and win over his environment. The psychologically mature person is the one that fate has endowed with the natural human qualities to rise above the conditions of his being and to impose control over it and modify it as he sees fit regardless of what others think. Being an animal, the human being possesses certain natural qualities normal for his species. He is temperamental and impulsive, and thus given to violence, passion, stubbornness and irrational actions. He desires to mate but not just to produce children. He fights life as it is and he works most to survive.

He senses that he is alone and endangered and seeing strength in numbers, he seeks to fit others to the needs of himself. The drive for self-preservation is instilled in him and the only way to be what he is, is to be selfish, placing his needs before all others with the "possible" exception of his own family. He must overcome his fears and inhibitions to his won satisfaction.

He must fulfill his primal lusts and desires. A human being free from guilt and frustrations closely approaches the ideal of the mature personality. Unhampered expression of the impulses might lead to his destruction but it is necessary to his health. He must not temper his striving for pleasure. He performs when he is motivated for not to do would leave him less than a man. He is free from the threats and negative reactions of others and does not fear for his own psyche. In other words, he is confident of being a law unto himself, the source and inspiration of all of his actions and of good for others."

People who begin to think in the CP fashion are ones who are, for the first time in existence, becoming consciously aware of the fact that they are alive as human beings.

> "Now aware of the need to foster his individual survival, there comes to stage center, in his existence, *his* need for survival - a need which cannot dominate man until consciousness of self emerges as it does at this level. Concomitant with the emergence of self-awareness and its bedfellow, the need for survival, is the emergence of the intentional, the operant, the instrumental learning system. Also, man begins to adjust the environment to his needs and seeks a primordial form of existence which he can control for his personal survival, not just one of automatic reactivity."[133]

They know they *live*. Conscious awareness is a characteristic which comes into being in the third system of human development. It is not there prior to that period of time.

Origin of the Egocentric State

The egocentric existential state emerges from living in the tribalistic way where you are hemmed in by totems and taboos. They get themselves in a very serious difficulty and create this third set of problems for a human being and his existence. At this level the energy previously devoted to finding ways to satisfy man's physiological needs and to the maintenance of tribal ways, now released, awakens him to the recognition that he is a separate and distinct being. As a result, man's quest is no longer for tensional relief or the continuance of his tribe's established way of life. Although I have no explanation of why the human being is structured as he or she is, the data says that at the third level - whatever tissue it is in the brain of a person - which enables him to be aware of the existence of self is activated. So, at the third level the individual has developing in his- or herself his first real comprehension of the fact that he or she lives as a person, that "I am a self. I am something that is separate and distinct from the other things that there are in this world of ours." This person having just developed - or just developing - this full awareness of his existence, develops a new way of

---

[133] Graves, Clare W. (1970). Levels of Existence: An Open System Theory of Values. *Journal of Humanistic Psychology*, Fall 1970, Vol. 10, No. 2, p. 131-155.

life which we call the Egocentric Way of Living which is centered upon the power of self.

This Promethean, CP way of life, within the Levels of Existence point of view, is based on the prerogatives of the haves and the duties of the have-nots. Ultimately when this way of life, based historically on the agricultural revolution, is established, life is seen as a continuous process with survival dependent on a controlled relationship. Fealty and loyalty, service and *noblesse oblige* become cornerstones of this way of life. Assured of their survival, through fief and vassalage, the "haves" set forth on their power with life based on the right way to behavior as their might dictates it - as dictated by those who are in power. Ultimately, a system develops in which each acts out in detail, in the interests of his own survival, how life is to be lived; but hardly more than ten percent ever achieve any modicum of power. The remainder are left to submit.

History suggests to us that the few, and there were few in the beginning, who were able to gain their freedom from survival problems not only surged almost uncontrollably forward into a new way of being but also dragged after them, to the survival level, tribal members unable to free themselves of the burden of stagnating tribalistic existence. And history suggests that the few became the authoritarians while the many became those who submitted. The many accept the "might-is-right" of the few because by such acceptance they are assured survival. This was so in the past and it is still so today.

Additionally, each successive neurological system in the brain is activated by a specific set of chemicals, some of which we have fairly good knowledge of at this stage of development, and some of which we do not. This is akin to the atomic table of elements of chemistry wherein scientists laid out a picture of all of the elements that might exist in this world of ours, and said some had been discovered and some had not.

Once reaching the egocentric existential state, the individual has a new physiology. This is a new psychological being, a different psychological being endocrinologically. One of the major differences between the CP and the DQ systems is the ratio between noradrenaline and adrenaline in the individual.[134] We have pretty good evidence at this stage of the game that something in the noradrenaline chemical family is the neurological activating force at the third level. Something in the adrenaline family is the activating factor at the fourth neurological system. We can change a person temporarily from behaving in the third

---

[134] Lee, William R., Cowan, Christopher C., & Todorovic, Natasha, (Eds.) (2003). *Graves: Levels of Human Existence*. Transcribed lecture by Dr. Graves at the Washington School of Psychiatry. Santa Barbara: ECLET Publishing.

level fashion to begin to show behavior of the fourth level of behavior by simply changing the amount of noradrenaline and adrenaline in the system of the person. Right as I inject the adrenaline into the person in order to increase the ratio of adrenaline to noradrenaline, I will get the concomitant neurological activation and the concomitant change in behavior.

Although we immediately think of purposefully influencing this ratio, and although we can change a person temporarily, we cannot hold a person there. As with any developmental process, you don't produce it permanently by this method. These experiments are doomed to fail; that's not the way development takes place. So, you might temporarily get a higher level manifestation, but manufactured attempts will not hold permanently.

The First Truly Expressive System

Now, this is the first of the truly expressive systems and it is very different from that sacrificial type second system that we talked about in the previous chapter - the power of self to do this or to do that. It's the person who believes that being different from other animals, from inanimate things - that there is something very special about the self, and so the person develops this very egoistic way of believing and values anything that contributes to the self, and disparages anything that doesn't contribute to the self. If you look at the person at the third level in terms of his or her typical behavior, the person behaves in a manner to ensure that the self is not going to be controlled in terms of: struggling to gain freedom from others; to gain one's own power; one's own satisfaction; and, therefore, he or she ensnares, entraps, outwits, lives by outwitting others, by avoiding being caught at the time that he or she is very openly taking advantage of others. He behaves in terms of stubborn resistiveness to the idea of anything stronger than the self, anything better than the self, but shows obeisance when overpowered.

What is the psychology of this level? Well, it is a person who is given to impulsive, uncensored expression of his impulse life. You are dealing with a person who has a very marked tendency to frequent manifestations of uncontrolled hostility. This is a person that is full of the tendency to show concrete assertive negativism – "I'll do what I want to. To hell with you. If you want to stop me, stop me, buddy!" You are dealing with a person who is, at the least, passively resistant to what you are trying to do, so you've got to push him on all the while. 'Tie him down' psychologically because he has a very strong tendency to believe that any suggestion you are going to make to him is an attempt to subjugate him, so you just tie him in here and say: "Now look, yes, I am going to subjugate you, that's just what I am trying to do." You are trying to get this person to get control over his impulses. That is to become subjugated. If you don't lay down the rules, say what is going to happen, and see to it that it does happen, you are just never going to get this impulsiveness in this individual controlled.

You are dealing with a person who lives right here, and right now, and seeks immediate gratification, a person who is always saying: "What's in it for me?" If the person seeks immediate gratification, and if the person, in seeking that immediate gratification, does what you want the person to do, you've got to have somebody there to gratify them immediately - something there that is in it for him. This is why it is so important to get as close as you can in training to an individual relationship.

He thinks in terms of self-centeredness, in terms of controlling or being controlled, in terms of struggling to gain one's own satisfaction – to hell with others. This thinking is raw, impulsive, amoral, and uninhibited in character. There is no feeling of guilt; but there is a strong element of shame. There is a driving concept of heroism in this system. If the dragon is there, one must join battle with it even if one dies in the struggle, for less would make one less than a person.

This person believes humans exist in three classes: (a) the strong, far-seeing, anointed ones; (b) the desirous, motivated, but not far-seeing ones; and (c) the inherently weak and lazy masses who need and prefer directions. This system takes its form because of the normal distribution of risk-taking potential and the normal distribution of operant, intentional learning capacity - the dominant learning mode of the "P" neurological system. Through the exercise of strong risk-taking tendencies and superior capacity to learn by operant, instrumental or intentional learning, some are exceedingly successful, some moderately so, and many hardly at all.

The CP conditions for existence produce a fearful, insecure world for all. The power ethic prevails. There is open and unabashed aggressive expression of individual lusts by the 'haves,' more covertly and deviously by the 'have-nots.' It is a world driven by man's lusts and is seemingly noteworthy for its lack of a "moral sense." But this is an error, for at this level, where man is led to value the ruthless use of power, unconscionably daring deeds, impulsive action, volatile emotion, and the greatest of risk, morality is ruthlessness. It is the inhumane eye for an eye, tooth for a tooth variety, since he values conquest in any form and even war as the epitome of the heroic effort, as the entrance to immaterial Valhalla.

Driven by the need to maintain his existence, CP man manipulates his world and egocentrically interprets the reward or punishment feedback as good or bad for himself, which is his major consideration. He perceives that many people try but few succeed and, as a result, he comes to believe that the heroic (e.g., Homeric) deed is the means to his survival. He values heroism as the means, and the epic hero becomes his most revered figure. To the hero or victor belong the spoils and the right to exercise greed, avarice, envy, gluttony, pride (and sloth if not being heroic), for he has shown through his deeds that the gods or the fates see him as worthy of survival. Might is right. He who wins has a right to loot the world to his own ends and those who lose have a right only to the scraps that a hero may toss their way.

> The power ethic reveres he who can tell time what he wills and mean it, he who shows no fear of the world's wrath and assurance of its favor. Right is demonstrated in violent action - an aspect of this ethic which many see today, but few understand. In the power ethic, the more daring and horrendous the act of man, the more it is revered. It does not matter, within the power ethic, whether a man has plans for replacement of the system which he attacks. The heroic thing is to attack the system and if there is nothing present to be attacked then, if he is truly a hero, he will create a dragon to be destroyed, for even if he should die in the course of his attack, he is assured that he will live - live on forever in the words of men.[135]

This is not an attractive value system from other frames of reference, but for all its negative aspects, it is a giant step forward for man. Some men, in their pursuit of power, *do* tame the mighty river, *do* provide the leisure for beginning intellectual effort, *do* build cities, *do* assign occupational positions that directly improve the personal lot of some and indirectly spill off to the betterment of the miserable many. They are very necessary people. They are the ones who, because of their awareness of themselves, will do anything that is necessary to alter the world or other people in order to try to stay alive. So, in terms of progress, they were very important to building ancient aqueducts, to building the ancient roads that enabled other humans to travel.

---

[135] Graves, Clare W. (1970). Levels of Existence: An Open System Theory of Values. *Journal of Humanistic Psychology*, Fall 1970, Vol. 10, No. 2, p. 131-155.

Learning in the Egocentric State

If we look at working with this system in an educational capacity we need to understand the qualities of the teacher that must be present to ensure learning takes place. Your teacher must be a person who accentuates the positive, and ignores the negative. This person never punishes. The person stops behavior, but doesn't punish for its happening. If a person makes an error, or if he is in the course of making an error in what he is learning, then this teacher just stops the individual. He doesn't give any punishment if an error is made. He has the patience of Job, and says: "Do it again. Start it again." If the person makes an error, he stops him and says, "Start it again." He just keeps going until he gets the positive response, and then he rewards. And generally, it is better here if you can have some kind of extrinsic reward that you can immediately give upon the achievement of the desired behavior.

You better know B. F. Skinner's operant conditioning to handle this. Remember, Skinnerian principles say that if you really want to teach a person to learn something, reward has got to come immediately after the response, and immediately generally means almost in the thousandths of a second after the response; awfully soon after the response is made, or this guy is not going to learn to do it.

You need a teacher who has, as one of his or her fundamental beliefs, that you must keep a person busy and focused every minute and that idle hands get into trouble. The teacher has to believe that boredom is the human being's worst enemy. You need a teacher who, when the learner tries to gain some end by devious means, by lies, simply says, very quietly, "Who are you kidding? What do you think you are trying to get away with? Now, cut it out. Let's get back to work, no more of that monkey business." And he drops it right there. He never goes into "why did you lie?" Never goes into the reasons for the deviousness. He never starts to preach and never remonstrates. He just signals to the person: "I know you are lying. You are not kidding me. Now cut it out. Let's get back to work."

You need a teacher who is perfectly at peace believing, that if you have to discipline you just do it, and you never get into a discussion as to why you did it. You never get into a discussion as to what led up to the necessity of the discipline. So, you need a teacher, who, if there must be discipline they'll just discipline, and that's it. And, say no more. You need a person who in his own nature is highly structured and requires high structure in everything that he has anything to do with. Every detail is worked out. Every minute is laid out in a lesson plan, and it may be laid out in ten-minute sections or the like. He moves from one ten-minute plan to the next ten-minute plan like clockwork, and keeps going in that particular way.

Not only must the person be highly structured, but he must prescribe in advance the limits within which any kind of behavior is provided. It is, if you are doing the simple task of teaching these people to write, you have this as the sheet of paper and the teacher would say: "I want a margin of an inch and a quarter, inch and a half here. I want so much here. I want you down this far from the top, and up this far from the bottom." By God, if you started elsewhere the teacher would yank it out of your hand. Well, this is what you've got to do. Now, you structure it just like that, and if the kid starts to write outside the margin, you just come up take the paper away and say to him, "start over." He starts another piece of paper and if he doesn't follow instructions you take it away and start over again.

You have to do that. Why? Well, we said this, the person here has such a short attention span, by having everything structured, you never give him a chance to get away. You are always putting something in front of him, and you are always holding him right there. At the same time this teacher, who insists on setting the structure very, very tightly, must have the patience of Job to put up with taking twenty papers away from this kid before he starts to write in there. That kid, in this CP state, is going to push the limits right down the line. He'll do everything in the world before he'll give in and put that word inside that margin.

You see, what you are trying to teach him is control of his impulse life; he doesn't have any control over it. So, even though you have this very highly structured instructor, he must be able to put up with this learner trying over and over, and over again to push the limits. He must have incredible patience to repeatedly deal with the same thing without becoming upset. You must have a person who does not believe that if you are open and honest with other people, they'll be open and honest with you.

The last major characteristic this instructor must have is that of *never* admitting that he made a mistake in anything in his, or her, entire life. Particularly, never admit it to an underling. Never admit that you made a mistake. Never let the kid know you are or have been wrong. This kid is just sitting there for that opening, and if you come in and say that you did something wrong, that kid is going to ride you up the wall for the rest of the day. You have had it. You just don't make those mistakes.

At CP man is activated to learn by stimuli that can be used to satisfy specific need states such as hunger, thirst, and sex. The means to this kind of learning is operant conditioning or the "trial-and-error" learning method; that is, a person learns by making movements which, shortly after being made, bring about tensional release from the specific drive state. Learning takes place best when much activity is spent getting to the reward, the reward is presented soon after the act is performed, and the need state is very strong. For example, a CP personality can best learn to spell 10 words if (1) he spends a lot of time at the task, (2) he gets a candy bar or other food as soon as he has succeeded in learning how to spell the words, and (3) he is very hungry. The CP personality is egocentric, impulsive and hedonistic. For him the best answer to any problem is the one that brings him immediate pleasure regardless of what happens to anyone else.

Why would you drill? Because, Skinnerian studies show that for any habitual way of handling a machine, turning a wrench, doing a job, it must be redone, then immediately rewarded multiple times for it to become an established habit. So, it's almost essential to somehow or another set up training for the CP state, something that's awfully close to a one-to-one relationship. It's why we have such a terribly difficult time getting these people trained and getting them to function in an organization. We just don't have someone there to give them an immediate reward when they do what we want them to do.

In this state, with cognitive capacity increased but still limited and the operant learning system present to serve the need for survival of the individual, man proceeds into a sensory-motor exploration of his world. He begins to intentionally manipulate his world rather than passively accept it, and from this manipulation develops his third-level values.

Today, prison is often where you find your prime examples of third level behavior. It's a mix, according to the studies I've done in prison - about 33 to 35 percent of any adult prison population. It's a very, very difficult system to work with because our penal system is based upon the idea of punishment. Experiments have been done with mazes in which a person or an animal, in learning the maze, can learn it by reward or punishment, or reward and punishment simultaneously. That is, you can set up lights or bells to be touched or things of that sort in such a manner that any one of those ways can be used for learning to take place. If you have people who are operating at the third level, and they are moving through the maze, they find their way through it only by positive reinforcement. If you actually punish them, they just go on making the same error over and over and over again; they do not learn.

The conditions of existence mentioned earlier in this chapter activate the P system, that psychoneurological system which possesses the tissue specifically tuned to sense consciousness, and consciousness of self, and has the capacity to experience the feeling of shame. It also activates the operant or intentional learning system. The egocentric existential state learns predominantly through Skinnerian operant conditioning reward principles but does not learn from punishment. You can't punish them into behaving as you'd like them to. Can't do it. To use the punitive methodology with the CP is to invite uncontrolled, destructive acts upon the promoter of, or the instruments of the learning system. You can do it by rewarding them, and our values won't let us reward those who break the law or social norms. I don't know where they're going to end up; it's going to be a mess, for you can't get anywhere with punishment. That kind of thinking won't work.

To put a person who operates in the third level in prison with the expectation that somehow or another he will learn from that experience to alter his behavior is in my judgment the most hopeless thing in the world that you can do. You'll never get a person who operates at the third level to change his behavior by punishment. He basically can't feel it. He does not feel or comprehend punishment. Or, putting it another way, the neurological systems in the human organism that have the capacity to feel punishment are not activated in a person who operates in the CP state.

The person operating at the third level has a preponderance of noradrenaline in his system. Now, if this noradrenaline- or third level-dominated person is working the maze, and he's demonstrating that he can learn only by reward, and if he has adrenaline shot into him or her, immediately that person will begin to learn by punishment. The activation of the capacity to learn by punishment is a part of the *fourth level* system, not the third. *These people cannot learn by punishment.* They can learn only by reward; and they can learn only by rewards that are immediately applied after the desirable behavior takes place. This is something that theoretically is very possible to do.

What I am trying to say to you is: punishment doesn't work because the tissue in the head that is able to feel, to perceive punishment isn't activated. In the head you have tissue present, but just having the tissue does not produce the behavior. You have to have the concomitant chemistry. If the chemistry isn't there, the behavior doesn't come through even if the tissue that would make it possible for that behavior to exist is present. What you see in the third level is the tissue, but they don't have the chemistry. So, the behavior - learning by punishment - is not functionally present in the individual. He can't learn that way. It isn't that they are obstreperous; it is that they cannot learn by punishment. Neurologically it isn't possible, and chemicals play a role in that neurological aspect.

We are trying to base our approach to the problem on the idea that in some way or another, punishing "them" for that which "they" are doing will produce the desired results. I really don't see a solution. I see this as quite an impasse. When you have people operating at the higher levels, as the American public is, believing honestly in their own mind that punishment will sooner or later work if we only find the right one, you are almost doomed to failure when the reality is the punishment isn't going to work, no matter which method you use.

It is theoretically possible to use Skinnerian positive reinforcement techniques to change behavior, provided that you have the things that you had with Skinner. If you have a rat in a Skinner box, and can control that rat's behavior so that it is narrowed down to be able to do only the things that he can do in the confines of that rat cage, then the limited number of anything that he or she can do are so few that you can wait until in the course of his or her exasperation he does what one wants. Then you can immediately reward it.

But, even in a prison, you can't do that. It's just almost impossible to set up the conditions whereby: a) you get elicited, or spontaneously appearing, the good behavior; and b) you are able to reward it immediately. And you can't teach in any other way at this level. So, it's really very, very hard to conceive of any way in our prison systems that you can really go about the business of rehabilitating those in the CP state. Theoretically, yes; practically, it is terribly difficult.

That is because this person, the CP, operates by what we call the intentional learning system. This is the system which learns by reaching out to do something, intending to do something, which results in reward or punishment. This person soon gets the idea that some people in the world have it - what they intend to do turns out successfully - and other people don't have it. So, on the societal level, they order the world according to 'might is right,' into those who have and those who don't have - haves and the have-nots. They think that is perfectly right because the gods must be inspired by one person such that whatever he did turned out successfully; and they must have displeasure with the person whose action did not turn out successfully.

In the P dynamic neurological system we find a very different matter from the BO system. In the P dynamic neurological system new qualities come into play. The elements of reward and punishment, not necessary to the learning in the N system or the O system, are essential for learning in the C system. The response is more volitional than automatic, and there is a delayed time factor in conditioning in the P system, which is distinctly different from the character of the operation of the O dynamic neurological system. Contrary to the O system where simple contiguity, not delay in time, is sufficient to establish a bond, in the P neurological system both the sensory and motor neuron patterns must persist for reinforcement and thus conditioning to take place. But this is not the total story.

Much of this, which is related to what I am saying, wasn't even known until the mid-sixties. We didn't know really very much about the basic structuring of the brain and things of that nature until the sixties, and the second thing is illustrated in this manner: We have this very solid evidence that what activates neurological tissue in the brain is chemical in nature. But it is a horrendous research problem, to try to sort out what is the specific factor within the noradrenaline complex that actually activates the tissue, and that enables the individual to learn by reward and possibly blocks the learning by punishment. Biochemistry just hasn't progressed that far. It's not that people aren't hunting and searching, but it's the enormity of the problem.

Management of the Egocentric State

This third level spawns the first form of management, the first organized form of management that you find in human behavior. It is an *exploitative* form of management. These people are manageable only through Skinnerian operant conditioning principles. That is, you can manage them by manipulating rewards. But you are absolutely hopeless if you try and manage them by punishment.

To manage an individual centralized in the CP system you need a person who prefers to confront undesired behavior and just candidly say: "I won't have it," but who will not get into any discussion. The manager must operate dispassionately and simply say, "I told you not to do that." Of course, he starts up again and the manager repeats: "I said not to do that, I told you not to do it." The guy starts opening his mouth; the manager puts his hand right on his mouth, and stops him. "I am not going to discus this, I just told you not to do it. I just told you not to do it. Stop it!"

Your manager must be a person who accentuates the positive and ignores the negative. This person never punishes. The person stops behavior, but doesn't punish for its happening. If a person makes an error in what he is learning, if he is in the course of making an error, then this manager just stops the individual. He doesn't give any punishment if an error is made. He has the patience to repeatedly say: "Do it again. Start it again." If the person makes an error, he stops him and says, "Start it again." He just keeps going until he gets the positive response, and then he rewards. And generally, it is better here if you can have some kind of extrinsic reward that you can deliver immediately upon the achievement of the desired behavior.

Your manager must be perfectly at peace believing that if you have to discipline you just do it, and you never get into a discussion as to why you did it. You never get into a discussion as to what led up to the necessity of the discipline. I've seen this very often by coaches who are trying to handle some pretty rough kids as far as teaching them football or some ball game. The guy pulls something and he just benches him. He puts him down at the end and says absolutely nothing. The minute the guy does it again he yanks him, right in the midst of running a play in practice. The guy is supposed go out two steps, swing back and come in. He goes out two steps and swings in, and the coach just reaches up, grabs him and says: "Take your helmet off and sit down." That's it. No more.

He never asks: "What the hell is the matter with you? You didn't remember X." He just yanks him in that manner. Why? Now, remember what we said about the CP state? He has a tremendous tendency to react aggressively. If you yank him out and start saying something, he and the coach are liable to be in a fistfight in ten minutes and go at it for the rest of the afternoon. The guy will come right back at you. We have these requirements for the manager, coach or teacher, because we have a human being who is unbelievably egocentric, who is concerned with what's in it for me. We don't get into a discussion because in the person's egocentrism, in the person's short attention span, he can't hold himself in long enough to listen to somebody else. He won't let somebody else finish a sentence.

If we are going to send a CP out to work before the transition to DQ has taken place, then wherever you plan to place this person, you'd better align that organization correctly. Get *that* work organized in a way that will suit *that* person, or you are going to end up with a reputation of sending poor employees to *that* organization. You don't have a chance to win if you don't manage the person, the organization and the job correctly.

The tremendously important factor is to plan for disparate work activities every 20 to 25 minutes. You don't run much past that. Package your activities in 15 to 25 minute units. They need this variety. They cannot continue to work if they don't have it. If I had workers, for example, operating heavy equipment, I would try and arrange it in such a way that either every half hour he used the machine to do a different task or he got on a different machine, rather than keep him on any one machine for a half a day. I would be switching that person if I were trying to bring him along because, if you don't do that, he is going to get bored pretty soon and, depending upon where he's working, if you keep him on it for 45 minutes or so he is going to turn 'that machine' to run somebody off the road just for fun. He is going to get in trouble with it. So, you've got to keep switching tasks continuously and regularly or you are going to get into difficulty.

The most difficult thing that I have to get across to people who want to work with those centralized at this level is that I don't care what their work process has been. If they want to hire these people - in other words, if you want to take seriously hiring the hardcore, rough, tough unemployed—you'd better chop your work up into these units, or you will never keep these people on the job. The usual routine just won't do it. You've got to try to at least get somewhere between five to seven different activities. One good example of a job at this level is an outside deliveryman's job: he loads, he drives, he unloads, he takes in, he checks, and he comes back. You see, he's got five or six activities in there that he is switching among as he goes from store to store, house to house, or office to office. By not keeping them busy and interested, only the organization can lose. If you run them ten or 15 minutes beyond their time tolerance, you are not going to have anybody around. They will simply leave. Now, I don't know how they are going to leave, whether they are going to leave destructively, or whether they are just going to take an earth-moving machine somewhere, leave it running, and go without turning it off, and without caring.

Welfare wise, to the CP it is *my* welfare, *my* individual welfare that counts. The welfare worker's task is to develop a program for the rapid and almost immediate improvement of the particular client or client family's existence. There is no postponement capacity in the CP state, and he is unbelievably frustrated by the slightest inability to do something right now about improving his state. He wants the worker to re-order conditions right now that will enable him to show right away that he can, if conditions are right, be man or woman enough to foster his own survival.

If you are trying to get this hard-core group in a social program to get them back into the work force, there is one thing probably above anything else that you must always keep in the back of your mind: these individuals normally have a history of having reached out earlier to try to get into our world, and they never got there. They are absolutely, firmly convinced in their minds that we have the whole world organized to keep them out. You are fighting that mistrust to a paranoid degree, constantly. Every person along the line that you bring in to administer the program - the physician doing the examination, the recruiter, the person who is going to supervise them at work eventually and on—must understand how to work with these people. Operant conditioning requires numerous positive experiences before these people are going to buy something. Every human being along the line has got to be selected so that he provides this positive experience or you are going to lose this guy somewhere in the process. It's something that can be designed. We just don't stop and think about it this way. We don't use the E-C framework to think about it and organize the approach properly.

 This level of existence is more familiar to American managers than the previous two. The desired management style is Tough-Paternalistic. It communicates to the Egocentric subordinate a two-fold message: (1) that the manager probably could do a better job, and (2) the subordinate's capabilities are respected and, therefore, he may do the job. A subordinate at the Egocentric level knows how to do the job, shows pride and personal ability in the task (no matter the degree of skill, education, or knowledge required), and has to feel free to come and go as desired.

 The manager assigns tasks to subordinates at the CP level in this "tough" manner—providing enough specific detail to define the desired end results, establish limits to subordinate discretion, and set the completion date. The manager keeps out of things unless asked. The manager's trust is not blindly total, but based on performance. To blindly trust an Egocentric is to show you are a weak fool, not to be respected for your toughness, and to be taken advantage of at will—the subordinate's will. The manager must estimate how long the managed needs to prove the stated competence without resulting in successive risk or cost. At the end of this period, the performance is evaluated. If the task is right, the Egocentric is competent in that area. If the task is wrong or poorly done the Tough-Paternalistic style requires the manager to assign the employee to a task in line with the demonstrated competence or dismiss the employee if they are of no value to the organization. The development of increased competence on the part of the Egocentric employee is done by assigning that person to an apprenticeship position under a master with no specified training period or program.

Mismanagement of the third-level person can come about by applying a management style that is too restrictive - the typical authoritarian "Theory X" Manager.[136] This is a direct affront to the CP's pride, a putdown of competence, and a general "getting on my back" situation. Management of this sort will result in the individual leaving the organization. However, the parting will usually be violent and often focused on the immediate source of displeasure—the mismanaging manger. The departing Egocentric is not coolly calculating the "price" due for discomfort, but rather immediately expressing individual frustration and personal hate. If the individual is not able to leave, the manager will be subjected to a continuing barrage of overt hostility in which every weapon is used and little restraint is shown.

Another form of mismanagement is one in which the CP subordinate has no respect for the manager due to the manager's failure to establish the tough, competent, 'no fool' image. In this case, the subordinate will do exactly what that person pleases. Or, since there is no pride in being involved with such losers, the Egocentric will leave to seek out an organization (or manager) with opportunity for pride and excitement.

The assumption that humans exist in the three classes, (a) the strong, far-seeing, anointed ones; (b) the desirous, motivated, but not far-seeing ones; and (c) the inherently weak and lazy masses who need and prefer directions, spawns a form of organizational life where the *anointed* use the *masses* to accomplish the anointed ones' ends through the direction of the *desirous* at this level. This is the 'exploitative' form of management which presumes that those of demonstrated superiority have the right because they were "chosen" to organize and carry out, through power delegated to the desirous and the efforts of the lesser ones, whatever the anointed chooses. This management believes that the world - all its people and all its things - are there to serve the anointed one's ends. Only superior power can challenge in combat the organization's goals and means.

The anointed one, 'The Big Boss,' decides what is to be done, when it is to be done, where to do it, and provides the means to accomplish it. The Big Boss selects from the desirous the Work Bosses. The Work

---

[136] See McGregor, 1960.

Bosses decide how it is to be done, who is to do it, and how to get them to do it, etc.[137]

Readiness for Change

Interestingly, when the person lives successfully in this CP state and in living successfully begins to create problems for himself - namely, in living successfully the person begins to get other people angry at him for using the others to gain his own satisfaction, and for his ensnaring and entrapping others. Then this person has created the new problems for himself or herself. And if he or she is going to stay alive, he or she has got to begin to shut down a little bit on this egocentric behavior and begin to think a little bit about other human beings.

The egocentric way of life and its value system creates a new existential problem for man. The winner cannot but die, and the loser cannot but wonder why - why he is doomed to his miserable existence. Each must now face his inexplicable existential problem and find an answer, a reason for being which coalesces the two. Ultimately, third-level men see that, in spite of their manipulations, life seems not in their control. Egocentric values break down from the weight of the existential problems they create. "What is this all about? Why was I born? Why can't I go on living?" says the 'have.' "Why can't I find some success in life?" asks the miserable 'have not.' Eventually they conclude that life's problems are a sign indicating that if one finds the "right" form of existence the result will be pleasure everlasting."[138]

Well, as the theory goes, we are equipped by nature to deal with this problem because, as CP values fail to meet the test of time, both the 'have' and the 'have not' must explain why their new problems have come to be. The person begins to realize that his or her own third-level behavior is beginning to produce difficulty. This produces whatever the chemicals are in the brain that activate tremendous productions of adrenaline in the system. When this tremendous production of adrenaline is produced in the system it activates the tissue in the brain that is able to experience guilt. And so the person begins to feel guilty about his or her ensnaring, entrapping, egocentric behavior and begins to say, so to speak, "Well, I'd better sacrifice a little bit of myself to others if I am going to get along in this world."

---

[137] Further details on priniples of E-C management, leadership, and education are available in other publications. See http://www.clarewgraves.com
[138] Graves, Clare W. (1970). Levels of Existence: An Open System Theory of Values. *Journal of Humanistic Psychology,* Fall 1970, Vol. 10, No. 2, p. 131-155.

Out of this striving, they create man's fourth subsistence form for existence from whence emerges his fourth-level value system. Here man develops a way of life built around his explanation of his 'have' and 'have not' world as part of an ordered plan. He believes it is meant that some shall have in life and yet face death, that some shall have less and that the many shall not have. This shift from the egocentric existential state is a move to the lasting security level of need. He learns by avoidant learning. As he moves to this level, he develops a way of life based on the culminated conviction that there must be a reason for it all, a reason why the 'have' shall have so much in life yet be faced with death, and a reason why the 'have not' has to live his life in a miserable existence.

Conception of the Transitional CP/dq State

"My conception of the mature personality, as I suspect are all conceptions, is based on how this world is and the men we are. Though there are some who will profess to disagree with me, if they should really stop to think, they would agree that there are two facts of life upon which a conception of mature behaviour must be based. One is men are not born equal, though they are born dependent on one another. The other fact is that the strong must use the weak to fight this world and its other people in order to survive. Therefore, the mature personality insists that the world take cognizance of those realities.

To me the mature personality organizes to maintain his existence and the right way of life taking into consideration only those he must in order to survive. He sees to it that he organizes his world so as to improve his chances. He takes over and assigns roles to those less able to decide and sees to it they know what their roles are and live by them. He is meticulously careful to take care of those lesser ones who can help him so long as they are helpful but he realizes, because of his superior powers, that they are more expendable than he in the mundane of life.

He takes seriously his duties to those who depend on him but he does not overdo it lest he raise wishes in them they are not competent to fulfill. He leads them to do what is right by outstanding examples in his own life.

He maintains his position in the world as is appropriate for one of his competence by deed not by word, lest those who are dependent on him feel they be shamed in the eyes of others. He feels compassion for the fact that his dependent ones are not as he, but no undo qualms of guilt can enter into his decisions. His standards of action are high for himself and his kind but he readily recognizes the weaknesses in other men and his need to control them. So, he, through his superior competence sees to it that other people are organized so as to maintain the viability of that for which he is responsible. He enlarges his domain when it is to his advantage to do so and he is not overly hesitant as to how, if and when it becomes necessary.

He is ever watchful to his survival making arrangements whenever necessary, with whom ever necessary when they become necessary. These arrangements must take into consideration that the competent people in the world must care for the ones who are dependent on them.

He realizes that world could soon disintegrate into chaos if order were not impressed upon it. He knows the problem of unbridled lust in the lesser ones so he organizes so that normally the rules of living are quite strict upon them except as, through his largeness [*sic*], he provides them moment uninhibited exultation. It is by example in his own life that he brings forth the force for implementing his will. For example, any man worthy of his name, any woman worthy of being called a lady serves their human desires but in a manner that is properly formalized."

Notice the change that is coming in here. The individual is beginning to reign in his impulses and shows a beginning concern about the need for immediate gratification in others and their motivations around avoiding shame. This particular response shows that this person is just beginning to make the kind of transition with the response lying in two worlds. The awareness of guilt is sneaking in and the individual is becoming aware of, and questioning, unbridled lusts in the weaker. In respect to societal organization, a sense of order is seen to be required, but it is an imposition of morality with attempts to enforce formalistic prescriptions over the weaker and use them to one's own advantage. This individual begins to recognize that if you don't lay down the rules, say what is going to happen, and see to it that it does happen, you are just never going to get impulsiveness controlled in weaker individuals.

Just note as the individual is moving out of CP into the DQ. Now, when we are working, we don't stay with the simple designation of say, CP, DQ, ER. We have CP, and then the person who is centralized here —a transitional state—will be shown by upper case CP over lower case dq—CP/dq—and later by lower case cp over upper case DQ—cp/DQ— the exiting and entering phases.

In the CP state we had a human being who was unbelievably egocentric, who was concerned with 'what's in it for me.' We didn't allow for a discussion, because in the person's egocentrism, in the person's short attention span, he couldn't hold himself in long enough to listen to somebody else. He wouldn't let somebody else finish a sentence. The assertion of self was against outside power over him. That is changing as he completes his transition into DQ.

Conception of the Transitional cp/DQ State

> "There is little doubt in my mind as to what makes mature personality. I learned that at the end of my old man's switch and I'm not likely to forget it. The grown-up learns and particularly he learns nothing comes lest you put out first. Right is right and wrong is wrong and if you are going to be mature you better learn it, the sooner the better. It always has been this way and it will always be because that is the way it is. My old man learned it from his and his old man learned it from his father, and my kids are going to learn it from me because that is the law of the land.
>
> We were not put on this earth to get something for nothing. We were not put here to want or to wish for or to have evil thoughts. We were put here to do right and see to it that other people do right too. It is our duty to strike wrong whenever we find it. The mature personality knows what the rules are and he knows if he violates them he should get it. Life is a serious business with no place for frivolousness in it. He knows what he is allowed to wish for and he knows what is forbidden and he behaves accordingly. Any mature man has got his duties and he does them even if he does not want to because it would be wrong of him not to do so. If he does not the grown-up

knows he should be punished. There is no place for self-serving sentimentally in becoming of age.

One thing that bothers me about this work is what the kids said in class about God, heaven and the like. I didn't see a mature person seeing God as nice and loving. God is vengeful, he is to be feared. He is not some nice old grandfather-like guy. To me it is hell that you have got to fear more than you look for heaven. God says there are laws we must live by or He will see to it we pay for it in the future. That's what being fully grown is. The mature he is that guy who watches out for evil that is in us. He is the guy who learns to keep evil down and strive against it."

This particular response shows that this person is completing the transition with the response lying in two worlds—more in DQ than in CP. Notice that as the CP begins to drop out, this over-aggressive assertiveness is increasingly modulated because he is learning to bind his impulses tightly within. While CP learns when positive results accrue from impulse-driven, self-assertive, great risk-taking ventures, DQ quivers in fear lest action lead to condemnation/pain; hence, there is an aim to make the other person feel guilt for being what he/she is. We have an individual who is increasingly learning from punitive action, even for thoughts in the heart. Notice the increasing awareness of guilt with self-sacrificing obeisance rather than the previous heroic expressiveness.

For all its negative aspects, the CP value system is a giant step forward. Pursuing power, some men do succeed in taming the mighty river, or building a city or doing other things that improve the personal lot of some and indirectly help others. But the CP way of life and its value system create a new existential problem: The winners (heroes) must eventually die and their admirers wonder why, and why they themselves are doomed to a miserable existence. Both winners and losers seek a reason for their inexplicable fates.

Eventually, they conclude that life's problems are a sign indicating that if one finds the "right" form of existence, there will be pleasure everlasting. Man now comes to believe that the life is part of an ordered plan in which it is meant that some shall have more and some shall have less and all shall suffer and die. This conviction leads to the belief that the 'have' and 'have not' condition is a part of a directed design - a design of the forces guiding man and his destiny. Now man moves to the lasting security level of need and learns by avoidant learning. As he moves to the DQ level he develops a way of life based on the conviction that there must be a reason for it all, a reason why the 'have' shall possess so much in life yet be faced with death, and a reason why the 'have not' is forced to endure a miserable existence. And the answer comes: Life is a test of whether one is worthy of salvation. Thus, the saintly way of life, based on one of the world's great religions or great philosophies, comes to be. Here man creates what he believes is a way for lasting peace in this life or everlasting life, a way which, it seems to him, will remove the pain of both the 'have' and the 'have not.' Here he seeks salvation. Out of this mix develops the fourth level of human existence.

Chapter 10

The Absolutistic Existence — The DQ State

The 4th Subsistence Level

The DQ - Saintly Existential State

Theme: *Sacrifice self now in order to receive reward later.*

Alternative Theme: *'Sacrifice now to receive reward later'*

The *'Sacrifice now to get later'* Conceptions

Now, the fourth system - the absolutistic existential state - is incredibly different from the one which preceded it - almost a polar opposite. The person at this level believes that the prime value is obeisance instead of the expressivism of the third system. At this stage of ordered existence he focuses on adjusting to the world, this time not as he experiences it to be, but as he has come to perceive it to be. This sponsors a benevolently autocratic, moralistic-prescriptive form for managing all life, a way which must be religiously adhered to.

This system appeared, probably in its various forms, about 4000-6000 years ago when successful CP living, taming the mighty river, and accomplishments in building and organizing improved the lot of some - the 'haves,' but left the many with a miserable existence. It created the problem that the 'haves' confront when they are brought face-to-face with death and must give up the successful self-centered existence. "What is this living all about? Why was I born? Why can't I go on living?" asks the successful. The 'have-nots,' also facing the awareness of death, must explain why life has been such a miserable existence. "Why was I born to live this miserable existence?" asks the 'have not.'

Each must now face these inexplicable problems and find an answer, a reason for being which coalesces the two. He explains his have and have-not world, his life and death condition, as part of an ordered plan. It is meant that some shall have, that others shall have less, and that many shall not have. And there is meaning in why man shall live, why roles are determined, and why men shall die. The answer is: it is God or nature's designing. It is what the higher power prescribes it to be and no questioning of authority is permitted. It has all been planned this way. It is whatever the higher power says that it is and we must obey. The reason is to test, in many ways, if one is worthy of everlasting existence. At this time, he becomes a human awakened to inner man—physiological self and the external world. The capacity to philosophize beginning in the "Q" system of the brain is activated and the DQ, absolutistic existential state is born. This state gives rise to the fourth level theme of existence for this worldview: *Sacrifice the desires of the self now in order to get a lasting reward later.* And, it gives rise to its associated value system - the absolutistic sacrificial existential system.

This system begins to emerge when a successful CP existence creates a bi-polar set of problems, the problems of existence D. These problems result when the self-centered, hedonistic CP existence creates a problem for the 'haves' as well as the 'have-nots' because sooner or later there will be an awful lot of clashing going on. D problems are products of the increased activation of consciousness of self and others.

Awareness of these death problems activates the Q neurological system, a system specifically equipped to experience guilt; to learn through avoidant learning - punishment; to defer gratification; to control impulses; and to rationalize. The absolutistic state is a quest for a permanent peace. As DQ man sees it, that state is the tensionless state. Thus, his values repeat that which he valued at the animistic existential state, the absence of tension, but in a new form, a *saintly* existence.

The third level believes that, in some manner or other, life can go on forever; but at the entering stage of the fourth level, whatever it is that creates awareness of death begins to emerge. This is associated with guilt and plays a very definite role in structuring what we've come to call the absolutistic existential state which is sensitive to the feeling of guilt and, thus, to disapproval. Those centralized in the fourth system feel guilt for possessing forbidden thoughts or desires and believe the feeling of guilt and the act of atonement are the proper responses for wrong done to others. Those in the DQ state are the ones who struggle to free themselves from the feeling of guilt at selfishness thorough the acceptance of hierarchy. They believe in living in a world in which one person acts and the other person judges. The higher authority evaluates the struggling acts of the lower without taking the offending person's feelings into account.

The time does come when some men question the price they must pay for the later heavenly life. But historically, as in our time, when this quest begins man searches for his next higher value system and is accused of breakdown in his moral and ethical ways, e.g., the attack of the Romans on the early Christians. The absolutistic existential state emerges in man when he perceives that basic physiological needs are being met and will continue to be satisfied, but when he is still endangered by predatory man, predatory animals, and a predatory world. There is a flood of free energy in his system released from considered and continuous attention to maintaining physiological life. He is a human who becomes frightened by an influx of inner and outer stimulation he can neither comprehend nor control. He is in a state of frightened existence. Since he now perceives himself caught in a world of unpredictability and chaos, he strives with all at his command to achieve safety and security in this world.

To attain safety and security, he seeks to create an orderly, predictable, stable, unchanging world—one in which the unexpected does not happen. As he sees it, only complete denial of this inner world and complete control of it and the outer world can keep him safe from the many stimuli of which he has become aware. At the DQ level, he develops a way of life based on "Thou shalt suffer the pangs of one's existence in this life to prove thyself worthy in later life." This saintly form of existence comes from experiencing that living in this world is not made for ultimate pleasure - a perception based on the previous endless struggle with unbridled lusts and a threatening universe. Not only did the people begin to believe that in order for existence to continue there must be control of one's impulse life, there also developed the belief that this control must be absolute, that they must learn *the* rules for the control of the impulse life of the individual.

Peace in this world relates to safety and security, and the way to achieve this is to divine the immutable laws of living and submit to and obey them and, once having found them, let no change take place. Here he perceives that certain rules are prescribed for each class of men and that these rules describe the proper way each class is to behave. The rules are the price man must pay for his more lasting life, for the peace which he seeks - the price of no ultimate pleasure while living. What one must do is obey. What one must obey is the power that knows what it is all about. "This is the way it always has been; this is the way it is today; and such is the way it shall always be" is the lesson of life to be learned. People at the fourth level live by the principle, *sacrifice now in order to get later*, and this was, in fact, the theme that I found in all of the conceptions of mature personality that were expressed by what ultimately became this category of human behavior.

At this level man accepts his position and his role in life. Inequality is a fact of life. He believes that the task of living is to strive for perfection in his assigned role - absolute perfection, regardless of how high or low his assigned station. He believes that salvation will come ultimately to the man who, regardless of his original position, lives best by the rules of life prescribed for him. What one wants, what he desires is not important. What is important is that he disciplines himself to the prescription of his world.

Thus the prime value of fourth-level man is self-sacrifice. He who sacrifices best his wants in the way authority prescribes is most revered. We can see the same represented in the role of the leader and the led at the fourth level. Both work to establish a valued, protective, supportive alliance. The leader values the life that enables him, if necessary, to sacrifice himself in the protection of the followers. Those who follow value sacrificing in support of the leader. Both live by different *schema* varying from the same *thema*.

Thinking at this level is absolutistic: one right way and only one right way to think about anything. All others are wrong. In the absolutistic existential state, thinking is in a categorical fashion: black or white, good or evil, all or none, for me or against me. DQ assumes a right-wrong position in respect to everything, even an either-or conception of knowledge, and sees weakness in any person who takes a position and then changes.

This fourth, absolutistic existential state, the saintly way of life, seems to have given birth to the great monotheistic religions of the day. The world's great philosophies also come to be because in all of the formal monotheistic religions, in some of the much more rigid political systems, there is this very strong belief, very strong prime value, of obeisance to authority. This really is very new in human existence. We just didn't believe until about 5000 years ago that there is one power, be it the state or be it the individual or be it what it may - the king, the God, or what - that a person had to bow down to and behave in conjunction with. But, it's a very strong system and it believes that there is one right way and only one right way to behave.

Earlier forms of fourth-level values are typified in those of Medieval Europe or the Manchu[139] dynasty. In these *schema*, each man was assured, if he lived his role properly, that reward would come hereafter. But after knowledge and technology started to burgeon from the efforts of the few who achieved a fourth-level existence, the sacrificial value system took on a different schematic form. It took on the form of Kantian ethics, the Protestant ethic, or "Mao Think." These *schemata* strove to incorporate empirical evidence with absolutistic thinking. In this fourth-level *schema*, man values sacrificing at this time in this life to gain, at a later time, in this life or in some life after death.

At this level, man does not propitiate the spirits for removal of threat to his immediate existence; rather, he is on a quest for ever-lasting peace—Nirvana or Heaven. To man at this level, the means to the end must fit the end. Thus, they require the giving up of bodily and selfish desire in the here and now. The saintly, the monkish, the Christian form of existence must coalesce with whatever is the particular group's heavenly end. Typical means values are denial, deference, piety, modesty, self-sacrifice, and harsh self-discipline and no self-indulgence. In his new existential state, man's theme for existence is "one shall sacrifice earthly desires now in order to come to everlasting peace later." This theme gives rise to the sacrificial value system. Man focuses his earthly

---

[139] A document such as the sixteen maxims in the "Holy Edict" of Emperor K'ang-Hi which lays down prescriptions for good living and a ruler's path to serve the people can be found at: http://www.sacred-texts.com/journals/mon/kang-hi.htm

existence on the means to salvation—sacrifice of desire in the here and now.

At the saintly level (DQ), man develops a way of life based on "Thou shalt suffer the pangs of existence in this life to prove thyself worthy of later life." This saintly form of existence comes from seeing that living in this world is not made for ultimate pleasure—a perception based on the previous endless struggle with unbridled lusts and a threatening universe. Here man perceives that certain rules are prescribed for each class of men, and that these rules describe the proper way each class is to behave. The rules are the price man must pay for his more lasting life, for the peace which he seeks—the price of no ultimate pleasure while living. The measure of this worthiness is how much he has lived by the established rules.

Here he reveres the established, the lasting, the unchanging as he did in the BO state - not the lasting ways of his tribe, but the all-encompassing ways for all mankind. Man's search for his Nirvana will peak in his absolutistic sacrificial values, which if followed, will assure him that he will achieve the end which he values most, the end that is known as salvation. This end is the ultimate reward for living by the values which "the Power" has laid down as the basis of man's earthly behavior. These are learned through avoidance learning or Mowrer's two-factor learning theory. The most representative *schema* of this thematic form of valuing is to value life hereafter in the form of Nirvana, heaven or the afterlife. He becomes Fromm's (1955) "Hoarding Character" or Riesman's "Traditional Directed Man" and seeks those earthly ways of being which will provide, at some later time, that which he values - the reward for living right - the tensionless state.

The absolutistic level can be recognized in those who are very genuinely highly ideological people, highly religious people. Freud observed the fourth subsistence level of human behavior just as the early conditioning psychologists observed the second level.

Caught in an uncertain and fearful world, man at the fourth subsistence level works to construct an ordered, stabilized, and certain world in which the feared or unanticipated does not come to be. To live with his perception that life is precarious, that one exists in a world of ever threatening stimuli, man creates the constrictive ethic, an ethic which he must develop in order to deal with his state of frightened, over-stimulated existence. This is a suppressive, repressive, Freudian-istically explained ethic. Man in the fourth system values the suppression and repression of his inner life and a rigid ordering of the outer world. He prefers isolated local unit political institutions and absolutistic authority. The latter is usually divine, but it can be the absolute authority of nature. This point illustrates a significant aspect of the absolutistic state.

Of all the value systems that exist, the fourth-level system is one of the most confusing. This central-peripheral problem can be seen in many other forms. We can see it in the fourth-level value of hierarchical dominant-submission human relationships. To avoid this confusion one must keep in mind the thematic and schematic conception of value. The schematic representations of fourth-level values oft times appear diametrically opposed. Thus, they appear to be different value systems.

For example, the Moslems and Hindus, often enemies, share the same thematic value system within this point of view. The holy wars of the crusades stemmed from the same value system as the non-violence of Gandhi or Martin Luther King. They are the same because, centrally, they are alike in that all of them value sacrifice now for achievement of a better state later. Doctrinaire Catholicism and doctrinaire atheistic Communism are mortal enemies, yet within this point of view they are only polar opposite *schema* varying from the same central sacrificial *thema*. Peripherally, the schematic representations are so different that at many times in history wars have been fought over whose form of sacrificial values should prevail.

Time, for the fourth system, has stopped. The world is right as it is, as he now sees it to be, and should not be tampered with. Normally, he who is living a satisfying fourth-level existence is almost impossible to change. It would be like trying to change the political beliefs of an ardent John Birch society member. Why is it that orthodox communism has the problems that it has - whose communistic way is the *right* communistic way? Was it Lenin's or Stalin's? Whose communistic way is the right one? Was it Mao's? They all believed in absolutism, but it was absolutism that's different.

Now, this is at one and the same time one of the strengths and one of the great weaknesses of the fourth level, or the absolutistic way of living. If you believe there is only one right way, and if those beliefs out there with their different details developed in different parts of the world, and all have their own "one right way," then clashes will develop between these differing "one right ways." If you agree with it, and bow down to the higher power that defines what behavior is right and what is wrong within a system, things are just fine. If you vary, then you have a very, very difficult time with the fight that ensues. So, this is at one and the same time the most peaceful and the most warlike of all of the systems that we have.

As previously stated, the person living in the egocentric existential state, by living successfully, begins to create problems. The person begins to get other people angry at him for his entrapment and using others to gain his own satisfaction. He has to shut down some of his egocentric behavior and begin to think a little bit about other human beings. Well, as the theory goes, we are equipped by nature to deal with this problem. Because, as the person begins to realize that his own third level behavior (or her own egocentric behavior) is beginning to produce difficulty, it produces chemicals in the brain that activate tremendous productions of adrenaline in the system. This activates the tissue in the brain that is able to experience guilt, and so the person begins to feel guilty about his/her ensnaring, entrapping egocentric behavior and begins to say, so to speak, "Well, I better sacrifice a little bit of myself to others if I am going to get along in this world." Out of this mix the fourth level of human existence develops.

At this level, man perceives that living in this world does not bring ultimate pleasure, and also sees that rules are prescribed for each class of people. Obedience to these rules is the price that one must pay for more lasting life. DQ people generally subscribe to some dogmatic system, typically a religion. These are the people who believe in "living by the Ten Commandments," obeying the letter of the law, etc. They work best within a rigid set of rules, such as army regulations.

Examples of the DQ Existential State[140] – *'sacrifice self for reward later'*

Now you come to the person who is at peace with the absolutistic way of life, who feels comfortable there. Let's take a look at our first DQ conception.

DQ Conception #1 -

> "This assignment was to develop on our won and in writing, our personal conception of what is the psychologically mature person in operation. Dr. Graves, I have found this to be a most difficult task. It is my honest belief that what is a mature personality is determined by that power which determines good and evil in the world. God created man and God has indicated in His Ten

---

[140] CWG: These are written exactly as the person originally submitted them, complete with spelling mistakes.

Commandments the principles by which the human should live. It is not for me to decide what God pretended [I believe this is a Freudian slip and she meant 'intended']. If God had wanted man to decide he would have indicated that. He would not have "commanded". As a result one cannot easily fulfill this assignment. I have thought very much about how I could fulfill this assignment. The only way it can be done is within God's design. Therefore, since God did give man free will to choose, in this context, to be mature or immature, I have decided the only way I can fulfill the assignment is to decry [I believe she meant 'describe'] what I think God meant by each of his commandments. I do hope for your forgiveness if wrong of if this does not satisfy the requirements.

Thou shalt have no other God before me.

This commandment, in operation, questions the right of man to decide what the mature person is. This assignment, as stated to us, would place man before God because it would not be God who determines the mature personality. The mature personality accepts what God commands. He does not, in arrogance, take unto himself that which is not in his domain. The mature knows that God, in His omniscience, knows best. He lives for this rule.

Thou shalt not make any graven image.

The dictionary says this means one does not make an image of God in wood or in stone. This the mature person does not do. It is one reason why this assignment is an improper assignment, though I may be wrong, since the dictionary said no image in wood or stone. It seems to me if I sculpted my picture of the mature personality, I would be creating a graven image. This is because God created man in his own image. Thus an image of the mature human being would be a graven image of God.

Thou shalt not take the name of thy Lord thy God in vain.

This is what I have been c/trying to say [she has crying and has scratched it out and put in 'trying']. The mature personality operates so, as not to take the name of God in vain. He does not question what is the mature person. He accepts that it is what God says it is, because God says that is the road to everlasting peace and contentment.

Remember the Sabbath, keep it holy

The mature personality does on the Sabbath what holy means. He sets it apart and he devotes it to the service and worship of God. One sees that self is given to a sacred purpose.

Honor thy father and thy mother.

The mature personality does by word and deed honor his father and his mother. He does not criticize his parents since they are what God intended them to be. To criticize is to criticize God. The mature is thankful to his folks for having given him life and the opportunity to serve God in God's ways; he is not ungrateful like kids are today.

Thou shalt not kill

The mature personality does not kill. This is why so many people are unhealthy. They add to the commandment, except in the service of God. This is not right. God commanded, "Thou shalt not kill."

Thou shalt not commit adultery

This should be the easiest of all to fulfill because God gave man the will to control his impulses. Man knows what it is for. It is to produce children. So the mature personality accepts this even, for example, if the wife is barren, for if that happens, God intends that marriage to serve him in some other way.

Thou shalt not steal

I have heard some kids say, "How can I serve God if I am dead?" Therefore, if I am hungry God will not condemn me if I steal bread. This is not the mature personality in operation. The mature follows this commandment even if it means to suffer with the hunger of children. God tests man in many ways to see if he is worthy.

Thou shalt not bear false witness

Some who say they are mature personalities show they are (not?) through this commandment. They do not realize that not to bear false witness means not to fail to tell the truth even if the truth hurts. Its only meaning is not, "Don't lie about a person." The mature personality tells the truth. He is honest all ways and at all times.

Thou shalt not covet

To covet is to want, to desire. The mature personality does not covet. He suppresses desire and he does not question any why others have. If God intended him to have he would have given to him. If God gives, it is not because man needs or desires or wishes. It is because God has to see if it is used to serve God's purpose. The mature person does not covet, she accepts."

We note in this conception of the mature adult personality in operation the acceptance of prescriptions of higher power without questioning, acceptance of what is without wanting to change it, with tests of worthiness to be deserving of peace in afterlife. The tone implies absolute obeisance to rightful higher authority and the text is filled with shoulds, oughts and musts. There is no doubt about the source of rightful authority and guilt is centralized as a theme of existence.

DQ behavior shows a struggle to free self from the guilt of selfishness thorough the acceptance of hierarchy. He assigns roles which individuals are required to stay within. In this system a higher authority has laid down a class-ordered life. On the larger scale, the DQ state sponsors a benevolently autocratic, moralistic-prescriptive form for managing all life. Each is to live like father, like son, as prescribed in the design for living or running the organization. There is meaning in man's living, in the way roles are assigned, and why some men shall suffer and why all men must die. Fourth-level men believe life is a test of whether one is worthy of salvation, be this salvation occidental or oriental in flavor. All rewards, all punishments, all duties, all methods of performing duties are prescribed and must be religiously adhered to. He thinks in terms of punishment right now, and forever after, for wrong doing unless one repents.

Stringent 'Thou Shalts' and 'Thou Shalt Nots' for living are developed because man lays a strong hand on his impulses and imposes a rigid order on the world. It is the ethic of the Hindu Mystic, the Buddhist Monk, and the Christian Saint. An ethic of prescribed rules, attributed to some Divine-like authority which are the rules of achieving everlasting peace, everlasting life, be it in Nirvana, Jannah, Heaven, or the Happy Hunting Ground. Now, take a look at:

DQ Conception # 2 –

"Maturity can be defined as a ripeness as a fruition of determined potentialities, as a fullness of possible development. The word and the concept, as I see it, carry certain moral implications. When we say she or he is mature, we are passing judgments, the word carries an implied ought: maturity is good and one ought to be mature.

The mature ought to be what he can be and nothing more. The cardinal rule of maturity is that an individual must [n]ever seek vainly and erroneously to comp[l]ete himself falsely. He must never seek to find (lose himself) in the material world of things or hide himself in books or meaningless social activities. The mature individual never seeks to define himself strictly by roles. This, however, is only negative advice.

Positively speaking, the mature individual must (ought) transcend his animal desires and give its geist free range in order that it might seek the fullest possible actualization of its ideas.

The mature individual must not repress his animality (here used in a neutral context) because man is both geist and body, and in fact they are one. An individual geist can only actualize itself through a body. The body ought therefore be appreciated, respected, and cultivated to the fullest extent possible.

The mature individual must seek harmony between the symbolic system (as may be manifested by the intellectual rational ego), must realize its origins and limitations, while yet cultivating its powers. The mature individual must take stock of this emotive meaning structures and understand them. In this way the play of emotions and the subconscious will not produce existential anxiety in the mature individual and psychopathological stress will be avoided. The mature individual must take stock of his emotive meaning structures and understand them -- as opposed to vain attempts of others to comprehend, repress or ignore them.

The mature individual does not seek power or control of the environment. Since the mature personality realizes that his geist is but a particular manifestation of the Universal, he is aware that the same is true of all men.

Since personality is a process and develops through relationships, the mature individual must not bother himself with seeking absolute freedom. For him, it is a meaningless concept.

The mature individual realizes that the possibility of death lies always on the horizon and life per se is here and now. He will live his life, at any one moment, as if at the next death might bring an end to the projection of his ideals. This realization will not bring despair to the mature individual but rather will intensify his celebration of the joy of becoming. In the fullest sense, maturity is the ability to Be and Become; to know communion and realize the inevitability of reunion with the Universal."

See the black-and-white absolutism? Note the nodal DQ in the *existential jargon*. Maturity is prescribed according to a known universal order, that which differentiates the DQ system, specifically, from all the other systems is the belief that we are controlled by a divine being, a divine fixture-creature-being. A person will say, for example, that in the long run anything that happens in his world will be in line with the master plan of God. The person in the DQ system apparently has this conception of the universe: 'An all-powerful figure, variously named - all-powerful something or other - planned the universe, laid down the laws of the universe, and watches second by second as the days and hours go by as to whether or not the divine plan laid down is being followed. Then he delivers either reward or punishment on the spot or tacks this up on a score sheet to ultimately decide whether the person shall be rewarded or punished.' You see this in their description of commandments and directives where musts and oughts prevail, as well as the seeking of peace and contentment. Despite the existential lofty jargon, thoughts are redundant, repetitious, categorical, and judgmental.

According to the data, man in our DQ state values suppression and repression of his inner life and a rigid ordering of the outer world. He values isolated, hierarchical, local unit political institutions and will accept at most only a weak confederation of political units. Federalization he strongly rejects. His believes in some absolutistic, usually Divine authority, and in hierarchically ordered human relationships - that he is born into position in life and that he should not question his authorities' prescriptions. His authority is emphasized because the particular source of absolute authority varies from person to person. He believes that the world is full of dangerous forces stemming from within man's nature and existing outside his particular group. For those who are psychologically sophisticated, an interesting thing is suggested by the psychology of the absolutistic existential state: fourth-level man may be man as described within orthodox psychoanalytic circles.

The person at this level believes in the formation of absolute rules and their necessity for controlling the impulses of mankind. They show the capacity, which is not present in the previous system, of true interpersonal relations developing. Here he thinks in terms of others being taken into account, as people having needs and feelings which are different from the others; but such feelings are judged as the right feelings or the wrong feelings. They begin to show the capacity for pity. They begin to show that they have definite feelings for other people, but the way they show it is that they give a great deal of attention to the person if what the other person does is considered to be right because they assume a right/wrong position in respect to everything. They just ostracize or shun or shunt aside the person if they consider the individual to be doing wrong.

Kindness to *his kind* is valued, and tolerance toward the unbeknighted is expected. Life is a serious business here. Only institutionalized pleasure is permitted. He thinks in terms of tenderness, of giving, of living with - provided one lives by "my" authoritarian ways. In the long run, giving is always done in terms of giving now or doing now in order to get later, but only after one has learned the right. He values *his* absolutistic moral laws and the words 'should' and 'ought' are repeated often. He assumes an "either/or" conception of knowledge. Rules are black and white, and only the authority that he accepts (for instance, his church or political party) is proper in its definition of virtue and sin. *His* authority defines both. The DQ system has much in common with the BO system, but now it is man's higher authority—the ultimate authority - that sets the rules for life instead of his elders.

Learning in the Absolutistic State

So let us, first of all, ask ourselves: if I say that this theory says the most important factor determining the success of the educational process is the characteristics of the teacher, then what are the characteristics that should be in the trainer, or the teacher who is attempting to teach those in the absolutistic state? This person, first of all, should have high establishment status. Let me illustrate it to you this way: in a collegiate setting, your full professor, whether that full professor is really any good or not, should be teaching the class.

Expertise is not nearly as important in getting a message across as status. When I am going out among people of this kind and I am going to be introduced, I get out all of my degrees and everything I've done. When they introduce me they tell the audience that I am on the National Committee for Marijuana and Drug Abuse, that I am a consultant to the State Department and to the Health, Education and Welfare Department, and God forbid, I've been a consultant to this White House, and so on because high status is of the utmost importance.

If I was setting up a kind of program for these people, I would pick my trainer who is a consistent minded, direct type of person, not given to attempts at verbal control. Then, preferably, I would put them into a residential training setup where they are together day and night and where the trainer becomes mother and father and everything to them. Because someone has got to be there in the beginning of this process to deal with all the fears and all the guilts they have about their inferiority, about whether or not they've got enough on the ball to learn, and all their guilt for going beyond their parents. This teacher has to be an incredible father or mother to them. They must provide a basic classical psychoanalytic education. This education has to be carried on very much in private just as the psycho-analyst takes the patient into the sound-proof room and carries on in private and encourages all the fears and all the feelings that the individual has to come out. The trainer has to be able to do this sort of thing.

Now, this may not be practical. This means therefore, that you don't want to train these people in a short session. It means you might set up this sort of thing: a three hour training program in which, in essence, for the first hour the instructor encourages people to go on and to work and to try to learn that which is difficult. If a trainee begins to doubt, then turn this over to the other members of the group and say, "Now, you convince John that he can do it. You people talk with John about that."

They carry on a discussion. So, you have about an hour or so in which you encourage the people to learn, and then you review what they have just learned, or you have to present. It is best that this be presented in a direct lecture fashion, highly organized with the things broken down to their finest principles. The people should be immediately examined upon what they have learned. If they run into difficulty, they should be immediately encouraged to go on, and toward the end of the session the trainer deals with any fears that have come up about learning the material brought up in the middle of the session. So, about two thirds of your training, with these people, is, in essence, psychotherapy. Only about one third of it is content. About two thirds of it is dealing with the anxieties the people have as to whether or not they can learn it.

The Q dynamic neurological system seems, learning-wise, to follow the O. H. Mowrer two-factor or avoidant learning principles. People at the fourth level of existence contrast sharply with those at the CP level because they learn best through punishment rather than reward. At the DQ level, a person is extremely sensitive to punishment and is motivated, above all else, to avoid aversive stimulation. Punishment is a method one should never use if he wants effective, constructive learning from the impulsive, anger-prone, immediate reward-seeking person centralized in the CP system. But, when the DQ way of thinking is dominant in man, the most effective means to achieve desired learning is through punitive, aversive stimulation. For some reason related to the presence of an excess of adrenaline in the system, a person centralized in the DQ state is particularly attuned to aversive stimulation. Learning is accomplished best by getting him to avoid that which will lead to punishment. In other words, DQ people learn best when they are punished for doing the wrong thing, through rote repetition and instruction, and through a respected authority who provides appropriate punishment for transgressions.

The curriculum must build on what the person believes and it must not be very different. If the individual has an absolutistic conception, that which would influence that person to change, if that person were to change, would be an authority that the individual respects who had a slightly different point of view of an unimportant aspect of that person's thinking. Any differences must be little insignificant things. That is, a Catholic authority would influence a Catholic student if that Catholic authority had a different idea about eating fish on Friday than the church was professing at that particular time. You would never try to move a Catholic, a DQ Catholic, in the direction of thinking in an ER way, at that period in time, by suggesting to them that they should use birth control. That's too hot an idea. In a million years you would stay away from it. You would just close that person down completely if you tried to get them to change some of their utmost ideas by hitting at an idea which is deeply ego involved in the person.

These are the rules for teaching new material or helping them look at ego-involving issues in different ways: An authority must induce it. An authority must make a suggestion that is a minor change in the field of the person's life and never hit an important ego-involved idea. Close supervision with a prestigious instructor; it doesn't matter what the person's expertise is, but the person must have prestige in the eyes of the person or group that you are trying to teach.

You use techniques similar to those you used with CP to teach the closed DQ. Once the closed DQ has done something wrong, stopping him from doing it is as far as you go. If you go any further, that system is tight. That system will blow up on you, and you are going to be in difficulty. This person has a short attention span because he's got so many problems; he hasn't got any energy left with which to think about things. So, you've got to do the thinking for him.

You have to structure the world for him; at the same time, the instructor who insists on setting the structure very, very tightly must have great patience. Not only must the instructor be highly structured, but also he must prescribe in advance the limits within which any kind of behavior is provided. For example, if you are doing the simple task of teaching these people to write, it is for these people that you set up a structured learning environment with step-by-step instructions. That is, you have the sheet of paper and the teacher would say: "I want a margin of an inch and a quarter, inch and a half here. I want so much here. I want you down this far from the top, and up this far from the bottom." By God, if you started elsewhere the teacher would yank it out of your hand. Well, this is what you've got to do. Now, you structure it just like that, and if the kid starts to write outside of that, you just come up take it away and say to him start over. The problem you'll have the first time you take paper away is he is liable to burst out into tears. He won't do it a second time.

Management of the Absolutistic State

One of the first things that I study is the character of the work in the organization. How do they get the work done? Have they got CP work in this organization, or DQ work? Or how much CP work do they have to do, how much DQ? What kind of jobs do they have? That's the delimiting factor in an organization. The way you do the work determines the people you select to do the work, determines the style of the manager you select to mange them, determines the style of management that you have, determines the pay system, and the whole set of the procedures in the organization. If one finds a fourth-level organization, one implements action by continuous and constant supervision of those who are to use it. One, so to speak, stands over people to see that compliance is achieved.

Fourth-level being spawns paternalistic or benevolently autocratic management. In this system a higher authority has laid down a class-ordered life. Here management is based on the assumption that people are born into classes unequal in rank. Those chosen to be born with more have the vested responsibility to supply for the needs of others and to regulate them through fatherly concern. These prescriptions must be religiously adhered to.

At work, the fourth-level person responds to the authoritarian management style—moralistic-prescriptive. The saintly employee knows and accepts the subordinate position. The manager's role, in this person's mind, is to provide the routine, structure the task, define and clarify the regulations, and represent the organization. The routine clerical and administrative jobs found in the bureaucratic structure of large organizations are especially attractive to the saintly person. From this orderliness, and the saintly's submission to it, comes the individual security the person seeks and psychologically requires.

Each is to live like father, like son, as prescribed in the design for living or running the organization. Rules are prescribed for everyone and all things. Obedience and submission to the "order-of-things" is the price of a secure, lasting life. The world is seen as predictable, orderly, and unchanging, based on the predestined order set down by some external, often extra-human authority. It is one's duty to accept the order-of-things, not to question, struggle, or explore. Security comes through sacrifice and submission. To be properly managed, those in the absolutistic state must be managed through moralistic-prescriptive management.

Within this state of human existence the leader-follower relationship is consistent with the safety motive and the constrictive ethic. It, too, is a prescribed relationship, a relationship laid down in divine authority. He who lives at this level believes the role of each human is predestined. The leader leads because he is born to lead and the follower follows because his is predestined. Perceiving that position is ordained and believing that restriction is the proper way of life, the leader and the led develop a protective and supportive alliance for the management of human affairs. DQ behavior shows a struggle to free self from the guilt of selfishness through the acceptance of hierarchy. Fealty and loyalty, service and noblesse oblige are the keystones to organization relationships when both leader and led are at the fourth subsistence level.

The leader and follower in feudal, agricultural or limited commercial organizations have similar and congruent values which makes for viability; but such is not necessarily so in other instances where the values of the managers are similar to the values of those who are managed. At work he responds only to a managerial style which is appropriate for his psychology—only to rigidly prescribed and rigidly enforced rules.[141] Failure to manage him consistently with his expectations results in work deterioration. This deterioration appears in the form of neurotic behavior, psychotic behavior, or unconscious sabotage of the productive effort, [142] and a firm conviction that the manager is not fulfilling the managerial role of providing order and regulation. It becomes the DQ's duty to unseat this manager. Attempts will be made to recruit others in the work group to the crusade—to root out 'evil.' In the extreme, either the manager goes, thus vindicating the righteousness of the aroused DQ, or the organization by retaining 'evil' is also seen as evil. In this situation management should expect the conscious, willful commission of acts of sabotage and disruption of the most horrendous proportion. The resultant organizational chaos vindicates the DQ through the punishment of evil.

The considerable portion of the American work force at this level may, to some degree, explain the consistent percentage of personnel loss (through resignation and transfer) by organizations implementing a job enrichment program. The subordinate at the fourth level perceives the job enrichment program as personally threatening and laden with insecurity. Since this program comes from the highest organizational authority, the entire system must be full of 'evil' (read: lack of order). The Saintly flees to a haven of structure and order; a 'good' organization that has some moral fiber to it.

Note that the closed personality in this state just can't take stress. So, you have the same principles whether it's neurotic or whether it is a person who is unalterably closed for biological or other reasons. Try to construct in your mind the managerial environment that you have set up

---

[141] CWG: What Blake and Mouton call 9:1 management.
[142] Graves, Clare W. (1966). The Deterioration of Work Standards. *Harvard Business Review*. Sept.-Oct., Vol 4, No. 5, p 117-126.

for that person. Watch them until you see that person in equilibrium and see to it that you do not vary from that managerial environment for that person. They need a predictable work setting.

Let me illustrate it in this way: I had a very severe neurotic who was also one of the best auditors in a bank with which I was consulting. This woman was so severe that if she had paper on the desk and you just happened to be walking along and hit that paper and shift it, she would blow. Now, we're not going to do anything about that. We don't know how to change that kind of closed personality. It's a serious a problem. What do you do with this person? We did a very simple thing. We built a glass cage around her desk so that no one could ever hit her papers. We just did that simple thing.

Employees in the absolutistic existential state do not respond to autonomy and participation. When the opportunity for such is extended to them, they choose autocracy, not democracy - what we would expect of them? When attempting to get the employee to do something new it is the authority that must suggest the shift. The authority must accept that the person will reject the idea in the beginning. The authority must quietly insist on the person's considering the idea. The person will eventually accept it. Then you must consistently supervise the person in the process of the change.

The important thing is to be able to read whether or not this person is responding negatively or positively to what you are doing. If you see that you begin to get negative manifestations, backtrack just as fast as you can to try to find out what it is that you are doing to mismanage him. He reveres authority, and he believes the biggest sin that you can commit in this world is to question authority. But when he has dropped clues to authority indicating how to behave and authority doesn't behave that way, then you've got this person in a very serious situation. Now, all that you have from then on is a build-up of pressure. In any organization where there are people behaving ineffectively, in at least 85 percent of the cases this is the reason: management is not reading those people correctly.

Mismanagement at this level is failure to provide firm direction and structure. Many managers have misinterpreted Theory Y to mean that the only appropriate style is open, participatory, non-authoritarian, democratic management (an interpretation McGregor never would have accepted). This misconstrued Theory Y style of management is the surest way of mismanaging the saintly level person, a form of mismanagement so severe that it is guaranteed to produce physically ill and withdrawn DQ employees, disrupt organizational life and morale, and cause a decline in productivity.

If mismanagement continues, you will find that it begins to show itself in the system being unable to control itself. Namely, the disorder behavior, the behavior that is damaging to the organization, is going to increase. It's going to increase to the point that the individual actually endangers the very existence of the organization of which he is a part. It is the DQ who, when mismanaged, will take the ship down with him if he has to. He'll do something horrendous, go amuck. Or go after the people. Now, if this doesn't work, all he's got left to do is run from the situation.

If you have been managing successfully, then DQ management ultimately gives way, and one of the reasons is that nature does not place brains solely in the heads of predestined leaders. Some of the led get their share and some of these ultimately question their slavish existence. When successful moralistic-prescriptive management frees energy in the human system and when this increased energy is joined with the impelling reason of dissatisfaction, dynamic brain systems are activated which produce insights that propel man to a still higher level of human existence.

Readiness for Change in the Absolutistic State

Man tarries long enough here to order his existence so that it will assure his satisfaction at some later time - a way that, it seems to him, will remove the pain of both the 'have' and the 'have-not.' Here he seeks salvation. The rules are the price man must pay for his more lasting life, for the peace which he seeks - the price of no ultimate pleasure while living. After security is achieved through the absolutistic rules, the time comes when some men question the price. When this happens, the saintly way of life is doomed to decay, since some men are bound to ask why they cannot have some pleasure in this life.

This DQ to ER regressive disorganization of fourth-level values is seen by many people as the ultimate sign of man's depravity. Fourth-level man sees the ultimate destruction of all that is good in man as fifth-level wants begin to impel man to seek a new form of existence and a new value system. As man casts aside the inhuman, overly denying aspects of the sacrificial ethic, it is as if a feeling of independence surges up within him. The saints of the church, Godric[143], for example, could no longer stand their saintliness; and the current better-off Russian has started to employ the profit motive. Overcoming self's desires had to give way to what might be termed an Adlerian 'Will to Power.'[144]

But when the absolutistic existential state brings a modicum of earthly security to those who pursue them, their very success creates a new fifth-level existential problem for man which appears in the crisis stages between outmoded DQ values and ER values. Through those prescribed absolutistic rules, the time comes when some people question the price of sacrificial values, the price of the saintly existence. Why must life be only a time of denial? He questions why he was born to live only to find satisfaction later, or in an afterlife.

He cannot have enjoyment in this life so long as he is at the mercy of an unknown world, the servant of the universe rather than its master, so long as he does not express his independence from predetermined fate. Living by order, as in medieval days, seemed for a period of time to solve the problems of existence, then the plagues came in and upset people's lives regardless of whether they lived by the laws or not. People were faced with this kind of discrepancy that caused them to have to begin to think in another way. And so, in order to deal with the fact of having to explain why, even if they live the way 'my God,' 'my Lord,' 'my Power,' 'my Communist leader' says, things still didn't go well. They had to activate another way of thinking. When this question arises in the mind of man, the saintly way of life, the sacrificial ethic, is doomed for decay and readied for discard.

When man casts aside the inhuman aspects of his saintly existence he is charged with excess energy from security problems now solved as he sets out to build a life for pleasure here and now. As he perceives this, man begins again to try to adjust his environment to the self and begins the tortuous climb to the ER level, on through another period of transition to another level, now slipping, now falling in the quest for his goal. Such questioning helps to move man to the fifth subsistence level, the state of materialistic existence. As the ER values begin to emerge and the fifth level comes to be, DQ man views them as impious and the ultimate sign of man's depravity; the new independence of ER man is exhilarating to people caught up in the new values.

---

[143] Possibly St. Godric of Finchale (1170), a merchant who became a pious hermit and is still known as composer of some of the oldest English hymns.

[144] Graves, Clare W. (1970). Levels of Existence: An Open System Theory of Values. *Journal of Humanistic Psychology*, Fall 1970, Vol. 10, No. 2, p. 151.

DQ/ER Transition

In helping a person make the transition from the DQ to the ER system, we are trying to get this person who is just another nice, decent, run of the mill human being to become something distinctive with being what the society values. And so you have to have as a teacher or manager a model who represents 'making it' in society and getting all of the trappings of society; moreover, going on beyond there and distinguishing himself or herself in some manner. This is what the model person has got to be. And this model must be one who can be presented to the training people as having achieved outstanding performance in some way or another so that this person can begin to tease them on in the direction of outstanding performance. The outstanding performance has been achieved within the rules of the game.

So, you need a teacher who has very firm ideas as to how to go about accomplishing. You need a teacher who can show the people being trained that: "I started out here where you are. I didn't know any more than you do, but look where I am today. Look where I am." You have to have a person as a teacher who believes that one should strive for excellence within what his society defines as excellent, whatever the society's ideas of excellence are. This teacher is a teacher who has a tremendous capacity to exude warmth. It is a teacher to which the trainee would want emotionally to attach himself. But this person must be one who has a desire to become genuinely and personally involved with the learning individual.

In contrast to the previous instructor that we spoke of, this must be a person of remarkable verbal facility who seems to spend an inordinate amount of time in direct verbal interaction with people. One of the characteristics you look for is a person who will talk for hours with another human being about how desperate is the plight of the Bantu under Apartheid in South Africa, while sitting comfortably here with the trainee. One of the characteristics is that they love to talk about problems of long-term standing, and about what ought to be done about them, and how something ought to be done about them, but they keep it on a verbal level - they just talk, and talk, and talk.

You want a person very sensitive to intense human feelings, one who has great capacity to empathize. One of the beliefs of this teacher would be that troublesome behavior is the result of emotional difficulty. In contrast to the previous one, we have a teacher who is most willing to admit mistakes to subordinates and to the younger. Why? Because you want the trainee to learn what? That this person got to those heights after making all of these mistakes. So the trainee says, "I, too, maybe can get there. I haven't tried to step out because I'm afraid of making a mistake. But if he stepped out (or she stepped out) and got there and made all of these mistakes, my heavens, I too can get there." You want this.

The supervision here should be casual rather than strict. You need a person who is willing to take a chance with a decision by the trainee to try to do something which scares the living daylights out of the trainer. The trainer has got to exude: "I trust you. Go ahead, take your chance." A characteristic that is highly definitive here is that this trainer is often talking about "what a great satisfaction I get out of reaching the shy, the withdrawn, the isolated." They speak of those who are left out. The trainer has got to believe that there are *no* bad children, *no* bad students, *no* bad learners; they get in trouble because of forces beyond their control.

Now, this trainer must, as a first step to training this person, put an input into the individual suggesting: "You ought to be different. You really ought to try to go just a little bit further." In other words, letting the reach exceed the grasp. This teacher has to be the impetus to change. The teacher has to suggest - has to keep suggesting - that the person try to better himself. You are trying to upgrade a human being in essence here, and so you are to keep in mind that it is the teacher that has higher status and high expertise to the trainee, that must encourage the person to seek to be better. This teacher then must be very, very careful to interpersonally and privately work with this individual to get started. If you have a homogeneous group, you can work very well at the group level here because, if you get a number of open DQs together, one of the first things the teacher can do to begin to get them to learn in the direction in which he wants to go is to have them enter into a group discussion as to how each of them might think of using what the teacher might be bringing them to become distinguished.

These people love to learn by discussion. The teacher can use debate methods. The teacher should always incorporate competition into the learning. The teacher, in this particular situation, works almost day and night, so to speak, with the trainees in the beginning of the experience. You have a person who has learned before the teacher came into the situation that his way or her way of behaving has already been determined. You are now trying to get this person to believe in his own self-destiny rather than in a destiny determined by some divine fate or circumstances, or something of that nature. You are trying to get this person to be better than his parents, to aspire to have more then his parents ever had. And a lot of DQs are going to feel awfully guilty when you begin to suggest to them that they ought to aspire. So, you have to have a very close relationship.

To facilitate a transition, the teacher or manager must learn when to put the group on its own and begin to have them solve their problems in respect to the subject matter, through their own efforts. In other words, you go from the first step of the teacher working closely with the learners through their problems of learning 'what it is' and helping them learn it, to the teacher getting out of the picture, and saying: "Now, here's the problem. You help one another handle this," to the third step: "Here is the problem. Each one of you work this out yourself." The teacher has to withdraw from the situation.

When the teacher gets to the point in this learning situation that he or she does begin to withdraw, this teacher now has to have a tremendous capacity to handle feelings in another way, because the kids will turn on that teacher. The trainees will turn on the teacher, and begin to be almost irrational in the way they go after the teacher, because they would have learned by now that whatever the teacher is teaching, is not as simple as the teacher outlined in the beginning. And the minute they get here, they are going to get mad because "You led me down a road here, and you told me there were answers, and now I find out I've got to find the answers that you suggested to me in the first place were there." At that point, the teacher begins to move out. The transition, in essence, has begun.

This value system, like all others, seems not to satisfy man as he puts it to the test of time. Now you have the person beginning to independently operate against authority, which is what you were attempting to do; helping them standing on their own feet, making their own decisions. Notice these elements in the following conception:

DQ/er Conception (Exiting)

> "I shall open my conception with a short statement which will lay before you the basic facts of what a conception of mature behaviour should be. The statement will be about the assignment that we have been doing in class and the facts of my conception.
>
> 1. This class has been the worst of what I feared I would run into in college. It has been nothing but empty-headed theorizing and muddle-headed hemming and hawing. Why we have to spend four

weeks talking about what proper instruction would cover in one good lecture, I don't know.

2. It seems to me that it would be far more efficient for the facts of mature personality to be presented and then cover how to achieve it along with what happens if one does not. *[Note the subtly challenging reference to authority]*

3. Several times I have asked why such nonsense is allowed, why the time is being utterly wasted and why the instructor will not tell us what mature personality is.

4. Therefore, at the risk of incurring the instructor's displeasure, sir, my conception is what any clear thinking person knows mature personality is.

The Mature Personality

1. The mature personality is the clear thinking person who makes decisions on the basis of fact. The mature does not let emotion overrule his reason.

2. The mature personality thinks about the things that are important, not about a lot of muddle-headed abstractions. He stands for the tried and true and against those who through their muddle-headed thinking would question the established purposes and virtue of man.

3. The mature personality does not go off on tangents, he is clearly focused.

4. The mature personality is loyal, he respects those who know better.

5. The mature personality has "his reach beyond his grasp." He works hard, he does not waste time, he knows that reward should come only for effort.

6. The mature personality sees to it he is known by his deeds, what he does, not what is said and he knows that it is right for him to do so.

7. The mature personality lives by the rules of proper living and requires that all others do so lest there be chaos.

8. The mature personality seeks always to better himself, he is never satisfied with half measure.

9. The mature accepts the laws for living because it is only through their existence that one can be free.

10. The mature has goals in life, he is not hampered in his goal seeking or decisions by uncertainties. He knows where he is going.

11. The mature is open-minded. He listens to all sides so that when he makes a decision he has all the information necessary to make the best decision, the one he knows is right.

12. The mature personality is he who achieves on his own, through his own efforts, by following the established rules.

13. The mature personality is one who respects the established order in life. He is one who knows that established order does exist and he is one who strives always to know and to guide his life by that established order.

14. The mature personality is respectful of his duty and he does it. If he does not subscribe to what is being done he seeks to achieve the position where he can institute right.

15. The mature has the will to work. He does not waste time. He always finds something worthwhile to do.

16. The mature controls his thinking. He keeps his mind on what he wants and off what he should not think about.

17. The mature strives to express only positive emotions -- he uses negative emotions only to handle the evil in the world such as war or crime which he may need to hate so as to kill the evil.

18. The mature uses up surplus energy in work not in frivolity or sex or drinking or eating or the like.

19. The mature is undaunted by failure or misfortune. He believes success comes to he who keeps trying whatever his troubles may be. Every adversity has a benefit.

20. The mature is a master of his attitudes. He directs his thoughts and ordains through self-direction how to control his destiny.

21. The mature separates fact from fiction, fantasy from reality.

22. The mature believes the greatest value in life is to master the negative and animal emotions so as to do good for people even if they cannot or will not do good for themselves.

23. And finally--whatever the mature has accomplished he recognizes it is not enough. To do right he must set his standards high and seek ever and ever to achieve more, so the best be better."

Now, we begin to get an increase in the ER tendency coming in. Notice the little change in language that takes place here. He protests too much about freedom, autonomy, and individuality. There is a sense of turbulence and intrapersonal stress in self versus authority issues, while authority teaches the dictates of independence. We still have the core theme of 'sacrifice self now for later' but a self-designated, right-thinking person prescribes for others with an assertion of self against the deficiencies and errors of authority. Notice the criticism; we begin to see a disdain for authority which doesn't behave like proper authority should. Increasingly, authority shifts from external towards the inner authority of self and one's own right thinking mind.

He wants to listen to all sides so as to learn how to out-argue the opposition. Now, notice again, this change from absolutism in the direction of relativism; but it is not over to relativism, yet. There is still a proper way to live with a no-nonsense, non-theoretical, tangible, down-to-Earth approach. He rejects the ambiguity of confused thoughts; but "metaphysical certitude" prevails which is not defined in moral terms any more. He is struggling for and making the change while trying to hold onto ever-weakening authority anchors. This is why you would make this upper case DQ over ER—DQ/er. He still has that strong DQ element in him and the absolutism is beginning to disappear.

Here, we came out of a protocol that had a lot of shoulds in it, and there is still certainty. This is why you would still say that this is predominantly DQ with ER creeping into it. Now, let's get over a little bit further to where the ER is stronger than the DQ:

dq/ER Conception (Entering)

"I should like to preface my conception with a few words about the way this class is being conducted, and what I have to say is no shit. It is the straight stuff.

I'm a senior in college but I wonder how I got there. Maybe they did not want to embarrass the old man because I sure did not go for the crap those professors dished out the first three years. In fact, of all the time I have given to school this is the first class that ever acted as if there was some respect for the people who don't think the way profs or teachers do. This is what education ought to be, not that poll parroting stuff we always get demanded. You would think no one knows anything except profs from the way most of them operate. But that is enough of that! What I believe mature personality is, is detailed below.

The mature woman can be seen through her analogue, the mature animal. She does not look for trouble but she is ever alert to its possibility. She has her antennae at the ready.

She takes nothing for granted. There's no certainties in the world so she organizes her domain so as to control and amplify her chances for success.

When others interfere with her domain she does not necessarily react to destroy or seriously hare them but to get them under control so as to drive them from her domain, but react with vigor and fury she can if necessary.

She gets away with what she can which will foster her chances lest she be considered a fool.

She is friendly with whoever are with her but watchfully so because she knows it is human nature to take people if you can.

She is too rational to ask for or take on that which is certain trouble but she will take advantage of any situation which is about to foster her success.

She is the one who has control of her world or whatever her organization is because she is not only one who can plan but is one who insists on running her affairs. She takes no shit.

She is able to shift attitudes as necessary. No fear, no doubt, no shame can stand in the way of her carrying out what she sees as the best.

She does not get bound up by the old virtues crap because she knows life is what you make it to be, not what the sayers say it is. She knows that that which is best for her is best for all.

The mature does not cast people into molds. She knows her opinion is a good as anyone's because nothing is certain except the certainty of one's own experience.

The last thing the mature would do would be to let others manage her affairs. It is she who looks out for herself and her interests.

She watches her impulses but she has no fear for using them if her own best interests are endangered.

She does not spend time contemplating who she is or what it is all about. She knows and she knows, she knows.

Look at the change. The multiplistic thinking - many ways to do a thing but one best way - is strong. Diversity is present, but there lingers the feeling that there is a wrong to be eradicated. Shame and guilt have decreased dramatically but have not been eliminated. The absolutism is decreased with awareness of differing value systems, and varieties of thinking, although she copes with it through atomistic additive thinking which is argumentative toward, and oppositional to, authority. She attempts to brusquely cast the shackles of authority aside in favor of the authority of her own tried-and-true experience. The struggle is within the self and with authority, not the dragons of CP. Notice the strong negation of external controls coming in, wariness of others, controlled expressiveness as opposed to 'to hell with the consequences,' and attempts to remove ambiguity and establish truth through her own actions to control self and the environment, rather than through authority or a higher power. In reading this statement one can intuit that "the right" is learned by careful testing, not arrogant assault. She is anxious to grasp things not yet in hand and hungers for an opportunity to express herself.

I want to go back to the methodology that the instructor uses when attempting to train the people to move from the DQ to the ER state. I would suggest that it would be most advisable to have knowledge of and take advantage of all that David McClelland has done. McClelland is the master at putting the achievement motive into human beings; and so it would be very important to learn more about his methodology. It is spelled out well in a number of his writings.

This instructor uses all of the means possible to reward the person in front of the group. This is the instructor who sets up prizes to be won, the stars to be gotten, the Boy Scout Merit Badge, for example. This is a 4-H[145] - "To make the best better" - and all of the training methodologies that you find in 4-H. All of the methodologies that they have worked out in scouting over the years are the kinds of methodologies that are very appropriate. And notice how the Scoutmaster takes the group off to the woods and he spends the night with them. He goes into residence with them, so to speak. The 4-H leader gives his heart and soul to the 4-H youngsters day and night. There is nothing else in the life of the person. Those are simply models of this kind of training that have been around for a long time.

This is the human being who responds magnificently to learning what you measure on objective tests. So, you measure objectively when you are assessing this individual's performance. You try to set it up so that no matter what the individual accomplishes, just as soon as the individual has learned one thing, you push the individual out a little bit further, put another goal in front, and you always keep the reach exceeding the grasp of the individual.

On a child-rearing level we refer to this as 'accelerated unilateral' training, where the parent communicates to the child: "I love you, but I will love you more if you do more, and more. Now that you've done more I'm going to love you more tomorrow if you do more." He keeps rewarding the child for doing more, so you just pull the youngster toward this excellence of performance.

When the expertise comes, the individual can stand on his own feet against authority and you have accomplished the purpose of this kind of training. It is important to give thought to the seriousness of this and to

---

[145] 4-H is the youth education branch of the Cooperative Extension Service, a program of the United States Department of Agriculture. Each state and each county has access to a County Extension office for both youth and adult programs.

consider that the last thing you want to happen is for training to end here, because you are going to end up with this: It is notorious that along with moving the person from DQ to ER, the tendency to believe that "come what may, I must continue to have what I want" temporarily comes into the individual's life. It will be more permanent if you don't take steps to overcome it. So, they are led into this apparent immoral behavior. But I can say this with all honesty: I do not consider this immoral behavior at all, in no way whatsoever. This is normal, natural ER behavior. Every human being who passes through the ER system will behave in that manner. That is the norm.

Now, let's be careful about this. You'll never get advanced development without these people. It is the psychology of Richard Nixon that will make underdeveloped areas developed. You must have this kind of thinking for it to happen. It is what made, and I say this carefully, America great. America was built on people who behaved that way—one's own self-interest; do whatever you have to in fostering one's own self-interest, and spill off a tremendous number of things that improve the welfare of other human beings. But, if we do not ultimately train in such a manner that we move people on beyond this, then we get stalled here. This becomes the norm of living, rather than the means to the end of solving the problem of undeveloped physical resources.

It takes the ER mind to solve the problem of an undeveloped physical world. No other mind has ever been able to solve this problem. But if you leave it there, you ultimately get these very serious social problems. So is important that you think of the overall business to try to keep the human being moving.

The DQ to ER Transition and the Righteous Existence – DQ/er [146]

As we turn to the transition of man from a state of submission to the assertion of his selfish independence we come to what may be, in the eyes of many, the most dastardly of all I have to say. No words that I shall ever pen will be more condemned or less hailed than those which I shall now commit to paper. But be that as it may they must be written for the future of mankind may rest upon man's ability to extricate himself from living within "The American Ways of Life," those states

---

[146] This section is essentially as Dr. Graves wrote it prior to preparing the 1977 manuscript. The exact year of its writing is unknown.

for existence which come to be when the ER, the selfishly independent system of human behavior, begins to emerge.

This statement will be heretical to some, communistic to others and anarchistic to many. But let me explain what is meant by the assertion. This world, as we all know, is full of paradoxes, but of all that exist, the most paradoxical, it seems to me, is the one which arises when man's need for independence begins to emerge. As man starts his transition from the absolutistic form for existence, the ordered, authoritarian, submissive way of life, and as man moves through the stage of independence on into the sociocentric ways for being, five definable and describable states of existence emerge, one after another, in our ordered hierarchical way. These five states, each of which has a strong flavor of selfish independence in them, have brought more that is good to man and more that is bad for him than all states of existence which preceded them. No states of existence prior to these five have given man more power over the physical universe, more verifiable knowledge, or a greater increase in his material welfare than have they. But no states are more certain to pave the way for man's demise than these five unless we can move, at least the leadership of man, beyond these states where man believes that the epitome of human living lies somewhere with one or some of the ER states of existence.

I will grant, as you shall see, that it is the psychology of the existential states which have a strong element of selfish independence in them which split the mighty atom, waft away disease, and provide the means for material abundance for man. But it is these same states, with the same element of selfish independence in them, which lead man to exploit this world for his own selfish gain. He does so because he is temporarily deluded to believe that more is always there to be procured or to be replaced by something created by man's scientific ingenuity. If the leaders of mankind - industrialists, presidents, premiers and legislators - continue, operationally, to deny the negative aspects of the ER component; if they continue to assert, verbally and behaviorally, that any or a combination of the ER states is the *sine qua non* of human existence, then mankind is in for dire trouble in the future. Nothing can be more certain to lead to our destruction or to our reduction to lower level human states of existence than for us to continue under leadership wherein this kind of thinking directs human lives.

Thus, as we begin a study of the ER states, I suggest for your consideration that of all the things the world can ill afford, at this time in its existence, it is an exacerbation or continuance of "The American Way of Life," for "The American Way of Life" is an admixture of those existential states which come to be when the ER need for independence from authority and nature emerges in man. There are five states of human existence which have the ER flavor in them.

The first is in actuality more a DQ state than it is ER, for in it the need for independence is emerging within an absolutistic, authoritarian submission complex. The ER component is present, but it is subordinated within the DQ kind of thinking we have just previously examined. This we will call the righteous way of life, the *righteous* state of existence. It is the DQ over er state (DQ/er).

In the second state, the ER need for independence is the stronger force, but it is still held in tow by the lingering dq (dq/ER). We shall call it the *negativistic* way of life. The third of the states is the *nodal* ER way of life where man is going hell-bent for his own independent way (ER). "Clear the decks, full speed ahead, and the devil take the hind most" is its dictum. The fourth state, the *selfish* state of existence, comes to be when man begins to feel an infringement on his being by the wants of others. It is the ER over fs state (ER/fs). Here man still focuses on going his own way, but in a manner which, on the surface, appears concerned with others, but underneath operates to keep others off his back without feeling hostile to him. The last of "The American Ways of Life," one of which we are beginning to see much, is the *enticing* way of existence, the FS over er way (FS/er).   Here, in this state the last vestige of selfish independence is hanging on as man begins to become more concerned with others than himself. Here he behaves so as to get satisfaction for himself by being the jolly good fellow, the non-party pooper, and the cooperating colleague that his friends want him to be. It is these five states, these "American Ways of Life," that we shall now examine. We shall explore "The Righteous Existence," the DQ over er (DQ/er) state in this section.

The Righteous Existence – Its Existential State

The nodal DQ system is an authoritarian, dogmatic, rigid psychological state. The system is redundant, doing over and over what has been found wanting. It is filled with hidden feelings of hostility and aggression and has a strong element of guilt in its core. It is conservationistic, strongly driven toward closure, concrete, relatively simple in cognitive structure, tightly bound and resistant to change with strong drives within, but even stronger control forces over the drives. It is a tight, narrowly confined system of limited degrees of behavioral freedom which gives rise to a very righteous way for living.

In this transitional state, according to our theory, the component 'adjustment of the organism to the environment' is still stronger than the component 'adjustment of the environment to the organism,' but both are strong. Thus, the person in this state feels a need to express his selfish needs but in a setting wherein he must submit to authority. In this state, the avoidant learning system is still dominant, so the person must learn anew what to avoid so as to express himself the way in which authority approves. With the need to submit to authority stronger than the need to assert selfish independence, guilt will be felt when the selfish desires arise.

Thus, this person's existential problem is: "How can I handle this need for independent and selfish expression of all that is in me - desire, anger from blocked desire, and guilt for desire - in a setting where independence is forbidden and punished, and desire is akin to sin?" The answer is: "The Right Way, the way that authority prescribes, the way authority will not punish, the way that may not gain me overt approval but at least won't get me punished." Do what has to be done, but do it *their* way, authority's way is the answer. "That is the way to solve the problem," one's cognitive powers tell him. "Discipline yourself to expressing your desires the way authority says is the right way for you to express them; then you will not have to feel any qualms of guilt about letting your self through. Set yourself this goal and don't veer from it, then you will have created a non-disturbing mix of personal desire and authority's demand which enables you to avoid guilt. But remember, having to express yourself their way, rather than your way, will make you angry, so include some ways to handle this feeling such as working it off or condemning he who does not have the discipline you possess." So, of this mental state, regardless of the specifics of its source, the way to do all this becomes "The Righteous Way of Life."

The Righteous Way of Being

Righteous man is a man we all know. He is no stranger to any of us for we meet him everyday. He is that righteously conscientious bureaucrat who won't pass your automobile license application because you filled in a blank in legible long hand when the directions said print. "I am sorry," he says, pointing at the blank, "you see, it says print." He is that TV manufacturer's employee who says, when your tube quit on the twentieth day after installation, "You didn't send in your manufacturer's warranty card by the fifteen days specified, so the warranty is no good," even though he knows from whom, and when, you purchased the set. He is one of "The Silent Majority,"[147] one of those righteous achievement-oriented persons who strives to do better and better, then better and better and better what his authorities prescribe is the proper thing to do. For example, calling dissenters names when authority begins the game. He is the loyal selfless employee who does what he is told to do when he is told to do it, the way he is told to do it, who sees darned well that you do the same if you work for him. He is a man of the authoritarian submissive world. Higher authority rides hard on him and he orders about anyone below. He is the righteous, picayune, contempt-citing judge; the ever-watchful, ever-castigating mother; the rigidly moralistic father; the oh so proper hostess. He is the Marine's Marine. These people live in any town of any state in most parts of the most industrialized countries. They are the rigidly conforming, consistently rule-following persons who live in a tight little world of never venturing, never daring beyond the prescriptive injunctions of *their* external authority,

Righteous man believes in authority and obedience. He organizes work and living into tight little cells and sees to it that anyone who gets out of line receives immediately the appropriate punishment. 'Right is right, wrong is wrong, and if there is wrong it must stop right now before it leads to anarchy.' Of course, right is not what he has decided is right, or what he has learned or what the evidence shows is right. Right is what *his authority* says it is. This human has a policy about policies, and rules about rules. He will allow no deviation, not any deviation from the letter of the law and he believes in strict, immediate and righteous indignant enforcement when deviations arise. 'Produce, and produce it my way or perish' is his game. "We don't let anyone get away with anything around here," and "We do it by the book," are two of his favorite phrases.

I recall a recent experience with one of these proper, always correct human beings. It was the day of a home high school football game and I was helping some students get ready to serve refreshments. Soda was to be sold on this hot afternoon and it had to be cooled. But the barrels the administration had provided were full of holes. They could not contain the cooling waters of the melting ice. So I went to the school custodian to borrow the empty plastic barrels sitting unused in the school cafeteria. I rang the bell from behind the seven-foot iron gate protecting the custodian's inner sanctum from predatory souls like me. Growling, he came to the gate, castigating me for breaking the rules by even approaching the gate. When I explained the problem - what was desired

---

[147] From President Richard Nixon's 'Silent Majority' speech of November 3, 1969.

- and that the boys were selling the soda to purchase a new movie projector and camera for the school, he looked at me disdainfully and said: Permission to let me borrow the barrels would be to go against the rules. A request had to go to the administration, through the administration, to the dietician, and through her to him. It had to be done in writing (he spared me how many copies), had to be countersigned, and had to be done by Wednesday. And, it could not be done this day even if I went and got the respective countersigned signatures because the rules said Wednesday.

I explained the emergency, proffered a twenty-dollar bill as collateral and said if anything happened, I would go to the store, a short distance away and replace the barrels before the crowd had dispersed. Though I should have expected what was to come since I was in the process of writing this book, for a fleeting moment I hoped I was wrong. He lit into me that it was parents like me, with no respect for authority, who were causing all those dope problems; who were the irresponsibles always breaking the rules and leading to the destruction of America. Then, when he said he was damned sure I was the kind who would be off playing golf tomorrow (Sunday) instead of going to church as any rule abiding, authority respecting person would, I gave up the quest.

This righteous, self-assured, condemnatory, pompous, deprecatory attitude is typical of the early transitional state between nodal DQ existence and nodal ER being. In this ambivalent existential state we find the human who is deferential and ingratiating in respect to his superiors. Yet with subordinates, or those he sees as beneath him, or outside his authority hierarchy, he is aggressive and autocratic. He hides his buried angry feelings behind legalities and rules. Rules are rules and regulations are sacred, simply because his higher authority laid them down and, after all, his authority's rule is law.

We have seen a lot of this in recent years, especially directed toward the college youth. "Those damned college kids are immature. They don't know what it's all about," the righteous person says. "How long are we going to put up with their undisciplined behavior?" they ask. If those kids were mature enough, if there was one ounce of man or woman in them, they would quit all this foolishness and do what we put them in school to do. After all, how can a society hold together if you don't have "law and order." (That is, of course, the law and the order of the righteous who are the establishment of the moment) This is the baseball manager who forces the player to cut his hair before he enters training camp. Or, it is the football coach who lines up all the boys in the locker room and says as he shears them, "If you are going to play for me you are going to look like football players" - his definition, of course. These are the people who outwardly express righteous concern for the "character building" aspects of their sports and then, as they teach the players to slide with spikes seeking flesh and forearm seeking chin, they grin in glee. (May I say parenthetically to scotch any wrong ideas, I was a four-letter man and spent ten years as a coach.) Outwardly, these righteous ones preach character, but inwardly they take unconscious pleasure in every head that they pluck, every bone they hear crunch.

Righteous man is the skipper who runs a tight ship, the waitress who says, haughtily, "No substitutions" when you want the gravy left off the special of the day. He is the college professor who takes off points for spelling paedomorphic with an 'ea' rather than an 'ae' when he could have said it in a much simpler language in the first place. It is the dean who requires the student to fulfill what is for that student an educationally ridiculous requirement when the student has a most valid educational argument for a substitution. It is the college chaplain who sees as his major college goal to maintain the virgin penis, or the bridge player who says, in a friendly game, "But you said seven hearts and you can't change to seven diamonds because it is an insufficient bid," even if you did make a mistake.

In relation to authority, these righteous ones go so out of their way to impress their betters that their behavior extends beyond being deferential to almost being obsequious. In relation to their own lives, they are budgeted to the last dime and planned for this day, tomorrow, next week, and next years' Christmas presents. Home life and work life and play life as well are systematized and organized. Jobs are organized by rigid job descriptions. Duties are assigned and responsibility and authority are meticulously spelled out. Of course, the day's production may never get done because the boss isn't present to say what to do when some unforeseen occurrence not covered in the manual comes up. "But," he says, "I couldn't do it. I won't go beyond my job description, you know." At play, he takes up golf because the doctor told him he needed to relax, yet pursues it with such tenacity of purpose that he drives the casual golfer nuts with his ordered recording of every stroke, noting of every putt, proper swinging according to his pro approach to the game.

Righteous man seems to get lost in the minutia of doing. He is so systematized, so inflexible, so lacking in spontaneity that many people wonder, how can he be that way? But he himself seldom has a doubt, a doubt that is, so long as his authority is there to give him advice or counsel. He is forever seeking the advice of authority, the guidance of "the more experienced" which he so over-generalizes that even should his authority admit he does not know, this righteous one cannot believe it. Phenomenologically, man in the righteous state sees himself as a responsible, prudent person who is saving society from anarchy. He sees himself as loyal, honest, kindly, dependable, selfless and as a highly conscientious person. And the fact of the matter is, he is just that when all goes well for him. He patiently and diligently carries out the orders from above. He takes great pleasure when, because of his deferential diligence, the company House Organ writes him up as the model Acme Incorporated employee. Externally, he goes out of his way to do, and he does it organizedly and well.

Man in this existential state is punctilious and scrupulous. He sees himself, and others often times see him, as the paragon of virtue. But he is far more than this. He must always build more and more rules, develop more and more moral prescriptions to cover everything and anything that is the least new and different. And he must hold himself and everyone else to the letter of the law. The righteous gives respect, and he jolly well demands it, too. Emotional behavior, in any form, is to be damned. He even fails to recognize his own ranting when crossed by a subordinate (he would never rant at the most unscrupulous authority.) To him, what you might call *ranting* is righteous and proper indignation. It is what any right thinking man would do. It is not an emotional display. Under no circumstances can he let authority down, and under no circumstances will he allow disrespect to be shown to himself or to his authority. He lives in a world of the familiar, a world of 'it was done this way before, and it is to be done this way today,' no matter how changed are today's circumstances. He is always saying, "Now, let's stick to the facts. Let's have no speculation here." He is, as he sees himself, a clear-minded, right-thinking, unquestionably objective person.

Miserliness and penuriousness are not unknown in his behavioral repertoire. He has his little world and he wants to keep it and protect it from all possible incursions. "Mine is mine and yours is yours and don't you encroach upon my privacy." To encroach upon it is to bring forth his wrath. Ask him what his salary is or how much his home cost and see what happens. He gets along quite well in a mechanical, uncreative sense, so long as his well-ordered life is not disturbed; but any untoward stress is a serious threat to his equanimity, as anyone knows who has felt the brunt of his righteous, cutting tongue.

But please do not misunderstand. This man with his penchant for following prescriptions, for organization and efficiency is, at certain times, and in certain conditions of existence, a very necessary and valuable state for man's being. Man in this state is the perfect human organism upon whom to practice Frederick Taylor's 'scientific management.'[148] In fact, had not Taylor found his 'little Pennsylvania Dutchman' to demonstrate his conception of how to organize work, he would not have proven his point. Had it not been for others of the Dutchman's kind, American production in Taylor's day could never have become so eminently successful. This is emphasized so as to bring out again that each basic existential state is not an abnormal, necessarily undesirable state of affairs. It is not only a normal state of affairs, for certain conditions of existence, it is also a very necessary state for man to be in if certain human progress is to be made.

This form for being was not a detriment to America when its industry was beginning to burgeon, nor to Japan in its current state. In fact, those who have been striving to understand (a) the peculiarities in the Japanese character structure and (b) what there is about it that enables them to develop so fast industrially would do well to heed and study these words. But it is a detriment in much of America today. In fact, its existence is one of the most serious threats to America's peace and well-being. And it will one day, not too far away, become a detriment in Japan or elsewhere in the world where it exists. Dutiful, obedient, unquestioning, righteous man is to akin to the Judas Cow that leads others to go, unquestioning, to their slaughter. But he worries me today, for I fear he may awaken too late from his slumbering in properness and rightness to extricate himself from the human slaughter house into which his modern day Frederick Taylors, his all-knowing, not to be questioned authorities, have led him.

No one knew better the problems that accrue from this part of "The American Way of Life" than Frederick Taylor, and no one felt more that eventually it would have to go than the many of his guinea pigs who successfully operated within this way of being. In later years, Taylor was most forthright in speaking of the hate his methodology, the DQ/er management techniques, engendered in those upon whom it was used. Taylor told us how terrible it was to feel the hostility his methods engendered in those who followed without question, at least for a while, his organization for work. He knew well what was coming from those whose production increased say 180 percent when they truly realized their return for this increased effort was miniscule in comparison to what the company took as its share.

---

[148] Taylor, Frederick W. (1911). *The Principles of Scientific Management* (Chpt. 2). New York: Harper Bros..

Actually in E-C theory, Taylor's success with the 'Dutchman' and his like solved the existential problems of their lives and put them in a state of readiness to change. Then their realization of being used for the company's benefit became the dissonance in their field which spurred them to seek a higher level of being than the Taylor-like human automaton. This is one reason why this subsystem in "The American Way of Life" needs be laid aside. Its very existence on the American scene is one of the prime reasons why the seeds of violence are so widely sewn in our country. Righteous men profess a concern for their fellow man. But as they exercise their right way to get things done, they only temporarily improve the existence of their subordinates. They pay the employee more to take their orders, but they take a disproportionate return for the effort the employees have put forth. As a result a paradox is created. Improvement of the employee's state of existence reduces his fear and frees him to perceive that he is being taken. Thus he begins to show his resentment to his benefactor and his benefactor is insulted by his lessening appreciation. This builds into a vicious circle out of which our long series of labor management wars have developed. This is a situation we cannot long endure, and since its origin lies in the psychology of the Righteous State, then if we truly want to attack the problem of violence, this is one of its source points, which can be controlled provided we work to move man to a higher level of existence. But there are other reasons why righteousness must not continue to be the way for man to live.

One of the reasons stems from the psychology of the system. This is a rigid, tightly bound, singularly directed system which is always in a very tenuous balance - a balance which is sometimes maintained in very devious ways or sometimes explodes. In the second instance, out of this system comes Leopold-Loeb[149] horrendous crime, while out of the first instance arises the crime of the paragon of virtue who is unknown as a consorter with prostitutes, and as one who must unconsciously kill them. Also out of this system and its tenuous balance come many costly accidents and errors at work which organizations can ill afford.

Another reason I shall mention is that out of this system arises the ideological righteousness which has kept man, and still keeps man, on the brink or in the throes of war. So it is about time we moved beyond a way for living which has this as an integral part of its being. But it is the fourth reason which seems to be the most important one of all.

As long as man operates at this level, he will rear children so as to engender in them a strong element of hate. Thus, they will come into

---

[149] See Darrow and Levin.

adulthood and be studied, as by Freud and certain religionists, who will find in them this hostile, aggressive element which Freud named the death instinct and the religionists called original sin. This will, then, cause man to behave so as to bottle up what is seen as the innate perverseness of man. As a result, man will go on and on in the vicious cycle that leads to one man using another for his benefit, to horrendous crime and to war. It will prevent man forever from passing through the next two ER systems which he must get through if ever we are to learn that these negative aspects of man's behavior are induced and not necessarily innate.

For these reasons, I suggest this part of "The American Way of Life" must go. It must go because in its character as a system it sows the seeds for violence in ours or any society. If we want to be rid of the violence we know, and all that ensues therefrom, we must move man out of righteousness, through negativism and selfish independence, on into the higher states and those which come beyond. Mankind, in the more industrialized regions, can no longer afford the luxury of complete certainty of mind. Yet paradoxically enough, in other regions of the world where people need to solve lower-level existential problems, authoritarian certainty is the only possible way for people to move up. This paradox we must truly come to understand. It is not wrong for Righteous dictatorship to exist. It is necessary when certain conditions of existence accrue. The question is whether the existential conditions in Greece in 1970 warrant a military dictatorship.[150]

But, in America, at least most parts of it, and in much of the world, these conditions of existence have long since been passed by. Our need, that is the highly industrialized world's need, is not to know how to reestablish 'the good 'ole days' when man lived in the certainty of knowing what was right and that which was not. It is to know how to aid any man who is able or is striving to move up to do just that so as to leave behind the obsolescence of the righteous way of life. And our need is to fashion a way of existence whereby righteous man, who cannot change, still can have a meaningful place in a changing world. But let us look further at "Righteous Man," for there is still much we need to understand.

One aspect of righteous man's existence which should be abundantly clear by now is his love, marriage, and sex life. Quite obviously he will extend his ordered, idealizing way of existence to these realms. In fact, he orders them too much and so over-idealizes love and

---

[150] See Papandreou, Andreas (1970). *New Democracy at Gunpoint: The Greek Front.* York: Doubleday, and Vlachos, Helen. (1970). *House Arrest.* Boston: Gambit.

marriage that they become at times almost a mockery. Spontaneity is just not there. Marriage is an unalterable arrangement run on an authoritarian-submission basis, depending on which partner is dominant. Sex is to be pure and purposeful or duty bound, but not fun to be had, except that in this tight little system leakage quite often occurs in the form of perversion or other netherworldly affairs.

On the emotional and affective side, he is steadfast as a rock; but if one needs to move him from the position on which he stands, one finds the rock is anchored to the strata down below. He is practical if doing as is his bent, but resistant to creating if imagination is required. He is loyal beyond belief, but possessive to the nth degree. He is very patient and reserved, but quite suspicious and cold. When you go to his lectures at the university he is proper, always calm, and objective with every point well reasoned, every fact ordered in its place; but he is pedantic and dull as hell unless he wishes to scathingly bite at someone for disturbing his lecture by being one minute late. He believes a penny saved is a penny earned, and don't you try to get him to spend it lest you find his stinginess prevails. When life is going well he accentuates the positive, but when this world of ours is not all that he desires, then we find the negative comes quickly to the fore.

On an interpersonal level, if one does not disturb the sanctity of his rules, as I did with the custodian, righteous man is a polite, formal, very aware of his place, yet personable human being. But unfortunately for men who are different or who question the prescriptions of authority, man in the righteous state does not take a discriminating bite from the pork chop offered by authority; he swallows the whole hog. He accepts, *in toto*, the beliefs, preachments, and protestations of authority. He does so to such an extent that when authority changes the rules to say, as of now, 'let dissent be damned' where previously he said the rule was to allow its expression, the righteous one falls happily into line. When this becomes the rule, "The Silent Majority" becomes the arrogant voice of derision yelling in glee as authority says, through its 'effete snob,' insolent phraseology, "The rules are now: tear them apart! Let them have it! Shut them up!" Or their ultimate retort: "If you don't like it here - that is the way of our rules - then why don't you leave?"

When in position of authority, be it the school or university, the civil service position or in business, righteous man sets up rigidly defined external criteria for judging one's performance. At the college level, in the name of improving the intellectual atmosphere, I have heard them plead for or have seen them circulate petitions for a zero to one hundred point grading system or for a twelve point system when all research evidence indicates even the five point A, B, C, D, and F is notoriously unreliable. But at work, he sets up his standards for performance and unquestioningly accepts both their objectivity and their fairness. He believes he can, must, and does judge by objective criteria, even in respect to human behavior. Thus he protects himself when anyone should question his objectivity of judgment by one of the two major coping devices of the righteous man: rationalization and denial. When his judgment is questioned, he says most assuredly, "I simply applied the standards. You can't blame me for your failure to measure up. I don't set the standards, they do."

So far as righteous man is concerned, conflict must be dealt with promptly and with a strong hand. If one has conflict, the reason is 'soft leadership.' This man, when in position of authority, believes the way to get things done is to put the offender in a bind. The offender does as he is told or else he gets it. If it is the judge holding court, you shut up or you go to jail for contempt. If it is the defendant being righteous, you take his crap or you don't have any trial to carry on. If it's the student, he makes his non-negotiable demands. If it's the university president, he will talk to no one so long as the word 'demand' is being used. It is a win-lose world in which the righteous one lives, and it's only a matter of who wins as to who shall call the way the repression of the loser shall take place. Obviously this is a sorry solution to human problems because the victor must always increase pressure to keep the vanquished down, and the vanquished use all of their creativity, not toward human goals, but toward how to defeat the system under which the establishment of the moment is operating.

The pitiful thing about the win-lose psychology of righteous man is that other human beings get caught in the swirl of its vortex. Quieter, more constructively oriented people who can honestly see other ways are darned by the damners because they see that the castigator is not always right; but this means nothing to him, for he is never in doubt. In all seriousness, this problem is, at the time of this writing, a most distressing aspect of the American scene. What a shame it is that one must live today in a setting in which a Vice-President of the United States can see no more constructive way to make political hay than to resort to the methodology of the righteous man.[151] How better it would

---

[151] Probably a reference to Richard Nixon's Vice President, Spiro T. Agnew, who, beginning in the late 1960s, gave voice to words often prepared by Patrick Buchanan and William Safire for the administration. Agnew resigned in 1973 amidst a financial scandal related to his prior service as a Maryland state official. The Watergate affair followed a year later and led to Nixon's resignation from the Presidency.

be, not only for America but for mankind in general, if leadership could operate beyond this lower-level of existential being; but to bring this about is most difficult for oh-so-many reasons,

First of all, in a free society, the drive of righteous being - his strong achievement orientation and his ability to avoid allowing doubt to enter his mind - all mitigate against leaders coming to the fore who are not of this frame of mind. Secondly, of all the states of human existence by which man has come to live, hardly any is more difficult to change than is this state. Thirdly, we must face the facts of human existence, one of which is that no matter how much we might like that it be different, there are human beings so constituted that they cannot, within existing knowledge, be enabled to move beyond this road block to man's movement up.

These and other reasons face us today with one of the most serious of man's problems, namely, what does one do when he knows those who believe they are so right are just plain wrong? What does mankind do when that which he needs in order to exist is not righteous certainty of what is the way, but tremulous exploration in the direction of that which has never been?

Righteous man honestly believes that his rules - the rules - must be followed or chaos will ensue. He does not recognize that the ensuing chaos he is striving to avoid is that which would arise in himself and not that which he believes the behavior of other people will produce. This he cannot and does not see. He simply cannot see aggression in his words, "Those damned radicals. We ought all be rid of them," or in his hand as the righteous father says, "I am doing it for your own good" while he whales the hide off the kid. This exists, partially, because he avoids and disdains self-exploration. 'Why does a right thinking man have to look inside himself,' he asks? The fact of the matter is he scoffs at any such tender-minded introspection. A strong man, a good man, a right-thinking man knows his rightness; he does not have to probe why. And of him who does: "Well, I always thought there was something peculiar about Tom." "He's just not a man of his convictions," says the righteous, "or he wouldn't be questioning his stand."

All in all, the state of righteous existence is a most interesting one to explore, one which we could examine much more, but now we must ask, from whence does it come to be, how does it operate under stress and how best can one manage this system of behavior?

The Origins of the Righteous Existential State

As we have said, in all existential states nothing fails like success; therefore, successful saintly living creates the seeds of its own demise. Saintly man, provided he has the potential to move on, finds himself troubled by the conditions his saintly existence has created. Denial of self, abstinence, piety, bowing to his God's prescription for living improves immeasurably the conditions of the saint's existence. The diligent adherence to saintliness increases man's material well-being and as it does, it loosens within him those lustful human wants he has honestly cast aside, particularly his need for independence. This creates severe cognitive dissonance for saintly man. As long as he was truly miserable, it helped him to maintain his sanity to believe God meant it to be so in order to prove, by his endurance of it, that he was worthy of afterlife. *Having* was no problem for him so long as *not having* was a trial to test his worthiness for a more significant existence. But when adherence to the Godly prescriptions provides not assurance of the future but the beginning of affluence today, saintly man meets a most severe trial. For examples, Godrich and all the other saints who were the first to lay saintliness aside; he who has felt guilty over every little twinge of want, for every whimsical desire, a true existential problem is created when he begins to have. "How can I live," he asks, "when my life is so free of other living problems that I can feel sexual desire, or desire for independence from authorities' feelings when saintliness says it is wrong for me to feel these desires?" (The problem of celibacy in the Catholic Church today, for example.) "How can I explain my accumulation of worldly human things which I have promised to deny?" This is the ambivalent state into which man is cast when successful DQ living loosens within man those gnawing human wants which are an integral part of his nature,

Historically man's experience has brought him to know the woes of unbridled human wants, egoistic existences and other experience have taught him that denial, the saintly way, is the proper means to his ultimate satisfaction. Now man faces a new and different existential problem. Now he must ask, because of the conditions of his existence, how can I find a way for being when the need to express my human lustful desires is almost as strong as the belief they should be denied? How? His answer is: "Why, the way I've always done it, which is to create a new way for being out of this new existential state." So he proceeds to do just that.

Since he is spiraling back on his staircase to that position where the expression of the lustful drives of man is demanded, he must find a new and better way by which to handle them. Unbridled expression has proved wanting, and saintly denial is still a strong part of self. Thus, his new way for being recognizes that within self, strong forbidden desire is emerging, but in existential conditions where denial of self is still in the prime position. Of this existential mix - strong desires and belief they should be denied - he creates man's state of righteous conformistic existence.

The righteous state, like all other existential states, can be a way station on the way up, or it can be an equifinal resting place after a trip from the AN state. More probably, it is a state into which the person has been propelled by the over-demanding, over-controlling, over-accelerating, forced-maturing activities of the parental group. When the child is met with little or no approval when he tries to assert himself, when he is met with harsh and primitive and consistent discipline or consistently derisive deprivation of love if he disobeys, it makes cognitive sense for him to find a way in which to operate which the parents do not punish or condemn. And it is darned smart of him to adopt it, and only it, as the *right way* for living. If he did not do so, then he would be quite unable to function as a living human being. So in the developmental background of Righteous Man he learns first to avoid punishment, then he learns he can continue to avoid it if he does precisely that and only that which his parents do not punish. And out of this he learns not to stick his neck out, not to vary from that which works, not to do anything other than that which harsh experience has taught him is right - right in the sense that it is the right way to avoid punishment and guilt. Obviously such learning puts the person into a very narrow and circumscribed behavioral world, one where he has a limited number of behavioral options at his choice. Thus the question arises, what does "Righteous Man" do when *his right way* becomes inadequate to the task of living? In other words how does he behave when under stress?

Reaction to Stress in the Righteous System

Again, within E-C theory, what we have described is normal - a healthy state of affairs when certain conditions of existence prevail. Even those characteristics which seem negatively toned are but the normal responses to the ordinary stress of every day life. So, now it behooves us to look at the system when stress is more severe. Here, as in all systems, that which threatens the system, the symptomatic behaviors which arise, their meaning, and their purpose are specific to the system. So, first of all, we want to see what threatens the system.

This system is threatened when pressure is brought to bear upon the person to take a position opposed to absolutism, to the prescriptions of authority, or when there is ambiguity in the total field. This should not be a surprise to anyone, for the basis of the system is a highly ordered way of life built around the prescriptions of authority which are absolute and unquestionable.

With this in mind we want to look next at those coping devices which are used when the kinds of stress listed above, alone or in combination, throw the system out of equilibrium. We want to see what are the foremost devices the person settled in this system utilizes to restore his normal state of affairs, the normal DQ/er operational conditions.

Mild DQ system stress will increase the hostile feelings buried beneath the righteous one's facade. It will result in increasing his fear of punishment or disapproval which he fears will result if he expresses the hostility. His primary coping device is to increase the very proper kinds of behavior which have enabled him to avoid punishment in the past. If this does not reduce the threat and alleviate the negative feelings, he will displace his hostility on lesser lights. Or he may try to drive off the threat by driving away from himself those who are or he suspects may be the source of the threat. This he characteristically does by accusing them of mixing in his personal affairs, of attempting to pry, or of invading his privacy. In this manner he accomplishes two things. He gets rid of the threat and provides time for the threatening hostility to subside; and he prevents the threat from arising again by people learning to avoid him or at least "stay out of my personal affairs." To prevent the reoccurrence of threat, he restricts his routine even more than usual and holds fast to the known and the familiar. If he can't win by this he will set up, or strive to set up, new rules and regulations which will prevent the disturbing stimuli from occurring.

But if these basic coping devices do not work, if they do not remove the stress and leave him alone in his right little world, or if others do not know how to react to the system and thus do not hew to the rules for managing the righteous state, then more negative manifestations are precipitated. The sign that things are becoming rough are: anxiety will appear and be expressed, periods of severe doubt will arise, complaints directed at some other source arise, unconscious errors and mistakes or accidents arise, loss of control will ensue, temper will appear with periods of extreme outbursts. Then if the threat to the system continues to increase, bizarre obsessions and compulsions may arise, as may feelings of dissociation, conversion symptoms, phobic manifestations, hypochondriacal signs, or feelings of dejection. Or, if the stress continues, then the more serious systemic forms of pathology will ensue.

The righteous person becomes overtly anxious when he feels inner forces such as hostile feelings or desires about which he feels guilty threatening to break through. Here he fears that punishment which will come if they do. When he is overtly anxious, the usual way he handles it is to tie into his work whatever it may be. The housewife tears at the task of 'fixing up her home;' the husband drives himself at his work 'so as to see that everything is right;' and the student bears down to learn every insignificant detail 'so as not to miss a point.' If this absorption in work does not reestablish equilibrium, the righteous then uses that symptomatic device which is most congruent with his momentary existential state of being.

If what he needs is commendation, then he develops medical symptoms, hypochondriasis, and struggles on in *all the pain,* thus being commended for keeping the show on the road. If he perceives that facing the stress which is inciting his hostility is too much because if it continues he may erupt or be overwhelmed with guilt, then he avoids what it is by getting too tired or too sick to do the job. If the dynamics of the situation expect him to do what he believes will result in criticism of him, then he may develop private phobias, phobias the external observer does not know are present, phobias which enable him to avoid doing certain things, fear of sex relations or the like. But here all the external observer can see is a peculiar resistance to some quite usual human activity. Another time when the righteous will use a phobic device is when he is faced with having to do that at which previously he has failed - dating with boys, dating with girls. Here being afraid is better than being humiliated.

If he must make a decision where he cannot avoid going it alone without the aid or prior prescription of authority, then often he has a short-lived agitated depression. Here he both punishes himself for being angry at his deserting authority and he punishes authority and others by making them miserable about his depression. This intra, extra-punitive device is also used when the stress is fear of or anger over abandonment by his authority. But in both cases it is a very proper, very controlled agitated depression which is consonant with his existential state.

When the righteous utilizes conversion, he develops the more serious conversion symptoms: blindness rather than a pain in the back, paralysis of the legs rather than a tic. Here she develops frigidity and dutifully suffers through her husband's intrusion on her body. These conversion symptoms are noticeably different from those in other systems because of their severity and because the righteous scoffs them aside and doggedly carries on 'in the pain of it all.' Obviously two questions arise: Why severe? and Why scoff them aside? It seems that in this system the answer to the first is that the impulses welling up and about to break through are, for him, his cardinal sin, usually a desire to let authority have it. The answer to the second, "Well, what would you expect any right thinking, responsible, duty-following person would do? Why, he would carry on wouldn't he? How could any right thinking person do otherwise? He would never, not ever, shirk his duty."

Obviously, obsessive and compulsive behavior is the normal way of life in this righteous state of existence, but there are times when obsessive ideas and ritualistic compulsions become quite bizarre. Usually, in this state, this comes to be when the balance is so tenuous and the fear of expressing hostility and being caught so great that a constant leakage device must be used to maintain any semblance of systemic stability.

Hostile breakthrough, quite brutal in character, occurs when, because of current conditions, the energy for control is reduced to almost the least amount necessary to maintain the systemic balance and something unexpected happens or some unfeeling person pushes him beyond the limit of his righteous control. It is not too common for a breakthrough of explosive proportions to occur because hostility is rather generally leaked off in disciplining children, ranting at students, or condemning indolent, irresponsible employees.

Delusional behavior is rare because of how it arises. Usually the righteous will not make a mistake as to which authority to turn to for support. He is too cautious for that. But when he does, and either anticipates or experiences lack of support or disparagement, he may be given to a sporadic and disorganized display of persecutory delusions.

Depression is the ultimate solution to which he is apt to turn if things become too much for him to handle. Here he makes an agitated display for the approval he feels he is in danger of losing, or he makes his plea for a reestablishment of those conditions of existence in which he was in equilibrium. But in respect to the latter, again we find systemic disposition plays the major role. For the righteous, with his tendency towards over-control, holds himself tightly in tow when the death of a significant one occurs, only to tumble into despair months later as a result of some seemingly trivial matter.

There is one other device which the righteous utilizes, but I will reserve discussing it until the end of this chapter, for it has to do with the transition to the next existential state. So now let us look at managing the DQ over ER systems.

Managing the Righteous State

Obviously the Righteous Man will create a form of management congruent with his psychology, whether in a business, in the educational world as a teacher or instructor, or in the world of therapy. The Righteous Man decides what is to be done, by whom it is to be done, and when it is to be done. He is the planner, the director, and the controller. He is the teacher who says in words or in action: "I talk. You listen. I tell you what to learn. You learn it. I drill you in it and you take my exams to show that you know it. If you don't I'll tan the hide off of you."

The organizational structure is, as in all DQ states, pyramidal with a very rigidly ordered superior-subordinate relationship defined by the medium of rigid job description or the like. Decisions are made on high and are communicated mostly and formally in writing, though at times by direct order. If someone disagrees with that which is ordered and remains recalcitrant and is lower in the hierarchy, exhortation or persuasion might be utilized or, more often, being told to shape up or ship out squelches him. Discipline is defined and is swift and sure for any who break the rules. No "soft headed" human relations are exercised here, even though the righteous one may and often does see himself as a kind and humane task master, he is, he says, "doing it for your own good" because his experience tells him you will be better off if you do it his way. Challenge of authority is not permitted because the person is being paid to do as he is told. Rigid lines of responsibility, authority, and accountability are drawn, and woe unto he who oversteps the bounds of his assigned role. This is true even for the higher bosses unless he can make it stick, for this is a win-lose world. What the underlying wants, would like to do, or the like has nothing to do with what shall be done. The organization, the authority rules supreme. The assigned power of the moment decides and from there on the only thing left is to get it done.

In earlier days, and in some places today, organizational desires were forced by means of the final sanction, "If you don't like it leave. On second thought, you're fired!" Or, "I was going to flunk you anyhow." But today, at least in the workday world and in some protected position like civil service, tenured teaching, or protective labor contracts, the squeeze play is used. He shapes up as he is told to or he is informed his performance appraisal will be negative today, next year, and ever after. This, what Blake and Mouton call 9-1 management,[152] works today only where there is surplus labor or in a societal setting as Japan where the vast majority of people are in the DQ over ER states.

In fact, the two worlds in America where it can truly be exercised are in untenured managerial and administrative positions and in schools. It worked in the past when labor was surplus and unorganized and man was in a frightened or frightenable state, but it is quite difficult to implement in many parts of the world today because too many protections against arbitrary authority have been built into societies. Yet I have never attended a management or administrative meeting where some or many have not rued the day of its passing. At these meetings some have always said, if not in precise words in their meaning, "We sure could get things done around here if only we could use the tried-and-true methods of management. There's nothing wrong here that a good dose of discipline would not take care of."

But again, don't misunderstand me; this is not a bad form of management. It becomes bad only when it is used in a non-congruent setting. In fact it is a necessary form of management when the work force is in the CP state. And it is even a good form of management, if softened a little, when subordinates are in the righteous state. I mean by this that when people are in the conditions of the CP state, as we saw earlier, their psychology is such that only strict authoritarian ways will get the job done. And I mean that when people are in the DQ over ER states, benign autocracy is the means to the end of productive results. But, in either instance, if the recipient of the management or education or whatever is open and not closed, then this form of management is relatively short-lived. This is because its very success improves the state of existence of the recipient and causes him to begin to challenge its "papa knows best" way of doing things.

Thus managing the person in the righteous state is a matter of what his state is *within* the state of righteous being. If, so far as present knowledge is concerned, the person is unalterably closed within this state, then it is only fair and decent that this man, that all men in such a state of existence, be allowed to be. It is proper that they should be

---

[152] Blake, Robert and Mouton, Jane (1964). *The Managerial Grid: Key Orientations for Achieving Production through People.* Houston: Gulf Publishing Co..

managed by close supervision and control which is humane, not harshly punitive. They should be placed in positions, that is jobs, classrooms, study programs or the like, where their mechanical efficiency is of value, where holding to the rules is an asset for them, not a liability. They should be provided with clear and unambiguous directions as to what, where, when and how their responsibility is to be performed. And, once there, they should be protected from disruption or disturbance. They should be told clearly and unambiguously what the rules are and what penalties will be exercised for their violation.

If rules are violated, the penalty should be swiftly, quietly exercised with their privacy protected. If not, the person's guilt will unconsciously overwhelm him and drive him to commit some grievous error, have an accident or the like. For Righteous Man must be punished by himself or authority when he has done wrong, otherwise he cannot return to equilibrium.

If the person is closed down in the system, changing him is a very difficult thing to do. Basically the procedure is to reduce the threat to the system. Since threat comes from pressure to oppose authority or absolute rules and from an ambiguous world, then these must be reduced. Here one does not act as a punitive authority. He does not punish or condemn the person for anything he does. He takes a *long time* to assure the person in action he is a non-punitive, non- remonstrative authority. He becomes the epitome of the psychoanalytic father figure. After he has been accepted and has come to be trusted, he slowly teases, urges the person to test whether he will be punished if he talks about his bad desires or castigates authority. One does all this in a private setting to protect the person. One reassures him it is all right to express bad thoughts and encourages him to do so to the degree that does not frighten the person. Then as feelings are expressed, one provides other ways to express it in a controlled situation. But there is a problem here.

We have no way of really telling whether the person is alterably or unalterably closed except to provide him the opportunity to change. If he has that opportunity, in the proper setting as described above, and then does not change, we are left to conclude that he is unalterably closed. But if he opens up, if his shell is broken, then he is as any open DQ over ER person and we proceed to use the methods which now induce movement up.

If the person is now open, or in the righteous state as a way station on the way up, then gentle but continuously increasing disturbance of his *status quo* must be interjected into his field. But vacillatory response and error must be expected as he tests reality for moving up. He who aids this person must encourage him in every step out of his routine ways but never remonstrate, humiliate, or punish no matter the resulting behavior, particularly if it is evidence of freeing himself from authorities' prescriptions. Then, if this happens, reward him in the beginning but then intermittently. If he makes mild or serious errors as he makes his own decisions, work through with him quietly and considerately where his attempt went wrong and how the desired step can be taken without recurrence of that error, yet indicating all the while that errors are expected, that they are wanted, and that if they occur he will be protected from their consequences. But always, ever always, keep communicating the expectation that more mistakes will occur before he will feel secure in another way of life.

To help the person in the righteous state break his rule-bounded dependency, teeny-weeny steps, not giant steps, is a part of the way. One does not jump on his rule boundedness as in some reality therapies. One does not throw him to the wolves of a probing group experience. One does not toss him early in the process into an intra-psychic reorganization therapeutic situation. One first establishes a non-threatening, trustful relationship with the individual in mind. Then slowly, oh so slowly, backtracking whenever necessary, one picks some old outmoded rule or prescription which the person is still following, one which his authority has followed before and has now cast aside. Then he teases, urges and entices the person toward breaking it. He carefully and consistently protects the person from any harm or condemnation that might come to be for violation of the rule. Then gradually, oh so gradually, one encourages the person to dare a little more. Careful support and encouragement, ready backing off at the first sign that threat is being felt, is a procedure not to be broken when working with the righteous. Any attempt to probe down into the emotional and motivational dynamics of the state tends not to work unless the needed trust is previously established by the supportive kind of relationship described above. Even then, deep probing psychoanalysis for example, may not work because of the marked capacity of this state for avoiding significant exploration of its inner forces by surface intellectualization.

If we do not hew very closely to the rules for managing the righteous, we can easily precipitate this normal state into more negative manifestations. But negative manifestations are peculiar in this system. What we want to avoid is negatively returning to righteous behavior. What we want to see come is true negativism. We want to see him begin to fight against authorities' rules. But we must not hurry him on too fast lest the negativism settle into that of the catatonic like behavior where he rigidly shuts down on some or many of his motoric processes. We want to avoid this active kind of negativism and see arise the vacillatory kind or the passive kind where he quietly pursues, on his own, the condemnation of authority.

This peculiar negativism is the most seriously misunderstood of righteous man's symptomatic displays, the one so often referred to as the most serious of all when, within E-C theory, it is the truly healthy sign. When righteous man quits seeking commendation from the authority which he has previously revered and followed; when he begins to be negative, impulsive, erratic, and unpredictable; when he begins to transfer his hostility onto authority and away from self and no longer onto subordinates, then this behavior, which authority is bent on eradicating, means righteous man is growing. He is headed for the next rung in man's existential ladder. Would that righteous men could see that the Black militant, the disturbingly activist student, the insulting defendant in the courtroom, in the early stages of their negativism, are striving to grow, not destroy. Would that authority could see that at this critical point in man's emergence, a new state of being, the oppositionist negativistic stage - a higher-level stage, not a breakdown in values - is striving to become. Would that authority could see that now is the time to put the person on his own; now is the time to urge him to try to do and change things himself.

But this righteous man cannot do, for he does not understand E-C theory nor that growth is the discard of the righteous way of life for a temporary life of opposition, our next existential state.

ER

Chapter 11

The Multiplistic Existence — The ER State

The 5th Subsistence Level

Theme: *Express self for what self desires, but in a fashion calculated not to bring down the wrath of others.*

The *'Express self for what self desires without shame or guilt'* Conceptions

In the absolutistic existential state man questions why he was born to live only to find satisfaction later or in his afterlife. "Why can't man have some enjoyment now?" is a question he asks. He asks this question when a successful, fourth-level, ordered form of existence improves his state of being. When this question arises in the mind of man, the sacrificial ethic is doomed to decay, and it is readied for discard. But man's values are not gone, as our theory says, because man plods on to another level, now slipping, now falling in the quest for his goal—a better form of human existence. From such questioning he moves into the multiplistic existential state, the ER, fifth subsistence level, the state of materialistic existence which first appeared 600 - 700 years ago.

In my way of thinking, the Industrial revolution was a result of the failure of the more medieval forms of life to solve the problems of existence. When that occurred, the human had to develop a different way of thinking. You see, if you don't believe that the powers that be or The Power that is knows everything, knows all the rules as to how to live, then you have to begin to think that maybe you know something too, or at least somebody else knows something about how to live. So they started to switch. People who made this move began to switch from the absolutistic way of thinking to what we call the multiplistic existential state.

Now, the multiplistic way of thinking is very similar in some respects to the absolutistic where the person thinks there is one right way to think and the only one right way, and if you don't think that way you are going to get into serious trouble; whereas in the multiplistic state, man thinks there are many different ways you can think about something, but there is just one good way you should think about things. And this business of allowing for many ways to think about something allowed for people to experiment with the world in different ways. An experimental system developed, and so it was this thinking that led to the Industrial Revolution. Tremendous changes in human thinking took place at this particular time in existence.

It is in the ER state where man must assert his independence as a person. In the multiplistic existential state man strives not to conquer the dragonish world through raw, naked force as he did at the CP level, but to conquer it by learning its secrets. In the CP system of thinking it's the power of self; here, in the ER system of thinking, importance lies in the power of ideas, the power of ways and means of changing things, not raw power. They are both expressive systems and share this characteristic.

He tarries long enough here to develop and utilize the objectivistic, positivistic scientific method so as to provide the material ends to a satisfactory human existence in the here and now for those who merit it. Careful testing rather than arrogant affirmations or logical reasoning teaches him what is right. Materialistic values derive naturally from this *thema* in the multiplistic existential state. They are the values of accomplishing and getting, having and possessing. The authority of one's own tried and true experience replaces professed authority, or divisive authority.

This level emerges when the D problems of creating order, the need for lasting order and everlasting security, are fulfilled by the theophilosophical prescriptives of authority or when higher authority does not solve the problems of everlasting peace and creates the problem that God's word alone is not enough to achieve lasting order and security. Rigid, dogmatic, authoritarian leadership blocks those developing feelings of self which begin to emerge. This produces problems in the individual for having to adhere to authoritarian ways. And, it arises from the problem created by the fact of death, which a developing consciousness begins to question. This creates the E problems, the problems of needing to know more than God's word in order to handle pestilence and nature's vagaries. Expressing of self is seen as necessary to carry out what God designed but did not control.

This desire and need for self-expression, doubt about the prescriptions and answers of authority, and the fact that lower classes have little pleasure in life and the higher classes cannot be certain of afterlife, activates the R neurological system—the multiplistic existential state. The person asks: "Is this the only life I will ever live and, if so, why can't I have some pleasure in this existence?" This leads to the activation of the R system which provides for the beginning of dispassionate, objective, hypothetico-deductive, not moralistic-prescriptive thinking. This leads to thinking in an ER rather than the absolutistic, DQ, manner. That is, there are *many ways to think,* but only *one best way* rather than only *the right* or *the wrong* way.

At the multiplistic existential state, man's free will meets the barrier of external conditions as well as the assertion of the will by others. In the ER state man perceives that his life is restricted by his limited control of the physical universe and his lustful human drives. To satisfy the latter, his materialistic aim, he must conquer the first. Man's freedom of action emerges, not only one's own but that of others too, and of this is born man's materialistic state of existence. Rationalistic multiplistic man who "objectively" explores his world comes to be. The fifth level of existence spawns the pragmatic, utilitarian, power over man and nature values. The means to the end is rational, objective positivism, that is, scientism. At this stage, secular values become supreme. The power figure of the state, the business, the organization, rules. The objective mind, the rational mind, the mechanistic, the positivistic is revered. This pragmatic, scientific, utilitarianism is the dominant mode of existence in the United States today.

Fifth-level man seeks to analyze and comprehend: not to explain 'why,' but to learn 'how' so as to change what is. At the fifth level, he values equality of opportunity and the mechanistic, measuring, quantitative approach to problems, including man. He thinks it is right to receive and aspire beyond what one's assigned class permits. He values gamesmanship, competition, the entrepreneurial attitude, efficiency, work simplification, the calculated risk, the scheming and manipulation. Nothing is for sure until proven so. There are as many possible value systems as there are people evolving. But these fifth-level, self-centered values are not the "to hell with the other man," egocentric values of the third system. Here he is careful not to go too far. He avoids inviting rage against him. He sees to it that the loser gets more than scraps but never as much as he.

The theme of existence becomes: *Express self for what self desires but in a fashion calculated not to bring down the wrath of* [important or influential] *others*. Materialistic values flow from this *thema*. They are values of accomplishing and getting, having and possessing. An important means value is achievement of control over the physical universe so as to provide for man's material wants. This is the dominant mode of existence in America today.

The few, and there are few in the beginning, lift themselves to the fifth system through their own efforts. As a result, they see themselves as unquestionably superior to others. After all, they alone have brought themselves to this exalted position by superior use of their own energies —right? They were not born to be; they were made by their own efforts. Therefore, they conclude that they are indeed superior; they are destined to lead, not by Divine plan but by proven superiority.

Examples of ER Conceptions

The conceptions of this state are dogmatic, absolutistic for a period of time, pragmatic, but experimentalistic. Although man at the multiplistic existential state has lost the behavioral rigidity of the fourth system, he nevertheless retains the dogmatic component derived from his perception of self as all-powerful. If the person changed his opinion, he became absolutistic in another way. But whatever he said about the healthy personality at that time, that, by God, was it! Generally speaking, what is healthy is what works.

In the study, fifth-level man demonstrated above anything else a will to power. He values action and risk, force and energy. He believes in and demands complete loyalty to the secular power source and that one should "rule by the book" if one is in power. At the same time, he believes that the ends are more important than and justify the means—c*aveat emptor*—let the buyer beware—"business is business." Push it just as far as you can, and if the other guy gets hurt, well, just hope that you haven't hurt him so much that he is going to raise hell about it and get back at you. That's the way of thinking.

Belief in profit, rugged individualism, nationalism, and federalization are expressed in this system - one's own self interest prevails. This system pretends that "mine own self interest" is really the interest of others. It's most pronounced in the entrepreneurial thinker, in him who thinks he can come up with some new way of thinking, a new way of conducting business, a new way of doing anything, and if this works then he's got a right to it. So, it's the typical entrepreneurial marketplace way of thinking. It's the physician who is more a businessman than a physician. He is more interested in the price of his stocks that day or the real estate deal he's preparing to close than he is the medicine. It's very definitely an expressive system.

This is one nodal version of the typical fifth level:

Nodal ER Conception -

> "After giving rational thought to what is the mature personality I have come to the following list of characteristics which add up to what it is.
>
> 1. The major characteristic of the mature person is that he is an independently operating individual. He goes it alone, so there is no such thing as a mature person. There are only people who behave maturely in their various ways.

2. The mature does what has to be done. He is not held back in his actions or judgments by that which other people do or believe.[153]

3. The mature does not accept without questions existing data, theories or practices.[154]

4. He is energetic, outspoken and expressive of what he believes regardless of where others stand.

5. The mature does for himself and thinks for himself. He does not look to others for their guidance or support and he does not need their acceptance or acclaim.

6. The mature person is absolutely objective. He does not let his emotions interfere with what has to be done. He is an acting person who keeps feelings out of his actions. He goes by the facts as they are not by sentimentality. He does not get entangled in emotional problems, his or others.

7. The mature personality is goal directed. He knows what he wants to do and does what he has to, to get there. He does not resign himself to his fate or surrender to the inevitable.

8. The mature person does not conform to arbitrary standards. He conforms to what he has established to be right. He goes by his data until his data proves him wrong and then he changes however the data demand that he change.

9. The mature person is not afraid to do what has to be done. If a person has to be told his weaknesses, the mature person does so without being squeamish. He does not go out of his way to spare feelings. When people need to be shaped up, a mature person shapes them up. Wanting to be liked is not a weakness of the person who is mature.

---

[153] CWG: Notice the similarity to the third level, but that the extreme aggressiveness is not present. It's still there, almost the same kind of words, but it is a different inflection in them.

[154] CWG: Notice how different this is from the fourth level, where the person is supposed to accept what authority says.

10. The mature person does not feel guilty or ashamed for doing what rationally has to be done.
11. The mature person being rational and objective is a shrewd appraiser of that which is to his best interests.
12. The mature person accepts that he is human but he controls such tendencies when it is to his welfare to do so. He does not get sentimental and maudlin about such tendencies. He controls them himself.
13. The mature person has a reasoned, risk taking, calculating mind. He uses objective procedures to make his decisions. He places faith in that which he knows works, he does not get caught up in non-workable theory or speculation.
14. He is not afraid to stand alone, even in opposition to others, but he plans so as to have the best chance then goes ahead regardless of what others say or what effect it has.
15. The mature person is not afraid to get his hands dirty in order to do what has to be done. He plays hard when he plays and he plays to win, but he does not waste his time in activities which he sees as hopeless.
16. He is not satisfied with yesterday's ways unless he has found them to work and he holds to them only so long as he sees them to work.
17. The mature person is not one who resigns himself to his fate or surrenders to the inevitable. He changes his course rather than accept what works against him. He never gives up control to his environment. He seeks rather to get the control that will enable him to do what he knows needs to be done."

The fifth level is quite a different system. They don't think like the previous group that said there's only a right way to think about something and a wrong way to think about something. They don't think in an absolutistic fashion. They think in what we call a multiplistic fashion, meaning they accept that there are many ways of doing something. They will respond in ways which show a tendency to think in alternative ways. There are responses which show that the person accepts that there are more ways than one to do a thing, but there is one best way to do it, as contrasted to an absolutistic response.

They have a tendency to look at things in more than one way, but the decision as to how to look is always determined by what is good for the self. It always is based on the self-reference. One's own self-interest determines responses which show: "To thine own self be true."

They have a high, but not unrealistic, level of aspiration and a multiplicity of values which are acceptable based on context and expedience. They often lack conscience constraints while maintaining high autonomy and will tend to be independent operators without constraints of other people or authority—'an island unto the self.' The tone will show a tendency to want to express anger, but it is obviously modulated.

At the multiplistic existential level, interpersonal relations are very tenuous because of trust issues. They see life as an experience in which one should disassociate oneself from others. One should go it alone and have absolute self-sufficiency. It is important for one to stand on one's own feet. It is important that one not be dependent. It is important that one evidences his independence, his ability to think on his own. They are striving for complete autonomy. So, they think in terms of struggling out from under others or in terms of struggling to free self from others. They think in terms of struggling to free self from restriction, but not from what we call ego encroachment. They never yell about, "You're taking away my identity." They just say, "Get off my back. I don't want you trying telling me what to do."

They are critical and cynical, delivering cold, quantitative evaluation and often-harsh feedback to others. They have a disdain for empathy and, as opposed to the egocentric system, they will do odds-calculations and realistic probabilities, not brash risk-taking. If you know the ER level, you know that one of the primary characteristics of a person attempting to come fully into the ER level is to be stubborn as hell about changing his mind, and then suddenly he'll flip-flop. He never changes as a result of feedback, only self-generated choices. He will maintain self-evaluation, even in the face of negative information and evidence that his self-image is inaccurate.

The person at this level has moved beyond giving and receiving to objective viewing of self, of activity around self, and of one's own activities. He believes it is right for self to receive because guilt over receiving has been worked through. A person operating at the fifth level has no compunction whatsoever about taking whatever he can get. He doesn't feel guilty to sit at a supper table and take more from a little kid if the kid can be inveigled into giving up what he's got, well fine, go ahead and do it.

The person at the fifth level sees all life as a game and that the big task in the game is to figure out how to circumvent the rules in order to win. This person very frequently shows actions which others perceive as hostile. If you saw this person in operation you would say, "My God, how can a person behave in such a hostile fashion?" You go up to this person and say, "Jim, how can you behave that way? How can you be so mean?"

"I'm not mean," he'd reply. "There isn't a mean bone in my body. Never did a mean thing in my life."

You can sit there and see it yourself and say, "God, they're hurting these other people." The person has almost no capacity to perceive that he or she is hurting that other person.

Since fifth-level man values above all else the will to power, to action, to risk, the use of force and energy are its means. Since he believes that the power to change rests in the superior talents of the few, he scoffs at weakness and lack of drive. To him it is better to act and fail than suffer the ignominious shame of not having tried. To him the practical is so important that he ridicules the subjective or the ideal. But man at this level has much of the fourth level still within him. There is a moral overtone to his values. In the name of morality he assumes his rights, and in the name of morality he forces them onto others. This he believes is right because he conceives that 'God's' purpose is shown when success is brought to him who conquers the world.

One finds them as the divine right of kings, the unassailable prerogatives of management, and the inalienable rights of the parent. His values take many schematic forms since they were pragmatically established by those who gained power by exercising them - the theme 'survival of the fittest' rules. In fact, in the multiplistic state this Darwinian concept is seen as nature's signal that these power values are correct. But to other men this is not an ethic; it is prime immorality.

In many conceptions of value this ethic of selfish concern for one's own welfare through organization, manipulation and control is seen as man's most unhealthy behavior; whereas, in this point of view, we see it as a most necessary step forward in the moral growth of man. Certainly, it leads to war, in all its nastiest forms, as one figure or group in power sees his rights infringed by the rights which another person or group sees as their own. It places the masses in the position of a pawn in the power ethic of the few—but its positive side must not be overlooked.

Successful fifth-level men may improve immeasurably the conditions of human existence. They create wealth, techniques and come by knowledge for better human living conditions which accrue because man has now developed materialistic values. Thus, in the frame of reference of E-C theory, the crass materialistic values of the "The Status Seeker"[155] are not something to decry. Instead, they signify the improvement of the human condition. They are something we should work for lower-level man to come to have. They are not something we should condemn when they appear.

You have to look at the ER system and keep in mind that it is a way of thinking that opens the individual up for becoming what one would call quite highly successful in this world. It opens the person up for changing the world, and making it a better world, and conquering the problems of disease and poverty or appearing to move in the direction of conquering them. Science was part and parcel of multiplistic thinking. You couldn't possibly have any real science, as we know it, in absolutistic thinking, because science by its very nature is doubting. The allowance for many ways of thinking and for these many ways of thinking to be tested out must exist for there to be any kind of science; and this is what came with the emergence of the fifth level of human existence. So, it solves the problems of existence that are the fifth-level problems, the problems of getting the knowledge that is necessary to live not by the way that God says, not by the way that nature ordains or anything of that sort, but by the way that knowledge and information says that the individual should live. So, this accumulation of knowledge and information tremendously improves the state of human existence.

Many men see the regressive disorganization of fifth-level values as the ultimate sign of man's depravity. What Kant saw when the fifth-level emergence began led him to recoil and try to establish a new fourth-level scheme. It led Schopenhauer to his pessimistic view of man's values and Freud to the postulation of the Death Instinct. Fourth-level man sees, as did Freud, the ultimate destruction of all that is good in man as fifth-level wants begin to impel man to seek a new form of existence.

As man casts aside the inhuman aspects of his sacrificial ethic, it is as if a feeling of power surges through him—a feeling of power derived from the relative security of the absolutistic, ordered existence. In the

---

[155] Probably a reference to Packard, Vance (1959). *The Status Seekers: An Exploration of Class Behavior in America and the Hidden Barriers That Affect You, Your Community, Your Future.* New York: David McKay Company, Inc.

beginning this surge takes what fourth level calls an unethical form. The Saints of the church could not stand their saintliness and the current better-off Russian started to employ, clandestinely, the profit motive. Schopenhauer for one, tried to institutionalize this absolutistic to multiplistic transitional state; but, his pessimistic, giving up of self, overcoming selfish desire, form of values was not enough for men of the Adlerian "Will to Power." The Saints became more than unsaintly; they became hedonistic, greedy men. The communist worker demanded his share, and the communist farmer sought more than the commune. Here the world and all its things and its entire people become the tools of self interest. In the multiplistic state man's focus is on providing a better material life here on earth, not for later and not in the hereafter. In the course of using the world to his earthly self-interest he perceives ultimately that his actions produce some unwanted reactions.

One could propose, with descriptive design, that fifth-level values be called the Machiavellian system, the ethic of Might is Right. Machiavelli's time on earth coincided with western man's breakout from the dark ages, a time when occidental man started his tortuous climb from the ordered state of existence to higher levels of operation. It is perhaps more than chance that we call this period the Renaissance. It was indeed a rebirth for many of western man. They were reborn to be human, not just another cog in a tightly ordered metaphysical scheme. But we cannot rest by calling fifth-level values the Machiavellian system. At another time, in other places, the same emergence took place. Hegel schematized it another way, the American "Robber Baron" another and the Japanese diet and some Japanese government officials show it still in another form. Thus they spawn a modification of the power ethic, a state of existence derived from the individual's ability to produce at will and based on what can be called the *domestication* of power.

One should point out, at this stage, that failure to recognize Machiavellian principles as an ethic because of the usual restrictive interpretation of the word *ethical* may be a major reason why those who have attempted to find order in ethical systems have not been too successful. Within the conception of man presented herein, acceptance of Machiavellian principles as an ethical system, albeit difficult, is essential to understanding conditions in many organizations today.

He who lives by the power ethic believes that the power to change rests in the superior talents of the few, those few who are capable of using force to obtain desired ends. Power is virtue. It is better to act and fail than to suffer the ignominious shame of not having tried. To be in the throes of the power ethic, a successful organization can be established and maintained only through the cunning use of force. He believes that competition is the spice of life. He believes that those who demonstrate that they are superior in the use of power have the right to set the rules, make the laws and to force the weaker to pursue the ends outlined by the superior person. To him, it is right not to keep faith when to do so would harm his own self-interests. It is right to deceive and it is right to connive if such is necessary to achieve one's goal. Fraud and manipulation are necessary means to the end, and cruelty and fear are only tools to be properly applied. He organizes, directs and controls through the media of force and fear, while attempting to avoid the reaction of hate, never mind needing to be loved or liked. He values the practical, the utilitarian and scoffs at the theoretical or idealistic.

The few, and there are few in the beginning, who are able to gain their freedom from sacrificial values, surge uncontrollably forward into a new form of existence, a new value system. As they do so it seems to many that the world of morality has been torn asunder. But a positive sign must not be overlooked. As these few surge forward, and as some of them are successful in their Will to Power, they tend to drag after them, through their success, the masses unable to free themselves from the burden of staying alive—first into the fourth and later into the fifth level of existence. Thus, no matter what one's judgment of the power or pragmatic ethic, as described here, it can contribute much to the ultimate welfare of mankind. In fact, it seems the most necessary of all stages for man's movement to higher levels.

Fifth-level man is the man of action, the risk-taker. He is a practical man who accomplishes, through action, that of which he dreams. He worships the great god, Power. He uses his own power to organize the energy of others and things and, when successful, greatly improves the conditions of his existence. As a result of such success, he comes to believe that he is superior to others. He believes a successful endeavor can be maintained only by the cunning use of force, and that he, who is superior in the use of power, has a right to name the game, set the rules, define ends, etc.

In the ER state man enjoys mapping the territory of experience but shies from intense personal experiencing itself. He is uncomfortable sensing the whole as more than its parts. He prefers to add up his or her own conception of the parts and stick to that by breaking things into parts so as to understand and control them. Man at the ER level thinks beyond giving and receiving to objective viewing of self, others, things, activity around self and one's own activities.

He thinks in terms of real concern for others so long as such thinking does not hurt self. He tries to analyze and comprehend and in so doing to become impersonal and distant. He spawns a rational-economic, bargaining, self-promoting conception for managing life's problems. He sees the world in terms of intra-psychic separation from others. He thinks in terms of disidentifying self from earlier ways of thinking and doing and of rearranging things to suit self. He sees himself as struggling to free self from others. These are struggles to free self from actual restriction, not ego-encroachment. He lives so as to express self but by avoiding serious trouble when so doing. His actions are perceived by others to be hostile, but he is unaware of his hostility and denies its presence.

He believes he has the right to force the weaker to pursue his ends. He thinks in terms of it being right to receive and to aspire beyond what one's class is. He permits desire and action to go beyond one's status. Guilt over being and wanting recedes. He behaves in terms of not receiving or not following "the word." The life of man in the multiplistic system revolves around competition and achievement in a personal sense. 'Bend the rules, don't break them,' is the dictum. Promote the individual self but carefully.

Learning in the Multiplistic State

According to E-C theory, the Levels of Existence point of view, the psychology of the human being is an unfolding or emergent process marked by the progressive subordination of older behavioral systems to newer, higher-order systems. The human tends normally to change his psychology as the conditions of his existence change. And, the significant changes that take place are more on the order of how the person thinks than what the person thinks or what information he possesses. He learns differently and needs to be managed differently as he passes through each existential state. This holds true for the person living in the multiplistic, ER state.

Those at the ER level introduce situationalism and relativism into their way of thinking. To them there may be many answers to a problem, but there is one best answer. They think in terms of analyzing, and wanting to comprehend in an impersonal, objective, distant, rational, positivistic manner. They see life, and thus learning, as a game that has precise rules that if mastered will enable them to win the game. They think in terms of breaking things into parts, and they prefer to add up their own conception of the parts.

When the E neurological system centralizes and dominates man's behavior, when the ER, multiplistic state comes to be the way of life, man's learning changes once again from what it was at the absolutistic state. At this level it is what psychologists call the latent, the signal learning, system that must be utilized to direct man's learning. Once again man learns in an active manner, but not in the active, aggressive, immediate reward, no-punishment fashion of the CP system. At this level the patterning of stimulation, changing and challenging ideational content, and the degree to which outcomes meet the person's expectations are the major motivating factors.

At this level of operation man can wait for delayed reward if the learning activity is under his own control, not evaluated by ones in positions of authority, and replete with perceptual novelty. Here learning does not have to be tied to a specific need state, nor is it dependent on the amount of consummatory activity or immediate reward. The keystones are the opportunity to learn through his own efforts, the presence of mild risk, the individual's experience, and much variety in the learning experience. Here it is the work of D. K. Adams,[156] E. C. Tolman and his students, and Julian B. Rotter and his students, whose work must be mastered by he who develops learning systems for those centered in the multiplistic existential state.

Since the R system follows these principles, the individual must be allowed to experience things for him or herself in order to learn. That which influences the individual centralized at the fifth level to learn or change is the individual's own experience. They could also learn from a self-professed authority of an amateur who talked as if he knew something about a topic but really didn't know a damned thing about what he was talking about. Those at the multiplistic level would never pay any attention to anybody that knew anything about what was going on because authority must be challenged and questioned. Man in the ER state always has an opinion that came from my experience, or that came from what 'my barber says,' 'what my hairdresser says.' Some amateur that shouldn't even be having any experience in that area was an effective teacher and change agent for a person in the fifth level!

Management of the Multiplistic State

The success of this society to date has been because we had an accidental congruence between leadership that had a higher degree of

---

[156] Adams, D.K. (1954).

fifth-level characteristics in it and followers that had a higher degree of fourth level in their makeup. So, these people just fit perfectly. Here was a leader with tremendous need to accomplish something, that's the fifth level, and here is someone operating in the fourth level who has a tremendous need to follow someone else, to be dependent; it fit magnificently and made our society into the successful thing it is. But, we are in serious trouble with it today. We are in serious trouble because the leaders have continued to be at the fifth level, or to have a higher degree of the ER state in them, and the very success of their leadership has pushed a large mass of the followers on beyond that level and they can't stand that way of thinking.

So, we have leaders who are actually psychologically following and falling behind. They often make the assumption that multiplistic thinking is leadership. Of course that's leadership only of people who think in a particular fashion. "Men and women at the [fifth] level of behavior act and think in very different ways from [fourth]-level people. These ways are well known to most managers. An employee at the [fifth] level believes in the power of self. He believes that he can alter the established order through the exercise of his own will. He no longer sees himself as having to fit into some prescribed organizational design …He believes that those who can prove this hand of God through accomplishment deserve all that their success can bring them; those who fail are simply ordained to submit themselves to rules made by the favored few."[157]

This multiplistic existential system spawns bureaucratic management. Bureaucratic management is management based on the assumption that the world and its organisms are machines. Objectively arrayed knowledge provides for the control of organizations. Tested experience and objective knowledge will make for the properly designed machine, and keeping it well-oiled will make for productivity and gain profits. Management at the ER state is characterized by: simplification, specialization of function, objective qualification for position, interchangeability of parts, and objective evaluation of performance.

Those in the fifth existential state are very different persons than those in the fourth—they are readily open to change. The way to change the resisting fifth-level man was well illustrated in the Bell and Gossett case reported to you at last year's [Fourth Annual Value Analysis] conference.[158] You may recall Barry's speech of last year. He spoke of the cold reception the Bell and Gossett engineering department gave to

---

[157] Graves, Clare W. (1966). The Deterioration of Work Standards. *Harvard Business Review*. Sept.-Oct., Vol 4, No. 5, p 117-126.
[158] Society of American Value Engineers annual conference, 1965.

Value Engineering. I do not know if Barry was aware that intuitively he came by the psychological knowledge I have mentioned today, but certainly the Bell and Gossett situation illustrates magnificently how to induce change in resisting fifth-level people. He described the futility of his efforts, what a miserable experience it was, and told of how he devised a plan which subsequently changed the whole atmosphere of the company.

The plan he described requested the president of the company to positively and firmly lay down the law to Bell & Gossett people. The president defined the goal, laid down the rules, and then proceeded to use power to see to it they were achieved. The president, following Barry's suggestion, put the people in a new but reducible state of tension. The very thing we have said man most enjoys, solving new problems. Barry illustrated that when these new psychological principles were put into operation, albeit intuitively, that the people responded as the principles would predict. Or, in his own words: "All this changed the climate completely. We have at Bell & Gossett a working, engineering cost-reduction program."

But let me offer a word of caution. As I read the report, Barry was a most fortunate man. He used fifth-level methods to implement change in people who believed in the fifth-level way of life. If he had tried the same on sixth-level people, he would have been an unbelievable failure, and if such had been used on seventh-level people, those seventh-level people would long since have left Bell & Gossett for other organizations.

"When [fourth]-level people are under [fifth]-level management—or 9.1 management, as Blake and Mouton would call it—production soars, provided the managers are good organizers. But when 9.1 management faces [fifth]-level people, production is only as good as the bait management can contrive. I use the managerial grid terminology to make a point. The point is that the work of Blake and Mouton, a giant step forward in organizational psychology, has a serious weakness from the viewpoint of top executives and others who deal with not one but many types of employees groups and situations. The managerial grid approach treats the producer more or less as a constant, and places human variability only at the managerial level. My position is that productivity is a function of the psychology both of the controller and the controlled, plus certain situational factors. Therefore, there is more to handling deteriorating work standards than managerial training, as has so often been suggested in the past."[159]

---

[159] Ibid., (Graves, 1966).

If you have a need to change resisting fifth-level people so that your field may move on, don't be afraid of coercive persuasion. In fact, use it, but never ruthlessly - it doesn't pay - otherwise you just will not have any success in changing their way of behaving. Increase the pressure. Place them in a situation where new attitudes and new behaviors are demanding. Don't ask them to change—tell them to. Expression of ambition must be controlled, and being too open allows others to manipulate. Be discreet and never too trusting with a system of control which prescribes that managerially determined ends and means are proper and that it is necessary to accomplish organizational goals through coercion, reward and threat. This I call Directive Management.

The Directive Manager sees himself as superior to and as the organizer of the productive energies present in lesser men. He is convinced he engineers human behavior. He is amazingly successful when he is a good organizer, when the values of the working group are congruent with his Might is Right values, and when the working group is at the absolutistic existential state. Constrictive values make sense with Machiavellian ethics when the goal is to organize human effort toward the end that a leader prescribes. Thus, we hypothesize here that in an embryonic and developing industrial or political organization, it is dissimilar but congruent values that make for organization viability. But soon a devastating thing occurs; devastating, that is, to him who behaves by Directive Management, he who believes in "The Prerogatives of Management," he who believes in management by direction.

Successful Directive Management in an industrial setting improves the lot of the workers. To achieve his end the Directive Manager must train his people; such training increases their competence. Their competence in turn improves their living circumstances, and this results in more energy freed in their system. This enables them to question their directed existence and leads to organizational insight to fight the power of their Directive Managers. Thus, the workers themselves move to the fifth level and begin to operate within the power ethic.

When the managed in a Directive organization begin to operate by the power ethic, a long period of organizational instability is ushered in. In many such instances the vitality of the company is seriously threatened. We saw this, for example, with Ford in the thirties.[160] If management remains at the fifth level when the workers move from the absolutistic state to the multiplistic state, we have a situation in which the

---

[160] See: Burlingame, Roger (1956). *Henry Ford: The Greatest Success Story in the History of Industry*. New York: Signet Key Books. See also: Herndon, Booton (1969). *Ford: An Unconventional Biography of the Men and Their Times*. New York: Weybright & Talley.

values of the managing and the managed are similar, but this time the similarity of values is not congruent. The managers feel threatened with the loss of their power, fixate, and they try to counter the power move of the managed by over-systematizing that which is but moderately systematizable and by refining their measures of that which, to date, was not measurable. And the workers counter with all their new felt power can do.

This psychology produces an enigmatic situation when both leader and led are at the [fifth] level, for each believes in his God-given right to do as he pleases. Each believes that he who wins has the right to set the rules. Thus, a desire on the part of the leader to set the rules, which works so well when the [fifth]-level leader has [fourth]-level followers, now is challenged by a producer's determination to set the rules. The game of push and withstand-the-push comes into existence. A long-continuing war for organizational power begins, typified by periods of high productivity, resistance to production, and bargaining for the fruits of production. In fact, production becomes a matter of boom-or-bust. It booms when there is temporary agreement as to the rules of work: it busts when the parties tilt for a bigger share of the power pie. Production can be maintained only by giving to get, provided a satisfactory device such as an individual incentive system can be contrived. Quite often, however, contrived systems are short-lived because the real battle is for power in the organization—for material gain."[161] He who lives by the power ethic believes that the power to change rests in the superior talents of the few, those few who are capable of using force to obtain desired ends.

The employee centralized at the ER state expects compensation as a result of accomplishment. The job situation should allow for considerable flexibility and opportunity for individual initiative. The individual will approach rules and regulations as having no inherent sanctity to be maneuvered as the situation requires. The management style for the multiplistic level is bargaining management. The bargaining can be done between manager and employee in an overt and to-the-point fashion. The manager requires three essential items to manage employees whose thinking is in the ER state: A) rewards, B) sanctions, C) defined boundaries with latitude within the boundaries.

The overt bargaining between manager and managed begins by the organizational goals and objectives being shown to the employee. The multiplistic employee expects compensation as a result of accomplishment. The issue is not what the manager wants done, but

---

[161] Ibid., (Graves, 1966).

rather what is the payment offered. If the rewards are not attractive, management must, if continued employment of the individuals is desired, seek out better rewards. If the rewards are acceptable the boundaries (policy, resource levels, time, legal constraints, etc.) must be clearly communicated. The employee is then free to operate unrestrained within the boundaries. However, the manager must not tolerate their violation or hesitate to use the sanctions.

Once a bargain has been made the multiplistic employee will work diligently to attain the goals. There is no need to schedule activities, order and organize the efforts, and evaluate the changing status of the program since this person is "managing" all of that. They are self-managing and prefer not to be controlled. The only supervision required is to check for boundary violation.

Mismanagement at the materialistic level takes two basic forms. The first, and most common, is where the rewards are not worth the effort. This can be brought about by management: violating the terms of the bargain, engaging in punishment rather than correction, establishing narrow unrealistic boundaries, and having no worthwhile rewards or limited rewards. The result will be the departure of the employee from the organization. However, in departing the person at this level is likely to "take" some compensation for the trouble caused. The organization has lost a dynamic, innovative, and hard-working person who, if properly managed, could greatly contribute. The second form of mismanagement is in not setting boundaries and in not having or using the sanctions. The employee in the ER state will soon become the de facto manager and eventually the in facto manager.

Some managers, too many of them, try to copy what has been successful in other organizations where the managed begin to operate by the power ethic. They try to use Participative Managerial techniques, but the attempt aborts because Directive Managers can never truly allow participation. Thus they soon induce hate - which is the one thing a Directive Manager must avoid because hate ultimately consumes the vitality of any organism or organization in which it arises. If you mismanaged someone at the ER level, you are going to get a clinging vine that is the stickiest thing you ever had on your back. They are going to get on you. They are going to hang on, and you wish to God you could get that molasses off of your soul.

But other managers meet threat to their power by questioning their Might-is-Right way and begin their movement to the sixth level of existence. Movement to the sixth level of human existence occurs when the 'have nots' begin to threaten the power and prerogatives of the 'haves' and movement begins when the 'haves' begin to perceive that power alone does not please man. Man wants also to be liked, to feel he is accepted, to belong. Now as the belonging level of need emerges the sociocratic ethic, the team concept of work, the organization man idea, the "we must all think alike and all want the same" system of proper behavior develops.

Readiness for Change in the Multiplistic State

Fifth-level values immeasurably improve man's conditions for existence. He has learned how to live with want - AN through DQ - and how to overcome it - ER; but he has learned this for his self and his self alone. He has not learned how to live with his abundance, nor how to live when there are other men who still must live in want. He creates wealth and techniques, including the objectivistic, positivistic scientific method, so as to provide the material ends to a satisfactory human existence in the here and now for those who merit it. They lead to knowledge that improves the human condition. And from this arises his welfare concept, namely that welfare is for only the deserving or those who show in their efforts that they merit a little aid on the way. But never, not ever, must it violate the work effort and independent assertion of the self.

The solution of material problems, coupled with this perception, begins man's move into his sixth form of existence. Just as the individual at the third level got into the trouble and had to change, so does the person who's at the fifth level. He gets into trouble with being too successful and has to begin to try to solve the problem of explaining 'why I've got about everything in the world and nobody else has anything' or 'how I am going to get along in this world when other people are getting more and more angry with me because I've got more than they have. In fact, I've got more than I can use, and I'm getting pretty wasteful with it.'

We should not be misled to believe that fifth-level values are the end of man's growth or the sign of his ultimate moral decay. These values, too, will become suspect by man. The power ethic dooms itself to decay, with time, because it creates for man a paradox which he cannot abide. As fifth-level values result in the improvement of man's existence, life for him becomes worth living. But how can life be lived well if one must constantly fight others for one's survival? Man sees the need to get along with other men if the good life is to continue. It is not that he will give up all aspects of the pleasurable existence. It is rather that he will come to see that satisfying self alone, in a materialistic way, is not enough.

The ER to FS Transition

So, how do you move the ER to the FS state? You have to have a two-fold kind of set up for training: a) the person with both the prestige and the expertise sets up the program, and b) the actual training needs to be conducted by a peer of extreme competence in whatever it is you are training, an active training person having low prestige and high expertise, working for the person who has both. This is the biggest educational problem I am faced with in my college. I do not directly teach these people. My best previous students at the undergraduate level do the effective teaching. I do the organizing.

You must remember what is occurring here as you move from DQ. As you move from CP you are moving a person who has no respect for authority to DQ where he goes over the dam in respecting authority, then to ER where the person begins to negate authority and says: "I can stand on my own feet and solve problems." So, if you bring in as the active training person someone with high prestige who's going to be an authority, then this guy is going to buck everything you do. You go into the classroom with these people with high prestige and high authority, and that kid is going to sit out there and every time you say something, he'll say, "Prove it!" He's going to come at you and completely disrupt the operation because he is fighting himself loose from overly depending upon authority. That, in another sense, is what ER is doing - fighting to get loose of the shackles of authority. So, you have to have a non-authority figure as the active person who works with the learner. But this is the next phase: your trainer who is of low prestige and high expertise must be available to the learner, but he must not try to move in.

I do it in this way: I set up the things that are to be done and what's to be learned and give that assignment to my surrogate, a previous student. Then the surrogate takes over and delivers the assignment to the students. He gets out of the picture, but my surrogate also sees that the people carry out the basic work. He's got an office upstairs, and he says to them: "I will be in that office at certain hours if you ever want to talk to me about anything that you have been assigned to learn." From there on, you stay out of the learning process. This person cannot learn if his peer or an authority is watching. He must work out the problem privately and anonymously.

The surrogate must wait until the student decides to ask questions. Neither you nor the surrogate should interfere. If the master teacher does come in, you've lost this fellow; he won't learn what you are trying to get across. When he finally comes in for support, he will work the living tail off of that surrogate. They come to me, once they start to make contact, and say: "Doc, these kids are killing me! They are coming to me at night, they are coming to me every hour of the day. I can't get them off my back."

"That's your job, that's your job," I tell them. I won't see most of those students until the end of the term. I don't even evaluate them. The surrogate knows the rules, and the surrogate evaluates them. I don't make the decisions. I only play a role in grading when there is difficulty between the surrogate and the student; then the student can come to me.

Most of the time they will say to me at the end of the course: "Well, for the first time in my educational experience, I had something that was educational." And they say: "Doc, I never had a better course in my life; you've got the best course in the world." I haven't seen them since the course started!

The surrogate has to be at FS because he has to be willing to sacrifice self once they latch onto him. He has to have this tremendous empathy, and has to want to get along with the students. It will just floor you to experience the progress that is made under this kind of set up in contrast to the progress that comes otherwise. Never in your life will you have an experience that any human being learns so much more than you thought a human being would.

This person has worked himself away from authority. He wants to believe, above everything else, that he can stand on his own feet. When someone sets up an educational program which supports him in the direction of believing that he is good enough to solve his own educational problems, and he doesn't have to go to daddy teacher any more to do it, he says: "Somebody's respecting me for the first time in my life." And they come to me and say that. They say directly to me: "Now it's the first time I ever had a human being really respect me for the brain that I've got." Out of this they begin to empathize; they begin to have a feeling. They begin to like the surrogate. They begin to like me. They cease to be cold human beings. This rapidly generalizes to others, and the guy moves into FS. But the keys are: the master teacher organizes; the surrogate assigns; the surrogate makes himself available and waits until contacted; the student is allowed to carry out the learning anonymously.

One of the things that you run into is the further up the scale you go, the more you have an overall human being that is freeing up and being able to move further. So the chances are that fewer and fewer are going to fail. But this, to me, is a methodological approach which, if you ever try it out, is just 'damn close to magic.' I don't talk like that very often, but I tell you, it floors me. I have the administration and other people in the college come around every once in a while questioning the grades that these students have received. I always insist that they leave their work with me, whatever the results are, so when the Dean comes to me and questions, then I can say: "All right now, you just take a look at it. What are you going to give that guy?"

They'll say: "Well, how the hell do you get the quality of work out of this guy that no one else in the school can?" If you look at the student's record, everything else will be riding what I call 'the probation fence,' Ds and Cs. This will be the one A or B on the person's record, and it's genuine. I didn't give this person anything. All that's involved in this is basically paying attention to the psychology of this person, and seeing to it that the person who actively teaches when asked to teach is a peer of low prestige but high expertise, and a method which allows the person to learn anonymously.

Apparently there is an incredible hunger in the ER to learn, but we knock it out of him because we throw him into an ordinary classroom setting. He simply cannot take it. We have a lot of experimental evidence to support this particular thing. We've taken ERs and studied them in many different circumstances to see whether or not they work better alone, with groups, small groups, or in any other situation. This is a system-specific thing, and the only group that only learns in an anonymous situation.

In some manner, for some reason or another, their psychology is of such an order that they can't perform in front of other people. They love to come out in the open once they've got something licked. I used to coach golf, and when I ran into this with a golfer, I found that if the golfer was having difficulty, the only way to deal with him was to find himself a place to practice somewhere out on the back of the course and stay away from him until he'd got his hook or his slice or whatever it was solved. I'd never say a word to him about anything that he might do until he had gone out there quietly and by himself. In other words, I never tried to coach this guy. But if he came to me after he thought he had figured out why he was slicing, then I could support him. It's the type of thing that is system-specific.

Now, the problem you have in many training setups is that the trainer - the educator - wants to be right in there getting the satisfaction of doing something. Here, the training person is simply an organizer, that's all. He's got to go back and say, "There isn't anything that I actively did in interacting with this person that in any way brought about this person's learning. I didn't aid this person to learn." You've got to learn to get your satisfaction out of the results and not by being in on the production of the result.

Now, let's take a look at a conception that shows the movement out of ER with the entry of some FS—ER/fs. We take another half step up the ladder and notice some feeling for others is reasserting itself. She depends on her own competencies and abilities to achieve goals while the group begins to enter in as an element. She considers conforming to the reality of the group and recognizing the external importance. The ER is still predominant in that the abilities and competencies of the person prevail, and she views the potentials of the rational, objective self are unlimited. With FS entering there is an increasing awareness of her own emotions and viewing herself as the accurate appraiser of people and situations. There is still a denial of the need for others and an attempt to remain detached but the harsh criticality of pure ER is softening. Lets look at another example of increasing FS while ER loosens its hold:

Example #1 – The ER/fs Conception -

> "The psychologically mature person is the one who deals successfully with the environment, the one who has an unquestioned accurate and objective perception of one's environment and others and who is able to handle both successfully. The mature person takes both the conflicts and contradictions of life and turns them into experiences which are to her advantage.
>
> Of course dealing successfully and handling successfully presupposes a wider range of abilities and competencies than one might think at first and thus will not be achieved by many. But it is the true sign of maturity. It means a superior ability to exercise one's emotions so that these volatile features enhance rather than harm one's ability to perceive and achieve goals. Indeed, perceiving clearly is probably the best way to deal with any environment and at this the mature personality is superior. One might be tempted to assert that dealing with other humans to fulfill

one's personal need is really the only necessity in dealing with the environment. But I think other people are only one part of the environment, so the concept should include organizing other humans, the physical environment and one's own mind and one's own body to assure one's personal welfare.

The mature person is completely free of illusion. To her, mature means one must appraise others and self accurately, it means to be intelligent in any situation, even to being uninhibited as in sex, for it is intelligent to be so. The mature has that clear perception of reality which is based on objective evidence and her rational deductions. She must realize this reality and acts in her own best interests even if to do so requires her to take well thought out risks, even if it means to lose a friend.

The mature person says what needs to be said and does what needs to be done even if doing so may not be liked by others. The mature person is capable unto his or her self and does not need to depend on anyone. That is, the mature person adapts to the reality of the way things are but does not just accept them. If something isn't right or isn't working correctly as the mature person sees it, it is weighed against other factors. It is then labeled good, bad, right, wrong or whatever label is necessary. Then what the mature person does is to take intelligent action toward it, doing it if it is to one's advantage, avoiding it if it is not.

The truly mature person is the one who insists on total fulfillment with all actions determined by values directed at her own well being. She would always recognize the necessity of developing herself as an entity while appearing to conform to the reality of the group. She would not do so out of fear of punishment or lest she feel guilty or ashamed but out of the realization that she must do so to employ the realities and personalities around her to her own ends without arousing them."

In the shift from ER to greater FS, when FS is stronger than ER, as in this next case, we see the leaving behind of categorical certainty substituted for relativistic thinking. Notice the tentativeness in what to say and do with movement back towards an inner focus. There is a search for inner, unanxious peace and an unwillingness to commit fully to persons or ideas due to greater ambiguity and uncertainty. Emotional elements take the fore as the individual becomes more aware, accepting and open with his/her own internal processes. Companions, not DQ confidants, become central to the person with the increasing importance of people, friends and relationships interacting in an interdependent world. Authority becomes more of an equal than something to challenge, escape, or revere.

Example #2 – The er/FS Conception

"I suspect as I start this, that each human being, as he sits back, alone with himself, considers his character to be fundamentally okay, or at least, headed in the right direction with good intention. In the social market place this attitude most assuredly gives way to a more self-critical state of mind, a consciousness in which ideals to be aimed at are evolved - however, it seems that solitude breeds a kind of tacit self-consent. My problem then becomes this: should I describe myself or what I would like to be? On the other hand, as I consider the vague presence of some sort of evaluative force which seeks by means of this document to classify my personality, I would imagine that if I describe what I think I am, it would in that way be aided.

But the intent of the question with which I am faced, namely to define what I consider to be a psychological mature human being, seems to point toward the ideals of the social market place, the psychological goals and aspirations of self-critical man. What I am driving at seems to be this: there appears to be a gap within the nature of this "evaluative force" of which I speak between its consideration of the personality itself and the intellectualizations of this personality, between actual behavioural skills and the sorts of fantasies which the behaving being aspires to.

At this point, consideration of this question appears to me as crucial; yet for now a resolution of just who I should describe shall have to wait and I shall acquiesce with the supposed intent of this project, attempting to imagine my psychological ideal. I suppose the best way to approach such a consideration would be an outline of the dynamic sort of tendencies of the mature individual, then to be illustrated by the subject's attitude toward different realms of human experience - i.e. friendship, religion, authority, etc. Specifically, I envision the mature human as a vital, growing entity, potentially susceptible to change and influence at all times, experiencing happiness, suffering and developing. Since the self can only be a derivative of what is outside the self, since man's self consciousness, his "selfhood", seems necessarily to be socially founded, an obsession with individuality and autonomy appears a bit unrealistic, yet within its capacity as a reasoning entity, as an arbitrator of conflicting forces, the mature self finds its dignity, its separateness. Its peace is inner, unanxious over, and tempered to the realities of the outside. Social participation is motivated by enjoyment and a kind of personal curiosity, and not by a sense of quest. Emotionally, affection is esteemed, other emotions being a part of humanness. Rationality is valued as a means of growth, though owing to man's nature, by no means an exclusive means.

Regarding specific life's activities, physical activity, whether it be sport or manual labour, is seen as a fulfilling activity. Career goals of material, political or social nature are seen as insignificant. Consistent with this sketch of an overall attitude seems to be these opinions:

On friendship - Inner security is such that friendships are not of a dependent nature. Friends are viewed more as "companions in the world" than as necessary to the satisfaction of need. Large circles of friends are sought but not required. The ability to be affectionate without expecting or requiring its return is also a sign of maturity.

On authority - Authority as a social expedient and necessity is recognized and accepted, though social mores will not mold the individual in the sense of ruling him; critical evaluation on the part of the individual is here the final judge. In the case of political and economic sorts of imperatives, having to abide by them is neither a matter of hardship or pleasure.

On the mystic urge - often deemed the religious attitude, the theological need to explain the unknown - mystic, a-rational, Zen-like attitudes toward reality are recognized as legitimate. The complimentary of this general state of mind with the tendency toward rational understanding is seen as a whole view of reality. The concept of God as a moral force is virtually dismissed, and as a first cause determining force, respected though considered irrelevant for personal peace of mind.

As a final note, maturity also engenders a sort of overview of what such a paper as this has an object - i.e., something of a self-reflexive awareness of the relative nature of opinion; a recognition that although I can and must (because of my humanness) argue out of my own position, argumentation and opinion from other positions is equally valid in the sense of being understandable and defensible. But then again, it would appear that such a perspective cannot be humanly, vitally maintained and that we must therefore jump in and outside ourselves in the process of growth."

Now man begins his transition to Maslow's belonging level of need and to the sixth level of human existence. His values begin to change but, again, those who view man from other frameworks call this change bad. When his ER existential problems are resolved, man finds his material wants have been fulfilled by the over exercise of his need for independence. His life is good, and on the surface seems relatively assured. He finds himself master of the objective physical world, but a prime neophyte in the subjectivistic, humanistic world. He has achieved the satisfaction of a good life, but it has been achieved at a price - he pays the price of not being liked by other men for his callous use of knowledge for himself. He has become envied and even respected, but liked he is not. He has achieved his personal status, his material existence, at the expense of being rejected even by his own children who want no part of their parents' materialistic values.

Now, as the other side of man, his subjectivity, gnaws for its opening, a feeling of dependence emerges. It is a swing back to *sacrificing* some of self in order to take care of others. Remember back in the third level as the individual expressed himself, he got into trouble with other human beings and had to begin to try to solve that problem of coming into difficulty with them. If you have the problem of explaining to others why you are successful, mollifying others for being successful, then in order to do this you are going to have to think in some way other than the way the person thought in the fifth level. The solution of material problems, coupled with this perception, trips the sixth-level system and the person begins to stop thinking in terms of his own material success and begins thinking in terms of others again.

But once assured of *his* material satisfaction, he finds a new spiritual void in his being. For example, nearly all the people I find interested in 'consciousness' - and please don't misunderstand me here because some of you might be - are people who have lost their way in the ER to FS transition.

The cyclic aspect of this theory comes back in again. The need to belong, to affiliate himself rather than 'go-it-alone,' becomes central. This affiliative need, which is man's third form of belonging need, now organizes man's existence. As it does, the adjustment of the organism-to-the-environment process becomes dominant again and gives rise to a new *thema* for existence: *'Sacrifice some now so others can have too.'* So, it creates a whole set of problems, the F problems that come with being successful in this world.

Chapter 12

The Relativistic Existence – The FS State

The 6th Subsistence Level

The FS - Sociocentric, Personalistic, Sociocratic Existential State

Theme: *'Sacrifice now in order to get acceptance now.'*

Alternative Theme: *'Sacrifice now in order for all to get now'*

The *'Sacrifice self now to get now'* Conceptions

The sixth level, the relativistic existential system, first appeared 80-90 years ago.[162] It arises when the ER way of life solves the problems of living for many, more than any preceding way of life. Fifth-level values improve immeasurably man's conditions for existence. They create wealth and techniques. They lead to knowledge that improves the human condition. In the ER existential state man has fulfilled his material wants. His life is safe and it is relatively assured; but what of other men? The struggle for individuality, through expression of self and outer material existence, does not bring the happiness expected. It has left one alone in the world facing the problems brought by antipathy of others. This creates the F problems, the problems of coming to peace with aloneness, with one's inner self and with others. These problems, felt by those who profited from ER ways but who also sensed a widening gulf between the successful ones and those who have not shared the fruits of multiplistic living, increase markedly the activation of the right side of the brain - the equipment for subjective, non-linear thinking. These problems activate the S neurological system—the system for truly experiencing the inner, subjective feelings of humankind.

To fourth-level man, fifth-level values are akin to sin; to the sixth they are the crass materialism of "The Status Seeker." But in this frame of reference they are not values to condemn. They are values we should strive to enable lower-level man to experience, even though they are not values that will become permanent as the major establishment in America today seems to believe. Yet they, too, give way because they create a new existential problem for man. He has learned how to live with want and how to live to overcome it; but he has not learned how to live with abundance. He has achieved his status, his material existence at the expense of being rejected. Now he has a new problem and now he must seek a new way of life and a new value system. The successful want to be liked; and the passed-over want in.

This perception begins man's move to his sixth form of existence, to the state of the sociocentric being, to a concern with belonging, being accepted, and not rejected. Man becomes centrally concerned with peace with his inner self and in the relation of his self to the inner self of others. The belonging need arises as the *adjustment to the environment* component ascends to the dominant position. But this time, the conforming tendency - the adjustive tendency - is not to external stimuli or absolutistic authority. It is to the peer group. Man becomes concerned with knowing the inner side of self and other selves so

---

[162] As of Graves's writing in 1982, thus the 19th to 20th century transition.

harmony can come to be, so people as individuals can be at peace with themselves and thus with the world. The team concept, the 'we are all buddies, let us all break bread together' system of thinking develops.

Now he feels the need to belong to the community of man, to affiliate himself rather than to go it alone. When he finds his peers critical of his opinion, he'll change it. And the *thema*, "*sacrifice some now so that others can have now*" comes to be. Again, as in the BO and DQ states, man values authority, but not that of his elders' wishes, nor of his all powerful authority, the external standard he conforms to is the authority and the wishes of his contemporaries whom he values. He values pleasing his others, being accepted by them and not being rejected. What he values is what his contemporary group indicates it is right for him to value. Thus, I call these values sociocratic because the peer group determines the means by which this end value - community with valued others - is to be obtained. An external standard determines what is healthy, but it is neither absolutistic nor theocratic. It is: 'What the group of people I like say a healthy personality is, that's what it is.'

Two aspects of sixth-level valuing stand out. Here man values commonality over differential classification. To classify people into types or groups is to threaten the sociocentric's sense of community. The other aspect is his return to religiousness, which again he values as he did in the previous adjustive systems. But here he does not value religions, per se, or religious-like rituals or religious dogma. Rather, it is the spiritual attitude, the tender touch which he reveres. Notice, we went in and out of religion: we didn't have it in CP; we went into it in DQ; went out of it in ER; but we are back into it in FS. Sixth-level values with the theme 'sacrifice now in order to get acceptance now and so all can get now,' are a great step forward for man. They reflect the beginning of man's humanism, the demise of his animalism.

At the sixth level it is the feelings of man, rather than the hidden secrets of the physical universe, which draw his attention. "Getting along with" is valued more than "getting ahead of." Consumer goodwill takes precedence over free enterprise, cooperation stands out as more valued than competition, and social approval is valued over individual fame. Consumption and warm social intercourse are more valued at this level than are production and cold, calculating self-interest.

It is true that peripherally his values seem to shift without center but this, too, is an illusion. The group, valuing deeply interpersonal penetration and interpersonal communication, is constantly shifting its value base so that no shade of difference is left out. As the base swings to include this or that variation in some member of the group, the values appear to be built on shifting dunes of sand. But, the central core is not changing; it is a very solid thing. While he seems to be uncertain of what he values, this is more illusion than it is real. It is only the peripheral aspect which seems shallow, non-serious and fickle. The peripheral values are only swinging to the left, to the right and back to center. He values softness over cold rationality, sensitivity in preference to objectivity, taste over wealth, respectability over power, and personality more than things. He values interpersonal penetration, interpersonal communication, committeeism, majority rule, the tender, the subjective, the non-ordered formal informality, the subjective approach, avoidance of classification, and the religious attitude, but not religious dogma. Sixth-level man knows as well as man at any other level what he values, what is right, and what is wrong for him: it is being with, in with, and within, the feelings of his valued others.

FS considers the knowledge and he will think about it intellectually, but the choice, if there are alternatives, will be made on the basis of feeling. What he actually does may have absolutely nothing to do with the analysis that he's made. You'd go: "What the hell is going on here?" His conclusion doesn't follow his logic, because the conclusion is based on feeling and not on his logic. Intellectually, the FS individual considers many alternatives, but makes choice on the basis of feeling, not on the basis of information, knowledge or rule. This is important because it differentiates between FS and A'N'. For the A'N', conclusions will follow his logic. It may not be what anyone else has, but he's got his.

Look for behavior which indicates a chameleon-like character: "When I feel this way, I do this; when I feel that way I do that." The clue word being 'feel;' always the word *feel*. FS values indicate that people come first, so when control is necessary it *must* always be exercised *not* to hurt people. (Here you will see a difference from the A'N', to follow. For the A'N', if you have to exercise control and the exercising of it is going to hurt people's feelings, you regret having to do it, but you do it. You do it as decently as you can, but you do it.)"

Rather than the centrality of the life being authority as in DQ, hate and aggression as in the CP, my own self-interest as in the ER, the centrality of life for FS is people and friends. The individual speaks earnestly about community, intimacy, shared experiences, and other responses which show that centrality. They express a need to be "more connected" and feel alienated when others do not share his or her unique personal delights. Behaviorally, he shows an inability to commit self to others beyond one's group. Watch for the one thing this person is negative about - hurting other people. That's the only negation you seem to pick up.

Finally, listen for an unwillingness to change things. They have a belief that: "Things should be different, but I am not the one to start out changing these things. If there is change, it's got to be the group or something of that sort that brings it about, not me." He would actively support the group, not just go along. In other words, you get responses often which say, "Well, I don't know it all but, by God, I'll fight for what my people, my friends think is right" even though he says he doesn't know what's right.

The important thing, in my point of view, is that the data I have indicates that the aggressiveness of man as we know it appears in the third system - it comes in with the CP. And I can show you that there are chemical changes, even hormonal changes taking place in the body of man when he is under the influence of the CP system which cause him to be his most aggressive self, and that this aggressive self remains relatively strong in the human personality, though it takes on a different form, in the DQ system and in the ER system. I have not found aggressiveness in FS personalities. By the time the FS system is dominant in a personality, crime against the other person - crime against the other person's self - is not found. I have not found it in FS personalities.

Now, I have found crime against the self. I have found them taking drugs to the point of hurting the self. I have found suicide—aggression against the self. Suicide, the data says, is rather an odd one. Suicide is highest in the FS system. The data says that homicide as a behavior of man disappears as the transition is made into the FS system. This is a very interesting finding and suggests that if we could possibly work on the problems of human existence in such a manner as to get the mass of our people beyond the ER level of existence, then we would not have to worry about homicide crime anymore; this phenomenon will disappear.

I find that in the BO system the only basic reason for war that exists is that you have invaded my property. You don't have any ideological war. You don't have war for gain. You don't have anything of that sort. The person will fight like the dog fights when you come across whatever he has laid out as the perimeter of his property line. In the CP system man fights for the fun of fighting. He is an aggressive 'bastard' at that level of existence; that is his nature and this is what we must understand. In the DQ system he fights ideologically. In the ER system he fights for selfish economic gain. In the FS system he begins to question whether there is any purpose in any of these fights at all.

Examples of the Sixth Level

This system has been alternately called the Sociocentric Existence, the Interpersonalistic level, the Personalistic system, Sociocratic Values, the Sixth Subsistence level, the FS state and the Relativistic Existential State. It is a system wherein the individual thinks in terms of the rights of others' individualities rather than just in terms of one's own individuality. Others also exist as individuals in their own right, having their own, just as good, view of the world. Thus, man shows a greater degree of affective warmth and a greater ability to extend it to full appreciation of the individuality of the other person as he turns excessively to the exploration of the inner self and others, while focusing on relationships as a central aspect of living. Goals are related to the whole of one's group, not just one or some of the group. The individual absorbs self into the group and, in essence, becomes the group. The way people relate to others looms high in their consciousness. Here is a conception illustrating the nodal FS state:

FS Conception –

> "I can say what is my conception of the mature personality in one sentence but it would take reams of paper to clarify what I mean. So I shall, in this endeavor, express my thoughts in one sentence and then elaborate only upon the basis of what I mean.
>
> The mature personality is a participating, creative personality which in its operation does justice to every type of personality, every mode of culture, every human potential without forming anyone into typological molds.
>
> The mature personality provides a means for bringing relations of reciprocity and willing amity to the entire family of human beings. The mature provides for the interchange and utilization of the entire experiences of humankind. He or she lives in a moral world which tears down manmade barriers of law and custom widening the means of communication and cooperation between humans.
>
> The mature is a committed person, committing self to continuous self-development, and to intimate relations and cooperation with all people. He or she is

one who believes in face-to-face interaction and assessment, one who believes friendly eyes are the indispensable mirrors for reflecting what is. He or she believes in an absolutely open society where every nook, every corner is exposed to anyone who is curious. He or she behaves so as to demonstrate that every person may be freely heard.

The mature personality deliberately exercises choice which directs life toward allegiances, which are beyond the boundaries of natural communities and the organized state, and toward the ultimate hopes of mankind. He or she seeks to widen the ties of fellowship without respect to birth, caste or property, and disavows claims to special privilege or the exclusivity of leadership. He or she replaces Godly authority with the temporal authority of the time and the place. He or she softens the features which identify a person with a particular society or culture. To the mature, humanity is a unity of souls seeking salvation not a union of Catholics, High Episcopalians, Orthodox Jews or Baptists.

The mature is beyond sordid concern with his or her own survival and is focused on intensive cultivation of a belief in freedom, not a belief of freedom.

To the mature technology is for human needs, not power, productivity, profit or prestige and scientific endeavor is not for ruthless exploitation or desecration. Scientific endeavor is for depth exploration of all regions not just physical regions, so as to provide for the inner human knowledge that will assure human supremacy.

The mature indulges in the dematerialization of self, in self-transcending endeavors which reach beyond sordid concern with one's own survival, beyond the over-rational and irrational, beyond mechanical uniformity toward a concept of organic unity. He or she operates by the belief that we are all one and should seek to enhance human expression to provide for a world society based on human values. He or she believes one should know both the objective and the subjective and show the ability to face one's whole self and direct every part of it to a more unified development.

In summary, and in Freudian terms, the mature personality accepts its id, but does not give it primacy, and fosters the sure ego but does not allow it to depress the fullest expression of the ego."

Those centralized in FS believe man must live in a non-competitive way with other humans. At the FS level man becomes, centrally, a sociocentric being, a being concerned with the relation of his self to other selves. He becomes concerned with belonging, with being accepted, with not being rejected, with knowing the inner side of self and other selves so human harmony can come to be. And when he achieves this he becomes concerned with more than self and other selves. He becomes concerned with self in relation to life and the whole, the total universe. This manifests in the sixth-level concept of welfare, a concept many today abhor, for it is a concept of the right of all to the goods of a society, equally distributed with need, not merit, as its core.

Origin of the Relativistic State

Man—*Homo sapiens*—came to be about 100,000 years ago. The first level of existence went for about 60,000 years. Forty thousand years ago, the leading edge of second-level thinking started to appear. About 10,000 years ago the leading edge of third-level thinking started to appear. About 4,000-5,000 years ago the leading edge of fourth-level thinking came into existence. About 600-700 years ago (1300-1400 AD) the fifth level started to come to be, and about 80 years ago (1900 AD) the leading edge of the sixth level appeared. In my data, the leading edge of the seventh level started to appear around 1952 or '53.

He has achieved his status, his material existence at the expense of being rejected. The power ethic dooms itself to decay, with time, because it creates for man a paradox which he cannot abide. As fifth-level values result in the improvement of man's existence, life for him becomes worth living. But how can life be lived well if one must constantly fight others for one's survival? If you have the problem of explaining to others why you are successful, mollifying others for being successful, then, in order to do this, you are going to have to think some way other than the way the person thought in the fifth level. Man sees the need to get along with other men if the good life is to continue. This perception trips the sixth-level neurology and begins man's move to his sixth form of existence, to the state of the sociocentric being, to a concern with belonging, being accepted, and not rejected. The person begins to stop thinking in terms of his own material success and begins the swing back to thinking in terms of others again, sacrificing self-interest.

When some people see fifth-level values changing into the values of level six, again, they see decay all around them. In a sense this is true, because man transforming into sixth-level thinking lays authority aside, because he rejects strongly non-dignified non-human ways of living. Sixth-level values are those of "The Lonely Crowd,"[163] those of the chameleon-like "Marketing Character,"[164] but they are, within this point of view, a giant step forward for man.

To many, such as the materialistic establishment and philosophers like Ayn Rand, the ascendance of these values [relativistic or sociocentric] signify the breakthrough of man's most regrettable weakness, his delicate capacity for tenderness, his subjectiveness, his concern for others rather than his individuality. When "The Organization Man"[165] tries to fit in rather than take over, those who see values from an older frame of reference despair of such behavior.

Yet they are higher values because in them we find the many, not the few, valued, as at the fourth level. They are higher than the fourth level, for at least man's opinion, not just extra-human opinion, is considered. But they are called bad by many, particularly many scientists, because they value the subjective and relativistic rather than just the objective and the positivistic. At this level many feel that man has lost himself, and he has given himself up for social approval. But the E-C frame of reference says that this conclusion is an error. It says that man has simply subordinated his self-interest for the time being and that self-interest will return again in a new and higher form.

When the electrical executives contrived to allow all to live rather than kill off competition[166] as in "Robber Baron"[167] days, such was

---

[163] Riesman, David (1950). *The Lonely Crowd*. New Haven, CT: Yale University Press. Also, *The Lonely Crowd, Revised edition: A Study of the Changing American Character* by David Riesman, Nathan Glazer, Reuel Denney, and Todd Gitlin (2001). Yale Nota Bene.
[164] Fromm, Eric (1955). *The Sane Society*. New York: Rinehart.
[165] Whyte, William H. (1956). *The Organization Man*. New York: Simon and Schuster.
[166] Scandal in the early 1960s involving heavy electrical equipment manufacturers led by General Electric, Westinghouse, I-T-E and Allis Chalmers who were accused of conspiring to fix prices on government sales. See: Dennis W. Carlton and Jeffrey M.

called bad. It certainly cannot be called the best of man because the customer was the one who paid the bill. But, one can ask if it is not better than GE setting out, come what may, to competitively kill Westinghouse or Allis Chalmers. Similarly, Riesman infers that the "Other Directed" is not the best of men. Fromm (1955) looks askance at his "Marketing Character" and the fourth-level absolutist or the fifth-level individualist condemns the welfare state concept of sixth level man. But, our point of view asks: "Is it bad to think of him and just not think of me? Is it bad to aspire that all shall share the fruits of what the cumulative efforts of man have provided?"

"Yes," say many, but they say it through the imputation of malevolence to others. "If you let the other man have, he will get you in the end," they say. "If you do not provide for your own old age, then you should suffer the consequences of your own weak will," is another of their condemnations.

Others, operating in the materialistic way, have perceived that power alone does not please man and become aware of a desire to belong and be accepted by others, rather than hated or opposed.

After man has achieved basic personal and economic security, and after he has successfully challenged the established order, he again changes his psychological spots. (I am writing of long-term changes, of course—ones that usually require more than a lifetime.) He begins to become a sociocentric being. He becomes concerned with social, rather than basic personal or material matters. He now seeks for something other than survival, safety, order, or material gain. He seeks a congenial atmosphere, a comfortable work pace, and, as a result, his productive effort and output deteriorate relative to what they were at the [fourth] or [fifth] level.[168]

Sixth-level man objects strongly to authority's lead or pressure and professes revulsion against uniformity and homogenization. He follows the crowd's or peer's lead or pressure since emphasis is placed upon "getting along," accepting the authority of the group or the majority, and seeking status from others. Thinking shows an almost radical, almost compulsive emphasis on seeing everything from a relativistic, subjective frame of reference as he revolts against notions of quantity

---

Perloff, *Modern Industrial Organization*, p. 181-183, and Richard A. Posner, "The Social Cost of Monopoly and Regulation," *Journal of Political Economy*, 83:807-827.

[167] Josephson, Matthew (1934). *The Robber Barons*. New York: Harcourt, Brace, and Co. Also called "industrial statesmen" by those who suggest a different view of history, such as Allan Nevins.

[168] Ibid., (Graves, 1966).

and is rigidly against rigidity, judgmental about judgmentalism. He thinks in terms of goals which relate to all human kind rather than just to self, and in terms of living by what is unique for thee.

This other-directed individual believes he will find 'salvation' in belonging and in participating with others in what they want him to do. While sixth-level man has given up his dogmatism, he nevertheless rigidifies in a world of sociocentric thinking. "When man centralizes his values at the FS level, many feel that man has lost his 'self,' that he has given it up for social approval. But the frame of reference advanced here indicates that this conclusion is in error. It suggests that man has simply subordinated self interest for the time being and that self interest will return again but in a new and higher form, the A'N' form of existence.

All the problems created by the over-extension of the attack of the fifth level upon nature and nature's laws are accumulating while the person lives the sixth-level way. As this person lives in the sixth-level way, the world just gets in worse trouble. Keep in mind that this person is a much broader individual, much more perceptive of what is going on. He/she begins to perceive that all the ways people have lived by in this world have, in fact, created more problems for them than they have solved.

Up to this period of time the person was living in a world of abundance, where all kinds of raw materials existed. There was all kinds of space to conquer and move into. Now raw materials are disappearing, space is disappearing, and overpopulation that comes from the expensiveness of the people at the fifth level has come to be. Suddenly the person operating at the sixth level begins to realize that everything human beings have ever believed in is by and large wrong—that it has really led more to trouble than good. Thus, the sixth level begins to disappear. Sixth-level thinking that came in about the end of the 19th century should, if there's anything to this theory at all, be around for the shortest period of time of any of the ways of thinking that we have had previously.

Basic Operation of the State

Now the sixth-level state is a different one from the fifth. In the sixth level the person's struggle for individuality is over. One's own and others' individualities are recognized. When the person begins to think this way, the person is free from the *struggle* for life, free of the struggle for control, free from the struggle for ego definition, free of struggling to help others, free of the struggle for freedom, free from guilt, free of having to develop feelings for others. This person is much more affectively warm than any of the other systems that we have. They exude warmth for other human beings and they show a tremendous capacity to extend the right of the other person's full expression to that other person. They just wouldn't think of moving in on another person and in any way suggesting how that person should think or believe or behave.

As the sociocentric state begins to develop, the person begins to think in terms of being different from others, as living in different situations and in terms of not 'the one and the only way to behave,' not in terms of 'the best way to behave,' but in terms of 'the most appropriate way to behave in that particular situation.' He and she have found that some people survive living one way; some people survive living in another way.

So, it gives birth to what we call relativistic thinking; that is thinking in terms of behaving as the situation calls for, trying to get along with the unassailable laws of the universe, and in terms of trying to live in a way that many ways of thinking can live together at one and the same time. He thinks in terms of going beyond behaving as the self dictates, trying to conquer others, in terms of what God thinks, in terms of what the data says, instead of trying to think only in terms of what the self thinks or in terms of changing the world to suit the self. As this wave comes to its nodal point, the person begins to think in terms of defining the 'what has to be' rather than 'what should be,' or 'what can be' in terms of feeling with others. So, it's a much broader way of thinking about the world; but underneath it all you have to keep in mind that the person who is operating at the sixth level begins to believe that there is a way that he or she can learn to behave that can get along with all other people and can show appreciation for the thoughts and the feelings of others.

It's a very warm system, but the person gets all tied up in this business of attempting to express self or attempting to let others express self. Because he or she doesn't have to worry about trying to stay alive or trying to overcome the storm or other things like that, he sort of loses sight of the fact that he can do something to stay alive around here. As he switches over to this subjectivistic kind of thinking, an intuitive kind of thinking—he sort of gets away from the task of doing something about the very problems with which he is faced. As he tries to let everyone have their way, he loses sight of the fact that you just can't do that. That's something in this world that is just against the "laws of nature" which will get you into trouble if you are not careful.

I get scared to death when they enter the FS system and think that everyone in this world is nice. If we can get to the point that we solve the problem of getting up one more level so their eyes are open and they realize there are all kinds of people in this world who are not nice, we'll be better off. This is the problem that I'm faced with. It isn't the problem of the drug culture and the like. I sat around the other morning with a dozen young men graduating this year [1971]. Unless this economy changes incredibly, they haven't a ghost of a chance of getting jobs, paying taxes, having lodging, or getting food by just wandering around 'being happy.'

They see the world situationistically. They see it relativistically. In the relativistic existential state, individuals respond in ways which indicate 'others have their way and we have ours, and each to his own; it is not mine to judge.' If the central psychology of this system is to avoid rejection by society and others, then this is what the whole life of the person revolves around—avoiding rejection by the valued others. They talk about how important it is to have community; how important it is for there to be intimacy among people; how important it is that there be involvement; how important it is that people share experience, but if you observe them behaviorally they show an amazing inability to commit themselves to doing for other people. They're still very much interested in themselves but they are talking, almost glibly, about the need to share with others, the need to be with others, the need to get along with others. One of the things which is most characteristic about them is—and we see a great deal of this today—their inability to articulate: "Hey man, yeah man, that's it. We're with it boy, we really got it. You got the feel, man?" What the hell are they talking about? They cannot express, in an articulate manner, what their feelings are. He appears to affect a deliberate inarticulation and disdain for precise language.

You will find responses from both FS and ER which are similar. They both show negative sensitivity to control by authority. FS is sensitive to control by the peer group and the situation, whereas ER will go off alone in his own direction. At the FS *sociocentric level,* man becomes centrally a sociocentric being, a being concerned with the relation of his self to other selves. He becomes concerned with belonging, with being accepted, with not being rejected, with knowing the inner side of self and other selves so human harmony can come to be. When he achieves this he becomes concerned with more than self and other selves. He becomes concerned with self in relation to life and the whole, the total universe.[169]

Learning in the Relativistic State

Let us think about learning in the FS, sociocentric, relativistic existential system. At this level yet another functional neurological system dominates man's behavior. The S system follows the learning principles of what is today called modern Social Learning in the theory of Rotter and others and Observational Learning and the like as found in the work of Bandura and Walters. This is a learning system that I have not seen utilized as much as it might be by learning-systems people.

The learning system associated with it has been variously called the vicarious, the modeling or the observational learning system. All of these refer to an individual's acquisition of new knowledge and potential behavior through observation without receiving any direct external reinforcement for his own acts or without even making the observed response. This learning occurs when people watch what others do, or when they attend to the physical environment, to events, and to symbols such as words or pictures. It occurs when FS man observes the consequences that other people obtain when they behave one way or another without even engaging in the behavior he observes.

You are getting beyond the ER level where the human being is concerned with things material. You are getting beyond the human being that is concerned with just seeing to it that his belly is full and he's got a good house to live in. This human being has all these things. You are getting to a human being who is now free enough to really begin to do some very serious thinking, and he is going to do it about the here and the now. Those who think in an FS way are unhappy over the absence of personal relevance in any abstractions that are a part of learning. They think in terms of *sensing* and *apprehending* rather than in terms of *comprehending*. They tend to refuse to deal with anything that analyzes or breaks down a learning experience—thus a way of thinking not easy to handle within learning-systems thinking. If you are developing learning programs for those centralized in the FS existential state, you should attend particularly to the work of Bandura and Walters.

---

[169] Graves, Clare W. (1970). Levels of Existence: An Open System Theory of Values. *Journal of Humanistic Psychology*, Fall, Vol. 10, No. 2, p. 131-155.

The individual in the relativistic existential state wants to solve problems. The FS moves to solve problems through human philosophical thought, but FS wants to work *with* the teacher, leader, manager, etc. in this. Remember, the FS level is also the most egalitarian of the systems. Let me illustrate this to you in this manner. I have talked about the way one would be introduced to different groups. Now, when you get to the FS level, you don't get introduced with any of these trappings. If I am going out where I know there will be an FS group and the person says: "Well, now how should we go about introducing you?" I say: "We have with us tonight Clare Graves, he works at Union College." That's it.

Why? The person centralized in the FS system is going to judge whether I have expertise. I damned well better have it, or I am not going to get anywhere. The trainer working with those thinking in the FS state better know something, and they better have *earned* status. He better not have any status that comes from any other direction. You don't violate this egalitarian characteristic in the FS system. You're just another human being—and I am not saying this in any derogatory fashion—no matter who you are. You are valued by the FS if you have either the information or the attitude that is conducive to showing the FS that you understand what he is trying to do which is to unravel a tremendous problem for which there just isn't any easy answer. But above all, the methodology is openness, candidness, honesty and meeting the people with whom you are working on the level which says: "Look, you, too, have got a brain in your head; I'll help you with this problem" or "Please help me with this problem."

We now have our human up to the FS level and we are now teaching in order to make movement on to the A'N' level possible. Now, what are we dealing with here? The theory says, when we get the human being to the FS level, we have come to the end of one way of looking at existence. And now we have to take this human being, and sort of flip-flop this person and get him to see the whole business of life in an altogether different light from that which he has seen life before. We have to get this human to see that he or she has come to the very end of being able to solve problems by thinking the way the person thinks. We have to produce one hell of a jump, one tremendous change in the cognitive thinking of the human being.

This human, this FS human, has much clearer eyes in terms of seeing of what the world is all about than has the human beings who have preceded him at other levels of existence. We have a human who, with the psychology that is present, wants very much to attach self to the ideas of others, is driven very much from within to explore things of the here and now in a very serious philosophical fashion, exploring in essence the problems of the here and now in as almost a serious fashion as the philosophically minded people of the DQ world explored the problems of God and its meaning, the hereafter, and all of the things that developed back in those earlier times.

The person gets to this point, and begins to flounder. He tries drugs as a means to coming up with insights. This is what they are doing with this whole psychedelic business; they are trying to come up with something that will pull things together for them. Look at the language they use: "I want to get it together. I wanna' get it all together." So, at this point they try things such as meditation. They try biofeedback. All of them are good methods. Unfortunately, they are simply holding methods; they don't provide the philosophical framework that enables people to think differently about the problems. They enable them to handle their frustrations, and to build up some more knowledge about themselves and what they are troubled with; but, it is coming up with some new way of thinking about the problems, whatever they are, that we are confronted with.

Something is missing. FS man doesn't have a means to the end of trying to think about the things his innards tell him he wants to think about. The basic educational need is in the person. The trainer, the educating person, has to provide the framework for thinking that the person lacks. You offer a method, once you get to a point where the learner has a need to try to understand things in the here and now—things that have been felt, perceived, but not been quite able to put together – in a way that would focus in upon the idea that what is missing is the framework with which to think about the problem. I don't care what problem you are dealing with. The problem of the transition from FS to A'N' is the problem of coming up with a *new way to think about* the problems that the person is trying to solve; that is what this transition is.

We can't make the FS to A'N' transition—and please don't misunderstand me here because I am not trying to be egocentric—until some guy like me comes along with a new way of thinking about whatever the problems are, because somebody's got to supply the framework. This applies to any set of problems. The jump is to a new framework.

Now, we don't know at this stage of the game in the psychological world, as I have said, whether this kind of theoretical point of view is the answer toward the FS desire to make more sense out of things human. But you have to detail it with them. You have to lay it out before them. You have to provide those crucial points of dissonance in which they are brought up sharply to see how great is the need for a change in their way of thinking. Above all, the methodology is openness, candidness, honesty and meeting the people with whom you are working on the level which says: "Look, you too have a brain in your head."

New ways of thinking about particular problems enable the transition from the FS to the A'N' to take place. I don't care how fuzzy that framework is, if you have any kind of framework which you think may help the person put together things he feels the need to put together and make sense of, candidly and openly lay it on the line to the person, and say: "Test it out."

Management of the Relativistic State

Sixth-level man is a sociocentric being. In the personalistic, FS state, the manager must keep in mind that, for the employee, relating self to others and to one's inner self is central. He believes in belonging, adjusting, and togetherness. He is other-directed. Incentives stem from others and directiveness comes from the power of group opinion. If his group slows down at work, he slows down. If his group says change, he changes. If his group says fix prices, he fixes prices. 'Right' to him is to do as his group directs, and 'wrong' is to be or want to be different. Getting along, not rocking the boat is a must to sixth-level man. He is the strong promoter of "human relations" in industry. It is he who believes in the magic of the tender treatment, of participation, of the sanctity of the group approach, of the inviolability of majority rule, the nice word, the personal 'good brother' attention of the boss.

Today many managers—too many of them, for reasons that cannot now be detailed—tend to remain somewhere in the region of fourth- and fifth-level existence, while many of the managed are beginning to move through and beyond the level of existence of their managers. The managed are beginning to behave in the manner described by McGregor's Theory Y, but many of their bosses cannot accept the insights necessary to lift themselves to the level of responsive or integrative management required. On the one hand, the fixated fifth-level manager cannot overcome the fear of loss of his power, and the sixth-level manager's energy is consumed in the fear of being disliked. The former are increasing directive managerial controls and the latter are regressing thereto. These managers who blame their problems on labor that is too powerful, on government that intervenes, on foreigners that compete, or on unreasoning workers whose demands are ridiculous might better ask: "How do my values clash with the values of those whom I manage?"

As the belonging level emerges, the sociocratic ethic, the team concept of work, the 'organization man' idea, gathers force. FS spawns participative or consensus management. Management, here, is based on the assumption that the human is a group animal seeking above all else to be accepted in a community of humans important to him. Within this ethic, the rules created for proper behavior are the ways prescribed so that groups may function smoothly. When these rules evolve, incentives stem from others and directiveness comes from the power of group opinion. It provides each a voice in running the organization because this system believes nothing gets done until all the people involved agree; so the management brings all interested people together before a decision is made. This is done, though to others it appears tedious—almost interminable—before the process of discussion toward compromise produces a consensus. Through this procedure, all members align themselves behind the consensus goal. It is an ethic typified by passivity to what others expect one to do. He is good who can be persuaded to do as the organization desires, and he is good who quietly accepts the directive that he get into no trouble with the group and gets the group in no trouble. The belief is that the human will work best when he or she feels secure and a part of what is happening. He is bad who rocks the boat, who deigns to differ.

The individual is seen to benefit only through the elevation of the group as a whole. Thus, this management does not operate for the quick pay-off but for that which will provide the long run better competitive position. This is because a stable life for all is the prime value with quality far exceeding quantity as a value. Quality control is a prime means to organizational goals, so short-term setbacks are accepted in order to obtain long-term qualitative goals. It promotes self-discipline over self-expression; adequate means to do the work and to live over frills, ceremonies, social welfare and social interaction; the future over the present or the past; own group over outsiders; in-group cooperation over competition; and group over individual needs.

Thus, group membership is greatly valued – all individual values, morals, concepts, and ethics are derived from the group and can change overnight. Any non-group individual, thing, or concept has no valid claim to any consideration beyond what the group grants. There is an easy working relationship between management and labor because both believe one's importance is determined by the good reputation of the organization. Management and labor trust one another to make the right decisions, the decisions that will improve their group's competitive position.

The subordinate at this level is concerned with social rather than material matters. As a result the work place slows down as the employee seeks acceptance by others and a congenial atmosphere. An effective change agent here is a peer—never authority. Authority couldn't have any effect whatsoever. They object strongly to authority's lead or pressure, but a peer that the individual liked could effect change. It is the peer group that determines the means by which the valued end – community with other people he values – is to be obtained.

The appropriate management approach at this level is the group process. It requires that the manager be open to the group's values and become a group member. As a member of the group the manager has equal 'right' with all other group members to offer suggestions as to what the group should consider or do. The manager must be ready to go along with whatever everyone else in the group thinks is best. The manager must be open, nondirective, and participatory in the truest sense of the terms. The congruent form of management, Participative Management,[170] is consistent with this state. Participative management fosters the idea that organizations will prosper when all play a role in the decision-making process, when all have a say. It is a form of management that gives power to the managed and acceptance to those who run the organization.

Because there are strong needs to be accepted, the manager, therefore, accepts others unquestioningly. Group processes, consensus, majority rule, and sensitivity training are valued. Through the continued, within-group, participative stance of offering suggestions—trial ballooning—the manager attempts to provide the substitutive direction organizationally required. "If the [sixth]-level person is a producer, he slows down his work pace and turns to satisfying the needs which are now important to him—his *social* needs. This is why participative management must operate when the producer and the manager are at the [sixth] level."[171]

---

[170] See Blake and Mouton (Managerial Grid), MacGregor (Theory X and Theory Y), and Lickert (Four-Model Systems). The central idea is that empowered employees will feel better about their jobs and be more productive. [Extended into financials by Open Book Management. (Also see: Case, John (1995). *Open Book Management*. New York: Harper Collins.]

[171] Ibid., (Graves, 1966).

Participative-substitutive group process management will not increase human effort unless the group itself puts on the pressure; but it will keep effort from deteriorating more. It will substitute new means of production for the human physical means that the group, and interpersonalistic individuals, will not accept and have resisted. "The [sixth]-level employee no longer believes it is his moral duty to do his best, as does the [fourth]-level worker; nor does he believe that hard work is the measure of the man, as does the [fifth]-level producer. He believes there are other means to the end of living than hard work. The means which can be tapped for productive effort is the group effort. Being a social man and being subservient to his group, [sixth]-level man will readily follow the group's plan for revising work procedures and the like. But there is an inherent danger in this group-mindedness. [Sixth]-level people can become so enamored of group decision-making processes that they have one meeting after another and never get anything done. That is why management at this level must be what I call "substitutive" as well as participative. The group must work to substitute new ideas and new machines to compensate for the inevitable loss of sheer human effort."[172]

Managements' failure to "substitute" within group process management is increasingly seen, especially in public sector. In non-competitive work groups and organizations where the group or organization is at the sixth level, only participative, human relations techniques instituting Value Analysis[173] concepts will be effective – participative-substitutive group process for the relativistic existential state. "Participative management accepts the fact that the producer now has needs he must satisfy which are more social than material. These needs can be harnessed to productive effort, but sometimes the means seem roundabout."[174] The manager centralized in the relativistic state, at first, will most likely "[gravitate] to the Blake-Mouton 5.5 managerial style; that is, he shows intermediate concern for production and intermediate concern for people. And later this 5.5 style becomes the 1.9 style; that is, "keep the people happy and hope for production."[175] As a group member, the manager has equal right to personally reject trial balloons that are dysfunctional to the group, manager, or organization.

The proportion of employees at this level in organizations today is growing and will increase in the future. The negative results of attempts

---

[172] Ibid., (Graves, 1966).
[173] See Miles, Lawrence D. (1961).
[174] Ibid., (Graves, 1966).
[175] Ibid., (Graves, 1966).

to apply inappropriate managerial styles by managers who are unable or unwilling to manage in a participative-substitutive group process style are becoming apparent. This may go far to explain what we see occurring more and more in today's organizations where neither management nor labor leadership can manage a large percentage of the work force.

There are two basic forms that mismanagement takes at the interpersonalistic level. The first and currently most common is the use of a non-participatory management style. The manager in this case is seen as non-group by the FS subordinate and, therefore, someone having no rights to "manage" the group. In the best case the manager is just neutrally non-group and ignored. In the worst case the manager is negatively non-group, and a Directive Manager, resulting in a serious error of judgment. Today the management of many organizations views the increasing numbers of individuals at the FS level as evidence of people "going soft." If this interpretation is made and steps are taken to combat the attitudes with a directive, authoritarian managerial style (9.1), the result will be a disastrous form of mismanagement. Passive resistance of the worst order will arise, and productivity and performance will tumble. In the extreme, management having clearly shown itself as non-group, the entire organization could be brought to a halt through continued passive covert activity, or more active overt activity.

The second form of mismanagement is for the manager to join the group totally and unconditionally without the substitutive element. The sixth-level group will do as it pleases within and with the organization. If it is a highly qualified and skilled group, this won't present a problem. If not, viability is threatened because of similar values. The leader strives to entice the group to arrive at the managerially desired decision and the group strives to avoid a decision they fear others will not like. The time for decision-making is so slowed that the organization comes to a state of arrested development. Conferences are held, committees are constituted and informal meetings abound. When these fail, these believers in communication as the means to the organizational goals sharpen their communication techniques. Group Dynamics, Sensitivity Training, Learning through Listening, Conference Management Techniques, morale studies, feed-down, feed-up and feedback procedures are tried, but to little avail. After all, the goal of sixth-level people is to be liked, not to decide.

When FS managers manage DQ or ER level people in situations where there are no great pressures from competitors, management sometimes abdicates its responsibility, as well as its authority. Suppose the manager, because of the desire to be liked and not hated, tries to woo the producers. The ER level producers conclude that management does not have to watch cost, hence try to 'take' it for all they can get. And as this wooing takes place, DQ producers become disgusted because the leaders believe the followers should participate in decisions and the follower believes he should be told. The manager waits for participation and the managed wait for direction. In his desire to be liked, the leader loses his sense of energetic purpose. He must make it appear that his group decides and the group must not appear to push. Decisions should be made when all see alike, but such violates the variability in men. In this hopeless combination of dissimilar incongruent value systems the organization is stifled. Often, it dies.

One other form of mismanagement for the sociocentric employee is lack of honesty and openness from the manager and the organization. If the organization has a problem, candidly and openly lay it on the line to the person (as in education). If you don't have a solution, candidly and openly lay this on the line to the person, and say: "The problem is, we know what the problem is, but we don't know how to think about the problem that we've got." The FS with his group-centeredness is tremendously disposed to sit down and really do some thinking about this. And he will work by the hour in a group setting, exploring this, exploring that, going all over the place trying to find some kind of a solution. So, if you don't have it, you say so. You don't violate one thing of the utmost importance in the centrality of the FS system: this is basically a human organism that is becoming very honest; not completely and totally so—we're not perfect, human beings—but relatively speaking, in comparison with other levels of existence, this is an open and honest human being. If you don't meet that person at that level, you are dead.

Readiness for Change in the Relativistic State

Picture, if you will, FS man seated in a yoga position contemplating his inner self. He has completed the last theme of the subsistence movement of existence. There are no new deficiency motivations to rouse him from his meditations. In fact, he might well go on contemplating his navel to the day of his death, if he only had some suitable arrangement to care for his daily needs. And it is quite possible for a few FS individuals to live this way. But what happens when the majority of a population begins to arrive at the FS level of existence? Who is left to care for their daily needs? Who is left to look after the elaborate technology which assures their survival? If we return to FS man seated in his yoga position, we see that what finally disturbs him is the roof falling in on his head.

This roof can be called the A' problems—the ecological crisis, the energy crisis, the population crisis, limits to growth, or any other such thing which is enough of a disturbance to awaken FS man. Naturally enough, his first reaction will be that evil technology is taking over and that all the good feeling and greenery which made the Earth great is in the process of being wrecked forever. (We remember that attitude from the days when his father, ER man, had much the same erroneous notion.) FS man is correct in the sense that his entire way of life, his level of existence, is indeed breaking down—it *must* break down in order to free energy for the jump into the A'N' state, the first level of being. This is where the leading edge of man is today.

Using this framework to approach current American society, we can easily see an efflorescence of personalistic (FS) values in the popularity of such things as Esalen, yoga, the encounter group, the humanistic psychology movement, and participatory decision-making in management. By all these means and many others, personalistic FS man endeavors to achieve self-harmony and harmony with others. These individuals do not, of course, see their striving for harmony with the human element as merely a stage they are going through, but as the ultimate, the permanent, goal of all life. This short-range vision which views the current goal as the ultimate goal of life is shared by human beings at every level of existence for as long as they remain centralized in that particular level.

Using E-C theory, we see that the so called *generation gap* of the recent past was in reality a *values* gap between the DQ and the ER and the FS levels of existence. For example, many of the parents of FS youth subscribed to ER values which emphasize proving one's worth by amassing material wealth. To individuals operating at this level, it was inconceivable that their children might reject competition for cooperation and seek inner self-knowledge rather than power, position, and things. Worse yet to the ER parents was the devotion of these young people to foreigners and minority groups who, according to ER thinking, deserved their unfortunate condition because they were too weak or too stupid to fight for something better. Thus, the foreigners and minorities were characterized as lazy and irresponsible and the youth who defended them as lily-livered "bleeding hearts."

In turn, FS youth contributed to the confrontation because their civil disobedience and passive resistance offended their parents more than outright violence ever could have. These young people not only challenged Might (and therefore Right), but offered no new Might and Right to replace that which they mocked. Consequently, they were rightly (to the ER mentality) called anarchists, and it was widely said that such permissiveness was wrecking the values which made America great. Of course, our hindsight now tells us that America was not, in fact, "wrecked;" and today one can see a great many of the ER parents who protested against anarchy getting in touch with themselves at Esalen and advocating theories of participative management.

Another outgrowth of the transition of our society from ER to FS values was the de-emphasis of technology. Technology was the principal means by which ER man conquered the world. He did not, like his ancestor CP man, use force alone; but rather he attempted to understand the natural laws in order to conquer men and nature. Because of the close historical association of technology with ER values, the emerging FS consciousness could not help but view technology as a weapon of conquest. Thus, along with rejecting conquest, FS man rejected technology and in its place set up its exact opposite: Nature. In other words, the exploration of inner man and a return to nature (including all manner of idealized natural foods) replaced the exploitation of nature and other human beings in a quest for material wealth.

Since, at the sixth level, man values participation, the committee or group decision, and interpersonal relationships rather than going it alone, many such as Rand and Fromm fear that he has lost his self, that he has given up personal dignity for social approval. But this, I submit, is an error. Man has not given up his self; he has simply subordinated it for the time being. This is not the end of self-respect. It will return, our system says, only in a newer, higher form. Thus, man shows growth in placing self at a distance when reflecting on one's own actions.

Sixth-level values are a great step forward for man. They reflect the beginning of man's humanism, the demise of his animalism. As interpersonal relationships become safe and secure, sixth-level man comes to perceive that he has played his individuality for the chance of social acceptance. He finds that sacrificing self to obtain the good will of others takes from him his individuality. Eventually he finds this is a price too high to pay. A gnawing urge to be himself begins to work in his inner world and he begins to strive for his seventh form of human existence. Thus, man strives on seeking a new value system by which he can be a more inclusive man.

When he achieves this, he finds he must become concerned with more than self or other selves, because while he was focusing on the inner self to the exclusion of the external world, his outer world has gone to pot. So now he turns outward to life and to the whole, the total universe. As he does so he begins to see the problems of restoring the balance of life which has been torn asunder by his individualistically oriented, self-seeking climb up the first ladder of existence.

Rather than these changes continuing to get closer and closer together as Toffler[176] suggests, my own thesis is that there will be an acceleration up to the time that it produces very horrendous problems. When it produces problems of such a degree, things are going to have to slow down tremendously in order to deal with the resulting problems.

The accumulation of unsolved problems is such that it's actually going to produce the most dramatic change in human behavior that has yet occurred in all of man's history. The human brain is of the order of ten or eleven or twelve billion cells, on the average [now thought to be 100 billion neurons]. Each of those cells has the capacity for ten thousand interconnections. That's rather tremendous. Now, as I said earlier, Darwin never dealt with that. He never answered why we have that big brain. All the data I have presented say that in all of mankind's history up to this moment, relatively few of the cells have been called upon. The N cells, the O cells, the P cells, the Q cells, the R cells, the S cells—they have been called upon to date. But they make up very few of the total number of cells in the brain. What are the rest doing there? What about the idea of open-endedness?

We could show that these levels—AN, BO, CP, DQ, ER, FS, A'-N', etc.—are distinctly different neurological systems. And I could even go on to point out the locus of these spatially within the brain. This defense for the existence of dynamic neurological systems and for qualitative as well as quantitative differences as to how humans learn when each system is open and operant cannot be herein expanded, but these data do suggest that there is substantive evidence for the conception of a hierarchically arranged dynamic neurological system in the brain.

I have hypothesized that it is the activation in the brain of a tremendous number of those cells that have been there but doing nothing, and that they combine with the lower level systems to start human life all over again. The seventh level of human behavior is actually the beginning of human life all over again on a new and different basis. This accounts for why the brain is so big, and why the problems before us are solvable if we but manage to stay alive.

A seminar participant once said: "I seemingly foresee a fairly chaotic situation arising. As people in certain parts of the world develop

---

[176] Toffler, Alvin (1970). *Future Shock*. New York: Random House.

leadership whose level of coping becomes higher and higher and they deal with problems that are greater and greater in different ways, also advancing technologically at tremendously accelerated ways, whereas other nations have, uh, operate on lesser coping levels and have leadership whose coping system is on a lower level, and deal with problem on a much more aggressive ways. Then we are going to have a tremendous conflict at some point of things, you think?"

I replied, "May I say we are having a tremendous conflict, not that 'we are going to have.' We just haven't had it in as rough a form as it could possibly be."

He continued, "Well, I don't think that there is enough of a disparity between leadership in the more advanced or leadership in some of the lesser advanced areas of the world. Our leadership here, I would say, is primarily ER, and in the third world nations it is primarily CP. But I don't see it is that much as of disparity between the levels of leadership, as I would see between A'N' and DQ, or between A'N' and CP. So the danger is being kept aside momentarily, but as things begin to accelerate a little bit more we are going to create greater problems."

I concluded, "It's a great, great bomb we are living on. It may go off. I don't know that it will, but it can. As I say over and over again, there is no guarantee in existence. If thus and so occurs, that is, directed toward the solution of the existential problems that are now facing us, then things can go well for us in the future. It would take a lengthy period of time to right them, so we will have a long period when man, if he arrives leadership-wise at the seventh level nodal version, we'll be there. But, we have no guarantees that we're going to get there."

You see, as man moves from the sixth level, the level of being with other men, the sociocentric level, to the seventh level, the level of freedom to know and to do, the cognitive level of existence, a chasm of unbelievable depth of meaning is being crossed. The bridge from the sixth level, the FS level, to the seventh level, the A'N' level, is the bridge between getting and giving, taking and contributing, destroying and constructing. It is the bridge between deficiency or deficit motivation and growth or abundance motivation. It is the bridge between similarity to animals and dissimilarity to animals.

By now he has felt many times that he has arrived, but arrived he has not, nor will his arrival ever come to be. His forms for existence to date have required of him less than he has to give, his cognitiveness. He has not arrived because all previous forms of existence, all previous value systems restricted his most typically human characteristic, his cognition. But now with six basic existential problems solved, the cognitive realm opens wide and enables the leading edge of man to capture a glimpse of the future modes of life and values for mankind. Feeling an expansive sense of freedom, he emerges into the seventh level or First Being Level.

Chapter 13

The Systemic Existence — The A'N' State[177]

The 1ˢᵗ Being Level

The A'N' - Existential, Cognitive, Problematic Existential State

Theme: *Express self for what self desires, but never at the expense of others and in a manner that all life, not just my life, will profit.*

The *'Express self but not at the expense of others'* Conceptions

---

[177] A'N' was GT in earlier publications. With the conclusion that there are six basic themes which repeat, a thesis of this book, Dr. Graves began using the primes rather than the previous GT and HU for the last two systems appearing in his data. While that was only a hypothesis, as indicated earlier, the editors have chosen to use the primes since Dr. Graves used them in his later papers. The transition from the sixth (FS) to the seventh level marked the transition from "subsistence" levels to "being" levels, the second cycle through the basic themes.

A'N' is the first system in the second spiral of existence – the First Being Level. The seventh state develops when man has resolved the basic human fears, when man's need for respect of self, as well as others, reorganizes and revitalizes his capacities to do and to know. With this, a marked change in his conception of existence arises. Man has done previously and he has known previously, but now the purpose of his doing and his knowing changes radically.

The A'N' system is triggered by the second set of human survival problems – the A' problems of existence. These are the problems of the threat to organismic life and rape of the world produced by the third, fourth, fifth, and sixth existential ways. Thus, the A' problems are problems such as the need to substitute for depleting natural resources, overpopulation, difficulties of too much individuality, and the like—problems which require tremendous change in thinking of human kind in order to solve them. The A'N' state develops when man has resolved the basic human fears, when man's need for respect of self, as well as others, reorganizes and revitalizes his capacities to do and to know. The seventh level of human behavior is actually the beginning of human life all over again on a new and different basis.

With this, a marked change in his conception of existence arises. Earlier forms of existence constricted man's cognition. This characteristic is now sufficiently awakened to provide him insight into his future. Now, with his energies free for cognitive activation, man focuses upon his self and his world.

The picture revealed is not pleasant. Illuminated in devastating detail is man's failure to be what he might be and his misuse of his world, to focus upon the truly salient aspects of life. Triggered by this revelation, man leaps out in search of a way of life and a system of values which will enable him to be more than a parasite leeching upon the world and all its beings. He seeks a foundation for self respect which will have a firm base in existential reality. He casts aside the need to depend and seeks, instead, to be and let be—to be not dependent, not independent, but to be interdependent. He can be, and others can be, too. This firm basis he creates through his seventh-level value system, a value system truly rooted in knowledge and reality, not in the delusions brought on by animal-like needs.

The accumulation of unsolved problems is such that they will produce the most dramatic change in human behavior that has yet occurred in all of man's history. He sees now that he has the problem of life hereafter—not life now, not life after life, but the restoration of his world so that *life* can continue to be. The most serious problem of existence to date is now *his species'* existential problem. Thus at the seventh level, the cognitive level, man truly sees the problems before him if life, *any life,* is to continue.

At this stage the biochemical changes for this system are the 'radium' of E-C theory. My data say that something in the chemical complex producing fear in the organism plays a role, but that's a pretty slim clue. We've got a long, long way to go. The problem of the chemistry of the brain desperately needs to be looked at from within this point of view. Thus far, we can say that this system is triggered by the second set of human survival problems – the A' problems of existence. Second-order survival problems trigger into operation the systemic thinking process in the brain along with a marked activation of previously uncommitted cells. These cells of the Y system in the brain combine with the basic coping cells to form the first of the second order coping systems; that is, N plus some Y equals N' which greatly expands the conceptual thinking of man. This gives birth to the Problematic, Systemic or Cognitive Existential State, A'N'. His *thema* for existence in this problematic existential state is now: *"express self so that all others, all beings, can continue to exist."*[178]

As I have said, once we are able to grasp the meaning of passing from the level of 'being one with others' to the A'N' *cognitive level* of knowing and having to do so that *all* can be and can continue to be, it is possible to see the enormous differences between man and other animals. Thus far, man has been just another animal, a pawn in the hand of the spirit world, a sacrificer of self, an attacker of the world and other men, and a social automaton; but man has never been himself. Here we step over the line which separates those needs that man has in common with other animals and those needs which are distinctly human. But a knowledgeable existence is not enough. It must be subordinated in a higher form of reactive existence.

Many times man has felt that he has arrived, but arrived he has not, nor will arrival ever come to be. Thus, at the end of his first six-step trek, man finds he must return and begin again to travel the road by whence he has come. Man must return for some things to an autistic frame of reference. Thus, our seventh level of existence and our seventh-level value system are repetitions, in an advanced form, of his first level of existence and its reactive value system.

Man, at the threshold of the seventh level, where so many political and cultural dissenters stand today, is at the *threshold of being human.* He is

---

[178] Graves, Clare W. (1970). Levels of Existence: An Open System Theory of Values. *Journal of Humanistic Psychology*, Fall 1970, Vol. 10, No. 2, p. 131-155.

no longer just another of nature's species. And we, in our times, in our ethical and general behavior, are just approaching this threshold. Would that we will not be so lacking in understanding, and would that we not be so hasty in condemnation, that by such misunderstanding and that by such condemnation we block man, forever, from crossing the line between animalism and humanism.

Theoretically, he will move on to repeat his six stages to the benefit of cognitive man (A'N'), and then again to the benefit of compassionate man (B'O'), and so on. By then, man will, in all probability, have changed himself and will move infinitely on. The cyclic aspect of human behavior is not just in the systems cycling as you go from the *sacrifice-self* to the *express-self* to the *sacrifice-self*, and so on; but there is cyclic aspect in the overall system. It appears there are six basic systems of human behavior. When they're lived through, and if the human being is going to continue to exist, the human has to begin to think all over again in some new and different manner.

Despite this, when some people see sixth-level values changing into the values of level seven, once again, they see decay. In a sense this is true, because man transforming into seventh-level thinking values the enjoyment of this life over and above obeisance to authority. He strongly rejects non-dignified, non-human ways of living. It is seen as decadent because it values new ways, new structurings for life, not just the ways of one's elders. Oddly enough, many see this value system as decadent because it casts aside most absolutism; because it does not value self above others, but others having 'just as much as me;' and because it does not value others above self, it values all *and* self, not just the selected few.

It is seen as decadent because it sees many means to the same end, because it readily changes means, and because its ends are in conflict with those of lower level systems. A'N' thinking is in terms of the systemic whole, and thought is about the different wholes in many different ways. It strives to ascertain which way of thinking or which combination of ways fits the extant set of conditions. It is seen as decadent for it values new ways, new structures for life, not just the ways of one's elders, because it values others as well as self, because it values the enjoyment of this life over and above obeisance to authority, because it values others having just as much as me and because it values all and self, not just the few selected others, and thinks in terms of competence, not trappings. It thinks in terms of authority being centered in the person in terms of his/her capacity to act in this or that situation. It is not derived from age, status, blood, etc. It is situational. It must be earned and it must be given over to the superior competence of another.

This system, conceptualized as it is, seems to fall in the humanistic tradition. The theme is: *Express self for what self desires, and others need, but never at the expense of others, and in a manner that all life, not just my life will profit.* A'N' thinking is in terms of what is best for the survival of life, my life, their lives, and all life, but not compulsively; and 'what is best for me or thee does not have to be best for she or them. My way does not have to be yours, nor yours mine; yet I have very strong convictions about what is my way, but never such about yours.' In the FS and the A'N', they both look at things situationally and relativistically. From the sociocentric individual you get the feeling that he is not too sure where he stands, but the seventh-level individual knows full well where he stands. He's got his values; he's got his opinion. It may not be what anyone else has, and he might not share it with you, but if he's got expertise or knowledge in the subject then he's got an opinion.

Overview of System

The cognitive realm opens wide with six basic existential problems solved. This enables the leading edge of man to capture a glimpse of future modes of life and values for humankind. Once we are able to grasp the meaning of passing from the levels of subsistence to the levels of being, we may be able to explain the difference between what man has been and what he might come to be. Feeling an expansive sense of freedom, this human emerges into the Seventh Level or First Being Level unconcerned with social disapproval or any of the usual fears of the other levels. The problems of man today may fade away as, from this new perception, man searches for better, non-violent, and non-submissive ways of being.

Values here, at the Cognitive Existential State, are very different values. Seventh-level values come not from selfish interest but from the recognition of the magnificence of existence and from the desire to see that it shall continue to be. Because of its prime characteristic, dissolution of fear and compulsiveness, with marked increases in conceptual space, other people cannot readily empathize with seventh-level thinking. To seventh-level man, the prime value is life; thus, he focuses on the problems that its existence creates. This is why the prime need is for existence—existence of life, not self. Here, for the first time, man is able to face existence in all its dimensions, even to the point of valuing inconsistencies, oppositions, and flat contradictions. With this, a marked change in his conception of existence arises.

Those centralized in the cognitive existential state truly learn that life is interdependent. The world is seen kaleidoscopically with different views demanding different attention. Knowledge in A'N' thinking exists in different settings; knowers think in different ways. Thus, thinking is in terms of several legitimate interpretations. Several sets of values are legitimate, depending on the thinker and his/her conditions of and for existence. A'N' thinking is in terms of the systemic whole and thought is about many different wholes in different ways. Thought strives to ascertain which way of thinking or which combination of ways fits the extant set of conditions. The A'N' accepts and lives with the fact of differences and that one is relating to people who are different, and thus shows readiness to live with differences.

Since he values "life," the seventh level looks at the world in respect to the many problems that its existence creates—different wants in different species, different values in different men. He sees the world and all its things—all its beings and all its people—as truly interdependent. He sees them entwined in a subjective-objective complex. So he values pluralism. He values that which will enable all animals, all plants and things to be, and all mankind to become. His ethics are based on the best possible evidence as to what will benefit *all*—the majority, the needy, or the desiring is not enough. He values that which will do good for him and all the universe, but the peripheral aspects of what he values today may change tomorrow because as he solves one set of problems he seeks another in its place.

Formulation of the Theory

As I say above, I didn't stand on the mountaintop of Sinai and get the word of Jehovah to develop this theory. This point of view came about in very long series of studies. One of the things I did when I saw that there were people who think in a CP fashion, and people who think in DQ fashion—way back in the beginning before I even had this terminology—when I knew that some people thought in one way, other people thought in another way, and still others thought in yet a different way—I put them together in groups. I took a group of people who thought the same way, and I put them together in different kinds of situations then I observed how they operated. I went out in every day life, unbeknown to these people, and I would just mix and move around them and watch how they behaved and how they operated as human beings in the laboratory of life.

The laboratory in my department enabled me to put people, whom we now refer to as CPs, DQs, ERs, FSs, and A'N's into groups. I put them in situations where they were required to solve problems with multiple answers. I put a group of DQs in a room and they had an opportunity to solve problems that had multiple answers. I put a group of ERs in there, and they had the same opportunity. I put a group of FSs in there, and they had the same opportunity. And I put a group of A'N's in there, and lo and behold, when the results started to come in I found this most peculiar phenomenon: the A'N's find unbelievably more solutions than all the others put together. They found more solutions than the third plus the fourth plus the fifth plus the sixth. I found that the quality of their solutions to problems were *amazingly* better. Now that's a rather remarkable finding when you start to think about it. I found that the average time it took the A'N' group to arrive at a solution was *amazingly* shorter than it took any of the other groups.

Lets go back and look at the data that I am trying to explain. I had to explain why these people appear to be, in one sense of the word, so much more intelligent than other human beings. This is an incredibly different way of thinking. How can anyone be so apparently superior? I ran into these data and I thought at that point, "The whole damned study just blew up. All I've got here is just another measure of intelligence." I thought, "I'm just running into a point where these guys are finding more answers because they're simply brighter human beings."

So, I went back to test this. I used every known way of assessing the intelligence of human beings: the judgment of people who are supposed to know who is brighter or not; I used instruments; I used every possible way. I found that on the average, people who thought in an A'-N' fashion were no brighter than people who thought in a CP fashion. I found that the only thing that was different was a little bit of the range of intelligence. The lower end was not present. That is, I didn't have mentally retarded A'N's; but, I had people who operated and behaved in an A'N' fashion, if you want to use IQ reference, who had an IQ of less then 90.

The studies show that correlation between the E-C levels and IQ is about a .15 relationship. That .15 is accounted for by the fact that you at least have to be more than mentally retarded to get to the CP level and beyond. But at the CP and beyond, intelligence—IQ—just doesn't play a role in this at all. The question arises: So, what in heaven's name does account for this? Why, if a person is not more intelligent, can he solve problems better? What makes it possible for them to operate so much more effectively?

I found that the A'N's did not behave in a redundant fashion. They would try a solution to a problem; the evidence would pile up that it wouldn't work; they would discard it and go off and try another one. The people operating at any of the other systems would try a solution to a problem and you'd come back a half an hour later and there they were trying to use the same method that failed before. The A'N' never did that. When a method didn't work, that was it. He knew it didn't work and he just discarded it as a possibility. He didn't waste his time.

Why aren't they redundant? Because they are not afraid that they might have made a mistake in throwing out an attempted solution. They don't have these fears. They know full well that they did not make a mistake, so they just throw it out. They are not afraid to try a solution that other people would not try. They go ahead and attempt it.

We are trying to explain something remarkable here: A'N' man can solve problems better without being more intelligent. To explain this, I propose that two things, which were present in the second, the third, the fourth, the fifth and the sixth level have disappeared in human behavior when the seventh level comes to be. One of them is compulsiveness—the person is without compulsion. Ambition is shown, but there is not ambitiousness. Anger, even hostility, is present, but it is intellectually used rather than just emotionally displayed. One directs it, rather than allowing it to direct or drive the A'N' self. He does not feel that something has to be done. Let me use one of my favorite terms and see if you can get a feel for what I mean by it. The phrase that I use to describe the person who thinks in the seventh level way is: "the person is one who has ambition but is not ambitious."

For example, I heard [TV talk show host] Merv Griffin quizzing somebody about his goals:

> "I don't have any goals—unless just basically staying alive as human being and not contributing to the mess the human beings are in is a goal. Nothing I necessarily feel I want to accomplish, or there isn't anything I feel I must accomplish," said the guest.
> Merv looked at him and said: "But you've accomplished so much."
> "Well," he says, "yeah, it's true. I've accomplished a lot, but I don't have to. It doesn't matter to me whether I accomplish any more tomorrow or not."

What I find best explains the reason people in the A'N' level behave so much better, quantitatively and qualitatively, time-wise, etc., is this: they simply are not afraid. So, I offer this hypothesis for your consideration: this is the first human being that has lived since man became aware of himself, as an individual at the CP level, who has no fear. They are not afraid of not finding food and staying alive (AN). They are not afraid that they're not going to have shelter (BO). They are not afraid of predatory man (CP). They are not afraid of God (DQ). They are not afraid of not having status or not making it on their own in this world (ER). They are not afraid of social disapproval or rejection (FS). People who are not operating at the seventh level find this very difficult to comprehend. Fear is gone. There is no fear. You ask the person,

> "But, aren't you afraid that people won't like you?"
> "No," comes the reply.
> "Don't you want to be liked by people?" you might ask.
> "Yes."
> "But don't you have to be liked by people?"
> "No, I don't give a damn whether they like me or whether they don't."

The seventh level person would say: "If they like me, fine; but I am not afraid of being not liked. It's not going to make any difference whether I'm liked by them or not liked by them."

Apparently the A'N' human being has gotten beyond having the common basic fears of mankind. He doesn't quake and shiver when the boss comes in. If the boss comes in and if the boss is off base, then he says to the boss: "There is the door. Go." He is not scared of him. He is not afraid to tell him to go. You've got a human being who isn't afraid.

Now, we wouldn't deny, would we, that the fear element has a chemical factor in it? As we know, the brain hasn't changed structurally over the long period of man's history. But if you and I took all the fears that we have out of ourselves, and had all of that energy freed to activate our cognitive processes, look at what we might be able to do. So, if we move the chemical out of the brain what do you have left? I had to explain where that brain-power in the A'N' system came from, and it seemed to me that it came from this dissolution of fear. That would at least account for the extreme energization of the A'N' system and then, provide one possible explanation why they are so much more competent in solving problems.

So, the A'N' groups find more solutions because they aren't afraid to try more solutions. They scoff at standard operating procedure. They value getting done what they want to do without harming or using others in the process. In a sense, the individual is on a binge of personal esteem. He may or may not value what other men do. He really doesn't care. Now, that doesn't mean that they don't behave with caution in a dangerous situation, they do. But there is no fear. This type of thinking still involves anxieties, worries, and concerns, even some fears, but not in a manner bothersome to the person. No need is felt to overcome them. They do not intrude. One lives comfortably with them, tries to deal with them, but does not feel compelled to master them, though still thinking it would be nice if they were gone. They weren't stopped by: 'Well, you shouldn't,' or 'That's not the right way to think,' or 'You'll get in trouble if you think that way.' They found better solutions because, apparently, there was more brain-power brought to bear upon their thinking than you had in others.

I found that the solutions to problems that they came up with were qualitatively of a much higher order. That is what is represented in Exhibit XII. The space within the two lines illustrates that there are more psychological degrees of freedom in the A'N' system than there is in the space of the others combined. The area is greater than the sum of all these others, showing something very remarkable happens when the A'N' state of mind comes into existence in a human being.

In our problem-solving experiments, those centralized in the cognitive existential state, those behaving in the A'N' system, were significantly different behaviorally from both the FS and ER systems. This is why the A'N' system is portrayed as larger than the FS—because in my data these people were freer overall to behave in accordance with their own desires than they were in other systems. The A'N' system is represented as much larger than any other system because the data suggested that it be so conceptualized. So, the two prime characteristics of this system: lack of compulsiveness and absence of fear.

My data say that the ones who think in this way have a remarkable capacity for solving complex problems that other people can't get within a million miles of. This is just the kind of meat he is looking for, and that's what he wants to chew every day of his life. My evidence says this guy thrives on that kind of problem.

Exhibit XII

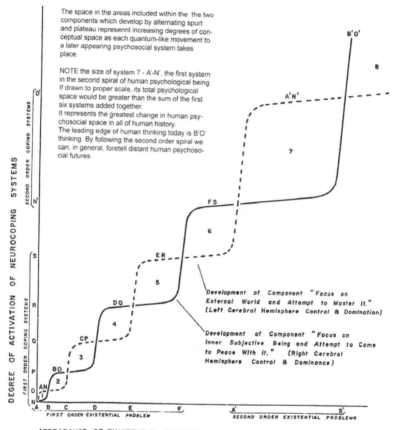

Does not a person at a higher level have a greater repertoire? Indeed he does. You see here in the picture (Exhibit VI, next page) that a person operating at this level has all of these coping means at his disposal. This is why you will find, as we get more into the problem of management and educational methods it is of the utmost importance that the training agent or the managing person be at a level higher then anyone in the group, if you have a heterogeneous group. Then he is more able to call upon the methods that are appropriate to anyone in the group. This is what we are lacking in our educational and organizational world today.

Exhibit VI (repeated)

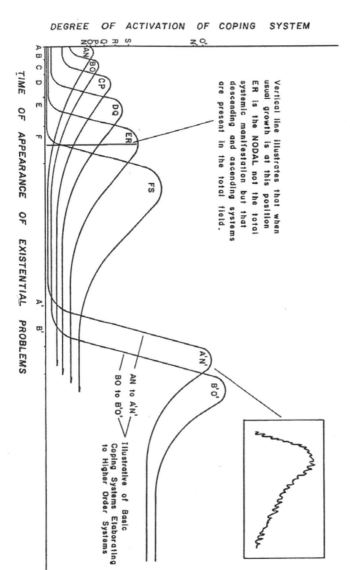

We have so many people who are directing the activities of others who are below at least some of the people who they are trying to manage or educate. In this kind of an incongruent situation it just won't work.

To the A'N', knowledge exists in specific settings. The settings differ and so do the knowers. Several interpretations of any phenomenon are always legitimate depending on the person, his point of view, and his purpose. To them, the teacher's job is to pose problems, help provide ways to see them, but to leave the person to his own conclusion as to what answers to accept. For the seventh level, change and learning would develop whenever new information came in regardless of the source of the information.

Concern is felt, but solutions do not have to be. Care for others is displayed, but one does not feel compelled to care for. Their thought is of being there to help and helping if helping is desired, but not helping to straighten out, to shape up, to gain power or control over. It is not what others think of him that counts. It is not what success or power or prestige he has that is important. Things done well are preferred, but if done poorly, it does not mean the end of the world. It is what he thinks of himself that is important.

The A'N' individual lives in a world of paradoxes. He knows that his personal life is absolutely unimportant, but because it is part of life there is nothing more important in the world. A'N' man enjoys a good meal or good company when it is there, but does not miss it when it is not. He requires little, compared to his ER ancestor, and gets more pleasure from simple things. A'N' man knows how to get what is necessary to his existence and does not want to waste time getting what is superfluous. More than ER man before him, he knows what power is, how to create and use it; but he also knows how limited is its usefulness.

As I said, compulsiveness is also gone in those centralized in this system. The person who thinks in the seventh level way is not compulsively driven to find sexual satisfaction. The person who thinks at the seventh level way can have a rollicking good time in bed if the opportunity is there; but if the opportunity never comes again, so what? It doesn't matter. It just doesn't matter! That which alone commands his unswerving loyalty, and in whose cause he is *ruthless,* is the continuance of life on this earth.

The data indicated that system seven people, those dominated by the A'N' system of personality, were much less rigid and far less dogmatic than other people. They solved problems not only more rapidly, they also found many more solutions to multiple answer problems, and they could change their point of reference unbelievably more rapidly than others.

Another important thing in this point of view is my data regarding aggression. My evidence says, when man operates at the higher level, though aggressiveness is not gone, it is subordinated; in such a large system it is relatively an insignificant thing. I mentioned the aggressiveness of man as we know it appears in the third system. It comes in with the CP system. And, as we noted, there are chemical and hormonal changes taking place in the body of man when he is under the influence of the CP system which cause him to be his most aggressive self and that this aggressive self remains relatively strong in the human personality, though it takes on a different form in the DQ system and in the ER systems. By the time the FS system is dominant in a personality, crime against the person and crime against the other person's self is not found, though I have found crime against the self. Now, in the A'N' system he's even gotten beyond it. At least my subjects have not shown any tendency to commit suicide, no matter how difficult things become for them. They haven't shown any tendency to immolate themselves in any form or to unduly harm their own bodies or others. The Seventh level, the systemic existence, is like the third and fifth levels in that man adjusts the world to himself; but unlike the third, the adjustment of the world is dealt with realistically, not egocentrically.

The seventh level is like the fifth in its emphasis on adjusting the world to the self, but it is not *just* for the self as it is at the fifth level. The welfare of others is considered in this system. The difference in the A'N', for example, from the ER, is that the person will defend his conclusion as long as he thinks it's the proper conclusion. The ER will hold on to it even after everyone in the whole world knows it isn't working – Nixon, for instance. Everyone knew his Viet Nam policy was failing and that darned guy held onto his conclusions firmly all this time. The A'N' will never do this.

Thus far, I've offered a rough chronometer of the evolution of these different systems. Although systemic thought started to emerge in physics literature around 1915, the leading edge of the seventh level, the problematic state, started to appear in significant amount in my data around 1952-1953. The subject population consisted of about 7 percent of them around that time. The thinking was present in rare cases earlier than that.

We have been in decreasing periods of time for the dominance of a system in human behavior up to this date. What the theory says is that the problems which have accumulated over the first six levels of human existence are so immense that we now have created a situation in which, as we approach the possibility of living by the seventh level way of life, we will begin a period which will again be a very long period as we try put this world back into order again. As I have said, my own thesis is that there will be an acceleration up to the time that it produces very horrendous problems. When it produces problems to such a degree, things are going to have to slow down tremendously in order to deal with them.

The A'N' way of life will be so different from any that we have known up to now that its substance is very difficult to transmit; it is the most difficult system of all to comprehend. Possibly the following will help: A'N' man will explode at what he does not like, but he will not be worked up or angry about it. He will get satisfaction out of doing well but will get no satisfaction from praise for having done so. Praise is anathema to him. He is egoless, but terribly concerned with the 'rightness' of his own existence. He is detached from and unaffected by social realities, but has a very clear sense of their existence. In living his life he constantly takes into account his personal qualities, his social situation, his body, and his power, but they are of no great concern to him. They are not terribly important to him unless they are terribly important to you. He fights for himself but is not defensive.

A'N' is a system that has only emerged in recent years in the behavior of people. A tremendous increase of conceptual space markedly changes the thinking of the human when operating at this level. Fear, but not anxiety, practically disappears. Compulsiveness is gone. A person has ambition, but is not ambitious. He or she has anxieties, worries, and concerns, even some fears; but they are not bothersome to the person. No need is felt to overcome them because they do not intrude. He or she thinks of how to deal with them so as to feel comfortable, but does not feel compelled to master them. The A'N' accepts that life is an up-and-down journey from problem to solution, with no mean point ever to be found.

The A'N' has no irrational doubt, but he does feel anxiety; he seeks to do better, but is not ambitious. People who operate at this level have ambition but are not ambitious. They are people who have strong concerns but 'don't give a damn,' and yet will 'work like hell' to help. They think of being there to help and helping, if help is desired. They never think in terms of helping to try to straighten a person out or to try to shape a person up or to try to control a person or to try to provide for a person.

He will strive to achieve—but through submission, not domination—and his conclusions will follow his logic. He enjoys the best of life, of sex, of friends, and comfort that is provided, but he is not dependent on them. These are people who have a very strong feeling of care for other human beings, but the last thing in the world they want you to do in any way at all is to reciprocate. For example, the person who operates at this level simply cannot abide compliments. Oh, they will accept them, but when they accept them they say under their breath "Oh, god, I didn't want that. I don't live to get complimented. I have no such desire for that kind of experience." It's a very different view of life.

They see the world as one great big system and that unless you attend to each and every part you're going to be in real trouble. There is no room in this person's thinking for selfishness. They see life in terms of life continuing hereafter, but they have no concern with a hereafter whatsoever. They are terribly concerned about the fact that life must continue to exist hereafter, in terms of what is best for the survival of life—my life, their life and all life—but not compulsively. When they talk about life, they don't mean human life, they mean all life.

They accept that the one thing you can be sure about life is that it's a problem. That's all there is to life. It's a bunch of problems and there is no other way to live it. Thus, at the seventh level, the cognitive level, man truly sees the problems before him if life, any life, is to continue.

Thus, his values here are of a very different order. Values at the seventh level came not from selfish interest but from the recognition of the magnificence of life and from the desire to see that it shall continue to be. To seventh-level man, the prime value is existence and thus he focuses on the problems that the nature of existence per se creates. For the first time, man is able to face existence in all its dimensions, both those which seem to be known and those which are unexplained, even to the point of valuing inconsistencies, oppositions and flat contradictions.

He values "life" and looks at the world in the context of the many problems that it creates: different wants in different species, different values in different men. He accepts and lives with the fact of differences and of relating to people who are different. He shows readiness to live with those differences and fascination with them. What one values is based on the best possible evidence of what will be good for him but not harm others. This value system prescribes that what one valued yesterday may not be what one values tomorrow. It prescribes that some values which were bad yesterday will be bad today, just as some values which were good yesterday will probably be good tomorrow because knowledge tells us this is so.

His 'means' values here are *accepting* values. He values the genuine acceptance of human nature as it is; he shuns artificiality and others' preferences for what it should be. He values all human appetites but is not a compulsive slave to any of them. He values spontaneity, simplicity, and ethics that 'make sense'—but not conventionality. Just continuing to develop is more valued than striving to become this or that. The activity is more important than any acclaim that may result.

He values solving problems more than fulfilling selfish desires and what must be done rather than that which he desires to do. Universality is valued over provinciality and broadness of view is preferred to pettiness. He values the long run of time, even beyond his life. Detachment is a value which replaces the objectivity of his ER days, and a few deep relationships mean more to him than broad acceptance by other men. Viable ends determine his behavior more than do the means to the ends. Above all else, he values democracy in the very deepest sense. He is not an egocentric—"Do unto others as you would have them do unto you"—but a "Do unto others as they would have done to them" democrat. To him there are many roads to Rome and what matters is not the path that is taken, but that one gets to Rome, to the continuance of all life.

Today seventh-level man, with his mind open for cognitive roaming, is developing the coming mode of life. Proper behavior in the seventh level of existence is the recognizant way. Its ethic is 'recognize—truly notice—what life is and you shall know how to behave.' That is the foundation stone of the existence ethic. The proper way to behave is the way that comes from working within existent reality. If it is realistic that one should suffer, then suffer he should. If it is realistic to be happy, then it is good to be happy. If the situation calls for authoritarianism, then it is proper to be authoritarian; and if the situation calls for democracy, one should be democratic. Behavior is proper if it is based on today's best possible evidence. He who behaves within such limits and fails or has to change should feel no shame. This ethic prescribes that what was right yesterday may not be seen as right tomorrow. And it prescribes that some behavior which was wrong yesterday will always be wrong, just as some behavior which was right yesterday may or may not be right today.

Management of the Cognitive State

An employee at the cognitive existential state is perfectly willing to have management set reasonable standards for quantity and quality of performance, but he is ends-oriented, not means-oriented. The cognitive goes into action only when he has a problem that really interests him. He appears to drop out, have no more verve, and not be creative any longer simply because the problems are of no interest to him whatsoever. Free of compulsions and anxieties of previous levels, this is a truly cooperative individual who, seeing the interdependence of all things, has no need for destructive individual competition but is capable of cold ruthlessness if the situation requires as long as it doesn't harm others.

The A'N' worker reacts negatively when required to ask an administrator's approval for materials he needs in order to be productive. He reacts positively when he can tell his supervisor what he needs to do a job and when the supervisor considers it his job to do as his subordinate says. The A'N' employee believes that he – not a superior – should make the decisions whenever he is competent to make it – and most A'N' workers know their supervisors are not as competent to make the decision.

People who operate at this level are typically competent regardless of their surroundings. They are free of the compulsions and anxieties of previous levels. Therefore, their productivity is not a function of those lower-level incentives. Threat and coercion do not work with them, because they are not frightened people. Beyond a certain point, pecuniary motives do not affect them. Status and prestige symbols, such as fancy titles, flattery, office size, luxurious carpeting, etc., are not incentives to them. Many of them are not even driven by a need for social approval. What is important to them is that they be autonomous in the exercise of their competence, that they be allowed all possible freedom to do what needs to be done as best they can do it. In other words, they want their managers to let them improve productivity the way they know it can be improved. They do not want to waste their competency doing it management's way simply because things always have been done that way.

The A'N' motivation is from within. He seeks a sense of personal competence and believes those having information about the current situation should lead—as the situation changes so should the leader—in a revolving leadership pattern. Because he will avoid any kind of relationship in which others try to dominate him, he must be approached through what I call 'acceptance management'—management which takes him as he is, accepts the fact that in his area of work he is competent and responsible, and supports him in doing what he wants to do.

If the cognitive employee accepts the assignment, it becomes the manager's responsibility to facilitate the accomplishment of the goals. In this system, the means to the end or organizational goals are restructured to fit the individual characteristics of the organizational member, rather than attempt to restructure the person to fit organizational needs. The manager's role is to rework the organization so that goals are achieved, utilizing people as they are, not as someone wishes them to be or perceives they should be. And what of the seventh-level man if he is resisting management's agenda? Leave him alone. Once you have discussed the possibility of change with him, and if the suggested change is plausible, he will get there on his own.

If the A'N' cannot accept the assignment, it is the manager's role to facilitate that person to another unit or organization where the assignments are acceptable. It is useless to try to get seventh-level man to subordinate his desires to those of the organization. The minute the larger establishment starts to put its tentacles around him, the A'N' begins to get strangled and he just backs off and watches for a while to see whether or not these tentacles are going to grow or whether they are going to be removed. If he cannot get the acceptance he desires, he will build a non-organizational oriented world for himself, retire into it, do a passable but not excellent job, and wait for managerial change to occur. He sits there and appears to contribute no more, because he's not going to waste his energy until he is sure that these tentacles are removed from the system. If he does not get the change and if he cannot move, he will surreptitiously put his effort to his desired end as he presents a passable front to management. In any case, whether the cognitive remains or departs, there is no sabotage and no crusade to combat evil. In fact, management that mismanages the A'N' often considers that person the ideal employee and is totally surprised at the subordinate's departure when a better situation becomes available.

The A'N' is informationally oriented, pragmatic, and seeks to do the best possible given the information on the present situation. Values and concepts are derived from current information. Those having the information on the situation should lead; as things change, so should leader—a revolving leadership pattern.

If the cognitive sees DQ and ER-driven people tear off to change the world, do things about perceived problems, and try to get things accomplished, the A'N' again just sits back and says: "All right, go ahead. Go on, but I'll pick up the pieces when you get done making a mess out of it." During this period of time the A'N's are just sitting back on their hind ends waiting for those people to make mistakes. They have their plans to do something when the time comes. When A'N' employees are autonomous and properly coupled with jobs that utilize their competence, one can expect optimum productivity from them.

Man at the cognitive or systemic existential state is a man many of you know very well but understand very little. He is anathema to most businessmen. The A'N' does well any job he takes on within his realm of competence, but as an employee or fellow worker, he is a pain-in-the-neck. He won't live by the rules. He will work when he wants to work, the way he wants to work, and where he wants to work; and if the boss or fellow worker does not like it, he does not care. Motivation comes from within as he seeks a sense of personal competence. They must do their own managing of their own work and of their own affairs. Their procedures must be their own, not those that tradition or group decision-making have established. He rebels against the idea that it is management's prerogative to plan and organize work methods without consulting him and without following his desires. As I said earlier, he will have no part of standard operating procedure unless, and to the extent, that it is valid.

Since the Cognitive believes that those with the knowledge should lead, who is more knowledgeable than the doer? He does not see himself bound by social convention. He is generally an excellent producer, both quantitatively and qualitatively, albeit a thorn in the side of the man who believes in organization and control. When the manager and managed are both cognitive it spawns a variable management form wherein managed and managing change according to the fit between problem and competencies needed to deal with problems. The appropriate managerial style is clearly facilitative, role reversal, and acceptance of the competent leadership of the doer. Facilitative management requires an open relationship between manager and subordinate. All the information, goals, resources, constraints, etc., are discussed.

My experience is that fourth- and fifth-level organizations, particularly, think that seventh-level people are unemployable. For example, in a fourth-level organization, the boss noted that there was a problem of morale. He asked his employees what the problem was. When they failed to reply, he said, "All right. I'm now instructing my personnel man to take 15 minutes with each of you to find out what this problem is. Line up for appointments." When he called one of the men over to make his appointment, a seventh-level person just got up and left! This man is quietly confident of his capacity to survive, come what may.

"What happens when [seventh]-level employees are supervised by managers who do not understand them – fourth-level authoritarian types, say, or fifth-level social leaders? The fact that the [seventh]-level employee is demonstrably tops as a producer does not save the day. He ultimately gets himself fired, squeezed out, or buried where his talent is lost. Intransigent management insists that he conform to the mold. He refuses, and, as a result, management loses creative excellence. The employees who stay are the mediocre ones who are willing to conform. This can be a particularly serious loss in advanced technology industries, professional service industries, and others where creative talent plays a major role (and where, of course, [seventh]-level employees are likely to be found)."[179]

One of the problems you have here is that the evidence seems to indicate that people who operate at lower levels see the values and beliefs of people at levels higher than theirs as immoral. (When I say higher I am referring to two systems above and beyond.) Generally, if a person is operating at a DQ or an ER level and runs into someone who thinks in an A'N' fashion, they'll end up calling him a CP—take him right down. They have that kind of difficulty. You simply cannot get away from it.

Cognitive level behavior is threatening to many who manage. The very thought that the manager is a facilitator or "that work can best be accomplished by the manager working for the managed, rather than by the supervised working for the supervisor, is far too "unconventional" for most bosses to ever accept."[180] Occasionally one of my students will, at the beginning of the year, come and tell me that he isn't particularly interested in Industrial Psychology, and will ask if I will help him to learn what he does want to learn. If I say no, he'll sign up for some other course and study what he wants to know on his own. Then when he needs my help he will, for instance, ask me to get some information from the library for him. People look at this a bit askance, but this man, in effect, is saying, "You've had a lot of experience with psychological literature—I haven't. It is much more efficient for you to find this information for me, rather than for me to waste my time going through ten journals, when you could find the same information in ten minutes."

---

[179] Ibid., (Graves, 1966).
[180] Ibid., (Graves, 1966).

The boss, too, must learn that he has to do what the seventh-level person wants him to do in order to get the job done. He must discard the idea that the prerogative of the boss is to organize the work and tell the person how to do it. This is going to be difficult for a lot of people and organizations to learn and to apply.

Possessing esteem of self, he is not concerned as to the opinion others have of him. He insists on an atmosphere of trust and respect. He expects to be truly integrated into the organization just as he is and resists coercion and restrictions. It is not what others think of him which counts, it is what he sees himself to be. The way to mismanage at this level is simply to fail to facilitate. So, to summarize, the Cognitive subordinate responds to mismanagement in three ways:

1. *Stays:* working within the organization to change the situation – the information of the situation indicates change is possible and probable.
2. *Submits:* remains in the organization (usually for personal economic reasons) by doing what is required in the manner required – the information says the situation must be tolerated. Change is not likely.
3. *Departs*: the information indicates that a better situation exists elsewhere.

For example, when I go to a corporation with plants all over the country and they say, "Well, if you are going to get anywhere with this idea you've got to demonstrate it somewhere in the company" I find out where their headquarters is. I say, "Get your map out. Where is the plant that is the furthest away from every other part of damned organization, particularly the corporate headquarters?" I'll find all the A'N's have gone out there.

So, if I am asked where to go to look for and to try to find A'N' people in any broad organizational set up, I would look at one of two places: a) the place which is psychologically most remote from the authority of the establishment, meaning that one place the 'establishment' cares least about; or b) one that is geographically most remote. The A'N's recognize the impossibility of trying to change closed minds, so they say, "Get away from 'em!"

Long 'sacred' channels of communication seriously hamper the productivity of A'N' people who want to be able to decide when they know; and when they do not know, they are motivated to seek out those who do. But their motivation becomes negative when they must waste time going through channels which require them to explain what does not need to be explained to people who do not need to have it explained to them.

Another important question to ask is: What kind of characteristics would an organization have in which A'N' would feel comfortable? One above all else: honesty and openness. The cognitive wants to go in and be able ask the employment manager, "How much do you make?" and the guy gets out his check and shows him. He wants to ask what the profit and loss figures were in the company last year and have the employment manager say: "The president told me that if anyone asks that to take him up to controller, sit down, and show him the books." They lay the books out before the guy. Honesty and openness, that is the thing that stands out.[181]

But the answer lies not in organization alone. For one thing, mass production, as we know it, has to go. Work must be creatively reorganized, while maintaining the constancy of large production at low cost. This must be done through work enlargement, dropping the ideas of mass production, and getting the human being back to producing something on his own, not just being a part of the total process. We must seriously consider how to re-organize industry to take care of these people. There is a movement in Union Carbide[182] to try to create an organizational structure in which seventh-level people can work; U.S. Steel[183] is working on this problem in its safety program.

Secondly, we must reorganize our work so that the methods engineers and the industrial engineering specialists work not in developing ideas to change the methods of manufacturing, but in working out the details of the working man's ideas. For example, a man with only a third-grade education recently discussed the problems of his job with me. He definitely operates on the seventh-level of behavior, and complained that the layout engineer persisted in laying out the work without even considering how he, the worker, had to perform it. He wanted the engineer to ask him how he wanted the job laid out, and then go back and work it out for him. The seventh-level person wants this kind of treatment from his boss.

---

[181] Subsequently popularized as OBM, open books management.
[182] Union Carbide, infamous for the 1984 chemical disaster in Bhopal, India, is now a subsidiary of the Dow Chemical Company. The 1972 long term plan included "strengthening the assignment of individual responsibilties and accountabilities, strengthening business management methods, allocating resources selectively in strategic planning units, and practicing good corporate citizenship at home and abroad."
[183] United States Steel.

Seventh-level people are appearing in increasingly larger numbers throughout our population. They are the very best people in an organization and you cannot afford to lose them. If the organization is more seventh level, your ideas will be implemented into action without undue effort on your part beyond that of disseminating your ideas. They are the best producers. They are the ones you can depend on to stand by you in a crisis. But if you're not in a crisis, they will work *when* they want to, *how* they want to, *where* they want to. In fact, the seventh-level evidence is before you already, but the question is – are you ready for seventh-level implementations?

Readiness for Change in the Cognitive, Problematic State

When man finally is able to see himself and the world about him with clear cognition, he finds a picture that is far from pleasant. Visible in unmistakable clarity and devastating detail is man's failure to be what he might and his misuse of his world. This revelation causes him to leap out in search of a way of life and system of values which will enable him to be more than a parasite leeching on the world, all its being, other lives and the future. He seeks self-respect with a firm base in existential reality.

A'N' man is developing the future modes of life and values for mankind. For A'N' man, the ethic is: "Recognize—truly notice—what life is and you shall know how to behave." The proper way to behave is the way that comes from working within existential reality. His values now are of a different order from those at previous levels: they arise not from selfish interest but from the recognition of the magnificence of existence and a desire to see that it shall continue to be.

A colleague of mine, John Calhoun of the National Institutes of Mental Health, has studied along this line, though he has studied population growth and decline rather than the way I've studied. Calhoun says his evidence indicates that for the movement from the seventh level to the eighth level to fully take place and to have an eighth-level form of human existence, the seventh-level actions must reduce the population of mankind as on the Earth at 2020 A.D. by one half.[184]

That's an enormous problem. It says that there's going to have to be some kind of, to play with words a little bit here, 'gentle ruthlessness' come into human governing to see to it that people with a strong internal desire to reproduce are simply prevented from reproducing, in

---

[184] Calhoun (1969).

order to get us out of this bind that we are in. The Chinese have more then halved their birth rate in the last generation. Though Mao was beyond fourth level, the Maoistic thinking[185] is trying to deal with seriousness of the problems of the second, third and fourth level living.

Well, as I say, this is Calhoun's work and Calhoun speaks of it in a very simple fashion. Just suppose you could reduce the population by half, how much of the energy problem would be solved? You'd have solved quite a bit, at least temporarily. How much of the food problem would be solved? You'd have solved quite a bit, at least temporarily. That's the way Calhoun speaks of it. His emphasis is neither to the environmental impact nor the psychological. To my way of thinking, he is simply saying that the environmental and the neurological go hand in hand, and if you don't do something about the environmental, if you don't do something about the source of the problems, what good does it do to have the neurological potential to solve problems?

I'm not saying there is sense of doom. I am just saying that there has to be an unbelievably radical change in our way of thinking for us to avoid a sense of doom. It is entirely possible within the structuring of the human brain that the radical way of thinking can take place. And history says to us that no matter how bad the problems have been, when the radical change in thinking was needed, it has always taken place. So, by extrapolation, it's not pessimistic; it's optimistic. We are coming to the point of the greatest psychological revolution we've ever known it.

Let us not be misled at this point. This theory says the future can never be completely predicted because it allows only for the prediction of the general and not the particular. According to my studies, it would be exceedingly presumptuous of the human race at this primitive state of its development, approaching only the first step of the second ladder of existence, to imagine that the future could be predicted in precise detail. I say this because my studies indicate that something unique and unpredictable, something beyond the general form of the next system, has always emerged to characterize each new level.

The present moment finds our society attempting to negotiate the most difficult, but at the same time the most exciting, transition the human race has faced to date. It is not merely a transition to a new level of existence but the start of a new "movement" in the symphony of human history. The future offers us, basically, three possibilities:

---

[185] Reference to the interval of Chinese policy guided by Chairman Mao Tse Tung and his followers prior to 1976.

1. Most gruesome is the chance that we might fail to stabilize our world and, through successive catastrophes regress as far back as the Ik tribe has—AN to BO.
2. Only slightly less frightening is the vision of fixation in the DQ/ER/FS societal complex. This might resemble George Orwell's *1984* with its tyrannic, manipulative government glossed over by a veneer of humanitarian-sounding doublethink and moralistic rationalizations. That is a very real possibility in the next decades.
3. The last possibility is that we could emerge into the A'N' level and proceed toward stabilizing our world so that all life can continue.

If we succeed in the last alternative, we will find ourselves in a very different world from what we know now and we will find ourselves thinking in a very different way. For one thing, we will no longer be living in a world of unbridled self-expression and self-indulgence or in a world of reverence for the individual, but in one whose rule is 'express self, but only so that all life can continue.' It may well be a world which, in comparison to this one, is rather restrictive and 'authoritarian,' but this will not be the authority of forcibly taken, God-given, or self-serving power; rather it will be the authority of knowledge and necessity.

The purpose of A'N' man will be to bring the earth back to equilibrium so that life upon it can survive, and this involves learning to act within the limits inherent in the balance of life. We may find such vital human concerns as food and procreation falling under strict regulation, while in other respects society will be free not only from any form of compulsion but also from prejudice and bigotry. Almost certainly it will be a society in which renewable resources play a far greater role than they do today: wood, wind and tide may be used for energy; cotton and wool for clothing, and possibly even bicycles and horses for short trips. Yet while more naturalistic than the world we know today, at the same time the A'N' world will be unimaginably more advanced technologically, a quantitative extension, for A'N' man will have no fear of technology and will understand its consequences. He will truly know when to use it and when not to use it, rather than being bent on using it whenever possible as ER man has been.

From the standpoint of values, we appear to be headed for a reversal, though in higher order form, of those values and beliefs we have held most dear, and in our institutional ways of living. A few things we might expect when man's life is ordered by A'N' thinking are:

1. Quality – not quantity – will become the measure of worth.
2. Reduction of use will be valued; growth will be devalued.
3. Freedom to operate in one's own self-interest will be replicated by the responsibility to operate in the interest of others.
4. The measure of educational success will not be quantity of learning but whether the education leads to movement up the existential staircase. Business and other organizations will be judged in the same way.
5. The boss will be the expediter of subordinates' desires rather than the director of their activities.
6. The political systems which let anyone run for office will be replaced by systems that require candidates to meet certain requirements for office.
7. A leisure ethic will replace the work ethic as the primary means of valuing a person. A man will be revered more for his ability to contribute in his non-earning time than in his earning time.
8. Work will be increased for the young and reduced for the older, while education is increased for the older and reduced for the younger.
9. Actions that promote interdependent existence will be valued more than those that promote the sanctity of the individual.
10. Unity with nature will replace unity with God.

Other values can be deduced in this manner: Take anything man has strongly valued in the first ladder of existence, reverse it, put it in higher-order form and you have the key to what this theory says. Study the Tasaday tribe of the Philippines, put their values and their ways into a technologically complex world and you have the immediate future of an A'N' world. Then follow this new form of the AN state of existence with a B'O' form and so on and you can develop a general picture of the remote future of man.

This theoretical point of view, its spiraling-like character, and the fact that A'N' is the seventh-level system will mean new institutional ways for human living will be created. The systemic existential state will create new governmental systems. Seventh-level man is going to create new ways of controlling the various forces in the universe of which we are a part. However, I cannot tell you the specifics. Why? Just step back four thousand years with me and ask the question in a different form. Say we had this theory, now ask, "What will DQ create?" Well, who would have guessed that what the DQ would have created was the concept of a monotheistic God. No one would ever have guessed that.

The psychological keynote of a society organized according to A'N' thinking will be freedom from inner compulsiveness and rigidifying anxiety. A'N' man who exists today in ever increasing numbers does not fear death, nor God, nor his fellow man. Magic and superstition hold no sway over him. He is not mystically minded, though he lives in the most mysterious of "mystic" universes.

There is a general aspect and a specific aspect of each system, and how magnificent. How magnificent it is that we can get a general view of the future, but we'll be always be caught in the same problem that they were caught in with the atomic table of elements in chemistry. They knew radium would be found. But there was nothing in the knowledge of chemistry that said when this element of this particular atomic weight is found that it would be 'radioactive.' So, we know that A'N' man will create new systems of governmental control. I can't tell you what the specifics are. That's why we are in so much trouble; we are trying to find the genius somewhere that can come up with the ideas to procreate these new forms of government needed at the present time. All of us know the forms we've got are not doing the job. We know we need new and different control systems, and we will create something along that line.

Because of this different way of thinking, human institutions at the A'N' level will become very different from what we have today. For instance, those processes and institutions which today are centralized would likely become decentralized, while those which are decentralized might become centralized. Since A'N' man performs only necessary work and then only in the way in which he sees fit, there is bound to be drastic change not only in the structure of work but also in the amount of work done, the location in time and space of the work, and the reasons for which it is carried out. As an industrial psychologist, I have already noted a dramatic rise in the number of A'N' individuals occupying positions which will make them heirs to corporate power. When their time comes, business will shift toward an A'N' outlook.

Our institutions of learning will undergo a similar transformation when the Systemic Existential State becomes prevalent. Today we endeavor to teach children to be what they are not. That is, we prevent them from reaching higher into the existential hierarchy by preventing them from acting out the levels of existence on which they are actually living. Education in an A'N' society would encourage all individuals to express their values as fully as possible, thus freeing the natural growth process from artificial constraints.

There would be no poverty and wealth in such a society, but this circumstance would not result from altruism or political conviction, but rather from A'N' man's conviction that equal access to a high-quality life is essential for everyone. Though he recognizes that all men are not equal, inequality in the necessities of life is to him an unnatural travesty on all life. The A'N' individual who had more than enough would not take pity on the poor nor would he envy a person who had more, but he would simply be very uncomfortable until both had a *necessary* amount.

Although there seems to be a lot of seventh-level thinking around today, I don't know of any society that is ordered in accordance with seventh-level thinking. It hasn't gotten that far. So, we really don't know whether or not we are going to get beyond the problems that have been created by the first six levels of thinking into the being levels of thinking. That is the second set of six ways of behaving that can develop over time—if man continues to exist on this earth.

If this thinking seems strange, we must remember that a description of today's FS humanity, typified by the Esalen Institute, would have seemed equally perverse and bizarre to those who were ER men twenty years ago. Those of us who survive long enough to live in a society ordered by the A'N' way of thinking—if such comes about—will find it perfectly natural.

But as magnificent as this value system may seem to those who can feel it, it is not, as so many have thought, the ultimate for man. As he bases his values on what information does for him, he finds in time that this, too, is a narrowly based system. There is much he can never know and much no man will ever know. Beyond it lies another value world that few men have yet to know.

Once man comes to the seventh level of existential emergence he will be driven by the winds of knowledge and human, not Godly, faith and the surging waves of confidence on to the B'O' and still higher levels of existence. The knowledge and competence acquired at the A'N' level will bring him to the next level of understanding, the B'O' level, from whence he will move, though today we cannot see how. But it will be on to the delight of tasting more of his emergent self. On this other side of his self he may become the doer of greater things or lesser things, but he will be doing human things.

If ever man leaps to this great beyond, there will be no bowing to suffering, no vassalage, no peonage. There will be no shame in behavior, for man will know it is human to behave. There will be no pointing of the finger at other men, no segregation, depredation, or degradation in behavior. Man will be driving forth on the subsequent crests of his humanness rather than vacillating and swirling in the turbulence of partially emerged man, blocked forever from becoming himself in the sands of time, and he will see welfare as to encompass all that is living, including self and other men and all other living things.

Chapter 14

The Intuitive Existence – The B'O' State[186]

The 2nd Being Level

The B'O' - Experientialist Existential State

Theme [tentative]: *'Adjust to the realities of one's existence and automatically accept the existential dichotomies as they are and go on living'*[187]

'Sacrifice the idea that one will ever know what it is all about and adjust to this as the existential reality of existence.'

---

[186] Dr. Graves did not attempt to summarize this state as his data was so sparse. The comments which follow are extremely tentative and represent only a superficial understanding of the eighth level, one which is still emerging.
[187] Fromm (1947).

In the latter part of my studies I had some people appear whose thinking about what was mature human behavior was different from any that I had previously experienced. As I looked into it, it was apparent that these few individuals—I've had only six of them in my data so far who have thought in this different manner—just didn't see the world in any of the other seven ways. They're beginning to think in a way that intuition, subjectivism plays a great deal more in their behavior than in any of the other systems. The conception you get here was a very interesting one: 'I'll be damned if I know.' You go into an almost mystical conception where the guy says he has sort of a *feeling* what a healthy human being is.[188]

They are most like the tribalistic, second-level people. In fact, they think in many respects in a higher order magical superstitious way about the world of which they are a part. Well, one cannot say anything that is more than speculative about eighth level behavior. One can say that in the course of my studies, I had people who thought in what I have come to call the seventh level, or A'N' way, and in the course of their thinking in that manner they changed and started to take on another way of thinking. Well, at that time, the so-called A'N' way of thinking was thought by most authorities—Maslow, Blake and Mouton, and others—to be the epitome of the way of thinking about human behavior. What are you going to do when you find that the epitome of the way of thinking is discarded and a new way of thinking that you have not seen before suddenly appears out of the blue?

I had to find some way of making sense out of this. When I look back over my data, what I first saw was that the seventh-level way of thinking had more in common with the first level way of thinking than any of the other five systems. It had more in common with autistic thinking than it had in common with two, three, four, five, or six. Therefore, the question rose in my mind: Can I make sense out of these six people whose thinking is very different from what I have found before? If I say seventh-level is mostly like one, (AN), then is eighth-level mostly like two (BO)? Well, I looked at my data and, lo and behold, eighth level was mostly like two. So, eighth level is a higher-level form of tribalistic thinking.

We are not very far along in this at this stage of the game, but my data simply doesn't hold together in respect to these six people who changed in the midst of my studies from thinking in what my judges classified as the seventh-level way. (Notice, I said 'my judges.' I did not do the classifying. My judges had classified a seventh level way which

---

[188] "1-2-3-4-5-6-7" *NEWSDAY*. Saturday, March 11, 1967.

then took on yet a new form of thinking.) I saw a lot of evidence of that in these six people, but I've never had enough people to do any systematic studies of them.

From this I hypothesized that the eighth level existed, and I had to begin to try to describe it a little bit by the evidence I had for it. What I found in the eighth level was that one thing above all else stood out, that these people thought the most stupid question you could possibly ask yourself was: "Do you know yourself?" These people said: "No one is ever going to know himself. 'Know thyself' is ridiculous. There is no way that one can ever know the permutations and combination of eleven billion cells with over ten thousand interconnections. It can't possibly be known."

So this eighth-level thinking appeared, and I simply tried to get an overall system that would rationalize all of my data. I had to try to conceive of man's brain structured so as to support the basis for my theorization. I had to build the six, upon six, upon six idea: that there are six basic coping systems we have just about used up; that the first new set of coping systems is about to take over; that it is made up of the basic neurological systems of the first level of human existence plus a mass of previously unused cells in the brain; and that the eighth system is made up of more unused cells in the brain, plus X and Y, just gives logical closure to what I am dealing with.

Emergence of B'O'

For those men who have come relatively to satisfy their need to esteem life, a new existential state, the B'O' state is just beginning to be. It emerges when problematic man *truly realizes* that there is much he will never know about existence. This insight brings man to the end of his first ladder value trek because now man learns he must return to his beginning and travel again, in a higher order form, the road by whence he has come. A problem-solving existence is not enough. It must become subordinated within a new form of autistic existence. This I call the intuitive existence after the eighth-level *thema* of existence, *'adjust to the reality of existence which is that you can only be, you can never really know.'*

These eighth-level experientialistic values are only beginning to emerge in the lives of some men. Two young people living together without the concern for all our technological trappings and all our prescriptions for dress and demeanor are not necessarily the rebellious, slovenly, dogmatic beatniks whose values are basically fifth level. That is a serious misinterpretation of the behavior at the eighth level. The fact that he is not concerned with proper behavior, the fact that he seems not to live by "the rules" is not angry non-conformity. It is that he values deeper human things more. It is that he follows his impressions, not an established order.

The eighth-level values we also call impressionistic. It is at B'O' where man must learn to fashion a life that honors and respects all the different levels of human being. Here again he adjusts to the world, to a world he will never really come to know. He values what he feels he should, not just what his knowledge tells him he should. Here man values those "vast realms of consciousness still undreamed of, vast ranges of experience like the humming of unseen harps we know nothing of within us."[189] He values wonder, awe, reverence, humility, fusion, integration, unity, simplicity, the poetic perception of reality—non-interfering perception versus active controlling perception, enlarging consciousness, and the ineffable experience.[190]

Since eighth-level man need not attend so much to the problems of his existence (for him they have been solved), he values those newer, deeper things in life which are there to be experienced. He values escaping "...from the barbed wire entanglement of his own ideas and his own mechanical devices..."[191] He values the "marvellous rich world of context and sheer fluid beauty and [fearless] face-to-face awareness of now-naked-life..."[192] Perceiving the world as somewhat beyond his ken, there is a serious, stable cast to the values of eighth-level man. Cooperation and trust are most seriously valued to the extent that he will withdraw from relationships that cannot be based on such.

Play, exhibitionism, receiving the plaudits of others, mean little if anything to man at this level. It is not that he cannot play, nor is it that he cannot or won't dominate. It is that he prefers serious endeavor and cares not to dominate. He does not value adjusting to the world as authority says it is; nor does he value the imposition of his self upon the world. What he values is adjusting to the world as he senses it to be.

At the second being level, B'O', man will be driven by knowledge and human faith. The knowledge and competence acquired at the A'N'

---

[189] De Sola Pinto, Vivian and Roberts, Warren (Eds). (1920). "Terra Incognita." *The Complete Poems of D. H. Lawrence* (Vols. I and II). New York, New York: The Viking Press.

[190] The reader will note the similarity of the seventh level values to some of the thoughts of Abraham Maslow. And he will note that this work is a revision and extension of many of Maslow's writings.

[191] Ibid., (De Sola Pinto, Vivian and Roberts, Warren, 1920).

[192] Ibid., (De Sola Pinto, Vivian and Roberts, Warren, 1920). *see* D. H. Lawrence

level will bring him to the level of understanding, the B'O' level. His problems, now that he has put the world back together, will be those of bringing stabilization to life once again. He will need to learn how to live so that the balance of nature is not again upset, so that individual man will not again set off on another self-aggrandizing binge. His values will be set not by the accumulated wisdom of the elders, as in the BO system, but by the accumulated knowledge of the knowers. But here again, as always, this accumulating knowledge will create new problems and precipitate man to continue up just another step in his existential staircase.

Personal experience has shown this person that no matter how much information is available, one can never know or understand all things. Reality can be experienced, but never known. The B'O' insists on an atmosphere of trust and respect to be integrated into the organization. He resists coercion and restrictions in a quiet, personal way—never in an exhibitionistic manner. They avoid relations in which others try to dominate and seek not to dominate others, but can provide firm direction as required.

Comments on the Conceptualization of B'O'

This system eight brings forth another way this conceptualization is basically different from the Maslowian conception of personality. To my knowledge, it is not only a system beyond any that has been suggested by other theorists—other systems-like thinkers—but it is also a system whose appearance raised for me a serious theoretical question: "What can it mean that in order for these data to be conceptualized I have to add another system beyond that which had been described by Maslow as the self-actualizing man?" The undeniable fact of its emergence in the course of the studies forced me to reconsider the long-standing conception of psychological maturity as a state which can be conceived to exist.

All the work done on self-actualization came under question. I had to weigh the total significance of the level eight emergence plus all the other data and finally settle on an open system—quantitative and qualitative change—as the meaning in human existence, not just a quantitative change with time. I had to open 'actualization' as a process and close down the idea that it is a theoretically achievable state or condition. I had to include the data of this new system with the rest of mine beyond the Maslowian apex. I had to reconsider the whole problem of the maturity of man and the meaning of human existence. It means that when Harvey, Hunt and Schroder see the abstract man as mature, Maslow sees the self-actualized man as mature, Fromm sees the productive orientation character as mature, Freud sees the genital character as mature, that they are subject—all of them—to man's greatest illusion: the illusion of psychological maturity.

According to my data, as I have said, maturity just cannot be considered an achievable state, even in theory. Maturity, instead, must be conceived as a possibly never-ending process, as a continuous emergence of newer and newer concepts of maturity, rather than as the theoretically achievable, most perfect state for human existence. The B'O' system of personality—the intuitionistic style of living—presents an amazing challenge to consider when it is studied. The central core of this style of living is that one shall adjust to the realities of one's existence and shall automatically accept the existential realities, called by Fromm *existential dichotomies* as they are: 'Thou shall passively adjust to these and go on living.'

This central core is amazingly like the central core of system two (BO) the first psychological system in the sense of man's adjusting to his world. It is more like system two than any other system. Yet at the same time, it is more unlike system two (BO) than any other system. At level two the organism has to passively adjust. The only way he survives is through the magnificent adaptability of his Pavlovian type conditioning reflexes. But at level eight (B'O') this passive adjustment seems to be chosen rather than determined. Men operating at this eighth level seem more able to chose—far less determined—than at lower levels of human existence.

Thus, if this observation—that level eight psychology is like and unlike the level two psychology at one and the same time—holds with further study, if level eight is but a much more complex form of level two, then a tantalizing question must be asked: Is nine a higher order three, and is ten a higher order four? Is this which we now think is man's nature, the character of his being, but the first ladder? If so, one can extrapolate that the ninth-level way of thinking will be a higher order of the egocentric, exploitative form of human behavior. Such speculation is not only possible but required in the meaning of my data.

Management of the Experientialistic State (B'O') [193]

It is useless to get a B'O' employee to subordinate his desires to those of the organization. Instead, management must fit the organization to him. Therefore, they must be approached, as in the cognitive case, through facilitative, acceptance management which takes them as they are, supports them in doing what they want to do, and accepts the fact that they are competent and responsible. Experientialistic employees take the work activities very seriously and are wrapped up in that which each personally wants to do.

Readiness for Change

If the conditions for the existence of man continue to improve, the day will come when B'O' will be the dominant value system of man. The time will come when all other values will be subordinated within their supra-ordination, but they too will pass away. Nor are they the ultimate in human values. They are only the latest to emerge from a long history of value change. They are only stepping-stones to later emerging value systems.

These eighth-level impressionistic values are only beginning to emerge in the lives of some men. If the conditions for existence of man continue to improve, the day will come when they will be the dominant value system of man. The time will come when all other values will be subordinated within their supra-ordination, but they too will pass away. When the time comes that the leading edge of man finds eighth-level values wanting and ready for discard, some men, somewhere, sometime, will accuse these new venturers of a breakdown of man's values.

Conclusion

We have come, momentarily, to the end of our analysis of values within our organismic, systems conception of man, to the end of man's value trek. The reader has the opportunity to judge the validity of our

---

[193] The reader will notice that these management descriptions are similar to those of the A'N' and FS systems. We have included as much of Graves's writing as possible on this subject since it has been of some debate and focus recently in new age, spiritual, transpersonal psychology, and consciousness circles. It is included so that the reader may come to his/her own conclusions on the basis of the existing (or the lack of existing) evidence, contradictions and emerging patterns of human behavior.

position. The theory presented is of course a sketch; it is not finished. Obviously, it is oversimplified with yet much to be tested before one accepts this point of view. Man does not necessarily move slowly and steadily as described. In our world of past and present, there are societies and people at all levels, and societies and peoples whose levels are mixed; but these and other complications, such as transitional state value systems, are complications to be dealt with elsewhere. All men do not progress, and some societies may wither and die. Man may never cross his great divide; but on the other hand, he may. And so the problem of ethical and moral decline lies, this theory says, not so much in the breakdown and discard of 'the old' as in the retention of existentially inappropriate values during a period of profound transformation in human existence.

So let us close by asking a serious question: Must man's blindness toward himself block him forever from crossing his great divide – the line between his animalism and his humanism? Or is there a view of mankind's nature which might allow us to reach for the light of hope rather than stumble on into the darkness of despair? Are man's many value problems not more than the accumulating signs of his depravity, or are they signals which, if perceived, will provide not only insights into a better tomorrow but also more appropriate means for attack upon mankind's distress?

Certainly today's man cannot be hurt if he does no more than search for the latter, rather than give in to the former. Let us not give up on mankind. Let us first re-examine our evidence. Let us not revert only to past solutions. Let us look forward for possible new approaches. Let us ask: Has this work reordered man's value behavior so as to provide for his future rather than prepare for his demise?

Section III

The Sum of All Our Days is Just a Beginning

Verification

CHAPTER 15

Verification

Twenty-five years of naturalistic observation, research and contemplation has produced an emergent cyclical conception of adult psychosocial development. Now the question is: Does this theory do what a theory should do? Does it fulfill the purposes that any theory should fulfill? One of the better statements of what a theory should do is that of Calvin S. Hall and Gardner Lindzey. In *Theories of Personality* they say:

> "... The theory itself is assumed and acceptance or rejection of it is determined by its utility, not by its truth or falsity. In this instance, utility has two components—verifiability and comprehensiveness. Verifiability refers to the capacity of the theory to generate predictions which are confirmed when the relevant empirical data are collected. Comprehensiveness refers to the scope or the completeness of these derivations. We might have a theory which generated consequences that were often confirmed but which dealt with only a few aspects of the phenomena of interest. Ideally the theory should lead to accurate predictions which deal very generally or inclusively with the empirical events with which the theory purports to embrace.
>
> It is important to distinguish between what may be called the systematic and heuristic generation of research. It is clear that in the ideal case, the theory permits the derivation of

specific testable propositions and these in turn lead to specific empirical studies. However, it is also manifest that many theories, for example, Freud's and Darwin's have had a great effect upon investigative paths without the mediation of explicit propositions. This capacity of a theory to generate research by suggesting ideas or even by arousing disbelief and resistance may be referred to as the heuristic influence of the theory. Both types of influence are of great importance and at the present stage of development within psychology are to be valued equally.

A second function which a theory should serve is that of permitting the incorporation of known empirical findings within a logically consistent and reasonably simple framework. A theory is a means of organizing and integrating all that is known concerning a related set of events."[194]

In this chapter I will examine the utility and incorporative value of the emergent cyclical conception by looking at its verifiability. Its systematic and heuristic value has been looked at in previous chapters and will oft times be referred to in this chapter. The problem of verifiability is of serious import to me. It is of serious import because my work is open to the criticism of contamination. During the time of my efforts, my work situation required that, for the most part, I work alone. By and large, with two slight exceptions, it was I alone who observed and conceived studies, developed methodologies, collected data, classified and analyzed data. When conceptualizing, I paid no attention to similar conceptions of others until after the emergent cyclical point of view had been conceived. With limited exceptions, during the research years, I tested the conceptual system myself. Therefore, when the problem of verifiability took center scene it was necessary to seek outside my work situation for means to really test the conceptualization. Fortunately, the literature provided useful information for this purpose. When I did search, I found many people had and have been working along a similar vein of thought. So in this chapter, I will use primarily the work of others to test for verifiability of the emergent cyclical conception.

---

[194] Hall, Calvin S. and Gardner, Lindzey (1957). *Theories of Personality*. New York: John Wiley & Sons, p. 13-15.

Support for Basic E–C Theory from General Psychology Sources

The first thing to test is the very heart of emergent cyclical theory. As I see it, the heart is the organismic side of the double-helix. If general and specific support cannot be found for my conception of the organismic side of the helix, then the whole structure tumbles. This is because the organismic, not the environmentosocial side, is the delimiting side of psychosocial development.

The environments of humans, the other side of the helix, vary enormously. But our best knowledge is that today only one species of humanity exists, *sapiens*. We do have in existence many other species of animals. We have dogs, cats, chickens, chimpanzees, and gorillas. But we have only one species structured, generally, as is *Homo sapiens*. Dogs live in as many environments as do humans, but the neuropsychological equipment of dogs is basic to dog behavior, it not basic to the behavior of *Homo sapiens*. So a crucial test of emergent cyclical theory is: Does the evidence from studies indicate that the organism *Homo sapiens* is structured systemically in the manner conceived in emergent cyclical-theory? More specifically: Is there substantive evidence to support the contention that the neuropsychological equipment, the N, O, P, Q, R, S, N', O' plus X, Y and Z is structurally and functionally as emergent cyclical theory says?

My version of emergent cyclical theory (I say my version because there may be other versions of which I am not aware) says that the brain should be conceived as a series of hierarchically and prepotently organized "dynamic neurological systems"[195] or cell assemblies[196] or the like. How else can one account for data like mine which say that one conceptual form of maturity and one form of existence follows another in an ordered, hierarchical, prepotent way? I see no other way than to suggest that the brain of *Homo sapiens* does in fact consist, in some structural way, of a hierarchy of prepotently ordered series of neuropsychological systems. These systems operate in a delimiting fashion to order the observed conceptions of maturity and forms for existence. But an assertion of conviction is not enough. One must get beyond assertion to data. So the question is: Do such data exist?

---

[195] Krech, David (1950). Dynamic Systems as Open Neurological Systems. *Psychological Review*, Vol. 57, p. 345-361.
[196] Hebb, D. O. (1955). Drives and the Conceptual Nervous System. *Psychological Review*, Vol. 62 (4), p. 243-254.

A search of the literature certainly suggests that this conclusion about the nature of the human brain is more than an assertion. (See Table IV) There is a plethora of data to support the contention. The data of Thorpe, Engen, Berlyne, Sharpless and Jasper, Jung and Hassler, Hernandez-Peon and Brust-Carmona, Segundo, and others suggest that the lowest order dynamic neurological system is the habituation system, the system whose keystone is that it functions (learns) not to respond after receiving repeated stimulation and exercising reaction to it. The N seems to be directed by our imperative, periodic, and physiological needs. It seems to control them and to respond only to changes in *intensity* of stimulation.

The second and apparently next higher order system O must consist of different tissue anatomically and must function differently because it responds only to the *frequency* of stimulation, something to which the first system does not respond. This assertion of emergent cyclical theory is supported by microscopic anatomical examination of what neurological tissue responds to what stimulation. Such examination reveals that tissue of the lowest-order system, the emergent cyclical N system, is structurally different from the tissue of the second-order system, the emergent cyclical O system. It is identified in the work of Morgan, Gastaut, Pavlov, Olds and Olds, and many others. It is characteristic of this system to act like the classical, the respondent-learning system. It seems to be a system in which learning takes place without volition or conscious awareness and from the simple association of stimulus and response in time and/or space.

Table IV

Six Levels of Existence and Motivational, Emotional, Learning and Thinking Subsystems				
Subsystem				
Level of Existence	Motivational	Emotional	Dominant Learning System	Way of Thinking
6th Subsistence	Love, Affiliation, Belonging, Approval	Depression?	Observational?	Relativistic
5th Subsistence	Adequacy, Competency	Manic Excitement?	Expectancy?	Multiplistic
4th Subsistence	Order and meaning	Guilt	Avoidant	Absolutistic
3rd Subsistence	Psychological maintenance (Locomotion, Exploration, Investigation)	Anger and Shame	Instrumental, Operant, Intentional	Egocentric
2nd Subsistence	Aperiodic physiological (Safety, pain avoidance, stimulation, activity)	Fear	Classical or Respondent	Animistic
1st Subsistence	Imperative, periodic physiological (Hunger, thirst, sex, sleep)	Distress and delight	Habituation	Autistic

A third, still higher-order system (the P system of emergent cyclical theory) seems indicated by the research which established the significance of previous events and positive reinforcement in learning. This third system in the hierarchy appears to be what others have called the operant, the instrumental or the intentional learning system. Here the work of Solomon and Brush,[197] Olds and Olds, and the Skinnerians seems definitive.

A fourth system, the avoidant system in learning theory, the system which responds dominantly to negative reinforcement, is suggested by the work of Horney, Hernandez-Peon, and particularly by Schacter and Latane.[198] One places it fourth in the hierarchy because of the elegant work of Schacter and Latane which demonstrates that learning by negative reinforcement is activated to the dominant position in the human learning hierarchy only after learning by reward.

Later systems are not as clear, but the fifth could well be the expectancy system of Rotter and the sixth, the observational system. Thus there is certainly strong evidence that psychosocial theory should be erected on a conceptual base built upon hierarchical structures in the brain.

There is also evidence to suggest that the neuropsychological system I have designated as Z, the hypothesized elaborating system in the brain, does exist. It is well documented that after birth countless numbers of cells in the brain are uncommitted. They are not tied in with any established functional system. Thus if the N, O, P etc. neuropsychological systems are basic coping systems, and if data for N' behavior exists, then N, O, P, connecting with some cells in the elaborating system, is a good explanation for the tremendous increase in conceptual space of the A'N' system over the sum of all previous systems. But there is more to the nature of dynamic neurological systems than each having its own core, its own anatomical structures sensitive to a particular type of stimulation and not sensitive to other stimulation, and its own learning system.

In keeping with Krech's (1950) original meaning of dynamic neurological system, each system gives rise to dominant needs and emotions. Each has its own unique biochemistry, its own values, its own way of thinking, but space does not permit full development of these aspects of emergent cyclical theory. So I shall but briefly touch upon what research seems to have shown.

Many investigators whose work I shall cite later have produced results supporting the systemic organization of motives, emotions, and

---

[197] Solomon, Richard L. and Brush, Elinor S. (1957). Experimentally Derived Conceptions of Anxiety and Aversion. In Jones, Marshall R. (Ed.) *Nebraska Symposium on Motivation*. Oxford: University of Nebraska Press, p. 212-305.

[198] Schacter, Stan, and Latane, Bibb (1964). Crime, Cognition, and the Autonomic Nervous System. *Nebraska Symposium on Motivation*, 12, p. 221-275.

ways of thinking. There is good evidence that the needs or motives are ordered per system somewhat as follows:

> Associated with the first, the N system, are the needs for satisfaction of the imperative periodic physiological needs. These are followed by the O needs, the aperiodic, not necessarily imperative, physiological needs. These are the needs for temperature control, pain avoidance, safety, sensory stimulation, general activity and the like. Next are the P needs, the needs for locomotion, exploration and investigation. These needs seem to assume dominance when the third system is activated and they operate in consort with the intentional, operant, instrumental or positive reinforcement learning systems. The fourth level needs, the Q needs, are for order and meaning. They are followed at the fifth level by the R needs, the needs for adequacy and competency. Then at the sixth level the S neurological system, the needs for love, affiliation, belonging and approval are shown by research to assume the dominant position.
>
> Research on emotion indicates that only distress and delight accompany the N system. In the second, the O system, fear seems to dominate. It is followed in the P system by the emergence of shame and anger as the dominant emotions. Guilt becomes dominant at the fourth level, in the Q system. But data is unclear as to the dominant emotion of the fifth and sixth levels. Yet there are some limited suggestions that manic excitement is associated with the fifth, the R system and a depressive tone with the sixth, the S system. Suicide increases markedly in the sixth system.
>
> Research on thinking indicates that at the N level, thinking is autistic in character. At the second level, the O system, thinking is predominantly animistic. Highly egocentric thinking is dominant in the P system, which is the third dynamic neurological system. Associated with the Q system of the fourth level is absolutistic thinking. Multiplistic thinking, à la the conception of Perry,[199] appears to be dominant in the R, the fifth level neurological system. The concept of relativism dominates the thinking of the sixth, the S system. And when the N' system is activated in the brain, its way of thinking is

---

[199] Perry, William G. Jr. (1970). *Forms of Intellectual and Ethical Development in the College Years: A Scheme*. New York; Holt, Rinehart & Winston.

systemic. In the B'O' system, thinking appears to be differentialistic.

Now two questions must be asked. The first is about support for the concepts of the X and Y systems which have been hypothesized. The other has to do with the environmentosocial side of the helix, the problems of living as a human being.

The first question is: "Is there evidence to support the presence in the brain of a general activating system which consists of subsystems that are a part of the psychoneurological equipment of the organism?" The answer to this is two-fold. First there is more than ample evidence for an activating system. This evidence is in the literature under precisely that heading. The evidence that there are subsystems in the general activating system is not as ample, but it can be found. The work of Funkenstein, Wolfe,[200] Hokfelt,[201] West,[202] and Schacter and Latane[203] certainly points to chemical differences in the P and Q systems. They do so by reporting that the proportion of noradrenaline to adrenaline is greater in the former (the P system) with this ratio reversed in the Q system. There is also suggestive evidence that the amount of thyroxin in the total system is disproportionately high when the R system is activated. But what can we say about support for the other side of the helix?

About the 'problem of existence' side of the helix, one must ask: What meaning can lie in a brain ordered as I have conceived? What light does this throw upon the problems of existence? Can it mean that each system lies in the brain to be activated, if necessary to deal with certain and not other problems of existence? Can it mean that higher-order systems lie latent in the brain, to be brought into play if and only when the process of living as a human being creates new existential problems?

Such indeed might be the reason for the N, O, P, etc. hypothesized ordering of the brain. The first neurosystem would be there to enable man to cope with the problems of life itself (the A problems). The second would be present to enable the human to have a safe and secure life once life is established (the B problems of existence). The third neurological system would enable him to cope with that specifically human problem, awareness of his own individual existence (the C

---

[200] Wolfe, R. (1963). The Role of Conceptual Systems in Cognitive Functioning at Varying Levels of Age and Intelligence. *Journal of Personality*. 31 (1), p. 108-122.

[201] Hokfelt, Bernt (1951).

[202] West, G. B. (1951).

[203] Schacter, Stan and Latane, Bibb (1964). Crime, Cognition, and the Autonomic Nervous System. *Nebraska Symposium on Motivation*, 12, p. 221-275.

problems of existence). The fourth would be the coping system that enables humans to deal with the problem that death must come even when life has been nothing but a period of misery and pain (the D problems of existence). The fifth system would enable him to cope and hold on when finally he has faced the realization that the only life one will ever have is this life on earth (the E problems). The sixth would enable the person to handle the threat in the realization of aloneness in this universe of ours (the F problems of existence). The seventh system would exist to enable the human to find some meaning in existence when finally it is realized that there is no lasting significance in his tribe, his own raw power, in his or her God, in a material existence on this earth, or in intimate relations with fellow human beings (the A' problems of existence). And who knows what significance lies in the existence of neuropsychological systems beyond the seventh?

In other words, if the brain is hierarchically ordered, as I have conceived it to be, it would enable a human to successfully and successively meet the hierarchically ordered problems of human existence. But all of this simply raises another question: "Since the dynamic neurological systems, after the first, are structures latent in the brain, what evidence is there to support the hypothesis that six factors operate to produce the emergence of each successive system?"

Support for the Six Factor Theory of Change

1. Potential.

Emergent-cyclical theory proposes that the first condition necessary for change from one existential state to another is potential. The next higher-level neuropsychological system must be present in the brain. There are many embryological studies which show that arrest of embryological development does occur. When autopsies are done, comparison histological studies show that when arrest occurs, systems which oft times develop later are absent. And the studies previously cited in this chapter lend credence to the hypothesis of a structural and functional hierarchy of potential systems in the brain.

2. Resolution of Current Existential Problems.

Support for the second change factor, resolution of existential problems at the level of centralization, is not as easy to come by. Yet there is much evidence to support that the human is certainly intelligent enough to put first things first. There is good evidence that the imperative, physiological needs are prepotent over those physiological needs of lesser importance, the aperiodic physiological needs. These are in turn prepotent over the lowest level psychological maintenance needs, those governed by man's third level neuropsychological equipment. Sorokins' *Famine in Russia* and the studies of the Ik[204] tribe in Uganda demonstrate this prepotency in reverse.

But E-C theory says potential and the resolution of existential problems are necessary but not sufficient conditions to produce emergence of succeeding levels of existence. This appears to be an aspect of change in which many have been in error. In fact, it is perhaps the belief that potential and the resolution of existential problems is sufficient to produce change that has led to the bad reputation of 'permissiveness.'

3. Feeling of Dissonance

According to my studies, and those of Festinger and his devotees; Kohlberg, Scharf and Hickey;[205] Blasi; Blatt (1969); and others, and as yet unpublished work of investigators like Fenton,[206] Mosher,[207] Lasher,[208] and Pindeo,[209] the evidence indicates that dilemmas or thought problems, or what Festinger and I call dissonance, is a third necessary change factor but not a sufficient condition for change.

Dissonance precipitates a crisis but it does not trigger the attempt to move to the next system. In fact, what it triggers is a regressive search through past ways of behaving for some old way or ways that can re-establish the previous steady state wherein existential problems were solved. This regressive search will end in arrest, regression or development for a definite reason. If the old existential problems are X, then no person in crisis can ever re-establish X. The person cannot do so because life is now being lived in the conditions X + 1 where 1 is the new problems of existence created by having lived in the X way.

---

[204] Turnbull, Colin (1972). *The Mountain People*. Simon and Schuster.
[205] Kohlberg, L., Hickey, J. & Scharf, P. (1972). The justice structure of the prison: A theory and intervention. *Prison Journal*, 51, p. 3-14. Kohlberg, L. Kauffman, K., Scharpf, P. and Hickey, J. (1974). *The Just Community Appraoch to Corrections: A Manual*. Cambridge, MA: Moral Education Research Foundation.
[206] Fenton, Edwin, Colby, Ann, and Speicher-Dubin, Betsy (1974). "Developing Moral Dilemmas for Social Studies Classes." Mimeogaphed. Cambridge, Mass." Harvard University, Center for Moral Education (cited in Mosher, Ralph (1980). *Moral Education: A First Generation of Research and Development*. New York: Praeger.)
[207] Mosher – not located.
[208] Lasher – not located.
[209] Pindeo – not located.

4. Gaining of Insights

That which stops this regressive search and puts the human in position to experience the emergence of the next set of neuropsychological coping equipment is the gradual production, toward a critical amount, of the chemical constituents which activate the next set of coping equipment. This activation of previously latent equipment provides for the development of insight, the fourth factor in the change process. Data in support of this lies, among others, in the work of Rensch, Funkenstein, Hess,[210] Wolfe,[211] Selye, Hokfelt,[212] Krech, and West.[213]

Of particular significance, herein, is the evidence, which ties into what I have said about:

1. The existence of hierarchically ordered structural systems.
2. The shift of dominance of the center of brain activation.
3. The appearance of a different biochemical complex.
4. Change of emotional tone concomitant with the shift.
5. The emergence to dominance or the subordination of previously dominant learning systems when the chemical complex changes.

When these changes are seen to occur concomitantly with changes in ways of thinking, judging, valuing and the like, then it does seem that there is support for the concept of "dynamic neurological systems."

In the totality of what I have said, this chemical side of the brain seems to operate somewhat as follows: When dissonance enters the psychological field of one who seems previously to have the problem of existence solved, the organism begins slowly to produce the new chemical complex. This starts the attempt to move to a new level of existence which can cope with the new existential problems X + 1. If conditions are right, this process proceeds slowly until it reaches a critical point. Upon reaching this critical point the jump to a new level

---

[210] Hess, E. H. (1959). Imprinting. *Sciences,* 130, p. 133-141. Pupilometrics. In N. S. Greenfield and R. A. Sternbach, (Eds.), (1972). *Handbook of Psychophysiology.* New York, NY: Holt, Rinehart, & Winston, p. 491-531. Hess, R. D. & Shipman, V. C. (1965). Early Experience and the Socialization of Cognitive Mode Children. *Child Development,* Published by the University of Chicago Press for the Society for Research in Child Development, Inc., 36, p. 859-886.
[211] Wolfe, R. (1963). The Role of Conceptual Systems in Cognitive Functioning at Varying Levels of Age and Intelligence. *Journal of Personality,* Vol. 31 (1), p. 108-122.
[212] Ibid., (Hokfelt, 1985).
[213] West, G.B.

of brain activation, an enlarged and new world of conceptual space, movement to a new level of existence takes place. *And all hell will not stop it once this critical point is reached.*

But again, insight, even in conjunction with potential, resolution of existential problems and dissonance, is not sufficient to produce control by the next level neurological system. Unfortunately, "Full many a flower is born to blush unseen and waste its sweetness on the desert air."[214] The reasons for this are obvious. A human being is not, nor ever will be, an island unto himself. There are others around whenever any insight is achieved. Most of them, though they share potential and may share the solution of current existential problems, will not necessarily share the dissonance; and few indeed will share the new insights. Thus, there will be barriers.

5. Barriers Overcome

'The Establishment' and its way of thinking must be overcome or move aside if insight is to begin to propel the quantum-like psychosocial jump. Tomes of support for this lie in essays on the atmosphere needed for psychotherapeutic change.

If this fifth factor in the change process is provided for, then and only then does the sixth factor, consolidation, come into action. It is the last factor in the change process.

6. Opportunity for Consolidation

Now if we add to our thinking that the hierarchically ordered brain systems are infinite, emergent cyclical theory provides some most remarkable insights into human existence. It provides the human with a reason for being in his or her existence no matter the previous existential problems solved. Life is a constant ordering, reordering and, at times, disordering of styles of existence. Man is always metamorphizing. Like the egg, to the larvae, to the moth, each new form of psychosocial being is contiguous with the old stage but is qualitatively as well as quantitatively different from it. Psychosocial man, his institutions, and his life are processes in transit from the earliest order of adult behavioral organization, through a series of way stations, to no knowable destination.

Through the E-C assertion that the solution of current existential problems creates a new set in their place, and through its depiction of the neuropsychological equipment, it provides a means to map out the natural history of man, a need cited by Elkind. It also provides a means

---

[214] Gray, Thomas. "Elegy Written in a Country Churchyard."

to approach the humanistic psychological goal of Bugental. Beyond this, by the overall task performed in this chapter, namely, welding together many disparate studies, it has placed in one conceptual framework facts derived from numerous studies in general psychology. And though I will not develop it now, E-C theory provides a means to begin to draw into one framework our many theories of human behavior.

So it appears to me that there is ample support for the position that human psychosocial behavior develops from the existential state of man. And there is support for the hypothesis that the emergent states are the map of human existence. They are the story of the never-ending quest of human emergence, what human life is all about and what it is meant to be. The encoded neuropsychological equipment of humans are the pylons upon which are erected new ways of psychosocial being appropriate to new existential problems. We are but one organism biologically. We are an infinite number of beings psychologically.

Support From Other Conceptions

Many people have thought about human development in a stage-like developing-systems fashion. Some like Ludwig von Bertalanffy, Lancelot Whyte, and Gordon Allport[215], have shown in their publications systems-like thinking but they have not gone on to develop conceptions of the systems. Others like Gerald Heard and Lewis Mumford have proceeded from reading to thinking, and from thinking to the construction of hierarchically ordered psychosocial systems. Still others have developed conceptions from experimental, clinical or other forms of systematic investigation. System conceptions of one form or another are presented in the published and non-published works of many people. (See Table VII a-g, p. 440-446)

They have conceived of development as a series of stages. But this plethora of published and unpublished material in this area has created a monstrous problem for the reader. There are as many languages for transmitting their thinking as there are contributors to this way of thinking. This was the prime problem I had to deal with when the emergent cyclical conception was conceived.

The problem is that there are almost as many languages as there are conceptions. The problem seems to stem, for the most part, from one fact. During the late forties, through the fifties and sixties and extending into the seventies many people, mostly independently of one another,

---

[215] Allport (1960), p. 39-54.

became disenchanted with the state of theory in the development psychosocial world. Many set out from many different directions and by many different means to investigate the region of their discontent. When they did so, by and large, they worked alone or in neat little, relatively isolated groups. Thus, when they started to conceptualize from the results of their library, clinical, experimental, or other research they found themselves with masses of un-rationalized data. Their information did not lend itself to rationalization within any then-existing conceptual system; or they found themselves dissatisfied with the capacity of the conceptual frameworks others had developed to express the meaning in what they found.

As a result of these conditions, most of the conceptualizers or investigators developed their own conceptual system within which to rationalize their information. This situation created a serious problem for me when I began to test my emergent cyclical conception through others' work.

Try as I could, and try I did (my first two published papers were an abortive attempt to rationalize my results through Maslowian thinking), I found no system which met the test of comprehensiveness as did the emergent cyclical point of view once I formulated it. I could not subsume my results and my conception within any systems-like conception I could find in the literature. All dealt with only some of the hierarchical systems my data had dictated. Some were truncated at both ends. Some closed off at the later appearing part of the hierarchy; some showed gaps, and some were otherwise not as comprehensive as emergent cyclical theory. None dealt with the total map of human existence and few had any way for conceptualizing the open-endedness of psychosocial development which I found necessary to hypothesize.

So I felt forced to make a decision. The decision was to translate, where possible, the systemic conceptualizations of others into the language of emergent cyclical theory. This was not done out of egocentricism but out of necessity. I could not subsume my results and my conception in the work of others. But I could, for the most part, subsume their information and their conception within my emergent cyclical conception. So in this section of this chapter I continuously translate their many languages into my emergent cyclical language.

Testing E–C Theory Through the Work of Harvey, Hunt and Schroder et al.

Harvey, Hunt and Schroder et al., have done many predictive studies based on their 1961 conception. They developed a conception which, in the middle toward the upper ranges of their hierarchy, can be used to test E-C theory. To a considerable extent they have found confirmation of their systems I, II, III and IV. Hunt, who found it necessary to hypothesize a Sub I system, a system which occupies a position just before their system, has modified their original conception I.[216] Their systems I, II, III and IV are essentially equivalent to E-C systems DQ, ER, FS and A'N' respectively. Hunt's modification is essentially equivalent to the emergent cyclical CP system. So I shall, in this section, use the work of this group to test the validity of E-C systems CP, DQ, ER, FS and A'N'.

The predictions based on the original Harvey, Hunt and Schroder conception have broken down in respect to their system III, the FS system of E-C theory. Therefore, it occurred to me that this reported problem and the changes made by Hunt and Driver and Streufert might provide crucial tests of their conceptualization versus the conceptualization of this book.

One problem, which arises, is in essence: Do the systems of psychosocial behavior differ only in a quantitative way or do they vary also in a qualitative manner? Another problem is: Are there only four systems or are there at least five as per Hunt, or are there more as per E-C theory? A third problem is: Is system IV, (roughly A'N' in E-C theory) the highest, the ultimate system, or is the hierarchy open-ended?

My position in respect to the first problem, the quantitative/qualitative problem has been stated previously. But I have not examined the other side particularly, as Harvey, Hunt and Schroder see it. Of it they say:

> "The question of whether a more abstract level of functioning is only a quantitative extension of a concrete level, and the two levels are hence continuous, as Murphy suggests, or is so quantitatively different from the more concrete functioning that it is discontinuous from it, as Goldstein and Scheerer maintain, is indeed an old – and yet unresolved – one.

---

[216] Hunt, David E. (1966). A Conceptual Systems Change Model and its Application to Education. In O.J. Harvey (Ed.), *Experience, Structure and Adaptability*. NY: Springer Publishing, Inc..

It is, among other questions, the problem of reductionism versus holism, or relatedly of quantity versus quality, issues with which psychology—indeed all of science—has spent much effort. Points of view on this issue, which most clearly separated the "Gestalters" and the "Structuralists", for instance, have not been agreed upon but only bypassed or overlooked in pursuit of a concern with different types of questions.

It seems to us that although, "...the stream of behavior" may be seen not "to flow smoothly, but to occur in easily perceived bursts and breaks." (Barker, 1957, P. 156) Such variation could as well represent a continuity as be expressive of a qualitative break.

Attribution of a discontinuity is probably a function of the aspect of behavior being observed or measured and the method by which the observation is obtained. It frequently results from concern with phenotypic expressions rather than with genotypic function and underlying process. The genotype may be expressed in phenotypic opposites: one person, for example, might show his insecurity by reacting very aggressively whereas another would reticently withdraw from contact with others. Thus, one investigator who was more concerned with functions of behavior might from the same behavioral manifestations infer what he considered continuities; another whose observations were of expressions of this function might infer such marked variability that he would attribute it to breaks and discontinuities ... due attention must be given to *what* it is that is being measured and the dimension of the observation. Very pertinent to this issue is the elaboration of William James on his assertion that objection to viewing the stream of thought or consciousness as continuous is "based partly on a confusion and partly on a superficial introspective point of view."[217]

It is my judgment, based on the data previously presented supporting the existence of qualitatively different "dynamic neurological systems," that the quantitative/qualitative problem is far less simple than the quotation above makes it out to be. There is far more to conceptualizing human behavior than making a choice between a

---

[217] Harvey, O.J., Hunt, David E. and Schroder, Arold M. (1961). *Conceptual Systems and Personality Organization*. New York: John Wiley & Sons, Inc., p. 27-28.

quantitative or qualitative format. The problem is more than to decide whether to base a psychosocial conceptualization on one or the other side of this age-old either-or problem. We must not be misled to believe the difference between one form of human behavior and another form of human behavior has to be seen from either the quantitative direction or from the qualitative point of view. It is entirely possible that it is not one or the other, but *both* that vary from one system of human behavior to another.

It would seem, from the following quotation, that Harvey, Hunt and Schroder have dismissed this alternative possibility because they say:

> "Our use of state in the present book refers to levels of cognitive functioning on what we assume to be a continuous dimension of concreteness – abstraction."[218]

Having made this assumption, they have found a problem with their data which might not exist if they had not made an either/or choice. Harvey expresses this problem in his 1966 book, *Experience, Structure and Adaptability,* where he says:

> "In all our studies System 1 [DQ] and System 4 [A'N'] representatives have differed as they should according to the theory ... with System 2 [ER] individuals following in between closer to System 1 [DQ] on some things and closer to System 4 [A'N] on others. The one source of inconsistency has been the response of System 3 [FS] representatives who on such things as evaluativeness, and categoricalness of TIB completions fall next to System 4 [A'N] (where they should be according to their assumed position on the concreteness-abstraction dimension), but who on authoritarianism and ability to change fall next to System 1 [DQ].[219] This inconsistency is, no doubt, due partially to a lack of clarity in the theoretical formulation of System 3 [FS] functioning which results in somewhat ambiguous criteria for scoring this system. Hence, we are much more equivocal in our view and interpretation of System 3 [FS] functioning than of the functioning of other systems."[220]

---

[218] Ibid., (Harvey, Hunt and Schroder, 1961, p. 24).
[219] CWG: This writer calls to the reader's attention that the second sentence above about System 3 (FS) is inconsistent with the theory.
[220] Harvey, O. J. (Ed.) (1966). *Experience, Structure & Adaptability.* New York: Springer Publishing Company, Inc., p. 47-48.

This problem is actually more serious than Harvey says because, as noted above, there is an inconsistency in both the results of System 2 (ER) and System 3 (FS). If one examines the statement above and at the same time observes the way the Harvey, Hunt and Schroder data in Table V is reorganized in Table VI, it will be found that the problem appears to be more than something wrong with the conceptualization of System 3 (FS).

Actually Harvey's statement shows System 2 (ER) close to System 1 (DQ) in some respects and close to System 4 (A'N') in other respects as well as System 3 (FS) being closer to System 1 (DQ) in some respects and closer to System 4 (A'N') in other respects. These failures to predict suggest that the problem is in the region of the total conceptualization rather than in the region of conceptualizing System 3 (FS). The point of this argument is that if one accepts their data or my data as the data are, then he will conceptualize so that systems vary both quantitatively and qualitatively and will not be caught in the fruitlessness of the age-old either-or argument. And the point is, that when one lets the data dictate the conceptualization as per Exhibit XII (page 431), there will be no inconsistency in the Harvey, Hunt and Schroder data. Rather there will be support for the much more complex conceptualization to the test one other Harvey, Hunt and Schroder quotation must be considered. They say:

> "As indicated in Chapter 4, developmental stages can be viewed in terms of two phases (Bemis and Shepard, 1956): the first phase including stages I and II and the second phase including stages III and IV. One implication of this "recapitulation" is that arrestation at stages I and III and at stages II and IV have generic similarities. Differences do exist in the abstractness of subject-object relatedness in system I and system III (particularly in respect to external and internal causation), but these systems are generically similar in that for both, judgments and behavior are anchored to external objects, such as rules, power and relationships. In a non-systemic sense the two forms of relatedness combine to describe behavior that, from an operational viewpoint is more "dependent."[221]

This quotation is presented because in my judgment it is the failure of Harvey, Hunt and Schroder to see either the total meaning in this relationship, or to carry through on it that has led them predictably

---

[221] Ibid., (Harvey, Hunt, and Schroder, 1961, p. 199).

astray. But we cannot tarry longer on this point. We must move on to the task of testing this conceptualization of adult personality, first through the medium of the Harvey, Hunt and Schroder data.

In summary, then, the Harvey, Hunt and Schroder position is that the systems of behavior vary quantitatively from one to another primarily on the concrete-abstract dimension. Whereas my position is that the systems vary in a much more complex manner from system to system. Particularly, my position is that there are qualitative, that is system specific, manifestations as well as quantitative differences. Thus, in the test to follow we shall examine their data in order to see if they support or refute the position of this book.

Their systems were established in a manner different from the way that mine were established. They utilized the 'This I Believe' test[222] to establish the existence of their conceptual systems. They report the validity of the TIB Test, but this is not the most important information for the purpose in mind here; for our purpose, the important information is:

a) Through their methodology they established four systems. All four are much like those I seem to have found.

b) Independently of one another the Harvey, Hunt and Schroder group and I studied the systems established through many common instrumental means.

c) Independently of one another we found remarkably similar results.

Since their data lend themselves to quantification, they are presented in tabular form in Table V. Most of the Harvey, Hunt and Schroder data has been summarized in the 1966 book of Harvey, previously referred to. Not all of their data is presented in Table V. This selection does not contradict the data presented in any way. It is simply more of the same. One manipulation has been performed, where possible, in order to foster presentation. The data have been transformed to rank order form. They studied four systems. They studied them through a number of dimensions. Table V presents their results with 'Stage IV' being the highest degree of the dimensions studied and 'Stage I' being the lowest degree. Where their findings did not show ranks are summated according to the Harvey summary and are distributed appropriately to each system. But before we proceed, let one matter be emphasized again. There are no

---

[222] Ibid., (Harvey, Hunt and Schroder, 1966, p. 46).

substantial differences except one between my total data and the data of the Harvey, Hunt and Schroder group. It is the conceptualization that differs. The one difference is that my data required breaking the Harvey, Hunt and Schroder System II into two systems. One is system ER in my conceptualization. The other is CP which is the system Sub I that David E. Hunt also said should be in the hierarchy.

Table V
Harvey, Hunt, and Schroder Characteristics of Systems Listing of Dimensions Studied Random Data Arranged by Rank Order

Roman numerals = Systems
4=s most of characteristic
1=s least of characteristic
*=s significant difference from other H, H, & S systems

DIMENSION MEASURED	Systems				
	H, H, & S	I	II	III	IV
	Graves	DQ	ER	FS	A'N'
Cognitive Complexity		1	2	3	4
Intelligence		2.3	2.6	2.4	2.7
Religiousness		*ii-iii-iv 4	*i-iii 1	*i 3	*iv 2
Authoritarianism		4	3	2	1
Dogmatism		4	3	2	1
Left Opinionation		*ii 1	*i 1.5	2	1.5
Right Opinionation		*ii-iv 4	*i 1	3	*i 1
Rigidity		*iii-iii-iv 4	*i-iv 3	*i-iv 2	*i-ii-iii 1
Deference		*ii-iv 4	*i 1.5	3	*i 1.5
Autonomy		*ii-iv 1	*i 3.5	2	*i 3.5
Aggressiveness		*ii 2	*i-iii-iv 4	*ii 2	*ii 2
Self-Causality		*ii-iv 2	*i-iii-iv 1	*ii 3	*i-ii 4
"Nettler" Anomie		*ii-iii-iv 3	*i-iii-iv 1	*i-ii 3	*i-ii 2
Self Concept		*iv 2	*iv 1	*iv 3	*i-ii-iii 4

Table V (cont'd)

Self Control	*ii-iii-iv 4	*i 1.8	*i 2.1	*i 2.1
Honesty	*ii-iii 4	*i-iii 1	*i-ii 3	2
Creativity – (Desire to be Different)	*ii 1	*i-iii 4	*ii 2	3
Kindness	*ii 3.5	*i-iii 1	*ii 3.5	2
Loyalty	*ii-iii-iv 4	*i-iii-iv 1	*i-ii 3	*i-ii 2
Independence	*ii 1.5	*i-iii 4	*ii 1.5	2
Machiavellianism	*ii 2	*i-iii-iv 4	*ii 2	*ii 2
Cue Utilization	*iv 1.7	*iv 1.9	*iv 2.4	*i-ii-iii 4
Influence on belief of Input-Deviant	*iv 3	*iv 1.9	*iv 4	*i-ii-iii 1
Redundancy	*ii-iv 4	*i 1.5	3	*i 1.5
Change of Set	*iv 2	*iv 2	*iv 2	*i-ii-iii 4
Relevancy of Questions	*iv 1	*iv 3	*iv 2	*i-ii-iii 4
Integrating Contradiction	*iv 1.7	*iv 1.9	*iv 2.4	*iv 2.4
Attaining New Concept Speed	*ii-iv 1	*i 3	3	*i 3
Denny Doodle- Bug Time	*ii-iv 4	*i-iv 2	*iv 3	*i-ii-iii 1
D. Doodlebug Help Sought	*iv 4	*iv 2	*iv 3	*i-ii-iii 1
Arguing Against Belief in Public and Private	*iv 1	*iv 2	*iv 3	*i-ii-iii 4
Arguing Against Belief in Private	*iv 1	*iv 2	*iv 3	*i-ii-iii 4
Arguing Against Belief 'in Public	2	1	3	4
Creating Novelty Appropriateness	*iv 1	*iv 2	*iv 3	*i-ii-iii 4
Maintenance of Belief - Input - Deviant	*iv 3	*iv 2	*iv 1	*i-ii-iii 4

Table VI
Harvey, Hunt, Schroder Data Rearranged
According to Graves's Conception

Dimension Measured	System				
HH & S Graves	I DQ	II ER	III FS	IV A'N'	Nature of Variation
1. Intelligence	2.3	2.6	2.4	2.7	None
2. Cognitive Complexity	1	2	3	4	Quantitative increasing
3. Dogmatism	4	3	2	1	Quantitative increasing
4. Rigidity	*2-3-4 4	*1-4 3	*1-4 2	*1-2-3 1	Quantitative increasing
5. Arguing Against Belief Public/Private	*4 1	*4 2	*4 3	*1-2-3 4	Quantitative increasing
6. Appropriateness of Solutions Created	1	2	3	4	Quantitative increasing
7. Relevancy of Questions	*4 1	*4 2	*4 3	*1-2-3 4	Quantitative increasing
8. Integrating Contradiction	*4 1.7	*4 1.9	*4 2.4	*1-2-3 4	Trend Quant and System Specific
9. Change of Set	*4 2	*4 2	*4 2	*1-2-3 4	
10. Cue Utilization	*4 1.7	*4 1.9	*4 2.4	*1-2-3 4	
11. Aggressiveness	*2 2	*1-3-4 4	*2 2	*2 2	System Specific
12. Self Causality	*2-4 2	*1-3-4 1	*2 3	*1-2 4	System Specific
13. Self Concept	*4 2	*4 1	*4 3	*1-2-3 4	System Specific
14. Self Control	*2-3-4 4	*1 1.8	*1 2.1	*1 2.1	System Specific
15. "Nettler" Anomie	*2-3-4 4	*1-3-4 1	*1-2 3	*1-2 2	System Specific
16. Desire to be Different	*2 1	*1-3 4	*2 2	3	System Specific
17. Machiavellianism	*2 2	*1-3-4 4	*2 2	*2 2	System Specific
18. Maintenance of Belief Input- Deviant	*4 3	*4 2	*4 1	*1-2-3 4	System Specific
19. Attaining New Concept Speed	*2-4 1	*1 3	3	*1 3	System Specific
20. Arguing Against Belief in Public	2	1	3	4	System Specific

Table VI (cont'd)

21. Independence	*2 1.5	*1-3 4	*2 1.5	2	System Specific
22. Integrating Contradiction	*4 1.7	*4 1.9	*4 2.4	*1-2-3 4	System Specific
23. Opinionation – Right	4	1	3	2	Cyclic
24. Loyalty	*2-3-4 4	*1-3-4 1	*1 3	*1-2 2	Cyclic
25. Religiousness	*2-3-4 4	*1-3 1	*1 3	*1-3 2	Cyclic
26. Honesty	*2-3 4	*1-3 1	*1-2 3	2	Cyclic
27. Deference	*2-4 1	*1 1.5	3	*1 1.5	Cyclic
28. Redundancy	*2-4 4	*1 1.5	3	*1 1.5	Cyclic
29. Kindness	*2 3.5	*1-3 1	*2 3.5	2	Cyclic
30. Autonomy	*2-4 1	*1 3.5	2	*1 3.5	Cyclic
31. Affiliation	3	*1-3-4 1	*1-2-4 4	2	Cyclic
32. Doodlebug Time	*2-4 4	*1-4 2	*4 3	*1-2-3 1	Cyclic
33. Influence on Belief Input - Deviant	*4 3	*4 2	*4 4	*1-2-3 1	Probably Cyclic
34. Relevancy of Questions	*4 1	*4 3	*4 2	*1-2-3 4	Probably Cyclic
35. Doodlebug Help Sought	*4 4	*4 2	*4 3	*1-2-3 1	Probably Cyclic
36. Arguing Against Belief in Private	2	2	4	1	Probably Cyclic
37. Authoritarianism	4	2	3	1	Probably Cyclic
38. Opinionation Left	*2 1	*1 1.5	2	1.5	Probably Cyclic

Examination of the data in Table V would appear almost unintelligible ordered as it is. Examine the dimensions as listed and you will see how disorderly the data appear to be. However, when ordered as per Table VI, these data dictate a conceptualization much more complex than the quantitative variation of one main dimension, concreteness – abstractness which is proposed by the Harvey, Hunt and Schroder group. This you can see by examining the data as they are ordered in Table VI.

Item 1, intelligence, shows essentially no variation over the systems. Thus, Harvey, Hunt and Schroder data says:

    a) Conceptualize adult behavior so as to allow for no variation in certain psychological dimensions. My data say the same thing except for systems AN, BO and CP which I explain by saying that an IQ of more than 70 or so is required to think beyond the CP system.

Items 2 through 10, dogmatism, relevancy and quantity of problem solving, vary on a quantitative scale. Thus, the Harvey, Hunt and Schroder data also say:

    b) Conceptualize adult behavior so as to allow for quantitative variation in some psychological dimensions.

My data say the same thing. Items 23 through 38 show a different kind of variation. Systems I (DQ) and III (FS) are a pair. Systems II (ER) and IV (A'N') are almost a pair. (The CP problem mentioned above requires the modification 'almost.') But, in both pairs the two are not alike in every way. Therefore, their data say:

    c) Conceptualize adult behavior in an alternating wave-like fashion allowing for the repetition of a theme. Again my data say the same thing.

Their data say also:

    d) Conceptualize adult behavior so that every other system is similar to but at the same time different from its alternate. Here again my data say the same thing, especially in saying CP is an alternate of DQ.

Now focus on the items in Table VI where significant differences are noted, and focus on items 11 through 22. Note the instances in which one system is significantly different from three systems, from two systems, etc. Note, also, that some of these differences vary significantly in one system only. Note also, in System FS, that it is characterized by a paucity of items significantly different from each of the other three systems. Thus, these data of Harvey, Hunt and Schroder say:

    a) Conceptualize adult behavior so that each system has its system-specificness, so that each system has a quality all its own. Once more my data say the same thing.

Also the data in Table VI say:

> b) Conceptualize adult human behavior so that systems DQ and FS are more externally controlled and so that systems ER and A'N' are self-expressive. My data say CP is also self-expressive.

And finally the data says:

> c) Increased degrees of behavioral freedom in each successive system, particularly at system IV. The purpose of Exhibit XII (repeated below) is to points a, b, c, d, e, f and g above.

In its entirety, Exhibit XII shows the emergence of the eight systems which research seems to have identified to date, the eighth only partially. It illustrates that they emerge as the basic components grow and develop under the stimulation of new existential problems. This growth is represented partially as quantitative change satisfying thus the (b) requirement above of the Harvey, Hunt and Schroder data. The components are represented to show periods of spurt and periods of plateau, a form of growth producing the wave-like repetition of theme/variation on theme demanded by the data and noted as (c) and (d) above, and the alternating wavelike and similar/dissimilar, at one and the same time, aspects of the data.

Solid lines representing the even-numbered systems indicate a similarity in the tendency of these to be tightly bound. The odd-numbered systems are represented by a broken line indicating each to be less tightly bound than the even-numbered systems. Thereby, (f) above, namely, that the even-numbered systems be externally controlled and conservative and that the odd-numbered systems be self-expressive and change-oriented, is expressed in the diagram just as the Harvey, Hunt and Schroder data indicate.

The transition points produced by the growth of the components plus the cross hatching represent each system having a quality all its own, which is the data of (e) above. Requirement (g) of the Harvey, Hunt and Schroder data, the charge to conceive adult human behavior in order to show increased degrees of behavioral freedom at each successive system, particularly at system A'N', is shown by increasing the size of each system. And, finally, the point (a) that some psychological dimensions do not vary over systems is represented by the constant shape of the systems.

Testing further by reading down the columns, we see that each system is centralized in a different way, that each is organized to a different end. The DQ system is rigid, strongly in control of self, much identified with the American motif, loyal and religious. ER is aggressive, self-motivated, Machiavellian, disloyal to authority, nonaffiliated with others, and so on. System FS is significantly different in its lack of difference (note the relative sameness of the rankings) except in the region—'need for affiliation'. And A'N' is the most different, not only in the content of the differences, arguing against beliefs, relevancy of approach, integrating contradiction, utilization of cues, etc., but also in terms of the quantity of significant differences from all other systems.

As we continue to look down the columns, we can see that the Harvey, Hunt and Schroder data support that each even-numbered system be considerably larger than its predecessor. This is shown in items involving self-expansiveness, which suggest that System A'N' should be represented as much larger over the FS system than ER is over the DQ system. System A'N' must be represented as showing many more degrees of behavioral freedom because it is, according to the Harvey, Hunt and Schroder data, far less rigid, far less dogmatic, much more able to solve problems, much quicker to solve problems, much more able to change points of view, etc. Examining further, we see why each even-numbered system is but slightly larger than its predecessor.

Exhibit XII *(repeated)*

A Double Helix Representation of the Oscillating, Spiraling Development of Adult Human Psychosocial, Existential States as the Brain Alternates Dominance by the Left Hemisphere, in Odd Numbered States, and the Right Hemisphere in Even Numbered States.

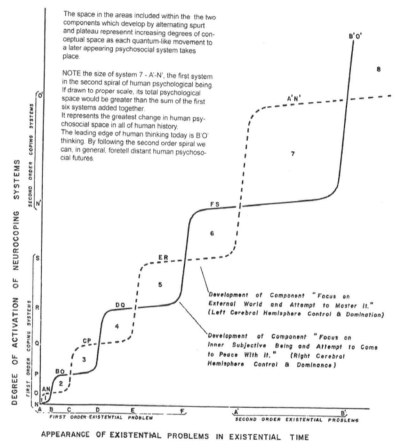

This is what must be because the Harvey, Hunt and Schroder data show the even-numbered systems to be constricting, consolidating systems, not growth systems. Yet, FS is in position six and is represented larger than ER because, when the Harvey, Hunt and Schroder data are ordered as per Table VI, it falls unquestionably between ER and A'N' just as my data indicated was its nature and its position in the hierarchy.

But, now, we have an additional testing problem arising from Harvey, Hunt and Schroder position. With time this group has diverged. This has been so in respect to Schroder, Driver and Streufert. They have come to accentuate structural differences in systems over and above content differences and thus force the question: How adequately does this conception fit with the Schroder, Driver and Streufert data? This is a most substantive question to answer because of the nature of their studies.

The question is difficult to answer because most of the Schroder, Driver and Streufert studies cover only what I call the DQ through A'N' systems. As they say, when writing of certain of their studies, "Unfortunately, none of the studies in these areas covers the entire range of stimulus complexity."[223] Though this problem exists there are several passages in their book which serve as a partial test of this conceptualization.

The first of these passages seems to support the contention that there is far more to the conceptualization of adult behavior than just quantitative differences from system to system. For example, I contend that the adult's psychology should be seen as an open system, as a system in which data processing characteristics change in more than a quantitative fashion from system to system; and I suggest that Schroder, Driver and Streufert seem to accept this when they say, while writing of a discrepancy in certain of their studies, that:

> "We could regard this divergence as mere error, but it fits into a very interesting picture that is beginning to emerge. We might consider the mind as an open system (following von Bertalanffy, 1952). It can handle only so much information. The point of interest is the manner in which it handles information ... when perception reaches a peak, a new mechanism comes into action. As load continues to climb, higher-order structures go in into action."[224]

This is, of course, the open system/new process point of view that I have expressed.

Another confirmation of the emergent cyclical conception has to do with change factors. Schroder, Driver and Streufert state from the studies of Brock (1962) and Suedfeld (1964) that:

---

[223] Ibid., p. 61.
[224] Ibid., p. 98-99.

> "The more concrete the attitude structure, the more likely it is that a single salient component of information will become central and that other informational units will become irrelevant. This implies—and research substantiates the implication—that if one can change the salience of certain classes of information, attitude change occurs. This can be accomplished by "authority" or by extreme stress, as in information deprivation followed by a message that thus becomes highly salient."[225]

This reference to authority as the instrument of progressive change is a direct confirmation of what was found to produce change in the DQ system of personality and is further confirmed by the work of Michael J. Driver, who found them to rely heavily on information handed down by external authority. Schroder, Driver and Streufert state that:

> "This approach provides a provocative point of view in the study of group structures. At the individual level, we have seen that concreteness implies increasing centralization of hierarchy (in values, for example), decreasing degrees of freedom in connectedness among parts, decreasing flexibility in ingetration, and so on. We believe that parallel phenomena occur in group structure. Concreteness in a group implies increasing increasing centralization of power, decreasing interpersonal communication, decreasing flexibility in role assignments, and so on. Information-processing systems in sociologically concrete groups would be expected to exhibit the constriction and rigidity of concrete systems in individuals."[226]

They support the hierarchical centralization of power and the fewer degrees of behavioral freedom of the DQ system while they support that the A'N' system pays far more attention to information regardless of source than does the DQ system; a point made earlier in this work:

> "(a) Information search and time spent in processing information are curvilinearly related to uncertainty and to external demand. (b) Abstract persons search for more information (about a figure) and spend more time in processing the information than do concrete persons. (c) Information search and information processing by abstract

---

[225] Ibid., p. 100.
[226] Ibid., p. 101.

persons increase more with increasing uncertainty than do search and processing by concrete persons. Since abstract individuals produce many integrations of the information given, and also require further information in order to examine the feasibility of each decision, the complexity of their decision processes should increase rapidly with increases in information input (in this case, with greater ambiguity of the figures). The concrete person's tendency to structure a stimulus field and to reduce the degrees of freedom available precludes much of this activity. (d) The asymptote of searching and processing time occurs at a lower level of uncertainty and external demand for concrete persons. (e) Searching and information processing time of abstract and concrete persons are most dissimilar in the middle ranges of uncertainty and external demand. (f) Abstract persons give more information in their decisions than do concrete persons. (g) Abstract persons are more likely than concrete persons to qualify their decisions with remarks indicating remaining doubt, uncertainty, and tentativeness.

We have shown that abstract persons in Driver's experiment (1962) tracked (differentiated) more discrepant information than did concrete subjects. The experimenter weighted the dimensions in terms of their representation in the decision making of the group. More evenly weighted dimensions would indicate that the group's decision making involved a better representation of all of the differentiated aspects of the interaction. Generally, even weights represent a better reflection of all environmental information in behavior, thereby improving the quality of the integration.

Driver found that for groups composed of abstract persons (as opposed to groups of concrete persons) there were more dimensions, and that these were more evenly weighted in decision-making. Information integration was significantly higher for abstract than for concrete groups."[227]

At another point in their book, they confirm the 'partial solution of existential problems' concept when they say:

---

[227] Ibid., p. 114.

> "It is possible that a person could use an integratively complex structure for handling interpersonal stimuli but have only a simple hierarchical structure for handling religious stimuli."[228]

But what of the wave-like manifestation of the emergent cyclical conception? What of its characterization of the systems as outer directed, inner directed, then again outer directed with a different focus, and so forth? What of the verbal characterization appended to the DQ, ER, FS and A'N' systems, those that Schroder, Driver and Streufert call low integrative complexity, moderately low integrative complexity, medium high integrative complexity and high abstract integrative complexity, respectively? Does or does not the data of Schroder, Driver and Streufert support my position? As has been said before, this is not an easy question to answer. To my knowledge, they report only one study (Streufert, 1966), which examines moderately low integrative subjects and medium high integrative subjects, the ER and FS systems of this work, and even this report is difficult to interpret. What they say is that:

> "Medium low [ER] subjects differentiated between situations in which the refuting source was close or distant—being more negative to the source in close interaction situations. This follows from the concern with differentiation of the self from absolutistic control."[229]

This seems to confirm that their lower integrative complexity (DQ) is seen as externally controlled (the last sentence in the quotation above). And the first sentence seems to say that their moderately[230] low integrative complexity (ER) is more self, more externally expressive. But, their statement about the medium high integrative complexity (FS) subjects is even more difficult to fathom in terms of answering the wave-like question. They say:

> "Medium high subjects [FS] made some distinctions regarding the closeness of interaction, but in addition, differentiated between judgments of the source in minority and majority situations. This also ties into the general hypothesis that, at this

---

[228] Ibid., pg 128-129.
[229] Ibid., p. 140.
[230] Schroder, Driver & Streufert, 1967, use the terms 'moderately' and 'medium' interchangeably.

level [FS], the standards of others have complex interacting effects on oneself in a noncategorical, nonabsolutistic way."[231]

As I interpret the above, it seems to say that their medium high integrative complexity (FS) subjects are other-directed but in a manner different from the categorical, absolutistic, low integrative complexity (DQ) subjects. Thus, I must conclude there is suggestive data from Schroder, Driver and Streufert which can be used to test the wave-like aspects of this conceptualization. Nevertheless, at another place in their book they use language which is in many respects both cognizant of content systemic differences and similar to the verbal characterization presented in this book.

> "As the structure advances to the level we have defined as moderately low integrative complexity, interpersonal attitude structures become less "content bound" and are used to process information about content in relation to the proximity or relevance of persons. The structure appears to have the potential to generate some variation in output (judgment, evaluation) as the object of the attitude (such as a refuting source) becomes more or less relevant (interaction, closeness, distance). However, few kinds of information are processed, the focus is egocentric, and the content is anchored in self-reference so that attitudes can swing from neutral to highly negative purely on the basis of personal relevance. Alternate views (hierarchical organizations) can be considered, but the structural properties for integrating these discrepant organizations (perceptions) are lacking. At this level, alternatives are available and can be maintained if the person can avoid close contact or interaction; for example, "He can keep his beliefs so long as he does not interfere with mine." Freedom is defined in terms of reference to a differentiated self: "It is what I want to do." It is as if the structure for maintaining these minimal alternatives is so fragile that a good deal of protection is required to prevent a return to a more concrete level of structure where the direction of the attitude determines what is right, and alternatives are wrong and considered a threat." [232]

However, at this point, they are writing more theoretically than they are writing from data collected in specific studies. Thus, I do not deem it

---

[231] Ibid., p. 140.
[232] Ibid., p. 134-135.

proper to make a case using these words of theirs to test this conceptualization. Their words are referred to only in respect to the questions raised because the reader may be interested in checking this matter himself.

There is one part of the data reported by Schroder, Driver and Streufert which may or may not stand in refutation of the conceptualization presented in this book. It is the data they present in respect to the distribution of intelligence over systems. You may recall that my data tended to differ little across systems except for AN, BO and CP, but they report that they found correlations of from .12 to .50 between integrative complexity and intelligence.[233]

This may or may not be a refutation of one aspect of their conceptualization. Our methodologies were different. Schroder, Driver, and Streufert used correlation techniques to study intelligence as it ranged over all of the systems.[234] I studied the distributional range of intelligence across systems. This discrepancy cannot be resolved at this time, but its existence raises a most important point in respect to the systems conceptualization of behavior.

The point is that older methodologies may well be inappropriate to behavior viewed from a systems perspective. We may find, as Murphy stated, that new views of man may well require new methods of exploration if we are to explore them. But this is a digression from our question of the moment: Do the Harvey, Hunt and Schroder data, do the Schroder, Driver and Streufert data, support or refute the conceptualization of this book?

I submit that most of the conceptualization of this book testable through their data is confirmed by it. In fact, one can say that the emergent cyclical framework fits better the Harvey, Hunt & Schroder and Schroder, Driver and Streufert data than does their own conceptualization. This can be seen by reviewing that which was tested and the reasons why the testing was done.

The decision to test E-C theory through the Harvey, Hunt and Schroder and Schroder, and Schroder, Driver and Streufert data was made for several reasons.

---

[233] Ibid., p. 122.
[234] Schroder, Driver and Streufert also mention that "low- and high-level information-processing systems can be equally intelligent" (p .10) confirming Graves's results. At another point they write, "Intelligence as measured by the group administration of the Otis, SAT and other intelligence tests, is significantly related to conceptual structure (.46 in the largest sample tested)." When they removed the low intelligence subjects from their experiment "the correlation was considerably reduced."(p. 121-122).

1. They are somewhat different conceptions of what psychosocial behavior is like. But they share the same basic assumption, namely, that psychosocial behaviour is the joint product of situational and dispositional factors. Thus a fair comparison of the basic and more peripheral aspects of the two conceptions can be made. So the first comparison should be between the basic aspects. This comparison shows that the Harvey, Hunt and Schroder and Schroder, Driver and Streufert conception does not systematize the organismic side of the double-helix. It does say much of the situational side but does not systematize it either. E-C theory systematizes both.
2. The two conceptions share several systems in common, I (DQ), II (ER), III (FS), and IV (A'N'). Hunt's version ads a fifth sub I (CP). The E-C conception adds two at the bottom, AN and BO, and one at the upper end, B'O'. E-C theory is also open-ended which is a matter Harvey, Hunt and Schroder and Schroder, Driver and Streufert appear to notice but move on. They equivocate in respect to open-endedness.
3. The Harvey, Hunt and Schroder and Schroder, Driver and Streufert people have reported several predictive and conceptual problems with their system. The E-C conception clears up these prediction problems.
4. The Harvey, Hunt and Schroder and Schroder, Driver and Streufert people theorize that the differences between systems is quantitative and not qualitative. E-C theory says the differences are both, and uses their studies to show that support is more on the E-C side.
5. The E-C development curve is a helix. The Harvey, Hunt and Schroder and Schroder, Driver and Streufert is a straight-line curve.
6. The E-C conception provides a framework by which the general aspects of future systems can be predicted. The Harvey, Hunt and Schroder and Schroder, Driver and Streufert conception offers nothing on this point.
7. The E-C conception posits a six-factor picture of the change process from one system to another. The Harvey group posits a much simpler change process.

8. The E-C conception includes within it the recent data that the two sides of the brain function differently. The Harvey-Schroder group do not.

But these are not the only tests to which the E-C point of view has been put. Verifiability has been tested in three other ways. One is by comparing the E-C conception to several other similar points of view. A second is through tests conducted in the author's laboratory. And the third is the test of application. Several people have been involved in testing the theory in institutional and work-a-day worlds.

E-C Theory Compared to Other Stage Developmental Conceptualizers

Table VII a–g compares the emergent cyclical conception to psychosocial systems as seen by others. The first five columns list the systems as per Graves's E-C theory. The left-hand column numbers the systems from 1 through 8, and the next lists them as nodal, exiting or entering states. The third column names the levels of existence, and the fourth lists the existential state of each nodal, exiting or entering system. The fifth column classifies them by their way of thinking, which my data said is the major way they should be characterized.

Under Others, systems-like conceptions produced by other people are numbered 1 through 23.

Column 1 (Table VII b) is the basic 1960 Harvey, Hunt and Schroder classification system. Column 2 lists the Harvey, Hunt and Schroder system as modified by Hunt; and column 3 lists the Schroder, Driver and Streufert version of the Harvey, Hunt and Schroder conception. These three versions of the Harvey, Hunt and Schroder conceptual systems were utilized in earlier parts of this chapter to test the emergent cyclical conception.

Table VII a — Graves Terminology

Number	Entering/Nodal/Exiting	Level of Existence	Existential State	Characteristic Way of Thinking
1	NODAL	1st Subsistence	AN	Autistic
1	Exiting		AN/bo	
2	Entering		an/BO	
2	NODAL	2nd Subsistence	BO	Animistic
2	Exiting		BO/cp	
3	Entering		bo/CP	
3	NODAL	3rd Subsistence	CP	Egocentric
3	Exiting		CP/dq	
4	Entering		cp/DQ	
4	NODAL	4th Subsistence	DQ	Absolutistic
4	Exiting		DQ/er	
5	Entering		dq/ER	
5	NODAL	5th Subsistence	ER	Multiplistic
5	Exiting		ER/fs	
6	Entering		er/FS	
6	NODAL	6th Subsistence	FS	Relativistic
6	Exiting		FS/a'n'	
7	Entering		fs/A'N'	
7	NODAL	1st Being	A'N'	Systemic
7	Exiting		A'N'/b'o'	
8	Entering		a'n'/B'O'	
8	NODAL	2nd Being	B'O'	Differentialist

Table VII b — Graves Compared with Other Theories

Graves Levels	1 Harvey, Hunt, & Shroder	2 Hunt	3 Driver, Steufort, Shroder	4 Riesman
AN				
AN/bo				
an/BO				
BO				
BO/cp				
bo/CP				
CP		Type Sub-I		
CP/dq				
cp/DQ				
DQ	Type I	Type I	Low integrative complexity	Tradition-directed
DQ/er				
dq/ER				
ER	Type II	Type II	Moderate/low integrative complexity	Inner-directed
ER/fs				
er/FS			Medium/high integrative complexity	
FS	Type III	Type III		Other-directed
FS/a'n'				
fs/A'N'				
A'N'	Type IV	Type IV	High abstract integrative complexity	Autonomous
A'N'/b'o'				
a'n'/B'O'				
B'O'				

Table VII c — Graves Compared to Other Theories

Graves Levels	5 Stein	6 Heard	7 Mumford	8 Ausubel
AN				
AN/bo				
an/BO				
BO		Coconscious	Archaic man	Ego omnipotence
BO/cp				
bo/CP				
CP	[Similar to] Type C	Heroic self-assertive	Civilized man	Crisis of ego development
CP/dq				
cp/DQ				
DQ	Type D	Aesthetic self-accusing	Axial man	Satellization
DQ/er				
dq/ER				
ER	Type C	Humanistic self-sufficient	New world man	Crisis of desatellization
ER/fs				
er/FS				
FS	Type B	Leptoid post-individual	World culture[1]	Desatellization
FS/a'n'				
fs/A'N'				
A'N'	Type A			
A'N'/b'o'				
a'n'/B'O'				
B'O'	Type E ?			

---

[1] Dr. Graves omits Mumford's Post-historic Man. See Mumford (1956).

Table VII d — Graves Compared to Other Theories

Graves Levels	9 Kohlberg	10 Sullivan, Grant & Grant	11 Perry	12 Selman
AN		Level 1		Zero
AN/bo				
an/BO				
BO		Level 2		
BO/cp				
bo/CP				
CP	1 Punishment & obedience			
CP/dq	2 Naive instrumental hedonism	Level 3		
cp/DQ	3 Good boy morality	Level 3 (conformist)		
DQ	4 Law and order morality		1 Duality	Level 1
DQ/er			2 Multiplistic prelegitimate	
dq/ER	5 Morality of democratic contract	Level 4	3 Multiplistic	
ER			4 Multiplistic relativism	Level 2
ER/fs			5 Relativism competing	
er/FS			6 Relativistic	
FS	6 Morality of individual principles	Level 5	7 Initial commitment	Level 3
FS/a'n'			8 Implications of commitment	
fs/A'N'			9 Commitment	
A'N'		Level 6		Level 4
A'N'/b'o'				
a'n'/B'O'				
B'O'				

Table VII e — Graves Compared to Other Theories

Graves Levels	13 Broughton	14 Isaacs	15 Calhoun	16 Loevinger
AN	Zero	Zeta		Presocial or Autistic
AN/bo				
an/BO				Symbiotic
BO	Level 1	Epsilon	1 Sapient Revolution	
cp/BO				
bo/CP				Impulsive
CP	Level 2	Delta	2 Living Agricultural Revolution	Self-protective
CP/dq				
cp/DQ				Conformist, malignant, fixated
DQ	Level 3	Gamma	3 Authoritarian Religious Revolution	Conformist
DQ/er			4 Holistic Artistic Revolution	Self-aware or Conscientious conformist
dq/ER				
ER	Level 4	Beta	5 Scientific Exploitive Revolution	Conscientious
ER/fs				Individualistic
er/FS				
FS	Level 4.5		6 Communication Electronic Revolution	
FS/a'n'				Autonomous
fs/A'N'				
A'N'	Level 5	Alpha	7 Compassionate Systems Revolution	
A'N'/b'o'				?Integrated?
a'n'/B'O'				
B'O'				

Table VII f — Graves Compared to Other Theories

Graves Levels	17 Fromm	18 Erikson	19 Bull	20 Peck
AN				
AN/bo		< Trust vs. Mistrust >		
an/BO				
BO	Symbiosis			
BO/cp				
bo/CP				
CP		< Autonomy vs. Shame & Doubt >	Anomy	Amoral
CP/dq			Heteronomy	
cp/DQ				
DQ	Conformity		Socionomy	
DQ/er		< Initiative vs. Guilt >		
dq/ER				Irrational Conscientious
ER			Autonomy	
ER/fs	Autonomy	< Industry vs. Inferiority >		Rational Altruistic
er/FS				
FS		< Identity vs. Role Difference >		
FS/a'n'				
fs/A'N'				
A'N'		< Intimacy vs. Isolation >		
A'N'/b'o'		< Generality vs. Self-absorption >		
a'n'/B'O'		< Integrity vs. despair > [not included by Graves]		
B'O'				

Table VII g — Graves Compared with Other Theories

Graves Levels	21 Schein	22 McGregor	23 Blake & Mouton	24 Howe	25 Drews
AN					
AN/bo					
an/BO					
BO					
BO/cp					
bo/CP					
CP		Theory X		Physical	Social Leader
CP/dq			9-1		
cp/DQ					
DQ				Power dependent	Studious
DQ/er					
dq/ER					
ER	Rational Economic		5-5	Equality seeking	
ER/fs					
er/FS					
FS	Social		1-9	Value oriented	
FS/a'n'					
fs/A'N'					
A'N'	Self-Actualizing	Theory Y	9-9		
A'N'/b'o'					
a'n'/B'O'					
B'O'					

Columns 4 through 25 (Table VII a-g) present 22 other versions of the developing systems point of view. The total list presented is not necessarily exhaustive. It is representative of how systems people have portrayed psychosocial development from a systems point of view.

to emergent cyclical theory. To see David Riesman's work in relation to mine, call to mind or study his *Faces in the Crowd* and *The Lonely Crowd*. His 'traditions directed man' is directed by the traditions for living into which he was born. He lives by adjusting to the ways that existed when he came into existence. He is outer-directed. Riesman's description seems to fit moderately a person seen by E-C theory as living in the DQ state of being.

Riesman's 'inner directed,' as I read Riesman, is driven from within to change things rather than to adjust to them. The human oriented this way is driven from within to change the outer world so as to put his/her imprint upon it. The descriptions Riesman presents of his 'inner-directed' person seem to me to fit the ER state of being.

His 'other-directed' man is like the 'tradition-directed' in terms of focus but he is not like him in terms of what he focuses upon. His focus is more interpersonal than ideological.

Thus, as a test of E-C theory, note that Riesman places his three types in a hierarchy. They move up from the tradition-directed, to inner- and then to other-directed. Therefore, his work supports the ideas of systems, hierarchy of systems, wave-like alternating change, repetition of *thema*, centralization of *thema* and specification of *thema* into *schema*. All of these have been posited as integral aspects of emergent cyclical theory.

Morris Stein's work, listed in column 5, was inspired by the personality theory of H. A. Murray. Stein had his chemist subjects rank order their needs as described in a twenty-item need descriptive questionnaire as per Murray's theory. From intercorrelation studies he came up with five systems which he called A, B, C, D and E. Though I cannot say that there is a one to one relation between his systems and those of E-C theory, I can say there is remarkable similarity between Stein's five types and five emergent cyclical systems. Stein's "C" system is, according to its key descriptive phrases, similar to a person in the nodal ER state:

> '...a person of driven achievement orientation...hostile aggressiveness...one who returns to master so as to demonstrate few if any weaknesses...a person without fear...who is argumentative...who perceives others as obstacles to be removed, surpassed, ignored...and one who takes pride in being impulsive ...' [236]

---

[236] See Stein, Morris, in White, Robert W. (Ed.). *The Study of Lives*. 1964, p. 281-303.

These are the same key characteristics I found in the emergent cyclical system CP.

Similarly, Stein's type "D" has much in it that I call DQ thinking. Type "C" is remarkably close to what I see as the ER orientation. Type "B" is again quite similar to the emergent cyclical FS system. Type "A" is close to what I have seen as the A'N' system, and Type "E" is similar to B'O'. Stein's work is particularly supportive of the descriptive aspects of the emergent cyclical systems CP, DQ, ER, FS and A'N'.

But there are other aspects of Stein's work that are important. One is that I never heard of Stein until after basic E-C theory was conceived. Another is that he used subjects who were chemists. As third is that his methodology was very different from mine. And fourth, his work derived from H.A. Murray's theory of personality, not from a stage theoretical person. These facts are quite important so far as theory validation is concerned. They are so important that I checked each of the contributors 4 through 25. What I found was that:

- many in the list of Table VII who have spawned systems conceptions of personality somewhat similar to E-C theory had no knowledge of, or intercourse with, one another before they spawned their conceptions;
- most of them spawned their conceptions from data collected through widely varying methodologies;
- their sources were as disparate as: Heard (history); Calhoun (rats and mice); Kohlberg (children from different cultures); and Graves (adults 18-61); and
- the bases of their work ranged from well-developed theories to no theory at all.

From this I conclude that when so many different people, from so many different directions traveling many different ways arrive at essentially the same destination at approximately the same time in history, something significant occurred. Namely, these remarkable facts tend to confirm that the systems point of view presented in this book is not an artifact of my somewhat peculiar methodologies.

The work of Gerald Heard and Mumford (columns 6 and 7) also tends to support the point of view of this book. Their work supports the thought that we had better give the systems approach to personality and cultural theory a good hard look. Their works are particularly important because they each arrived at five systems in common with E-C theory and in common with each other. They got there from data other than mine. Their data were historical and cultural changes that have taken place over time.

Both profess that the data of history support the evolutionary awakening of man's behavioral and mental capacities. Each describes five nodal systems. Heard's are Coconscious Man (BO), Heroic Self-assertive man (CP), Aesthetic Self-accusing man (DQ), Humanic Self-sufficient man (ER), and Leptoid Post-individual man (FS). Mumford's five are: Archaic (BO) man, Civilized (CP) man, Axial (DQ) man, New World (ER) man and World Culture (FS) man.

Neither includes AN man but this is understandable since this kind of human behavior (the behavior of the Tasaday) was not known to exist at the time they wrote their conceptions. Both of them see development as a phenomenon which will continue its systematic growth in the future. But Mumford accepts that development is open-ended while Heard takes the more traditional Utopian position.

Heard, along with Mumford, professes that the data of history support the evolutionary awakening of mental and behavioral capacities. He does so when he says:

> "...growth is in the nature of the minds of man. Consciousness evolves just as does the brain structure the consciousness precipitates."[237]

Or when he says:

> "Man can hope to change himself constructively because there is a power of unexpended growth in him. He does grow in consciousness, learn from experience, and make sense of an increasing area of consciousness."[238]

The meaning in Mumford's words is seen to be quite similar, for he says:

> "In carrying man's self-transformation to this further stage, world culture may bring about a fresh release of spiritual energy that will unveil new potentialities no more visible in the human self today than radium was in the physical world a century ago, though always present..."[239]

And then, as he continues, he supports the open-endedness of the E-C conception. Mumford says:

---

[237] Heard, Gerald (1963). *The Five Ages of Man.* New York; The Julian Press, p. 27.
[238] Ibid., (Heard, 12).
[239] Mumford, Lewis (1956). *The Transformations of Man.* NY: Harper Torchbooks, Harper & Row, p. 192.

> "Even on its lowest terms, world culture will weld the nations and the tribes together in a more meaningful network of relations and purposes. But uniform man is himself no terminal point. For who can set the bounds to man's emergence or to his power of surpassing his provisional achievements? So far we have found no limits to the imagination, nor yet to the sources on which it may draw. Every goal man reaches provides a new starting point, and, the sum of all man's days is just a beginning."[240]

On this point Heard does not agree with the E-C point of view or that of Mumford. He says in his section *On the Further Direction of Psychophysical Evolution*:

> "in brief, the really possible Utopia would be this world experienced by a psychophysique at full aperture."[241]

But it is Heard who supports directly the wave-like spiral of systems, for he says:

> "... man's history has followed an oscillatory spiral as he alternates between the exploration of his environment (and the expansion of his power in it) and investigation of his subjective being (and attempt to achieve peace with it) but the spiral has accelerated greatly in the speed of its ascent."[242]

Then he says:

> "Man's story is specifically the winning of an increasing awareness, purpose, intuition and objective. In short, man's history is the record of how he has gained in the intensification of consciousness, of self-understanding. It is a psychological story. For the spiral evolution of the psyche is the theme of the human venture. It is the clue to man's varied and successive behaviors, to the interpretation of his activities. It is the key to the explanation of his conflicts, his constructs, his orders and revolts, his catastrophes and recoveries, his breakdown and resumptions."[243]

---

[240] Ibid., (Mumford, 249).
[241] Ibid., (Heard, 332).
[242] Ibid., (Heard, 284).
[243] Ibid., (Heard, 5).

The more indirect words of Mumford which support this point are:

> "At all these stages in the development of the self, only a small part of man's potentialities were consciously represented in image or idea. Fortunately, the repressed or neglected aspects, even in primitive society, were not effectively excluded from living experiences. However well fortified the inner world, some of the outer world is constantly breaking through, making demands that must be met, offering suggestions that, even if unheeded, produce a certain effect. So, too, however heavy the crust formed by external nature, by human institutions and habits, the pressure from the inner world would produce cracks and fissures, and even from time to time explosively erupt."[244]

Charlotte Buhler, writing on the change in the concept of homeostasis, also verifies the two component cyclic aspects of this conception when she says:

> "The main revision of thought lies in the recognition that homeostasis, or else the basic tendencies of the organism need to be redefined so as to cover the tendency to *change* besides the tendency toward *maintenance*. Both are seen as being equally primary tendencies." [245]

Another point confirmed by Heard is that man's personality and culture are far more than movement from more simple to more complex ways of satisfying physiological needs through condition. In respect to this his words are:

> "… nor can man be understood, and his story explained by saying he is an accident of economy, that all his culture has risen from physiological necessities. It is true that his art and his science have aided his physical survival, but only because his curiosity has forced him to pursue knowledge of his environment. Human history, if we are to understand it, is psychological history. Man's works and his instruments are the silt lines of his mind's currents, the tide marks of his consciousness."[246]

---

[244] Ibid., (Mumford, 1956, p. 176).
[245] Buhler, Charlotte (1959). Theoretical observations about life's basic tendencies. *American Journal of Psychotherapy.* 13, 3 p. 561-581.
[246] Ibid., (Heard, 1963, p. 21-22).

Ausubel's conception (column 8) is important both from a confirmation and disconfirmation point of view. In one sentence he supports the E-C contention that development is a continuous and continuing organism-environment interaction. But it may be that he takes issue with the E-C position that a biological blueprint delimits development. His words are:

> "Ego development is the outcome of continuous biosocial interaction. There is no predetermined course or sequence of events which reflects the unfolding of a detailed blueprint designed by inner impulses."[247]

He proceeds to lay out five states which he says are typical in human development. He leaves me thoroughly confused as to whether his position does or does not confirm E-C theory.

The works of Kohlberg (column 9), Sullivan, Grant and Grant (column 10), Perry (column 11), Selman (column 12), Broughton (column 13), Isaacs (column 14), Calhoun (column 15) and Loevinger (column 16) are of another order.

The eight stages of Erikson (column 18) are useful for testing only in that his eight stages do seem, in an overlapping way, to follow the general thought of the E-C conception.

Bull's work does not seem to be too concerned with theoretical matters. But the fact that he found no development after age 13 in girls and age 15 in boys may reflect the inadequacy of non-helixical, non-spiraling conceptions of development. Also, that his subjects did not see cheating as much of an offense could confirm that in the second spiral of existence, as it comes to be, value and all other judgments are made on a new and different basis.

Peck's work (column 20), as I see it, is more of historical than theoretical importance. Schein,[248] McGregor, and Blake and Mouton (columns 21-23), are listed as systems contributors from the organizational and non-abnormal applied world of thought. But there is one thing of theoretical importance in Schein's work. His conception of Complex Man says that the Self-actualizing man of Maslow is not the epitome of development, a matter that Kohlberg is beginning to accept.

---

[247] Ausubel, David P. (1952). *Ego Development and the Personality Disorders: A Developmental Approach to Psychopathology*. New York: Grune & Stratton, p. 44.
[248] Schein, Edgar H. (1978). *Career Dynamics: Matching Individual and Organizational Needs*. Redding, MA: Addison Wesley Publishing Company; see also (1971) The Individual, the Organization and the Career: A Conceptual Scheme. *Journal of Applied Behavioral Science*, No 7.

Howe (column 24) is listed as one of the first if not the earliest persons to lay out systems of development in descriptive form. Drews[249] (column 25) is listed because of her Stanford Research Institute summary of the hierarchical systems position.

But now it is time to return to my testing of emergent cyclical theory through the works of other conceptualizers. And I shall do so by picking up with Kohlberg's work (column 9 in the list).

Kohlberg's studies of moral development are quite important as a test of the E-C conception. This is because E-C theory says there is nothing approaching morality, as we commonly think of it, until the nodal CP system appears. If this position is not supported, then the emergent cyclical conception is in trouble. But Kohlberg's conception, Type 1, finds no concept of duty or morality except in terms of concrete rules enforced by restraining outer power. He says also that his Type 1, the punishment and obedience orientation, shows little concern for others beyond avoiding taboos. What the Type 1 values is power and if you have it, you set the rules for others and are not bound by them yourself.

As I see them, Kohlberg's Types 2, 3 and 4 confirm the exiting, entering and nodal aspects of E-C theory. I see his Type 2 as the CP/dq exiting third level subsystem. I see his Type 3 as the cp/DQ subsystem, the entering version of the DQ system. His Type 4, which conforms to avoid authority's censure and its resulting feeling of guilt, as Kohlberg describes it, is the nodal DQ system in operation. Type 5 appears to me as dq/ER morality, and in Table VII you find a gap until the FS system slot. This is not surprising to me because I have found the ER entering subsystem dq/ER particularly antithetical to conventional morality. The nodal and exiting ER subsystems are the same, but respectively less so. E-C theory says that moral development should not return in full blossom until the FS system. And I read Kohlberg's description of system 6 as the FS system.

Furthermore, E-C theory says Kohlberg's system for classification should become blurred, run out or be in need of supplementation beyond his level 6. His classification scheme has no satisfactory way for dealing with a second spiral of existence operating on a new and fundamentally different *basis* for living. That this is true is supported by the recent attempt of Kohlberg to handle his problem by beginning to

---

[249] Drews, Elizabeth (1971).

write about a seventh system.[250] Therefore, it seems reasonable to conclude that Kohlberg's work stands in confirmation of E-C theory.

Column 10 lists the work of Sullivan, Grant and Grant. The first confirmatory matter of importance is that they postulate what I have called the AN system. They are the first people in this review to postulate the existence of this system. And they describe it very much as it is described in E-C theory. In fact, they make the same mistake I was making until after 1962, namely, describing that this group, if adults, were always in trouble. In 1963 I postulated that a steady state brand of what I call the AN existential state must have existed in man's past because the logic of Emergent-Cyclical theory, as then developing, made no sense without its having once existed.

But this is not a criticism of Sullivan, Grant and Grant, nor a disconfirmation of E-C theory. It is simply that the existence of the Tasaday was not known until 1967. Sullivan, Grant and Grant, along with twelve others, designated a Level 2, a BO existential state. They also recognize Level 3 behavior. But as I interpret their words, their Level 3 (cons), Level 3 conformists and Level 4 are transitional rather than nodal systems. When I use the Sullivan, Grant & Grant descriptions to test their fit with the E-C framework, I find their "Level

---

[250] Editor's Note: Kohlberg retracted this claim following the writing of this book and Graves's death. In Kohlberg, Lawrence (1983). *Moral Stages: A Current Formulation and a Response to Critics*. S.Karger, Basel (Switzerland), he writes: "We no longer claim that our empirical work has succeeded in defining the nature of a sixth and highest stage of moral judgment. The existence and nature of such a stage is, at this moment, a matter of theoretical and philosophic speculation." (p. 9) Kohlberg, et al., explain the reason for this further when they, "point out that the case materials from which we constructed our theoretical definition of a sixth stage came from the writings of a small elite sample; elite in the sense of its formal philosophic training and in the sense of its ability for and commitment to moral leadership ... While both philosophical and psychological considerations lead us to continue to hypothesize and look for a sixth moral stage, our longitudinal data have not provided us with material necessary to (a) verify our hypothesis or (b) construct a detailed scoring manual description which would allow reliable identification of a sixth stage. Until 1972, our conceptualization and test manual definition of Stage 6 was based on our 1958 cross-sectional and ideal-typical method for stage scoring [Kohlberg, 1958]. This method classified as Stage 6 high school and college responses which are now scored as Stage 5, Stage 4, and occasionally even as Stage 3 in the Standardized Issue Scoring Manual [Colby et al., 1983a]. The material that was formerly scored as Stage 6 is now scored as substage B at one of these lower stages (60) ... In the absence of clearer empirical confirmation of a sixth stage of moral judgment, we are led to suspend claiming that our research provides support for a number of psychological and philosophic claims which Kohlberg [1971] made in his article *From Is to Ought*." In Colby, Anne and Lawrence Kohlberg (1987). *The Measurement of Moral Judgment*. Cambridge University Press, p. 60 & 63.

3 (cons)" are CP/dq. Their Level 3 conformists are cp/DQ and their Level 4 is dq/ER. I find this confirming rather than disconfirming because of what is said about pathology in Exhibit IX (p. 179) In it, emergent cyclical theory says delinquent behavior is most apt to arise from subsystems which function c, c' or c" (gamma) etc. The behavior we call delinquency is not apt to spring from b, b', b" (beta) etc. functioning.

The mode of functioning next most apt to produce delinquency according to the E-C conceptions is b" (exiting CP beta) functioning. This is so because of the composition of the components of the three subsystems Level 3 (cons) CP/dq; Level 3 conformist cp/DQ and Level 4 DQ/er. Both the CP and ER components have strong non-conforming tendencies, with the CP tendency stronger than the ER. That is, both have strong "focus on the external world and attempt to change it."

So CP/dq and cp/DQ should be delinquency-prone systems. The b" should be next in line because it is a system in which there is a very strong conforming tendency but a weaker but very brash non-conforming tendency. The cp/DQ, though dominantly conforming, has in it a significant amount of the most aggressive kind of thinking found in any system. The b" delinquency should be of a different character than in CP/dq or the cp/DQ subsystems. It should be compulsive delinquency breaking through impulsively and oft times horrendously, now and then, when the strong DQ component is temporarily overwhelmed, when the superego breaks down and the id shoots through.

Conversely, Sullivan, Grant and Grant's Level 5 should be a nodal system relatively free of aggressive delinquency. Relative to the E-C framework their description of Level 5 seems to be the nodal FS existential state in which I have found crimes against property and other persons almost to disappear. This confirms the E-C conception because FS psychological space has reduced raw aggressive tendencies to a minor part of the total system. But there is a kind of "delinquency" which is prevalent in the FS state that is rarely found in the systems beyond FS. It is "delinquency" against the self: dope, suicide and the like.

Sullivan, Grant and Grant's Level 6 seems quite close to emergent cyclical A'N'. Their Level 7 is either the nodal B'O' system or one with strong B'O' components in it. Sullivan, Grant and Grant also confirm much of what has been said about the change process and the need to establish congruency in order to effectively manage. So, overall one can conclude that far more in the work of Sullivan, Grant and Grant confirms the E-C position than disconfirms it.

But I should not leave Sullivan, Grant and Grant without using their work to put the total E-C framework to the test. To remove myself from this test and thus avoid contaminating it, I offer the words of Loevinger as she describes her view of what development is all about according to Sullivan, Grant and Grant. Loevinger's words are:

> "Development proceeds in the direction of increasing involvement with others, increasing perceptual and cognitive discrimination, increasingly accurate perception, and more effective operation. At each of the successive development levels, they describe a core problem, the characteristics of children [adults] fixated at that stage, typical anxieties and potentialities for delinquency."[251]

E-C theory agrees with all of this with one slight exception. My data do not entirely agree with "development proceeds in the direction of increasing involvement with others." My data say this statement applies to the development of Subsistence Level, even-numbered BO, DQ and FS systems, not systems CP and ER. Also my data indicate that Being Level systems stray slightly from Loevinger's words about this developmental dimension.

Test by Perry's Data

The conception of William Perry (column 11) does not include the first three behavior systems identified by other investigators. But this is not a criticism. His sample, Harvard college students, would not be expected to behave in the AN, BO, or CP fashion. As a conception, and as I see it, Perry's framework tends more to confirm the subsystem aspect of the ER point of view than any other conception listed in Table VII. Beginning with Perry's Position I (DQ), his framework follows step by step each nodal, exiting, and entering subsystem until it runs out just before what would be the E-C nodal A'N' system. But this should not be passed by because it is a disconfirmation. Perry says his Position 9 logically rounds out his framework. I would say only the addition of a Position 10 would accomplish this.

---

[251] Loevinger, Jane (1976). *Ego Development*. San Francisco, Jossey Bass, p. 105-106.

But all in all, as I read Perry's work, and those who have written from it, like Anthony Athos, I find remarkable cross-confirmation of the philosophy, nature and content between Perry's system and my own.

Test by Selman's Conception

Robert Selman's conception, based on reasoning about interpersonal relations, is compared to the E-C conception in column 12. It derives from answers to six interpersonal dilemmas and interviews. My interpretation of his Levels 1, 2, 3 and 4 says there is much in common with existential states, DQ, ER, FS and A'N' respectively. But I do not feel sufficiently apprised of his work at this time to seriously discuss whether it confirms or disconfirms the E-C conception.

Test by Broughton's Conception

The conception of John Broughton is, to me, a particularly crucial test of the emergent cyclical point of view. It is a crucial test because his conception of human development was arrived at in a careful philosophical and scientific fashion. Mine was arrived at with no concern for philosophical matters and minimal concern for "established scientific" ways. Thus, a serious test of E-C theory is: Does philosophically careful and "scientifically proper" work confirm or disconfirm the emergent cyclical conception? The answer, I believe, is positive. This is said because column 13 shows only two slight variations between the ordering of his "natural epistemologies" and the E-C nodal stages. The first slight difference stems from his designation of his first stage as zero. Neither his description of a child at the zero stage nor the data I have on the AN state agrees with the use of the appellation zero to designate the first level.

The other point pertains to Broughton's equivocation about the stage after his Level 4 system. The equivocation leads him to call it Level 4 1/2. But the data I have collected, and the data of all who have described this systemic position, suggest there is no need to equivocate. The weight of the evidence says call it Level 5 because that is what it is.

So, to me, Broughton's work provides important confirmation. A meticulous investigator and thoughtful philosopher finds essentially the same nodal framework at which I arrived in a more cavalier fashion.

Test by Isaacs' Conception

The conception of Kenneth S. Isaacs[252] significantly contributes to the task of testing E-C theory. This is because few conceptions provide the opportunity to test both nodal and detailed aspects as well.

Isaacs's method is to collect the fantasies of people produced in response to the Thematic Apperception Test. Then he classifies the fantasies and analyzes the resulting categories. His work produced six levels of operation which he named Zeta, Epsilon, Delta, Gamma, Beta and Alpha. To test through his system, I shall work from his descriptions and comment on confirmation as I move along.

Isaacs' Zeta Level is essentially what I have discerned as the AN existential state. He agrees that the person operating at the Zeta level is rare today except in illness or stress. The person does not affectively distinguish self from others. S/he shows no distinctions between self and others, sees no distinction between self and other objects, between human and non-human, or between animate and inanimate objects. Zeta humans have few rules for living and the ones they have are not very effective for living. They differentiate but little in the environment than other people do. All of these are characteristics of the AN state according to my data.

At the Epsilon level, the person does differentiate self from others, but barely. S/he sees no possibility that people can planfully interact to solve their problems. Feelings, gratifications and satisfactions are all from within the self not related to others. Feelings are just accepted as givens and there is no idea that the actions of other humans may be the cause of them. These are very similar to what I have found in the BO state.

At the Delta level, third in his hierarchy, it is as if the person were awakening. Here people see the world in terms of getting from or being deprived, in terms of controlling or being controlled. People at this level seem to be out to get more and will do whatever is necessary to get it. They will snare, entrap, enslave, or anything necessary to get, or to avoid being caught. They comply only with fear and are stubbornly resistive. They show such emotions as shame, disgust, fear and anger, but not guilt. This confirms what was said in Chapter IX about the emotional components in the P neuropsychological system. Isaacs' description of perception at this level also confirms the perceptual component of the P system.

---

[252] Isaacs, Kenneth (1956).

Isaacs' Gamma Level is quite like the emergent cyclical DQ state. The more tender emotions of pity, sympathy and tenderness are fully present. Guilt, which E-C theory says is *the* key emotion of the Q neuropsychological system, is clearly present according to Isaacs, who says: "Other signals of attainment of Gamma level are guilt over Delta tendencies, and disapproval of Delta tendencies in one's self and others."[253]

Particularly important is the confirmation of the ER system's position as fourth in the hierarchy. First, he says that objectivity has arrived. Then he confirms the focus of the ER state with the words:

> "The focus at this level is with a final intra-psychic separation of self from others. In the process of attempting to disidentify with and rearrange the various aspects of earlier identifications, there may be a struggling against others who may temporarily personify the forces fighting within the self."[254]

Also, Isaacs' words that the Beta (ER) struggle for freedom resembles but is not like the Delta (CP) struggle for freedom, confirms the cyclic thematic aspect of E-C theory.

Disconfirming evidence is that Isaacs appears not to find the sixth (FS) level.[255] This I say because his description of his Alpha level appears to be more like the emergent cyclical A'N' than like the FS system. Also disconfirming are Isaacs' words about the Alpha system. They seem to suggest that he sees the Alpha level as the "ultimate" level, which is markedly disputed by the E-C conception.[256]

---

[253] Ibid., (Isaacs, p. 22).

[254] Ibid., (Isaacs, p. 24).

[255] Editors' Note: Isaacs refers to Beta both as "a state of being able to stand off from oneself and view the activity around one's self, including one's own activity, with some perspective," (p. 23) which implies objectivity and the rationality of ER. At the same time, Isaacs reports that the "Beta struggle is with the internal." He emphasizes empathy, sympathy and tender feelings in Beta (Table 5, p. 35) and "relating through empathic capacity" (p. 24), descriptors consistent with FS; whereas Graves's ER system is described as having disdain for empathy and emotion. Isaacs's particular focus is on affect, the degree of, and ability to, interrelate with others, feelings for others and the quality of interacting. Isaacs points out (2005) that his approach, Relatability, is both like and unlike Graves's work, and that he doubts the direct correlation of the two despite some similarities. Instead, he views E-C theory and Relatability as complements.

[256] Editor's Note: Isaacs sees movement towards the Alpha, with its increased relatability, as a movement towards greater maturity; whereas Graves shows conceptions of maturity articulated differently within each of the systems.

Isaacs's work confirms, along with 17 other conceptions in Table VII, that shame and not guilt is a part of the third developmental system. It confirms that the emergence of guilt occurs in the fourth system. It confirms that guilt decreases in the fifth system. And it confirms the cyclic and family of systems of the E-C conception.

Test by John Calhoun's Conception

The conception of John Calhoun[257] (column 15) is of single importance as a testing ground for E-C theory. First, to my knowledge, his is the only conception of this kind derived from the study of infrahuman organisms. He used his population studies of rats to procure the data for his conception. Secondly, his conception pertains to the psychological development of the species. Third, as shown in column 15, his systems follow the E-C framework with the exception that he has an additional system between 4 and 5. Fourth, he is the only person of whom I know who not only utilizes the extending systems concept of E-C theory, but also has an explanation for it, namely, the systematic decrease in population. Furthermore, the details of his system are quite similar to E-C theory with the exception of the one system previously noted.

Test by Jane Loevinger's Conception

The last conception I shall use to test the E-C point of view is that of Jane Loevinger. Her work is, to date, the classic review of the stage developmental explanation of behavior. But before I begin the test, a few clarifying remarks are required.

Beyond doubt I find Loevinger's work more pregnant with significant meaning than others, with the possible exception of the totality of the Harvey, Hunt, Schroder, Driver, Streufert, et al. group. Yet I am hampered in testing the stage aspect of E-C theory through her work. Unfortunately, I do not find the ordering of her stages entirely clear; nor do I understand the verbal labels and the descriptions of her stages and levels as well as I would like. Thus the comparison I show in

---

[257] Calhoun, John (1968). "Space and the Strategy of Life." Unpublished paper presented at the American Association for the Advancement of Science 135th Annual Meeting, Dallas TX. (1970) "Levels of Existence re Gravesian Philosophy: Random Notes by John B. Calhoun for evening seminar discussion." (1971) "R$_x$Evolution, Tribalism, and the Cheshire Cat: Three Paths from Now." unpublished paper, NIMH: Unit for Research on Behavioral Systems, Laboratory of Psychology. URBSDOC No. 167.

column 16 is the best I can arrive at, though my desire is that it be better.

I take as a basis for depiction of her position her statement on page 14 of her book, *Ego Development* where she says that her hierarchy is now a ten-point scale, whereas once it was four, and "I do not foreclose further evolution." I would say that those words confirm the extending, possibly ever-evolving, aspect of the E-C conception. Secondly, she writes in Chapter 11 of both stages and transitions which at times she describes as levels. I see this as a partial confirmation of the E-C transitional stages which I represent as periods in which the person enters, goes into a nodal stage, then exits therefrom.

Therefore, to test whether the E-C stages are substantive, one must find a reasonable fit between her stages with the AN, BO etc. nodal stages of E-C theory. And one must find some fit between those phases of development which she terms transitions or levels. To do this, one should indicate what her developmental stages seem to be. Thus, accepting her words that she now sees ten steps in the developmental process, I infer that the following is the order of their development.

Table VIII

Loevinger's Steps	Step or Stage	Step/Transition/ Level	Step According to E-C
1	Presocial or autistic		AN
2		Symbiotic	an/BO
3	Impulsive		bo/CP
4	Self-protective		CP
5	Conformist, malignant, fixated		cp/DQ
6	Conformist		DQ
7		Self-aware or conscientious conformist	DQ/er
8	Conscientious		ER
9		Individualistic	ER/fs
10	Autonomous		FS/a'n'
11	Integrated		? A'N'/bo ?

From this comparison, and as I see it, Loevinger's work confirms some aspect, stage-wise or transitional wise, of 10 of the 22 states and sub states of E-C theory. Loevinger seems to agree that, in my language, all the existential states I have posited are developmentally present in either stage or transitional form. She seems to agree that AN, CP, DQ, and ER are nodal stages. We seem to agree as to the nature of the progression but not entirely as to her identification of the nodal stages beyond the four noted. We also do not agree as to the exiting and entering sub-stages. But these, it seems to me, are minor disagreements to be worked out by further research. In other words, I see much in Loevinger's ten developmental demarcation points which confirms E-C theory. However, I have shown very skimpy evidence that she confirms the existence of an FS state. There are also some salient differences between the terminology she appends to the ten steps in her scale and the meaning I have depicted of some of the nodal existential states of E-C theory. We agree that states AN, CP, DQ, and ER seem to exist. We don't see them entirely the same way.

There is, in fact, so much in Loevinger's work that confirms the emergent cyclical point of view that I shall only sample, from here on, to show some of the regions of agreement. Loevinger agrees that a stage developmental point of view has remarkable facility for subsuming, in one framework, many other theories and much psychological knowledge. For example, she cites, as I do, that Bentham's pleasure-pain principle[258] is 'Self-protective' (ER psychology) and that Skinner's hedonism and schedules of reinforcement is the same. She sees Thorndike's work as 'Conformistic' (DQ psychology) attempts to seek for reward and avoid punishment. Both of us see Sullivan's 'avoidance of anxiety by seeking self esteem as distinct from esteem in the eyes of others'[259] the same way. Both of us see the 'Conscientious' in her system, DQ/er in mine, as transitional. Each of us sees Adlerian theory as crossing two stages: social interest and self-interest. However, she sees self-interest as 'Self-Protective' (CP psychology) where I see the ER version of self-interest. Both of us see Freud as a mastering system and Kohlberg's and Adler's later work seeking for unity and coherence.

---

[258] Bentham, Jeremy (1962). In John Bowring (Ed.), *The Works of Jeremy Bentham*. London: 1838-1843; reprinted New York, 1962.

[259] See Sullivan, H.S., in Loevinger, Jane (1976). *Ego Development*. San Francisco; Jossey Bass, p. 419. The actual words in Loevinger are, "The avoidance of anxiety was the predominant motive in formation and maintenance of the self-esteem."

Loevinger sees growth as a dialectic[260] just as E-C theory does, though we see the dialectic a bit differently. Each of us sees a *thema* for each stage of development, for Loevinger says of this: "each stage of ego development embodies a view of human motivation and interpersonal reaction consonant with its own mode of functioning."[261] We particularly agree on a point many others might dispute. That is: "Ego development is growth and there is no way to force it. One can only try to open doors."[262] We agree that the problem of practical application goes far beyond producing change in a level, a questionable approach at best. It has more to do with establishing congruence than with promoting growth.

We agree that change efforts can be led only by people of a higher level, that a person operating at any level may become a patient, and that therapy may reopen the way to new growth but cannot produce the growth. We agree, in Loevinger's language, that a modest rise in ego development, or in E-C language, a modest movement up the levels of existence will not do mankind much good. For societal good to ensue, we must hope for movement to E-C Being Level Systems. Finally, two last points of agreement which cross-confirm are that both of us would say:

1. Politically raising a politician's ego level would probably ensure loss of an election *(earlier-appearing)*.
2. Persons at a higher level have access to the modes of reasoning of those at lower levels and conversely, those at lower levels can only translate the motives of persons at higher levels into their own lower level *(later-appearing)*.

So, all in all, I would say there is remarkable cross confirmation of two points of view of two people who have not met nor communicated with one another.

The Work of Joel Aronoff

Finally, I turn to two other studies which support the emergent cyclical point of view. The first is the Saint Kitts study of Joel Aronoff, an investigator who is a significant contributor to this field of study. Aronoff tested the Maslowian theory of need in relation to the occupational and cultural institutions of the cane cutters and fishermen

---

[260] Ibid., (Loevinger, p. 422).
[261] Ibid., (Loevinger, p. 423).
[262] Ibid., (Loevinger, p. 426).

on that Caribbean island. Though his work cannot be as directly related to emergent cyclical theory, it is in the same trend of thought. Aronoff tested the validity of the Maslowian hierarchy and found it possible to show substantial relationship between Maslow's hierarchy and the form and character of occupational life on the island. According to the E-C point of view, time would be a certain reordering of the occupational life of the islanders as their way of life solved lower-level problems and new problems appeared. This was substantially supported by Aronoff's research.

The Work of Douglas LaBier

The other study is one done in my own laboratory. The study was carried out by Douglas LaBier.[263] The idea as to what and how to test was provided by Graves. Supervision and design was done by W. C. Huntley and the study was carried out by LaBier with Graves totally out of the picture after the idea of what to test was presented.

The idea was as follows: The E-C conception proposes that the personality of the mature organism tends to move continuously, as the conditions of human existence change, if there is potential in the organism. Where the potential is present the personality tends to metamorphize a new form or quality, each of which is contiguous with but centrally different from the previous stage. He operates differently not only in that more brain cells are operant or activated but also in that brain systems or networks become activated to permit ways of thinking, perceiving, valuing, learning, believing, etc., which were not present before. Consequently, one can view the psychology of the mature organism as an unfolding or emergent process marked by the progressive subordination of older systems in favor of newer higher order systems. Therefore, if one is to test the substance of this position, one must (a) devise a means to operationally define the system, and (b) devise a means to put the progressive hypothesis to the test. The means selected was the perceptual readiness test.

Much argument exists in respect to the perceptual readiness test. So, the literature in respect to it comes from: Postman, Bruner and McGinnies through Bricker and Chapanis, Solomon and Howes, Postman and Schneider, etc. This review brought forth the factors necessary to control.

---

[263] LaBier, Douglas, C. W. Graves, and W.C. Huntley (1965). *Personality Structure and Perceptual Readiness: An investigation of their Relationship to Hypothesized Levels of Human Existence*. Unpublished paper, Union College.

Operationalizing E-C theory was done by drawing on the work of Harvey, Hunt and Schroder, Milton Rokeach, and Gough and Sanford. Rokeach's Dogmatism Scale and the Gough-Sanford Rigidity Scale were used.

In terms of E-C theory, the Harvey, Hunt and Schroder studies, Rokeach's concept of open and closed systems of belief distinguishes existential states DQ and ER from states FS and A'N'. Thus the Dogmatism Scale allows one to separate and operationally describe behavior associated with states DQ and ER, on the one hand, and states FS and A'N' on the other.

To separate DQ from ER and FS from A'N', the 60 items of the Dogmatism Scale were interspersed with the 21 items of the Gough-Sanford Rigidity Scale because the latter measures resistance to change of single beliefs, sets, or habits, whereas dogmatism refers to change of systems of belief. Therefore, certain score combinations of high or low dogmatism with high or low rigidity should represent the following existential states.

Existential State	Combination
DQ	high rigidity – high dogmatism
ER	low rigidity – high dogmatism
FS	high rigidity – low dogmatism
A'N'	low rigidity – low dogmatism

It is hypothesized that the DQ fourth-level system is closed in total belief systems as well as rigid in particular activities and thus would yield a questionnaire score high both in dogmatism and rigidity which are theoretically, as I have said, characteristic of the DQ state. ER behavior (fifth level), on the other hand, while still closed in belief systems, manifests flexibility in particular actions, the typical multiplistic way of thinking.

With movement to the FS state, emergent cyclical theory says the person sheds his/her closed system of belief, is able to change, adapt, or move to different kinds of belief systems. However, being an even-numbered system—system six—rigidity is demanded within the particular beliefs system adopted. Then at the A'N' stage, E-C theory says both rigidity and dogmatism recede to produce a system unburdened by adherence to particular acts or particular belief systems.

So, it was hypothesized that if one operationally defines and designates certain existential states, as per above, a subject whose thinking it thereby designated as representing a particular state will recognize words representing the dominant thinking of the state more quickly than the words representing other states.

The stimulus words used and ordered according to the four most common states in our society are listed per state below. These four states were used because we were limited by subject availability. They were undergraduate college students. Appropriate controls according to the Postman et al. work were exercised.

DQ	ER	FS	A'N'
Safety	Power	Social	Esteem
Submit	Action	Adjust	Being
Order	Useful	Fashion	Express
Obey	Practical	Together	Free
Security	Risk	Team	Indulge

The choice of the words was dictated by the content in the original conception of maturity, the base line data of E-C theory.

The twenty words were tachistocopically shown to the subjects in random order. Each word was exposed two times for .01 second. If the subject failed to recognize the word, it was again exposed two times at .02, .03 seconds, etc. at exposure times increasing in steps of .01 second until recognition occurred. However, beyond the exposure time of .10 second, it was necessary to increase the exposure steps from .01 to .10 second, because the tachistoscope employed was not calibrated for .01 second increments beyond the exposure time of .10 second.

The subject was instructed to respond to every exposure whether or not the full word was distinguished. A full record of the subject's pre-recognition response was maintained thus for each subject.

The mean recognition time for the 5 words representing the hypothesized level was calculated and compared with the mean recognition time for all twenty words. The results are listed in Table IX.

In addition, the mean times of recognition for words representing each of the four hypothesized existential states were calculated. Statistical tests of significance of association between hypothesized states and times of representative word recognition were performed and found to be significant. These additional results are shown in Table X.

The data of Tables IX and X. indicate that the subjects recognized the words of their hypothesized state at a mean recognition time which was quicker than the mean recognition for all 20 words. Moreover, when one plots the mean recognition time of each group of words for each subject, one finds that the speed of recognition of each group of words for each subject increases as the subject's hypothesized state is approached and then decreases in a roughly constant manner. These are shown in Exhibits XV-XVIII.

Table IX
MEAN RECOGNITION TIME TO WORDS REPRESENTING EXISTENTIAL STATE DQ, ER, FS & A'N', AND MEAN RECOGNITION TO ALL WORDS OF HYPOTHESIZED DQ, ER, FS & A'N' SUBJECTS

		Level 4 words	all words
	1	.010 sec.	.031 sec.
Hypothesized Level 4 or DQ Subjects	2	.280 sec.	.380 sec.
	3	.042 sec.	.079 sec.
		Level 5 words	all words
	1	.042 sec.	.101 sec.
Hypothesized Level 5 or ER Subjects	2	.680 sec.	.845 sec.
	3	.054 sec.	.065 sec.
		Level 6 words	all words
	1	.076 sec.	.111 sec.
Hypothesized Level 6 or FS Subjects	2	.098 sec.	.137 sec.
	3	.010 sec.	.021 sec.
		Level 7 words	all words
	1	.046 sec.	.120 sec.
Hypothesized Level 7 or A'N' Subjects	2	.014 sec.	.031 sec.
	3	.030 sec.	.037 sec.

Table X
Mean Recognition Time of 12 Individuals (3 at Each Level) Hypothesized DQ, ER, FS & A'N' Subjects to Words Representing States DQ, ER, FS & A'N'

Hypothesized Level	Subject #	States			
		4	5	6	7
Hypothesized Level 4 or DQ Subjects	1	.010	.022	.032	.058
	2	.280	.340	.420	.480
	3	.042	.064	.089	.132
Hypothesized Level 5 or ER Subjects	1	.156	.042	.060	.144
	2	.880	.680	.920	.900
	3	.076	.054	.064	.066
Hypothesized Level 6 or FS Subjects	1	.156	.082	.076	.130
	2	.168	.144	.098	.138
	3	.022	.016	.010	.014
Hypothesized Level 7 or A'N' Subjects	1	.250	.122	.082	.046
	2	.052	.034	.024	.014
	3	.038	.040	.040	.030

Thus, for most subjects, the time required for recognition of the words for the states on either side of the subject's hypothesized state undergoes a constant increase. From there, one may speculate that these data represent the role of selective perception for areas which have varying degrees of value or meaning for the subject. This supports the progressive subordination aspect of the E-C conception. That is, if each different stage of existence follows an ever-emergent or unfolding pattern and eventually becomes subordinated to newer emerging systems, then certain aspects or portions of both later and earlier appearing states of existence will be present within the individual. So, if the relative times of recognition can serve as a basis for speculation, then it appears that tendencies toward the behavior of states both below and above one's own undergo a decrease with each succeeding state.

One area of observation open to view but not quantifiable which confirms the nodal, open, arrested, closed and transitional aspects of the E-C point of view can be seen through visual inspection of the line graphs of Exhibits XV, XVI, XVII, and XVIII.

Exhibit XV
Hypothesized DQ Subjects – Set A

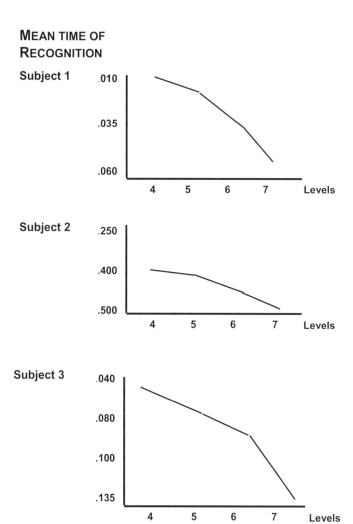

Exhibit XVI
Hypothesized ER Subjects – Set B

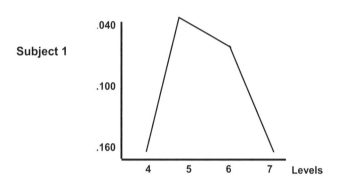

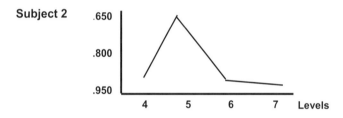

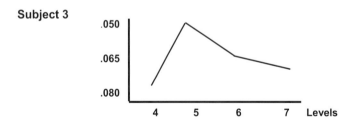

Exhibit XVII
Hypothesized FS Subjects – Set C

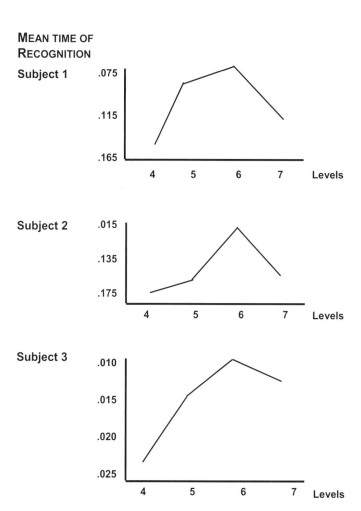

Exhibit XVIII
Hypothesized A'N' Subjects – Set D

MEAN TIME OF RECOGNITION

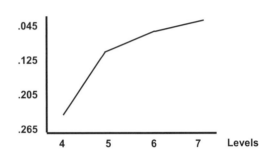

Subject 1

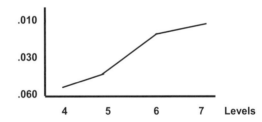

Subject 2

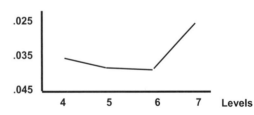

Subject 3

All subjects whose speed of reaction to system sensitive words is plotted in Exhibits XV-XVIII. Exhibit XV would be judged to be nodal open DQ personalities according to E-C theory. Each responds to the DQ words most quickly, to the ER words second, the FS words third, and the A'N' words fourth. But the three subjects in Exhibit XVI are of a different order. Only subject 3 shows a typical open ER personality. In this subject's graph, the quick reaction to the DQ words shown by the previous three subjects is much slower. The ER words are responded to most quickly with the response to the FS words second most rapid and the A'N' words third.

Subjects 1 and 2 of Exhibit XVI show quite different patterns of reaction. Reaction to the DQ words is slowest of all. The ER words are reacted to most quickly but not much more quickly than the FS words and speed of reaction to the A'N' words is a little faster than to the DQ words but noticeable slower than the ER and FS words. This person, according to E-C theory, would be seen as in an ER/fs state of transition from the ER nodal state to the FS nodal state. He is an exiting ER. Subject 2 in Exhibit XVI provides a third pattern. This subject's speed of reaction is almost the same to the DQ, FS and A'N' words. The only words to which quick reaction is shown are the ER words. This pattern has been found to typify the closed form of an arrested ER existential state.

The subjects whose word reaction patterns are plotted in Exhibit XVII show a transitional exiting pattern (subject 1), an open pattern (subject 2) and an arrested pattern (subject 3). Subject 1 provides a curve much like the ER/fs transition state in Exhibit XVI but the position of the leading and following components is reversed. E-C theory would see this pattern as one entering the er/FS existential state. Subject 2 is very slow in responding, if he responds at all, to the A'N' words, but does respond, though slowly, to the DQ words. His speed of response to ER words is faster. To the FS he responds most quickly but then drops suddenly off, quite unlike the open pattern we have seen in other subjects plotted.

In Exhibit XVIII, Subjects 1 and 2 both show the typical open A'N' pattern but subject 3 displays a pattern of response not previously seen. This subject's response is most quick to the A'N' words but responds more quickly to the DQ words than to the ER or FS words. This pattern is typical of many scientifically or technologically trained people who have opened up in almost all respects except religious absolutism.

Verification

CHAPTER 16

The Broader Meaning of the Concept

Now that the level of existence conception of adult personality has been presented we must ask what is the broader meaning of this concept? Just what does it express? What it expresses is that there are various modes of standing out in this world, various general modes of existence which follow one another in an ordered way, and various ideas as to what is the best of human existence. It is a concept which makes statements about actually and theoretically-appearing forms or configurations of existence. It says that human existence contains numerous, probably infinite, modes of being precisely rooted in the multifold potentiality of man's hierarchically structured brain and the varying conditions for human existence. Since the emphasis of this concept is on the human being as he emerges in psychological time and in psychological space, then it is what the conception says about the process-like character of man's systems that must be divined if ever man's personality or culture is to be known so as to effectively treat many of man's problems.

In this conception, neither mature personality nor Utopian culture is an ultimately discoverable state or condition, nor is the quality of human life. They are organic processes determined by the mutual interaction of the conditions present in the total system that has emerged to date; and they are processes of a dynamic organic, not static, mechanistic nature. Within this conception, the personality of an individual is only the position he is at in his movement from earlier appearing stages of existence to later appearing stages of existence. The personality of an adult or the state of a culture may be moving at a rapid pace or at a speed which, for practical purposes, can be called non-movement or stabilization. They can, in fact, be seen as moving up and down, first this way and then that way. They may be bouncing, so to speak, in a disorganized way or they may be tightly centralizing around some core at some particular level of existence.

According to this conception, man can never know his total self, and man can never fulfill his total potentialities. He can know only the self that has emerged, and he can express only the potential that has been activated to date, and his level of emergence limits what he sees as that which life should be. Even if certain self-systems have emerged, this total self, total in the Spearman sense, he may not know because knowing self is a function of relating to a world which permits the expression of the emerged self. Yet, as contradictory as it may seem, at certain stages of existence, man will believe that he can come to know himself, and at certain stages man will believe that the expression of potential is not only possible but necessary, while at other stages he will consider such beliefs to be ridiculous.

At each stage of human existence the adult man is off on his quest of his holy grail, the way of life by which he believes men should live. At his first level he is on a quest for automatic physiological satisfaction. At the second level he seeks a safe mode for living, and this is followed, in turn, by a search for heroic status, for the power and the glory, then by a search for everlasting peace, a search for material fulfillment in the here and now, a search for personal fulfillment here and now, a search for integrated living and a search for spiritual peace in a world he knows can never be known. And, when he finds, at the eighth level, that he will never find that peace, he will be off on his ninth-level quest. As he sets off on each quest, he believes he will find the answer to his existence, and as he settles into each nodal state he is certain he has found it. Yet, always to his surprise and ever to his dismay he finds, at every stage, that the solution to existence is not the solution he thinks he has found. Every state he reaches leaves him discontented and perplexed. It is simply that as he solves one set of human problems he finds a new set in their place. The quest he finds is never ending. He learns that the most crucial fact about existence is not how to exist but that it emerges, that it is always developing in time and in space and will never be defined at any one point or any one time in life unless one becomes a closed personality. What he learns is that which Goethe wrote about in *Duration in Change*.[264] He learns that:

---

[264] von Goethe, Johann Woflgang (1803). Also translated "Constancy in Change."

> The hand of yours that once so nimbly
> Moved to do a deed of grace –
> The structural form is there no longer
> Another now is in its place.
> All is changed. The new hand bearing
> Now the name the other bore
> Came like a wave that rose and, falling
> Joins the elements once more.

This level of existence conception of adult human behavior sees human life as a coherent developmental process of successive equilibrations, successive styles of living. But let us not be misled. A level is not, in reality, an attainable state. A level is a theoretical state of equilibrium. It is a state toward which a human who has certain dynamic systems open moves when in relatively stabilized conditions of existence. Levels are constructs. They are not realities. They are constructs to be seen more like the constructs of absolute zero and absolute vacuum rather than as actual existential states. They are not to be viewed as forms of human behavior which actually exist. They are the base points from which the living, behaving human being varies. In other words, a level is a theoretical balance between a more advanced stage which is emerging and a preceding stage out of which an adult has emerged. Thus, a person can be said to be in a level only when he remains a relatively unchanging psychological being in a relatively changing world.

The person who tends to persist in showing one form of behavior when the world about him changes is the one who most approaches the theoretical picture of a level. This person we call a closed level three, a closed level four, a closed level five, etc. We can see how closely he approaches the theoretical picture by first of all testing for closure, then by examining the closed person's behavior in relation to the theoretical description of the level. This testing for closure is done by the application of four criteria. They are:

    I. the behavior of the closed person is displayed in inappropriate circumstances, is over generalized;
   II. the behavior of the closed person is insatiable;
  III. the behavior of the closed person shows an undue response to frustration; and
  IV. the behavior of the person is inflexible.

On the other hand, an open personality tends to change as the world changes and changes the world as his open personality changes. The open personality moves in the direction of more effective adjustment to the new realities of existence. This open personality would not tend to show the typical picture of a level as much as the closed person would. His behavioral level would be shown as the momentarily dominant trend in the flowing process rather than as the almost pure representation of the theoretical behavioral form (Exhibit XIX).

Whether a personality is open, arrested, or whether it is closed is a function of the potential in the person, the developmental history of the organism and the current environmental circumstances. To be open, a personality must, of course, possess potential for higher-level behavior and must have had, as well, a past history and current conditions of existence conducive to the state of openness. A closed personality can be closed because it can't go any further; that is, it has no higher level capacity to emerge into. Or it can become closed because the historical psychosocial life circumstances have restricted it from being in any other state than that into which it has developed. The arrested personality, on the other hand, is one which possesses the potential for growth; has, to a point, adequate historical psychosocial circumstances, but is caught in current world conditions which present barriers to its movement on. But there is much more that we must examine in order to develop a more complete feeling for the level of existence conception of adult behavior. One of these additional areas is the nature of the organism as seen from this conceptual point of view.

The organism as seen, herein, is a generally preprogrammed, complex energy system. This preprogrammed system interacts with the environmental system to produce successive thematic styles of being – existential states AN, BO, CP, etc. – which are specified by individual differences, individual history and individual current circumstances into the schematic form for existence of the individual person or cultural system. This total biosocial system tends, normally, to be open, but the nature of the organism is such that it can operate throughout a lifetime in a relatively closed state of psychological affairs. Though we refer to the human part of this large system as preprogrammed, we do not mean predetermined, nor do we mean purposeful striving toward some goal or end. We mean simply that the organism is made up of a series of systems which supraordinate one after another, thereby placing certain broad general prescriptions on our degrees of behavioral freedom. We mean that man's nature is to alternate through spurts of growth and periods of consolidation, through cycles of external concern and inner

Exhibit XIX

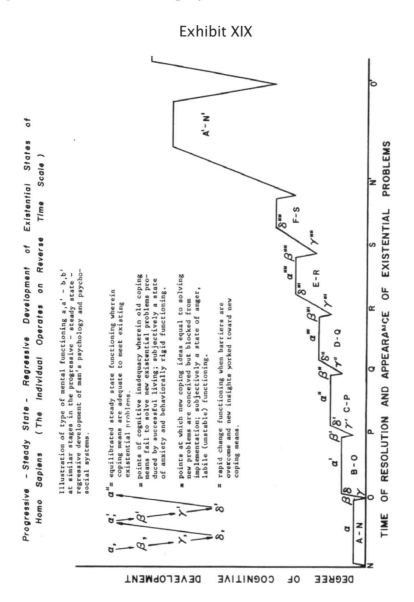

spiritual contemplation. And we mean that man's nature is to open up as the conditions for his existence improve. In other words, man's nature is how he happens to be structured brain wise and otherwise and what this structuring is revealed to be as it unravels in time and in space as the conditions for existence change. That is all we mean by saying man is a preprogrammed complex energy system. In general, 'whither thou goest, I go,'[265] though we know not why.

According to this conception we do ourselves a disservice by arguing whether man's nature is good or bad, active or reactive, mechanical or teleological. Man's nature is emergent. What man is cannot be seen before. We can see it only insofar as it has been revealed to us by his movement through the levels of human existence. And, what has been revealed to us, so far, is that in some way or another man's nature is all of these and more. Our very conception envisages that new aspects of man are now before us which were not seen before, and that the man that man now is will go on proliferating into new forms if the conditions for human existence continue to improve.

What seems to be revealed to us about man's nature is that he can settle into a state which on the surface makes it appear that he is good. He can, for example, be the apparently kind, loyal, self-controlled DQ constellation of level four revealed in Table I. Or, he can be in a state which readily lends itself to a bad interpretation, the aggressive, unkind, Machiavellian-like constellation of the level three and five, CP and ER systems. He is an organism whose behavior can appear to be mechanistic, as when he is dominated by the AN or CP systems of his behavior can appear to be a striving to be, to have a teleological aspect when he operates in a DQ or FS system. He can seem to be predominantly an active organism when he operates in one of the odd-numbered systems, or, he can be seen to be a passive, reactive organism when he settles into the equilibriums of one of the conservationistic, even-numbered systems.

What we see about man's nature from this conceptual viewpoint is that his nature allows forever new ways of standing out, of existing in this world. What we see is that these various modes for existence lead investigators to necessarily see the nature of man display itself in different behavioral constellations. We see these different behavioral constellations lead to different questions as to the nature of man's nature from which different answers must result. What the data behind this conception seem to say is that man's nature, as revealed so far, makes him an enigma; what the interpretation of the data seems to say is that when we come to see more of man's nature revealed, we will find it more enigmatic. But enigmatic or not, it is our task to make sense of

---

[265] Paraphrase of Ruth 1:16 in the Bible.

man as his emergence reveals, more and more, the nature of his self to us.

One thing we seem to see is that man's basic need is very simple. It is to exist, not to succumb; and to exist in whatever specification of the general form he can with emerging potential at his disposal, in the circumstances he is in. We cannot say that man is striving to become his total human self as he moves from one level to another. We cannot say that he is attempting to totally self-actualize. What we can say is that at each level he is striving to be what he can be there, and at each level he believes that what he should be is what he has emerged to be to date. He is striving to be what he can be within the general form of existence, the *thema* for living, that is open to him at his level of emergence in the conditions of existence he is in.

But, why is he so striving thus? Because he must, that's why. Because if he does not find a specific way of being within his general possibilities, he will cease to exist. And if this be circular reasoning, then so be it; for who am I to argue with what my data say? There is no deeper meaning in all of man's behavior than that he behaves according to the dictates of his nature and experience. Man does not strive to become; he does not strive toward some ultimate goal. He strives no more than to be what he can be in the realities of his existence. He strives only to exist.

One of the realities of existence, according to this conception of man's personality, is that his brain consists of hierarchically ordered systems which can be inactive, partially active, subordinately or supraordinately active. Therefore, when some systems are inactive or subordinated, man must, in order to be, develop a mode of existence which will enable him to live even though a part of his brain is not activated or is subordinated. If a particular system is supraordering, then the reality of his existence is that he must develop styles of living which are consonant with it being the dominating system. If he does not do this, then he will be in dire trouble so far as his existence is concerned. The fact that man, as the conditions for his existence change, moves through systematic behavioral forms, is neither purposeful nor remarkable, nor divinely planned nor ordered. It is only that being human-like and not dog-like, man displays human ways of behaving and not dog ways. The levels of which we speak are, therefore, but the common hierarchically ordered general ways of behaving that humans have for adjusting to their existential realities.

Levels of human existence come to be when human beings, possessed of certain human potential, live in a world of certain experience. If we have the potential to function in the presence of certain experiences, than we will develop, in a general way, a common *thema* for existence in these experiences. If there is a limitation of human potential or a limitation of optimum experience, then our level of emergence will be restricted. We are so structured, brain-wise, that we must reject or assimilate experiences which are a part of the reality of our existence. If we assimilate the experiences, then we must accommodate our way of being to this existential reality—if we are to exist. As we have to accommodate more and more to internal and external changes in existential reality. We change or the style of existence that is ours begins to wither away and die, and our very existence becomes threatened. When our world is relatively unchanging, we have nothing new to assimilate, nothing new to which we must accommodate. Thus, in such circumstances, we come to a relative equilibrium with our world and remain basically stabilized in a level of human existence. When so stabilized, we will see the world only through the tint of the level of human existence at which we have arrived.

Higher levels of human existence, thus, are not some preformed ideal toward which man strives, nor toward which he is drawn. Man is not his intentions, nor is he his past. He is what a human can be, with his equipment, in the conditions for existence that he is in. With his emerged equipment in the conditions he is in, it makes sense to him to look at the world the way he does at whatever level he happens to be centralized. A level of human existence, thus, is no more than one's most sense-making way of looking at one's existence—for the one who has the potential he has and who is living in the conditions of existence he is in. Levels, then, are simply a description of the natural movement of man, the organism structured as he is, in the process of assimilating and accommodating to change.

I am not saying in this conception of adult behavior that one style of being, one form of human existence is, inevitably and in all circumstances, superior to or better than another form of human existence, another style of being. What I am saying is that when one form of being is more congruent with the realities of existence, then it is the better form of living for those realities. And, what I am saying is that when one form of existence ceases to be functional for the realities of existence, then some other form, either higher or lower in the hierarchy, is the better style of living. I do suggest, however, and this I deeply believe is so, that for the overall welfare of total man's existence in this world, over the long run of time, higher levels are better than lower levels and that the prime goal of any societies' governing figures should be to promote human movement up the levels of human existence.

In this conception, man's personality, if normally progressing, will change in shape, not just in size, from one level to another. The personality, as the conditions of existence change, constantly forms levels of integration which are both quantitatively and qualitatively different from the totality out of which they have evolved. An adult personality is thus like an itinerant traveler on a journey to where he does not know. Like the traveling man, personality tarries now and then to feel out where it is and to see if it has arrived. But, the personality finds to its dismay that to be where it *is* is not where it wants to be. As it becomes comfortable where it is, it finds the self disturbed by the boredom and problems created by its stay. It finds the self dissatisfied with the existence that has induced the halt. So ultimately, the open personality travels on, knowing only where it has been, and that where it has been is not where it was seeking to be. And blindly on this open personality travels, often forgetting where it has been as it begins to glimpse the next stop on the journey.

Each way-stage of adult man's psychology has, stylistically, its way and time integrating the whole. It is characterized by a period of preparation, a period of achievement of relative equilibrium, and a period of disintegration as preparation takes place for movement to a higher stage. To understand a personality we must comprehend the totality of his system. This totality is a totality in the sense of the momentary total state of the organism. It is the organization around which the psychological man is centralized in the levels of human existence now. This totality of the moment, that is an adult man's personality, operates by the minimaxing principle of Von Neuman.[266] At any moment in time, the whole may be dominated by minimizing the growth or change tendency and by maximizing the conservation tendency. At another moment in time it will be the maximizing of growth that rules while the conservative tendency is minimized. This is one way the cyclic aspect of personality can be seen.

To work with this totality one must understand what W. Ross Ashby means when he writes of "The Law of Requisite Variety."[267] This law states that any controlling device must have an order of complexity at least similar to that of the system with which it deals. If it does not

---

[266] Von Neuman, John and Morgenstern, Oskar (1947). *Theory of Games and Economic Behavior.* Princeton: Princeton University Press.

[267] Ashby, Walter R. (1958). Requisite Variety and its Implications for the Control of Complex Systems. *Cybernetica*, 1 (2).

have an order of complexity similar to that with which it deals then the control means will be ineffective. Thus the totality of the system dictates the controls that should be applied to it. But as the system, adult personality or culture changes, as according to this conception, in its saccadic, regressive-progressive, step-like, quantum-like manner, and becomes a different totality, then the question of proper controls changes also. This, of course, has marked implications for psychotherapy, education, management, and government.

A central aspect of this conception is that man is more a problem-solving organism than a pleasure-seeking being. The solution of man's existential problems at a level produces dissonance, triggers insights, and opens up a new way of behaving, indicating that *Beyond the Pleasure Principle,* as Freud wrote of it,[268] is not a destructive tendency in man but a change tendency, a growth tendency. This organism, man, behaves by the principles of pleasure, the principle of conservation only secondarily to the change—the growth principle. This is why this conception has taken the double-goal form into which it has been cast, a form of thinking about human behavior and Freud's dualism which sees dualism in a different light than has been seen previously. For example, one authority who has written in this vein is William Gray who says:

> "I would add that the goal of our species is even more one of continuously attempting to increase our effectiveness in problem solving, in discovery, and in being curious. To have such a goal would mean that the human species behaves in accordance with the goal of growth. I would, however, think that a principle of conservation does enter the picture for humans in the form that has been classically described as the instinct for self-preservation. In terms that are more consonant with general systems theory I would like to state this principle as one of conservation of safety acting as a modifier of the more basic drive to grow continually in ability to increase information negentropization.
>
> Essentially what one wishes is the maximization of increase in ability to negentropize information effectively, and minimization of the danger of such processes going beyond the existing set of limitations in the degree of change than can be tolerated in essential variables. One must add that the sets of parameters describing the most desirable "mix" in such a mini-maxing system are not to be considered fixed for all

---

[268] Freud, Sigmund (1942). *Beyond the Pleasure Principle.* London: Hogarth Press.

times, [recall this author's previous words on health, maturity, and management of human affairs] but subject to a series of step-like or quantum-like changes in time... The notion of the double goal system as described above has been reached from the two Bertalanffy principles of "open system" and "steady state." It is also possible to arrive at a similar notion starting from an expanded view of cybernetic theory, [and from data as this author has shown] in which equal consideration is given to the previously neglected area of positive feedback."[269]

An expanded view of cybernetics would give equal weight to both types of feedback.

"In systems of any degree of complexity, networks serving the function of mutual causality would contain both types of feedback and would have to be constructed in a manner to allow for quantum changes in time of the sets of parametric values. Systems so constructed would have double goal characteristics similar to those previously described...

The presence, then of double-goal oriented processes makes possible the development of systems of ever increasing complexity. With this comes the danger that the concordant increase in discrete information (fact and theory in psychology) may become overwhelming, with the result that the process of complexity increase may become self-defeating. If this is to be avoided, ways must be found of organizing complexities into systems supraordinal to these complexities."[270]

This is what I am attempting to do through the level of existence concept. I am attempting to take on an almost disorganized mass of complexities, the information and theorization about human behavior, and order it into a supraordinal system. This is why this model follows General Systems thinking. It does so because as Gray goes on to say:

"General systems theory serves as an excellent model in this regard, in the sense that it finds supraordinal principles that bring together as parts of a larger whole concepts and information previously regarded as compartmentalized and isolated ..."[271]

---

[269] Gray, William. Source not located in Dr. Gray's writings or papers.
[270] Ibid., Gray.
[271] Ibid., Gray.

Some of these supraordinal principles derived from the studies "that bring together, as parts of a larger whole, concepts and information previously regarded as compartmentalized and isolated,"[272] are listed below so that you can see the principles behind the section that is to follow. The pertinent ones are:

1. Adult personality is characterized by three principle attributes: organization, dynamic flow of processes, and history.
2. In the course of man's history, brain potentials—hierarchically ordered dynamic neurological systems—have accumulated which unfold progressively during the history of the race or the history of a person as potentials for behaving.
3. These systems are determined by the mutual interaction of the conditions present in the total man-environment system, by the interplay of processes, not solely by the awakening of mysterious potencies.
4. Earlier, the dynamic interplay produces systems which are more automatic, more mechanistic.
5. Later, the dynamic interplay produces systems which are more fluid, more organic.
6. The systems tend toward openness but can, to a certain extent, congeal into machine-like systems, that is, closed systems.
7. These systems represent both a continuum and a discontinuum.
8. Change is not the rule. Lack of change is not the rule. If there are no disturbances, no change can appear to be the rule. If there is disturbance, change may be seen to be the rule.
9. No higher stage is, in all respects, radically different from its preceding stage. Yet a higher stage may be, in others, quite radically different from a preceding stage even though it is built on the proceeding stage.
10. When change does ensue, old elements take on new subjective meaning in new systems.
11. There are both general and specific aspects to each stage —the *thema* and the *schema* for existence.

---

[272] Ibid., Gray.

12. There are general and specific factors which propel the organism from one stage to another.
13. The formation of systematic concepts for living at a level is the product of common problems, common mental devices for approach to problems, and the human desire for closure.
14. As man solves the problems of existence at a level, dissonance is created; new brain systems, if present, are activated; and, when activated, change his perceptions so as to cause him to see new problems of existence.
15. Systems are separated by a chemical-type switching means such that, for a long time, higher systems appear not to order experience, thus providing the illusion that *a system* is *the form* that human existence should take on.
16. The whole is the actual state of the total, developing, interrelated system at a given time.
17. To make possible an increase in order, that is, movement up the hierarchy, a supply of energy is necessary.
18. The necessary supply of energy for increase in order comes from a resolution of existential problems at a level.
19. If certain movement toward a new level has passed a critical point, displacement into a negative environment is no longer able to stop it.
20. One cannot see the possibility of higher levels until he has reached the degree of control over current problem that makes other possibilities possible.
21. The organism constantly seeks conditions for existence in which it can perform to its emerged best with optimal comfort.
22. The organism strives toward behavior within a level which has a feeling of comfort, ease, fitness, adequacy, and properness.
23. What is seen as the nature of man at a given time depends upon a wealth of specific psychological time-determined, psychological space-determined events.
24. Man is so programmed that each time he discovers a new and different way of living he will act as if this is *the* discovery and he will act if it is the last discovery that will be made.

25. Human nature does not exist in the tissues of the human being. It comes to exist in the bio-chemical-social-environmental field.
26. Levels of existence are created by man's functioning—if it is man's physiological needs that are functioning as figure, while others are ground, he will create a schematic form of existence specified for thematic physiological functioning.
27. The lower does not disappear; it is integrated into and subordinated to the higher.
28. In general, levels tend not to persist as lasting structures. It is the principle of levels as a *process* that persists.
29. The adult human tends to develop from a state of automatic reactivity, through controlled reactivity to active, spontaneous behavior, to??
30. The adult tends to develop from a state of few behavioral possibilities, through stages of limited behavioral possibilities, to states of many behavioral possibilities, to??
31. The adult tends to develop from behaving in order to get, through stages of different kinds of getting, to behaving in order to be, to??
32. The adult consciousness tends to develop from a no time-space-cause stage, through a limited time-space-cause state, to an extended time-space-cause state, to??
33. The adult human tends to develop from not knowing, to magical knowing, to egocentric knowing, to absolute knowing, to experimentalistic knowing, to relativistic knowing, to systemic knowing, to??
34. The adult tends to develop from being at the mercy of the world, to believing he is subordinate to the power of the world, to believing he is in control, to believing he must cooperate with the world, to??

Significance of the Conception

From this conceptual viewpoint and some of the preceding propositions, adult personality is to be viewed not as a recognizable cross section but as a vertically oriented multidimensional trend phase which leads us toward certain significant reorganizations of our view of human problems. If adult personality and its relatives, healthy personality and healthy culture, are processes passing through definable nodal stages; if there is a psychology of man particular to each stage; then our tasks as scientists and practitioners must take a decided change. As scientists, we must seek those better models which represent this process, and we must seek to know more the principles for change involved in the process. We must strive to represent more adequately what these stages are, how they develop, what encourages or arrests the developing process, and we must seek further for keys to predicting what new stages are yet to appear. And as practitioners we must reexamine our approach to man's many problems.

In the scientific psychological world, the world of pure psychological investigation, we must ask some new questions about some very old problems. Assuming that adult man's psychology develops in a step-like manner through hierarchically ordered stages, we must reconsider, for example, man's psychology of time, space, causality, and materiality, something the European existentialists and phenomenologist have been doing, though not within a highly ordered framework of thought. Within this point of view, we would quit asking 'how does adult man perceive time, space and materiality?' as if such questions might lead to some general laws to be discovered. We would not ask, 'What is creative man like?' nor 'What is the nature of the creative process?' We would ask instead: 'How does man, at one level in his hierarchy of systems, perceive of time, space, causality and materiality?' We would ask: 'What is the way one perceives of time, space, causality and materiality within a level and what is an abnormal perception of the same?' We would ask: 'How does biologically mature man perceive time, space, causality and materiality when one system dominates his behavior in contrast to when other systems higher or lower in the hierarchy dominate his thinking?' In an area like creativity we would ask: 'What is the creative process like at one level, what is it like at another level, and what is the nature of that which man creates when he is at one level in contrast to the nature of that which he creates when he is at another level?' In fact, the whole world of general psychology, from psychophysics on, would be open to reinvestigation from within this changed conception of adult personality. But this is not the only world that would be open to reconsideration.

If psychological development is an ever-evolving, step-like process, our ideas about so-called unethical behavior would assuredly change. We would see that value and ethical systems come, and that value and ethical systems go, in a highly ordered way. We would cease trying to preach what is mature ethical behavior and we would question what we are doing when we try to mold the 'properly moral' person. We would see that what we normally call 'the breakdown of morality' is one of two things. On the one hand, moral and ethical breakdown would be seen as the turbulent behavior of man as he strives to discard an old, once appropriate system of values, and strives to find a new system of values more appropriate to his changed conditions of existence. On the other hand, moral breakdown might be what a person centralized at a one level of existence sees in the value system of one at a higher or lower level of existence.

If we see psychological maturity as a step-like process having no ultimate end, then we would reconsider our approach to the problems of psychopathology. We would not seek a general set of principles which would differentiate the operation of the pathological person from he who is *the* psychologically mature human being. We would look, instead, for the kinds of pathology which are typical to a particular stage in the maturing process. We would look for the system-specific principles of treatment which move the pathological person to the open form of his stage of maturity, and then for the principles that would enable him to move to the next existential state if he is capable of such. But if he is not capable of movement, we would look for a way to dignify his existence where he is. At the same time we would seek to prevent his taking on a pathological form in the next level of maturity. From this point of view, we would not argue whether behavioristic therapy is better than psychoanalytic therapies or either better than Rogerian therapy. We would ask: 'For what system of behavior is what therapy appropriate? For what way-stages along the existential staircase do we not yet have appropriate therapy?'

The same would hold for labor-management relations and for the human problems of business and governmental organizations. We would not continue seeking that magical Theory Y, participative, or 9.9 form of management applicable to all men at work. We would be seeking for ways to organize work when one form of management can be congruent with a heterogeneous work force. We would begin to ask: 'How can we best utilize the qualities a man has in his existential state?' rather than 'How can we change him to fit the level preferred by the organization?' On a philosophical level, we would ask whether it is the function of an industrial organization to manage mainly for economic gain or more for human growth? And probably we will ask: 'In the long run, is economic viability possible only when we manage for human growth?'

There is still another broad region of human behavior which could be valuably reconsidered within the meaning of this concept. The whole world of human knowledge and human products could be reexamined. Political science, hard science, art, music and literature—all would be open to investigation as they, and attitudes toward them, have evolved and as they have changed as man's level of existence changed. Take literary criticism as an example. Would we not need to ask, 'From what level of existence do the percepts of the critic arise? Is the critic judging the literary effort from within the existential state of the writer, or does his criticism suggest that only the criteria which stem from his position on the existential staircase be used to judge a literary production?' And we would ask, 'From what level does the literary production emanate and how well does it portray the character of its existential source?'

The meaning of this concept may well cast a different light upon the immediate, as contrasted to the future, goals of a society. If a society is more homogeneous and at lower levels, its goals must be more narrow, more concrete, and more immediate than the broader more abstract, more remote goals we have seen the United States attempt to promote in some nations—for example, democracy in Viet Nam. If a society is like ours—quite heterogeneous—then our goals must be at one and the same time concrete and abstract, immediate and remote; but this is not where the only problem of societal goals lies. By and large, many do not argue as to promoting human welfare as a goal. What they argue about is: 'What is human welfare' and 'the means to the end.' It is here that this way of thinking has further significance.

Let us take a generally lower level society, Ethiopia, for example. A narrow concrete goal is already extant in their country. It is to improve their food production. But how much do those who strive in that direction consider that the Ethiopian farmer maybe psychologically locked into his transitional third-level farming methodology? How much do the goal promoters know of how to change, by Pavlovian and Skinnerian psychological principles, the farming methodology of the Ethiopian by virtue of a mixture of respondent and operant conditioning? How much do they realize that demonstration, exhortation, persuasion, and promise of later reward are not the proper means to the end of getting an Ethiopian farmer to switch to a but slightly changed though much improved way of plowing?

In our more heterogeneous society, the problem is not basically the same as in a lower level society. There is a great problem with the establishment of our goals. We are generally for human growth and development, but we don't know for certain what we mean by it, nor how to bring it about. This is particularly evident when we examine "Goals for Americans" presented in the 1960 President's Commission on National Goals.[273]

The paramount goal as stated in that report "is to guard the rights of the individual, to ensure his development and to enlarge his opportunity,"[274] a goal which is partially subscribed to by this conceptual system but one which, in many respects, is seen in a different way from that presented by the President's Committee.

These differences begin to stand out when we note the commission also said the "aim is to build a nation and help build a world in which every human being shall be free to dedicate and develop his capacities to the fullest." Within this point of view, one cannot conceive that the normal human will develop his capacities to the fullest. Such a belief is the delusion of the FS way of thinking. This is not possible in an infinitely emerging psychological world. Instead, according to the level of existence point of view, the aim should be to build a nation and help build a world in which every human being is free to develop in an ordered way from one level to the next and on as future levels emerge, if he is so capable, or to grow intra-systemically if he is not possessed of the necessary potential.

The above is not a semantic play. On the contrary, it is a very serious difference because of principles 17 and 18 above which state, namely, that movement up levels requires a supply of free energy and that this energy comes from the resolution of certain existential problems particular to the level of existence. It points our attention in quite a different direction than the staged goal of the President's Commission.

Principle 19—if the movement toward a new level has passed a certain critical point, displacement into a negative environment can no longer stop it—brings into focus a different kind of problem that we have today. It would appear that throwing out DQ authority by the offspring of white, middle-class parents and the throwing off of materialism by young affluents are both beyond the critical point. To try to pull them back to the values of times past, as some are wont to do, can only come to naught.

These are but two examples of six revolutionary level changes occurring concomitantly in our society at this time which may be

---

[273] President's Commission on National Goals [Eisenhower]. (1960). *Goals for Americans*. New York: American Assembly, Columbia University.
[274] Hummel, Dean L. and Bonham Jr., S.J. (1968). *Pupil Personnel Services In The Schools*. Rand McNally and Company, p 3.

controllable only by radically changed national planning rather than by repressive "law and order" measures. I will detail and have more to say of these six revolutionary changes because herein lies the error in "The Greening of America" thinking.[275]

Other goals stated by the President's Commission which need to be reconsidered are: to "promote the maximum development of his (the citizen's) capabilities," to place "self-fulfillment at the summit," and to see that "the very deepest goals for Americans relate to the spiritual health of our people." These need to be reconsidered because all the principles listed question self-fulfillment, maximum development and support a change to new and different fulfillment and ever continuing development. Then, on the spiritual side, principles 29 through 34 suggest "spiritual" to be of a very different order than previously we have considered it to be. It is different because the principles indicate that what is "spiritual" in human existence is now and will be forever changing and, particularly, that only people centralized in even-numbered systems have true spiritual concern. But we cannot tarry too long on these points. We must move on because there are still many other problems, foreign and domestic, which we might well reconsider from within the levels of existence point of view.

On the foreign side, if we should come to view psychosocial maturity as a process rather than as an achievable state, we might perceive the underdeveloped nation plight in a very different light. We would not look at an underdeveloped nation and ask: 'How can we get this nation to behave in a manner we consider politically mature?'—democracy if Americans are the viewers, communism if the Russians[276] are the viewers? We would ask instead: 'At what stage in the process of nation-like maturity are the people in this underdeveloped country? Are they more homogeneous or more heterogeneous level wise? In what existential state is its leadership centralized? Is the relationship between the leader, the led and the political organization congruent?' We would ask: 'Are we, in our foreign policy, promoting congruency or are we promoting an impossible task for the leadership of said country? Are we, or are we not, asking the leaders to develop and administer a political organization congruent with the psychology of their people?' We would ask: 'What is the political form most congruent for this country—confederation, authoritarian federalization, democratic federalization, etc.?' We would not ask, 'How do we aid it to become democratic now, but how can we help it become what it is ready to become so that later it

---

[275] See Reich, Charles (1970).
[276] A reference to "the Russians" as of 1977 when the Soviet Union was still intact.

can become other than what it is now, and thus move up the hierarchy of political organization?' We would not ask: 'How can we convince Red China to become less hostile and more democratic?' We would ask: 'What can we learn about the existential position and existential problems of Russia and China which will help us develop different, though congruent, approaches to the Chinese and Russian situation?'

On the domestic side, think of how we might reevaluate the problem of poverty from within the conceptual change. If those who are poverty stricken are at several different levels of existence, and thus operate by widely varying psychological principles, not only from poverty-stricken to poverty-stricken, but in contrast to the non-poverty-stricken, would not our approach to poverty change? The new approaches would, by and large, be very different from what they have been. For example, we would not try to teach or aid the poverty-stricken to live by principles of maturity of those much higher in the hierarchy. Rather, we would ascertain the level of operation of the particular poverty stricken person, or poverty-stricken group, and would apply those principles which would enable movement from the kind of psychological being he is, from the level of maturity he has achieved, to the next level he can become.

For example, let us look at three of our welfare problems: providing food, providing adequate medical services, and providing housing. We are not truly aware that our past welfare practices have really been successful and thus, in being successful have, as this theory says, created new and monstrous problems for us. Our provision of food and other necessities, and our attempts to provide medical services have worked very well for many, but they have not achieved our desired goals. Instead of enabling many people to become self-sufficient—our goal—we seem to have arrested their development and made them more dependent. Instead of improving their health, we seem, too often, to find the means we have provided are not utilized as we envisioned they would be. But these problems we might well correct if we should see, from within the levels of existence point of view, why we went astray and what we need to do to get on a better track.

Principle 4 says earlier-appearing, that is, lower-level systems, are more automatic, more mechanistic. Principle 12 says there are general and specific factors which propel the organism from one stage to another. Principles 17 and 16 say certain problems, not other problems, must be solved in order for movement to take place; and principle 6 says systems can congeal into closed states under certain conditions. Attendance to these principles and the broader aspects of them suggests previous welfare practices have both met and violated the character of lower level systems, and thus promoted change—but toward closure not openness!

We have in principle, though not properly in operation, a sound system for moving man through the first two existential states. We have a totally inadequate system for moving man through the third to the fourth level of existence, and we will never get the hard work, self disciplined DQ to ER ethic emerging until we develop a proper CP to DQ welfare system.

If one understands the mechanical, concrete immediate character of lower level behavior and the necessary factors for promoting readiness for change, he would not practice our basically sound, lowest-level welfare principles as we have practiced them. Many welfare recipients operate within lower-level systems where change can be promoted only by knowing well the psychology of such systems. These systems operate on the principles of immediacy. They are systems wherein time and space concepts are very limited. They are systems which change when classical and operant conditioning principles are applied to them. But our past practices have not heeded these characteristics of lower-level systems very well, particularly the development of a CP welfare system built around operant conditioning procedures.

We have provided food or access to food so that the recipient gets a lot at one time, or has to exercise his means to food through his own planning efforts. Both violate his psychology and according to conditioning principles fixate his behavior rather than change it. To establish readiness for change by solving the food problem, the food has to come to the lower-level person everyday, regularly over an extended period of time. It can neither come in a first-of-the-month windfall nor can his own day-to-day planning satisfactorily distribute it to himself. Here, our problem is not providing food in both the proper amount and nutritional quality. The problem is how to develop a continuous distribution system.

The medical service problem is quite similar. The lower-level system must be tuned up to move up to higher levels. It must become physiologically sound. But lower-level people, having limited awareness, lack of available energy and the like, limited concepts of time, space and cause, simply are not psychologically prone to go to and procure the services available. It is not even enough to provide facilities in their immediate neighborhood because their psychology locks them into their past way of living so they cannot, so to speak, get out of their home and go across the street for service. Here, the levels of existence point of view says we need medical and paramedical teams which move, by way of mobile basic medical laboratories, directly to and then into their homes if ever we are to establish a state of readiness to move lower-level people. And then there is the problem of adequate housing for our poorer people. Nowhere is the level of existence point of view more violated than in this region, except in the total absence of a welfare design for people centralized at the third level of existence.

We are generally *for* human growth and development, but we don't know how to bring it about. If we knew, we would never attempt to provide *better* housing for second or third level poverty stricken by destroying *existing* housing, no matter how bad, *before* housing is built. Humans whose behavior is centralized at the second or third level do not have the postponement capacity necessary to wait for future reward. The means to the end of *satisfying* lower level people's desire for better housing must not, according to this conception, be based on a promise of things to come. We must, instead, according to this thinking, reverse our process. If we are to meet the lower-level psychology of many poor people, we must not tear down existing houses that are really not habitable or rehabilitatable. We must, instead, survey our cities for empty lots, and empty, but reconstructable buildings and we must build on them and restructure them.

This we must do because lower-level people live in a world of immediacy. Immediacy is a prime need at these lower levels. If we do this then we can move families to their new homes rather than displace them. But this is not enough for transferring lower-level people to better housing conditions. Another aspect of lower-level psychology is to be psychologically locked into one's territory. Therefore, any urban renewal or university expansion which cuts into lower-level space will be strongly reacted to by those whose existence is precarious. Obviously these two lower-level characteristics seriously complicate urban renewal planning. We simply must think our way around such problems if we are to renovate our cities in terms of lower-level psychology rather than contrary to it. If we do not heed this information, we can expect more hostility and more resistance to other non-attending, though well-intentioned, urban renewal, poor housing, and replacement plans. And, if we do not develop a third level, CP welfare system, we are lost.

Now let us take education as a means to our goal. Here, whether in the university or the lower grades, levels of existence principles say we constantly violate the means to the end of a society where all are educated by what is best for them in our schools, at all grade levels; we have students who need and parents who desire different kinds of education. Yet, I know of only one school, university-wise or elementary-wise, that utilizes the means to the end suggested by this conception.[277] Where do we find universities, elementary, or secondary systems organized so that the level of existence of the student determines the form, content, and methodology of his education? Where can we find the needed schools based upon the kind of thinking expressed in this concept? To my knowledge they barely exist and mostly are not even in the planning stage.

From this point of view we would take a very different look at our university discontents and drop-outs. We would not ask how can we get them to accept an educational form which is appropriate for certain levels of existence but apparently not for the level of existence our discontented young minds are at. We would ask, instead: 'How should a university's organization be restructured so that its form becomes congruent with the level of existence of what so many call 'our psychedelic monsters,' as well as the other levels of existence extant in a university?' In all of education, we would seriously reconsider what education is and how to bring it about. We can see those alternatives if we develop our educational thinking from certain basic assumptions stemming from the principles of the levels of existence conception of man's development.

Let us assume, from this point of view, that the aim of an educational institution is to take the student from thinking levels of lower complexity, if competent, to thinking levels of higher complexity. Then, if we can ascertain what are the higher levels of thinking complexity and their hierarchically ordered relationship, and if we can ascertain what educational intervention techniques are necessary to move a person from one level of thinking normality to the next level of thinking normality, then we can prescribe, better than we have, the means to meet the ever-emergent ends of a heterogeneous society; and we can develop techniques to assess the progress toward that goal at both the institutional and student level.

When one begins to see the problem of goals, and organizing to promote certain goals, from within this point of view, three aspects of current planning seem possibly in error. One is the type of planning which conceives that the ultimate society is the one for which we should plan. A second is to plan a society around the percepts of only one level of existence. And the third is the type of planning which seeks to return to the past. Each of these forms of planning are erroneous from an infinitely evolving point of view, the point of view of this book.

---

[277] See Drews (1968a) for some references to possible schools.

It seems inferred in the ideas of some people whose words I presented earlier—for example, Herbert Hoover, and former editor of the *Cleveland Press*, Louis B. Seltzer— that we have erred because we have failed adequately to plan for a fourth-level DQ type of society. Mr. Hoover, in that 1951 speech at the Iowa Centennial Foundation, made a plea for society to return to the old days when we had "incorruptible service and honor in public affairs." He asserted we could make the world over again if we would but "try out some of the old virtues." Mr. Seltzer, in his editorial entitled, "Can't We Tell Right From Wrong?" decried the movement of many in our society from the DQ to the ER system of behavior. And he inferred that we should plan for a return to the old. He said something has happened to us, something serious. He said,

> "…though we have gained much in the past century, it is possible that what we have lost is more important than what we have gained, that we have lost something we once had and that what we have gotten in its place is corruption, loose behavior, dulled principles, subverted morals, easy expediencies."[278]

This kind of planning suggestion is with us at the time of this writing as it was in 1951 when Mr. Hoover and Mr. Seltzer spoke. But it did not then, nor does it now, take into account that as man's behavioral systems emerge there are times when he seems, in terms of past morality, to go from good to bad, those times when man moves from an even-numbered to an odd-numbered level of existence. But this should not cause us to plan for going back. It should lead us to re-examine what it means to human life to cast aside constrictive ethics and to replace them with more higher-level ways of valuing.

Another system which some planners are wont to maximize is typified by what Maslow called the 'belonging system.' This is a type of plan which strives to homogenize man, to make all men existentially alike. Such planning would strive to draw all lower-level people up into this system, would arrest the higher-level bound and would retract those now at higher levels into its constrictive form. It would plan to have all people live by its "other directed" form of being which is quite contrary to the nature of an ever-emergent organism.

---

[278] Seltzer, Louis B. (1951). "Can't We Tell Right From Wrong." Editorial, *Cleveland Press*.

Still a third system which some like Herman Kahn[279] would chose to maximize is the fifth level, ER, positivistic, mechanistic, objectivistic System where 19th century physical science concepts rule supreme and corrupt the world of man. Little more need be said of this type of plan because Lewis B. Mumford[280] levels a more devastating criticism upon this form of planning than this author could ever write.

The other basic form of planning—planning for the mature society—is just as erroneous from the levels of existence point of view. It simply should not be thought about. It simply cannot be conceived of in a system of thought which sees man's behavior to ever evolve rather than to approach its apex.

Future planning must be pluralistic for a long time to come, and possibly forever. This is so because at no time in the foreseeable, or intermediate, future can one conceive of all people at one level, and because it is very difficult to conceive that a process which is ever-evolving will ever get all people to the same position on the existential staircase. Above all else, future planning must take into account that there is not *A* consciousness revolution taking place in the world. Instead, there are five fully developed revolutions in full process and two others operating to a lesser degree.

Nowhere is our planning more in error than where people are planning as if the only revolution taking place today is the emergence of Consciousness III. Book upon book, article upon article have been written about this revolution in man's consciousness and what to do about it, but nowhere in our annals is there greater evidence of liberal-minded ethnocentrism running rampant. These liberals seem to see only the ER to FS revolution, or else contaminate their thinking by mistaking the DQ to ER revolution as the same as the revolution toward Consciousness III. As a result, these mistaken ones will never truly understand, nor effectively meet, the antipathy between the 'hardhats' for the 'hippies' or the 'curse upon both of your houses' by the Black power movement.

Of the first revolution, we know very little. What it is like and what it portends, in adult human development, was, until recently, buried in the history of man. In fact, the existence of it was only a theoretical hypothesis when the levels of existence point of view first took its current form. But fortunately for those like me who drew the hypothesis that this level of existence had to exist, even though scholars like Mumford and Heard said it did not, the Tasaday have given at least

---

[279] Kahn (1960).
[280] Ibid., (Mumford, 1956 see: Chapter 7).

partial credence to it. The discovery strongly suggests that the AN to BO revolution must be a part of man's development and must be the first revolution of man's consciousness. So, now that we have brought dissonance into their field, perhaps it is true that what is being revealed today is what the AN to BO revolution is all about. But since we know so little of what is happening in 'Tasaday life,' I cannot write of what this revolution is like because I do not have the data for it. What I can do is say that emergent cyclical theory says it is the first consciousness revolution. I can hope that those who are bringing dissonance into Tasaday life are doing so with an intuitive understanding of how to implement positive, not negative or regressive, change. I should like to think that if or when the critical point is reached, the jump will be to the positive BO consciousness of Margaret Mead's, Arapesh type[281] and not the negative form of the Alorese.[282] Above all else, I hope the intrusion into Tasaday life does not produce another group of Ik.

The second revolution for which we need to plan and positively help to take place is the BO to CP change—a revolution occurring in several African nations. Responding appropriately to this second-level revolution takes all the patience higher-level man can muster. This revolution with its heroistically assertive, paranoically flavored overtones is not easy to handle because of its extreme militancy and brutalistic aggression—the norm when tribal consciousness is supplanted by the emerging CP state of mind.

According to this theory, the third revolution should be the easiest of all to discern, but it is the one we seem to understand the least so far as aiding it to consummate is concerned. This change is from the aggressive, self assertive, 'I'll look out for me to hell with others, or at least go down in the glory of having faced the dragon' way of life to an authority obeying, aesthetic way of life. Black Muslim, puritanical aestheticism with all the good and all the bad that goes therewith (witness the Prison Riots[283]) is a modern example of this type of revolution. But our failure to solve our prison problem is evidence of

---

[281] Mead, Margaret (1970). *The Mountain Arapesh II: Arts and Supernaturalism*. Garden City, NY: Natural History Press, p. 491. This book was published with 2 other volumes, *The Mountain Arapesh* and *The Mountain Arapesh III: Stream of Events in Alitoa*. The books were originally published in *Antropological Papers of the American Museum of Natural History*, volume 36, 37, parts 3, 1938, 1940.

[282] Du Bois, Cora Alice with Kardiner, Abram and Oberholzer, Emil (1944). *The People of Alor: A Social-psychological Study of an East Indian Island*. Minneapolis: University of Minnesota Press.

[283] Wicker, Tom (1975). *A Time to Die*. New York: Quadrangle Books.

our inability to plan constructively for this consciousness revolution when it is the order of the day.

The fourth revolution involves changing DQ to ER consciousness, changing from authority-bound, authority-respecting, authority-beseeching behavior to 'mine own directing, mine own calculating self' interest. The active, anti-middle class establishment, flag besmirching hippie hated by the 'hard hat,' is an example. This 'hard hat' is hanging on to his hope for fulfillment of the American dream by holding tight to the last vestiges of authority. He hates the hippie for being one half-step ahead on the way to self-sufficiency. Actually, both are a part of this revolution. The 'hard hat' disguises his revolt in labor union attacks on authority, while the hippie stands alone as he tramples authority into the muck and mire. The odd thing about this revolution is that neither recognizes his relation to authority for what it is. The 'hard hat' is in the throes of his last defense of the establishment and soon, if he continues to grow, he will step into the shoes of the openly attacking hippie. But the hippie does not know that he is not trying to get rid of authority per se. Rather, he is attempting to substitute his self as the authority in place of the authority of the establishment. This authority-hating, authority-baiting, flag-desecrating revolutionist is really fighting to get a strong foothold on the materialistic existence so as to point to his success as the evidence of his right to authority. Negativistically, both charge ahead toward the nodal ER consciousness though they are a half a step apart. And each will find when he achieves the values of the self-sufficient, self-made man he will become the object of scorn and derision by those who have entered into the fifth revolution in man's consciousness.

The fifth revolution strives to supplant the objectivistic, materialistic, marketing, 'I have gotten here myself' orientation with a subjectivistic, spiritualistic, 'Greening of America,' humanistic consciousness. This revolution throws off the trappings of the affluent life but maintains a strong grip on its foundation. Thereby, this revolutionist retains reams of time to trip through Esalenic experiences at Big Sur or in the inner sanctums of other growth experiences.

The character of this revolution is very necessary for man when his consciousness begins to perceive what is the ER negative spilloff on the world of man. Possessed of a still-present need to explore, but repulsed by what ER tampering with the outer world has wrought, the FS revolutionist turns to the exploration of his inner self because there, he believes, peace from the endangerment brought to man from the ER way will be found. But, like all the revolutions that see the good life just one step ahead, the FS revolutionist, too, will find self-realization is no more a panacea than any other magic potion has been.

This revolution is not, as the Consciousness III proponents are wont to believe, man on the threshold of the ultimate realization of his truly human self. It is not the door to the house where the epitome of human experience resides. It is not the dream home in which he will settle down forever to feast on the aromatic pleasures emanating from the greenery around. It is, instead, the prelude to the last dying gasp of individualism. It is the entrance into that state of consciousness from whose disillusionment man ultimately will learn the hardest lesson he has had to master to date. As this existential state comes in and plays itself out, in the dusk of its day, FS man learns an emotionally devastating lesson. He learns that to become his total human self was not why he was born, that becoming himself is only a myth.

Out of this state of consciousness he will learn, from the meaning in any or all of his growth experiences, that Consciousness III is not the culminating theme in man's symphony of life. And, out of it he will learn that this is the shortest theme of the first six themes in the symphony of man. The FS state of consciousness is the end of the beginning and the beginning of the new—a new symphonic movement built on man's realization that he is a systemic being, not an individual person. This realization is the psychological herald of the sixth revolution which is looming up before the societies of man today.

This sixth revolution, the FS to A'N' revolution, is, society-wise, the one with which we must succeed if we are to be able to handle the problems extant in the five other revolutions I have cited. I say societal-wise because there is a seventh revolution of consciousness in its embryonic form, the A'N' to B'O' revolution, but little is known of it except as I have spoken of it, individually and theoretically, at an earlier point in this book. Societally, it is the FS to A'N' revolution that is attempting to reshape our organized ways for living and conducting the affairs of man.

During this sixth revolution, man sees (those who are there) or will see (those who are yet to reach it) that living must be restructured and must begin anew on a different basic premise. He sees what his first ladder of existence and its basic premises, individualism and the supremacy of man, have wrought in this revolution; he makes that long reach for the second ladder of existence where all must begin anew, yet not anew. He recognizes that he must begin anew by resurrecting *life* to the center of the scene. Just as man was one with all life when in the AN state, so again must man become one with all life, but in a new and higher order form. Just as behaving automatically in tune with one's biophysical promptings and in accordance with nature as provided, was the basis for existence in untutored, technologically naive AN man, so must A'N' man relearn to live again by biophysical promptings in the natural world that nature provides, but, now, in a world of vast knowledge and technological sophistication.

In the course of this revolution, he must rid himself of many once useful but now outmoded values and beliefs, of many mis-garnered notions which were responsible for his climb up the first ladder of existence. Now he must learn to cast aside majority rule and learn it is the factor of knowledge and not the quantity of votes that is right. Now he must learn that to believe in the equality of men is to believe fallaciously. But, in so doing he must truly learn to respect any man or anything regardless of the quantitative or qualitative differences that exist. Now he must learn that winning is not everything, nor is it the only thing. He must learn that life and its continuance is the important thing—not your life, not my life—at the same time that he learns there is nothing in this world more important than your life or my life. And, if this characterization of this revolution seems heretical, if it seems to throw out all that is good and yet retain the best, and if what I have said seems so contradictory as to be nonsensical, just keep in mind that striving to learn, to be at peace with this mixed up kind of thinking, is why this is called the most significant of the six revolutions in consciousness I have described thus far.

If man accomplishes this revolution—and this is yet to be seen—if man reorganizes society within this seemingly peculiar way of thinking, he will have crossed his great divide, the demarcation point between those things he has in common with animals and those things which are uniquely human. But, as he does so he will, in a sense, return to the beginning because the A'N' state is just a higher order form of the AN state, and if he solves his problems of existence in this higher order AN state his next big revolution will be from the A'N' way of life to the B'O' form which, following the design of this book, is the second order form of the BO state.

Societies of man may never achieve this revolution. On the other hand, they might. If they do, then the whole world of values and purposes will be seen in a different light, and what is psychological maturity will take on a different hue. This, to me, is the most significant of all the aspects of the level of existence point of view. What can be more significant to man than to see and accept that the values of Individualistic man of fifty years ago, those values which made modern society what it is today, are no longer the values by which man should live today? And what can give more purpose to existence than the never-ending quest for that new set of values which will be consonant with each new set of existential conditions? What can make life more zestful than to ever have to reach for values and new purposes; to always have our reach in life exceeding our grasp?

If there is a never-ending tendency, beyond the pleasure principle, and if we have, in general, provided a map to this ever-changing process, then we have helped provide everlasting significance to the lives of all generations of mankind. And we move toward making systematic sense of the words in D. H. Lawrence's "Terra Incognita" wherein he says:

> "There are vast realms of consciousness still undreamed of
> vast ranges of experience, like the humming of unseen harps,
> we know nothing of, within us.
> Oh when man escaped from the barbed-wire entanglement
> of his own ideas and his own mechanical devices
> there is a marvelous rich world of contact and sheer fluid beauty
> and fearless face-to-face awareness of now-naked life
> and me, and you, and other men and women
> and grapes, and ghouls, and ghosts and green moonlight
> and ruddy orange limbs stirring the limbo
> of the unknown air, and eyes so soft
> softer than the space between the stars.
> And all things, and nothing, and being and not-being
> alternately palpitate,
> when at last we escape the barbed-wire enclosure
> of '*Know Thyself*,'" knowing we can never know,
> we can but touch, and wonder, and ponder, and make our effort
> and dangle in a last fastidious fine delight
> as the fuchsia does, dangling her reckless drop
> of purple after so much putting forth
> and slow mounting marvel of a little tree."

Ten Points Excerpted from Dr. Graves's Workshop Handouts[284]

The emergent, cyclical, double-helix theory describes, explains, and suggests means for managing the biopsychosocial development for the species *Homo sapiens*, or any individual member of the species. As a model for exploring healthy mature adult psychosocial behavior, the research of Clare W. Graves proposes:

1. *That the human being, though but one biological organism, has developed, to date, seven fixated exiting, eight open nodal, and seven entering states plus mixed states.* These are progressively developing psychosocial systems because *Homo sapiens* is an almost infinite psychological being which changes systematically as the world changes in the course of living.

2. *That these nodal systems are, normally, hierarchically ordered, prepotent and upwardly spiraling.* The biopsychological development of the mature human is an unfolding, emergent, oscillating process marked, normally, by the progressive subordination of older, lower order, less complex biopsychosocial systems to newer, higher order, more complex biopsychosocial systems. The process moves in a complex wave-like, progressive, nodal, regressive fashion and may fixate at certain progressive or regressive points. Each wave develops slowly to the point of inflection, then rapidly ascends to its nodal form, then begins a slow descent to the point of deflection where a precipitous fall ensues as the next wave starts slowly to ascend.

3. *That the biopsychosocial development of the mature human arises from the interaction of a double-helix complex of two sets of determining forces,* the environmentosocial determinants (the Existential Problems of Living) and the neuropsychological equipment of the organism (the Neuropsychological Equipment for Living). Each system develops from the interaction of these

---

[284] The two presentation handouts from which this synopsis is derived were prepared by Chris Cowan for Dr. Graves and under his direction for use in seminars and conferences in 1981 and 1982. Parts of these documents are also embedded in the text in Section II of *The Never Ending Quest*.

hierarchically ordered, parallel, and prepotent sets of forces. Adult psychosocial development is a flowing process in which the solution of current existential problems creates the next set of existential problems to be solved and, in their creation, produces complex chemicals which activate the next set of neuropsychological coping equipment consisting of the information processing means for detection and solution of the created set of existential problems.

4. *That these systems alternate their mental focus in a cyclic, oscillating, dominant fashion.* Every other psychosocial system is like, but at the same time, not like its alternating partner. Systems 2, 4, and 6 etc., are predominantly obeisance, conservative systems; but each obeys different authority sources and obeys and conserves in different ways. Systems 1, 3, 5, and 7 etc., are predominantly change systems, but how to and what to change is different in each odd-numbered system. Cerebral dominance in the odd-numbered systems is by the left hemisphere of the brain and in even-numbered systems is by the right hemisphere of the brain.

The first system is slightly differentiated to favor focus upon the external world and how to gain and expand power over it (left hemisphere brain domination). Then, alternating thereafter upon focus on the inner subjective world and how to come to know and come to peace with it in even-numbered systems (right hemisphere brain domination), then back to focus upon the external world and how to change it in subsequent odd-numbered systems with the aim and means of each systemic end changing in each alternately prognostic system.

5. *That when the human is centralized in one state of existence he or she has a psychology which is particular to that state.* His or her feelings, motivations, ethics and values, biochemistry, degree of neurological activation, learning system, belief systems, conception of mental health, ideas as to what mental illness is and how it should be treated, conceptions of and preferences for management, education, economics and political theory and practice are all appropriate to that state. A person may show the behavior of a level in a predominantly positive or negative manner.

6. *That these alternating systems show variation for psychological dimensions.* There is little mean variation for dimensions such as intelligence and temperament. However, certain psychological dimensions such as ideological dogmatism and objectivity emerge with a particular system in the hierarchy of systems, then decrease or increase systematically in subsequent systems. And certain psychological dimensions such as guilt, as a felt emotion, emerge with a particular system in the hierarchy then, in subsequent systems, vary quantitatively in an increasing or decreasing cyclic, wave-like fashion.

7. *That increasing degrees of behavioral freedom, increasing degrees of choice emerge with each successive level;* but the degree of increase is greater in odd-numbered than in even-numbered systems. Still, each movement up the Levels of Human Existence has resulted in an increase in the conceptual space of *Homo sapiens.*

8. *That each system has a general theme for existence which typifies it,* such that each central theme for existence is particularizable into almost an infinite number of ways for peripheral expression. Adult psychosocial life is a developing, emergent process which can be likened to a symphony built on six basic themes which repeat, in higher order form, every set of six. The first six tell the story of adult psychosocial development in a world of naturalistic abundance. The second order systems tell the story of how psychosocial development will take place in a world of naturalistic scarcity.

    In human existence, our species begins by stating in the simplest way those themes which will occupy us through history with almost infinite variations. These themes for living (AN, BO, CP, etc.) change as the human solves current problems of existence and, in their solution, creates new problems of existence. Every seventh system shows a degree of change in excess of the sum of all six previous changes.

9. *That humans tend normally to change their biopsychosocial being as the conditions of their existence change.* Each successive stage, wave, or level of existence is a state through which developing people

pass on their way to other states of being. In some cases, a person may not be genetically or constitutionally equipped to change in the normal upward hierarchically ordered, more complex direction when the person's conditions of existence change. A person may stabilize (existential conditions being right) at any one or a combination of levels in the hierarchy. He or she may, under certain circumstances, regress to a system lower in the hierarchy. And a person may settle, for specifiable organistic or environmental reasons, into what appears to be a fixated and relatively closed system rather be in the usual, open state of development.

10. *That at this point in our history, the societally effective leading edge of humanity, in the technologically advanced nations, is currently finishing the initial statement of the sixth (FS) state of existence* (modern Japan); and the United States (though temporarily stalled in a regressive phase) is beginning again with the first theme in a new and more sophisticated form of survivalistic living, the seventh, the A'N' existential level. That is, some humans have reached the point of finishing the first and most primitive *spiral of existence,* the one concerned with basic survival, with the development of individual independence, and with the ways of existence to foster it. But, at this time, human life is beginning to experience threats to existence created by the cumulative effect of the first six ways of being, namely, the creation of a whole new set of survival problems. Thus, some humans have started to think about and some of them are well into thinking according to the ways of a second spiral of existence, the *being level* systems. These humans have truly started to think of the interdependence of existence rather than an individualized independent existence. Thus we see that the six themes for existence may constantly repeat if humanity continues to exist and in existing constantly solves and constantly creates new problems of existence. Such a stately succession of themes and movements is the general pattern of the levels of existence.

Bibliography and References

(Although the original bibliographical notes were lost, the following list, compiled by the editors, is contemporary with Dr. Graves's writing of the core manuscript through 1977. It sources quotations and tracks major sources he was likely to have relied upon, based on the existing text.)

4H "4-H is the youth education branch of the Cooperative Extension Service, a program of the United States Department of Agriculture. Each state and each county has access to a County Extension office for both youth and adult programs."

ACE (American Council on Education) One Dupont Circle NW, Washington, DC 20036. Publisher of the College Board examinations (now SAT – Scholastic Aptitude Test).

Adams, Donald K., Mowrer, O.H., Ammons, R.B., Snygg, Donald, Butler, John M., Spence, Kenneth W., Cattell, Raymond B.,Wickens, Delos D., Harlow, Harry F., Wittenborn, J.R., Maier, Norman R.F. (1954). *Learning Theory, Personality Theory, and Clinical Research: The Kentucky Symposium.* New York, Wiley.

Adler, Alfred (1927). *Practice and Theory of Individual Psychology*, New York: Harcourt, Brace, and World.

_____ (1929). *The Science of Living.* New York: Greenberg.

_____ (1931). *What Life Should Mean to You.* Boston: Little, Brown.

_____ (1939). *Social Interest.* New York: Putnam.

_____ (1946). *Understanding Human Nature.* New York: Greenberg.

Adorno, T. W., Frenkel-Brunswik, Else, Levinson, Daniel J., and Sanford, R. Nevitt (1950). *The Authoritarian Personality.* New York: Harper & Row.

Ahammer, Inge M. (1973). In Baltes, Paul B. and Schaie, K. Warner, et al. *Life-Span Developmental Psychology*: *Personality and Socialization.* Academic Press.

Allen, JR., & West, L. J. (1968). Flight from violence: Hippies and the green rebellion. *American Journal of Psychiatry*, 125(3), 364-370.

Allport, Gordon W. (1937). *Personality: A psychological interpretation.* New York: Holt, Rinehart, & Winston.

_____ (1955). *Becoming: Basic considerations for a psychology of personality.* New Haven: Yale University Press.

_____ (1960). *Personality and Social Encounter.* Boston: Beacon Press.

_____ (1961). *Pattern and Growth in Personality.* New York: Holt, Rinehart, and Winston.

Ambrose, J. A. (1960). The development of the smiling response in early infancy. In B.M. Foss (Ed.), *Determinants of Infant Behavior.* London: Methuen & Co., Ltd.. American Psychological Association. Ethical standards of psychologists. Washington, D. C.: APA, 1963.

Aronoff, Joel (1967). *Psychological Needs and Cultural Systems: A Case Study*. Princeton, NJ: Van Nostrand.
Ashby, Walter Ross (1956). *An Introduction to Cybernetics*. London: Chapman & Hall.
_____ (1960). *Design for a Brain*. (2nd ed.). New York: Wiley.
_____ (1958). Requisite Variety and its Implications for the Control of Complex Systems. *Cybernetica*, 1 (2).
Athos, Anthony (1968). *Behavior in Organizations, a Multidemensional View*. New York: Prentice Hall.
Ausubel, David P. (1952). *Ego Development and the Personality Disorders: A Developmental Approach to PsychoPathology*. Grune & Stratton.
_____ (1968). *Educational Psychology: A Cognitive View*. New York: Holt, Rinehart & Winston
Baltes, Paul B. and Warner K. Shaie (1973). *Life-Span Developmental Psychology. Personality and Socialization*. NewYork: Academic Press.
Bandura, Albert (1969). *Principles of behavior modification*. New York: Holt, Rinehart & Winston.
_____ (1997). *Self Efficacy: The exercise of control*. New York: Freeman.
Bandura, A. and Walters, R. H. *Social Learning and Personality Development*. New York: Holt, Rinehart, and Winston, 1963.
Bard. P. & Rioch, D. (1937). A Study of Four Cats Deprived of Neocortex and Additional Portions of the Forebrain. *John Hopkins Hospital Bulletin*, 60, p. 73-147.
Barker, Roger G. (1957). Structure of the Stream of Behavior. *Proceedings of the Fifteenth International Congress of Psychology, Brussels, Amsterdam*. North Holland Publishing, p. 155-156.
Barron, Frank (1954). Personal soundness in university graduate students. *Publications in Personality Assessment and Research*. No. 1. Berkeley: University of California Press.
_____ (1963). *Creativity and Psychological Health*. Princeton: D. Van Nostrand Company, Inc. .
Bartlett, Frederic C. (1932). *Remembering: A Study in Experimental and Social Psychology*. Cambridge: Cambridge University Press.
Bavelas, Alex (1948). "Mathematical model for group structures." *Applied Anthropology*, p. 7.
_____ (1950). Communication Patterns in Task-Oriented Groups. *Journal of the Acoustical Society of America* 22, p. 725-730. [Professor of Psychology, founder of the Group Networks Laboratory at MIT in 1948, pioneer in group communications and social networks at MIT.]
_____ (1950). Bavelas et al. Human communications systems. *Quarterly Progress Report*, Research Laboratory of Electronics, M I T, July, p. 81-86.
_____ (1952). In H. von Foerster (Ed.), Communication patterns in problem-solving groups. *Cybernetics - circular, causal and feedback mechanisms in biological and social systems. Transactions of the eighth conference*. New York: Josiah Macy, Jr. Foundation.

Bibliography

_____ (1963). Teleconferencing: Background Information. *Research Paper P-106*, Institute for Defense Analysis, p. 4.

_____ (1948). A mathematical model for group structure. *Human Organization*, 7:16-30.

_____ (1950). Communication patterns in task-oriented groups. *Journal of the Acoustical Society of America.* 22:271-282.

Bavelas, Alex and Barret, Dermot (1950). An Experimental Approach to Organizational Communication. *Personnel* 27, p. 366-371.

Bentham, Jeremy (1962). In John Bowring (Ed.), *The Works of Jeremy Bentham.* New York.

Bergson, Henri L. (1913). *Time and Free Will: An Essay on the Immediate data of Consciousness.* New York: Macmillan.

_____ (1946). *The Creative Mind.* New York: Philosophical Library.

_____ (1954). *The Two Sources of Morality and Religion.* (First published in France, 1932) Garden City: Doubleday, Anchor.

Berlyne, Daniel E. (1960). *Conflict, Arousal, and Curiosity.* New York: McGraw Hill.

_____ (1967). Arousal and Reinforcement, *Nebraska Symposium on Motivation.* University of Nebraska Press, Vol 15, p 1-110.

_____ (1970). Novelty, complexity, and hedonic value. *Perception and Psychophysics*, 8, November, p. 279-286.

Bingham, W. E., & Griffiths, W. J., Jr. (1952). The effect of different environments during infancy on adult behavior in the rat. *Journal of Comparative and Physiological Psychology*, Vol. 45, p. 307-312.

Blake, Robert R. and Mouton, Jane S. (1964). *The Managerial Grid: Key Orientations or Achieving Production through People.* Houston: Gulf Publishing Co..

Blasi, Arthur (1976). Concept of development in personality theory. In Jane Loevinger, *Ego Development: Conceptions and Theories.* San Francisco: Jossey Bass. p. 29-53.

_____ *Self, Ego and Identity: Integrative approaches.* New York: Springer, p. 226-243. [Ref to 1971 in *Journal of Personality Assessment* 2001, Vol. 77, No. 3, Pages 541-567 "A Critical Review of the Validity of Ego Development Theory and Its Measurement." John Manners Gilmore and Kevin Durkin.]

_____ (1980). Bridging Moral Cognition and Moral Action: A Critical Review of the Literature. *Psychological Bulletin,* 88, p. 1-45.

Blatt, Moshe (1969). "Studies on the Effects of Classroom Discussions upon Children's Moral Development." Ph.D. dissertation, University of Chicago. Ann Arbor, MI: University Microfilms.

Blatt, Moshe, Colby, Ann, and Speicher, Betsy (1974). Hypothetical Dilemmas for Use in Moral Discusison. Cambridge, MA: Harvard University Center for Moral Education. Mimeographed.

Blatt, Moshe, and Kohlberg, Lawrence (1975). The Effect of Classrooms' Moral Discussion upon Children's Level of Moral Judgment. *Journal of*

Moral Education. 4: 129-61 [also see *Recent Research in Moral Development*, edited by Lawrence Kohlberg and Eliot Turiel, New York: Holt]

Blatz, William E. (1966). *Human Security: Some Reflections.* Toronto: University of Toronto Press.

Blatz, William Emet and Bott, Helen McMurchie (1928). *Parents and the pre-school child.* London; Toronto: J.M. Dent.

Blos, Peter (1941). *The Adolescent Personality.* New York: Appleton.

_____ (1962). *On Adolescence: A Psychoanalytic Interpretation.* New York: Free Press.

Bott, Helen McMurchie and William E. Blatz (1930). *The management of young children.* New York: William Morrow & Company.

Boas, Franz (1911). *The Mind of Primitive Man.* New York: MacMillan (Free Press, 1963).

Bowlby, J. (1958). The Nature of the Child's Tie to his Mother. *International Journal of Psychoanalysis*, 39, p. 1-24.

Brackbill, Y. (1958). Extinction of the Smiling Response in Infants as a Function of Reinforcement Schedule. *Child Development*, 29, p. 115-124.

Brady, J. V. (1960). Emotional behavior. In J. Field (Ed.), *Handbook of Physiology. Sect I Neurophysiology. Vol. III.* Washington, D. C.: American Physiological Society.

Bricker, P. D., and Alphonse Chapanis (1953). Do incorrectly perceived tachistoscopic stimuli convey some information? *Psychological Review*, 60, p.181-188.

Brock, T. C. (1962). Cognitive Restructuring and Attitude Change. *Journal of Abnormal Social Psychology*, Vol. 54, No. 4, p. 264-271.

Brogden. W. J. (1951). Animal Studies of Learning. In S. S. Stevens (Ed.), *Handbook of Experimental Psychology.* New York: Wiley, p. 568-612.

Bronson, Gordon (1965). The Hierarchical Organization of the Central Nervous System: Implications for Learning Processes and Critical Periods in Early Development. *Behavioral Science*, Vol. 10, No. 1, Jan. 1965, p. 7-25.

Broughton, John M. (1975). The Development of Natural Epistemology in Adolescence and Early Adulthood. Unpublished doctoral dissertation, Graduate School of Education, Harvard University.

_____ (1987). An Introduction to Critical Developmental Psychology. In J. M. Broughton (Ed.), *Critical Theories of Psychological Development.* New York: Plenum.

Bruner, J. S. (1957). On Perceptual Readiness. *Psychological Review*, 64, 123-152.

Bruner, J. S., Matter, J., & Papanek, M. (1955). Breadth of Learning as a Function of Drive Level and Mechanization. *Psychological Review*, 62, 1-10.

Bruner, J.S. and Postman, L. (1947). Emotional Selectivity in Perception and Reaction. *Journal of Personality,* 16, 69-77.

Bugental, James F. T. (1963). Humanistic psychology: A new breakthrough. *American Psychologist*, 18, 563-567.

Bibliography

_____ (1965). *The Search for Authenticity*. New York: Holt, Rinehart and Winston.

_____ (1967). *Challenges of Humanistic Psychology*. New York: Psychology. Psychological Service Associates, Los Angeles: McGraw-Hill Book Company.

Buhler, Charlotte (1930). *The First Year of Life*. New York: Day.

_____ (1933). *Der Menschliche Lebenslauf Als Psychologisches Problem (The Course of Human Life as a Psychological Problem)*. Leipzig: S. Hirzel, (2nd ed., Gottingoen: Hogrefe, 1959).

_____ (1959). Theoretical observations about life's basic tendencies. *American Journal of Psychotherapy*. 1959, 13:3, 561-581

_____ (1962). *Values in Psychotherapy*. New York: Free Press.

_____ (1964).The Human Course of Life in Its Goal Aspects. *Journal of Humanistic Psychology*. Spring 1964. p. 1-18.

_____ (1968). The course of Human Life as a Psychological Problem. *Human Development,* 11 (3), p. 184-200.

_____ (1968). *The Course of Human Life: A Study of Goals in the Humanistic Perspective*. Charlotte Buhler and Fred Massarik, (eds.) New York: Springer Pub. Co..

_____ (1972). *Introduction to Humanistic Psychology*. Bellmont, California: Wadsworth Publishing Co., Inc..

Bull, Norman J. (1969). *Moral Judgement from Childhood to Adolecence*. Beverly Hills, CA: Sage Publications.

Burlingame, Roger (1956). *Henry Ford: The Greatest Success Story in the History of Industry*. New York: Signet Key Books.

Butler, R. A. (1954). Incentive Conditions Which Influence Visual Exploration. *Journal of Experimental Psychology*, Vol. 48, p. 19-23.

Calhoun, John B. (1962). Population Density and Social Pathology. *Scientific American*. February, p. 139; (See: *Environment and Population: Problems of Adaptation*. New York: Praeger Scientific, 1983).

_____ (1963). *The Ecology and Sociology of the Norway Rat*. Public Health Service Publication No. 1008 U.S. Dept. of Health, Education, and Welfare, Public Health Service.

_____ (1968). Space and the Strategy of Life. Unpublished paper presented at the American Association for the Advancement of Science 135th Annual Meeting, Dallas, TX.

_____ (1969). Promotion of Man. Unpublished Paper. URBSDOC 146, Bethesda, MD.

_____ (1970). Levels of Existence re Gravesian Philosophy: Random Notes by John B. Calhoun for evening seminar discussion.

_____ (1971). Rx Evolution, Tribalism, and the Cheshire Cat: Three Paths from Now. Unpublished paper. URBSDOC 167. Bethesda, MD: Unit for Research on Behavioral Systems, Laboratory of Psychology, NIMH.

_____ (1973). Metascientific Research. 16 April, 1973, URBS Doc 219.1 unpublished paper, NIMH: Unit for Research on Behavioral Systems, Laboratory of Psychology.

Calvin, John (1949). *Institutes of the Christian Religion.* 8th Ed. Translated by John Allen. Grand Rapids: Eerdmans. (Also quoted by Robert Coles in The New Yorker for January 3, 1970, p. 63).

Camus, Albert. (1955). *The Myth of Sisyphus.* New York: Random House, Vintage Books.

_____ (1957). *The Rebel: An essay on man in revolt.* New York: Knopf.

_____ (1964). *Carnets.* Paris: Gallimard.

Christie, Richard (1970). *Studies in Machiavellianism.* New York: Academic Press.

Coleman, James C. (1969). Hierarchy in the Brain: Implications for Learning and Critical Periods, Psychology and Effective Behavior. *Behavioral Science.* Vol. 10, p. 7-25.

College Board Exams (known today as the "SAT" - Scholastic Aptitude Test). The College Board Headquarters, 45 Columbus Avenue, New York, NY 10023-6992.

Condorcet, Marie Jean Antoine Nicolas Caritat, marquis de (1822). *Esquisse d'un tableau historique des progrès de l'esprit humain.* Paris: Masson et Fils.

Cone, John D. and Hawkins, Robert (Eds.), (1977). *Behavioral Assessment: New Directions in Clinical Psychology.* NY: Bruner/Mazel.

Conel, J. LeR. (1939). *The Postnatal Development of the Human Cerebral Cortex. Cortex of the Newborn.* Cambridge, MA: Harvard University Press.

_____ (1941). *The Postnatal Development of the Human Cerebral Cortex II. Cortex of the One-Month Infant.* Cambridge, MA: Harvard University Press.

Darrow, Clarence (1932). *The Story of My Life.* New York, NY: Grosset's Universal Library.

Darrow, Clarence and Crowe, Robert E. (1923). *Attorney Clarence Darrow's Plea for Mercy and Prosecutor Robert E. Crowe's Demand for the Death Penalty in the Loeb Leopold Case: the Crime of a Century.* Chicago: Wilson Publishing Co..

Darwin, Charles (1859). *On the Origin of Species by Means of Natural Selection, or the Preservation of Favoured Races in the Struggle for Life.* London: John Murray, Albemarle Street.

Dewey, John (1920). *Reconstruction in Philosophy.* New York: Henry Holt and Company.

_____ (1929). *Experience and Nature.* New York: W. W. Norton & Company.

Dell, P. C. (1958). Some Basic Mechanisms of the Translation of Bodily Needs into Behavior. In G. E. W. Wolstenholme & C. M O'Conner (Eds.) *Symposium on the Neurological Basis of Behavior.* Boston: Little, Brown.

Doty, R. W. and Giurgea, C. (1961). Conditioned reflexes established by coupling electrical excitation of two cortical areas. In J. Delafresnaye (Ed.). *Brain Mechanisms and Learning.* Oxford: Blackwell, 1961.

Doty, R. W. (1969). Electrical stimulation of the brain in behavioral context. *Annual Review of Psychology,* 20, p. 289-320.

Doty, B. and Daiman, R. (1969). Diphenylhydantoin effects on avoidance conditioning as a function of age and problem difficulty. *Psychos. Sci.*, Vol. 14, p. 109-111.

Doty, B., & Doty L. (1966). Facilitating effects of amphetamine on avoidance conditioning in relation to age and problem difficulty. *Psychopharmacology*, Vol. 9, p. 234-241.

Drews, Elizabeth M.

_____ (1962). Dialogue on Communication. In Hitchcock, A. (Ed.), *Guidance and the Utilization of New Educational Media: Report of the 1962 Conference*. American Personnel and Guidance Association. Washington, D.C., 1-47, 63-68.

_____ (1963). The four faces of able adolescents. *Saturday Review*, 68-71.

_____ (1964, 1965, 1966). *The Creative Intellectual Style in Gifted Adolescents*. Vols. I, II, and III. Lansing, MI: Michigan State University.

_____ (1968b). Fernwood, a free school. *Journal of Humanistic Psychology*, 8(2), n.p.

_____ (1966). The Creative Intellectual Style in Gifted Adolescents, Report II; Report III; Portland, OR: Northwest Regional Educational Research Laboratory, 1966.

_____ (1972). *Learning Together*. Englewood Cliffs, NJ: Prentice-Hall.

Drews, E.M., and Lipson L. (1971). *Values and Humanity*. New York: St. Martin's Press.

Driesch, Hans Adolf Eduard (1905). *The history & theory of vitalism*. Authorised translation by C. K. Ogden (1914). Rev. and in part rewritten for the English ed. by the author. London: Macmillan and Co..

_____ (1929). *The Science and Philosophy of the Organism. The Gifford Lectures Delivered Before the University of Aberdeen in the Year 1907*. 2nd Edition. London: Adam and Charles Black.

_____ (1925). *The Crisis in Psychology*. Princeton: Princeton University Press.

_____ (1927). *Mind and Body*. New York: L. MacVeagh, The Dial Press.

_____ (1929). *Man in the Universe*. New York.

Driver, Michael J. (1960). The relationship between abstractness of conceptual functioning and group performance in a complex decision making environment. Unpublished masters thesis, Princeton University.

Edwards, Allen L. (1957). *The social desirability variable in personality assessment and research*. New York: Holt, Rinehart and Winston.

_____ (EPPS) Edwards Personal Preference Scale. The Psychological Corporation.

_____ (1967). Edwards Personality Inventory. (EPI), Science Research Associates, Inc.

Edwards, A. L. and Abbott, R. D. (1972). The R scale and acquiescent tendencies on scales consisting of items from the CPI, EPI, and PRF. *Psychological Reports*. 31, p. 303-306.

_____ (1973). Relationships between the EPI Scales and the 16 PF, CPI, and EPPS scales. *Educational and Psychological Measurement*, 33, 231-238.

_____ (1973). Relationships between the EPI scales and the EPPS and PRF scales. *Journal of Consulting and Clinical Psychology*, 40, 27-32.

Elkind, David (1971). Cognitive Growth Cycles in Mental Development. *Nebraska Symposium on Motivation*. Lincoln, NE: University of Nebraska Press.

_____ (1975). Recent Research on Cognitive Development in Adolescence. In Dragastin, S.E., and Elder, G. H., Jr. *Adolescence in the Life Cycle: Psychological Change and the Social Context*. New York: Halsted Press.

Elkind, David and Flavell, John H. (Eds.) (1969). *Studies in Cognitive Development: Essays in Honour of Jean Piaget*. New York: Oxford University Press.

Engen, T., Lipsitt, L. P., Lewis, P., and Kaye, H. (1963). Olfactory responses and adaptation in the human neonate. *Journal of Comparative and Physiological Psychology*. Vol. 56, p. 73-77.

Engen, T and Levy, N. (1956). Constant-Sum Judgments of Facial Expressions. *Journal of Experimental Psychology*. Vol. 51, p. 396-398.

Erikson, Erik Homburger (1950). *Childhood and Society*. New York: Norton.

_____ (1959). Identity and the Life Cycle: selected papers. *Psychological Issues, Monograph No. 1*. New York: International University Press. (see "Growth and Crises of the Healthy Personality.")

_____ (1964). *Insight and Responsibility*. New York: Norton.

_____ (1968). *Identity: Youth and Crisis*. New York: Norton.

Eysenck, Hans J. (1947). *Dimensions of Personality*. London: Routledge and Kegan Paul.

_____ (1952). *The Scientific Study of Personality*. London: Routledge and Kegan Paul.

_____ (1953). *The Structure of Human Personality*. London: Methuen.

_____ (1959). Learning Theory and Behavior Therapy. *Journal of Mental Science*, 105: 61 75.

_____ (1963). Eysenck Personality Inventory.

_____ (1967). The Dynamics of Anxiety and Hysteria: An experimental application of modern learning theory to psychiatry, (3rd imp. 1st-1957).

_____ (1967). *The Biological Basis of Personality*. Springfield: C. C. Thomas.

_____ (1970). *Readings in Extraversion-Introversion: Theoretical and Methodological Issues*. New York: John Wiley and Sons.

Eysenck, Hans J. and Rachman, S. (1965). *The Causes and Cures of Neurosis: An Introduction to Modern Behaviour Therapy based on Learning Theory and the Principles of Conditioning*. San Diego: R. R. Knapp, Educational and Industrial Training Service.

Fenton, Edwin, Colby, Ann, and Speicher-Dubin, Betsy (1974). "Developing Moral Dilemmas for Social Studies Classes." Mimeogaphed. Cambridge, MA.: Harvard University, Center for Moral Education (cited in Mosher, Ralph (1980). *Moral Education: A First Generation of Research and Development*. New York: Praeger. p. 223)

Festinger, Leon (1954). A theory of social comparison processes. *Human Relations*. 7:117-40.

_____ (1957). *A Theory of Cognitive Dissonance*. Stanford: Stanford University Press.
Festinger, Leon and Aronson, E. (1960). The Arousal and Reduction of Dissonance in Social Contexts. In D. Cartwright and A. Zander (Eds.), *Group Dynamics*. Evanston, IL: Row, Peterson, p. 214-231.
Festinger, L., Riecken, H.W. and Schachter, S. (1956). *When Prophesy Fails*. Minneapolis: University of Minnesota Press.
Flavell, John H. (1969). see Elkind.
Forgays, D. G. (1962). The Importance of Experience at Specific Times in the Development of an Organism. Paper presented at the meeting of the Eastern Psychological Association, April.
Forgays, D. G. and Forgays, J. (1952). The Nature of the Effect of Free-Environmental Experience in the Rat. *Journal of Comparative and Physiological Psychology*. Vol. 45, p. 322-328.
Frankl, Viktor (1946). *Man's Search for Meaning*. New York: Washington Square Press.
_____ (1959). *From Death Camp to Existentialism*. Boston: Beacon.
_____ (1967). *Psychotherapy and Existentialism*. New York: Washington Square Press.
Freud, Sigmund (1933). *New Introductory Lectures on Psychoanalysis*. New York: W.E. Norton Co., Inc. 1965.
_____ (1938). Brill, A. A., (ed.) *The Basic Writings of Sigmund Freud: (Psychopathology of Everyday Life, the Interpretation of Dreams, and Three Contributions To the Theory of Sex)*. New York: The Modern Library
_____ (1912). Release of On the Dynamics of Transference, On the Universal Tendency to Debasement in the Sphere of Love and On Beginning the Treatment.
_____ (1912). A note on the unconscious in psycho-analysis. S.E., 12:260-266.
_____ (1912). Contributions to a discussion on masturbation. S.E., 12:243-254.
_____ (1912). On the universal tendency to debasement in the sphere of love. S.E., 11:179-190.
_____ (1912). Recommendations to physicians practising psycho-analysis. S.E., 12:111-120.
_____ (1912). The dynamics of transference. S.E., 12:99-108.
_____ (1912). Types of onset of neurosis. S.E., 12:231-238.
_____ (1901). Psychopathology of Everyday Life. Translation by A. A. Brill (1914). Originally published in London by T. Fisher Unwin,.
_____ (1923). The Ego and the Id. In J. Strachey (Ed. and Trans.), *The Standard Edition of the Complete Psychological Works of Sigmund Freud* (vol. 19, p. 3-66). London: Hogarth Press .
_____ (1933). *New Introductory Lectures on Psychoanalysis*. New York: W.E. Norton Co., Inc. 1965.
_____ (1948). *Beyond the Pleasure Principle*. London: Hogarth.

Fromm, Eric (1941). *Escape from Freedom*. New York: Holt, Rinehart & Winston.
_____ (1947). *Man for Himself: An Inquiry into the Psychology of Ethics*. New York: Rinehart.
_____ (1955). *The Sane Society*. New York: Rinehart & Co.
_____ (1959). Values, Psychology and Human Existence. In A. E. Maslow (Ed.), *New Knowledge in Human Values*. New York: Harper.
_____ (1960). *The Fear of Freedom*. London: Routledge.
Funkenstein, D.H. (1955). The physiology of fear and anger. *Scientific American*, 74:192-193.
Funkenstein, D.H., King, S.H. and Drolette, Margaret E. (1953). The Experimental Evocation of Stress. Presented 18 March 1953, to the Symposium on Stress, AMSGS, WRAMC, Washington, D. C. From the Dept. of Psychiatry, Harvard Medical School, the Dept. of Social Relations, Harvard University, and the Dept. of Biostatistics, Harvard School of Public Health.
_____ (1957). *Mastery of Stress*. Cambridge: Harvard University Press.
Gastaut, H. (1958). Conditioned reflexes and behavior. In G. E. W. Wolstenholme & C. M. O'Conner (Eds.), *Symposium on the neurological basis of behavior*. Boston: Little, Brown.
Gaustaut, H., & Roger, A. (1966). Les mecanismes de l'activité nerveuse supérieure envisagds au niveau des graades structures fonctionnelles du cerveau. In H. H. Jasper & G. D. Smirnov (Eds.), *The Moscow colloquium on electroencephalography of higher nervous activity*. Montreal: EEG Journal.
Gloor, P. (1960). The Amygdala. In J. Field (Ed.). *Handbook of Physiology*. Sect. I, Neurophysiology. Vol II.. Washington, D. C.: American Physiological Society.
Goethe   (see von Goethe)
Goldstein, Kurt (1939). *The Organsim: A Holistic Approach to Biology Derived from Pathological Data in Man*. New York: American Book Co.
_____ (1940). *Human Nature (in the Light of Psychopathology)*. Cambridge, Mass.: Harvard University Press.
Goldstein, Kurt and Scheerer, M. (1941). Abstract and Concrete Behavior - An Experimental Study With Special Tests. *Psychological Monographs*. Vol. 53, No. 2, p. 110-130.
Goldstein, Kurt and Scheerer, M. (1947). Goldstein-Scheerer Test of Abstract and Concrete Thinking.
Gough, H. G. (1961) The Adjective Check List. Palo Alto, CA: Consulting Psychologists Press.
Gough, H. G., & Sanford, R.N. (1952). Rigidity as a Psychological Variable. Unpublished manuscript, University of California, Institute of Personality Assessment and Research.
Gray, Thomas (1751). "Elegy Written in a Country Churchyard." London.
Gray, William (1977). *General System Precursor Formation Theory*. Cambridge, MA: Aristocrat.

Bibliography

Gray, William, Duhl, Frederick J. and Rizzo, Nicholas D. (Eds.). (1969). *General Systems Theory and Psychiatry*. Boston, MA: Little, Brown and Company.

Gray, William and Rizzo, Nicholas D. (Eds.). (1973). *Unity Through Diversity: A Festschrift for Ludwig van Bertalanffy*. New York: Gordon and Breach.

Graves, Clare W. (1959). An emergent theory of ethical behavior based upon an epigenetic model. Unpublished paper, Schenectady, NY.

_____ (1961). On the Theory of Ethical Behavior. Paper presented at the First Unitarian Society of Schenectady, NY.

_____ (1962, November). Implications to Management of Systems-Ethical Theory. Proceedings of the 3rd Annual Values Conference. Schenectady, NY: Value Analysis, Inc.

_____ (1964). Levels of Human Existence and their Relation to Value Analysis and Engineering. Proceedings of the 5th Annual Values Conference. Schenectady, NY: Value Analysis, Inc.

_____ (1965, February). Value systems and their relation to managerial controls and organizational viability. Paper presented at the College of Management Philosophy, The Institute of Management Sciences, San Francisco, CA.

_____ (1966). Deterioration of Work Standards. *Harvard Business Review*, Boston, MA: Sept.-Oct., Vol. 44, No. 5, p 117-126.

_____ (1967). On the Theory of Value. Paper presented at the National Institutes of Mental Health, Washington, DC.

_____ (1969, March). Motivation-wise, executives are reluctant dragons. Keynote address presented at the Institute on Motivation and Productivity of the Public Personnel Association, The Hudson-Mohawk Training Directors Society, The Industrial Training Council, and The Capital District Personnel Association, Albany, NY.

_____ (1970). Levels of Existence: An Open System Theory of Values. *Journal of Humanistic Psychology*, Fall, Vol. 10, No. 2, p. 131-155.

_____ (1970, May). Personal dimensions of student disaffection. Paper presented at the 175th anniversary celebration of the founding of Union College, Schenectady, NY.

_____ (1970, May). The Levels of Existence and their relation to welfare problems. Paper presented at the Annual Conference Meeting, Virginia State Department of Welfare and Distribution, Roanoke, VA.

_____ (1971, March). Levels of Existence related to learning systems. Paper presented at the Ninth Annual Conference of the National Society for Programming Instruction, Rochester, NY.

_____ (1971, October). A Systems Conception of Personality: Remarks by Clare W. Graves on his Levels of Existence Theory. Presented at the Washington School of Psychiatry, Washington, DC. Transcription and handout compiled in Lee, William R., Cowan, Christopher C. and Todorovic, Natasha (Eds.) (2003). *Graves: Levels of Human Existence*. Santa Barbara, CA: ECLET Publishing.

_____ (1971, November). How Should Whom Lead Who to Do What? Paper presented at the YMCA Management Forum of 1971-1972, Downtown Branch YMCA, St. Louis, MO.

_____ (1971). Untitled Presentation. Annual Meeting of The Association of Humanistic Psychology.

_____ (1973, March). Let Us Bring Humanistic and General Psychology Together: A Research Project Needing to Become. Paper presented at National Institutes of Mental Health, Washington, DC.

_____ (1973, October). Seminar Notes. Presentation at the Quetico Centre, Ontario, Canada.

_____ (1974). Human Nature Prepares for a Momentous Leap. *The Futurist.* April, 1974, p. 72-87.

_____ (1974). Seminar recordings, Quetico Centre, Canada, June, 1974.

_____ (1978). Notes for "Up the Existential Staircase: A seminar on the Development, Nature, Meaning and Management of The Levels of Existence, Emergent, Cyclical, Double Helix Model of Adult Human Psychosocial Coping Systems." Unpublished paper.

_____ (1978). Levels of Complexity. Paper presented at North Texas State University, Denton, TX.

_____ (1980). Seminar at the National Values Center in Dallas, TX, December 1980. (audio tape)

_____ (1981, May). Summary Statement: The Emergent, Cyclical, Double-Helix Model Of The Adult Human Biopsychosocial Systems. Paper presented to the World Future Society, Boston, MA.

_____ (1982). Seminar handout. Unpublished paper.

_____ (2001). *ECLET: Emergent Cyclical Levels of Existence Theory: A Workshop with Dr. Clare W. Graves* [Audio tape]. Santa Barbara, CA: ECLET Publishing. (1974)

_____ (2001). *Reflections* [Audio tape]. Santa Barbara, CA: ECLET Publishing. (1980)

_____ (2001). *The Psychological Map* [Audio tape]. Santa Barbara, CA: ECLET Publishing. (1980)

Graves, Clare W., Huntley, W. C., and LaBier, Douglas (1965). "Personality Structure and Perceptual Readiness: An Investigation of their Relationship to Hypothesized Levels of Human Existence." Unpublished paper, Union College. Unpublished paper.

Graves, Clare W., Madden, Helen T., and Madden, Lynn P. (1970). The Congruent Management Strategy. Unpublished paper based on an industrial study.

Guyton, A. C. (1961). *Textbook of Medical Physiology.* Philadelphia: Saunders.

Hall, Calvin and Lindsey, Gardner (1957). *Theories of Personality.* New York: John Wiley & Sons.

Hampshire, Sir Stuart (1959). *Thought and Action.* New York: Viking.

Harlow, H. F. and Zimmermann, R. R. (1959). Affectional Responses in the Infant Monkey. *Science,* Vol. 130, p. 421-432.

Hartmann, Heinz (1958). *Ego Psychology and the Problem of Adaptation.* New York: International Universities Press.
_____ (1964). *Essays on Ego Psychology: Selected Problems in Psychoanalytic Theory.* New York: International Universities Press.
Harvey, O. J. (Ed.) (1966). *Experience, Structure and Adaptability.* New York: Springer Publishing Co..
Harvey, O.J., Hunt, David and Schroder, Harold M. (1961). *Conceptual Systems and Personality Organization.* New York: John Wiley and Sons.
Havighurst, Robert (1948). *Developmental tasks and education.* New York: David McKay Co..
Hawkins, Robert P., Peterson, R. F., Schweid, E. and Bijou, S W. (1966). Behavior therapy in the home: amelioration of problem parent-child relations with the parent in a therapeutic role. *Journal of Experimental Child Psychology,* 4:99-107.
_____ (1972). It's time we taught the young how to be good parents (and don't you wish we'd started a long time ago?). *Psychology Today,* 11:28-40.
_____ Cone, John D. & Hawkins, Robert P. (1977). *Behavioral Assessment: New Directions in Clinical Psychology.* New York: Brunner/Mazel Publishers.
Haymuy, T. P. (1961). The Role of the Cerebral Cortex in the Learning of an Instrumental Conditioned Response. In A. Fessard, R. W. Gerard, & J. Konorski (Eds.), *Brain Mechanisms and Learning.* Springfield, Illinois: Thomas.
Heard, Gerald (1941). *Man the Master.* New York: Harper and Brothers.
_____ (1963). *The Five Ages of Man.* New York: The Julian Press, Inc..
Hebb, Donald O. (1949). *The Organization of Behavior: A Neuropsychological Theory.* New York: Wiley.
_____ (1955). Drives and the CNS (central nervous system) *Psychological Review,* 62, 243-254
_____ (1958). *A Textbook of Psychology.* Philadelphia: Saunders.
_____ (1937). The innate organization of visual activity: I. Perception of figures by rats reared in total darkness. *Journal of Genetic Psychology,* 51:101-126.
_____ (1966). *A Textbook of Psychology.* Philadelphia: Saunders.
Heider, Fritz (1958). *The Psychology of Interpersonal Relations.* New York: John Wiley & Sons.
Hernandez-Peon, R. and Brust-Carmona, H. (1961). The Functional Role of Sub-cortical Structure in Habituation and Conditioning. In Fessard, A., Garard, R. W., and Konorski, J., (Eds.). *Brain Mechanisms and Learning.* Springfield: Thomas.
_____ (1966). In R.W. Russel (Ed.). *Frontiers in physiological psychology.* New York: Academic Press.
Herndon, Booton (1969). *Ford: An Unconventional Biography of the Men and Their Times.* New York: Weybright & Talley
Herzberg, Frederick I. (1959). *The Motivation to Work.* New York: Wiley.

_____ (1955 and 1966). *Work and the Nature of Man*. Cleveland: World Publishing Cleveland.
Hess, E. H. (1959). Imprinting. *Science*, 130, p. 133-141.
_____ (1972). Pupilometrics. In N. S. Greenfield and R. A. Stembach (Eds.) *Handbook of Psychophysiology*. New York: Holt, Richard & Winston, p. 491- 531.
Hess, R. D. and Shipman, V. C. (1965). Early Experience and the Socialization of Cognitive Mode - Children. *Child Development*. Published by the University of Chicago Press for the Society for Research in Child Development, Inc., 36, p. 859-886.
_____ (1967). Cognitive elements in maternal behavior. In J. P. Hill (Ed.), *Minnesota Symposia on Child Psychology* (Vol. 1). Minneapolis: University of Minnesota Press.
Hess, W. R. (1936). Le sommeil. C. r. *Soc. Biol.* Paris 1931, 107, 1333 and _____ Hypothalamus und die Zentren des autonomen Nervensystems: Physiologie, Arch. f. Psychiatrie, 1936, 103, 548. Cited in Ransom, S. W. and Magoun, H. W. The hypothalamus *Ergbn. Physiol.*, 1939 41, 56-163
Hess, E. H. (1965). Attitude and pupil size. *Scientific American*, 212 46-54.
Hess, E H and Polt, J M (1964). Pupil size in relation to mental activity during simple problem solving. *Science*, 143 p. 1190-1192. Cited in Ransom, S. W. and Magoun, H. W. The hypothalamus *Ergbn. Physiol.*, 1939 41, 56-163
Hinde, R. A. (1962). Sensitive Periods and the Development of Behavior. In S. A. Barnett (Ed.) *Lessons from Animal Behavior for the Clinician*. London: National Spastics Society Study Group and Heinemann Medical Books, Ltd..
Hokfelt, Bernt (1951). Noradrenaline and adrenaline in mammalian tissues; distribution under normal and pathological conditions with special reference to the endocrine system. Stockholm: Zetterlund and Thelander. (In *Acta Physiologica Scandinavica*, v. 25, Supplement 92)
_____ (1971). Catechol Conent of the mammalian (including human) suprarenal from foetal to adult stages. Scandinavian Physiological Congress, Abstracts of Communications. *Acta Physiologica Scandinavia*, v. 25, Supp 89, p. 41-43.
Hoover, President Herbert. 1951 speech at the Iowa Centennial Foundation.
Horney, Karen (1939). *New Ways in Psychoanalysis*. New York: W. W. Norton & Co. Inc..
_____ (1950). *Neurosis and Human Growth*. New York: W. W. Norton & Company.
Howe, M. J. A. (1970). *Introduction to Human Memory*. New York, Harper & Row, Publishers, Inc..
_____ (1970). Repeated presentation and recall of meaningful prose. *Journal of Educational Psychology*, 61: 214-19.
_____ (1975). *Learning in Infants and Young Children*. London: McMillan.

Howes, David (1954). On the Interpretation of Word Frequency as a Variable Affecting Speed of Recognition. *Journal of Experimental Psychology.* Vol. 48, p. 106-112.

Howes, D.H. and Solomon, R.L. (1951). Visual duration threshold as a function of word-probability. *Journal of Experimental Psychology*, Vol. 41, p. 401-410.

Hudgins, C. V. (1933). Conditioning and voluntary control of the papillary light reflex. *Journal of General Psychology*, 8, p. 3-51.

Hunt, D. E. (1961). Manual for judging free responses from Situational Interpretation Experiment. Unpublished manuscript.

Hunt, David E. and Sullivan, Edmund V. (1974). *Between Psychology and Education.* Hinsdale, IL.: Dryden Press.

Hunter, Evan (1954). *The Blackboard Jungle.* New York: Simon & Schuster.

Hunter, W. S. and Hudgins, C. V. (1934). Voluntary activity from the standpoint of behaviorism. *Journal of General Psychology*, 10, p. 198-204.

Hymovitch, B. (1952). The Effects of Experimental Variations on Problem Solving in the Rat. *Journal of Comparative and Physiological Psychology*, Vol. 45, p. 313-321.

Ionesco, Eugene. *The New Yorker.* 1960, p.47.

Isaacs, K. S. (1956). Relatability: A Proposed Construct and an Approach to Its Validation. Unpublished doctoral dissertation. University of Chicago.

_____ (2005). Unpublished tapes and personal conversations with the editors. (Also see *Uses of Emotion: Nature's Vital Gift.* Westport, CT: Praeger, 1998.)

Isaacs, K.S., Alexander, J., and Haggard, E. A. (1963). Faith, trust and gullibility. *International Journal of Psycho-Analysis*, Vol. 44.

Jaspers, Karl (1955). *Reason and Existenz.* New York: Noonday Press.

_____ (1964). *General Psychopathology.* Chicago: University of Chicago Press.

Jefferson, Thomas (1905). *The Writings of Thomas Jefferson.* In Andrew Lipscomb, A. Andrew and Albert Ellery Bergh (Eds.) Washington DC: The Thomas Jefferson Memorial Association.

Jersild, A. T. (1946). Emotional Development. In L. Carmichael (Ed.) *Manual of Child Psychology.* New York: Wiley.

Josephson, Matthew (1934). *The Robber Barons.* New York: Harcourt, Brace, and Co..

Jung, Carl G. (1959). Psychological Aspects of the Mother Archetype. In *Collected Works.* Vol. 9, Part 1: Archetypes and the Collective Unconscious. New York: Bollingen Series XX.

Jung, Carl G. (1959). Phenomenology of the spirit in fairy tales (R. F. C. Hull, Trans.). In H. Read et al. (Series Eds.). *The collected works of C.G. Jung* (vol. 9 pt. 1, pp. 207-254). New York: Pantheon. (Original work published 1948).

_____ (1961). *Memories, Dreams, Reflections.* New York: Vintage Books.

_____ (1964). *Man and His Symbols.* New York: Dell Publishing.

_____ (1969). The Structure and Dynamics of the Psyche. *Collected Works*, 8. Princeton, NJ: Princeton University Press.

_____ (1969). Psychology and Religion: West and East. *Collected Works*, 11. Princeton, NJ: Princeton University Press.

_____ (1970). Aion. Researches into the Phenomenology of the Self. *Collected Works*, 9, 11. Princeton, NJ: Princeton University Press.

_____ (1970). Mysterium Coniunctionis. *Collected Works*, 14. Princeton, NJ: Princeton University Press.

_____ (1971). Psychological Types. *Collected Works*, 6. Princeton, NJ: Princeton University Press.

_____ (1972). *The Collected Works of C. G. Jung*. (20 vols. ed. by H. Read, M. Fordham, G. Adler, NY, 1953. Translated by Richard Francis Carrington Hull. Bollingen Series XX. Princeton: Princeton University Press.

Jung, R. and Hassler R. (1960). The Extrapyramidal Motor System. In J. Field, (Ed.), *Handbook of Physiology*, Section I: Neurophysyiology, Vol 2, Washington D.C., American Physiological Society, p. 863-927.

_____ (1960). The extrapyramidal motor system. In J. Field, (Ed.), *Handbook of Physiology*. p. 863-927. In J. Field, Magoun, H. W. and Hall, V. E. (Eds.) Section I: Neurophysiology Vol. II Baltimore, MD: Williams & Wilkins, p. 781-1439.

Kahn, Herman (1960). *On Thermonuclear War*. Princeton, NJ: Princeton University Press.

Kahn, Herman and Wiener, Anthony J. (1967). *The Year 2000: A Framework for Speculation on the Next Thirty-Three Years*. New York: MacMillan Co..

Katz, Joseph in Baltes, Paul B. and Schaie, Warner, et al. (1973). *Life-Span Developmental Psychology: Personality and Socialization*. New York: Academic Press.

Keats, John (1818). Letter to John Hamilton Reynolds from Keats, May 3, 1818. In Rollins, Heyder Edward (Ed.) (1958). *The letters of John Keats*. Cambridge: Harvard University Press.

Kendler, Howard (1968). *Basic Psychology*. 2nd ed. New York: Appleton-Century-Crofts.

Kleitman, N. and Engelmann, T. G. (1953). Sleep Characteristics of Infants. *Journal of Applied Physiology*, Vol. 6, p. 266-282.

Klir G. J. (1969). *An Approach to General Systems Theory*. New York: Van Nostrand Reinhold Company.

Kluckhohn, Clyde and Murray, Henry A. (Eds.) (1948). *Personality in nature, society, and culture*. New York: Alfred A. Knopf.

Klukhohn, Clyde (1951). Values and Value-Orientations in the Theory of Action. In T. Parsons (Ed.) *Toward a General Theory of Action*. Cambridge.

Kluckhohn, Clyde. (1962). In Richard Kluckhohn, (Ed.), *Culture and Behavior*. New York: Free Press.

Koch, Sigmund (1954). In W. K. Estes, S. Koch, K. MacCorquodale, P. E. Meehl, C. G. Mueller, Jr., William N. Schoenfeld, & William S. Verplanck (Eds.), *Modern Learning Theory: A Critical Analysis of Five Examples*. New York: Appleton-Century-Crofts.

_____ (1956). Behavior as "intrinsically" regulated: work notes towards a pre-theory of phenomena called "motivational." *Nebraska Symposium on Motivation.* Lincoln, NE: University of Nebraska Press. p. 42-87.

_____ (1951). The current status of motivational psychology. *Psychological Review.* 58, 147-154.

Kohlberg, Lawrence A. (1964). Development of Moral Character and Moral Ideology. In M. Hoffman and L.W. Hoffman (Eds.), *Review of Child Development Research,* Vol 1, New York: Russell Sage Foundation, p. 383-431.

_____ (1966). Cognitive-Developmental Analysis of Children's Sex-Role Concepts and Attitudes. In E.E. Maccoby (Ed.), *The Development of Sex Differences.* Stanford, CA: Stanford University Press.

_____ (1969). Stage and Sequence: The Cognitive-Developmental Approach to Socialization. In D.A. Goslin (Ed.), *Handbook of Socialization: Theory in Research.* Boston: Houghton-Mifflin. [NY: Rand McNally in Mosher].

_____ (1975). "Scoring Manual – Revised." Cambridge, MA: Harvard University Center for Moral Education. Mimeographed.

Kohlberg, Lawrence, Kauffman, K., Scharf, P., and Hickey, J. (1972). The Justice Structure of the Prison: A Theory and Intervention. *Prison Journal* 51:3-14.

_____ (1973). *The Just Community Approach in Corrections: A Manual.* Niantic Connecticut: Connecticut Department of Corrections.

_____ (1974). *The Just Community Approach to Corrections: A Manual.* Part II, Manuscript. Harvard, CT: Moral Education Research Foundation.

_____ (1976). In Thomas Likona (Ed.), *Moral Development and Behavior; Moral Stages and Moralization.* Holt, Rinehart and Winston, CBS College Publishing.

Kohlberg, Lawrence and Kramer, R. (1969). Continuities and Discontinuities in Childhood and Adult Moral Development. *Human Development*, Vol. 12, p. 93-120.

Kohlberg, L. & Turiel, E. (1971). Moral development and moral education. In G. Lesser, (Ed.), *Psychology and educational practice.* Scott Foresman.

Krasner, Leonard and Ullmann, Leonard P. (Eds.) (1965). *Research in Behavior Modification: New Developments and Implications.* New York: Holt, Rinehart and Winston, Inc..

Krech, David (1950). Dynamic Systems as Open Neurological Systems. *Psychological Review*, Vol. 57, p. 354-361.

_____ (1956). Dynamic Systems as Open Neurological Systems. In *General Systems,* Vol. 1, p. 144-154.

Krech, David and Crutchfield, R. (1948). *Theory and Problems of Social Psychology.* New York: McGraw-Hill.

Krech, David and Klein, George S. (Eds.) (1952). *Theoretical Models and Personality Theory.* Durham, NC.

Krechevsky, I. (1937). Brain Mechanisms and Variability I: Variability Within a Means-Ends-Readiness. *Journal of Comparative Psychology*, Vol. 23, p. 121-138.

Kris, Ernst (1952). *Psychoanalytic Explorations in Art.* International Universities Press.

_____ (1975). *Selected Papers of Ernst Kris.* New Haven: Yale University Press.

Kroeber, Alfred L. (1953). *Anthropology Today: An Encyclopaedic Inventory.* Chicago: University of Chicago Press.

Kuhlen, Raymond G. (1968). Developmental changes in motivation during the adult years. In B.L. Neugarten (Ed.), *Middle age and aging.* Chicago, IL: University of Chicago Press.

_____ (1970). *Psychological Backgrounds of Adult Education.* Syracuse, NY: Syracuse University.

Kuhlen, Raymond G. and Thompson, George G. (Eds.) (1952). *Psychological Studies of Human Development.* New York: Appleton-Century-Crofts, Inc..

_____ (1959/1963). *Psychological Studies of Human Development* (2nd edition). New York: Appleton-Century-Crofts (See also Pressey and Kuhnen).

Laing, R. D. (1969). *Self and Others.* New York: Pantheon Books.

_____ (1970). *Knots.* New York: Pantheon Books.

_____ (1971). *The Politics of the Family and Other Essays.* New York: Pantheon Books.

Laszlo, Ervin. (1972). *Introduction to Systems Philosophy: Toward a new paradigm of contemporary thought.* New York: Gordon & Breach Science Publishers.

_____ (1972). *The Relevance of General Systems Theory: Papers presented to Ludwig von Bertalanffy on his seventieth birthday.* New York: George Braziller.

_____ (1972). *The Systems View of the World.* Oxford: Basil Blackwell.

Laszlo, E. and Wilber, J.B. (Eds.) (1970). *Human Values and Natural Science.* New York.

_____ (1971). *Human Values and the Mind of Man.* New York.

Lawrence, D. H. (1947). *The portable D.H. Lawrence.* Diana Trilling, (Ed.) New York: Penguin Books.

Lee, William R., Cowan, Christopher C., and Todorovic, Natasha (Eds.) (2003). *Graves: Levels of Human Existence.* Santa Barbara, CA: ECLET Publishing.

Legum, Colin (1961). *Congo Disaster.* Baltimore: Penguin.

Letter to the editor (name withheld) (1970, March 7). *Schenectady* (NY) *Gazette* .

Levin, Meyer. (1956). *Compulsion.* New York, NY: Simon and Schuster.

Levine, S. (1962). The Effects of Infantile Experience on Adult Behavior. In A. J. Bachrach (Ed.), *Experimental Foundations of Clinical Psychology.* New York: Basic Books.

Locke, John (1690). On Civil Government: An Essay Concerning Human Understanding. See also J. W. Gough, (Ed.), *John Locke's Political Philosophy; Eight Essays* (2d ed. 1973).

Loevinger, Jane (1966). The Meaning and Measurement of Ego Development. *American Psychologist.* March, p. 195-206.

_____ (1976). *Ego Development.* San Francisco: Jossey Bass.

Loevinger, Jane and Ruth Wessler (1970). *Measuring Ego Development*. San Francisco: Jossey-Bass.
Looft, William (1973). Personality and Socialization. In Paul B. Baltes and Warner Schaie, et al. *Life-Span Developmental Psychology*. Academic Press, p. 47-52.
Lowenstein, Rudolph M. (1953). *Drives, Affects, Behavior*. New York: International University Press, Inc..
Lowenstein, Rudolph et. al. (1966). *Psychoanalysis: A General Psychology Essays in Honor of Heinz Hartmann*. New York: International University Publishers.
Lyons, Joseph. (1963). *Psychology and the Measure of Man*. New York: Free Press of Glencoe, Crowell-Collier Publ. Co.
Machiavelli, Niccolo. *The Prince*. Chapter 17.
Maddi, Salvatore (1972). *Personality Theories: Comparative Analysis*. Homewood: Dorsey.
_____ (1967). The Existential Neurosis. *Journal of Abnormal Psychology*. 72:311-25.
Mahabharata. (1953). *The Ramayana and the Mahabharata*. Translated by Romesh C. Dutt. London: J. M. Dent & Sons.
Maier, Norman R. F. and Schneirla, T. C. (1949). Mechanisms in Conditioning. *Psychological Review*, Vol. 49, p. 117-134.
Maier, Norman R. F., Solem, Allen R., and Maier, Ayesha (1964). *Supervisory & Executive Development*. New York: John Wiley & Sons, Inc..
_____ (1963). *Problem-Solving Discussions and Conferences*. New York: McGraw-Hill.
_____ (1967). Assets and liabilities in group problem solving: The need for an integrative function. *Psychological Review*, Vol. 74, No. 4, p. 239-249.
_____ (1970). *Problem Solving and Creativity in Individuals and Groups*. Belmont, CA: Brooks/Cole Publishing.
Malinowski, Bronislaw (1944). *A Scientific Theory of Culture and Other Essays*. Chapel Hill, NC: University of North Carolina Press.
_____ (1960). *Freedom & Civilization*. Bloomington: Indiana Univ. Press.
_____ (1954). *Magic, Science & Religion*. New York: Doubleday Anchor Book.
_____ (1961). *The Dynamics of Culture Change*. New Haven, CT: Yale University Press.
Manchu Dynasty (1904). See "The Holy Edict of K'Ang-Hi" translated by Paul Carus, with (Daisetz) Teitaro Suzuki. *The Monist: A Quarterly Magazine Devoted to the Philosophy of Science*. Volume XIV. Chicago: The Open Court Publishing Company.
Mao, Chairman (1958) Introducing a Co-operative. [and initiating the Great Leap Forward leading to the Cultural Revolution] April 15, 1958 in *Selected Works of Mao Tse-Tung*. Vol. IV. 1965 Peking: Foreign Language Press.
Maskin, Myer (1960). Adaptation of Psychoanalytic Techniques to Specific Disorders. In Jules Masserman (Ed.) *Science and Psychoanalysis Vol, III*.

Psychoanalysis and Human Values. New York: Grune & Stratton, p. 321-352.
Maslow, Abraham H. (1943). Toward a Psychology of Being; A Theory of Human Motivation. *Psychological Review*, Vol. 50, p. 370-396.
_____ (1954). *Motivation and Personality*. New York: Harper.
_____ (1959). *New Knowledge in Human Values*. New York: Harper & Bros.
_____ (1962). *Toward a Psychology of Being*. Princeton, NJ: D. Van Nostrand Co..
_____ (1962). Some basic propositions of growth and self actualization psychology. In *Perceiving, Behaving and Becoming. A New Form for Education*. Washington, D.C.: Yearbook of Association for Supervision and Curriculum, Development.
_____ (1964). *Religion, Values, and Peak Experiences*. Columbus, OH: Ohio State University Press.
_____ (1965). Humanistic Science and Transcendent Experiences. *Journal of Humanistic Psychology*, 5, p. 219-227.
_____ (1967). A Theory of Metamotivation: The Biological Rooting of the Value-life. *Journal of Humanistic Psychology*, Vol.7, p.93-127.
_____ (1967). Self-actualizing and Beyond. In Bugental, J.F.T. (Ed.), *Challenges of Humanistic Psychology*. New York: McGraw-Hill.
_____ (1968). The Farther Reaches of Human Nature. *Journal of Transpersonal Psychology*, Vol.1, p.1-9.
_____ (1968). Human Potentialities and the Healthy Society. In Otto, Herbert (Ed.) *Human Potentialities*. St. Louis: Warren H. Green, Inc.
_____ (1971). *The Farther Reaches of Human Nature*. New York: Viking.
Masserman, Jules (Ed.) (1960). Psychoanalysis and Human Values. *Science and Psychoanalysis Vol. III*. New York: Grune & Stratton.
May, Rollo (1950). *The Meaning of Anxiety*. New York: Ronald Press.
_____ (1953). *Man's Search for Himself*. New York: Norton.
_____ (1961). *Existential Psychology*. New York: Random House.
May, Rollo, Angel, E., and Ellenberger, H. F. (Eds.) (1958). *Existence: A New Dimension in Psychiatry and Psychology*. New York: Basic Books.
McGregor, Douglas (1960). *The Human Side of Enterprise*. New York: McGraw-Hill Book Co..
McGraw, M. B. (1943). *The Neuro-Muscular Maturation of the Human Infant*. N.Y.: Columbia University Press.
Melzack, R., & Scott, T. H. (1957). The Effects of Early Experience on the Response to Pain. *Journal of Comparative and Physiological Psychology*, Vol. 50, p. 155-161.
Mehrabian, Albert (1968). *An Analysis of Personality Theories*. New York: Prentice Hall.
Menzies, R. (1937). Conditioned vasomotor responses in human subjects. *Journal of Psychology*, 4, 75-120
Merleau-Ponty, Maurice (1963). *The Structure of Behaviour* (Alden L. Fischer, Trans.). Boston: Beacon Press.
_____ (1962). *Phenomenology of Perception*. (Colin Smith, Trans.). New York: Humanities Press.

Miles, Lawrence D. (1961). *Techniques of Value Analysis and Engineering.* New York: McGraw-Hill Book Co..
Miller, G. A., Galanter, E., and Pribram, K. H. (1960). *Plans and the Structure of Behavior.* New York: Holt.
Millon, Theodore (1967). *Theories of Psychopathology.* Philadelphia: WB Saunders Co..
_____ (1968). *Approaches to Personality.* New York: Pitman Publishing Co..
Moltz, H. (1960). Imprinting: Empirical Basis and Theoretical Significance. *Psychological Bulletin,* Vol. 57, p. 291-314.
Morgan, C. T. (1951). The Psychophysiology of Learning. In S. S. Stevens (Ed.), *Handbook of Experimental Psychology.* New York: Wylie, p. 758-788.
Mosher, Ralph L. (1976). "A Three Democratic School Intervention Project." Unpublished proposal to the Danforth Foundation, Boston University.
_____ (1978). A Democratic High School: Damn It: Your Feet are Always in the Water. In Norman A. Sprinthall and Ralph Mosher (Eds.) *Value Development…As An Aim of Education.* Schenectady, NY: Character Research Press, p. 69-116
Mosher, Ralph L., and Sprinthall, Norman (1971). Psychological Education: A Means to Promote Personal Development through Adolescence. *The Counseling Psychologist* 2: 3-82. (see also Sprinthall)
Mowrer, O. Hobart and R. R. Sears (1939). *Frustration and aggression.* New Haven: Yale University Freer.
Mowrer, O. Hobart (1947). On the dual nature of learning: A reinterpretation of 'conditioning' and 'problem-solving.' *Harvard Educational Review,* Vol. 17, p. 102-148.
_____ (1951). Two factor learning theory: summary and comment. *Psychological Review,* Sept., 58(5):350-4.
_____ (1953). *Psychotherapy, Theory and Research.* The Ronald Press Company, J. Dollard, L. W. Doob, N. E. Miller.
_____ (1953). The new group therapy. In *Kentucky Symposium: Learning Theory, Personality Theory, and Clinical Research.* Princeton: Van Nostrand, 81-90.
_____ (1954). Ego pscyhology, cybernetics, and learning theory. In *Kentucky Symposium.* New York: Wiley. (also in Adams, et al., *Learning Theory and Clinical Research.* New York.)
_____ (1954). A psychologist looks at language. *American Psychologist,* Vol. 9, p. 660-694.
_____ (1960). *Learning theory and the symbolic processes.* New York: Wiley.
_____ (1960). *Learning theory and behavior.* New York: Wiley.
_____ (1960). "Sin," the Lesser of Two Evils. *American Psychologist,* 1960, 15(2), 113-118.
_____ (1964). *The New Group Therapy.* Princeton, New Jersey: Van Nostrand.
_____ (1966). Ego psychology, cybernetics and learning theory. In O. H. Mowrer, (Ed.), *Morality and mental health.* Chicago: Rand McNally.

Mowrer, O.H. and C. Kluckhohn (1944). A dynamic theory of personality. In J. McV. Hunt (Ed.), *Personaloity and the behavior disorders.* New York: Ronald.
Moynihan, Daniel Patrick (1973). *The Politics of a Guaranteed Income: the Nixon Administration and the Family Assistance Plan.* New York: Random House.
Munn, N. L. (1946). Learning in Children. In L. Carmichael (Ed.), *Manual of Child Psychology.* New York: Wiley.
Mumford, Lewis (1940). *Faith for Living.* New York.
_____ (1922). *The Story of Utopias,* (reprint in 1940).
_____ (1926). *The Golden Day.* New York: W. W. Norton and Company.
_____ (1944). *The Condition of Man.* New York: Harcourt, Brace & Co..
_____ (1946). *Values for Survival: Essays, Addresses, and Letters on Politics and Education.* New York: Harcourt, Brace.
_____ (1951). *The Conduct of Life.* New York: Harcout, Brace & Co..
_____ (1955). *The Human Prospect.* Boston: The Beacon Press.
_____ (1956). *The Transformations of Man.* New York. Harper and Row.
_____ (1967). *The Myth of the Machine: I. Technics and Human Development.* New York: Harcourt, Brace and World.
_____ (1970). *The Myth of the Machine: II. The Pentagon of Power.* New York: Harcourt, Brace, Janovich.
Murphy, Gardner (1947). *Personality: A Biosocial Approach to Origins and Structure.* New York and London, Harper & Row.
_____ (1958). *Human Potentialities.* New York: Basic Books Inc..
_____ (1965). Human Natures of the Future. In Walter D. Nunokawa, (Ed.), *Human Values & Abnormal Behavior.* Chicago: Scott, Foresman.
Murray, H. A. (Ed.) (1938). *Explorations in personality: A clinical and experimental study of fifty men of college age by the workers at the Harvard Psychological Clinic.* New York: Oxford University Press, p. 530-545.
_____ (1951) Toward a classification of interactions. In T. parsons and E. A. Shils (Eds.), *Toward a general theory of action.* Cambridge, MA: Harvard University Press.
_____ (1971). *Thematic Apperception Test: Manual.* Cambridge, MA: Harvard University Press.
Nance, John (1975). *The Gentle Tassaday: A Stone Age People in the Philippine Rain Forest.* New York: Hartcourt Brace Jovanovich.
MacLeish, Kenneth (1972). Stone Age Cave Men of Mindanao. *National Geographic Magazine,* 142 (2): 219-249.
Neissen, H. W., Chow, K. L., and Semmes, J. (1951). Effects of Restricted Opportunity for Tactual, Kinesthetic and Manipulative Experience on the Behavior of a Chimpanzee. *American Journal of Psychology,* Vol. 64, p. 485-507.
Nietzsche, Friedrich (1956). *The Birth of Tragedy and the Genealogy of Morals.* New York: Doubleday & Company.
_____ (1968). Thus Spoke Zarathustra (Walter Kaufmann, Trans.). *The Portable Nietzsche.* New York: Viking Press.

_____ (1973). In Solomon, Robert (Ed.). *Nietzsche: A Collection of Critical Essays.* Garden City, New York: Anchor Books.

_____ (1901). *Will to Power.*

Nixon, Richard M. (1969). The "Silent Majority' Speech." Televised address from the White House, November 3.

Olds, J. (1956). *The growth and structure of motives.* Glencoe, Ill.: Free Press.

Olds, J. and Olds, M.E. (1961). Interference and Learning in Paleocortical Systems. In A. Fessard, R.W. Gerard, and J. Konorski, (Eds.) *Brain Mechanisms and Learning.* Springfield, IL: Thomas.

_____ (1965). Drives, rewards and the brain. In F. Barron, W. C. Dement, W. Edwards, H. Lindman, L. D. Phillips, T. Olds, & M. Olds. *New directions in psychology II.* New York: Holt, Rinehart & Winston.

Olds, M. E., & Olds, J. (1962). Approach-escape interactions in rat brain. *American Journal of Physiology*, 203, 803-810.

_____ (1963). Olds, M. E., & Olds, J. Approach-avoidance analysis of rat diencephalon. *Journal of Comparative Neurology*, 120, 259-295.

_____ (1964). Olds, M. E., & Olds, J. Pharmacological patterns in subcortical reinforcement behavior. *International Journal of Neuropharmacology*, 2, 309-325.

Paine, Thomas (1942). *Age of Reason: Being an Investigation of True & Fabulous Theology.* Willey Book Company. (See also Conway, Moncure D. *Life of Thomas Paine.* New York: G. P. Putnam's Sons, Vols. 1-4. 1894-1896.)

Papandreou, Andreas (1970). *New Democracy at Gunpoint: The Greek Front.* York: Doubleday.

Parsons, Talcott and Shils, Edward (Eds.) (1951). *Toward a general theory of action.* New York: Harper & Row.

Pavlov, Ivan P. (1927). *Conditioned reflexes.* London: Routledge and Kegan Paul.

_____ (1950). *Selected works.* London: Central Books.

_____ (1960). *Conditioned Reflexes: an Investigation of the Physiological Activity of the Cerebral Cortex.* (Andrep, G., Trans.). Mineola, NY: Dover Publications, Incorporated.

Peck, Robert and Havighurst, R. (1960). *The Psychology of Character Development.* New York: John Wiley.

Pechman, Joseph A. and Timpane, Michael (Eds.) (1975). *Work Incentives and Income Guarantees: The New Jersey Negative Income Tax Experiment.* Washington, DC: Brookings Institution.

Perry, William G., Jr. (1970). *Forms of Intellectual and Ethical Development in the College Years: A Scheme.* New York: Holt, Rinehart, and Winston.

Piaget, Jean (1929). *The Child's Conception of the World.* NY: Harcourt, Brace Jovanovich.

_____ (1932). *The Moral Judgement of the Child.* NY: Harcourt, Brace Jovanovich.

_____ (1936). *The Origins of Intelligence in Children.* Paris: Delachaux & Niestle. (Republished: New York: International University Press, 1952).

_____ (1954). *The Construction of Reality in the Child.* New York: Basic Books.

_____ (1964). Development and Learning. In R. E. Ripple & V. N Rockcastle (Eds.), *Piaget Rediscovered.* Ithaca, New York: School of Education, Cornell University.

_____ (1972). Intellectual Evolution from Adolescence to Adulthood. *Human Development* 5: 1-12.

Piaget, Jean and Szeminska, A. (1952). *Child's Conception of Number.* London: Routledge & Kegan Paul.

Piaget, Jean and Inhelder, B. (1958). *The Growth of Logical Thinking from Childhood to Adolescence.* New York: Basic Books.

Pirsig, Robert M. (1974). *Zen and the Art of Motorcycle Maintenance: An Inquiry into Values.* New York: William Morrow & Co..

Platt, John R. (1966). *The Step to Man: The Evolving Nature of Man Social and Intellectual What he is and What he May Become.* New York: John Wiley & Sons.

Polanyi, Michael (1958). *Personal Knowledge.* Chicago, IL: University of Chicago Press.

_____ (1959). *The Study of Man.* University of Chicago Press.

_____ (1964). *Science, Faith, and Society: A Searching Examination of the Meaning and Nature of Scientific Inquire.* Chicago, IL: University of Chicago Press, Phoenix Books.

_____ (1966). *The Tacit Dimension.* Garden City, NY: Doubleday.

_____ (1968). Life's Irreducible Structure. *Science,* 160.

_____ (1974). *Scientific Thought and Social Reality.* M. Polanyi and F. Schwartz, (Eds.) International Universities Press,.

Postman, Leo, Bruner, J. S., and McGinnies, E. (1948). Personal Values as Selective Perception of Danger Signals: 21 factors in perception. *Journal of Abnormal and Social Psychology,* Vol. 43, p.142-154.

Postman, Leo (1953). Perception, motivation, and behavior. *Journal of Personality*, 22, 17-32.

Postman, Leo and Schneider, Jay S. (1951). Personal Values, Visual Recognition, and Recall. *Psychological Review*, Vol. 58, p. 271-284.

Pressey, S. L., and Kuhlen, R. G. (1957). *Psychological development through the life-span.* New York: Harper & Row.

Rand, Ayn (1936). *We the Living.* New York: Macmillan.

_____ (1943). *The Fountainhead.* Indianapolis: Bobbs-Merrill.

_____ (1946). *Anthem.* Los Angeles: Pamphleteers, Inc..

_____ (1957). *Atlas Shrugged.* New York: Random House.

Rank, Otto (1958). *Beyond Psychology.* Mineola, New York: Dover Publications.

Ramayana (see Mahabharata).

Razran, G. (1955). Conditioning and perception. *Psychological Review*, Vol. 62, p. 83-95.

Reich, Charles (1970). *The Greening of America.* New York: Random House.

Rensch, Bernhard (1959). *Evolution above the Species Level.* New York: John Wiley and Sons.

_____ (1971). *Biophilosophy.* New York: Columbia University Press.

Riesen, A. H. (1958). Plasticity of behavior. Psychological series. In H. F. Harlow & C. N. Woolsey (Eds.) *Biological and Biochemical Bases of Behavior*. Madison: University of Wisconsin Press.

_____ (1961). Stimulation as a Requirement for Growth and Function in Behavioral Development. In D. W. Fiske & S. R. Maddi (Eds.), *Functions of Varied Experience*. Homewood, Illinois: Dorsey.

Riesman, David (1950). *The Lonely Crowd*. Garden City: Doubleday.

_____ (1952). *Faces in the Crowd: Individual Studies in Character and Politics*. New Haven and London: Yale University Press.

Roberts, E. (1960). *Biochemical maturation of the central nervous system and behavior: Transactions of the third conference*. New York: Josiah Macy Foundation.

Roe, Ann (1956). *The Psychology of Occupations*. New York: Wiley.

Rogers, Carl R. (1942). *Counseling and Psychotherapy: Newer Concepts in Practice*. Boston: Houghton Mifflin Company.

_____ (1951). *Client-Centered Therapy: Its Current Practice, Implications, and Theory*. Boston: Houghton Mifflin.

_____ (1961). *On Becoming a Person: a Therapist's View of Psychotherapy*. Boston: Houghton Mifflin.

_____ (1963). Phychotherapy Today or Where do we go from here? *American Journal of Psychotherapy,* Vol XVII, No. 1, p. 5-16.

_____ (1969). *Freedom to Learn: A View of What Education Might Become*. Columbus, Ohio: Charles E. Merrill Publishing Company, p. 1057-1066.

Rogers, Carl R. and Burrhus F. Skinner (1956). Some Issues Concerning the Control of Human Behavior: A Symposium. *Science* Vol. 124 (November), No. 3231, p. 1057-1066. (Also published in L. Gorlow and W. Katkovsky (Ed.), *Readings in the Psychology of Adjustment*. New York: McGraw-Hill, 1959; and in Evans, R. I. *Carl Rogers - the Man and His Ideas*. New York: Dutton, 1975.)

_____ (1960). American Academy of Arts and Sciences, Conference on Evolutionary Theory and Human Progress: Conference C, The Individual and the design of culture, Dec 2-4, 1960. Mimeographed transcripts, p. 75-6, 79.

_____ (1963). Psychotherapy Today or Where do we go from here? *American Journal of Psychotherapy*. Vol XVII, No. 1, pages 5-16.

Rokeach, Milton (1960). *The Open and Closed Mind*. New York. Basic Books.

_____ (1960). *The Nature of Human Values*. New York: Free Press.

Rotter, Julian B. (1954). *Social learning and clinical psychology*. New York: Prentice-Hall.

_____ (1955). The role of the psychological situation in determining the direction of human behavior. *Nebraska Symposium on Motivation*. Lincoln, NE: University of Nebraska Press, p. 245-269

_____ (1960). Some implications of a social learning theory for the prediction of goal directed behavior from testing procedures. *Psychological Review*, Vol. 67, p. 301-316.

_____ (1966). Generalized expectancies for internal versus external control of reinforcement. *Psychological Monographs*, 80, (Whole No. 609).
Rousseau, Jean-Jacques (1755). *The Social Contract and Discourse on the Origin of Inequality.* New York: E. P. Dutton, 1950.
_____ (1907). *Rousseau's Emile, or Treatise on Education.* New York: D. Appleton and Company.
_____ (1953). *The Confessions.* New York: Viking Penguin.
_____ (1959). In B. Gagnebin and M. Raymond (Ed.), *Oeuvres complètes.* Pléiade.
_____ (1971). *The Social Contract.* Baltimore: Penguin Books.
Samuels, I. (1959). Reticular Mechanisms and Behavior. *Psychological Bulletin*, 56, 1-25.
Sanford, Nevitt (1970). *Issues in Personality Theory.* San Francisco: Jossey-Bass.
_____ (1973). Personality and Socialization. In Baltes, Paul B. and Schaie, Warner, et al. (Eds.), *Life-Span Developmental Psychology.* Academic Press.
Schacter, Stan and Bibb Latane (1964). Crime, Cognition, and the Autonomic Nervous System. *Nebraska Symposium on Motivation*, Vol. 12, p. 221-275.
Scharf, P. and Hickey, J. (1974). (see Kohlberg, L., Kauffman, K., Schar, P, and Hickey, J. *The Just Community Approach to Corrections: A Manual.* Cambridge, MA: Moral Education Research Foundation.
Scharf, P. and Hickey, J. (1976). *Just Community programme.*
Hickey, J. & Scharf, P. (1972 and 1980). *Toward a just correctional system.* San Francisco: Jossey-Bass.
Scharf, Peter (1973). Moral Atmosphere and Intervention in the Prison. Ed.D. dissertation, Harvard University.
Schein, Edgar H. (1956). The Chinese Indoctrination Program for Prisoner of War. *Psychiatry,* 19 (1956): 149-72
_____ (1961). *Coercive Persuasion.* New York: Norton.
_____ (1965). *Organization Psychology.* Englewood Cliffs, NJ: Prentice-Hall.
_____ (1971). The individual, the Organization and the Career: A Conceptual Scheme. *Journal of Applied Behavioral Science*, Vol. 7, No. 4, p. 401-426.
Schroder, Harold M., Driver, Michael J., and Streufert, Siegfried (1967). *Human Information Processing: Individual and Group Functioning in Complex Social Situations.* New York: Holt, Rinehart & Winston, Inc.
Scott, J. P. (1958). Critical Periods in the Development of Social Behavior in Puppies. *Psychosomatic Medicine*, 20(1), 42-54.
_____ (1962). Critical Periods in Behavioral Development. *Science,* Vol. 138, p. 949-958.
_____ (1963). The Progress of Primary Socialization in Canine and Human Infants. Monographs of the Society for Research in Child Development, 28 (1), p.1-47.
_____ (1967). The Development of Social Motivation. In D. Levine (Ed.), *Nebraska Symposium on Motivation.* Lincoln, Nebraska: University of Nebraska Press, p. 111-132.

Scott, W. A. (1965). *Values and organizations: A study of fraternities and sororitites.* Chicago: Rand McNally.
Segundo, J. P., Naquet, R. and Buser, P. (1955). Effects of cortical stimulation on electrocortical activity in monkeys. *Journal of Neurophysiology*, Vol. 18, p. 236-245.
_____ (1960). Apelbaum, J., Silva, E., Frick, O., and Segundo, J. Specificity and biasing of arousal reaction habituation. *Electroencephalography and clinical Neurophysiology*, Vol. 12, p. 829-840.
Seiler, John with Ralph Hower (1967). Organizational Inputs. In John A. Seiler, Richard D. Irwin (Ed.) *Systems Analysis and Organization.* Homewood, IL. Richard D. Irwin, Inc..
Selman, Robert L. (1974). "A Developmental Approach to Interpersonal and Moral Awareness in Young Children: Some Theoretical and Educational Perspectives." Paper read at the Montessori Society National Seminar, Boston.
_____ (1975). "The Development of Social-Cognitive Understanding: A Guide to Educational and Clinical Practice." In Lickona, Thomas (Ed.), *Morality: A Handbook of Moral Development and Behavior.* New York: Holt, Rinehard, and Winston.
_____ (1975). "The Development of Social-Cognitive Understanding: A Guide to Educational and Clinical Practice." In Thomas Lickona (Ed.), *Moral Development and Social Issues.* New York: Holt, Rinehart and Winston.
Selman, Robert L. and Byrne, D. F. (1972). "Manual for Scoring Role-Taking Stages in Moral and Social Dilemmas." Cambridge, MA: Harvard University Center for Moral Education. Mimeographed.
Selman, Robert and Lieberman, Marcus (1974). "The Evaluation of a Values Curriculum for Primary Grade Children Based on a Cognitive-Developmental Approach." Paper presented to the American Educational Research Association, Chicago, April. Mimeographed.
Selye, Hans M.D. (1946). The general adaptation syndrome and the diseases of adaptation. *Journal of Clinical Endocrinology*, 6, 117-230.
_____ (1950). *The Physiology and Pathology of Exposure to Stress.* Montreal: Acta.
_____ (1956). *The Stress of Life.* New York: McGraw-Hill.
_____ (1974). *Stress Without Distress.* Lippincott.
Seltzer, Louis (date not located). "Can't we tell right from wrong?" *Cleveland Press*; Cleveland Press Collection, University of Cleveland.
Shakespeare, William. *As You Like It.* Act II, Scene 7.
Shaie, K. Warner (1973). In Baltes, Paul B. and Schaie, Warner (Eds). *Life-Span Developmental Psychology: Personality and Socialization.* Academic Press.
Sharpless, S. and Jasper, H.H. (1956). Habituation of the Arousal Reaction. *Brain*, Vol. 79, p. 655-680.
Shaw, T.E. (Trans.) (1935). (aka Colonel T. E. Lawrence) *Odyssey* (of Homer). London: Oxford University Press.
Sheldon, William and Stevens, S. S. (1942). *The Varieties of Temperament.* New York: Harper & Brothers.

Skinner, B. F. (1956). Some Issues Concerning the Control of Human Behavior: A Symposium. *Science*, Nov. 30, Vol. 124, p. 1057-1066.
_____ (1956). A case history in scientific method. *American Psychologist*, 11, p. 221-33.
_____ (1971). *Beyond freedom and dignity*. New York: Knopf.
_____ (1948). *Walden Two*. New York: MacMillan Publishing Co..
Skinner & Rogers (see Rogers)
Soloman, R. L. and Howes, D. H. (1951). Word frequency, personal values and duration thresholds. *Psychological Review*, 58, p. 256-270.
Solomon, Richard L. and Rush, Eleanor S. (1957). Experimentally derived conceptions of anxiety and aversion. In Jones, Marshall R (Ed.), *Nebraska Symposium on Motivation*. Oxford, University of Nebraska Press, p. 212-305.
Sorokin, Pitirim A. (1937-1941). *Social & Cultural Dynamics, Vols. I-IV*. New York: The American Book Company.
_____ (1941). *The Crisis of Our Age*, New York: E.P. Dutton & Co. Inc..
_____ (1942). *Man and Society in Calamity*. New York: E.P. Dutton & Company Inc..
_____ (1947). *Society, Culture, and Personality: A System of General Sociology*. New York: Harper & Brothers.
_____ (1947/1962). *Society, Culture, and Personality: Their Structure and Dynamics*. New York: Harper & Brothers.
_____ (1948). *The Reconstruction of Humanity*. Boston: Beacon Press.
_____ (1950). *Social Philosophies of an Age of Crisis*. Boston: Beacon Press.
_____ (1954). *The Ways and Power of Love: Types, Factors and Techniques of Moral Transformation*. Boston: Beacon Press.
_____ (1957). *Social and Cultural Dynamics: A Study of Change in Major Systems of Art, Truth, Ethics, Law and Social Relationships*. Boston: Porter Sargent Publisher.
_____ (1964). *The Basic Trends of Our Times*.
_____ (1966). *Sociological Theories of Today*. New York.
Spearman, Charles E. (1904). General intelligence objectively determined and measured. *American Journal of Psychology*, Vol. 5, p. 201-293.
_____ (1927). *The abilities of man, their nature and measurement*. New York: Macmillan.
Spence, Kenneth W. (1944). The Nature of Theory Construction in Contemporary Psychology. *Psychology Review*, Vol. 51, 47-48.
_____ (1956). *Behavior theory and conditioning*. New Haven: Yale University Press.
_____ (1960). *Behavior Theory and Learning*. Englewood Cliffs, NJ: Prentice-Hall.
Sprinthall, Norman A. and Mosher, Ralph L. (1969). *Studies of adolescents in the secondary school*. Cambridge: Harvard University Center for Research and Development on Educational Differences. No. 6.

Stellar, E. (1960). Drive and Motivation. In J. Field (Ed.), *Handbook of Physiology*. Section I: Neurophysiology. Vol. III. Washington, D. C.: American Physiological Society.
Stein, Morris I. (1963). Explorations in Typology. In White, R. W., *The Study of Lives: Essays on Personality in Honor of Henry A. Murray*. Atherton Press, A Division of Prentice-Hall, Inc., p. 281-303.
Stein, M.I. and Neulinger, J. (1963). A typology of self-descriptions. Paper presented at the Conference of Role and Methodology of Classification in Psychiatry and Psychopathology. Washington, D.C.
Streufert, Siegfried (1966). Conceptual structure, communicator importance, and interpersonal attitudes toward conforming and deviant group members. *Journal of Personality and Social Psychology*. Vol.4, p.100-103.
Suedfeld, Peter (1964). Birth order of volunteers for sensory deprivation. *Journal of Abnormal Social Psychology,* 68, p.195-196.
_____ (1964). Conceptual structure and subjective stress in sensory deprivation. *Perceptual and Motor Skills*, 19, p. 896-898.
_____ (1964). Attitude manipulation in restricted environments: I. Conceptual structure and response to propaganda. *Journal of Abnormal Social Psychology*, 68 (3), p. 242-247.
_____ (1971). *Attitude Change*. Chicago: Aldine/Artherton, Inc..
Suedfeld, P., Grissom, R. J., & Vernon, J. (1960). The effects of sensory deprivation and social isolation on the performance of an unstructured cognitive task. *American Journal of Psychology*, 77, p. 111-115.
Suedfeld, P., & Vernon, J. (1964). Visual hallucinations in sensory deprivation: A problem of criteria. *Science.* 145, p. 412-413.
Suedfeld, P., Vernon, J., & Goldstein, K. M. (1964). The relationship between sensory deprivation and social isolation on the performance of an unstructured cognitive task. Eastern Psychological Association paper.
Sullivan, C., Grant, M.Q. and Grant, J.D. (1957). The Development of Interpersonal Maturity: Apps to Delinquency. *Psychiatry,* 20, p. 373-385.
Sullivan, H. S. (1953). *The Interpersonal Theory of Psychiatry*. New York: Norton.
Sutherland, John Derg (1959). *Psychoanalysis and Contemporary Thought*. New York Grove Press.
_____ (1968). *The Psychoanalytic Approach*. Edited by John D. Sutherland. Contributors: Elizabeth Bott and others. London: Institute of Psycho-Analysis.
_____ (1994). In Jill Savege Scharff (Ed.), *Autonomous Self: The Work of John D. Sutherland*. Library of Object Relations, Rowman and Littlefield Publishers.
Taylor, Frederick W. (1911). The Principles of Scientific Management. From Chapter 2 of *Scientific Management, comprising Shop Management, The Principles of Scientific Management and Testimony Before the Special House Committee*. New York: Harper Brothers.

Terzuolo, C. A., & Adey, W. R. (1960). Sensorimotor Cortical Activities. In J. Field (Ed.), *Handbook of physiology.* Section I: Neurophysiology. Vol. II. Washington, D. C.: American Physiological Society.

Thistlethwaite, D. (1951). A critical Review of Latent Learning and Related Experiments. *Psychological Bulletin.*

Theobald, Robert. (1963). *Free Men and Free Markets. Proposed: A Guaranteed Income.* Clarkson N. Potter, Inc.

Thoreau, Henry David (1958). In Walter Harding & Carl Bode (Eds.), *Thoreau, H. D. Correspondence.* New York: University Press.

Thorndike, Edward L. (1913). *Educational Psychology: The Psychology of Learning.* New York: Teachers College Press.

_____ (1914). Unity scale for measuring educational products. Proceedings of the Conference on Educational Measurement. Indiana University Bulletin, 12, 10.

_____ (1931). *Human Learning.* New York: D. Appleton-Century.

_____ (1932). *The Fundamentals of Learning.* New York: Teachers College, Columbia University.

_____ (1935). *The Psychology of Wants, Interests, and Attitudes.* New York: D. Appleton-Century.

_____ (1940). *Human Nature and the Social Order.* New York: Macmillan.

_____ (1943). *Man and His Works.* Cambridge, MA.

Thorndike, Edward L, Bregman, E. O., Cobb, M. V., Woodyard, E. (1926). *The Measurement of Intelligence.* New York: Teachers College, Columbia University, 1927.

Thorndike, E., Bregman, E., Tilton, J.W., and Woodyard, E. (1928). *Adult Learning.* New York: Macmillan.

_____ (1932). *The Fundamentals of Learning.* New York: Teachers College Press.

_____ (1935). *The Psychology of Wants, Interests, and Attitudes.*

Thorndike, Edward L. and Lorge, Irving (1944). *The Teacher's Word Book of 30,000 Words.* New York: Columbia University Press.

Thorndike, Robert L. (1949). *Personnel Selection: Test and Measurement Techniques.*

_____ (1955). *10,000 Careers.*

_____ (1964). *Concepts of Over- and Under-Achievement.*

Thorpe, W. H. (1963). *Learning and instinct in animals.* London: Methuen.

Tillich, Paul (1952). *The Courage to Be.* New Haven, CT: Yale University Press.

Toffler, Alvin (1970). *Future Shock.* New York. Random House.

Tolman, Edward Chance (1922). A new formula for behaviorism. *Psychological Review,* Vol. 29, p. 44-53.

_____ (1932). *Purposive behavior in animals and men.* New York: Century Co., Appleton-Century-Crofts.

_____ (1948). Cognitive maps in rats and men. *Psychological Review*, Vol. 55, 189-208.

_____ (1951). Operational Behaviorism and Current Trends in Psychology. In *E.C. Tolman: Collected Papers in Psychology.* Berkeley: University of California Press. p 89-103.

_____ (1951). A psychological model. In T. Parsons and E. A. Shils (Eds.), *Toward a general theory of action.* Cambridge, MA: Harvard University Press, p. 279-361.

_____ (1952). A Psychological Model. In T. Parsons and E. A. Shils (Eds.), *Toward a General Theory of Action.* Cambridge, MA: Harvard University Press.

_____ (1959). Principles of Purposive Behavior. In S. Koch (Ed.). *Psychology: a Study of Science.* Vols. 1 and 2. New York: Holt, Rinehart and Winston.

Travis, A. M. and Woolsey, C. N. (1956). Motor Performances of Monkeys after Bilateral Partial and Total Cerebral Decortications. *Journal of Physical Medicine,* Vol. 35, p. 273-310.

Tsanoff, Radaslov A. (1942). *The Moral Ideals of Our Civilization.* New York: E.P. Dutton & Co., Inc..

Turnbull, Colin M. (1972). *Mountain People.* New York: Simon & Schuster.

Ullman, L. P. and Krasner, L. (1965). Introduction. In L P. Ullman & L. Krasner (Eds.), *Case studies in behavior modification.* New York: Holt, Rinehart & Winston.

_____ (1969). *A psychological approach to abnormal behavior.* Englewood Cliffs, NJ: Prentice Hall.

Vlachos, Helen. (1970). *House Arrest.* Boston: Gambit.

von Bertalanffy, Ludwig (1959). Human Values in a Changing World. In A. H. Maslow (Ed.), *New Knowledge in Human Values.* New York: Harper.

_____ (1968). *General System Theory: Foundations, Development, Applications.* New York: George Braziller, Inc..

_____ (1967). *Robots, Men and Minds.* New York: George Braziller, Inc..

von Goethe, Johann Wolfgang (1803). "Constancy in Change."

von Neuman, John and O. Morgenstern (1944). *Theory of Games and Economic Behavior.* Princeton University Press, Princeton.

Wallace, Alfred Russel (1869). A Review of Principles of Geology by Charles Lyell. *Quarterly Review,* Vol. 126, p. 359-94.

_____ (1891). *Darwinism: an Exposition of the Theory of Natural Selection with Some of Its Applications.* London: Macmillan & Co. (Reprint: A.M.S. Press, New York, 1975).

_____ (1895). *Natural Selection.* New York: MacMillan and Co., p. 197.

_____ (1911). *The World of Life. A Manifestation of Creative Power, Directive Mind and Ultimate Purpose.* New York: Moffat, Yard.

_____ (1913). *Social Environment and Moral Progress* New York: Funk & Wagnalls.

Walters, R. H. (See Bandura)

Watson, John B. (1913). Psychology as the behaviorist views it. *Psychological Review,* 20, p. 158-177.

_____ (1914). *Behavior: An introduction to comparative psychology.* New York: Henry Holt & Co.

_____ (1919). *Psychology from the Standpoint of a Behaviorist.* Philadelphia: J. B. Lippincott Co.

_____ (1930). *Behaviorism.* Revised Edition. Chicago: University of Chicago Press.

Watson, John B. and Rayner, Rosalie (1920). Conditioned emotional reactions. *Journal of Experimental Psychology*, 3(1), p. 1-14.

Welker, W. I. (1961). An Analysis of Exploratory and Play Behavior in Animals. In D. W. Fiske and S. R. Maddi (Eds.), *Functions of Varied Experience.* Homewood, Illinois: Dorsey.

Werner, Heinz (1940). *Comparative psychology of mental development.* New York: International Universities Press, Inc..

Werner, H. and Kaplan, B. (1963). *Symbol formation: An organismic developmental approach to language and the expression of thought.* New York: John Wiley.

_____ (1978). In Barten, S.S., & Franklin, M.B. (Eds.), *Developmental processes: Heinz Werner's selected writings, Vols I & II.* New York: International Universities Press.

West, G. B. (1951). Can adrenaline potentiate the action of noradrenaline? *Journal of Pharmacy and Pharmacology.* Sept 3(9):571-5.

_____ (1952). The analysis of pharmacopeial samples of adrenaline; a limit test for nonadrenaline in adrenaline. *Journal of Pharmacy and Pharmacology*, 1952 Feb:4(2):95-7.

_____ (1955). Adrenaline and Noradrenaline. *Journal of Pharmacy and Pharmacology.* 1955 Feb;7(2):81-98.

West, Louis Jolyon (1964). Psychiatry, 'brainwashing,' and the American character. *American Journal of Psychiatry*, Vol. 120, p. 842-850. (Professor and Chairman of the Department for Psychiatry and Behavioral Research, Director of the Neuro-psychiatric Institute of the University of California, Los Angeles.)

_____ (1962). Lysergic Acid Diethylamide: Its effects on a Male Asiatic Elephant. *Science,* Vol. 138, No. 3545, 7, Dec., p. 1100-1102.

_____ (1968). See also: Allen, JR., & West, L. J. Flight from violence: Hippies and the green rebellion. *American Journal of Psychiatry*, 125(3), p. 364-370.

White, Leslie (1949). *The Science of Culture: A Study of Man and Civilization.* 2nd edition. New York: Grove Press.

_____ (1959). *The Evolution of Culture.* New York:McGraw-Hill.

_____ (1959). The Concept of Culture. *American Anthropologist*, vol. 61, no. 2, p. 239 (quoting Lowie, 1917 *Culture and Ethnography.* Boni and Liveright, New York. Martin, Paul S.).

_____ (1966). The Social Organization of Ethnological Theory. *Monographs in Cultural Anthropology,* Rice University Studies, 52:4, p. 1-66.

Whyte, Lancelot Law (1948). *The Next Development in Mankind.* New York: The Universe of Experience.

_____ (1962). *The Next Development in Man.* New York: Mentor Books.

_____ (1965). *Internal Factors in Evolution.* New York.

_____ (1973). The Structural Hierarchy in Organisms. In William Gray and Nicholas D. Rizzo (Ed.), *Unity in Diversity: A Festschrift for Ludwig von Bertalanff.* New York: Gordon and Breach, p. 271-285.

Whyte, William H. (1956). *The Organization Man*. New York: Simon and Schuster.
White, Robert. W. (1959). Motivation Reconsidered: The Concept of Competence. *Psychological Review*, No. 66, p. 297-333.
_____ (1963). *The Study of Lives: Essays on Personality in Honor of Henry A. Murray*. New York: Atherton Press, p. 280-303.
Wicker, Tom (1975). *A Time to Die*. New York: Quadrangle Books.
Wittgenstein, Ludwig Josef Johann (1965). *The Blue and Brown Books (Preliminary Studies for the Philosophical Investigations)*. New York: Harper, 1965.
_____ (1966). *The Philosophical Investigations: A Collection of Critical Essays.* George Pitcher (Ed.), Garden City, NY: Doubleday.
Witkin, H. A., Lewis, H. B., Hertzman, M. K., Machover, P., Meissner, Bretnall, and Wapner, W. (1954). *Personality through Perception*. New York: Harper.
Witkin, H. A. (1962). *Psychological Differentiation: Studies in Development*. New York: Wiley.
Wolfe, R. (1963). The Role of Conceptual Systems in Cognitive Functioning at Varying Levels of Age and Intelligence. *Journal of Personality*, 31 (1), p. 108-122.
Wolff, Werner (1943). *The Expression of Personality: Experimental Depth Psychology*. New York: Harper & Bros.
_____ (1950). *Values and Personality*. New York: Grune and Stratton.
Woolf, Leonard (1931 and 1940). *After the Deluge: A Study of Communal Psychology.* (2 vols) New York: Harcourt, Brace and Company.
Wriston, Henry M., et al. (1960). *Goals for Americans: The Report of the President's Commission on National Goals*. Englewood Cliffs, NJ: Prentice Hall.

INDEX

A

AN, **199** 167, 182, 184, 428, 449, 454, 456, 457, 458, 461, 480
  concept of space and time, 201
  CP and, 209
  DQ guilt, 208
  ER relationship with, 209
  examples, 202
  management of, 211-212
  motivation, 200
  pre-cultural, 55
  transition from, 213
A'N', 365, 184, 421, 428, 433, 448, 455, 456, 459, 465, 509
  A' problems of existence, 359
  as seen from DQ or ER, 385
  change, 189
    readiness for, 388
  character of a society, 392
  compulsiveness, 377 *see* compulsiveness
  contextual knowledge, 377
  feelings, 340
  formulation of the theory, 370
  intellectual doubt, 137
  learning, institutions of, 392
  less fear, 373
  management, 375, **382**-388
    mismanagement, 385, 386
  motivation, 382, 386
  overview, 368
  systemic thinking, 380
  transition, A'N' to B'O', 389
  values A'N', 368, 369, 370, 380, 383, 388, 390-391
absolutism, 62, 65, 68, 69, 76, 87, 78, 108, 110, 130, 147, 184, 254, 263, 309, 310, 314, 316, 317, 320, 338, 409, 435, 436
  absolutistic existential state *see* DQ
acceptance, 79, 231, 346
  prescriptions of authority, 261
Adams, D.K., 320
adjustment, 285

environment to the organism, 201, 285, 378
organism to the environment, 214
more effective, 476
Adler, Alfred, 144, 146, 272, 317, 462
  see will to power
Adorno, T. W., 124
adrenaline, 245 *see* noradrenaline
adult
  behavioral system, 1, 120
  educational problems, 4, 6, 39
  mature, 42, 171 *see* behavior *and* conceptions *and* mature *and* personality *and* psychological personality, 488
  psychological development
    15 key points, 129
  vertical orientation, 488
affect, 227, 293 *see* emotions
  deliberate inarticulation, 348
Africa, 204, 219
age, 34, 35, 36, 346, 367, 452
  see research, subjects
aggression, 68, 92, 98, 123, 233, 312, 362, 419, 448, 455, 500
  CP, 227, 241, 249, 341
  DQ, 284, 287, 292, 295
  FS against self, 341
  cp/DQ, 455
  disappearance, 125
  express self, not at expense, 96
  subordinated in higher levels, 378
aggressiveness, 122, 124, 125, 312, 424, 426, 430, 480
  appearance of, 341
  CP, DQ, and ER, 378
  homo homini lupus view, 22
Ahammer, Inge M., 34, 37
Allport, Gordon, 417
Alor people, 500
Amazon, BO living in, 219
ambiguity (DQ), 278, 280, 298, 303
  and (ER), 332

America, 13, 290, 302
  Greening of, 493, 501
American
  Robber Barons, 317
  cities, 224
  dream, 501
  Goals For, reconsidered, 492
  motif, 430
  society, 359
  Ways of Life, 282
American Council on Education, 123
anger *see* emotion
animistic existence *see* BO
approach, 33-50
Arapesh, 500
Aronoff, Joel, 463
arrested, 136, 207, 211, 357, 473, 478, 494 *see* open *and* closed
Ashby, W. Ross, 483 *see* General Systems Theory
assessments (of E-C theory)
  understand what to assess, 69
  verbal of BO, 220
Athos, Anthony, 457
Attica Prison riot (1971), 500
Ausubel, David P., 442, 452
authority, 77, 264, 266, 312, 327, 345, 346, 430, 501
  absolutistic (usually Divine), 263
  disdain for, 74
  ER and FS negative to, 349 [CP?]
  extra-human, 268
  Godly, 89
  oppositional to, 79
  righteous man in, 293
  social expedient as, 87
autistic (automatic) existence, 199
  see AN
autonomy, 87, 124, 270, 278, 314, 382, 384 *see* individual
awareness, 41, 88, 217, 408, 494
  see self
  cognitive, 148
  conscious, 230
  death, 182, 252
  differing value systems, 280
  emotions, 330
  guilt, 247, 249
  own existence of, 211, 412

B

BO, 215, 182, 184, 428, 449, 456
  animistic existence, 216
  entering from AN, 213
  existential state, 170
  learning, 219
  management, 220-224
    mismanagement, 221
    motivation, 218, 220
    negatively, 221
  transition, BO to CP, 500
  tribalistic, 55, 217
  values BO, 218, 222, 223, 398
B'O', 395, 190, 391, 448, 455
  change, readiness for, 401
  characteristics, 396
  comments on conceptualization, 399
  emergence of, 397
  Experientialist Existential State, 395
  limited data, 191
  management, 401
  values B'O', 397, 398-399
Baltes, Paul B., 34
Baltes, Paul B. and Shaie, Warner K., 37
Bandura, Albert and Walters, R.H., 350
Bandura, Albert, 17
Barker, Roger, 420
barriers *see* change, six conditions
Barron, Frank, 54
Bavelas, Alex, 118
behavior *see* emergent cyclical theory
  aberrant, 17
  adult, 12, 13, 27, 142, 428-429, 477, 480
  behavioral freedom, 188, 429, 430, 508
  breakdown in, 12-13 *see* immoral
  change in, 19, 34, 35, 81, 97, 106, 138, 140, 232, 238-239, 361, 416, 475, 483 *see* change
  confusing and contradictiory, 1, 91, 123, 127 *see* confusing
  cyclic aspect, 368
  deficiency, 26
  delinquent, 455
  delusional, 300

behavior *(continued)*
  dysfunctional and functional, 45
  emergent state, 141
  emotional, 289
  evil, 24
  fixate, 495
  forms of, 97, 140, 144, 163, 180, 421, 477
    unforeseen, 148
    emergent, 141, 142
    pathological, 137
  hierarchically ordered, 30, 114, 185
  immature, 11, 18, 24, 31, 42
  immoral behavior, 31
  infinite process, 37
  interrelated with character, 109
  mature, 16, 18-19, 22, 27-28, 43, 45, 46, 74, 92, 142, 489
    classes of, 47, 126
    conception of, 149
    non-conforming concepts, 149
    study of, 55, 109
  moral, 21
  neurotic, psychotic, 269
  new model, 142
  principles which govern, 152
  psychosocial, 185-188, 419, 438, 506
    theories of, 417
  standard for evaluation, 155
  systems, 124, 145-146, 295, 422, 423, 424, 437
  theory of, 3-5
behavioral sciences, 3
  behaviorism, 16, 20
  behaviorists, 16-21, 201
  conception, 20, 21, 22
  humanistic, 27
  modeling, 16, 17, 18, 19, 20, 350
  reinforcement, 17, 19, 20, 21, 240, 461
    negative, 409
    positive, 238, 239, 409, 411
  therapy, 490
becoming, 155
being levels, 163, 169, 174, 363, 456, 463, 509 *see* A'N' *and* B'O'
  Being Level I, II, III Systems, 163
    first, 365, 369, 440
    second, 395

belonging, 26, 147, 148, 189, 326, 334, 335, 338, 344, 347, 349, 353, 354, 410, 496
Bentham, Jeremy, 461
Bergson, Henri, 153
Berlyne, Daniel E., 408
biochemistry, 29, 30, 410, 507 *see* brain
biopsychological development, 506
bio-social ecological systems, 193
Black Muslim, 20, 500
Black Power movement, 499
Blackboard Jungle, The, 224
Blake, Robert R. and Mouton, Jane, 302, 322, 356, 396, 446, 452
  managerial grid, 322, 490
blank slate, 31
Blasi, Arthur, 414
Blatt, Moshe, 414
Blatz, William, 17
Blos, Peter, 6
Boas, Franz, 14
Boy Scout merit badge, 281
brain, 36, 163, 164, 167, 170, 207, 174, 258, 407, 475, 481 *see* dynamic neurological systems
  activation, 338, 360, 367, 415, 416
  awakening, 216
  basic structure, 240, 373, 449, 479
  cells, 174, 202, 361, 367, 397, 410, 464
  chemistry and dissonance, 415, 487
  chemistry, 258, 367
    fear, 367, 373 *see* emotions
    guilt, 258 *see* emotions
  elaborating system, 410 *see* Z
  general activating system, 412
  hemisphere dominance, 164, 186, 187, 338, 438, 507
  hierarchical and systemic, 37, 361, 407, 410
    hierarchically ordered, 413, 416, 475, 481
    systemically ordered, 37
  large brain of humans, 37, 174, 361, 407, 410
  possibility of latent systems, 412
  psychochemical, 131
  tissue in for self-awareness, 230
  uncommitted cells, 174
Bricker, P.D. and Chapanis, Alphonse 464

Brock, T.C., 432
Bronson, Gordon, 37
Broughton, John, 444, 452, 457
Bruner, Jerome, 6, 464
Brust-Carmona, H., 408
Buddhist
  monk, 261
  principles, 22
Bugental, James F.T., 53, 54, 417
Buhler, Charlotte, 34, 451
Bull, Norman, 452

C

CP, 225, 182, 184, 230, 427, 446, 448, 455, 458, 461, 478, 493
  and AN, 209
  aggressiveness, 378
  approach to living, 228
  change, readiness for, 245
  classification of humans (as strong, desirous, weak), 233, 244
  dominant-submissive, 226
  distinct self, 226
  examples, 228
    conception #1, 228
    conception #2, 229
    transitional CP/dq, 246
    transitional cp/DQ, 248
  impulses, control of, 236
  learning, 235
    punishment, 238
    reward, 235
    teacher, 235
  management, 227, 240-245
    mismanagement, 244
  motivation, 233, 247
  origin, 230
  psychology of, 231-233
  social issues, 242, 244
  state, 240
  transition CP to DQ, 241, 246, 247, 248
  value system, 234, 237, 245, 249
Calhoun, John, 6, 190, 388, 389, 444, 448, 452
  on population, 388
  test of E-C by, 460
Calvinist, 21, 23

Canada, 219
Camus, Albert, 140
category *see* conceptions *and* behavior *and* levels of existence
  expres self, 96, 97, 112, 126, 127, 137
  sacrifice now, 101, 254
categorical
  certainty, 331
  thinking, 68, 69, 71, 86, 255, 263, 436
Catholic, 100, 218, 266
  doctrinaire Catholicism, 257
  celibacy, 296
  authority, 105, 266
caveat emptor, 311
change, 486, 507-509
  see behavior change *and* conceptions
  attitude toward, 75
  behavior *see* behavior
  beliefs, 257
    single, 465
    systems of, 465
  central *see* conceptions, central
  closed
    belief system, 465
    mind, 386
    personality, 270, 303, 476
  conceptual, 154-155, 379
  conditions for change (six), 30, 103, 104, 105, 107, 170, 171-172, 413-416
    barriers, 26, 88, 104, 106, 107, 172, 180, 223, 416
    consolidation, 104, 107, 172, 415, 479
    dissonance, 104, 106, 172, 180, 353, 414, 484
    regressive search, 223, 414
      see regressive
    insight, 104, 105, 106, 172, 180, 415, 484
      specific to category, 106
    potential, 30, 104, 107, 170, 171, 213, 412, 476, 481
      biochemical, 367
      genetically equipped, 30, 509
      neuropsychological, 170
    resolution (solutions), 104, 106, 113, 413
      existential problems to, 171

change conditions resolution *(continued)*
    DQ, 432
    ER, 321-323, 324
    FS, 353, 354-355
    A'N', 383, 386
        particular to the level, 492
    support for six-elements view, 413
  conditions *for* existence, 104, 207, 479, 480
  conditions *of* existence, 29, 30, 155, 181, 213, 319, 464, 482, 490
  cultural, 449
  difficult to stop once started, 492
  direction of, **100**, 106, 113, 156
  environmental, 170
    change or adjust to, 184-185, 447
  excess energy required, 222, 492
  four demarcation points in: a, b, c, d, (also alpha, beta, gamma, delta), 178
  fixation, 180
  intellectual climate, 150
  instigators for sub-types, **100**
    external authority, 100, 102, 105, 109, 270, 278
    information, 102, 377
    need to know principles, 489
    own actions, 81, 321-322
    peer pressure, 101
  long term, 346
  managing, 384
  organismic-environment complex, 151
  personality, 477, 483, 484
  point of reference, 189, 378
  principles of, 489
  process of, 107, 170, 270, 438, 455, 482
  progressive or regressive, 99, 114, 148, 160, 178, 484, 506
  psychology, 29 *see* psychology
  regress, 107, 113, 178, 180, 185 *see* regressive
    AN to, 202
    DQ to ER 'regressive' disorganization, 271
    societal, 390
  responsibility for, 19
  readiness, 35, 157, 222, 291, 495
    see change, redinness *in* BO, CP, etc.
  social, 170
  step-like, quantum-like, 484, 485
  systems, 188
  tendency, 481-482
  values, 31, 334, 370, 402
China, 12, 17, 494
  Red Guards, 12
Christian, 253, 262
  ethics, 261
  form of existence, 255
  Roman attack on early, 253
class, 254, 256, 258, 310
  class-ordered life, 268
  CP sorting, 233, 244
  middle, 492, 501
closed, 136, 270, 302, 303, 465, 468, 473, 476-478, 488, 494 *see* open *and* arrested *and* systems
  behavior, 477
  closed system, 29, 30, 149, 303, 465, 486, 509
  minds, 386
  unalterable, 269, 302
  DQ, 267, 269
  ER, 472
cognition, human characteristic, 362
cognitive, 129, 351 *see* psychology
  activation, 366
  awareness of the self, 148 *see* awareness *and* self
  brain substance, 202
  capacities, 162, 237
  complexity, 129
  dissonance, 296
    see change, conditions, six
  employee, 383
  inadequacy, 178
  level of existence, 362, 367
  man, 223, 224, 367, 368
  processes, 373
  realm, 363, 369
  state, undifferentiated, 223
  structure, 284
communism *see* cultural systems
competition, 57, 274, 310, 318, 319
  cooperation more valued than, 339, 354, 359
  fixing in electrical industry, 345
  non-competitive, 344, 382

complexity, 148, 149
    controlling device, 481-482
    see systems
    integrative, 435-437, 441
    stimulus, 432
    thinking, 497
compulsion, 299, 300, 380, 390
    compulsiveness, 300, 346, 369, 374, 378, 392, 455
    without, 372, 381, 382
conceptions of mature personality, 11, 52, 55, 59-89, 98, 128, 149, 156, 185-187, 407
    additional categories added, 125, 126
    approach to, 33-37, 40-47, 54, 92-93, 125, 406, 417
    categories, 59-89, 128
        express self, 56
        express self to avoid shame
            entering, 57
            nodal, 59, 228-230, 461
            exiting, 60-62, 246-248, 456
        express self calculatedly
            entering, 76-77, 279-280
            nodal, 79-80, 311-313
            exiting, 81-83, 330-331
        deny self, 56, 92
        sacrifice self for reward later
            entering, 62-63, 456
            nodal, 65-67, 69-71, 254, 258-263
            exiting, 72-74, 275-278
        sacrifice self to obtain now
            enter, 84-86, 332-334
            nodal, 88-89, 342-344
    change of, 186
    change in conceptions, 99, 102, 106, 137, 366, 370 *see* change
        case of Linda S., 110-112
        case of Mike M., 110
        self-actualizing people, 148
        sub-type, 52, 60, 98-99, 101, 103, 104, 112-114, 148, 160, 278, 280
    central change in, 64, 71, 99, 103, 104, 107, 114
    classification, 30, 56, 59-89, 92-93, 114, 128, 134-138, 155-137, 254
    examples included in the text, 60-89
        B'O' (discussion), 399
        CP/dq transition, 60-62, 246

cp/DQ transition, 57, 248, 455
DQ/er, 72-74, 275-278
dq/ER, 76-77, 279-280
ER nodal, 79-80, 311-313
ER/fs, 81-83, 330-331
er/FS, 88-89, 332-334
FS, 88-89, 342-344
hierarchy of, 127, 128, 149
open-ended series of, 191
open minded conceptions, 102, 191
personality systems in miniature, 97-98
say about versus think about, 69
systematically organized, 137
    judging the conceptions, 93
conceptual framework revised, 92
conceptual space, **181**, 369, 379, 508
    odd/even systems, expansion in, 189
conceptualizations of adult personality
    information overlooked, 36
    perspectives
        psychoanalytic, 21
        homo homini lupus, 21, 25, 31
        behaviorist, 16, 18-20
        Gravesian, 31
        humanistic, 24, 26, 141, 359
        Life Span psychologists, 34
        Third Force, 24, 28
    what adults say personality is, 56
conceptualizers, 36, 37, 144, 145, 146, 418, 453
    behaviorists 19-20
    existential, 141
    Harvey, Hunt, and Schroder, 419-439
    other conceptions, 417-418
    phenomenological, 141
    projecting self into, 54
    psychologists 12, 115, 30, 34, 36-38
    stage developmental conceptualizers, 439-464
conditioning, 37 *see* behaviorism
conditions *see* change, conditions
    of and *for* human existence, 176
    for existence, 162, 166, 475
    of existence, 162, 166, 508
Condorcet, Marquis de, 24
conflict, 15, 119 *see* data, conflictual
    between members of groups, 119-120

conflict *(continued)*
  between theories, 142
  between theorists, 14, 38, 48
  righteous man and, 294
  controversy and, 13, 38, 51, 91, 133
  confusion and contradiction, 14, 51, 91, 138
Congo, 224
congruence, 30, 211, 301, 482
  higher education, 497
  management and governance, 320, 323, 324, 355, 490, 493
  rather than promoting growth, 463
  values, 269, 358
consciousness, 218, 220, 226, 270, 342, 398, 449, 488, 500
  Consciousness III, 20, 499, 502
  interest in, 335
  new forms emerge, 19
  self-consciousness emerges, 85, 182, 201, 226, 230, 252
  revolutions in, 223, 226, 309, 335, 360, 497, 499-502
consolidation, 417 *see* change
coping, 30, 180, 362
  cells and equipment, 367, 416, 507
  devices, 298
    of righteous man: rationalization and denial, 294
  means, 178
  systems, 161-162, 173, 397, 411
    activating - X, 161
    elaborating - Z, 161
    supporting - Y, 161
crime, 74, 291, 292, 378
  against self, 378, 341
  against property, 455
  homicide, 341
cultural institutions, E-C as theory of, 33
cultural system, 131, 478
  autocracy, 270, 302
  communism, 155, 257, 493
  democracy, 155, 270, 381, 491, 493
culture, 4, 24, 39, 126, 151, 159, 160, 163, 166, 175, 186, 188, 191, 449, 451, 475
  change in, 178, 483
  development, 15
  drug, 349

food gathering, 202
healthy, 489
less developed, 126, 202
nature of, 154
theory, 14, 15, 150, 153
Utopian *see* Utopian
ways of man (and personality), 176
world, 442, 450
cybernetics, 484
cyclic, 36, 113, 129, 147, 185, 335, 368, 427, 451, 459, 483, 507 *see* emergent-cyclical

D

DQ, 251, 183, 184, 252-305, 413, 421, 428, 433, 435, 446, 448, 449, 453, 456, 462, 465, 480
  absolutistic characteristics, 255
  AN and, 208
  authority, 263
  readiness for change, 271
  conception, 258, 262
  examples, 258
    conception #1, 258
    conception #2, 262
    DQ/er conception (exiting), 276
    dq/ER conception (entering), 279
  guilt, 253 *see* guilt
  learning, 265-267
    objective testing, 281
    teacher, 265
    closed DQ, 267
  leadership, 254
  management, 261, 267-271, 290-302
    mismanagement, 270
  motivation, 266, 304
  obeisance in, 252
  see obedience *and* obeisance
  orderly world, 94, 253, 256
  Righteous Existence, DQ/ER, 282, 284, 285
    managing, 301-305
      mismanagement, 325-326
    origins of the righteous state, 296-297
    reaction to stress, 297-301
    organizational structure, 301

DQ *(continued)*
    win-lose psychology, 294
    self-sacrifice, 254
    see sacrifice self
    state, 266
    teacher or manager, 273
    see teacher
    transition DQ to ER, 272, 273, 275, 282, 285, 287, 317, 501
    values, 246, 252, 253, 255, 257, 271, 272
Darwin, Charles, 37, 51, 52, 174, 361
Darwinian concept, 315
data (in the Gravesian work), 2, 51-90
    see Verification, 405-473
    A'N' difference, 371, 374
        rigidity and dogmatism, 377
    B'O' cases, 396, 399
    3 basic kinds of, 46
    conflictual and confusing, 114, 115, 116, 123, 142
    forms of human existence not included in the data, 55
    gathered prior to 1962, 129
    messages in, 134-138
        structuring a language, 137-138
    questions arising from, 71
    perplexing results
        functioning and production, 94-96
        opposed categories, 93
    rationalizing, 7, 133, 418
    tachistoscope, **466, 468-471**
deference (to authority), 124, 254, 287
delinquency, 455
democracy *see* cultural systems
denial, 294
dependence, 74, 334
depression, 299, 300, 409, 411
designation of levels *see* nomenclature
developing nations, 126
development, 29, 33-35, 37, 57, 69, 113, 129-131, 150-153, 163, 176, 172, 405, 477, 489, 499, 506-509
    barriers to, 35
    cognitive stage, 7, 29 *see* cognitive
    conceptualizations of, 34
    continuing process of, 35, 452
    cyclic, oscillating movement in, 113
    direction, not a state or form, 151
    emergent states in, 20
    fixate, regress, new form, 160
    process of, 7, 151, 185
    psychological, 2, 33
        adult, 129
        ever-evolving, step-like process, 489
        results from interaction, 166
    psychosocial development, 405
        environmentosocial-organismic field, 166
        complex wave-like, 178
        double-helix, 174
        organismic as delimiter, 407
        resultants of interaction, 167
        spurt-like, plateau-like, 178
        systems, 506
        systemic, 188
        social, 1
    stage-like, 417
dialectic, 463
dictatorship, 292
differentiation, 28, 182
    self from others, 201
disintegration, 15, 62, 483
    see equilibium
dissenters, 366
dissonance *see* change conditions
dogmatism, 68, 77, 93, 123, 189, 258, 284, 309, 347, 397, 428, 430, 465, 508
    Dogmatism Scale, 122, 465 *see* Rokeach
    rigidity and, 377, 465
dominant-submissive, 226, 256
Doty, R.W., 220
double-helix, 131, 160-162, 174, **187**, 406, 437, 504
    environmentosocial forces, 160
    organismic forces, 160
Drews, Elizabeth, 6, 452
Driesch, Hans Adolf Eduard, 153, 154
Driver, Michael J., 432
dynamic neurological systems, 161, 361, 412, 414, 419, *see* Krech
    structures latent in the brain, 412

E

E-C *see* emergent cyclical
ECLET (emergent, cyclical levels of existence theory). *see* emergent

ER, **307**, 184, 309, 421, 428, 435, 447, 449, 453, 456, 459, 462, 465, 501
  AN and, 209
  change, 321
    readiness for change, 326
  closed, 472
  examples, 310
    nodal ER conception, 311
    example #1, ER/fs conception, 330
    example #2, er/FSr conception, 332
  five states of existence, 283
  interpersonal relations, 314, 334
  learning, 319
  management, 315, **320**-326, 357
    mismanagement, 325-326
  motivation, 320
    self-motivated, 430
  transition ER to FS, 327, 334, 341, 360, 472
  values ER, 272, 309, 310, 311, 314, 315, 316, 317, 326, 334, 338, 344, 359, 360
education, 13, 29, 482, 507
  see learning and AN, BO, CP, etc.
  A'N' society in, 392
  broader meaning for, 496
  experience, 328
  forms appropriate to levels, 497
  in the person for FS, 352
  methods, 375
  move to more complex levels, 497
  subsidized, 64
  success, 391
Edwards Preference Inventory, 124
egalitarian, 351
ego, 68, 70, 442
  definition, 347
  development, **461**, 463
    see Loevinger
  ego-less (in A'N'), 379
  encroachment, 314, 319
  involved, 267
  superego, 455
egocentric, 22, 60, 78, 225, 248, 258
  see CP
egoistic, 209
elaborating system, 162, 165, 173, 410
  see Z
Elkind, David, x, 31, 416

emergence, 1, 2, 29, 141, 159, 185, 223, 319, 397, 417, 476, 480, 506
  behavior, 141 see behavior
    higher levels of, 148
  ends, 497
  growth, 160
  levels of, 30
  man's nature, 480
  organism, 500
  psychosocial systems, 5
  process, 465, 508
  stages, 7, 20
emergent cyclical (theory of adult biopsychosocial systems development)
  34 principles of E-C theory, 486
  adult personality and cultural institutions, 175
  basics of, 167, **168**
  compared to stage conceptualizers, 418, 439
  compared with other theories, **440-446**
  conception 2, 29, 33, 56, 160, 167, 405
  double-helix model see double-helix
  formulation of, 370
  model, 159, 163
  or unfolding pattern, 468
  points in the process of life, 166
  psychological life space of, 163
  spurt and plateau, 188
  support from general psychology, 407
  theory, 166, 506
    adult of, 51, 196, 417
    formulation of, 369
  personality and cultural institutions, 33
  wave-like manifestation, 113, 176, 435, 506
    spurt-like, plateau-like, 178
    successive equilibrations, 477
  formulation of, 370
  movement, 113
emotion, 29, 70, 87, 103, 412, 502, 508
  AN, 208
  A'N', 372
  affection, 87
  affective, 293

emotion *(continued)*
  distinguish self, 202, 459
  person affective, 227
  warmth, 342, 348
 anger, 11, 22, 72, 180, 201, 266, 285, 299, 459
  intellectually used, 375
  modulated, 314
 control over, 108
 CP and, 227, 233
 delight, 393, 409
 disappear, 205
 disgust, 227, 358, 458
 DQ and, 262, 273
 ER/fs 'great' appraiser of, 330
 FS, 338, 339, 340, 348, 349
 fear, 15, 57, 59, 60, 64, 141, 201, 233, 249, 366, 409, 458
  abandonment, 299
  barrier of, 107, 379
  being disliked, 353
  chemistry of, 367, 373
  demise, of our, 2, 392
  dissolution in A'N', 369, 372, 373, 379, 390
  expressing hostility, 300
  frightened DQ existence, 253
  inferiority, 265
  influx of stimulation, 253, 256
  loss of self, 360
  of powers, 141. 353
  punishment, of, 298, 299
  reduces, 291
  resolved, 366
  shame of, 58, 60, 130
  sex relations, 299
  social disapproval, 369
  tool as, 318
 grief, 227
 guilt, 58, 62, 64, 68, 92, 100, 129, 227, 249, 253, 265, 319, 458
  see conceptions *and* express self
  adrenaline and, 245, 258
  awareness of, 247, 249, 285
  change, 60, 247, 275, 280
  express self without, 105, 107, 110, 112, 114, 115, 116, 119, 120, 121, 123, 124, 307
  first appears, 129, 460
 fourth level (DQ), 208, 209, 249, 253
 free self from, 265, 269, 314-315, 347
 lack of, 227, 233, 458
 hate, 201, 227, 244, 318, 325, 340, 357, 447, 501
  Taylorism causing, 290
 hostility, 25, 232, 244, 284, 290, 298, 319, 372, 496
  transfer onto authority, 305
 jealousy, 201
 over-reactional (in BO), 218
 pseudo-emotions
  depression, 299, 409, 411
  discomfort, 244
  excitement, 244, 409, 411
  frustration, 95, 106, 201, 242, 244, 352, 477
 rage, 227
 Righteous control, 289, 304
 sensitivity to, 273
 sub-systems, 409
 shame, 58, 60, 78, 81, 92, 126, 130, 226, 233, 238, 247, 280, 315, 380, 392, 409, 445, 458
  see conceptions, express self to avoid shame
  ashamed, 11, 128, 313
  fear of, 62
  unashamed, 110
empathy
 disdain for, 80, 81, 314, 328,
 others' difficulty empathizing with A'N', 369
 required for DQ/ER teacher, 273
Engen, T., 408
entering, **56**, 57, 62, 76, 84, 506
 see nodal *and* exiting
environment
 side of development, 161
environmentosocial conditions, 160-167, 171, 407, 412
 see psychological space
 determinants, 506
 environmentosocial-organismic field, 166
 forces, 163
epistemologies, natural, 457
equilibrations, 477

equilibrium, 29, 270, 482, 483
  even-numbered systems, 480
  levels as theoretical state of, 477
  out of, 298
  restoring earth's by A'N', 390
equipment *see* brain *and*
neuropsychological
  risk-taking, chronological time and
    space-perceiving, 226
Erikson, Erik Homburger, 6, 23, 49,
  452
Esalen Institute, 393, 501
Establishment, the, 11, 12, 17, 22, 222,
  416
ethics, 2, 6, 29, 255, 354, 370, 381, 498,
  507
  Kantian, 255
  Judeo-Christian, 22
  Machiavellian, 323 *see* Machiavelli
  power ethic, 233
  system, 317, 489
Ethiopia, 489
evolution, 151, 378
  as process, 51
  psychological, 389
existential, 29, 365
  dichotomies, 112
  jargon, 263
  Means for Living, 162
  problems, 106, 162, 183, 492, 494
    in time, 160
    resolution and creation, **183**
  realities, 481, 482
  staircase, 195, 391, 399, 490, 499
    see ladder
  state, 162, 167, 175, 188, 417, 439
    development of in time, **479**
    AN, 167, 171, 207, 212, 454, 458
      see AN
    BO, 170, 179, 191, 454 *see* BO
    CP, 224 *see* CP
    DQ, 253, 258 *see* DQ
    DQ/ER 'righteous existence,'
      282-305 *see* DQ
    ER, 309, 338, 473 *see* ER
    FS, 350, 455 *see* FS
    A'N', 365, 367, 189 *see* A'N'
      cognitive, 369, 370, 374, 382,
        384
    B'O', 191, 368 *see* B'O'
      intuitive existence, 395, 397

  source of, **193**
existentialists, 140, 489
exiting, 56, 60, 72, 81, 506
  see entering *and* nodal
experience
  BO, 218
    stimulus-response, 220
  B'O', 399
  educational *see* education
  CP operant conditioning and many
    positive, 243
  factor in conception change, 52
  human, 53, 60, 202
  level-specific to activate neurology,
    170
  own (ER), 78, 81, 100, 101, 320
  peer group (FS), 102
  shared (FS), 340, 349
  students in the research, 46
  to reject or assimilate, 482
  tried-and-true (ER), 280, 309
experiential, 5, 169, 395, 401 *see* values
express self, 57, 128 *see* conceptions
  to hell with others, 57, 59, 60
  calculatedly, 76, 79, 81
  but not at the expense of others,
    103
Eysenck, Hans, 144, 146

F

FS, 337, 184, 349, 421, 428, 435, 449,
  455, 456, 459, 462, 465, 480, 492, 501,
  502
  basic operation, 347
  change, readiness for, 358
  readiness for change, 358
  examples, FS conception, 342
  learning, 350
    teacher, 351
  management, 353-358, 359
  mismanagement, 357-358
  origin, 344
  transition, FS to A'N' 352-353, 362
  values, 334, 339, 340, 342, 345, 347,
    359, 360, 368
faith, 183
  human, not Godly, 393, 398
  keep, 318
fear *see* emotion

federalization, 263, 311, 491
feedback from others, 81
feelings *see* emotions
   inner subjective, 338
   judging feelings, 264
Fenton, Edwin, Colby, Ann, and Speicher-Dubin, Betsy, 414
Festinger, Leon, 414
Five Ages of Man, 6 see Heard
Flavell, John H., 34
force field, 162 *see* existential state
Ford Motor Company, 323
4-H, 281
framework, 3-4, 15, 16-17, 25, 30, 32, 145, 208, 334, 353, 417, 457 *see* conceptualizers *and* behavior
   behavioral, 145
   conceptual, 36, 92, 99, 123, 145, 417, 418
   E-C, 243, 437, 438, 454, 455, 456, 460
   explanatory, 51
   thought, 489
   Perry, 456
Frankl, Viktor, 36
French Canadians, 219
Freud, Sigmund, 31, 49, 68, 144, 146, 256, 292, 316, 400, 462, 484
Freudian
   ethic, 257
   psychoanalysts, 21
   slips, 68, 259
Fromm, Erich, 191, 256, 346, 360, 400, 441
Funkenstein, D.H., 411, 415
future 1, 2, 11, 15, 129, 142, 144, 163, 354, 356
   mankind's 53, 282, 283, 391
   modes of life, 363, 369, 388
   multiple, 499
   possibilities, 362, 389-390
   prediction, 389, 438
   sustainable, 390

G

Gandhi, Mahatma, 257
Garden of Eden, 214
Gastaut, H., 408
General Systems, 6
   controlling device complexity of, *see* complexity
   mini-maxing, 484
   model, 163
   principles and E-C theory, 486
   theorists, 149
   theory, 150, 152, 153, 159, 484
generation gap, 359
goals, *see* America
   related to all human kind in FS, 347
God, 13, 51, 63, 65, 71, 87, 101, 135, 141, 201, 207, 252, 255, 272, 296, 321, 352, 373, 392, 393, 414, 420
   master plan in DQ, 263
   righteous man, 296
   word of, 309, 316
Godric, 272
Goldstein, Kurt, 6, 145, 147, 149, 419
Gough, H.G. and Sanford, R.N., 123, 465
Gough-Sanford Rigidity Scale, 464
governing, 388, 390
   A'N' approach, 391
   DQ values for, 263
   figures, prime goal of, 484
   new systems of, 391-392
Graves, Dr. Clare W., 22, 65, 147, 196, 216, 234, 351, 439, 448, 464
   consulting, 265
   workshop handouts, 506
Gray, Thomas, 415
Gray, William, 483, 484
great divide, 190, 402, 503
Greece, 292
Greening of America, 492, 501
see consciousness, Consciousness III
Griffin, Merv, 372
growth, 26, 148, 463, 491, 496, 501
   biological, 34
   consolidation and, 189, 479
   devalued, 391
   economic viability and, 490
   emergent phenomenon, 160
   healthy, 26
   life, 209
   limits to, 359
   man's, 211, 326
   mature behavioral systems, 148
   see behavior
   means of, 85

growth *(continued)*
  moral, 315
  motivation, 362
  odd numbered systems, 189
  phenomenon, 148, 160
  population, 388
  principles for managing, 211
  psychological, 35, 189
  sign of, 15, 16, 17, 360
  tendency, 483, 484
guilt *see* emotions

H

habituation, 200, 219, 408, 409
Hall, Calvin S. and Lindzey, Gardner, 405
harmony, 344, 349, 359
  organization of current state as 'maturity,' 155
Hartman, Heinz. *see* psychoanalysts
Harvard Business Review, 196
Harvey, O.J., Hunt, David and Schroder, Harold M., 6, 134, 135, 400, 419, 438, 439, 465
  characteristics in model, 424
  concreteness-abstraction, 421
  data, **424** and rearranged, **426**
  verification with approach, 419
Harvey, O.J., 6, 421
Hassler, R. 407
haves and have-nots, 227, 233, 326
Havighurst, Robert, 6, 34
Hawkins, Robert, 17
Heard, Gerald, 6, 36, 134, 417, 448, 449, 450, 451, 499
Hebb, D. O., 407
hedonism, CP tendency toward, 228
Hegel, G.W.F., 317
Heider, Fritz, 6
helix, 2, 4, 71, 407 *see* double helix
Hernandez-Peon, R., 408, 410
Herzberg, Fred, 23
Hess, E. H., 415
hierarchical
  rise of existential problems, 160
  systems, 36
  systems perspective, 29
  ordered stages, 489
  organization of systems, 173

hierarchy, 2, 128, 136, 151, 413, 419
  behavioral hierarchies, 147
  emerging personality, 91
  personality systems, 151
  systems in the brain, 481
Hindu, 261, 257
Hoarding Character *see* Fromm
Hokfelt, Bernt, 412, 415
Homer's *Odyssey*, 126
homo homini lupus see conceptions of adult personality
Homo sapiens, 33, 161, 164, 174, 180, 407, 506
homogeneity
  group, 274
  societal, 491, 493
homogeneity to heterogeneity, 152
homogenization, 346, 498
honesty, 358
Hoover, Herbert, 498
Horney, Karen, 144, 410
hostility, 25, 137, 292, 298, 305, 494
  avoiding to self in ER/fs, 384
  CP tendency to manifest, 232
  intellectually used in A'N', 372
  perceived by others of ER, 315, 319
  world as life condition, 166
Howe, M.J.A., 453
human, 169, 202, 209 *see* existence *and*
behavior *and* conditions *and*
development *and* personality
  awakened to inner man, 252
  behavior reconceptualized, 142, 154
  being, 155, 166, 189
  drives, lustful, 296, 309
  existence, 155
  existential helix, 2
  faith in, 393
  group animal, 354
  knowledge reconsidered, 491
  living, ER as 'epitome' of, 283
  mature, 138, 142
  nature
    objective and subjective sides, 36
    revised conception of, 136
  needs, distinctly human, 189
  philosophical thought, 351
  relations, 301, 353, 356
  survival, 172
  symphony with six themes, 396
    see six themes

human *(continued)*
 threshold of being, 367
 variability, 322
 wants, 296
Human Needs Foundation, 7
humanism (vs. animalism), 190, 200, 339, 360, 368
humanistic
 Conception *see* conceptions of adult personality
 weakness of, 28
 goal, 417
 subjectivistic world, 334
 tradition, 368
humanness, 24
Hummel, Dean L. and Bonham Jr., S.J, 490
Hunt, David E., 6, 419
Huntley, W.C., 464

I

Idi Amin, 13
Ik tribe (Uganda), 204, 390, 414, 500
immature *see* behavior *and* mature
immediacy, 495, 496
impulsive, 58, 59, 64, 232, 233, 237, 266, 305, 448 *see* CP
independence, 75, 130, 271, 272, 278, 282, 292, 308 *see* ER
Indian tribes, 219
individual, 176 *see* autonomy
 individualism, 227, 311, 316
 last gasp of, 502
individuality, 85, 278, 338, 342, 347, 360
 obsession with, 87
Industrial Revolution, 308
information, 36, 383, 399
inhumane human state, 205, 209
insights *see* change conditions
integrated living, 476
integration, 483
 A'N' into organization, 386
 knowledge of all, 13
integrative
 complexity, 435-437, 441
 management, 353
intelligence, 124, 128, 129, 186, 371, 428, 437, 508 *see* studies

 boredom as result, 226
 learning takes place without, 220
intentionality, 226
interdependence, 75, 182, 184, 272, 308, 314, 370, 509 *see* ER
 authority teaches dictates of, 278
 desires for, 296
 feeling of, 271
 need for, 130, 283, 284, 278, 284, 296, 334
 selfish, 282, 283, 284, 285, 292
 ultimate sign of depravity, 272
interdependence, 184, 332, 366, 382, 391, 509
Ionesco, Eugene, 135
Isaacs, Kenneth, 444, 452, 458, 460
Israeli Kibbutz, 17

J

James, William, 420
Japan, 290, 302, 509
 government, 317
Jaspers, Karl, 204
Jefferson, Thomas, 24
job enrichment, 23, 269
Josephson, Matthew, 346
Journal of Humanistic Psychology, 196
judgmental about judgmentalism, 347
Jung, Carl, 36, 146, 408

K

Kahn, Herman, 499
Kalahari Desert, 203
Kant, Emanuel, 316 *see* ethics
Katz, Joseph, 34, 35
Keats, John, 138, 139, 140
Kendler, Howard, 20
King, Rev. Martin Luther, 257
Kluckhohn, Clyde, 15
knowledge, 159, 220, 316, 321, 338, 366, 393, 398, 503
 A'N' in specific settings, 377
 about adult behavior, 1
 accumulation of, 185, 399
 DQ either-or, right-wrong conception of, 255
 ER callous use of, 334
 leadership and A'N', 118, 384

knowledge *(continued)*
  man's, 3, 155, 491
  power of, 390
  FS consideration of, 340
  self, 352, 359
Koch, Sigmund, 145
Kohlberg, L., Hickey, J. & Scharf, P., 414
Kohlberg, Lawrence, 6, 21, 34, 414, 445, 448, 452, 453, 454, 462
Krasner, Leonard, 17
Krech, David, 165, 407, 410, 415
Kris, Ernst, 23 *see* psychoanalysts
Kroeber, Alfred L., 145
Kuhlen, Raymond G., 34

L

LaBier, Douglas, 464
labeling *see* nomenclature
labor, 354, 355
  contracts, 302
  leaders and members, 13
  management relations, 353, 354, 355, 357, 490
  management wars, 392
  strike behavior, 13
ladder of existence, 361, 389
  see existential staircase
  first (subsistence levels), 361, 389, 391, 502, 503
  second (being levels), 389, 502
Law of Requisite Variety, 483
Lawrence, D.H., 398, 504
leadership, 118, 119-120, 295, 321, 362, 384, 493 *see* AN *through* A'N'
  authoritarian, 309
  change, 118, 120, 382, 383, 463
  congruence, 320
  different levels of coping, 361
  falling psychologically behind, 321
  man of, 283
  no concept, 201
  political, 294 *see* governing
  revolving, 137, 382, 383
  soft, 294
  success of, 321
  vying for, 116

learning, 30, 165, 186, 214, 217, 391, 409, 464, 507 *see* AN, BO, CP, etc.
  and education
  associative, 141
  avoidant, 246, 249, 253, 256, 385, 410
  change to latent, signal, 320
  fractionated, 13
  hierarchy, 410
  intentional instrumental, 202, 233, 238, 239, 409
  observational, 350
  process, 266, 328 *see* habituation *and* operant *and* Pavlovian
  punishment, by, 239, 240
  social-learning, 37
  systems, dominant, 409
  two-factor theory, 146, 256, 266
Legum, Colin, 224
Lenin, Vladimir, 257
Leopold-Loeb murder case (1924), 291
letter to Schenectady *Gazette* , 210
letter pairs *see* nomenclatures
level(s), 402, 477, 481, 487, 489, 492
  see conceptions *and* hierarchy *and* emergent cyclical *and* AN *through* B'O'
  constructs, not obtainable states, 477
  Gravesian eight, 147
  human existence of, 1, 29, 33, 38, 56, 146, 169, 409, 440, 475, 476
    conceptual needs for, 160
  personal organization of, 176
  sense-making way of looking, 482
  subsistence compared, **409**
  Maslow's original 5, 147
Lickert, Rensis, 355
life circumstances, 148, 476
life problems of species, group, individual, 161, 165
Life Span psychologists, 6, 34
Locke, John, 17
Loevinger, Jane, 6, 444, 452, 456, 460-464
Lonely Crowd *see* Riesman
Looft, William, 34, 37
Lowenstein, Rudolph M. 23, *see* psychoanalysts
Luzon, Phillippines, 219

M

Machiavelli, Niccolo, 23, 317, 425, 426, 430, 480
  principles, 317, 324
Maddi, Salvatore R., 21
magic, 217, 218, 222, 353, 392, 502
Mahabarata, 126
Maier, Norman, 115
majority rule, 503
Makaha, Hawaii, 134
Malinowski, Bronislaw, 14
man see Homo sapiens
  supremacy of, 502
  problem-solving organism, 484
management, 3, 6, 29, 196, 490, 507
  see AN, BO, CP, etc.
  adult behavior of, 33
  congruent with levels, 30
  participative, 325, 354-355, 356, 360, 490
  revised through E-C theory, 490
managerial means, 33
Manchu dynasty, 255
Mao Tse Tung [Zedong], 12, 17, 255, 257, 389
Marketing Character, 345-346 *see* Fromm
Maslow, Abraham, 5, 6, 24, 25, 26, 49, 140, 145, 147, 149, 396, 398, 400, 452
  ability, 25
  belonging system, 334, 498
  doubts about hierarchy, 147
  self-actualizing person, 148, 399, 400, 452
Maslowian, 27
  conception of personality, 399
  hierarchy, 27, 147, 464
  position, 27
  terminology, 147
  theory tested by Aronoff, 463
  thinking, 418
materialism, 23, 334, 339, 492
  see ER *and* conceptions
mature *see* behavior
  assumptions about, 148
  behavior, 16
    conforming and non-conforming concepts of, 149
  life for tomorrow, 17
  ways of, 11
  condition or process, 38
  personality
    criteria for, 41, 155
    views of, 399
  state, 39
May, Rollo, 141
McClelland, David, 281
McGregor, Douglas, 244, 270, 353, 446, 452
Mead, Margaret, 500
meaning of the E-C concept, 491
medical service problem (for lower levels), 495
meditation, 352, 358
Mehrabian, Albert, 180
Menzies, R., 220
methodology, 47, 406, 448
  see research *and* data
  change data, 105
  observations, 370
  research design, 44
  summary, 91
Millon, Theodore, 25
Mills, Wilbur, 210
Mindanao, Phillippines, 28, 127, 169, 203
Mittelman, James H, 13
model, 37, 142, 149, 159, 160, 174
  see emergent cyclical *and* personality
  building, 147
  ten basic criteria for model of mature personality, 155
morality, 52, 62, 318, 443, 453, 498
  conventionality, 453
  CP, 233, 247
  E-C theory, 453
  ER, 315
  immoral behavior, 31, 351
  Kohlberg, 453
  meanings of breakdown, 490
  problems of, 6
Morgan, C.T., 408
Moslems, 257
motivation, 109, 409, 463, 507 *see* needs
  apppropriate to state, 29, 507
  deficiency and abundance, 128, 347, 358, 362
Mowrer, O. Hobart, 146, 256, 266
Moynihan, Daniel Patrick, 212

Index

Mumford, Lewis B., 1, 134, 184, 417, 442, 448, 449, 450, 451, 499
Murphy, Gardner, 140, 142, 143, 149, 152, 153, 154, 156, 419, 437
Murray, H.A., 15, 447, 448

N

Nance, John, 28, 127, 169
needs, 30, 41, 189, 367, 410
  affiliative, 335 *see* belonging
  conceptual for E-C theory, 160-161
  deficiency and abundance, 26, 508 *see* motivation
  gratification, 28
  imperative, periodic, physiological, 211, 413 *see* needs, physiological
  lower level and higher level, 27, 28
  Maslowian, 27, 148
  of others, 268, 354
  open, systems of
  ordering of per system, 410
  organizational, 383
  physiological, 26, 167, 170, 199, 200, 202, 203, 204, 211, 216, 230, 253, 408, 411, 413-414, 451, 488
  safety and security, 218, 253
  satisfaction to fixate behavior, 28
  social *see* needs, affiliative
  subsistence, 163
  survival, 148
neurochemical, 5, 231, 238, 412
  changes for A'N', 367
  switching subsystem, 165
neurological systems, 203, 238, 361, 397, 408, 410 *see* dynamic neurological systems *and* brain
  activation, 29, 300
  hypothetico-deductive, 309
neuropsychological
  equipment for living, 161, 167, 169, 173, 174, 180, 407, 414, 416, 417, 506
    N, 172, 185, 200
    O, 170, 408
    P, 172, 226, 409, 459
    Q, 253, 459
    R, 182
    S, 338
  N', 407, 410
  dogs, 407
  for living, 161, 167, 173
  species, group, individual, 161
  potential, 163-164, 170, 413
  system
    X, Y, and Z, 165, 167, 410-412 *see* X *and* Y *and* Z
never-ending...
  process of emergence, 400
  quest (of human emergence), 4, 417, 504
New Jersey income support plan, 212
Nietzsche, Friedrich, 140 *see* will to power
Nixon, President Richard, 282, 378
nodal, 56-57, 59, 65, 69, 72, 79, 88, 170, 176, 191, 203, 348, 449, 453, 455, 456, 457, 458, 461-462, 467, 476, 489, 506 *see* entering *and* exiting
  system, 191, 449, 454, 455, 506 *see* AN, BO, CP, etc.
  stage, 457, 461, 462, 489
  state, 170, 176, 473, 475
nomenclature (designation of systems), 161, **169**, 248
  entering-steady state-exiting, **192**
  lower case letters in Exhibit IX, 178
  letter pairs (AN, etc.), 166
  numbers, 439, 440
    odd and even, 429
    odd and even systems, 149
  organism (helix 2): N, O, P, Q, R, S, then primes (N'), plus X, Y, Z, 162
  primes (A', N', etc.), 161, 365
  problems of living (helix 1): A, B, C, D, E, F, then primes (A'), 161
  psychosocial development, 166
  upper and lower case, 191, 248
non-violent, 369
noradrenaline and adrenaline, 231-232, 412 *see* adrenaline
  adrenaline, 245
  noradrenaline, 238, 240
numbering of Gravesian systems *see* nomenclature
New York teachers' strike (1968), 20

O

obedience, 286, 443, 453
  disobedience, civil, 359
obedient, 294, 290
obeisance, 67, 75, 130, 227, 232, 249, 252, 255, 261, 368, 507
  when overpowered, 226
obsessive and compulsive, 300
Olds, M.E. and Olds, J., 408, 410
open, arrested, closed, 270, 476, 478
  see personality *and* open *and* arrested *and* closed
open, 136, 302, 303, 399, 478, 486, 490, 495, 506, 507
  see closed *and* arrested
  DQ, 274, 303, 473
  ER, 473
  A'N', 473
  man's nature, 478
  minded, 102, 191, 381
  pattern, 472
  personality, 477, 482
  Rokeach's concept, 465
  system, 29, 30, 148, 149, 361, 432, 485
  to change, 321-322
open-ended, 148, 361
  development, 445
  hierarchy, 136, 138, 419
  theory, 190, 438, 449
open-mindedness, 102, 191
operant conditioning, 213, 223, 224, 226, 235, 237, 238, 240, 495
organicist, 149, 151, 153
organism, 127, 154, 212, 321, 367, 415, 478, 480, 506 *see* behavior *and* development *and* conditions *and* Homo sapiens *and* personality *and* potential
  biological, 2
  equipment for living, 161, 167
  organism/environmental complex, 151, 160, 166
  preprogrammed, not predetermined, energy system, 478
  organism-environment interaction, 452
organismic, 150, 165, 407
  based needs, 15 *see* needs
  complex, 161
  -minded psychologists, 154 *see* Driesch
  side of double helix, 161, 406, 437
organization, 3, 116-119, 221, 237, 241-242, 244, 261, 267-268, 310, 355, 490, 493
  characteristics for A'N', 386-388
  forms *see* CP, DQ, ER, FS, A'N'
  operations of, 1-2, 301-302, 323, 354, 383
  societal, 247
  structures (diagrams), **117**
  subject groups, 137
  viability, 3, 4 323, 357
Organization Man, 326, 345, 354
origins of the E-C studies, 38
Orthodox, 21
oscillating, 113, 125, 129, 506, 507
  see double-helix

P

Packard, Vance, 316
Paine, Thomas, 24
paradox, 377
Parsons, Talcott and Shils, Edward, 15
participative *see* management
pathology, 180, 205, 490
  behavior, 137
  over- and under-development of systems, 160
  treatment appropriateness, 490
Pavlov, Ivan, 146, 219, 220, 407, 491
  behavior, 214
  classical conditioning, 202, 219
Peace Corps, 221
Pechman, Joseph A. and Timpane, Michael, 212
Peck, Robert, 6, 452
permissiveness, 22
Perry, William, Jr., 6, 411, 452, 456
personality, 151-153 *see* conceptions
  attributes, 486
  culture and, 176, 178, 186, 188, 191, 451, 489 *see* culture
  cyclic aspect of, 483 *see* cyclic
  dimensions, 128, 129
  healthy
    change instigators for, 100

personality *(continued)*
    psychometric data for 4 sub-
       types, 122
  levels of integration forming, 483
  relativism and hierarchy, 151
  systems, 115, 448, 484
    as momentary, 166
    General Systems, 153
  mature, 39-44, 56
    describable state or condition or
      process of becoming? 38, 41
    existing conceptions of, 41
      see conceptions of mature
      personality
    reference points commonly
      used to describe, 41
    hierarchical rise of, 91
      see hierarchy
    theories, 6, 14, 150
      see conceptualizations
      confusion in, 38
      reconceptualizing, 40
  travels of personality, 483
  valuing of, 340
  variables, 175, 176
  vertically-oriented multi-
    dimensional trend phase, 488
  ways of being, 128
phenomenologists, 141
phobias, 299
physiological, 169, 202, 207, 213, 216, 230, 252, 409, 459
  life space, 166
  needs, 148, 200, 450, 488 *see* needs
  tension, 200
Piaget, Jean, 6, 34
political, 12, 29, 294, 507
  conviciton, 392
  dissenters, 366
  dictatorship, 292
  institutions, 257, 263
  legislative process, 13
  organization congruent with the people, 493
  politicians' level, 294, 463
  power, 87
  science, 491
  systems, 255, 390
  values, 323
population, 181, 358, 388, 460
  adult prison, 237

  growth, 387
  over-population, 347, 365
positivistic presentations with symptoms and hostility, 137
Postman, Leo, 464, 466
Postman, Leo and Schneider, Jay S., 464
Postman, Leo, Bruner, Jay S. and McGinnies, E., 464
potential *see* change, conditions
poverty, 13, 210, 211, 316, 494, 496
  and wealth, 392
power(s), 13, 22, 88, 234, 249, 316, 340, 346, 359, 376, 378, 446, 466, 476
  see CP *and* expressive
  assigned, 301
  centralization of, 433
  cognitive, 285
  corporate, heirs to, 391
  delegated, 244
  domestication of, 317
  ethic, 233, 317, 323, 324, 326, 344
    of the few, 316
    pragmatic, 318
  exercised by others, 226
  group opinion, 354
  higher, 67, 78, 183, 254, 257, 280
    prescriptions of, 261
  ideas rather than raw power, 308
  is virtue, 317
  loss of, 324, 353
  over man and nature, 310
  over physical universe, 283
  own, 141
  political, 87
  position, 227, 231
  raw, 308, 413
  restraining outer, 453
  ruthless, 233
  second level values of, 218
  self, 231, 232, 321 *see* self
  singular, 255, 256, 263
  that be or The Power, 308
    see power, higher
  threat to, 326
  to change things, 315, 318, 324
  to the managed, 354
  use of, 318
  will to, 311, 317, 318
  values, Darwinian support of, 315
pre-cultural ways, 55

predatory (CP), 223, 226, 253, 286, 372
prepotent, 161, 173
prison populations, 237
principles (aligned with General
  Systems Theory), 486
problem solving, 115, 189, 428, 430
problem(s), 11-32
  bi-polar of DQ, 252
  existence of, 2, 509
  see existential problems
  plural, not singular, 173
  solutions precede, 184
  solutions creeate new, 173
process, 40, 416, 432, 506
  see change *and* development
  actualization, 399
  anabolic and catabolic, 202, 211
  becoming, 38
  change, 103, 415, 455 *see* change
    critical points in, 180
  cognitive, 372
  continuing, 35, 231
  creative, 489
  decision-making, 355, 356
  development of, 7
  developmental, 461
    see development
  emergent, 29, 464
  ever-changing, 2
  ever-evolving, 499
  flowing, 166, 478
  group, 355, 356
  infinite, 2, 172
  internal, 332 *see* emotion
  learning, 37, 39, 328
    see learning *and* BO, CP, etc.
  levels as, 488, 489
  motoric, 305
  organic, 475
  organism-to-the-environment, 335
  psychological, 202, 205
  psychological maturity as, 39
  rather than state, 493
  step-like, 489
  successive equilibrations, 477
  systematically ordered, 98
progressive-steady state-regressive,
  178, **179**, **479**
Promethean, 231
Protestant ethic, 255
psycho-organismic principles, 30

psychoanalysts, 21, 23
  see conceptualizers
psychoanalytic circles, orthodox, 264
psychological, 409, 489
  affairs, muddled state of, 91
  being(s), 2, 103, 162, 231, 417, 477,
    506
  change, 319, 346
  degrees of freedom, 374
  development and age, 33, 35-36
  dimensions, 428, 430
  existence, 2
  field, 415
  goal, 417
  health, changed concept of, 151
  keynote for A'N' society, 391
  locked to ways and/or territory,
    491, 495, 496
  life space, 163, **164**, 166
  maturity, 2, 36-39, 40, 92, 103, 490,
    503 *see* conceptions *and* emergent
    cyclical
    definition will change, 2
    no such single thing as, 136
    nature of species, group, or
      individual, 162
    need to survive, 148, 414
  non-existence, 202, 209
  paradigms, 38
  positioning along the double helix,
    162
  principles, varied, 494
  revisions to consider to, 42-44
  revolution, greatest, 388
  space, 160, 169, 173, 176, 178, 180,
    182, 189, 455, 475, 489
    effects of changes in, 176
    time, 160, 178
  species, 460
  state, differentiated, 28
  test results, 123
  time, **113**, 127, 160, 163, 176, 178,
    185, 475, 487
psychology *see* conceptualizations
  adult, 29, 31-33, 36, 45, 55, 124-
    125, 127-131, 151, 153, 160, 432,
    483, 486-489
  all systems represent the whole, 32
  cognitive-developmental stage, 7,
    29
  contribution to of E-C, 7

psychology *(continued)*
  developmental, 6, 35
  existential states of *see* AN, BO, CP, etc. *and* existential states
  general sources for testing E-C, 407
  humanistic, 7, 24-28, 359
  open-ended, 136
  particular to state, 29, 507
  previous research, 93
  problems with, 34-36, 142, 145
  questions for, 489
  reconsideration of, 489
  state or process, 40
  unfolding, 29
  win-lose, 294
psychologies, 29 *see* conceptualizations
psychometric studies, **100** *see* studies
psychopathology, 152 *see* pathology
psychosocial systems, nesting, **171**
  behavior *see* behavior
  development *see* development
psychotherapy, 6, 14, 30, 266, 463, 484, 491 *see* therapy
  appropriate to state, 29
punish, 213, 235, 237, 285, 297
  self, 95, 303
punishment, 220, 234, 237, 238, 240, 253, 261, 263, 266, 269, 298, 443, 453, 462
  CP inability to feel, 238
  righteous man and, 303

Q

qualitative and quantitative, 165, 166, 384, 418, 419-420, 501
  behavior change, 97
  change through systems, 399, 415
  differences in learning, 361
  themes change, 72
  variations in groups, 176
quantitification, FS reaction against, 346
quantum-like jump, 29, 107, 160, 415, 482, 483
questions asked in studies, 42
quotations, popular Gravesian
  "At each stage of human existence…," 475
  "…an unfolding or emergent process marked by…," 319
  "I am not saying…," 482
  "The psychology of the adult human being…," 29
  "This level of existence conception…," 477
  "…personality…an itinerant traveler…," 483

R

'radium' as metaphor for E-C, 367, 392, 450
Ramayana, 126
Rand, Ayn, 345, 360
rationality, 84, 340
rationalization, 107, 294, 418
reactive, 199 *see* AN
reconceptualization (of personality, culture, and maturity), 40, 154, 159
  personality, 155, 159
redundancy, 120
redundant, 68, 69, 71, 120-121, 263, 284
regressive, 72, 99, 107, 113-114, 178, 185, 223, 271, 316, 414-415, 484, 500, 506, 509 *see* change, conditions
relationships
  controlled for survival, 231
  dominant-submissive, 257
  hierarchically ordered human, 263
  importance, 332, 343, 360, 381, 398
  organization, 269
relativistic, 338, 346, 349, 369, 488
  existence, 337-338, 342, 350-351, 356 *see* situational
  thinking, 86, 147, 331, 348
relativism, 411, 443 *see* situational
  cultural, 151
  entering ER move toward, 278, 319
relevancy
  of approach study, 120, 430
  of questions, 425, 426, 428
religious(ness), 130, 252, 256, 339, 430, 473
  attitude, 87, 340
  beliefs, 218
  in conception of mature, 89

remoteness (and A'N'), 385
Rensch, Bernhard, 415
repertoire, 375
  behavioral, 289 *see* behavior
research, 4-5, 38-40, 191, 240, 294, 405, 406, 462, 506-509
  approach, 44-49
    phase 1, generate conceptions, 44
    phase 2, classification, 46, 51-52, 93
    phase 3, exploration of categories, 47, 147
    phase 4, library research, 48, 127, 406
  methodology, 464
  judges, 47
  questions, 42-43
  subjects, 44, 54, 64
  suggested by other theories, 38, 410, 418
  three assumptions to test, 54
resultant (of forces' interaction), 160, 162, 167, 169
reward, 64, 67, 108, 122, 220, 234, 25, 237, 323, 462, 496 *see* sacrifice self
  learning by, 410
  operant conditioning, 239, 255, 266, 281, 304
  punishment and , 240,
    see punishment
  punishment or, 263
revolutions, 499
  see consciousness, revolutions
Reynolds, John Hamilton, 138
Rhodesia, 13
Riesman, David, 256, 345, 346, 446
right-wrong position (of DQ), 255
rigid, 430, 465 *see* dogmatism
  leadership, 309 *see* leadership
rigidity, 122, 189, 258, 377, 424, 426
  FS rigid opposition to, 347
  scale, Gough-Sanford, 465
  wave-like variation, 123
ritual, 217, 222, 339
  see thinking, ritualistic
Robber Baron *see* America
Roe, Ann, 147
Rogers, Carl, 14, 27, 145, 146
  therapy, 490
Rokeach, Milton, 122, 123, 135, 465

role
  assignment,433
  in life, 254, 255, 261, 262
  predestined, 268
Rotter, Julian, 320, 350, 410
Rousseau, Jean-Jacques, 24
rules, 110, 286
  absolute, 264
  circumvent, 315
  DQ, 258
  of righteous man, 295
  set by winner at ER, 324
Russia, 272, 317, 493, 494
  Russian Academy of Pedagogical Sciences, 17
ruthlessness, 233, 382, 388

S

sacrifice self systems, 83, 122, 128
  see conceptions
    sacrifice self now to get reward later, 62, 65, 69, 72 *see* DQ
    sacrifice self now to obtain now, 84, 88 *see* FS
saintly existence, 251, 253, 256, 272, 296 *see* DQ
Sanford, Nevitt, 34, 35, 122, 123, 465
scarcity, 22, 506
Schacter, Stan and Latane, Bibb, 410, 412
Scharf, P. and Hickey, J., 414
Schein, Edgar, 451, 446
schema , 165, 169, 254, 255, 256, 447, 486 *see thema*
schematic
  basis for model building, 149
  forms and values, 219, 255, 257, 315, 478, 488
Schopenhauer, Arthur, 316-317
Schroder, Harold, Driver, Michael and Streufert, Sigfeid, 432-439, 460
Schroder, Harold, 6
scientific, 489
  explanatory system, 140
  management, 290
  method, 309
  mode of existence, 310
  thought, 149, 154, 283 *see* thinking
Scott, W.A., 122, 125

Index

second spiral of existence *see* spiral
Segundo, J.P., 408
Seiler, John, 157
self-actualization, 42, 148, 399, 480
  beyond, 147 *see* conceptions *and* express self *and* sacrifice self
  deficiency in the term, 42
  style and degree of, 41
self-actualizing man, 25, 49, 148, 399, 452 *see* Maslow, Abraham
  change of conceptions by, 148
  concept of, 49
self, 110, 285, 344, 347, 476, 502
  aggressive in CP, DQ, ER, 341, 378
  as all-powerful, 311
  attack, 95-96
  attitude toward, 41, 42
  authority higher than, 67
  awareness, 148, 169, 182, 201, 217, 226, 234
  -centeredness, 227, 233, 252, 310
  concept of, 205
  control of, 430, 480
  emergent, 393
  -esteem, 147, 462
  free, 261, 269, 314, 319
  idea of, 184, 311
  -interest, 22, 282, 314, 317, 339, 340, 345, 347, 360, 391, 462
  physiological and external, 252
  power of, 141, 231, 232, 308, 321,
  protective, 444, 461, 462
  reflective, 87
  respect of, 366, 388
  -righteous, 68, 210
  search for, 52, 141
selfism (CP), 226
Selman, Robert, 443, 452, 457
Seltzer, Louis B., 498
Selye, Hans, 415
Shaie, K. Warner, 34, 37
shame *see* emotions
Shakespeare, William, 138
Sheldon, William and Stevens, S.S., 123
significance of the E-C conception, 488
Silent Majority, 286, 293
six themes, 161, 396, 502, 509
  see AN, BO, CP, etc. *and* conceptions
situational, 319, 367, 368 *see* relativism

factors, 438
Skinner, B.F., 17, 31, 49, 52, 145, 146, 235, 237, 238, 462
  principles, 18, 235, 240, 491
  positive reinforcement, 239
  psychology, 491
Skinnerians, 410 *see* conceptualizers
social, 222, 346, 355
  approval, 339, 345, 347, 360, 382
  change in a developing society, 491
  Goals for Americans, 492-493
  homogeneous or heterogeneous, 491
  institutions, 176
  learning, 16, 37, 350
  marketplace, 86
  participation, 85
  planning, 3, 497
social *(continued)*
  problems, 282
  program, 243
  questions to ask, 493
  reorganization, 503
  stability, 217
  system, 141
sociocentric, 283, 337-363, 338, 339, 342, 344, 345, 349, 369 *see* FS
sociocratic ethic, 326, 354
Solomon, Richard L. and Howes, D.H., 464
Solomon, Richard L. and Brush, Elinor S., 410
solutions *see* change, conditions, resolution *and* existential problems
Sorokin, Pitirim, 414
South Africa, 13, 273
Spearman, Charles E., 154, 155, 476
Spence, Kenneth, 145, 146
spiral
  existence of, 191, 391, 506, 509
    A'N' as beginning a second spiral, 191, 366
    first and second, 174
    first, 167, 170, 509
    second, 173, 174, 178, 184, 189, 366, 452, 453, 509
  systems, 450
spirits, 216, 217, 218, 221, 223, 255
spiritual, 92, 110, 335, 339, 476, 479, 493, 501 *see* religious *and* DQ *and* FS *and* sacrifice self now

spiritual *(continued)*
  attitude, 339
  thinking, 110
  values, 21
  void, 335
Stalin, Joseph, 257
Stambaugh, John, 52, 53
status, 41
  Status Seeker, 316, 338
steady state, 29, 178, 180, 185, 222, 414, 454, 485
Stein, Morris, 14, 442, 447, 448
step-like manner of psychological development, 489-490
stimulation, 320, 409, 429
  aversive, 266
  influx of, 253
  intensity and frequency of, 408
  repeated, 408
  type of, 410
stress
  closed DQ, 269
  interpersonal, 278
  reaction to, 95, 112, 114, 137, 180, 202, 278, 295, 458
  righteous system, 289, 297, 301
studies (in Graves's research), 122-131
  authoritarianism, 122, 124, 186, 424, 427
  dogmatism-rigidity, 122, 123, 147, 186, 424, 426, 465
  freedom to behave, 114, 115, 186
  intelligence and temperament, 122, 123, 124, 128, 186, 371, 424, 426, 428, 437
  preference (Edwards), 122, 124
  psychometric, 100, 121, 122, 125
  relevancy of approach, 120, 429
  supplemental
    interaction, 119
    problem solving, 115
  quality and quantity of solutions, 121
  values à la Scott, 122, 125
subordination of older systems, 29, 464
Subsistence Level Systems, 163, 184, 191, 216 *see* Being Level systems *and* spiral of existence, first
sub-types *see* nodal *and* entering *and* exiting

subjectivity, 201, 334
Suedfeld, Peter, 431
Sullivan, Harry Stack, 462
Sullivan, C., Grant, M.Q., and Grant, J.D., 443, 452, 454, 455, 456
Sutherland, John, 36
symphony (of human history), 130, 389, 502, 508 *see* six themes
Systemic, 440
  development, 188
  existential state, 365, 378, 384, 392
  forms of behavior, 163
  organization of neurological structures, 37
  stability, 300
  thinking, 191, 367, 378
systems *see* behavior *and* conceptions *and* psychosocial *and* personality *and* sacrificial / expressive *and* X Y Z
  activating, 162, 172, 180, 185, 412 *see* X
  belief, 131, 465, 507
  belonging, 148
  biopsychosocial, 478, 506
  change, pace of of, 176
  closed, 29, 30, 149, 465, 486, 509
  cognitive, 36
  complex variation in, 423
  conceptual, 36, 78, 126, 133, 145, 160, 406, 418, 423, 439, 492
  conceptualizing mature, 147
  coping, 161, 165, 174, 185, 367, 397, 410
  cultural, 131, 155, 476
  differences and similarities, 128
  double-goal, 485
  E-C as supraordinal, 485
  elaborating, 162, 165 *see* Z
  ethical, 489 *see* ethics
  feedback, 485
  hierarchical, 36, 114, 127, 149, 151, 149, 186, 188, 418, 447, 453, 481, 489
  ideological, 140
  incentive, 324
  integrating the whole, 483
  N,O,P,Q,R,S plus X,Y,Z, 174
  number, 128
  order of appearance, 128
  perceptual, 131
  potentially open, 30

systems *(continued)*
  rationalizing data for, 148
  saltatory development of, 160
  specific and general, 112
  study of change in four, 98
  structural differences, 432
  sub-systems, 409
    alternating, 188
    beyond B'O', 190
    even-numbered, 188, 429, 430, 431, 493, 508
      externally oriented, 188, 435
      tightly bound, 188
    odd-numbered, 188, 429
      internally oriented, 188, 435
      loosely bound, 188
    six, 161, 163, 185, 189, 368
    supporting, 162
    variations of form, 161
  subsistence and being levels, 162, 174, 509
  surges, calms, rigidifies, 60
  value, 78, 213, 257, 280, 358, 362, 402
  valuing others, 147

T

tachistoscope study, 463, 465
  dogmatism/rigidity, 464
  words tested, 465
Tasaday, 28, 127, 169, 203, 391, 448, 453, 497
Taylor, Frederick, 290-291
teach, 18, 39, 236, 239, 267, 492
  dictates of independence, 278
  indirectly, 327
  what children are not, 391
teacher, 13, 20, 235, 241, 265, 273, 275, 328, 351 *see* AN, BO, etc., learning *and* education
  accentuates positive for CP, 235
  avoids competition for DQ, 274
  authority as, 267
  expertise, 329
  handles feelings, 275
  impetus to change, 274
  importance of, 265
  logical reasoning as, 309
  pose problems, 376
  status of, 265, 273
  tenured, 302
technology, 255, 360
  behavior, 19
temperament, 121, 124, 129, 162, 186, 508 *see* studies
tendency, 86, 468
  alter existing structure, 149
  binding – loose or tight, 188, 429
  CP, 232, 241
  conforming in FS, 338, 455
  defensiveness when criticized, 136
  dominant/submissive, 226
  ER, 314
  growth and conservation, 483
  maintain existing structure, 149
  never-ending (beyond pleasure principle), 504
  non-conforming in CP and ER, 456
  thinking in alternative ways, 314
  toward ER in exiting DQ, 279, 282
  toward organizing and stabilizing, 149
tentativeness, 86
territory, 78, 201
  mapping experience, 318
  pschologically locked into, 496
thema, 165, 169, 183, 186, 219, 254, 255, 257, 309, 310, 335, 339, 366, 397, 447, 463, 481, 482, 486 *see schema*
thema and *schema*, 254, 447, 486
thematic and schematic, 257
thematic
  aspect of E-C theory, 459
  cyclic aspect of E-C, 459
  form of valuing, 256, 257
  physiological funcitoning, 488
  styles of being, 478
theme for existence, 72, 508
Thematic Aperception Test, 458
Theobald, Robert, 212
theory *see* emergent cyclical
  adult behavior, 3 *see* behavior
  formulation of, 369
  seeking complements, 31
  Theory X, 244
  Theory Y, 270, 490
therapy, 25, 301, 463
  see psychotherapy
  behavioristic, 490
  congruent, 30

therapy *(continued)*
  opens way but does not produce growth, 463
  Rogerian, 490
  psychoanalytic, 490
thinking, 30
  see conceptions *and* mature
  about man's problems, 2
  atomistic additive, 76, 280
  Black Muslim
  centralization, 57
  cerebral, 187
  cognitive, 351
  conceptual, 366
  Darwinian evolutionary, 37
  educational, 497
  "Establishment" way to be overcome, 418
  existential, 6
  for the group, 116
  General Systems, 6, 149, 152, 159, 485
  "Greening of America" thinking, 493
  idinal raw, 58
  independent, 75
  industrial, 221
  levels
    absolutistic, 147, 254, 316, 411
      DQ, 448
      moralistic-prescriptive, 310
    animistic, 411
      BO, 181
      tribalistic, 396
    autistic, 147, 411
    differentialistic, 412
    egocentric, 233, 411
    multiplistic, 76, 280, 316, 321, 411
      ER, 359
      hypothetico-deductive, 309
    relativistic, 86, 147, 331, 348, 411
      FS, 184
      FS delusion of full development, 492
      sociocentric (6th level), 345, 347
      subjective, non-linear, 339
    ritualistic, 217-218, 222, 339
      see BO
    systemic, 411

    7th level/A'N', 367, 368, 369, 392, 396
    8th level, 396, 397
    9th level, 400
  learning systems, 350
  Maoist, 388
  might-makes-right, 227
  mixed sub-types, 57
  organicists, 149
  phenomenological, 7
  psychological, new, 142
  quantitative, 110
  raw, 64
  rational objective, 84, 110
  research on, 410
  right-thinking, 74, 278, 295
  scientific, 146, 149
  stereotypical, 217
  systems-like, 417
  subsystems (six levels of), 409
  time of appearance, 344
  way of, 352, 409, 440
Third Force *see* conceptions of adult personality
Thoreau, Henry David, 138, 139
Thorndike, Edward, 462
Thorpe, W.H., 408
thyroxin, 412
Tillich, Paul, 140
time, 180 *see* psychological time
  factor in conception change, 52
  psychological, not chronological, 160
  leading edge of mankind moved, **181**
  scale of individual emergence reversed from that of species', 178
Toffler, Alvin, 361
Tolman, Edward Chance, 145
tradition, 127, 215, 218, 219, 222, 383
  ways, 221
Traditional Directed Man, 441, 447
  see Reisman
transition(s), 86, 87, 188, 429, 454, 461, 468
  see conceptions *and* AN, BO, CP, etc.
  sub-types, 56
  systems, 191, 195
trust, 22, 314
Tsanoff, Radoslav, 53
Turnbull, Colin M., 204

typology: E-C not a typological theory, 173

U

Uganda, 13, 414
Ullman, L.P., 17
ultimate psychological or cultural state, 155
unethical behavior, 489 *see* immoral
Union Carbide, 387
United States Steel, 387
Utopian, 17, 49, 154, 172, 449, 474

V

Value Analysis, 321, 356
value system, 253, 271, 275, 318, 338, 360, 368 *see* behavior *and* express self *and* sacrifice self
   A'N' (7th level), 366, 367, 380, 393
   BO (2nd level), 214
   B'O' (8th level), 401
   CP, 234, 245, 249
   DQ (4th level), 246, 252, 257
   moral breakdown, 490
   sacrificial, 255
value systems, 78, 280, 310, 362, 489
   higher level, 213
   incongruent, 358
   transitional state, 402
values, 2, 6, 19, 29, 30, 31, 238, 410, 490, 501, 503 *see* AN, BO, CP, etc.
and change
   absolutistic sacrificial, 256
   as value systems, 213
   bodily-based, 21
   breakdown, 29, 223-224, 305, 345, 360, 368, 401
   casting aside old, 20, 308
   change, 31, 339-340, 345, 354, 368, 370, 401
   commonality over differential classification, 339
   dissimilar but congruent for viability, 323
   from one's own experience, 78
   future, 363, 369, 391
   'generation gap,' 359
   individualistic, 503
   managed and manager's, 269, 323-324
   mature, 29
   means, 255, 381
   never-ending quest for new, 504
   phenomenistic, 219
   pluralism, 370
   reactive, 213
   return to religiousness, 339
   sacrificial, 256, 257, 272, 308, 318
   Scott's, 122, 125
   secular, 310
   traditionalistic, 218
valuing others, 147
verbal interaction, capacity for, 273
verifiability, 405, 406
   tests of, 439
verticality, 488
Viet Nam, 378, 491
violence, 3, 59, 213, 229, 291, 292, 359
   non-violence, 357
vitalism, 153, 154, 159
von Bertalanffy, Ludwig, 14, 417, 432, 485
von Goethe, Johann Wolfgang, 476
von Neuman, John, 483
von Neuman, John and Morgenstern, Oskar, 483

W

Wallace, Alfred Russel, 37, 174
Walters, R.H., 17
war, 13, 234, 291, 315
   for organizational power, 324
   reasons for, 341
   stress of, 202
   World War I German soldier, 204
Watson, John, 17
wave-like, **113**, 176, **177**, 178, 186, 188, 428, 435, 447, 450, 506, 508
   see emergent-cyclical conception *and* psychosocial development, complex variation, 129
ways of being, 128
welfare, 205, 211, 242, 494, 495
   facilitating movement through existential states, 495
   housing, 496
   human welfare as a goal, 491

Werner, Heinz, 6
West Virginia, 219
West, G.B., 412, 415
what versus *how* a person thinks, 135
White, Leslie, 14
Whyte, Lancelot, 417
Whyte, William H., 345
will to power, 311, 317, 318 *see* Adler *and* Nietzsche
win, 228, 298, 319
  -lose, 184, 294, 301
  circumvent rules to, 315
  winning not everything, 503
Witkin, H.A., 27
Wolfe, R., 412, 415

X

X - activating system, 162, 165, 167, 172, 174, 180, 185, 397, 407, 412
see Coping Systems

Y

Y - supporting system, 162, 165, 167, 174, 366, 367, 397, 407, 412
see Coping Systems
Y system and A'N', 367

Z

Z - elaborating system, 162, 165, 167, 173, 174, 406, 397, 410
see Coping System